FOURTH EDITION

Community Organizing and Development

Herbert J. Rubin
Northern Illinois University

Irene S. Rubin
Northern Illinois University

PEARSON

Boston   New York   San Francisco
Mexico City   Montreal   Toronto   London   Madrid   Munich   Paris
Hong Kong   Singapore   Tokyo   Cape Town   Sydney

Senior Editor: *Patricia Quinlin*
Series Editorial Assistant: *Nakeesha Warner*
Marketing Manager: *Laura Lee Manley*
Production Editor: *Pat Torelli*
Editorial Production Service: *Modern Graphics, Inc.*
Composition Buyer: *Linda Cox*
Manufacturing Buyer: *Debbi Rossi*
Electronic Composition: *Modern Graphics, Inc.*
Cover Administrator: *Joel Gendron*

For related titles and support materials, visit our online catalog at www.ablongman.com.

Between the time website information is gathered and then published, it is not unusual for some sites to have closed. Also, the transcription of URLs can result in typographical errors. The publisher would appreciate notification where these errors occur so that they may be corrected in subsequent editions.

Library of Congress Cataloging-in-Publication Data

Rubin, Herbert J.
  Community organizing and development / Herbert J. Rubin, Irene S. Rubin.
—4th ed.
     p. cm.
  Includes bibliographical references and index.
  ISBN 0-205-40813-3
  1. Community development—United States. 2. Community
organization—United States. 3. Social action—United States. 4. Community
power—United States. I. Rubin, Irene. II. Title.
  HN90.C6R73 2007
  307.1'40973—dc22
                                                              2006037691

Printed in the United States of America

10 9 8 7 6 5 4 3 2   11 10 09 08

CONTENTS

PREFACE

Community organizing and social action are about mobilizing people to work together to solve shared problems. People learn that problems have social causes and that collectively fighting back is a far better approach than passive acceptance or personal alienation. Development comes about as people increase their capacity to pressure government and businesses, obtain goods and services, and build and sustain democratic organizations. Through organizing and development, people gain the confidence and tools to collectively resolve societal problems.

Since organizing is difficult and sometimes frustrating work, why would someone choose to become an organizer? Some people do so because of individual experiences. Maybe their family and neighbors have been made ill by a chemical dump; perhaps their disabled child has been denied access to needed services. Others are outraged by injustice, watching the treatment of gays or seeing people sleep in doorways and huddle over subway grates to get a little warmth. Some feel it wrong that recent immigrants are denied human dignity and respect. Activists are motivated by the unkept promises that all people are equal before the law, are free to practice their religion, to speak their minds, to vote, to travel, and to have access to jobs and housing. Organizers fight to make those promises a reality.

This book is for social change activists who propose to spend their energy working to solve shared problems and mobilizing others to join the battle. Though the craft of organizing is best learned from first-hand experience, a text such as this suggests skills that organizers will need. We discuss theories and models of organizing and present hundreds of examples. The book explains what has been tried, what has worked in the past, and what is likely to work in the present. Throughout the text we integrate the experiences of organizers and activists with academic knowledge about communities, the political system, organizations, and social mobilization.

We balance descriptions of stirring protest actions and visible projects with the behind-the-scenes routines that make such work possible. Social mobilization campaigns are the dramatic, visible side of social action, as when civil rights activists confront police, who push them back with fire hoses and bare-fanged dogs. Less dramatic but equally visible are the changes that come about when community development corporations replace old buildings used as crack houses with clean, safe, affordable housing. These visible and newsworthy events are the culmination of many months of steady effort in mobilizing people, creating and sustaining an organization, finding money, and mastering a changing and often hostile political environment. Activism is motivated by anger or empathy, but to succeed, mastery of a variety of technical skills is required.

Reflections of the Fourth Edition

The core philosophy of the fourth edition sustains ideas in the earlier editions, that organizing is about empowering people within democratically run organizations that create capacity to bring about a more equitable and just society. In organizing, community refers to more than a geographic place to include the wide variety of bonds that link people together. We point out that problems come about because some are benefiting at the cost to many others and that the perceptions of problems and their solutions often define the actions that can be taken.

Though our philosophy remains the same, we have prepared a major rewrite to respond to the conservative times in which we now live. To better ground the reader in the broad world of social activism, we have added Chapter 2, which describes the infrastructure of organizing—the people, ideas, and shared examples of success—and Chapter 3, which provides in much more detail than in previous editions the similarities and differences between the major models of social activism. We more strongly argue on the importance of *progressive organizing* that focuses on changing underlying and inequitable social, economic, and political structures.

To encompass these changes, as well as to update examples while making a smoother presentation, we have reorganized the text. Part One introduces the overall model of progressive organizing, describing the core premises in Chapter 1, illustrating a wide array of examples of effective social actions in Chapter 2, and introducing a variety of models of social activism in Chapter 3. Part Two presents the three pillars of progressive organizing: empowering individuals, building community, and establishing social change organizations.

In Part Three, we examine social problems. Chapter 7 indicates that problems are socially framed and illustrates how these understandings affect what government policies come about in response to the problems. Chapter 8 sketches the history of organizing while Chapter 9 moves to the here and now, presenting the research techniques through which present-day activists discover and document problems their communities face.

Part Four discusses building capacity. Capacity refers to the skills and resources needed to accomplish tasks. Capacity emerges from the numbers of those involved in activism and the courage and strength of the local leaders as described in Chapter 10. Capacity expands through building effective organizations as discussed in Chapter 11. Skills and resources are shared as people meet with one another, learn from each other and expand their enthusiasm for fighting back—the topic of Chapter 12. Each new organization does not have to learn from scratch as assistance can be obtained from an array of support organizations as discussed in Chapter 13.

The next two sections detail the two complementary approaches to social activism. In Part Five, we focus on social mobilization, first presenting broader principles of this more aggressive approach in Chapter 14, and in Chapter 15 discussing how to mobilize people to join the battle. In Chapter 16 we examine how social action organizations can pressure government using both lobbying and electoral techniques. When these fail, more aggressive power tactics are required as illustrated in Chapter 17. Chapter 18 discusses litigation, media relations, and negotiations, techniques that complement both conventional political actions as well as more disruptive confrontations. To expand power, individual social change organizations build coalitions that orchestrate action campaigns as discussed in Chapter 19.

In Part Six, we detail the economic and social production model. Chapter 20 describes the premises underlying this model and presents numerous illustrations of the projects that are accomplished. Chapter 21 discusses the skills needed for planning, funding, implementing, and managing social production projects.

The Epilogue is more personal in that we present both our concerns about present-day social activism and suggest approaches for effectively continuing the battle to bring about a more just society.

We acknowledge the helpful suggestions made by the reviewers of this new edition: Gary Lounsberry, Florida Gulf Coast University; and Paula Nesoff, La Guardia Community College.

H.J.R.
I.S.R.

PART ONE

Progressive Organizing

In this section we present the values and goals of progressive organizing while illustrating the successes that have occurred. In Chapter 1 we point out why organizing is vital though indicating that there are many complementary paths to follow in the fight for economic and social justice. Chapter 2 presents a series of *narratives of the possible*, vignettes of successful organizing and renewal efforts. Chapter 3 introduces the large variety of social change models, showing their similarities and differences while concluding that all are complementary paths to the shared goal of bringing about progressive change.

CHAPTER

1

Organizing and Development for Progressive Social Change

To combat social and economic injustices, people join together in community-based and issue-focused organizations. Citizens rally in support of living wages, affordable housing, and quality education. Grandmothers, mothers, and daughters, as well as committed men, march to preserve the right of women to control their own bodies; supporters of immigrants unite with labor to outlaw sweatshops; neighbors join with health professionals to protect themselves from the menace of toxic wastes. A few neighbors in a one-time push demand a stop sign to make their children's walk home from school safer while hundreds of thousands join on the Mall in Washington, D.C., to demonstrate in opposition to the war in Iraq or for immigrants' rights. Community organizations partner with city hall to build affordable housing, church volunteers help the homeless, person by person, while statewide and national advocacy organizations lobby for public programs to provide the billions needed to expand the supply of affordable housing. When neighborhood organizations, issue organizations, and national advocacy groups come together on a single issue they form a social movement.

Success has a human face. Dying individuals and their families are comforted with hospice care set up by community groups. But success is also counted in terms of the increasing number of minorities who own their own homes because action organizations battled economic racism.

Success takes time to achieve. Campaigns can persist over decades, even generations, and involve millions of people, such as has occurred in battles for racial justice or to broaden legal rights for minorities, workers, women, and gays.

This book describes how people with a shared vision can bring about progressive social change by working together. We describe what has been accomplished, why the efforts are worthwhile, what obstacles are faced, and what tools and skills are needed.

Progressive Organizing

People organize for many reasons—to protect the environment, to combat racial prejudice, to end wars, to gain workplace rights, to allow women choice, to reduce discrimination and to protect minorities, among hundreds of important issues. But

3

organizing is also done by those who resent what others have gained and want to return to an unfair past. Right to life organizations have redoubled their efforts to deny women choice. Social conservatives work to reduce rights gays have gained. While workers organize to gain a living wage, better health care, or affordable homes, businesses pressure government to help destroy unions, lower corporate taxes, reduce regulations, and be allowed to exploit the environment.

The skills of organizing are the same almost irrespective of the cause. Learning activism is much more than mastering skills; it involves learning why action should be taken and why doing so is worthwhile. Activism is living out one's values. For us that means fighting for **progressive social change** by

> implementing *economic justice*—to combat the severe economic inequalities that leave many individuals ill-housed, ill-fed, lacking medical care, deprived of access to schooling
>
> striving for *social justice*—to assure that people, irrespective of their race, ethnicity, gender, religion, or sexual orientation, are treated in an equal and fair way
>
> protecting *civil liberties*—to preserve and expand constitutionally guaranteed political and individual rights, while battling those seeking to reduce such rights to preserve their own power
>
> respecting the *environment*—to become caretakers rather than exploiters of the earth

Progressive organizing is about defending the weak from the strong, sharing resources to eliminate human hardship, and striving to promote an equitable society. Organizations promoting progressive social change bring together men and women; gay and straight; white, black, brown, and red; those with only modest English language skills and limited formal education; and activists with advanced degrees. Progressive social activists work to build a world in which individuals are treated fairly, with respect, and as equals, no matter what position they occupy, while opposing the concentration of wealth in businesses or personal fortunes that enables a few to dominate government, denying access to others.

Those working for progressive change care about the ways in which their goals are achieved, insisting that actions be guided by a democratic open process. Progressive activists keep in mind the connection between separate issues. To increase the income of people while seriously harming the environment, or to have one ethnic group gain economically while exploiting another is not part of the progressive approach. Progressive activists recognize that individuals differ in their personal abilities but emphatically argue that no one should be limited in their opportunities or treated disrespectfully because of their gender, race, ethnicity, sexuality, or social class. Progressive organizing is about ending the structural barriers that allow social and economic injustice to persist.

Accomplishing Social Change Through Organizing and Development Efforts

Activism begins for a wide a variety of reasons. An individual might get angry at a personal injustice and fight back, perhaps because of a racial slur or being passed over for a job because of gender. Others guided by religious beliefs want to put their faith into action. Some people respond to first-hand experiences—a wheelchair-dependent individual noticing how the world ignores those with disabilities; others fight for abstract rights—the freedom to speak for a person holding an unpopular idea, or battle to eliminate prejudices and stereotypes that are simply wrong.

People share with one another both the problems they face and the solutions reached through extended **narratives of success** that communicate that while battles might be long and hard, victories are possible. Slowly but surely people recognize that alone they cannot overcome pervasive economic or social inequality but instead must join with others in a wide variety of organizations. *Social action organizations* directly pressure government and businesses both by lobbying and with confrontations to change laws, policies and regulations, to redirect resources to people and communities in need, and to enhance civil and human rights. *Economic and social development organizations* struggle to remedy failures in the capitalist economy by providing goods and services that are otherwise unavailable, especially to the poor. Economic and social development organizations exemplify a humane capitalism, setting up firms in which workers have a say, or by providing social services that empower by teaching people how to help themselves rather than always deferring to what experts say they must do. *Network organizations* coordinate the actions of other social change organizations while *national advocacy coalitions* and *support organizations* ferret out information about problems, share this information widely, help organizations learn from one another and themselves lobby politicians and regulators.

Progressive social change organizations unite communities of people who live near one another, bring together those who share a common background or heritage, and focus the power of those who collectively face a persisting problem to enable them to have an increased say over decisions and actions that affect their lives. In doing so an infrastructure for social change is organized.

> **Organizing** entails working with people to help them recognize that they face shared problems and to discover that by joining together they can fight to overcome these problems. Organizing builds upon and strengthens interpersonal, social, and community relationships while establishing ongoing organizations that enable people to sustain collective actions.

When individuals and organizations in many locales simultaneously fight back against a shared problem a **social movement** emerges. Social movements are

> collective challenges by people with common purposes and solidarity in sustained interaction with elites, opponents, and authorities. (Tarrow 1994, 3–4)

Organizing enables people and their communities to gain the capacity to take actions for change, a capacity that we label as development:

> **Development** entails the creation of personal and collective resources that enable people to fight back and to take charge. Development comes about when individuals gain the self-confidence that they can succeed and the skills and material resources to collectively undertake the actions required to materially and socially improve their lives.
>
> Development involves building and strengthening social change organizations that focus power. These organizations share knowledge, teach technical skills, create bonds of trust between people, and provide a setting in which people motivate one another by sharing narratives of both oppression and of successes. Social change organizations focus the power of many against the wealth and privilege of the few.

Overall, development is about building capacity for sustained change and empowerment.

> Taken together, organizing and development involve empowering groups of individuals within a community in ways that enable them to better control decisions, projects, programs and policies that affect them both individually and collectively.

Why People Must Organize

Through organizing, people join together and learn that problems they face stem from broader social, cultural, or economic forces and not from personal failings. Discovering they are not alone, people forge a shared understanding that challenges the myth that decision makers are right simply because they are in formal positions of power. Organizing builds the confidence necessary for democratic involvement, while establishing organizations that address a wide range of social and economic problems. Organizing empowers both individuals and the communities to which they belong.

But why must people take the time and make the effort to organize? Cannot individuals solve the problems they face by themselves? And, when individuals fail won't government step in to help those in need? The simple answer is no and no.

Problems Are Pervasive

Problems abound that affect economically and socially disadvantaged people yet are ignored by those in power. People are ill-housed, lack medical care, and work for poverty level wages. Health care costs keep going up, while more than 40 million individuals, many of them children, have no medical insurance. The combined burdens of child rearing and earning a living are falling increasingly on women, but women have difficulty getting jobs that pay enough to support a family. Employment in unionized manufacturing jobs has virtually vanished, while white collar workers fear layoffs as their companies downsize. In general as we enter a postindustrial era, those who are better off get even richer, the poor fall further behind, and the middle shrinks in size.

Problems magnify one another. Persistent racial and ethnic discrimination force the poor, minorities, and newly immigrant groups to live in high-crime neighborhoods that lack decent schools, abound with health hazards, and whose economic base has virtually disappeared. Immigrants come into the country and are exploited as a low wage labor force; once here they face language barriers and discrimination in obtaining services.

Individuals alone simply lack the wherewithal to help themselves escape from the consequences of complex and linked problems.

Problems Are Based on Structural Failings and Cultural Values that People by Themselves Cannot Combat

What at first appears to be a personal problem often stems from broader structural failings. An unemployed person can search for a new job, but what happens when those that can be found pay so poorly that people cannot support themselves? People try to find their own housing but often housing costs exceed what those working in the service sector can afford to pay. Better jobs require a quality education, yet public funding is lacking to improve schools, especially in poorer communities. People want to help themselves, but an individual cannot change the structure of the housing market nor force conglomerates to pay living wages.

But it is not simply the structure of the economy that makes it difficult for individuals alone to fight back. Deeply ingrained cultural beliefs curtail people in their battle against social inequalities. Cultural beliefs favor the rich over the poor, business over labor, male over female, and people from more established or whiter ethnic groups over those of color and newer immigrant groups. When faced with culturally supported racist or homophobic challenges, what can one person do? Turn a cheek and accept it? Pick a fight by himself or herself against all the prejudiced people? The sense that problems are not solvable and so must be accepted is a deeply ingrained part of our culture, reinforced by laws that maintain the status quo. To change persistent cultural beliefs requires collective action over a long period of time.

Government Is More Accessible to the Rich and Powerful

Governmental support is vital. Social Security and Medicare enable the elderly to live more dignified lives; the Community Reinvestment Act slows disinvestment from poor communities; while the Americans with Disabilities Act helps create a more humane society. Civil rights violations are federal offenses. Government programs fund AIDS prevention and treatment, help support affordable housing, and protect the environment. Local governments work to revitalize neighborhoods, can pass living wage ordinances, and establish human relations ordinances to combat discrimination based on race, ethnicity, color, and sexual orientation.

However, public sector programs did not come about because of a spontaneous awakening of responsibility among officials. Progressive programs are adopted only after people organize and battle for them, often against determined opposition. Without such pressures pharmaceutical companies will insist on lax standards and automobile companies will delay in making cars more efficient. Laws to end discrimination against women, minorities, and gays came about only after concerted organized efforts to battle the dominance of cultural conservatives. Without pressure from progressive organizations, government would tilt toward the privileged, enacting tax cuts for the rich or refusing to spend money on social services. Without collective efforts those already in power prevail.

Government claims to be accessible to all, but gaining access is the problem. The rich and businesses that provide campaign contributions find it easier to reach officials. Further, contacting government requires taking time off from work, then negotiating a labyrinth of complicated bureaucracies; the rich and businesses hire lawyers and full-time lobbyists to do these tasks. Without the actions of progressive organizations, government would only hear from large businesses and the wealthy and continue to minimize, if not ignore, the seriousness of problems that affect the rest of us.

People Are Intentionally Disempowered

Problems abound, government rarely voluntarily provides a solution, the economic and social structure tilts toward the privileged, while cultural values reinforce the idea that the system is just and to fight back is futile. This palpable unfairness would suggest that people, either out of disgust or desperation, would rebel—yet few do. Organizing is required to overcome this passive acceptance and perceived sense of helplessness.

Some problems simply appear to be beyond one's scope of action: What can be done when a company whose headquarters is thousands of miles away decides to shut down a local plant and the manager is as surprised as the workers? Whom do you fight when a loan firm charges predatory rates and is able to do so because it is a subsidiary of a large out-of-state bank that is regulated elsewhere?

Worse yet, people blame themselves for problems they experience. Battered women and victims of rape often erroneously accept self-blame. "If I had been a better wife, prepared tastier foods, perhaps he would not have hit me." Or, "Maybe my clothes were too provocative; the police said I shouldn't have been walking by that park at night." Such self-blame makes it hard to convince people to organize to pressure the police to arrest abusers and rapists. Until individuals understand that they are not at fault, but rather that the problems occur because of broader economic or social forces, or cultural beliefs, they cannot constructively respond.

Fear of retaliation is another reason that many people do not raise their voices in opposition. Retaliation may include arrests of those who speak up, cruelly disseminating false rumors to ruin the reputations of those who dare to rebel, or actual physical harm. People who marched for civil rights faced hostile police who dispersed them with water cannons and set dogs to attack them. Bosses fire people who are identified as troublemakers, and then work to prevent the person from being hired elsewhere. The impact of such actions is not lost on those who remain.

People also fail to fight back because they accept the idea that those in authority are right and that questioning that authority is wrong. The president of the company, or president of the nation, for that matter, must know best, or why else would he (and on occasion she) be president? As Piven and Cloward describe, those with wealth or political power have set up an

> elaborate system of beliefs and ritual behaviors [that] . . . defines for people what is right and what is wrong and why; what is possible and what is impossible. . . . Because this superstructure of beliefs and rituals is evolved in the context of unequal power, it is inevitable that the beliefs and rituals reinforce inequality, by rendering the powerful divine and the challengers evil. (Piven and Cloward 1977, 1)

By defining what is right, what is wrong, what is possible, and what must be accepted, those in power exercise a dominance without the necessity of physical or economic force.

Antonio Gramsci (1973) labeled the ability of those in power to frame how others think an *intellectual hegemony*. Workers are taught and end up believing that business people have a natural right to do with their firms as they please. Wives often accept the idea that their husbands should make the important family decisions, regardless of the consequences for themselves and their children. For decades gays felt the need to stay in the closet fearing both retribution and in many ways themselves accepting the cultural value that they were different. In general, people accept the idea that those in power should not be opposed, even when what they are doing seems harmful to others. Both literally and figuratively people accept that "father knows best."

A further reason why people feel helpless is that they are financially or socially dependent on precisely those who benefit from their subordination. Citizens understand that their families are being poisoned by dirty air, undrinkable water, and tainted food and worry about the effects of industrial wastes on their health, but are unwilling to antagonize the companies that provide their jobs. Wives who are abused stay in a marriage because they cannot figure out how to support themselves and their children without their husband's income. African Americans recognized the continual abuse they received, but how can you fight your employer even if he or she is a racist?

People feel vulnerable when they think they are alone in facing a problem and feel that if they speak up they will be picked off, defused, or ignored. This sense of isolation might come about because of a physical separation, when those with disabilities are unable to come together or when women are trapped at home. People are also isolated because social distance makes it hard for those from different backgrounds to join in a common struggle. Women work to oppose sexist structures, but the gap between poor African American women and middle-class white women weakens the ability to come together.

Organizing is required to battle these many forms of disempowerment.

Today Progressive Victories Are Threatened by an Organized and Effective Backlash

Successful progressive campaigns have helped redress the imbalance between rich and poor and reduce racial and gender inequality. In our own lifetimes (we were born in the mid-forties), we have witnessed laws that supported racial discrimination nullified, while the rights of women to control their own fertility has expanded. Those with disabilities have gained clout through the Americans with Disabilities Act; legal discrimination against gays has been reduced. Activist organizations now can pressure banks to end discrimination against poor neighborhoods. Community controlled economic development organizations provide affordable housing and increased job opportunities in the inner city.

Activists recognize that much more needs to be done, and there is now a firm base on which to build. With discrimination based on race and gender now illegal, the next step in the battle is bringing about more equal salaries and access to top positions. Unfortunately, gains achieved are now threatened and complaisance that past victories will remain is misguided. Today, progressive organizing is on the defensive as conservative forces, in a coordinated, organized backlash against gains made in social, gender, sexual, and economic justice seek to bring back the inequalities of the past. Much effort is required just to stay in place.

Social conservatives have battled against the rights of women and cast aspersions on gay activists, while denigrating minority religions and cultural beliefs. Men whose jobs and status are threatened (by outsourcing or downsizing) are taught that their problem came about because minority groups and women have advanced and become resentful. The conservative backlash encourages resentment of government; it encourages the belief that taxes are bad, social programs are harmful, and regulation of business and the environment hurts the economy. With government revenues reduced because of tax cuts that benefit the rich, and what is left over spent on an expanding military budget, the social safety net is torn asunder.

In recent years this conservative backlash has accelerated because elected officials, even those who claim to be liberal, fear to oppose this organized movement. More liberal politicians such as Bill Clinton weakened the social safety net and enthusiastically supported globalization. Conservative politicians run for office and win with an anti-feminist, anti-minority, anti-poor agenda, all the while ignoring what multiculturalism implies for our future. Once in office these individuals claim government programs do more harm than good, work to cut taxes and in doing so dry up the resources required to help the less fortunate.

How have we reached this point? Many ordinary, working class individuals sincerely feel threatened by the changes of the last two generations, while religious conservatives have deeply felt convictions that changes in gender roles or the acceptance of gayness are wrong. As higher paying jobs disappear, both the working poor and increasingly the middle class become fearful, defer to business, and refocus attention on a perceived moral decline. Resentment drives the backlash.

Individuals look for reasons for their fears and, hearing only a divided message from progressives, accept the voices of social conservatives. Right-wing talk radio pushes this message by attacking the gains of women, blaming the poor for their own misery, and questioning the possibilities of multiculturalism, while claiming that a-religiosity is the root of any of our problems. Coming together as part of a backlash, conservative foundations seek to bring about a return to a mythic past by channeling their millions into the political battle at the highest levels, subsidizing free-market economics departments and magazines. . . . Then there are the think tanks, the Institutes Hoover and American Enterprise, that send money sluicing on into the pockets of the right-wing pundit corps . . . furnishing them with what they need to keep their books coming and their minds in fighting trim between media bouts. A brigade of lobbyists. A flock of magazines and newspapers. A publishing house or two. And, at the bottom, the committed grass roots organizers . . . going door-to-door organizing their neighbors, mortgaging their houses even, to push the gospel of the backlash. (Frank 2004, 207)

Progressive organizing is necessary to respond to the conservative backlash that seriously threatens the progress of the previous generations.

Shared Characteristics of a Variety of Approaches to Progressive Organizing

Many paths can be followed to bring about progressive social change. *Traditional neighborhood organizing* brings together people to battle problems within a geographic area—deteriorating housing, crime, decaying roads, the lack of public transportation. Others organize for *economic betterment*—to increase the minimum wage, obtain health care, battle sweat shops, combat homelessness, or lessen the harm of globalization—often in alliances with organized labor. With *identity organizing*, also known as *new social movements*, people come together to demand respect and human rights for those who share a common, personal characteristic—being a woman, being gay, having a common ethnic background, being elderly, or being labeled as disabled. With *issue organizing*, people, irrespective of where they live or who they are, join together in response to a shared concern—child abuse, environmental deterioration, homelessness, third world poverty, or the pervasive threat of war, among many other persisting problems. *Faith-based organizations* bring people together who are already united within their churches, synagogues, mosques, and other places of worship. In contrast, some sectarian groups feel that organizing should be based on issues because faiths often divide on fundamental beliefs such as the role of women, or responses to the gay and transgendered movement.

Tactics vary. Many activists totally distrust elected officials, bureaucrats, and owners and managers of large businesses and will sup with them only with a very long spoon; meanwhile others feel it's fine to partner with government and businesses, and readily accept funds from large banks. For some, lobbying public officials is the way to go, while others favor rallies and demonstrations or even more raucous actions to force the issues. **Direct action** organizations favor "in-your-face" confrontations with the power structure while **economic and social development organizations** solve problems by building homes, providing job training, or community social services.

Our belief is that the problems are so immense and the solutions so uncertain that no one approach provides all the answers but rather the progressive movement should selectively blend and apply a variety of approaches. Blockade Wall Street if that is needed to call attention to economic callousness; but also help people form their own businesses to escape from poverty. Set up a tent in the central park to demonstrate the plight of the homeless; but put on a suit and tie and negotiate with bankers for the funds to build affordable housing.

We feel that all progressive approaches to organizing and development, from the most radical to the most accommodative, share the following seven characteristics.

Organizing and Development Are about Recognizing and Solving Problems

Organizing and development are about solving the problems, not causing disruption for its own sake, or enhancing egos. Some problems are visible and obvious: inadequate neighborhood services, gaps in health care, racist or sexist structures, buildings that are inaccessible to the less physically abled. Others are less immediately visible, such as the slow decline in the standard of living as businesses ratchet down workers' wages.

To motivate organizing, a problem must not be seen as stemming from something that cannot be changed. The subservience of women to men or blacks to whites is not ordained but upheld by unjust cultural rules (and laws) that have been altered. Recognizing that change is possible is core to organizing work.

To come together people must understand that others too face the same problem. For years, wheelchair-bound individuals were kept in isolation from one another and felt they were each alone with their problem. Organizing requires moving from the "I- suffer-or-I- have-a-problem perspective" to understanding that problems are shared and stem from societal neglect. Seen personally, a worker in a low-income job lacks the income for clean and safe housing. Seen socially, the problem is that wages are too low and federal money is spent for arms rather than for affordable housing. Diseases are most decidedly personal, but can be socially caused when government allows industries to contaminate the environment with carcinogens.

Through Organizing Efforts Both People and Communities Are Empowered

As we describe in detail in Chapter 4,

> Empowerment is a psychological feeling that individuals have when they feel they can accomplish chosen goals; it is also political or organizational strength that enables people to collectively carry out their will. Empowerment occurs when ordinary people discover that they have the capacity to solve the problems they face, control the means to do so, and have final, authoritative say in decision making. (Perkins 1995)

Further

> Empowered individuals are willing to and able to assert their collective wills, even when faced with the opposition from the established political or economic structure. (Jennings 1990)

Empowerment is both a means through which organizing is accomplished and a core goal of organizing and comes about by orchestrating battles to enable ordinary people to obtain power as—the " 'have-nots' battle the 'haves' " (Alinsky 1969): Power is the ability to affect decisions that shape social outcomes.

For the haves, power comes from owning businesses and property, from occupying key political positions, from controlling public and private police forces, and by convincing the broader society that they have a legitimate right to make decisions for others. When ordinary people begin a contest to obtain power, they lack wealth, rarely control force, and must contend with widespread cultural beliefs that business or government is automatically right. Battles occur over

- *How a problem is defined or framed.* Are people blamed for being poor because of their unwillingness to work or is there an understanding that poverty comes about when firms maximize their profits no matter the consequences?
- *How are decisions made?* Should decisions be made by politicians beholden to big businesses, big businesses on their own, or should a more democratic system prevail?
- *Who has the capacity to carry out the decisions that are made?* Should government or businesses do things for or to people, or should people themselves implement the decisions that they have made together?
- *Who benefits from a solution?* Do only a selected few benefit or does the broader public? Are some people considered to be deserving of benefits and others not?
- *How are societal resources allocated?* Should the rich continue to get richer or can a more just system for allocating resources be worked out?

People obtain power step by step—first by discovering that problems are shared, next by building action organizations, and then seeking to bring about a change. Small victories encourage larger efforts, as people master needed skills and enthusiasm and confidence increases. Empowerment *bootstraps* as people enhance their sense of self and their own abilities and understand that together they have the capacity to bring about changes. These efforts create a political understanding as

> ordinary people construct a broader analysis of politics; they shift from a non-ideological stance to an ideological stance, from defining themselves as non-political to defining themselves as political, from having a deep faith in the established political system to developing a critical political analysis. This critical perspective . . . creates the potential for grass-roots activists to play a more active and militant role. (Krauss 1988, 259)

Successful Organizing Expands upon Interpersonal Relations to Build Community

Organizing both builds upon and strengthens interpersonal relationships through building community. When people come together in an identifiable way a community emerges, sometimes of those who live near one another, and other times of those who share a background characteristic of ethnicity, gender or sexuality, or religious faith.

Some communities are of those who face a common concern—a fear that the environment is being despoiled or a need for affordable daycare—or of people who suffer from a particular disease.

Within communities people learn that they share problems. Women discover that other women also have been steered away from good jobs. In chatting with those on the block, neighbors discover that black, white, Hispanic, Asian, gay, and straight all suffer when the city fails to repair the streets or shut down a crack house. As people identify with a community and are willing to work for the shared cause, power expands.

Feeling part of a community enables people to battle the imposed myth of "rugged individualism," that encourages selfishness. This myth of rugged individualism deceptively suggests that an individual is truly free only if he or she is independent of others. This myth convinces people that it is wrong to join together to fight back. Being unwilling to fight back, they are disempowered, as is shown in some workers' response to forced unemployment:

> Although they do not necessarily feel that their joblessness is their own fault, they retain other individualistic reactions. For example, they feel that going out to look for work for themselves is more effective than group political activity in their own behalf and that of their jobless colleagues. Being particularly vulnerable to feelings of worthlessness and depression, the unemployed feel an unusually strong need to be self-reliant. (Gans 1988, 78)

But such individualistic action does little to battle underlying causes.

Personal Concerns Are Balanced with Collective Needs

Successful organizing balances the personal motivations of why people become active with collective concerns. Feminists expressed the understanding that what initially seems individual often stems from problems with political or economic structures with the phrase *the personal is the political*. Paulo Freire (1980) termed discovering the structural basis of problems as *conscientization*, while C. W. Mills (1959) created the label *sociological imagination* to describe when people recognize that their personal problems reflect pervasive economic or cultural forces.

Only rarely will individuals join a movement because of concern about some potential harm to the collectivity (although there are important exceptions in civil liberties and environmental movements). People join because of a *self-interest* and then discover that self-interest need not preclude working with and helping others. An individual's home might be deteriorating because loan money for repair is not available and then discover by working with others that banks are systematically discriminating against their neighborhood.

Self-interest is different from selfishness. Selfishness is about asking where is mine and damn the others. Self-interest reflects the understanding that few individuals, other than saints and driven ideologues, work only for others. Instead, people initially struggle for their own concerns, but learn through participation in social activism that their problems are shared and that a common solution must be found. *Organizing is about turning self-interest into collective concern.*

Community Empowerment Comes about by Building Organizations and Activist Networks

Successful organizing leaves in place an ongoing structure of formal organizations and activist networks. Social change organizations range from small groups of neighbors helping each other on up to national organizations pressing to change federal laws. They can take a wide variety of forms—from an affinity group set up for mutual support among a handful, to fully incorporated, economic and social production organizations that seem very much like capitalist businesses. Formal organizations have names and are located in a given place: the South Side Neighborhood Organization, ACORN, West Side Community Development Corporation, the National Community Reinvestment Coalition, the Logan Square Neighborhood Association, Kensington Welfare Rights Organization.

Organizations coordinate the actions of numbers of people, employ staff that provides expertise, focus their full attention on an issue and follow it over time. Social change organizations strongly communicate to those in positions of political and economic power that organized people are here, and we care about the matter and plan to persevere until progress is made. In addition, organized power is seen in ongoing *networks* that link individual activists together—both those concerned about a specific issue, and then (through overlapping membership in separate networks) people more generally concerned with progressive change.

Actions Reflect Progressive Social Values and Promote Democratic Empowerment

In organizing and development the means for achieving change must be consistent with progressive values. Using violence or underhanded politics might resolve a problem but be entirely inconsistent with bringing about democratic change. The process of solving problems and empowering people and communities—the means—should anticipate and reflect—*preconfigure*—the ends desired. Help from benevolent, progressive politicians is appreciated; but if solutions are simply provided from above, empowerment does not occur. Advantaging one racial or ethnic group at a cost to another is not a progressive solution, even if by so doing serious problems are overcome for one group. Social change organizations focus power to accomplish a shared, progressive agenda, not to enhance the ego of their leaders, or worse yet to try to dominate others the way oppressed people have been dominated in the past. As feminist organizers emphasize, this power is about accomplishing a shared goal, not the power to dominate others.

Progressive organizing brings about a more democratic society. As Saul Alinsky, one of the icons in community organizing, stated:

> Every conceivable effort must be made to rekindle the fire of democracy. . . . A people can participate only if they have both the opportunity to formulate their program, which is the reason for participation, and a medium through which they can express and achieve their program. . . . The universal premise of any people's program is "We the people will work out our own destiny." . . . Can there be a more fundamental democratic program than a democratically minded and participating people? (Alinsky 1969, 196–197)

Democracy involves the informed participation of a large number of people in making and carrying out decisions that affect them and doing so through a fair and transparent decision-making process.

In working to bring about a better society, social change organizations themselves must carry out their actions democratically. At the very least, decision making should be done in ways that strongly encourage all those affected to participate, perhaps through a vote. In organizations in which people know one another and have developed respect for each other, democracy is present when they talk through issues and plans extensively and build toward a consensus that both respects and accounts for the opinions of others (Mansbridge 1980).

Building democracy and acting democratically becomes both a means and a goal of progressive social change. Democracy, though, is quite fragile and what destroys democracy most easily is lack of use. If people feel alienated and powerless—and thereby do not use the democratic rights they have—democracy dies. People who do not believe they can exercise power will not fight against infringements of their rights or the rights of others.

But democratically determining what is of value is far from simple and requires taking time to *reflect upon* what the goals should be and why these ends are valued:

> What constitutes economic justice? For example, does economic justice require equality of income? of opportunity? of assuring that all can obtain a minimum standard of living and if so what is this standard?

> What constitutes social justice? How far do such rights extend? For instance, is the goal ending persecution of gays or does social justice require gay marriages?

> How are civil liberties obtained? What if the rights required by one group by their very nature infringe upon those required by another?

> To what extent can the environment be fully protected? The larger the human population the more severe the environmental impact. Does environmental protection require extreme programs of population control?

None of the answers to these, and many similar ones, are easy. In organizing, time must be set aside to allow reflection so activists can ask themselves why we have taken certain steps, what is it we are trying to bring about, and if the goals are truly worthwhile.

Successful Social Action Requires Understanding the Broader Economic Cultural and Political System

Social action is stimulated by immediate needs, but the strategies followed are shaped by the larger economic, political, and cultural factors. Through local campaigns, activists work to eliminate a drug house or battle the glass ceiling that limits opportunity for women. But how problems are solved depends on understanding why some people have little choice but to turn to selling drugs, or in grasping the broader cultural values and economic structures that sustain gender inequality in spite of the palpable harm it does. Why does the political system allow the massive inequality in income and in life opportunities to be maintained? Organizing is often done to combat racism, sexism, and homophobia, but campaigns need to be based on understanding why it is culturally acceptable, at least in some circles, to perpetuate these injustices and learning who benefits by doing so.

Systemic forces—the globalization of industry, the aging of our society—affect local actions. A battle to keep jobs at a nearby plant might come about because of decisions made by the World Trade Organization. In multicultural neighborhoods, local alliances change depending upon federal immigration policies. Environmental disputes over American forests are influenced by decisions of capitalists in foreign countries whose companies demand raw materials. Activists need not be experts in geopolitics, macroeconomics, and goodness knows what other abstruse field, but they do have to understand that local actions are embedded within broader economic, social, and political fields.

In addition, how problems are understood and what actions are considered proper depend upon the ideas, understandings, and perspectives—the **framings**— through which people perceive the world. Do people consider problems as personally or socially caused? Are government social programs labelled as charity, capitulation to special needs, or as part of a larger battle for economic justice? Do people consider protests a legitimate way of calling attention to grievances or are they the caterwauling of a few malcontents?

Conclusions

Organizing begins with the belief that change is possible, necessary, and through collective efforts can be brought about. Organizers help create the sense that change is possible, work to show the way, and in doing so help move the world as it is to one that it should be (Chambers, 2003). To do so a variety of complementary approaches are followed, including **social mobilization approaches** (rallies, demonstrations, and protests) as well as **social production approaches** (providing services, building homes, and creating jobs).

While organizing efforts are often stimulated by the here and now, solutions must respond to the broader economic, cultural, and political environments. Helping individuals one by one is commendable and an important first step, but over the long run will accomplish little unless the broader structures of social and economic inequality are addressed. The way to fight for workers' rights differs when conservative Republicans are in office than when labor-leaning Democrats are in charge.

Solving problems is crucial but the means by which they are solved is also important. Progressive organizing is motivated by the vision of a more equal, democratic, and empowered society but how you get there is as important as where you end up. Progressive action must enhance democracy, show respect for people, and their opinions, and encourage the diversity within our society, and as such should anticipate—preconfigure—the society activists hope to bring about.

In social change work, practical advice learned from experience is reinforced by academic knowledge. Experience teaches what works and what does not, while academic knowledge helps in understanding the broader principle of how society is structured. *Community Organizing and Development* tries to combine both academic knowledge and experience to help future activists and social change professionals better understand their praxis.

CHAPTER

2

A World of Action:
A World of Hope

Social activism comes about as people discover that they share the same problems and learn that by joining together they can make what is wrong right. Doing so requires the capacity—the set of knowledge, skills, and an organizational base that are the tools for implementing change. But more than tools are required; action will not occur unless people have the hope that their efforts will pay off.

Sustaining hope in the current conservative, roll-back-the-clock-on-change environment can be challenging. The national government is systematically destroying social programs and pushing for policies that benefit the rich. Globalization of industry and finance strengthens those who control capital while lessening the power of working people. Affordable housing is hard to find, health care costs escalate, while old age becomes a time of insecurity rather than of pleasant leisure. Developers in cahoots with city officials displace the inner city poor to make room for upscale gentrified housing. Under the pretense of protecting people from terrorists, officials reduce civil liberties. Discrimination persists as women slam up against glass ceilings at work, people of color end up paying higher interest rates than do others, while homophobic prejudices plague the gay community. The conservative media shouts out that the poor and downtrodden are to blame for their own ills while suggesting that government programs encourage rather than cure problems.

Yet, hope must be maintained as apathy and acceptance are the weapons of those in power. Activists build on the belief that change is possible as César Chavez, a successful organizer of migrant farm workers, proclaimed "Si se Puede" [Yes, it can be done] (Castillo and Garcia 1995, xiv). This belief is reinforced by the knowledge that in the past and continuing on today, social change efforts have succeeded.

An Activist's Tour of the World of Social Change: Activities and Accomplishments

Activists are not fools—they recognize that multibillion dollar corporations have incredible clout; that paid lobbyists in pinstriped suits have easier access to government than do working men and women; and that those in power play upon racial, gendered, and, at times, sexual fears to distract from struggles for economic and social justice. But activists are also congenital optimists believing that struggle will pay off, whether seen in the large marches to preserve women's freedom of choice or involving hundreds of thousands of women and men to quieter changes that take place when a community development corporation rebuilds a neighborhood house by house. Hope is reinforced as historic and present-day successes are shared through **narratives of the possible**, oft repeated stories of what has been and is still being done.

Most prominent are the public demonstrations, the flamboyant protests through which people call attention to their cause: In Seattle a few years ago, a coalition of environmentalists, workers' rights people, labor unionists, and for better or worse, anarchists, came together and shut down the city to show the harms from globalization; or in May 2004, hundreds of thousands, perhaps almost a million, women and men gathered on the Mall in Washington, D.C., to proclaim their belief that women have a right to control their own bodies. This orderly demonstration was covered on the national press and television, reasserting support for the gains of a generation ago.

Some narratives of success are seen in smaller events that focus a spotlight on persisting problems. For instance,

> After two years of unsuccessful fighting to get the legal marriage age in Utah changed from fourteen to sixteen in order to deal with the problem of girls being married off to adult men as polygamous wives, [Justice, Economic Dignity, and Independence for Women] . . . staged a marriage ceremony between a very old man and twelve-year-old girls in the state capital rotunda. . . . The girls wore frilly white wedding gowns at least one size too large and stuffed with pregnancy pillows to play up their childishness, and the old man in a tuxedo could have passed for the oldest man in the West. . . . The law was changed within a week. (Sen 2003, 88–89)

Actions differ in militancy and drama: Clergy, community activists, and community members solemnly carry candles and bow down in respectful prayer as they picket parks overrun by drug dealers, trying to shame the police to enforce narcotics laws; in contrast, marchers in an anti–Ku Klux Klan demonstration carry a vulgar poster reading "Narrow minded fucking Nazis, stick your hoods up in your asses" (Crespo 2002, 143). To call attention to the AIDS epidemic, ACT UP brought together in a march business suited gay men, drag queens in full regalia, and the Lesbian Avengers, women who strode bare breasted. In May of 2006, organizations of immigrants put together massive demonstrations to protest anti-immigrant legislation. Estimates were that well over a million were involved with hundreds of thousands marching in Los Angeles and Chicago. Orchestrating this effort required coordination among hundreds of small, grassroots organizations.

Street theater makes matters visible: Activists dressed as hungry sharks chasing poor families perform outside of a bank that buys predatory loans; coffins are placed in public squares to represent those who have died in wars; the Mall in Washington, D.C., was once filled by a giant quilt commemorating victims of AIDS. To coincide with the Boston Marathon, transportation calculated how long it took low-income people to commute to work by bus in contrast to the speedier transit serving the wealthier neighborhoods. Then, wearing transit equity t-shirts, they showed up on marathon day to present the results to the state officials (www.ace-ej.org/tru/busmarathon).

Some demonstrations are intentionally disruptive. For instance, activists including the "black bloc" of anarchists

> moved into the streets to disrupt the movement of buses to the Republican National Convention. Traffic was snarled. Groups of people dressed as goats, clowns, and billionaires surrounded delegates. Police cars were attacked, and hundreds were arrested and many beaten. (Wood and Moore 2002, 30)

Often actions publicize a problem and at the same time point out a solution. For instance, the Gray Panthers in Denver where

> Many elderly senior center participants, especially those with disabilities, had been unable to get from their bus stop to the senior center . . . before the light changed. The Panthers organized a demonstration in which some three hundred seniors, many of them with canes and wheelchairs, all attempted to cross with the light at the same time. The ensuing traffic tie-up effectively made its point, and the officials reversed themselves by giving into the Panthers' original demand. (Staples 2005, 183)

Publicity is used to remind people that problems persist even though others claimed they have been solved. To show that racism was still around in New Orleans, the Greater New Orleans Fair Housing Action Center sent matched pairs of white and African American males into Bourbon Street bars and discovered that the bars were more likely to charge African American customers more for a drink (Foster 2005).

Activist organizations provide people with immediate assistance. After Hurricane Katrina, activists—especially from organizations such as PICO and ACORN—were on the scene, organizing displaced people to demand a return to their homes, and making sure they were not deprived of vital services while living displaced. Social change organizations help protect the poor and elderly from economic fraud. With refund anticipation loans, unscrupulous tax preparation firms provide their clients with an immediate loan based on the expected tax refund, but charge a usuriously high fee for doing so. ACORN has led demonstrations against this practice in sixty cities while itself offering low-cost tax preparation services (ACORN 2005, February).

The narrative of the possible is seen in more subdued ways. In poorer areas in cities, large colorful murals are painted on retaining walls, in underpasses, and on sides of larger buildings, replacing what had been graffiti with vivid scenes of community triumphs—a portrait of a park reclaimed from drug dealers, or images of cultural pride—a local leader rallying workers to fight against sweatshop labor. Often these murals are painted by neighborhood teenagers guided by local artists moving energy from mischief into constructive assertions of cultural pride. Numerous community economic and social development organizations build homes and work to provide jobs in poor neighborhoods, having built well over half a million affordable housing units. In San Francisco architects worked with community groups to design modernistic apartment buildings to house the homeless. Economic production organizations have set up supermarkets in neighborhoods lacking quality stores, and run job training programs that move the unemployed into jobs. Throughout the country, both community groups and social service agencies facilitate microenterprises, small businesses that help people escape from poverty (Sherraden, Sanders, and Sherraden 2004).

Activists battle megacorporations such as Wal-Mart to keep them from displacing established local businesses, sometimes by lobbying city councils not to provide special benefits, or, more recently in Chicago, pressing the city council to adopt a policy mandating that big box stores pay living wages. At times, this work is done through political pressure but other times raucous actions occur when, for instance, Ruckus, a national activist group, set up a quarantine line around where Wal-Mart officials were meeting while shouting through a bull horn, "Would all Wal-Mart Managers please proceed to the decontamination station . . . so you can be served with a notice of quarantine and be brought in line with ethical business practices . . . " (e-mail list from Ruckus Society).

Social change groups partner with government. Working with the police, community members form Neighborhood Watches to rid their area of gangs and drugs. But poor neighborhoods are also where an increasing number of ex-offenders end up, without jobs, lacking training, and finding society unwilling to offer them a helping hand. In response, the community organizations help these individuals find housing and work to provide them with job training (Scally 2005). In Chicago, community groups worked with the transit authority to refurbish a train station into a multi-use community building adjacent to newly constructed affordable housing. Activist social workers in San Francisco helped poor individuals living in single-room occupancy buildings set up tenants associations that enabled them to manage the properties (Minkler 2005, 280).

Activist groups combine lobbying actions with background research to pressure government. For example,

> In Cleveland, Environmental Health Watch, an environmental policy nonprofit [group] and Cleveland Tenants Organization began working closely together four years ago because of a growing awareness about lead poisoning and other health consequences of substandard housing. Together they visited more than 250 homes . . . documenting lead and asthma-related environmental health hazards . . . through this work, these organizations won a new municipal ordinance that addressed lead paint dangers and strengthened their policy advocacy concerning housing measures to reduce asthma. (Scott 2005, 21)

Separate tactics are relied upon to battle the same problem. In Washington, D.C., professional activists working for environmental organizations present detailed, statistical scientific studies to the Environmental Protection Agency on the dangers of dioxin; while in a more dramatic and personal presentation on the harms of dioxin, women from the Seattle Lesbian Avengers march bare breasted with a magic marker sign written on their chests that says "No dioxins in my cunt" (Crespo 2002, 173).

Actions are often about preserving gains of the past. In the late 1970s, activists pressured the federal government to pass the Community Reinvestment Act (CRA) that requires banks to reinvest in poor communities. But over the years bank regulators have been less willing to strongly enforce the rules. In response, activists have set up national coalitions with local organizations monitoring what banks do in the home towns, while national advocacy coalitions with staffs of lawyers, urban policy experts, and other technicians monitor the Washington scene and rally people to battle when regulations are being weakened.

Local and national efforts are combined. In Kansas, where immigrants staff many factories, yet lack access to public service, community groups demonstrated, demanding that both immigrants and their children have rights to education, drivers' licenses, and fair treatment at work (Muhammad 2005). Meanwhile national organizations such as the National Council for La Raza or the Center for Community Change work at the federal level to push for laws that treat immigrants in an equitable manner.

Organizing efforts take place electronically. Demonstrations are announced and posted on protest.net (www.protest.net) while organizations notify members by e-mail on what actions to take or provide automated systems for writing letters to those in office. During a four-hour period we received three electronic announcements of actions to take—one to support housing access in Illinois, another for rights for retirees, and the third a request to sign a letter to oppose federal legislation that would weaken protections against predatory lending. In Illinois a state coalition of housing organizations had been pushing for legislation that would forbid landlords from rejecting tenants based on the tenants' source of income. Real estate interests opposed and the battle was close. When on the last day the vote came down to a handful of legislators, housing activist organizations electronically contacted their members in the swing-vote districts to call up their legislators to encourage them to vote the right way.

Legal actions, legislative lobbying, pressures at the ballot box are increasingly part of the repertoire of social change work. For instance, when the public transit service in Los Angeles favored an expensive Metro Rail that served wealthier people yet neglected the bus system that served the poorer, minority areas of Los Angeles County, the Labor/Community Strategy Center and the Bus Riders Union sued in court and

> forced the [transit board] to sit down with the BRU and negotiate. What emerged was a consent decree that ordered the [transit board] to stop discriminating against its bus riders and to correct the bus-rail service disparities it knowingly created. (Mann 2004, 46)

State, national, and local organizations hold lobby days in which their members appear en masse on Capitol Hill in Washington, D.C., or at state capitols. To strengthen their political clout, dozens of community organizations in the summer and fall of 2004 joined together in a GOTV (Get Out the Vote) campaign, seeking to register those from poor communities, minority neighborhoods, and even the homeless. In 2004 in precincts targeted for GOTV efforts voter participation increased 7 percent in comparison to precincts in which community organizations were not working (Center for Community Change 2004).

Faith-based activist organizations such as PICO work with local affiliates to pressure government to redirect programs to those in need:

> Peninsula Interfaith Action won support from the Mayor of East Palo Alto for a redevelopment project that would create a new supermarket, affordable housing and a pre-employment training center on vacant land. In March 150 people gathered for a prayer service to build support for the project. PIA . . . held a clergy led prayer service and action in front of city hall and across the street from a four-acre vacant lot where res-

idents envision getting a supermarket built along with affordable housing and a pre-employment training center built for their community. The current landowner wants to sell the land to the highest bidder, but PIA has called upon the city to use its redevelopment money and powers to make this vacant parcel serve community needs. The Mayor attended the prayer circle and agreed to work with the clergy. (PICO Network News, April 20, 2005)

Through lobbying, combined with public demonstrations, activists work to expand housing programs. For instance, in many areas housing trust funds are in place that provide a dedicated source of money for deep subsidies for affordable homes. To set up these funds requires campaigns that combine providing factual information on housing needs with political pressure on those who can establish such funds and have been successful in hundreds of places. In another effort to support housing in Chicago, advocates both demonstrated at city hall and lobbied individual aldermen for more affordable housing and

> Before the end of the campaign, more than 250 community organizations, churches, synagogues, community centers, issue organizations, and other groups had endorsed the Affordable Housing bill. Most contacted local aldermen asking for support .... Some turned out large numbers of community residents at crucial moments. (Hertz n.d., 37)

The city with the Mayor's full support passed a bill providing hundreds of millions of dollars for affordable housing.

In Los Angeles, a large coalition of organizations coordinated by the Southern California Association of Nonprofit Housing brought together housing advocates and labor and religious groups to form Housing L.A., which after a three-year campaign won a hundred million dollar housing trust fund. The activists lobbied those in office, garnered support from candidates, and used direct action techniques.

> Housing LA organized weekly lobbying visits to City Hall. . . . ACORN sponsored a march and rally with 400 tenants. During the holidays, when Housing LA knew the Mayor's proposal was forthcoming, the campaign picked up the pace. . . . Housing LA celebrated a "Home for the Holidays" event on the steps of City Hall, with a symbolic building of a house that represented the jobs created by housing production. The major speakers were the building trades and service union representatives. ("Three-Year Housing LA Campaign Culminates in Largest City Housing Trust Fund" 2002, 3)

Through persistent campaigning, community groups gain a place at the table. In Boston, the Dudley Street Neighborhood Initiative, an organization that orchestrates both direct action and community renewal programs, has a powerful say on any renewal tasks the city proposes for its neighborhood (Medoff and Sklar 1994). The Texas IAF is involved in numerous issues from schooling to job training to building communities in multicultural neighborhoods and is consulted by city governments when public programs impact the neighborhoods in which this multiracial, multicity community organization is involved (Warren 2001). In rural areas, community development organizations such as Coastal Enterprises Incorporated in northern New England, or Impact Seven in Wisconsin, provide expertise in job training and business development efforts that rural government lacks.

Some local activist organizations concentrate on school improvement programs; while on a national level, education activists examine the consequences of President Bush's No Child Left Behind program. In Miami, a local community group joined forces with environmental organizations to fight the heavy metal pollution that impacted schools. In Philadelphia a student-controlled organization fought to ensure that inner city schools receive adequate supplies, while in Sacramento community groups pressured the school board to set up a teacher home visit program to battle high dropout rates and poor attendance (Center for Community Change 2005). In Texas, the Texas Industrial Areas Foundation formed an ongoing statewide alliance to reform education, especially in Spanish-speaking areas (Shirley 2002) while in Chicago, community members sit on local school councils that can hire and fire school principals (Fung 2004).

Throughout the nation sustained campaigns to increase economic justice are seen, often involving coalitions between community groups and labor. In Hartford, labor works hand-in-hand with neighborhood groups to battle job losses (Simmons 1994), while in New York community groups and labor have organized green grocery workers (Ness 1998). Immigrants' rights groups work in partnership with progressive unions to organize immigrant laborers in their fight against unpaid wages, nonpaid overtime, and intolerable working conditions while asking why laborers receive such a small proportion of the price of the clothing in their wages (Louie 2001, 249).

National organizations carry on the fight. The Center for Community Change coordinates the battles to stop congress from further lowering support for the core welfare program, Temporary Assistance for Needy Families (TANF). In publicizing the Housing Wage—the amount of money a person has to earn to afford a modest two-bedroom apartment (a wage that in 2004 averaged $15.37 per hour; www.nlihc.org)—the National Low Income Housing Coalition documents the extent of the housing crisis.

Activists battle for a "living wage"—income sufficient to be above the poverty level—with campaigns having been carried out successfully in 123 cities, counties, and among other public entities (www.livingwagecampaign.org/). With success in hand, coalitions expand efforts to broader concerns for economic justice. For instance, in Los Angeles, an interfaith network pushed for the living wage. After its passage,

> Clergy and Laity United for Economic Justice (CLUE) continues to mobilize strong religious support behind ongoing worker struggles. For example [downtown hotels] balked at an agreement with the unions to gradually raise housekeepers' wages . . . while workers staged temporary walkouts, CLUE dispatched small teams in full ministerial garb to deliver brief sermons on workplace fairness while ordering coffee at several hotel dining rooms. On April 8, 1998, an interfaith procession of sixty ministers, priests and rabbis marched through Beverly Hills. They deposited bitter herbs outside of the Summit Hotel, which still had not signed the [union] agreement and

offered milk and honey to the two that had. Two months later, the Summit signed. (Reynolds 2002, 161–162)

Campaigns have changed state minimum wage laws. For example, in 2004 even though Florida supported the Republican ticket, ACORN was able to gain 72 percent voter support for a referendum to raise the state minimum wage that the activist group had gotten on the ballot (Atlas 2005).

In many locales, economic predators convince people, often older, widowed ladies, to take out a mortgage at outrageous rates. To battle this practice, housing organizations join with advocacy groups to picket the economic predators, while at the same time setting up statewide coalitions to lobby legislators to make such practice illegal. In a similar way battles are joined to end high-cost payday loans. To call attention to such problems, detailed statistical analyses are prepared and submitted to regulatory staff, while other activists work to make the issues quite public. In California,

> community groups . . . follow a money trail of oversized dollar bill footprints leading from the Wells Fargo Bank . . . a nearby Money Mart. There, a giant check for $55 million will be presented—the amount that Wells Fargo funds Money Mart to make 460% interest rate loans. . . . [meanwhile]
>
> The California Reinvestment Coalition released a new study in March titled The Financial Divide: An Uneven Playing Field. This study exposes how bank financing has supported the growth of high-priced payday lenders in California. Wells Fargo is one of the chief culprits. (California Reinvestment Coalition, and Community Reinvestment Coalition of North Carolina 2005)

Grasping What Has Been Seen: Building toward an Infrastructure for Social Change

After this whirlwind tour, let us step back and examine what it means. The first impression is of the tremendous variety and scope of collective actions, varying from the quite personal issues—of fair wages—to global matters of war and peace. Some issues require immediate action, for instance, a lockout of immigrant workers from a sweatshop. Others reflect ongoing social schisms based on gender, sexuality, or ethnicity that have lasted over the centuries. Some organizations form to fight for very focused concerns—a tenants' union, for instance, working to keep rents reasonable in one city; other organizations fighting for broad principles, such as the work of the Southern Poverty Law Center to protect minorities from racist actions or the efforts of the American Civil Liberties Union to defend free speech.

Many of the issues reflect underlying structural inequalities. Whether an organization is fighting for a better school in a poor minority community, or a living wage, or to end sweatshop labor, or to end predatory lending, the battle comes about because of persisting economic inequalities. Efforts to achieve gender equality or to stop homophobic prejudices are necessary because of a long tradition of conservative hegemony that sustains inappropriate hierarchies while denigrating nonmainstream groups. The narratives point out the complicated political structure that shapes how organizing occurs with most issues being concurrently fought on local, state, and national levels. Local venues might work to assure equal rights, for example, for gay couples, while at the state level arguments occur on whether such rights are protected by the state constitution. Meanwhile conservatives at the federal level push for a constitutional amendment that would undo any gains made elsewhere. To handle this multitiered battle, local organizations unite in state and national coalitions.

We have also seen a wide variety of complementary approaches. Some organizations work for **social equity** by pressuring government agencies and businesses to provide benefits to their members and constituents. For instance, in the past, organizations of the aged such as the Gray Panthers gained economic benefits for the elderly while nowadays activists in Janitors for Justice work to secure fair wages and terms of employment to workers (many immigrants) in the service industry. Other organizations work to bring about **social justice**, concentrating on civil liberties, civil rights, and the protection of the environment, struggling to reduce discrimination against gays and lesbians or to protect the civil rights of minorities and women.

Some activists focus on the **economic and social** needs of individuals and communities. Support organizations help people with cancer or heart disease or those who are victims of spouse or alcohol abuse. Some economic and social production groups work to restore neighborhoods through encouraging business growth or teaching the underemployed how to form businesses.

Another approach is about encouraging people to **identify with others in their community**, develop a collective pride, and then work together on shared concerns. Identity organizations might battle discrimination against Native Americans or Asian Americans while gay activist organizations help their members recognize that being homosexual or lesbian is not a stigma. Organizations that differ widely on the tactics they use, such as the confrontational Voces Unidas or Southwest Industrial Foundation and the business-oriented Texas Association of Mexican-American Chambers of Commerce (Márquez 2003), all speak up for the rights of the ethnic groups they serve. Finally, many organizations work within defined **geographic areas**, battling here and now problems facing a physical community, perhaps battling crime or the neglect of landlords or working to restore a commercial strip.

The tour makes apparent that social change organizations rely on a wide variety of tactics. These tactics vary from **direct actions** in which people join together to embarrass and compel those in power to respond to community needs, to **economic and social production** approaches which build upon capitalistic tools in ways that benefit those in need. Both direct action and social production activities are about accomplishing the same end of social betterment, though following different means.

An Infrastructure for Collective Action and Social Change

As our tour indicates, an **infrastructure for collective action and social change** is now in place and provides a strong foundation for progressive organizing and development work. The term *infrastructure* can refer to something physical or social that then acts as an underlying foundation for subsequent efforts. For instance, the physical infrastructure of a city includes roads, bridges, electric and gas lines, wiring for the Internet, water supply, and waste processing plants, while the organizational infrastructure is found in the competence of the quality of the educational system.

This infrastructure for collective action consists of the numerous organizations that provide a repository of knowledge and expertise on what to do, an expanding pool of experienced activists, as well as the coalitions, training, and support organizations that help build the capacity for change. In addition, the infrastructure circulates the narrative of success, the symbols that change is possible and, by working together, can be brought about.

People

Trained, informed, dedicated individuals are core to the social infrastructure for social change. In the past social change work has been linked to a handful of well-known figures—Saul Alinsky for neighborhood work, Dr. Martin Luther King, Jr. for civil rights, César Chavez for farm worker organizing, Gordan Means for the American Indian movement, Shel Trapp and Gale Cincotta as supporters of the Community Reinvestment Act, Gloria Steinem as one of many feminist leaders, Maggie Kuhn for the elderly, Mitch Synder for the homeless, and so on down the line. Today this list has dramatically expanded to include thousands, perhaps tens of thousands, of individuals who are paid social change professionals, as well as hundreds of thousands who are unpaid volunteer activists.

Direct action organizations employ thousands of full-time professionals. ACORN alone has hundreds of *organizers*, staffing over 85 offices, and a survey found that just the hundred-plus faith-based organizations examined now employ over 450 social change professionals (Warren and Wood 2001). Around 500-plus professional organizers attend the annual gatherings of the National Organizer Alliance, and about the same numbers show up as economic justice fighters at the conferences of the National Community Reinvestment Coalition. National People's Action unites over 300 local groups, each with professional organizers. Numerous others work full time organizing for the environment, for women's rights, to protect speech, to maintain the separation of state and religion, to defend consumers against indifferent companies, and to argue for workers' rights.

But far more individuals are involved in social change work than the direct action organizers. No aggregate numbers are available, but we suspect those involved in progressive economic and social development work far exceeds the number guiding direct action. Thousands of developmental activists lead the estimated 4,500 community-based development organizations, while like numbers are involved in community mental health and health services. Elsewhere, individuals involved in community development banks, community legal assistance, consumer credit counseling, or those who maintain shelters for the homeless or for abused or abandoned women, as well as those running community theaters or cultural and art centers are part of the social change infrastructure.

In addition, social change activists work for coalitions, trade associations, technical assistance providers, and training institutions. Some of these individuals prepare data or orchestrate arguments that are presented to regulators and legislators or are shared by computer lists with hundreds of activists throughout the nation. Others do the backup statistical work that enters into the policy debate. Editors of publications—some physical, others electronic—that keep activists informed of what is happening are part of the social change field as are community development trainers, instructors in direct action, and even academics who teach community organizing.

In addition to the thousands of paid professional social change activists, hundreds of thousands of volunteers are mobilized in social change work. For some, mobilization might involve little more than appearing at a meeting, or participating in a demonstration. But for many, mobilization entails a long-term commitment to a cause, through serving on a supervisory board, going door-to-door for that cause, signing petitions, or showing up repeatedly at public meetings.

Social change activists are tightly networked. They meet one another at meetings, demonstrations, conferences, and training sessions, and call each other (or nowadays e-mail). At meetings, or during actions or training sessions, activists share the tricks of the trade and develop new perspectives on old problems. Much networking is informal, Joe meets Mary at a meeting, learns that Mary has organized people to build a shelter for abused women that is linked to job training programs, wants to do the same, and so calls and asks for help, and, more likely than not is invited to visit and learn from Mary's success.

Organizations

Dedicated, knowledgeable people are core to the social change infrastructure. In addition, thousands of social change organizations spearhead direct actions, implement economic and social production projects, or provide social services.

This organizational infrastructure is most visible in hundreds of local organizations. In Boston the Dudley Street Neighborhood Initiative coordinates community planning, direct action, and economic and housing development programs (Medoff and Sklar 1994). In the poorest area of Newark, NJ, New Communities Corporation has built hundreds of apartments; shopping malls; and job training, health care, and assisted living facilities; along with other social and economic services for community residents. Throughout the nation, local chapters affiliated with ACORN conduct campaigns for affordable housing, to bring out the vote, to argue for living wages, for improved schools, and for virtually any issue that affects lower-income people. Years ago, ACORN's Philadelphia chapter started a squatters' campaign to sit in and take over abandoned housing. Today ACORN has a well-established housing affiliate that obtains, refurbishes, and provides homes to those in need. In Texas, local organizations in separate cities are linked together through the Texas IAF and coordinated joint campaigns, such as those working to bring about quality education of minorities (Shirley 2002). In Oakland, California, the multiracial neighborhood group Pueblo pressures city officials not to neglect the needs in the city's poorest neighborhoods (Wood 2002).

Many community organizations are small groups that work only in one neighborhood. But these smaller, local organizations gain strength by being part of broader **action networks**, such as ACORN, IAF, DART, PICO, Gamaliel, Neighborhood People's Action, among others, or as part of **housing and economic development networks,** such as those sponsored by the Enterprise Foundation or the Neighborhood Housing Service. Organizations in a network share a similar philosophy on what tactics to follow, attend common training programs and conferences, and set up webs of affiliations through which activists help one another.

In **coalitions**, organizations that sometimes work on different tasks, or disagree on what tactics to follow, come together temporarily to accomplish a shared purpose. Ethnically based neighborhood organizations, economic justice groups, legal assistance service agencies, direct action organizations, and consumer groups have set up coalitions to battle predatory lending. In Chicago, several dozen neighborhood housing organizations—some providing affordable homes for sale, others renting property to lower income people—formed the Chicago Rehab Network, while Housing Action Illinois unites a variety of groups interested in affordable housing throughout Illinois. In North Carolina, several groups work together in the Community Reinvestment Coalition of North Carolina, dozens of local organizations are part of the California Reinvestment Coalition, while nationally 600 groups, including community bankers, housing developers, numerous advocacy groups, and direct action groups have banded together in the National Community Reinvestment Coalition (NCRC) to defend the Community Reinvestment Act.

On occasion, the separate organizations in a coalition set up a permanent meta-organization, a **coalition support organization**, to coordinate joint activity. For instance, in Washington, D.C., the Consumer Federation of America (a coalition of 300 organizations) maintains a strong D.C. presence. The 600-plus-member NCRC has a staff of several dozen, while Housing Action Illinois's staff of five seeks to coordinate housing activists throughout Illinois. Coalition organizations carry out the shared goals of their members. The National Low Income Housing Coalition, for instance, is "dedicated solely to ending America's affordable housing crisis" (www.nlihc.org). To do so, this coalition support organization itself tracks legislation, shares what is learned with members, and monitors the broader political environment.

The services provided by support coalition organizations are often similar to those offered by **trade associations**. Trade associations are membership organizations that provide technical services, hold conferences, and set up networks between members. National trade associations frequently employ policy advocates and research analysts who gather data on the shared issues and then prepare this data so that members can use it in lobbying regulators and elected officials.

In addition, specialty organizations that provide both information and training are part of the social change infrastructure. In Chicago, the Woodstock Institute analyzes detailed data on bank issues while working to document predatory lending. Nationally, the Center on Budget and Policy Priorities analyzes the impact of the federal budget on programs that affect lower-income people. The Center for Community Change trains activists from extremely poor neighborhoods and produces an array of reports on progressive social and economic programs. These specialty organizations circulate information to national coalitions, networks, and trade associations, while their staff often testify in front of regulatory bodies and legislative committees. In this way, information becomes a tool to support change.

Spreading the Narrative of the Possible

The social change infrastructure is built up of people who care and know what to do as well as the organizations that have the capacity to carry out needed efforts. But technical knowledge and organizational capacity are not enough if people fail to believe that success is possible. Part of what the infrastructure of social change does is convey this possibility.

As both community activists and activist teachers have shown, this sense of the possible is communicated through first-hand narrative accounts (Forrester 1989; Freire 1970; Throgmorton 1996). These narratives shared in publications, at meetings, or in private conversations are down to earth, based on actual experiences, and contain concrete details. At times, narratives are spread in one-on-one encounters, as when an organizer knocks at the door of a community member, listens to the concerns expressed, and then communicates a narrative of the possible. "Yes, I understand how landlords like yours neglect repairs, a mile away, people like yourself got together, formed a tenants' group and marched on the home of the landlord shaming her into fixing up the apartments." When activists and social change professionals meet, they talk shop, sharing with each other what they have done and how an action was made to succeed or an economic development project was brought to fruition. "We scheduled the march on Sunday right after church, since many people from the neighborhood were already together, the pastor supported the issue, and so we had the buses parked outside of the church."

The infrastructure for social change helps diffuse these narratives. Numerous training academies that are set up teach techniques of direct action or ways of carrying out economic and social development projects, and also provide settings at which people share stories of success. Meetings sponsored by networks, coalitions, and trade associations are structured around peer-to-peer learning in which examples of how they succeeded abound. Gatherings held at meetings of the National Organizers Alliance encourage personal exchange; conventions and training sessions involve give and take among those who have accomplished a project and those who are planning similar activities.

Annual meetings of networks, trade associations, and coalitions are often built around a central collective action that then becomes the narrative of success for subsequent years. Conferences of ACORN always hold a direct confrontation with a major figure, usually a Washington-based elite, that is then discussed in newsletters and becomes an icon for later actions. Organizations schedule policy conferences in both state capitols and the national capitol during which people are encouraged (and taught how) to lobby their elected officials. After doing so, they return to a common area, a hotel room, a church facility, or at times, if elected officials are cooperative, a room in the capitol, and share with each other stories of the encounters with elected officials. These stories become part of the narratives of success. Conferences of economic and social production organizations include tours of successful projects that then are discussed as illustrations of what can be done because it already has been done by others.

Numerous newsletters sent out both electronically and by snail-mail detail personal accounts of victories. Every other week ACORN electronically releases a description of half a dozen actions taken by its members; PICO does so monthly. NPA publishes *Disclosure*, a newsletter that provides both news of the networks and illustrations of what separate affiliates have achieved. Economic and social production organizations share their victories in widely distributed magazines and newsletters, again with many being on-line. The Enterprise Foundation and the Center for Community Change prepare reports on social and economic production projects that detail how neighborhood groups brought about changes. A Housing Trust Project might appear to be a complicated undertaking but the possibility of bringing one to fruition is seen in the examples of success described in the *Housing Trust News Letter*. And, for those who have more time, in recent years many leading social change activists have written first-hand descriptions about what they and their organizations have accomplished (Chambers 2003; Gecan 2002; Sen 2003; Stout 1996; Trapp n.d.).

These shared narratives of the possible prevent people from spending needless time reinventing the wheel. More important, narratives of the possible show that change is possible and can be brought about by people no different than yourself.

Conclusion

This chapter shows that a wide array of approaches has been followed to bring about change, which demonstrates the possibility for continuing success. Victories are important but so is having a system for sustaining them and that is what the infrastructure of social change is about.

CHAPTER

3

Models for Implementing Progressive Social Change

Commonalities, Differences, and Reconciliations

In this chapter we systematically examine the variety of approaches taken to bring about social change, first in terms of their overall **goals and purposes** and then contrasting which **empowerment tactics** each approach uses. Next, we examine a series of **social change models** that offer separate paths for achieving social change goals (Hyde 1996; O'Donnell and Karanja 2000; Rothman 2000; Shragge 2003; Smock 2003; Weil and Gamble 2005; 1995). Different approaches are taught as part of a broader **culture of social change** within the separate **institutional networks** that both mobilize people to act while teaching them how to do so and when and why.

Grouping Social Change Actions by Goals and Purposes

The purpose of a specific social change organization can range from keeping a neighborhood clean on up to working for world peace. Table 3-1 organizes this wide variety of goals and purposes classifying them in terms of the **problems** faced and the **scope of solution** sought. Problems simply refer to the matters that engage those in the organization, varying from protecting the neighborhood, speaking up for an ethnic group, and addressing poverty, among many other concerns. But how those in an organization seek to solve a problem, the scope of solution, differs widely from providing quick fixes to pushing for broad changes in the society.

Sometimes the solution sought is just for the **specific** here and now **problem**—to shelter homeless people in the city or to work with individual victims of sexual discrimination. Other organizations feel that problems come about for multiple reasons and want to address these reasons all at once through **sectoral solutions**. For example, activists might want to improve education in a minority community and problems occur because of lack of funding of the schools and family disruptions that make

TABLE 3.1 Goals and Purposes of Social Action Organizations

Problems Faced	Scope of Solutions		
	Resolution of Specific Problems	Sectoral Solutions	Economic, Social, or Political Transformation
Geographic Place (neighborhood, community)	Improving and making safer parks; crime patrols	Community building approaches—physical repair while expanding social institutions	Moving toward collective responsibility and away from rampant individualism; having an empowered community organization in place
Social and Physical Infrastructure (schools, health facilities, housing transportation)	Repairing or building new homes in a community; expanded schools; better access to medical care	National affordable housing programs; single-payer health system with wide geographic spread of health facilities	Integrative social planning, not piecemeal decision making (anti-sprawl; keeping jobs near housing)
Social or Cultural Identity (gender, ethnicity, sexual identification, disabled)	An effective system in a company or a community for adjudicating gender, racial, sexual discrimination	Supportive programs for women, minorities, or the disabled	A world without prejudice in which people are judged on their accomplishments; acceptance of multiculturalism rather than white Christian hegemony
Economics (jobs, employment, economic distribution)	Job training programs; microenterprise development programs	Community economic development programs—coordinated infrastructure repair, job training, business attraction, school-business linkages	Revamped tax, income, and educational structures that promote a more egalitarian distribution of income; end of corporate hegemony; humane capitalism
Human Services (education, health, assisted housing, support services)	An assisted housing project; English as a second language program; community health programs	Immigrant assistance programs—housing, language, job training, family transition	Accepting housing, education, health care, support services as human rights for which the collectivity is responsible
Social Justice/ Human Rights (civil rights, immigrant rights, speech rights)	Enforcing fair housing legislation; defending a whistle blower	Coordinated educational, religious, and civic programs that encourage tolerance	An open and accepting society and end of cultural bullying
Environment (pollution, conservation, open space)	Clearing up a toxic waste dump; preserving wetlands	Regional planning programs that minimize the impact on land through nonsprawled development; mass transit systems	Putting quality of life over short-term economic profits

TABLE 3.1   Continued

Problems Faced	Scope of Solutions		
	Resolution of Specific Problems	**Sectoral Solutions**	**Economic, Social, or Political Transformation**
Conflict Resolution (intergroup, international)	Pressuring to end a particular war; harmony meetings between those from different groups	Community reconciliation boards; ongoing international peace conferences	Reduction in nationalistic sentiments
Political Transformation	Supporting a candidate for office; insisting on a citizen comment time at a city council meeting	Acceptance of social change organizations as having a place at the table; openness in government rules in place and enforced	Changing electoral rules so that money is less important for obtaining office

it harder to study, all compounded by the racism that assigns less-qualified teachers and obsolete books and equipment to schools that minorities attend (Center for Community Change 2005). Actions are needed on all fronts simultaneously.

Some activists feel that trying to solve problems one by one misses the broader picture, as all that is being done is attacking symptoms while ignoring the underlying political, economic, or social structures that enable inequities to persist. Helping people get job training or chasing out drug merchants from a park or battling racist or sexist stereotypes is important but does little to bring into question why the economy is so imbalanced, or hope so lacking that people sell poisons or that after years of civil rights efforts racism and sexism persist. Organizations that confront these broader questions follow a **transformative** or radical approach seeking to change underlying social, economic, political, or cultural structures that allow problems to persist (Hanna and Robinson 1994; O'Donnell and Karanja 2000; Reisch 2005). Is it the unbridled capitalism that allows workers to be easily fired or jobs to be sent abroad? To what extent does the cultural baggage—of ceremonies, symbols, holidays—that are part of a white, Christian, more male than female dominated society work against creating an equitable multicultural society? As such, a transformative, or radical, approach

> requires an analysis of the root causes of inequality, injustice and oppression, with a particular emphasis on examining the fundamental distribution of resources and power . . . radical community organizing . . . focus(es) on economic issues, especially on how capitalism affects the ability of community members to gain access to the basic necessities . . . radical organizers promote a redistribution of resources and power at the community and societal levels. (Reisch 2005, 290–291)

At its extreme, transformational strategies imply revolution.

Families of Empowerment Tactics

To accomplish social change goals, a wide variety of tactics are followed that fit into broad groupings: **social mobilization (SM)** (or equivalently **direct action [DA]** or **power based** or **protest** or **confrontation**) and **economic and social production (ESP)** (often called **development**) approaches. With social mobilization tactics, activists persuade, pressure, and at times coerce those in government or big businesses to change policies and programs. These power-based models (Gecan 2002; Smock 2003) are about pushing ideas on others, sometimes by lobbying and other times through confrontation through an orchestrated **campaign**. With the **economic and social production** (or **development**) approach, social change organizations carry out **programs** and **projects** either by themselves or in partnership with the business community or the public sector.

Social mobilization and ESP tactics represent extremes with several other approaches, as seen in Table 3-2. In each of the approaches, tactics can differ in their *intensity, commitment*, and *scope of involvement*. For instance, in a hunger strike, an individual puts his or her life on the line to symbolize an important cause, showing both intensity and commitment. In contrast, thousands and thousands might sign a petition or address a letter to congress, an action of broad scope but one of minimal intensity and commitment. With the chance of arrest, or worse, being involved in demonstrations, picketing or boycotts display both commitment and intensity. Community building efforts that focus only on repairing a handful of apartments while ignoring the gang problem that has discouraged re-investment illustrates an approach that lacks the scope to bring about sustained change. The first of three in-between models is that of **civic engagement** in which activists accept the legitimacy of current political structures and, working within the system, try to substitute their own agendas (Hart 2001). With **administrative engagement tactics**, activists participate in organizations, such as a city planning committee, that those in power have set up but then try to assert their own power. Being on a police review board or a citizen advisory commission on school change enables people to effect actions, although usually just to a limited degree. Under the **civic and service partnership** approach, services and programs are carried out by nonprofit organizations (Salamon 1995), though often in partnership with business or government, but doing so in ways that not only seek to accomplish a project but to empower people in doing so.

Categorizing the Variety of Social Change Models

Table 3-3 briefly describes a wide variety of social change models, ranging from an ad hoc gathering of neighbors, to national issue-based organizations that have worked for generations on issues such as improving the environment or combating racism or sexism. The exact categories are less important than realizing that both a wide variety of approaches are available and that the approaches do change over time. For

TABLE 3.2   Families of Empowerment Approaches

Social Change Tactic	Description	Illustrative Tactics	Variety in Intensity and Scope
Social Mobilization and Power	Use of disruptive, pressureful (usually public) actions to compel changes Social activists independently set up demands that those in power are pressured to carry out Activists set the agenda those in power implement	Marches, demonstrations, picketing, economic boycotts, litigation courts, strikes, sabotage	Can vary from legal marches with permits, to vandalism Might involve a single person as a symbol with a hunger strike, to the millions involved in the civil rights movement; can be seeking to solve a narrow problem or be a stage in broader social and political transformation
Civic Engagement	Nondisruptive involvement in the political or regulatory structures Activists try to influence current policies that those in power implement	Petitioning government, petitioning regulatory agencies, lobbying, publicity campaigns Supporting candidates for office	Campaigns can involve full-time efforts, while a petition can be undertaken with little more effort than checking a box on a web page National Get Out the Vote campaigns involve millions; while speaking at a city council meeting might be done alone
Administrative Engagement	Working in an official advisory capacity to governmental or regulatory agencies Those in power have set up the structures, though input is provided by activists	Community and sectoral planning efforts, being on advisory and review boards	Mostly done as a part-time volunteer effort Task is usually focused on one issue area with delimited responsibilities
Civic and Service Partnerships	Working with either the public sector or businesses to provide goods or services Activists set up goals within constraints posed by those in power; often expertise and funding provided by government	Community building efforts; becoming the contractor for social service or development work; community health clinics; neighborhood watches	Varies from advisory role on joint planning bodies to full-time work as a contract social service provider Focused on a particular task usually for a delimited period of time

(continued)

TABLE 3.2   Continued

Social Change Tactic	Description	Illustrative Tactics	Variety in Intensity and Scope
Social and Economic Production	Community-controlled provision of social services, housing, employment, and business development Activists determine the overall agenda that might or might not be limited by government resources	Self-help projects; support groups; housing production and economic projects run by Community Development Corporations; micro-enterprises; worker ownership, cooperatives	At one extreme there are small independent self-help projects, support groups, or isolated communes; at the other community ownership of large-scale economic enterprises In addition to building a project, also working to train and hire employees from the community to run the project

TABLE 3.3   Organizational Models for Social Change

Model	Brief Description
Ad Hoc Neighborhood Group	Friends and neighbors coming together to solve an immediate problem and then periodically meeting to push for neighborhood needs
Community Power Organization	Permanent place-based organization that advocates for neighborhood concerns; gains power from broad community membership
Network Advocacy Model	Permanent network of community power organizations united through common philosophy
Multiracial Community Power Organization	A community power organization that explicitly tries to unite those from separate ethnic and racial groups in common efforts
Faith-Based Organization	An organization that is either based within separate religious congregations or an organization whose members are motivated to act because of religious faith
Radical Community Organization	A permanent place-based organization that advocates for broader structural change
Radical Social Action	Usually a loose confederation of individuals who believe that disruption is required to bring about needed systemic reform
Consensus-Building Community Organization	A place-based organization that brings together different local constituency groups
Settlement House Model	An organization often sponsored by middle class individuals to provide services to poorer neighborhoods
Progressive Social Service	A social service agency run by professionals, but one that adopts a social change perspective

Model	Brief Description
Community-Building Organization	An organization, often sponsored by government or foundations, that unites other established community organizations in efforts to rebuild a local economy and infrastructure
Sectoral Organization	An organization, often a coalition, of separate groups that are focused on solving one problem, often through a variety of distinct means
Citizen Involvement Partnership	Often government-sponsored organizations meant to obtain citizen input for community planning, or in administration of public agencies such as schools or police
Community Economic Development and Housing Organization	Community-concerned and often community-controlled organization set up to build homes or create jobs in neighborhoods of need—often set up as Community Development Corporations
Alternative Social Service Model	An organization that provides social services varying from helping people with substance problems to rape counselling, but does so with heavy involvement of both the community while using former clients as peer providers of the services
Issue-Based Advocacy Model	A organization that mobilizes large numbers of people to focus on a specific issue, often doing so through both local and national branches
National/State Advocacy Model	An organization run with a professional staff that advocates for its individual members with state or national legislative or regulatory bodies
Women-centric Model	Membership organization that follows feminist ideology and usually focuses on issues of concern to women
Identity Organization	Organizations set up to promote pride and to gain social and political rights and recognition for identity groups
Progressive Politics Model	Electoral organization that supports progressive candidates
Coalitional Advocacy Model	A state or national (or sometimes citywide) organization that speaks for its members, made up of other organizations rather than individuals
Concurrent Identity and Issue Organizing	Either a membership or a coalitional organization that focuses on issues that disproportionately impact specific identity groups

instance, in different eras, settlement house work has ranged from using a community power approach, to progressive social services, to being so passive one would question whether or not it should be considered as working for social change at all (Fabricant and Fisher 2002).

A single type of organization can be concerned about a variety of issues. A women-centric group might fight low pay for women or sexual harassment or demand abortion rights. Similarly, the same type of problem might be of concern to the separate organizations, each seeing it in their own way. To a neighborhood group, a broken sidewalk might be a problem for the city to solve; for an economic development group one that its own staff can fix; while a community power organization might treat the problem as an example of how the community is neglected and use this neglect as a base to motivate organizing.

How important is it which model is followed so long as improvements come about? Does it matter if a women-centric organization brings into being a homeless shelter, or the same shelter is sponsored by a faith-based group or a neighborhood association? In each case, a homeless person is helped; but with some approaches all that is being done is patching up a small mistake, while others see the problem as stemming from more fundamental societal flaws.

Still, there is room enough for all to be engaged in social change work. Flamboyant individuals are unlikely to enjoy handling the financial minutiae in a community development finance organization while more accommodative souls probably would not want to work for an organization engaged in in-your-face confrontations. If you think the system is violently sexist, rotten to the core, and needs its shame shoved in its face, join up with the Lesbian Avengers. Believing that capitalism will work for the poor if only given a chance, you learn the technical skills and you set up a Community Development Finance organization and join the sedate National Community Capital Association. Motivated by faith and a concern for your fellow congregants, sign up with IAF affiliate; or, if more concerned with matters of race or ethnicity, become active in a multicultural group such as the Center for Third World Organizing. If you feel that the economy is biased against the poor, work locally with ACORN on its Living Wage campaigns, or become involved with United for a Fair Economy nationally.

If one model doesn't work, set up your own. For instance, feminist and women-centric models emerged in response to a rejection of the hierarchical Alinsky approaches (Hyde 2000; 2005) and then on their own, refocused political action not just to include concerns about public institutions but also including issues of the home and family (Sen 2003, liv).

Social change models differ in terms of how each responds to three broad concerns: (i) whether to focus more on direct action or ESP efforts; (ii) be concerned more on the here and now or on transforming the system; and (iii) have more direct membership involvement or work through a professional staff. In addition, as shown in Table 3-4, models differ in the relative importance of ideology in determining what actions to take.

Action Focus

Action focus or *purpose* varies widely. Traditional neighborhood organizing emphasizes improving a place while issue-based advocacy organizations work on a single issue—the environment, housing, peace, living wages, preservation, civil and speech rights, among many others. Identity organizing works to help those who share a characteristic such as gender, sexuality, ethnicity, or ableness, to battle oppression targeted at those with the shared characteristic while working to create pride among their members. Community power models are about solving problems but during so in ways that empower members by gaining a place at the table where decisions are made.

TABLE 3.4 Characteristics of Social Change Models Part One

Model Characteristic

Model Type	Preferred Empowerment Tactics	Focus: Emphasis on Issue/Identity, Place, Person, or Building Power Organization	Ideological Motivation; Macro–Social Change Ideology; Microempowerment Ideology	Preconfigurative	Role of Social Change Professionals and Members	Mobilization Tactics
Ad Hoc Neighborhood Group	Situationally contingent	Place	Pragmatic	No	Rarely participate	Door knocking; networking
Community Power	Power; direct action; civic engagement, administrative engagement	Place and organization building	Either pragmatic or transformational; microempowerment	Can be, but not core	Professional organizer and leadership development	Personal recruitment and institutional recruitment
Multiracial Community Power	Power, direct action; civic engagement, administrative engagement	Place and organization building	Transformational; microempowerment	Yes	Professional organizer and leadership development	Institutional recruitment then personal
Progressive Social Service	Economic and social production	Issues facing people but sometimes extends to place	Pragmatic	No	Professionally dominated	Trying to empower clients, but clients nonetheless
Community Building	Economic and social production	Place	Pragmatic; consensus	No	Leadership mixed with professional involvement	Representatives from community institutions
Citizen Involvement Models	Civic engagement	Place or issue	Status quo	No	Often not involved	Volunteers or appointees
Consensus-Building Community Model	Economic and social production	Place	Consensus	No	Leadership mixed with professional involvement	Representatives from community institutions

(continues)

TABLE 3.4 Continued

Model Type		Model Characteristic				
	Preferred Empowerment Tactics	Focus: Emphasis on Issue/Identity, Place, Person, or Building Power Organization	Ideological Motivation; Macro–Social Change Ideology; Microempowerment Ideology	Preconfigurative	Role of Social Change Professionals and Members	Mobilization Tactics
Economic or Housing Development	Economic and social production	Place or persons	Pragmatic but with some transformational	Somewhat in terms of redistribution of wealth	Organizations run by professionals with community boards	Community institutions
Alternative Social Services	Economic and social production	Persons or place	Pragmatic with some transformational; personal empowerment	Somewhat if peer counseling involved	Professionals dominate though members become active	Often client based
Sectoral	Economic and social production	Issue within place	Pragmatic	No	Professionals more dominant	Institutional recruitment
Faith-Based Model	Social mobilization; civic engagement, administrative engagement, production	Issues are means for building empowered organization	Reinforcing religious values	Can be but not always	Balance between social change professionals, clergy, and members	Groupings of congregations
Issue-Based Advocacy Model	Social mobilization; civic engagement, administrative engagement	Issues	Varies can be pragmatic but also transformative	Can be but not always	Balance between professionals and members	Individual recruitment, often through networks
Issue/Identity Advocacy Models	Social mobilization; civic engagement, administrative engagement	Issues but with a focus on racial or class implications	Transformational	Membership is transformational	Balance between professionals and members	Often joint individual/organizational mobilization

National Advocacy Model	Social mobilization; civic engagement, administrative engagement	Issues	Can be pragmatic; at times transformative	Rarely	Heavily dominated by professionals	Recruiting members more than activists
Women-centric/Feminist	All tactics	Issue as it affects identity	Feminist transformative	Intended as pre-configurative	Leaders dominate with professionals as most staff	Individuals through networks
Radical Community Organizing	Social mobilization	Place though emphasizes larger issues	Transformative	Intended as pre-configurative	Leaders dominate with professionals as most staff	Individuals through networks
Radical Social Action	Disruptive social mobilization	Issues	Radically transformative	No	Activist coteries with minimal permanence	Individuals through networks and publicity
Progressive Politics	Civic engagement	Issues	Mildly transformative	No	Professionals run with active leaders	Individual recruitment
Coalition Advocacy	Social mobilization; civic engagement, administrative engagement	Issues	Mildly transformative because of mixed membership	No	Professional leaders work with local professional leaders	Organizational membership
Network Advocacy	Social mobilization; civic engagement, administrative engagement	Issues	Depends on philosophy of network can be transformative	Perhaps depending on how network makes decisions	Balance between professionals and leaders	Organizational membership

Empowerment Tactics

Empowerment tactics range from violence to working with bankers and business people. Frequently the tactic chosen depends on little more than what seems to work. Call up city hall, complain about the schools and if politicians listen, so much the better; if not, activate thousands to picket downtown. Other times, though, tactics are chosen to mesh with the underlying analysis of what's wrong with the society and what solutions are appropriate (Smock 2003). For those who accept that the political and economic system is more or less on target, though needing some adjustments, less militant approaches are the way to go. But for those believing core structures in the distribution of wealth or power or in privileging of specific identity groups are rotten, providing a service does little, while working within the system is but mere tinkering when major transformations are required.

Once an organization settles upon a particular empowerment tactic, it is likely to continue its use, in part because people join because of their comfort level with the tactic. A community development corporation that works with business and government partners is unlikely to attract a revolutionary activist. A national advocacy organization whose tasks involve understanding the technical minutiae that go into banking regulations requires staff with law degrees and technical expertise in banking, not those adept at sabotage.

Ideology

Models differ in whether or not they reflect an *underlying ideology*. An ideology is a set of beliefs about what society should be as well as paths that should be followed to bring about that society. Ideologies answer a multitude of questions. Is change about reform or is social transformation required? When proponents of particular models label themselves as "progressive," "faith-based," "transformative," "socialist," "communitarianism," or "feminist," they are implying an ideological approach.

For some, the goal is to solve problems, period, a **pragmatic approach**. But increasingly the models are shaped by underlying ideologies, some with a political-economy slant, another that builds on identity, and a third based on faith.

Political-Economy Ideologies. Political economy ideologies focus on understanding the ways in which the distribution of wealth and political power set up structures of control. One variant of the political economy approach is that of *progressivism* that argues for democratic involvement while at the same time shows deep concern about economic inequality (Hart 2001; Moyer 2001; Osterman 2002). Progressive ideology, though, downplays the importance of cultural and religious factors in asserting social control (Hart 2001). Rather than being anticapitalistic, progressive ideology accepts capitalism but does so by promoting what Reynolds terms the "high-road to economics" in which businesses seek out profits but in ways that help workers and communities (Reynolds 2002, ix–xvi)—what Rubin and Sherraden have termed "humane capitalism" (Rubin and Sherraden 2005, 476)

In previous generations, *radical community organizing*, a type of political-economy approach, was associated with socialist and even communist beliefs. Today radical community organizing still is about economic concerns but in a less revolutionary way, and it encourages democratic, nonviolent, direct actions to point out economic injustice (Fitzgerald and Rodgers 2000). In addition, while economic issues are core, the radical organizing extends beyond economics to include concerns about gender, race, and sexuality.

At the opposite extreme among political-economy ideologies are the approaches such as consensus organizing that accept the status quo and belief that the system can be made to work:

> consensual organizing strategy tends to see the fundamental goal as rebuilding community, forging a sense of unity among fragmented elements, and gathering resources to perform specific community tasks (Fisher 1994, 188)

Identity Ideologies. Ideologies that emerge from identity organizing concentrate on those structural injustices that impact identity groups. Feminist ideology rails against gender imbalances, gay ideologies against homophobia, ethnic ideologies against cultural, racial, or ethnic discrimination. Feminist ideology questions why males are privileged over females, gay-theory (or queer theory as it is called by its proponents) why heterosexuality over homosexuality. Further, identity ideologies promote understanding of the world through alternative frameworks known as **standpoints**. Standpoint theorizes a shared sense of humaneness, mutual respect, the importance of building relationships, and the value of developing the empathy that allows seeing the world from an another point of view—gay rather than straight, female rather than masculine, disabled rather than abled, or from the point of view of those from different ethnic groups.

Within this broader ideological framework, refinements appear. Women-centric ideologies argue against relying on raw power and advocate bringing about change through consensual processes, though one that is seen through the lens of gender that then is modified through racial and class experiences (combining from Hyde 1987; Hyde 2005; Shragge 2003, 64; Smock 2003). Other identity ideologies argue that change occurs in different ways that reflect the separate social experiences of distinct ethnic groups (Roth 2004). The shared history of slavery gives a very different slant to action than does a history of economically motivated immigration.

Faith-Based Motivations as Ideology. Faith-based ideologies build on both the beliefs from religion and existing relations between those of the same faith to suggest organizing strategies. For instance, Ernie Cortes, an IAF organizer, will quote scriptures to evoke concerns on economic and racial justice while arguing that faith "need not mean a specific religious belief, but instead involves an affirmation that life has meaning, that religion communicates meaning and people have an obligation to future generations" (Cortes 1996).

Some faith-based ideologies find scriptural justification for militantly fighting to bring about radical transformation. Liberation theology, for instance (Smith 1991), questions private ownership of property especially when owners oppress the poor. For activist clergy, faith not only sustains action but necessitates it. As the Gamaliel leader Pastor Dennis Jacobsen argues

> Like it or not those summoned to do justice must carry this burden. Like the prophets of God, they see and feel the world differently from others. . . . It seems that those whom God summons to do justice have no choice but to act on their calling. (Jacobsen 2001, 97)

Our own clergy person, an ordained rabbi and social activist, describes:

> I have taken on the equally "religious" task of personally responding to the call for action that I find in our [religious] texts, trying to resurrect an oft-neglected system of civil law and helping others to make social justice a conscious part of their Jewish practice and Judaism a conscious part of their activism. (Jacobs 2004, 25)

Contemporary faith-based ideology, a "theology of organizing" (Warren 2001), finds motivation for action in deep personal values that argue for economic justice (Warren 2001, 57–61).

Preconfiguring.   With some social change models, the way an activist organization itself works and how it is structured must reflect the values that the organization is promoting for the broader society. When this occurs, organizations are said to *preconfigure* social change. For example, an underlying organizational goal might be to bring about a society in which the opinions of all, irrespective of class, race, or gender, are heard with respect. But if the organization is set up in a strict hierarchical way, only the voices of those at the top might matter and the organization fails to preconfigure social change goals. Instead, the organization might want to determine actions through consensus decision making, that is, obtaining an overwhelming consent from the membership. An organization that is about promoting multiculturalism but run only by white upper class graduates of Ivy League schools does not preconfigure changes in social hierarchies. Organizations that pay their staff too little, or that are housed in inexpensive quarters that are not accessible to the disabled, fail to preconfigure progressive goals.

But one can go too far. For instance, the civil rights and economic justice organization SDS believed strongly in the consensus that its members would talk well past the time for which action would have been effective; similarly, some white-dominated feminist groups show so much concern with procedural matters that they sometimes never get around to taking actions that would benefit minority women (Roth 2004).

Role of the Social Change Professional.   Social change organizations are built up of professional activists, organizers, and local leaders, as well as less active members. Models differ in the ways in which responsibilities are divided, especially between paid professionals and volunteers. At one extreme, ordinary members play a small role; for instance, national advocacy organizations are run by paid social change professionals. At the other end are the informal neighborhood groups that are dominated by local leaders and have no professional staff.

Balances need to be sought. Many organizations hire professional staff but one of the staff's chief responsibilities then becomes training people through **leadership**

development to empower members. Another way of maintaining balance is to ensure that organizations are run by a strong board of directors of elected volunteers that set overall policy that is then implemented by the social change professionals.

Mobilization Tactics. As we describe in Chapter 15, models differ in how they encourage people to become involved. In some, members are signed up, one by one, through door knocking efforts called *canvassing*. Or appeals to join are made at locales that attract those most likely to be interested in the issue. A shelter might provide a place for recruitment to a homeless rights group, while mobilizing in the gay rights movement initially takes place at gay bars. Other models mobilize through bringing together existing organizations, especially religious congregations or civic groups. Both canvassing approaches and congregational organizing are about *relationship building*. In contrast, with national advocacy models recruitment is a far more passive enterprise with those interested in the cause signing up, oftentimes through electronic means.

Models differ in what they say to encourage people to join. Some appeal to shared faith or ideology, a reaching out to those who agree on broad principles of social or economic justice. Others build on the self-interest of members, arguing that by working together people can obtain better homes or access to medical care. Issue-based advocacy organizations recruit those who are already concerned about the matter—whether saving the whales, or protecting speech rights, or getting the bums out of office. Recruitment to identity organizations comes about by arguing that people who are similar to one another—women, members of specific ethnic or cultural groups, those facing disability, gays, lesbians, bisexuals, or transsexuals—have to unite to combat the discrimination they collectively and individually face.

Institutional Networks and Cultures of Social Change

Many organizations that follow the same model are linked within what we term an **institutional network**. Within these networks, such as ACORN, National People's Action Network, Gamaliel Network, PICO, the IAF, Consensus Organizing Network, and NeighborWorks Network, organizations develop a **culture of social change** based upon shared values, beliefs, and preferences about which tactics to use. The culture is reinforced through common training programs and frequent dialogue, especially at annual meetings. More generally, institutional networks have the following characteristics:

Communications and Linkages
1. Sustained communications between the organizations while working on a common problem
2. Conferences and meetings to discuss approaches to social change, provide technical information, publicize successes, and recruit to the network
3. A shared ideology on why problems occur and what constitutes an appropriate solution

Systems of Support

4. Help for those in the network to build capacity from other organizations in the network
5. Support in formation of new organizations
6. Ongoing training for organizers and other social change professionals
7. Training for volunteer activists

The Network Itself Sets Up a Coordinating Organization

8. A name for the network
9. Central and, perhaps, regional offices
10. An incorporated nonprofit organization that coordinates the network
11. An established training academy
12. An ongoing, paid professional staff working for the network organization itself

The tightness of the linkages between organizations within networks differs. Some networks provide little more than technical assistance, while in others affiliated organizations work in lock step to carry out actions decided by the network. Some local organizations are members of several networks, for instance being part of National People's Action, yet receiving training from an economic and social production network.

Network organizations themselves differ markedly. At one extreme, the organization might be little more than an informal gathering of like-minded individuals who come together to share concerns, such as what takes place with the National Community Building Network. At the other end, some network organizations are themselves activist organizations, employing staff, running training academies, undertaking campaigns, and actively seeking to recruit affiliated organizations.

To give a better flavor of the different institutional networks, we briefly describe four families of institutional networks: (a) faith-based neighborhood networks; (b) power-based community networks; (c) economic and social production networks; and (d) issue- and identity-based networks.

Faith-Based Neighborhood Networks

A variety of institutional networks are organizations based upon religious congregations as well as other stable community institutions. Among the better known of these faith-based networks are the Industrial Areas Foundation (IAF), the Direct Action and Research Training Center (DART), the Gamaliel Foundation, and the PICO National Network.

Organizing in these networks comes about through building *relationships*, first between the network organization itself and local congregations, next between the local congregations that form the community action organization, and finally between the separate action organizations themselves. Most faith-based networks train organizers, some insisting that all affiliates only employ organizers that have gone through such training. Many of the network leaders are motivated by explicit religious beliefs (some are ordained) while the vocabulary of action uses religious terminology and allegories.

Still the network's goal is not promulgating religion, but instead using theology to motivate working for a social justice agenda through what is termed *value-based* organizing. For instance, the Gamaliel Foundation was originally set up as a religious mission to help black homeowners in Chicago facing discrimination. Another faith-based network, PICO, is a 35-year-old federation of approximately 50 organizations that "brings people together based on faith and values not just issues or anger . . . and teaches the art of compromise and negotiation." Many of the activists are clergy who have received instruction in intensive training sessions (some in English, others in Spanish) (http://www.piconetwork.org/). A third faith-based network, DART (the Direct Action Research and Training Center, based in Miami and founded in the early 1980s), helps build new community organizations, works with immigrant groups, and offers a four-month training school for organizers (a week in classes and the rest as a field trainee). Many then work in one of the twenty-two DART affiliates (www .thedartcenter.org).

The Industrial Areas Foundation (the IAF) founded in 1940 by the legendary Saul Alinsky, is the oldest of these networks. As described

> The IAF is non-ideological and strictly non-partisan, but proudly, publicly, and persistently political. The IAF builds a political base within society's rich and complex third sector—the sector of voluntary institutions that includes religious congregations, labor locals, homeowner groups, recovery groups, parents associations, settlement houses, immigrant societies, schools, seminaries, orders of men and women, religious, and others. And then the leaders use that base to compete at times, to confront at times, and to cooperate at times with leaders in the public and private sectors. (www.industrialareasfoundation.org/iafabout/about.htm)

The philosophy and approaches of the IAF are the best documented of the various networks.

The IAF as an Illustration of Congregation-Based Organizing.

In 1939, Saul Alinsky set up the Back of the Yards organization to work within a neighborhood of exploited immigrants in Chicago. A year later, with the help of both the Catholic church and Chicago philanthropists, Alinsky formalized his approach by setting up the Industrial Areas Foundation as both a fund-raising and training organization. During Alinsky's lifetime IAF work reflected his choice of direct action tactics while pushing the pragmatic idea that organizing is about immediate problem solving not political transformation (Warren 2001, 42 ff). On Alinsky's death, Edward Chambers, an Alinsky discipline, took over the IAF and transformed the handful of organizations into today's extended network.

Today the IAF is a national network of fifty-six separate organizations that are clustered into seven regional groupings, with the linkages between IAF organizations in the southwest, especially Texas, being especially close. Each separate chapter reflects the local ethnic and racial composition, though almost all are built up in poor communities. The IAF tries to empower people from the communities—local leaders—who work with the professional IAF organizers in campaigns to pressure the political system increasingly through economic and social production efforts (for example, building homes) (www.industrialareasfoundation.org/). All IAF chapters collect dues from member organizations to reduce dependence on outside funding. Each local organization pays the salary of a professional, IAF-trained organizer (that today number in the hundreds), who in turn works with local members to develop leadership skills. IAF provides extended ten-day training programs, on-site training, and issue-focused training, and in addition sponsors retreats.

Using religious discourse as the basis for directing social change, IAF leaders contrast the "world as it is with the world as it ought to be" (Chambers 2003; Jacobsen 2001). Churches and congregations provide the political base of IAF organizations for, as senior IAF organizer Ernie Cortes said, "[churches] are virtually the only institutions in society that are fundamentally concerned with the nurture and well-being of families and communities" (quoted in Osterman 2002, 93).

Local IAF affiliates are built up from congregations, as well as from other established community institutions—schools, parent teacher organizations, homeowners groups. Linkages are built between separate congregations that then join together in political pressure tactics as well as in community renewal projects such as the Nehemiah housing project. In addition, much time is spent building relationships through one-on-ones with individuals to motivate them to join in later action all the while, in Cortes' words, "reweav[ing] the social fabric" (Cortes 1996). Much of IAF action is motivated by the "iron rule": "Never, ever, do for people what they can do for themselves. [though recognizing] it is a very difficult rule to follow" (Rogers 1990, 15). However, observers have commented that in practice this rule is not always enforced as the IAF professional organizer is often dominant in setting the direction for IAF chapters (Osterman 2002, 69).

City-wide IAF organizations such as COPS in San Antonio and BUILD in Baltimore gain political clout by mobilizing large numbers of people who in turn pressure politicians by inviting them to show up at their churches and respond to questions. Strength is increased through creating statewide coalitions, such as those in Texas that have successfully increased funding for schools as well as the quality of education (Shirley 2002). Power is extended by linking together organizations that can contact separate officials. For example, in Chicago, the IAF affiliate United Power in Action has 330 dues-paying member organizations that influence a wide variety of public officials from many separate communities (Chambers 2003, 118).

In the past, IAF tactics followed the flamboyant direct actions of Alinsky: sit-ins, humorous in-your-face confrontations, and putting politicians on the spot in accountability sessions. Nowadays far more subdued tactics are the norm and seem effective, perhaps because of the ever-present threat of direct actions. IAF chapters are involved in various work: small neighborhood improvement programs, efforts to bridge racial gaps in communities, living wage campaigns, housing development programs, neighborhood renewal efforts, and job training for the poor and minorities. IAF chooses actions based on pragmatic considerations—that is, what is best for the members—and not on broader ideological concerns. As stated on IAF's web page, "The IAF is non-ideological and strictly non-partisan, but proudly, publicly, and persistently political." Over time, especially in Texas and in Baltimore, IAF affiliates have become part of the permanent political landscape and are consulted by those in office.

Power-Based Community Networks

Power-based networks such as ACORN, National People's Action (NPA), or organizations associated with the Center for Third World Organizing differ from faith-based networks in several important ways. Power organizations recruit individuals one by one and spend more time on solving problems than on relationship building, though the latter remains important. Similarly, while faith-based organizations battle racial injustice, many power-based organizations are guided by a core ideology that argues that racism is fundamental to other issues of economic and social injustice. For example, the Center for Third World Organizing, a training center for power-based organizations,

> has supported the creation of multi-racial, multi-ethnic organizations and campaigns; fearlessly challenged racist policies and practices of the state and other significant institutions; and has continuously sought opportunities to build bridges among a wide range of communities and activists of color. . . . We believe race permeates every aspect of our social existence, and has major influence on the way that identities, institutions, and society as a whole are shaped. Racial inequality is a fundamental characteristic of our social order—often interlocked with other systems of oppression like class, patriarchy, and xenophobia—that affects the organization and distribution of social resources, including power, privilege and wealth. (CTWO web page)

Let's describe in more detail two power-based networks: the tightly integrated ACORN network and the more loosely affiliated group of organizations that constitute the National People's Action network.

ACORN. ACORN, nowadays one of the best known and most active of the networks, grew out of the civil rights and welfare efforts in the sixties. Initially ACORN borrowed the direct action tactics of civil rights organizers though also emphasizing spending time in organizing building, almost irrespective of the immediate issues. Unlike the IAF, though, ACORN builds organizations by recruiting dues-paying members one by one (as we describe in more detail in Chapter 15), doing so in poorer, usually minority, neighborhoods. Members are expected to be active and participate, not just sign up and expect others to do the work.

By 2004 ACORN had affiliates in eighty cities (in contrast to forty just two years before) with a membership close to 200,000 families. In addition to its local affiliates, ACORN operates several national offices, including a headquarters in Brooklyn, NY, and a Washington, D.C. lobbying office, as well as an organizing center in Arkansas (ACORN Annual Report 2004). ACORN has also spun off several national sister organizations such as the ACORN Housing Corporation that builds affordable homes and is closely associated with progressive media outlets and unions such as Service Employees International Union.

ACORN's action agenda is avowedly political and progressive, some might say radical, using direct action, for example, sitting in at abandoned homes to demand better housing, and running large-scale demonstrations. Major issues have included affordable housing, concerns with welfare support, living wage campaigns, locally responsive schools, and voter registration, but ACORN chapters also take on the small neighborhood issues of parks and stop signs. Recently ACORN has been a leading participant in the battle against predatory mortgage lending and pay-day loans. ACORN has coordinated statewide campaigns, successfully pushing for a higher minimum wage in Florida, and was very active in registering voters and getting them to go to the polls for the 2004 election. Many of the ACORN chapters are located in cities affected by hurricane Katrina and are working to assure that redevelopment efforts are beneficial to the poor communities it serves. ACORN also provides services to its members, such as tax preparation, and has worked to set up and run charter schools.

To train local leaders and organizers, ACORN runs a week-long program three times a year, once in Spanish. ACORN members are also encouraged to attend an annual legislative and political conference in Washington, D.C., that provides training and includes an on-the-hill action day in which people press their representatives on political and economic concerns. In addition, ACORN holds a national conference to share experiences, to allow people to network, to hear speakers on pressing social issues and, most important, to orchestrate a major march or demonstration on a national target, for instance, a bank that has been ignoring poor communities.

ACORN's ideals and practice have not always been in sync. Though demanding racial and gender equality, until recently ACORN's staff had not reflected the diversity found in the communities it serves; but that is now changing. ACORN also had a reputation of not being willing to work with other organizations, but recently it has joined coalitions, especially on the living wage campaign and get out the vote efforts (Tait 2005, 114–115). Finally, while ACORN tries to maintain financial independence by surviving on members' dues, it now accepts grants from banks and foundations, especially for economic and social production work.

National People's Action.   Many of the local organizations affiliated with NPA appear similar to ACORN groups: They are neighborhood based, rely upon direct action, are multiracial, overtly political, and quite progressive. Unlike ACORN, whose own organizers recruit for local chapters, NPA is an affiliation of over 302 independent local organizations that have chosen to join the coalition, often after establishing themselves on their own. ACORN affiliates are secular groups; IAF affiliates are congregation based. NPA coalition members vary from congregation-based groups, to neighborhood organizations, to issued-based social change organizations.

NPA came about when several Chicago neighborhood groups, inspired by the IAF model, joined together to respond to the extreme redlining their communities were facing. Led by Gale Cincotta and Shel Trapp, the Chicago organizations made contact with neighborhood groups in other cities that also were experiencing similar problems and by doing so stimulated the national campaign that eventually brought about the Community Reinvestment Act.

Individual member organizations in NPA work on their own varying issues: immigration reform, affordable housing, jobs programs for young people, anti-crime efforts, or other issues that members suggest during the initial door-to-door mobilization effort.

When door-knocking, you take what someone gives you and test it out with other people. When you get three or four on a block pointing out the same problem, you respond "Okay, let's have a meeting about that." You don't make a decision, you just test it out at a series of encounters and if the test proves positive you go. I call this process "fishing" where you ask people what they want to see changed or improved (Trapp n.d., 25)

The NPA network promotes a national agenda that focuses on economic justice and neighborhood preservation, while at the same time keeping close watch on CRA as banks and conservative politicians seek to gut this crucial act. NPA accepts that local issues reflect national problems, that multiracial organizing is vital, that Washington does not know all the answers, that people learn from one another by peer-to-peer training, and that direct action is effective (Trapp n.d., 58–61), though violence is to be avoided (Trapp n.d., 87). National issues are debated in lively discussions at NPA's annual conference held in Washington, D.C., that provides attendees with background needed for action and as its highlight includes a dramatic direct action, usually a march on the home of a ranking federal official—the Secretary of HUD, Chair of the Federal Reserve Board, House or Senate leaders, or on the offices of a Washington agency whose policies need to be made more neighborhood friendly. NPA actions have a gung-ho rallying spirit, complete with campaign songs and feisty sloganeering.

NPA affiliates send their leaders and organizers for training at the National Technical Information Center (NTIC)—an affiliated direct action training center and research center. In addition, NPA organizations can contract with NTIC for specialized training. NTIC helps guide local campaigns by preparing and circulating technical reports on the background of issues, for example, what to do to preserve CRA or how to battle predatory lending. NTIC has worked closely with other organizations, supporting the rights of those with disabilities, economic justice organizations, environmental justice groups, tenants' organizations, as well as social service organizations wanting to do community organizing.

Economic and Social Production Networks

A large number of community-based organizations provide social services, housing, and economic development programs within neighborhoods of need. These ESP organizations require technical information on how to do their work as well as economic subsidies to make their efforts possible. To lobby for funds and to set up training programs, many economic and social production organizations join coalitions, such as the Coalition for Human Needs or trade associations such as the Association for Enterprise Opportunity.

Other networks assist local organizations directly involved in physical development projects. For instance the Local Initiative Support Corporation (LISC), Enterprise Foundation (a nonprofit private organization), and the NeighborWorks America® (NWA, a government-sponsored organization help local housing organizations) offer financial support for housing projects, run conferences that provide peer-to-peer training, produce formative newsletters, and offer more formal training institutes, as well as sponsor conferences. NeighborWorks America provides a series of training modules throughout the year in different sites that culminates with participants receiving a certification as economic and housing developers. These network organizations maintain active web pages and libraries with technical data.

Both LISC and Enterprise Foundation maintain a government relations office, encourage network members to lobby, and themselves testify on major issues confronting the housing community. As a government-sponsored organization Neighbor-Works America is more curtailed in its direct lobbying, though it does provide a wealth of information needed for congressional decision making. In addition, the individual nonprofit organizations associated with NWA have formed their own lobbying network.

Some ESP networks promote an underlying ideology. For instance, the Consensus Organizing Institute argues for partnerships between government, social services, business, and nonprofits with the goal of

> building consensus and unity among all segments of the community: neighborhood residents, bankers, business people, religious leaders, politicians, and government officials. No one is to be embarrassed, no resentments rubbed raw . . . consensual . . . organizing strategy tends to see the fundamental goal as rebuilding community, forging a sense of unity among fragmented elements, and gathering resources to perform specific community tasks. (Fisher 1994, 188)

This work is often led by community development corporations that work to physically repair the neighborhoods (Beck and Eichler 2000).

Issue and Identity-Based Networks

Over time, hundreds and hundreds of social change organizations have come into being, to fight about specific issues or to protect those in an identity group. These organizations work to preserve open space, expand access for those with disabilities, oppose racism, advocate for better schools, protest business fraud, help minorities and immigrants, or perhaps work to bring about affordable housing. Women gather together in local organizations to fight against a sexist boss or demand more gender-responsive employment policies.

Many of these local organizations handle problems on their own. When that is not the case, they look around for help and discover that help is available informally, nowadays often through electronic means. Much of modern-day feminist action has been coordinated through discussion networks and conferences (Roth 2004) while disability activists have found meetings at university centers good settings for sharing common problems and working out collective strategies (Fleischer and Zames 2001). Sometimes safe, secure locales are required in which to conduct such conversations; for example, the Highlander Center during the civil rights era provided a locale to talk about racial justice in a racially integrated environment.

Periodically, such peer-to-peer contact has resulted in the formation of a national organization. Some of these organizations have little more than a volunteer coordinator, often one whose time is donated. For instance, local groups wanting to ensure that public transportation is available for lower income communities came together in the Transportation Equity Networks coordinated by the Center for Community Change. Other times, more formal organizations with their own staff are set up, such as the NAACP or the National Council for La Raza. The Consumer Federation of America is concerned with consumer rights, the National Community Reinvestment Coalition with supporting the Community Reinvestment Act, and the National Low Income Housing Coalition with working for affordable housing. When formalized, these organizations become **support coalition organizations** that spend all their time lobbying on the federal level, providing backup information for local organizations, and, when resources permit, helping local organizations in their individual campaigns.

Tensions between Advocates of Separate Organizing Models

With the wide variety of approaches that guide social change models, disagreements inevitably occur. Some reflect little more than the follies of the human ego. Strong-willed personalities who become activists can rub each other wrong, while rivalries come about as organizations contend for the same limited pot of money from the few foundations that support social change work.

Other more fundamental differences periodically divide those involved in social change work, ranging from the underlying motivations for action, how well the organizations preconfigure social change, to the ways in which the separate organizations cope with tensions created by racial, gender, and class inequalities.

Transformative Actions or System Repair

Some social change activists argue that the overall social, political, and economic system must be questioned, while others claim that the structure, while far from perfect, can be repaired. A handful argue for *revolution* while at the opposite end are those who promote *consensus organizing*, claiming that problems can be resolved by building partnerships between government, business, and community members. Those who push for system repair pontificate that people supporting more radical transformation are grandstanding, or worse yet, encouraging severe repression. Those preferring the revolutionary route have demeaned people willing to work with government or businesses as sell-outs or pawns.

Most activists are in-between, feeling that the long run goal should be a transformation into a more just and equitable society, but this goal is accomplished step by step. You don't ask for the socialistic revolution. Instead you work for economic equity through making housing affordable or setting up a universal medical care system.

A version of the revolution versus system repair debate can be seen in the divide between proponents of power-based community organizing and supporters of the economic and social production approach (often called development). Organizing models emphasize the battle over power, see the world as a conflict between the haves and have-nots, work through confrontations, and mainly mobilize volunteers. In contrast, community development models are about building homes and businesses, encouraging cooperation with the capitalist sector, and are run through paid staff, though consulting with volunteer community members. (Stoecker 2003, 495)

In recent years reconciliations have occurred. For instance, as Peirce and Steinbach note, "You've got to have both tree shakers and jam makers to make community development work." The bricks and mortar organizations require the additional resources that organizing groups have been able to pressure financial institutions and local and state government to provide (Peirce and Steinbach 1987, 22). For instance, as James Capraro narrated,

> when the effects of predatory lending first became evident in our community, we simultaneously launched a major anti-predatory lending campaign through [the neighborhood organization] and the [development group]. . . . By raising predatory lending as an issue and disclosing some of the actors involved [the neighborhood organization] made it easier for [the development group] to . . . acquire houses. Conversely, by rehabilitating houses and occupying former vacancies with families [the neighborhood group's] members achieved greater payoff from the organizing campaign. (Capraro 2004, 154)

A related tension in the models can also be seen between those who are working as movement activists (that is, concentrating mostly on the issues) and those that are doing local organizing. As Stoecker explains, "in contrast to social activism, where an activist chooses an issue and tries to recruit adherents, in community organizing the organizer recruits people to the local organization and the people choose the issue" (Stoecker 2003, 494). Eric Shragge elaborates:

> One tension for me was between my background as a community organizer and my role as movement activist. The former teaches two things that conflict with the latter. First an organizer tries to balance his or her ideology and values with the demands of group cohesion . . . almost by definition there are compromises made. In the context of a social movement, it is more permissible . . . to polarize questions even if they appear to be divisive. (Shragge 2003, 29)

Tensions in Organization Building

The very way organizations are built can be problematic. At the extreme, some argue why waste time on the formality of organization building when all that is required is getting people out to object to a military action, or just to get a few neighbors together to protest a proposed industrial annexation? In sharp contrast, in IAF types of models, building an empowered organization is often more important than resolving any particular issue.

Other problems occur. Basing neighborhood organizations on churches does activate people who already share strong bonds, but the very connection to a church can mean that certain issues—women's rights for choice, for instance—might now be out of bounds. Similarly, integration and solidarity within an organization is sometimes easiest to build when people share a common identity—of pride in being black, or being part of the deaf culture, or living in the Beverly neighborhood. But building organizations based on identity can force one identity group against another, leading to battles between black and white, red and brown.

Another concern is how important it is to create a formal organizational structure with ongoing internal bureaucracy (Jasper 2004, 7). A lack of structure can cause chaos in a campaign, while too much structure can create delay and discourage community members from becoming involved. Similarly, models differ on the role of the professional working for the organizations. Concern is shown in balancing the expertise and knowledge of professional organizers, social activist technicians, and social workers with empowering others.

Race, Class, and Gender Tensions

A major mission of progressive social change organization is in ending racism and sexism and reducing profound economic inequality. Unfortunately, social change organizations themselves can be beset by these pervasive problems. As Osterman reflects:

> Race has always been a challenge for American progressive social movements. Sometimes race has been utilized by the opponents of progressive politics to keep potential allies apart. . . . Even if we put such episodes aside, it has proved hard to build broad-based progressive movements that include different races. (Osterman 2002, 75)

Historically some neighborhood associations were set up by one ethnic group to "defend" the community against another. Roth describes how feminists divided along ethnic and racial grounds (Roth 2004), while Leondar-Wright points out the complexity that occurs when social change organizations are simultaneously beset by racial, class, and gender divisions (Leondar-Wright 2005). In addition, people from different social classes develop cultures of organizing that can conflict with one another and as a result

> because of these class-based cultural differences, working- and middle-class movements have difficulties perceiv[ing] these common interests and working together. The middle class is prone to seeing the working class as rigid, self-interested, narrow, uninformed, parochial, and conflict oriented. The working class tends to perceive the middle class moralistic, intellectual, more talk than action, lacking common sense, and naive about power. (Rose 2000, 73)

Organizers often come from middle-class families, but social change efforts are more likely among the poor, leading to numerous misunderstandings. People from different social classes use language in distinct ways, differ in their comfort with speaking, and do not share a common knowledge base. People of greater wealth tend to have much more flexibility in their schedules and can meet when working class people cannot. Further, the formality of meetings and the abstract nature of some issues introduced by the middle class contrast with the concrete approaches of working class people and the poor (Stout 1996, 117–135).

Progressive organizers work to end divisive issues. Through carefully designed coalitions, individuals from separate ethnic groups are better able to work together. More recently the gap between unions, communities, and neighborhood organizations has been bridged by an emerging understanding of how poor peoples' unions, rather than the old established unions, speak for minority groups, not just white males (Rose 2000; Tait 2005). The lessons of multicultural organizing in which traditions of each group are respected, while differences acknowledged, have spread from training centers such as the Center for Third World Organizing (Wood 2002, 113–115). Most important, the willingness to confront these issues head on and begin dialogue on how race, gender, and class can divide those who should be working together has begun (Leondar-Wright 2005).

Conclusions

In these first three chapters we have presented complementary descriptions of what progressive organizing is about. In Chapter 1, we defined what is meant by progressive organizing; in Chapter 2, we presented narratives of successful action and described how an infrastructure of change is now in place.

In this chapter, we provided a more formal overview of this infrastructure of change, highlighting a wide variety of approaches ranging from quiet neighborhood partnerships to disruptive in-your-face actions. We argue that though models differ, each offers a partial, complementary path to bring about progressive change.

The Three Pillars of Progressive Organizing

Progressive social action is about creating a society in which people do not want economically, in which education, housing, and medical needs are met, honest work receives fair pay, and old age is a time of satisfaction—not fear. In such a society, inequalities in opportunity, treatment, and respect based on race, ethnicity, gender, sexual orientation, age, or other personal characteristics will disappear. But to bring about these changes requires a fundamental revamping of the underlying economic and social structures.

In Part Two we discuss three pillars on which successful organizing rests—encouraging empowerment, building communities, and establishing democratic social change organizations. Empowerment describes the confidence of individuals and communities to shape their own destinies and comes about when people feel that their efforts count and can bring about desired ends. Community is how people are linked through proximity, common interests, or shared backgrounds, while organization refers to a formal grouping with a defined purpose. An empowered person is willing to fight back, a united community projects political power, while organizations employ people who can orchestrate others to act.

In Chapter 4 we examine how the wealthy, big business, and many in political office seek to disempower ordinary people and then how people fight back in part by coming together in communities in which people share responsibility for one another. In Chapter 5, we examine what is meant by community, how community bonds develop, and how, by feeling part of a community, people gain the capacity for change. Chapter 6 examines social change organizations, formal groupings of people with a shared goal, and ongoing procedures for acting together. Organizations enable people to gain skills needed to fight back, focus energies for action, and provide continuity in long-term battles.

The three pillars of empowerment are closely linked. Personal empowerment, community building, and organizational development *bootstrap* with success in one activity making it easier to accomplish the next. Expanding organizational capacity empowers members, while individuals who feel empowered are more willing to join in shared action. A just, civil society comes about when people feel empowered, feel part of a supportive and helpful community, and have the capacity both as individuals and as members of an organization to shape their lives.

CHAPTER
4

Empowering Individuals

Empowerment occurs when individuals feel they have the capacity to solve problems, control the means to do so, and as a group have authoritative say in decision making (Perkins 1995). Empowered individuals are willing and able to assert their collective wills to "gain control over their lives" (Perkins and Zimerman 1995, 570). With *individual or psychological empowerment*, people gain the confidence in themselves while with *collective empowerment* people share expertise, support one another, and as a community become a recognized voice. People must be aware that they are able to bring about changes and gain pride from so knowing. As Linda Stout has argued,

> If individuals don't have a secure sense of their own personal power, the power they gain through the organization will not stand up under pressure or opposition. (Stout 1996, 113)

Empowerment is "both an outcome and a process" (Banach, Hamilton, and Perri 2003, 85) in which successes obtained by being part of a social change organization reinforces the personal confidence that change is possible. Empowerment *bootstraps* as through shared victories "people empower themselves" (Lee 2001, 60) and through doing so have confidence that they will succeed in future actions.

Care is needed, though, to avoid being seduced by a false sense of empowerment. Conservative voices have tried to equate empowerment to individual self-help rather than the ability to control a broader structure. Self-help does empower as people no longer feel helpless, but without affecting structural change the ends of empowerment have not been accomplished and end up creating "depoliticizing implications" (Hart 2001, 119).

Empowerment contains a psychological component—how people feel about themselves, a cultural component—shared perceptions about the ability to take action, and a structural component—a capacity for battling those in privileged positions. In addition, people

> are empowered to the extent they understand that their own access to social power exists through organization, through the strength of relationships among individual members in that organization, and through active participation in their organization and subsequent reflection on their involvement. (Speer and Hughey 1995, 737)

Empowerment is achieved collectively.

Psychological empowerment occurs as people who understand that there are collective solutions to problems begin to fight back. Rather than living passively as a tenant in public housing, residents empower themselves by setting up elected tenants' councils to improve living conditions. People who successfully pressure elected officials to enforce zoning ordinances and prohibit obnoxious uses of property become empowered. Residents who patrol their own neighborhoods to drive out drug hustlers feel empowered. As people learn they can use collective power to control their own world and to escape subordination from others they feel empowered.

Empowerment also occurs as people gain a material and social stake in society. As Herbert Rubin was told by a community developer:

> When people have a decent place to live, to go home everyday, their ability to deal with every other issue that's out there is greatly increased. I don't have to worry about where I am going to live, what I am going to pay for rent, I can move onto that next step and worry about a whole lot of other things. . . . It is a self-actualization thing (Rubin 1994, 413).

The pride of ownership and the learning that goes into maintaining property are all empowering. People who own homes for the first time have more stake in the community, and are more willing to fight to protect the neighborhood.

Empowerment links the personal and the political, enabling people to escape from the humiliations they feel when they are put down by others. When a man puts down a woman or ignores the input from a member of a minority group, the humiliation is intensely personal, but the cause is embedded in institutional structures of domination, and the remedy has to be collective (Hooks 1989). Those who have suffered from sexism or racism need to see that what at first seems personal is something that happens to many others, and must be battled collectively.

Finally, people are empowered when they control the environments in which they live. That means that cars do not speed through residential streets endangering children; it means that toxic waste does not drift in from a nearby incinerator; it means that the neighborhood is not a marketplace for drugs or prostitution. Empowerment comes about when neighbors working with neighbors create a safe community and keep it safe. It also means that the residents of the neighborhood own its businesses and homes, and that the money spent by the community does not leave the community, stripping it of resources.

In this chapter we examine the psychological aspects of empowerment. We begin by describing how those in privileged positions work to disempower others through manipulating cultural values that discourage people from fighting back. Next we discuss consciousness raising, procedures through which people learn that they are not alone, that problems are structural and not their own fault. We conclude by describing ways in which empowerment bootstraps as success in one area encourages future efforts.

The Battle for Personal Empowerment

But why do people remain disempowered? Why don't people recognize their own situations, organize, and battle for economic and social justice? How can the few maintain their positions and disempower the many, especially without the use of physical force? In part the answer is termed a *mobilization of bias*, a set of sustained beliefs that justify those in privileged positions maintaining those positions. This bias stems from the

> set of structures including norms, beliefs, rituals, institutions, organizations and pro-
> cedures ("rules of the game") that operate systematically to benefit certain groups and
> persons at the expense of others. (Bachrach and Botwinick 1992, 14)

Raw force disempowers, but at great cost in time, energy, and wealth. Instead of raw force those in privileged positions work to perpetuate a set of beliefs, taught in schools and demonstrated through everyday interactions, to convince others that underlying rules and structures are right and just. As people accept these cultural understandings they lose the will to fight and accept that the status quo must be right. This willingness to capitulate occurs because people feel they are alone with their problems, or feel looked down upon and so are unwilling to even try. When this happens, "a society . . . is robbed of the will to understand its own pain, sickness, suffering and dying" (Rappaport 1985, 15).

Empowerment occurs as people confront these imposed cultural rules that favor the rich, those of lighter skin, the owners of large businesses, and those in government. But becoming empowered by battling cultural rules is far from easy, as the rules are set up to convince people they cannot succeed. Let us examine an assortment of ways through which those in privileged positions seek to disempower others.

How the Mobilization of Bias Disempowers

To begin, many do not battle back because they are afraid, or blame themselves for the problems they face. People fear retaliation if they act and are terrified of what those on whom they are economically dependent might do. People hesitate to fight back since they are often isolated from each other, and think that they are alone; and many are disempowered as they themselves accept the belief that wealthy and powerful people deserve to be in charge.

Imbalances in the wealth disempower. When a few control an overwhelming proportion of the society's wealth, they have resources to hire others to maintain the political and economic status quo. Meanwhile those of lesser income must work full time and lack the hours to fight back themselves or the money to hire others to represent them. When people are ill-housed or ill-fed, or missing money for medicine, their first priorities are self-preservation, not building an organized community. People recognize that the air they breathe is foul, or the water has a funny taste, but fear speaking—being told (and believing) that their jobs depend upon companies being able to foul the environment. Those in need, especially individuals from minority groups, often receive worse education than others, depriving them of empowering knowledge.

When people are blamed for their problems humiliation often renders them powerless. *The organization of consent* tricks people into competing against each other rather than against those in power. Further, when people buy into the *legitimacy of the stratification* by class, race, or gender they implicitly accept inequality and make it hard to fight back. *Learned inefficacy* convinces people they lack the capacity to succeed.

Ironically, once people understand how they have been disempowered through the mobilization of bias, their motivation for fighting back increases. When people are humiliated, they are also angered. They see from their experiences in the unemployment lines and the kind of treatment they get in clinics or when public officials reply to them snidely that they are being intentionally put down. When people who are in wheelchairs know they are bright and able and can work but everywhere they turn there are unnecessary obstacles in their path, they recognize prejudice. People know what is happening to them, but accept the situation, because they feel powerless to change it. *Organizing is about building on these sparks of resistance to overcome the mechanisms of disempowerment—to build ways of battling back.*

Disempowering through Humiliation and Self-Blame.

To distract from the social or cultural causes of problems, people are taught to blame themselves for the bad things that happen. Those who work come to accept their low wages as a reflection on their lack of skills or personality and with self-blame fail to look for the unfairness in how people are paid. Worse yet, people might interpret problems as humiliations to be hidden, not acted upon, with a sense of shame keeping them from joining together. Not all that long ago, a disabled person would stay at home; people would go without adequate food rather than to admit to others that they could not earn enough to feed themselves; gays stayed in the closet. Those who feel humiliated are kept both isolated and powerless.

Self-blame distracts from understanding social causes and as such is encouraged by those who want to preserve the status quo. *Blaming the victim* disempowers by denying people any reason to look for causes beyond their own behavior. Police and the courts blame women who have been raped for "asking for it" by dressing sexily or going to a man's apartment. Marchers who are beaten by onlookers or police are told if they hadn't protested, violence would not have occurred. The poor who feel they are at fault for earning so little do not ask who is benefiting from their low salary and long hours. Instead they bear the guilt along with the problems.

Still another variation of this tactic of disempowerment is *blame shifting* in which people are told that their solutions will create even worse difficulties for which those who complain would be at fault. For instance, instead of the owners of polluting factories accepting responsibility for poisoning people, the owners shift blame by claiming that if they were forced to clean the air, the cost of installing scrubbers would make the firm declare bankruptcy, throwing large numbers of people out of work.

To battle disempowering humiliation and self-blame, activists set up safe environments in which to talk about problems. Battered women can do so in shelters, for instance, and in the shelters learn from each other that they are not to blame for provoking abuse (Schillinger 1988, 469). Blame shifting is fought by providing people with the facts of the matter, that clean factories can be profitable.

A sophisticated form of blaming the victim is the *culture of poverty* argument that is used to disempower large groups of people, especially minorities. The culture of poverty argument, one that often borders on racism, claims that culturally supported behavior within an ethnic community is the reason that groups face problems. Those using the manipulation of a culture of poverty argument claim that poor people of a given ethnic group are so caught up in the here and now they fail to save, or help each other start businesses, so that the ethnic economy fails to improve. Blame for problems is shifted to the culture of the ethnic group and away from those who benefit from economic inequalities.

Culture of poverty arguments are fought through exposing their underlying racism. People in minority communities know that they do help each other with emergencies while understanding that friends and neighborhoods cannot help them with startup capital since they, too, lack the funds. In discussion groups, activists make the structural basis of the problems clear, for instance the fact that banks tend to be far less willing to loan money in poor, minority communities than elsewhere so that capital is simply missing.

Disempowering through the Organization of Consent.   Humiliation and self-blame disempower by manipulating people's psychological vulnerabilities. Through the *organization of consent* people accept the cultural value put forth in schools, the media, and in daily life that justify their subordination. These values glorify competition over cooperation, promote individualism over shared responsibility, and communicate an image of capitalism that exaggerates its benefits and ignores its problems.

People are taught that to get ahead they have to compete with one another and please the boss rather than cooperate with each other. At schools, similar competition occurs, when high grades are limited, or when praise is provided for only the selected few. In general, work, school, and sports are portrayed as competitions in which many vie with one another but only a few actually win. Superstars in sports make fortunes, while those who tried and failed work at service jobs; both blue- and white-collar workers lose their jobs, as top executives earn hundreds of times more than ordinary employees.

In multicultural cities, politicians play on a logic similar to the organization of consent by emphasizing the competition between neighborhoods to play off one ethnic group against another. By accepting the belief that politics is about dividing up a limited pool of resources, neighborhood politicians ignore the broader question of why the poor communities receive only the table scraps and the larger projects remain downtown.

This ideology of individualism and competitive capitalism is taught in school and reinforced in movies, literature, and at work. People who can barely make the rent payment imagine being the landlord. Instead of joining a rent strike, individuals try to get a job collecting rent from others, while fantasizing about owning the building. If you identify with the boss, you are unlikely to organize a protest against him or her. This framing is reinforced when the privileged call attention to the exceptional individuals among the disempowered who do succeed. A brilliant child of a migrant farm laborer might become the chief of staff of a major research hospital, but this prestigious position is far more likely to be held by the son (sexism intentional) of a person already well off.

In battling disempowerment caused by the organization of consent, activists must help people understand that the game is fixed, that opportunities are structured according to pre-existing statuses, and that there are institutional barriers that need to be removed. As a renter, you can't become the landlord while working at a minimum wage job with no possibility of savings.

Disempowering through Obscured, Internalized Stratification.   Disempowerment is reinforced by pervasive cultural values that rank people by gender, race, ethnicity, class, wealth, and sexuality, with men favored over women, light-skinned over dark, northern European ethnic groups over others, rich over poor, and straight over gay. These values are reinforced in institutions—schools, places of work, in movies, and even in places of worship—controlled by dominant groups.

White males are privileged often in ways that neither they nor others explicitly recognize and end up disempowering others when they themselves unconsciously assume that they are in charge. Status put-downs can be explicit as occurred in a female led campaign to stop an incinerator from being built during which

> activists began to recognize their shared gender oppression as they confronted the sarcasm and contempt of male political officials and industry representatives who dismissed the women's human concerns as "irrational, uninformed and disruptive." (Stall and Stoecker 2005, 205)

But many do not recognize such stratification or worse yet they accept it and in doing so are disempowered. As working class activist Linda Stout describes,

> Another way oppression affects us is through what we call internalized oppression . . . . what happens to our self-image when we who are oppressed by race, class, and/or gender inequalities accept the societal messages about being "less than": less smart, less deserving, less valuable. . . . These messages are internalized and we feel bad about ourselves. Internalized oppression leads to a lack of self-esteem, even self-hatred, and the hatred of others like us. It reinforces the silencing of low-income and working-class voices, and the voices of women, people of color, and gay, lesbian and bisexual people. (Stout 1996, 89–90)

Yet, even when people recognize that they are being looked down on because of their lower status, it can be difficult to raise the issue and break down the pretense. Bringing concerns with race or gender or economic status to the forefront of an argument is awkward, because culturally we pretend such stratification is irrelevant.

Empowerment comes about when people are willing to fully confront, both with themselves and others, how their status—race, gender, ethnicity, age, size—is influencing the encounters that occur. Recognition is crucial before the disempowering perspective can be fought. For example, in a battle between poor minority women and hospital administrators over the closing of women's health clinics,

> a spokesperson for the hospital attacked the demands of the protesters, telling them, "You don't 'demand' of doctors. You wouldn't make demands of your husbands"

(Morgen 1988, 105). This reply made it clear that the protesters were viewed as patients and as wives, two subservient roles whose arguments were treated as illegitimate, regardless of their content. What had begun as a feeling of being denied access to the decision to close the clinics was transformed through direct contact with the doctors and the hospital into a recognition . . . that "they think we are stupid and unworthy of having our views taken seriously." (Morgen 1988, 104)

The hidden mechanisms of disempowerment were made apparent and could be then publicized.

Disempowering through Learned Inefficacy.   Another form of disempowerment comes about through *learned inefficacy* that is present when people falsely accept the belief they are not competent to fix a problem and as such become apathetic. Learned inefficacy is reinforced as people accept the myth that only experts or those with money or degrees have the skills to succeed. In that way, people are convinced that to contact government requires expensive lawyers or arcane knowledge of bureaucratic and legislative procedures or that starting a small business is an impossible task. By believing they will fail.

Learned inefficacy is reinforced by those in power. Officials might tell citizens that they should not comment on the issue at hand because they don't know the history of it. Bankers justify denying loans to small businesses in poor neighborhoods by arguing that such businesses are bound to fail. People learn from newspapers and classrooms that business lobbyists control decision making and conclude that there is no point in participating.

Learned inefficacy builds upon the sense of incompetence that is reinforced through the ordinary occurrences in life. Public schools impress upon students that if they have no natural talent for something they should not try to do it. Rather than a place where people learn confidence in their ability, school becomes a series of narrowed possibilities with expectations from students being low, especially in inner city schools. Fearing failure and embarrassment, young people learn not to try.

Television reinforces the elimination of possibilities by showing the poor and stigmatized in a negative way. Programs show African Americans as drug dealers, not successful business people. Pictures of inner city neighborhoods emphasize empty lots, dilapidated housing, and unemployed young men hanging out on the streets. Television rarely presents stories about poor people starting their own firms or community groups building new homes to revitalize their neighborhoods, or single mothers getting college degrees, one course at a time. People who live in poor communities see these biased televised portraits of their neighborhoods and conclude there is not much possibility for change.

Linda Stout details how poorly educated, lower income people fear to organize and feeling they lack the tools and skills to do so are stymied by what she terms "invisible walls." People with lesser education fear their language is inadequate for public discourse, erroneously assume that personal experiences do not make up for what they missed in formal education, and have such hectic work schedules that finding time to get together proves problematic (Stout 1996, 117–140). Ironically, this sense of inefficacy can inadvertently be reinforced by well-meaning, socially motivated organizers with good educations who want to solve problems for people rather than empower people to collectively solve problems themselves.

The battle to overcome learned inefficacy begins by building capacity as people learn step by step how to accomplish the smaller changes that teach them skills that then can be used to obtain the larger goals. Confidence to do so is gained through sharing *narratives of success*, stories of how others in similar class, ethnic, gender, or sexual statuses themselves overcame similar problems.

How the Mobilization of Bias Disempowers Those Who Try to Fight Back

Social control through learned inefficacy, fear of humiliation, self-blame, and the organization of consent disempowers people before they even try to fight back. But what about those who have the spunk to try to fight back and be empowered? In these cases, those in power try to slap down activists and prevent them from acting. A wide array of techniques are employed to try to disempower individuals who dare to fight back. We will illustrate four of them.

Disempowering through Attacking the Messenger and Ignoring the Message. The first approach is for those in power to attack the messenger rather than deal with the message itself. One way is to negatively label anyone who dares to point out a problem as a "whiner," or "malcontent" or as recently happened to one of the authors when he spoke out, a "shrill voice" implying the person simply likes to complain for the sake of attracting attention. Similarly, a "gadfly" is portrayed as some sort of minor irritant, a lightweight whose comments can be ignored, or brushed off, while a "whistle blower" is demeaned as a "tattle-tale."

Another approach is to attack the personal credentials of the activist. A person who lacks education is shamed for that lack, yet at the same time an educated activist is put down as a manipulative intellectual. Activists who are expert are accused of showing off. Personal attributes of activists such as being gay, or being a single mother, or receiving welfare assistance are mentioned by those in power even if they are totally irrelevant to the matter at hand. With "guilt by association" or "guilt by previous issue arguments" an activist who is active in one issue is tarred by his or her association with another. How can you speak for neighborhood development when in the past (forgetting it was several decades ago) you protested the war in Vietnam?

Activists should respond to personal attacks but keep the focus on the issue at hand. "It doesn't matter if I dropped out of school or if I have a Ph.D., the official banking data shows that getting mortgages in the Alden Neighborhood is far harder than elsewhere." "Whether or not I am a single mother, my child is still hungry and her school is overcrowded."

Disempowering through Personalization.   Personalization occurs when those in power play on the insecurities of people who are just beginning to have the courage to become involved. Those in high positions argue that they—elected officials or heads of businesses—represent the general interest and that members of a social change organization are worried only about their personal concerns. A request for a company-sponsored daycare facility might be put down by management as a selfish attempt on the part of women (not men) to have someone take over their responsibilities. Or when environmentalists argue with a city council to preserve open space, pro-development council members attack the group, arguing that the environmentalists want the luxury of the park for their own recreational purposes and are indifferent to the jobs development creates.

Disempowering through personalization can be effective, because one of the major reasons people do become involved is because of personal concerns. Organizers and activists try to teach those who face injustices that personal matters do count—not for selfish reasons but because they reflect broader social inequities. You're working in a sweatshop for twelve hours a day because officials won't enforce fair labor laws.

Organizing is often about showing that the personal is the political, exactly what those in power try to portray as illegitimate.

The Zero-Sum Argument and Disempowerment.   Another manipulation is for those in power to play upon the belief that resources are zero-sum, that is, gains by one group can only occur if they are compensated by losses from another group. Public officials sometimes promote the idea that there is only a limited amount of money for community groups and to fund one would be to deny another while businesses claim that to give in to demands of environmentalists would require cutting jobs. Zero-sum arguments are used by those who oppose affirmative action—if we hire women or minorities, well-qualified white men will not get jobs. In the past, in the U.S. South, the zero-sum logic was used to convince poor whites who were only slightly better off than poor blacks, that if black people were to gain, the whites would lose out. This approach encouraged virulent racism and distracted from the overall unfairness of an economic system that made so many whites and blacks poor.

This logic has now been extended in ways that hurt social programs. For some time, conservatives tried to cut federally supported housing programs and failed. But in 2004, a new tact was tried, building on both a blame shifting and a zero-sum argument. An activist mocked the logic of the conservatives:

> You want more money for public housing? Sorry, the cost of vouchers is making us cut public housing. . . . More money for lead safety? Sure wish we could, but those vouchers are eating up all our dollars. . . . because of vouchers, we had to cut funds for permanent housing for other people with disabilities in half. And those vouchers are so darn expensive, we had no choice but to agree to give up CDBG altogether. . . . The zero sum game is a fiction. We must campaign strenuously to stave off these cuts. (Crowley 2005, 1)

Such disempowering tactics are meant to create contention rather than cooperation between those who should be allies by making it more difficult for them to work together.

System Bias as Hidden Disempowerment.   System bias or the more encompassing term of ecological power (Stone 1976; 1989) occurs when "the power-wielder is effective without having to engage in direct action to prevail over opposition or to prevent opposition from developing" (Stone 1976, 105). System bias is a subtle way of controlling by hiding how decisions are actually made while a related but even more subtle form of disempowerment involves what is called nondecisions (Bachrach and Baratz 1963). A nondecision means that important questions about the allocation of resources or actions of government are never asked, there is no forum for their discussion, so that contention over these issues cannot possibly take place.

System bias occurs since elected officials and business people know one another and are financially mutually dependent. Because of the ongoing relationship, those in office absorb the values, goals, and ideas from business people and those values end up shaping political decisions. How does a politician learn about the long-term costs of pollution when his or her friends are from the business community and always talk about the new jobs they will bring? The result is a general tilt of government toward business and wealthy citizens with others simply being kept out of the decisional loop.

System bias also occurs when many of the decisions that are made that favor business are done quietly, without any public airing. Government transactions with the business community are kept secret, not necessarily because of any corruption, but because of the shared belief that business won't deal with government if negotiations are made public. Further, in these dealings language disguises the system bias. Public officials argue that when cities provide money to help businesses the money spent is an "investment." In contrast, help to the poor is labelled as "subsidies" or "welfare" and considered to be money targeted for the benefit of individuals, with no benefit to the collectivity.

Combating Personal Disempowerment

Those in power frame understandings so that ordinary people will believe that fighting back is both wrong and difficult to do. Through socialization at school and work, and then through reinforcement in the media, in literature, and even in places of worship, people are taught that hierarchy and inequality is legitimate, that individualism is more important than shared responsibility and that most people lack the ability and knowledge for political engagement. Further, the structure of a capitalistic economy works to preserve inequalities with workers being afraid of bosses while those who are the most pressed are most likely to lack the economic resources to reach out to government.

Organizing is about improving individuals' confidence in their ability to challenge the status quo while at the same time creating a capacity to do so. But activists who begin to organize are caught in a catch-22: Before collective action can be started people have to feel empowered enough to try. To escape from this *disempowerment trap*, a step-by-step path is followed that builds upon smaller successes to gain confidence to undertake larger efforts. As explained by Gutierrez and colleagues,

> Among the ways to enhance feelings of self-efficacy are personal mastery of a new activity, seeing a similar person master this activity. . . . Both individual capacity and

supportive social environments are necessary for confidence to develop. Confidence can be built by organizing activities intentionally focused on the development of new skills [while] it is important that "failure" be understood as a normal and even expected part of the developmental process. (Gutierrez, Lewis, Nagda et al. 2005, 346–347)

Organizing creates a cycle of empowerment that begins with a simple action. Just coming together in a community meeting shows that people can unite, while successfully holding a meeting at which politicians are held accountable shows even more power. This increased sense of personal empowerment morphs into collective capacity. But how does one start this process of bootstrapping?

Doing so involves three steps. The first step is termed **consciousness raising** during which people learn through shared, reflective discussions that problems are societal, not individual. In the next stage—**capacity building through bootstrapping**—people learn new skills and apply them to specific problems and discover that change, albeit small and focused, is possible. With **collective empowerment** people establish the organizations that continue the collective mission.

Consciousness Raising

To the extent to which people feel problems are personal, their own fault, and neither shared nor social, they remain disempowered. This sense of powerlessness is fought by learning to understand that personal problems are often society-based, building upon what C. Wright Mills (Mills 1959) termed the

> **sociological imagination** . . . *the ability to understand the relationship between what is happening in people's personal lives and the social forces that surround them.* (Sullivan 2003, 9)

To develop this understanding people come together in consciousness raising sessions, talk about what bothers them, and in doing so discover that problems are shared and others like themselves are victims.

Consciousness raising involves active listening to others and being willing to share personal experiences in a group. Women talk together and discover that, regardless of their income or education, men stereotype them as emotional, incomprehensible, spending machines. Neighbors who have tried to buy homes and were turned down for mortgages meet in a group, talk over their situations, and learn that their failure to get the money was not simply due to a slight blemish on their credit records but instead that banks seem always to find something wrong with the applications from anyone from their community.

This learning, what Paulo Freire termed critical pedagogy, goes far beyond mere discussion. Consciousness raising is directly linked to actions meant to combat the problems discovered. As Freire argued,

> it is only when the oppressed find the oppressor out and become involved in the organized struggle for their liberation that they begin to believe in themselves. This discovery cannot be purely intellectual but must involve action; nor can it be limited to mere

activism, but must include serious reflection: only then will it be a praxis. (Freire 1970, 52)

Gays employed in a firm get together and share insights on the humiliations that they receive, but only when they unite and battle back do they learn the extent of the problem they collectively face. For instance, gay activists in a firm seek out health benefits for their partners and when doing so are put down and firmly told, "NO, benefits are only for heterosexual couples." This shared experience in discovering that there is no support for their concerns makes clear to them the extent of societal oppression and motivates actions.

The ongoing dialogue and active listening that occurs as people share experiences with one another helps build analytical capacity about how economic and social structures oppress, a process Freire termed a *critical consciousness*. These actions raise a willingness to ask the deeper questions on how and why subordination is maintained. Women and minorities recognize that white men have a better chance at obtaining higher positions at work. Through further reflections, through critically thinking about the issues, people begin to ask why white men have better contacts for getting the jobs or are taught in school the skills needed for higher level positions while people of color and women are not. Thinking has moved from the immediate problem to the underlying structures that disempower.

Capacity Building through Bootstrapping

Capacity building is the antidote to learned inefficacy, the belief that one should not try because failure is inevitable. Capacity building has two components. One is the knowledge and skills on how to build organizations, carry out campaigns, or implement economic and social improvement. The second component of capacity building is the belief, based on experience, that effort will be rewarded, that people working together have the power to carry out a task.

Capacity building can be bolstered in a variety of ways. Through conducting training programs and through encouraging schools to improve their curriculum, community organizations help people learn new skills. These skills are reinforced through practice, whether in running meetings, organizing campaigns, or in teaching how to run and manage property. For instance, studies of tenant management in low income housing shows that "involving residents in the management and ownership of low income housing leads to an increased sense of control and ownership, two key aspects of the notion of empowerment" (Van Ryzin 1994, 250). Capacity building involves acquiring both the skills and the confidence to try.

Capacity building is reinforced through success. Initial campaigns or projects in which a community member has participated and which reached a satisfactory outcome create the belief that further efforts will work. As explained by a member of an organization for the disabled, successful actions build capacity:

Before the project I felt helpless about the decisions that were affecting my life. But then we visited our legislators at the Capitol and learned that letters and phone calls are taken seriously and can be effective in decisions. (Checkoway and Norsman 1986, 270).

Celebrations of victories are a form of capacity building.

Self-Assertion as a Step in Capacity Building. After people recognize that problems are shared and structurally caused, the next step is self-assertion through which people give vent to their anger. Individuals learn to talk back to a landlord, demanding and getting heating and plumbing repairs for one apartment and, better yet, discover that it is even more empowering if tenants of a whole building together pressure the landlord to provide improved housing conditions. These acts of self-assertion combat the cultural belief that owners have a right to charge what they want or allow a property to get run down.

Resistance involves not backing down when confronted with an evasive answer or not being intimidated by an authority figure. An employee may publicly insist that the boss clearly set forth job responsibilities or express a preference for being called Mrs. Jones, rather than Betty. Individuals may demand information from banks about where housing loans are being made. Organizers work hard to encourage people to speak out in public, to find their voice, and talk back (hooks 1989)

Capacity Building Bootstraps toward Empowerment. Bootstrapping toward empowerment involves two more steps. The first is to carry out an activity that has low costs but that yields a victory. For example, the organization gets a politician who has avoided constituents to show up at a meeting, and perhaps convinces city hall to put in a needed stop sign. With this victory in hand, the group then moves on to larger issues, such as neighborhood safety. To bootstrap successfully, activist organizations must carefully choose issues that are important enough to engage people, teach lessons on how to conduct actions, yet at the same time be winnable. In addition, initial actions should be designed to encourage many people to pitch in, such as having the group repair a deteriorating home, or walking to city hall en masse and demanding that the police chief explain why no action has been taken to close the dope house.

Framing the Agenda. Capacity is expanded by putting forth an agenda that makes invisible problems visible and in doing so combating system bias. A public demonstration or a media campaign is about turning what has been treated as nondecisions into issues that now must be faced. Few politicians or bureaucrats advocate poor housing, loss of jobs, neglect of AIDS patients, leaving the homeless on the streets, isolating the elderly, polluting the environment, poorly educating the young, or ignoring migrant workers. These are problems that, once raised, people will agree should be solved. But because the costs of solving these problems is perceived as too high, those in power try to assure that there is no forum in which they can be discussed. Community and social change organizations focus public attention on these issues, putting them back on the public agenda.

Setting a public agenda is empowering in two ways. The success of getting the broader community to see the issues in a favorable light is a milestone; and combating the system bias that kept the issues off the public agenda gives group members a new sense of possibilities.

Conclusion

Empowerment begins as people recognize that they are not alone, that those in privileged positions gain from problems that others face, and that these problems are shared. The march toward empowerment continues as people learn the skills and then put these skills into practice in social change campaigns. Empowerment increases when people recognize that they share responsibility for one another and collectively can bring about change. While working together they can expand the sense of community, a mutuality of obligation to one another. People learn that by helping others they also help themselves. To build on this sense of mutual obligation, people set up *formal social change organizations*—gather and concentrate resources of money, time, and expertise—to resolve problems. When organizations are in place that are guided by their membership, people no longer feel they lack control and feel empowered.

Community and *organization* are a means for building both personal and collective empowerment. As people strengthen the bonds of community they discover their own capacity and through the ability to work with others feel empowered. Organization members learn respect and tolerance and how to cooperate with one another. Ultimately, people discover that battling back against disempowerment is not simply for themselves or their families, but is part of their responsibility to a shared and evolving community.

In this chapter we have discussed the concept of empowerment. In the next two chapters, we examine the other pillars on which the empowerment cycle is based—through strengthening community and by establishing social change organizations.

CHAPTER

5

Building Community to Create Capacity for Change

Community describes the ways in which people either consider themselves or are defined by others as linked together and sharing a common fate. Community linkages can come from living near one another, sharing a personal characteristic, or having a strong belief held in common. In general, community describes the ways in which people define themselves as part of socially constructed groups, rather than seeing themselves as isolated individuals. Within a community, individuals can access the **social capital**, "the stocks of social trust, norms, and networks that people can draw upon in order to solve common problems" (Lang and Hornburg 1998, 4). Being part of a community can imply an obligation to help one another and share responsibilities. But what constitutes community can change as the sense of belonging is constantly being **constructed** and reconstructed as people redefine what constitutes a particular community and what obligations are created through belonging.

The Variety of Community Bonds

Community refers to many different forms of linkage. In **social networks** people might merely know one another and share little more, while in **helping networks** people are linked to one another and are willing to offer assistance: small loans, baby sitting, help in combating alcoholism, a place to stay when funds are short. **Electronic networks** describe people who are loosely connected on the Internet who provide help and information to one another within an area of shared interests. In contrast, **affinity groups** are closely knit face-to-face personal linkages between a few individuals who deeply trust one another to provide support during trying times, for example, when facing arrest as part of a demonstration. **Activist networks** refer to people connected by their willingness to battle on an issue.

A **perceptual community** consists of people who are seen by others as sharing a common belief or characteristic and as such might not even know one another personally. Such communities can be based upon shared **ascriptive attributes** such as place of birth, gender, or having a common racial, ethnic, or language background.

When people with shared ascriptive characteristics come together they create a **solidarity community**—perhaps as African Americans, Italian Catholics, or people of Croation descent—and feel joined by common history, rituals, customs, or beliefs.

In **identity communities** people intentionally choose to define themselves as part of a community. A surname of Cohen would usually label a person as part of a Jewish solidarity community irrespective of what the individual felt. But for that person to be part of a Jewish identity community, he or she would have to accept that label and act in ways that show he or she is a member of that group, perhaps by working to keep traditions alive. People can decide to identify as part of identity communities that focus on issues relevant to the labelled group as, for instance, identifying as feminists, gay activists, or part of a "deafness culture" or as a member of the disability community (Fleischer and Zames 2001).

But the meaning of being in an identity community is **constructed**, that is, negotiated with others, rather than being a clearcut matter. Does identifying as gay refer to only sexual orientation, or does it include a broader set of cultural beliefs that define a shared lifestyle? Does identifying as deaf refer only to lack of hearing, or does it entail being a member of a linguistic culture based on American Sign Language?

A **community of interest**, or **issue community**, is more focused than an identity community, though oftentimes what is being promoted as the interest might be the values of an identity community. Communities of interest come about for the very purposing of battling a problem that those in the community share and understand in a similar way; for instance, within a solidarity community the shared interest might be in preserving a religious tradition. Issue communities are **social constructions** as potential activists reach agreement through both overt and tacit negotiation on how to understand an issue so that separate, distinct issue communities might emerge on the same matter.

Finally, community can refer to a **geographic place**—a neighborhood, a large housing complex, or a park where the homeless congregate, perhaps even a small city. Some geographic areas become home to those who are part of solidarity communities because they share the need for a common house of worship or for specialty foods, or simply to meet one another because of sexual orientation. But geographic proximity need not imply that a community exists, as sometimes people just live in an area because it is affordable or convenient.

Community membership is not a given but instead is a **constructed concept**, emerging only as people agree on what belonging means. To what extent do people initially of African descent, but who came to the United States from Haiti or the Dominican Republic, define themselves as members of the same solidarity community as other African Americans? Does someone from Japan identify as an Asian American or as a Japanese American? or neither? or both? A person is born a female, but chooses whether to be a feminist. Even what neighborhood entails can be a construct, as boundaries shift as ethnic groups come and go or the value of housing changes from block to block.

Community membership differs in intensity, from affinity groups where people can quite literally put their lives in each other's hands, to some neighborhoods where those living next door do not even recognize each other. In helping communities, especially when support is provided on intimate matters, personal trust is necessary. But in issue communities many people might not know one another at all. Would you leave a child with a stranger?

Further, identifying with a community in no way implies a willingness to join in social change work. Those in a religious community offer one another support when people die or on matters of faith, but do so out of religious obligation, not as an effort to change the world. In contrast, membership in issue communities—those working to preserve freedom of choice, or fighting for a minimum wage or to preserve the environment—is primarily about fighting for change, even when those in the community are united only on this one concern.

Building and Strengthening Communities: The Path from Social Bonds to Social Action

Activists *build on* existing communities' bonds to unify people, while at the same time work to *strengthen bonds between people* to create the sense of we-ness that forms the mutual responsibility to undertake collective actions. Organizing is often about building on a shared sense of community and then turning the linkages felt into an obligation to join in collective action. People who are part of a Spanish-speaking community know that organizing is about building on this to unite people to combat the economic and personal discrimination that those of Spanish speaking descent face.

Let us explore the ways in which people are linked together within networks and geographic communities as well as in solidarity and identity communities. After doing so we will examine how the concept of social capital suggests ways in which people can support one another within communities and in doing so eventually work on shared issues.

Reinforcing Social Networks

Networks describe linkages between people. Networks can involve casual acquaintances, indirect links between two people who have a common acquaintance, or the many connections of those in a solidarity community located in one neighborhood. In addition, nowadays networks, especially issue networks, emerge electronically, as people interested in a shared concern—to fight against homelessness, to advocate for living wages, to preserve speech rights, among hundreds of issues—link together on the Internet.

Network connections influence the decision whether to join in social change actions. When individuals decide whether or not to join in collective action they will ask others in their immediate social networks for approval, even if these individuals are not involved in the activity. For instance, many civil rights activists became fully committed to the battle for racial justice only after getting support from their friends and family (McAdam and Paulsen 1993). More generally,

> networks create an initial disposition to participate . . . network functions . . . right before prospective members join a social movement organization by offering those

who are culturally sensitive to the issue an opportunity to participate . . . networks create a link between political potential and a movement organization (and) define different structures of meanings which affect the intensity of participation. (Passy 2001, 186–187)

Networks are then strengthened as people join together in a cause. For example, ideologically committed individuals joined the civil rights movement and moved to the South. Once there, many lived together (for their own protection) in safe houses and in doing so formed strong network attachments that were later evoked when the same individuals joined in other efforts.

Networks differ in intensity and extent. Members of a teenage gang are tightly networked to one another and communicate on all matters, while community activists in a small town might know each other well, join together on a variety of social change issues, yet might not even know what one another does for a living. In contrast, some networks involve quite casual linkages as when you ask a friend to recommend a quality tradesperson and then hire that person to perform a task.

But even these indirect, loosely linked networks can provide a base for organizing as **liberated networks** (Wellman and Leighton 1979) to create the indirect connections that provide communication channels along which support for collective action can emerge. A neighbor talks with another about a bad intersection, while local store owners discuss difficulties customers face in finding parking. Through the loosely structured liberated networks, the neighbors and the store owners discover each others' concerns, come together, note that a traffic study is required, and together pressure city hall to bring the study about. A neighborhood organization has begun.

Special language is used to describe the intensity and scope of social networks. **Social glue** refers to "the degree to which people take part in group life [and also] the amount of trust or the comfort level that people feel when participating in these groups" (Lang and Hornburg 1998, 4). When social glue is strong, people are linked through many different ties, perhaps doing business together, going to the same churches, participating in the same service clubs, and sharing the same ethnic traditions. Social glue is typically strong in solidarity communities. In more casual networks, social glue is weak, for example, in neighborhoods occupied primarily by renters who come into the community for a short time and then move elsewhere, or in commuting suburbs where people live in one place, work in another, and patronize businesses in still another place.

However, even when social glue is strong, those in the networks might not be amenable to organizing with others. For instance, if people in a tightly linked local network share a belief that ordinary workers can never fight back and that's the way the world is, each member of this network will reinforce with one another this disempowering belief. Strong social glue can build a coherence in a belief, but in this case a belief that disempowers by limiting information on the possibility for action.

In contrast, the phrase **social bridges** describes network linkages to the world outside of the immediate set of acquaintances. Social bridges (Granovetter 1973) open up a wide world of alternative knowledge beyond people's immediate experiences and "are vital because they not only connect groups to one another but also give members in any one group access to the larger world outside their social circle through a chain of affiliations" (Lang and Hornburg 1998, 4). Middle class people who meet each other in college and later live in different cities, but maintain contact, form a social bridge as do community activists who meet one another at national conventions.

When people are closely bound together, that social glue is strong, but where social bridges are lacking, as often occurs within solidarity or identity communities, organizing is difficult except on the matters that already link people. People will work to defend their cultural traditions but are harder to mobilize on issues that seem more distant. Similarly, within many poor communities social glue is strong, people know one another and readily help each other. But there tend to be fewer social bridges, limiting resources for action. People in poor neighborhoods might want to aid one another in finding jobs, but lack the contacts—the social bridges—to employers outside of the neighborhood. Building social bridges then becomes a core part of organizing work.

Neighborhood as Community

Neighborhood refers to a physical place, whether several blocks in a city or a large housing complex. Neighborhood organizing is about creating a shared responsibility to help improve both the physical place as well as the lives of those who live there. Because of geographic proximity, those in a neighborhood confront varying common problems: poverty, heavy traffic, poor schools, street crime, lack of affordable housing, floods, or closing of local stores. Neighborhoods are easiest to organize when those who live there face an immediate problem, for instance, recognizing that homes will be destroyed if the city and state construct a planned highway.

But defining what constitutes a neighborhood is far from easy. Geographic neighborhoods might be distinguished from one another by being separated by major highways, large parks, or busy shopping malls. Other neighborhoods are defined as the service area for a grammar school, a parish, or a community center. In older cities, neighborhoods might be remnants of areas set up to house workers for major industrial activities, such as the animal slaughtering that occurred in the Back of the Yards or the rail car construction in the Pullman area in Chicago. In larger cities, many neighborhoods were originally small villages that later were incorporated into a growing metropolis. In suburban areas and growing cities, the boundaries of neighborhoods are often those of the subdivisions that were built at the same time by housing developers. City governments might designate a geographic area as a neighborhood. Chicago, for instance, has seventy-some named neighborhood areas, as does smaller Minneapolis; officials in Dayton, San Antonio, Birmingham, and numerous other cities have divided their cities into neighborhood planning areas (Berry, Portney, and Thomson 1993).

Neighborhoods can be defined in terms of the prominent groups that live there, for instance, gold coasts as the enclaves of wealth, Bohemian neighborhoods, or as places that welcome gays. Often neighborhoods are labelled by the dominant ethnic group, though ethnic dominance of a community is often transient. Today with the major exception of African American neighborhoods and a handful of Hispanic areas (Massey and Denton 1993), few neighborhoods are racially, ethnically, or culturally homogeneous, at least, beyond the block level. In the sixties, the African American community of Watts in Los Angeles erupted in urban protests; thirty years later the same neighborhood again flared, this time called South-Central and predominantly occupied by Hispanic Americans. Today city neighborhoods must deal with multiple ethnic/cultural groups sharing a common space (Goode and Schneider 1994).

Urban and suburban neighborhoods are constantly in change, sometimes as a result of the movement of jobs, other times in response to ethnic and racial antagonisms, and most recently because of increased immigration. Unfortunately some neighborhood organizations have come about for the very purpose of opposing newer groups. In these places, there can be tensions over what language should be spoken in stores, government, social service agencies, or who owns the stores. Customs can divide. For instance, eye contact among Koreans, who own stores in predominantly African American neighborhoods, has quite a different meaning than it does for the black inhabitants, leading to misunderstandings (what is seen as politeness by one group is seen as a snub by another). Other times a successful meld of different cultures does appear. In one neighborhood we studied, older inhabitants of Polish origin were strongly objecting to the use of Spanish by the newer immigrants. Yet, these same individuals worked closely with the newer arrivals to pressure the school board to provide the classrooms needed by the increase in Spanish-speaking children.

Neighborhoods can represent places of ethnic pride that speaks against dominant power structures. For instance, a African American area, Bronzeville, had developed in Chicago as a result of racial segregation and subordination. However, three generations later when the opportunity came about to renew the neighborhood as a historic district and by doing so attract tourist trade, those living there reinvented a neighborhood history of Black Pride that provided them with a shield against the dominant white power structure:

> Heritage development, and the Bronzeville heritage specifically provides residents with the opportunity to make a stand against the encroachment of the city and white developers. But historic Bronzeville is also a constructed identity, a strategic re-imagining of community used to unite the community and galvanize its support for development. (Boyd 2000, 113)

Probably the easiest neighborhoods to organize are those that already have a reputation for activism and attract residents who choose community involvement. The Cedar-Riverside neighborhood in Minneapolis lured individuals interested in establishing alternative economic and social systems (Stoecker 1994); the Castro community in San Francisco has been open to people associated with the gay lifestyle; many college towns such as Madison, Wisconsin, or Berkeley, California, are well known for activist neighborhoods. Areas such as the Five Oaks neighborhood in Dayton, Ohio, form

> an "ideological community" . . . That is, residents choose the neighborhood in part because of its urbanness and diversity and because they consciously seek a neighborhood that will serve as a community. (Majka and Donnelly 1988)

Such places encourage innovative experiments in organizing. In contrast, other neighborhoods are about defending their inhabitants from outsiders and are unlikely places for progressive organizing. People might move to "gated communities"—neighborhoods that are homogeneous (middle or upper class) and intentionally cut off from those who are different from themselves (Blakely and Snyder 1997).

Sometimes local governments make it easier to organize by decentralizing decision making to the neighborhood level. Under Mayor Flynn in Boston and Mayor Washington in Chicago, City Hall provided neighborhood organizations with say over public decisions. In Chicago, neighborhood groups help govern schools and work with police (Fung 2004). In other cities, zoning, land use, and large infrastructure projects, and, in some cases, parts of the city budget must be approved by a recognized community organization, usually elected by neighborhood residents (Berry, Portney, and Thomson 1993). Research has shown that

> city government sponsored neighborhood associations, **if given genuine power over local affairs** (emphasis Rubin), appear to be more effective in involving and empowering disadvantaged minorities and generating a deeper sense of community than the voluntary organizations usually stressed in the civil society argument. (Foley and Edwards 1997, 559)

But questions are raised on whether those who are active in the neighborhoods are truly representative of others living there. In stable neighborhoods, those participating in government-sponsored organizations do reflect the views of community members, but this is not the case in poorer, less stable neighborhoods (Swindell 2000).

Progressive organizers are particularly interested in minority neighborhoods, especially those that better off individuals have left. Many of these neighborhoods, though poor, are often stable, with rich traditions and helping networks that provide a foundation for organizing work. But some, labelled as a hyperghetto, are harder to organize as it

> has lost much of its organizational strength—the "pulpit and the press," for instance have virtually collapsed as collective agencies—as it has become increasingly marginal economically; its activities are no longer structured around an internal and relatively autonomous social space that duplicates the institutional structure of the larger society and provides basic minimal resources for social mobility. (Warcquant and Wilson 1989, 15)

Scholars argue on how many neighborhoods actually fit the extreme of the hyperghetto that have in them an array of overlapping problems. These neighborhoods are characterized by many female-headed households, deteriorated physical structures, low levels of education, lack of jobs, and high crime rates (Jargowsky 1997). In addition, individuals living in poor communities are less likely than others to be socially connected to those who have contacts for jobs or services (Tigges, Browne, and Green 1998). Yet, as Felton Earls, one of the co-researchers in Chicago's project on human development, stated:

> We found in poor neighborhoods that people had very dense social networks. They were sharing food and money sometimes. They definitely knew each other and knew each other by name, but when the time came to . . . call the police, or go to city hall or [when residents were asked] "Do you think your neighbor would stop that child from

carrying a gun and joining a gang?" that's when these dense networks seemed paralyzed. (Williams 2004, 7)

Fortunately, recent research has shown that the number of the poor living in neighborhoods with such extreme difficulties has dropped from 17 percent to 12 percent (Kingsley and Pettit 2003, 1).

Neighborhoods are also arenas of social conflict that come about in battles over territory or prestige. One neighborhood we studied had half a dozen rival Korean clubs. Within the clubs the social ties were strong, but rivalries between the clubs precluded them from working together even though individuals shared a common ethnic culture. Conflicts may show up as fights between street gangs over turf, or the use of playgrounds and hanging places such as taverns, ethnic "ownership" of particular churches, or stores and restaurants that cater to the preferences of one ethnic group over another. Ethnic groups contend over the symbolic and material ownership of neighborhood space, battling over whose stores, churches, or social mores should dominate. Such battles make organizing quite difficult.

Solidarity, Identity, and Issue Communities as Evolving Social Constructs

What is considered as a community is often a social construct; that is, it emerges from a shared and socially created definition. Am I a member of an affordable housing network because I support affordable housing and know others who do so, or is further action required? Just because I live on Hyde Park Boulevard, does that mean I identify with the Hyde Park community?

Identity communities, solidarity communities, and issue communities are social constructs. Identity communities come about as people define community membership in terms of shared characteristics varying from a common hobby or avocation, a disability or disease, or, of course, a common heritage, culture, language, or the like. Solidarity communities are constructed as people see themselves, or are labelled by others, as being part of the same racial or ethnic group, or who accept that they share a similar history, cultural traditions, language, or religion, even if that shared history or culture is mostly a fabrication. An issue community emerges as people frame—establish and accept a shared social definition of—the causes and preferred solutions of a social problem.

Solidarity ties are usually based on birth, and for some are seen as given, not something that evolves. You are born from Irish, or Ethiopian, or Thai ancestry, or your religion of birth is Hindu, Catholic, Dutch Reform, or whatever. But such identities evolve over time. Certain Orthodox Hasidic Jews who live together in urban neighborhoods consider Conservative Jews as less religious and not truly of the same faith, and hence not part of their solidarity community. Slavic groups who were antagonistic to one another in Europe accepted a common cultural identity in the United States as part of their effort to unite to gain political clout (Kornblum 1974). Similarly, ties within identity communities—being a feminist, or gay, or disabled—come about only after people construct (define) what membership in that community entails. Are lesbians necessarily feminists? Can a person be considered part of a progressive community yet still oppose abortion rights?

With solidarity communities, cultural pride and ethnic identity provide the social glue that enables people to come together. People are likely to give to charities sponsored by their solidarity group, even if the contributors don't foresee that they themselves are likely to need support. Or people of a given ethnic neighborhood may rally when a hurricane devastates their ancestral homeland, collecting food and clothes in local churches.

Members of solidarity communities reinforce their connectedness through shared rituals, holidays, festivals, and evocations of a common history. To build a sense of community within a solidarity group, organizers encourage social events during which members relate shared historic sufferings to one another. Such narratives replay past traumas and humiliations: forced migrations for Native Americans, incarceration in concentration camps for Japanese Americans during World War II, slavery for African Americans. Similarly, the oppression of gays, or the callousness of the broader society that fails to accommodate those who are wheelchair-bound, or the shared put-downs that women receive become the glue that links people within an identity community. These historic, mutual experiences can be simultaneously a cause for pride—we went through all this and survived—as well as a cause for rebellion. Native American organizers build solidarity within the group by narrating how mainstream society stole Native American lands and deceived members of the group. Then by orchestrating actions on these same lands, demand that government must now restore traditional hunting, fishing, and land rights that it had taken away.

By reframing how the past is understood, solidarity groups turn prior humiliation into a source of pride. Felix Padilla describes how an activist Puerto Rican ideology came about by emphasizing differences in values from the dominant Caucasian groups:

> An essential feature of this ideology is the rejection of "white definitions" and myths of subordination and their replacement by Puerto Rican definitions. . . . This ideology defines Puerto Ricans as possessing precisely those human qualities in which dominant white America is so morally deficient, and some of the very qualities by which white America defines this subordinate group are transformed from denigration to approbation. (Padilla 1987, 65)

Those who self-label themselves as belonging to a solidarity community are more likely to share linkages than are strangers. Still each generation constructs anew what parts of a shared past to emphasize on which to build these linkages. Do African Americans emphasize the experience of slavery or the unrecognized triumphs of the past or both? Is black culture seen as complementary to, a predecessor of, or separate from white culture? Do American-born Japanese build their identities around a shared culture that emphasizes courtesy, calmness, and loyalty to the group over the individual—values that go back to the old country? Or do they emphasize the abuses of the imprisonment during World War II, events that underscore their common history in the United States? Is language something core to the cultural identity, as occurs among some Spanish-speaking groups, or is religious practice the defining characteristic of group membership and identity?

As ethnic groups construct or reconstruct definitions of who they are, certain symbols (either older historic ones or those newly invented) become the focus around which organizing takes place. Places take on symbolic value as ethnic churches, associations, restaurants, and other locales associated with the cultural group become their place to meet, to share information, or to do organizing work.

By forging new symbols and accentuating the bonds that foster solidarity, the organizing campaign itself becomes part of the re-creation of community. The African American civil rights movement was built on pre-existing solidarity bonds, but the terrors of working together in a hostile environment strengthened cultural linkages (McAdam 1994). Separate groups of Asian descent in the United States worked to create solidarity in their own groups—among Chinese Americans, Japanese Americans, or Filipino Americans—but their organizing showed the need to construct a broader overarching sense of an Asian American identity to obtain political power (Wei 1993). At times, though, the broader community comes together in response to anti-Asian racism, while at other times only the narrower interests of the separate solidarity communities of Chinese, Japanese, Philippino, or Vietnamese descent predominates. (Võ 2004). As the American Indian Movement began to chalk up impressive successes, more people of Native American descent identified as "Native American" when asked by the U.S. census, in part because they now could receive benefits, but also because the skillful use by organizers of Native American symbols and ceremonies created pride of being a Native American. Solidarity communities provide a basis for organizing work while successful campaigns increase pride in being part of the solidarity community.

The very construction of what constitutes a community can provide motivation for action. In East Los Angeles

> "the media's projection of an image of the Eastside community as undesirable and dangerous has persisted over the last three decades" (Pardo 1998, 66). Upset by this negative construction of a Hispanic community, women activists, who knew each other through both parish and gendered activities worked to portray the neighborhood as a place of cultural pride, constructing an image of place that deserves respectful treatment by outsiders that then became a motivation for others to join. (Pardo 1998, 98)

But even within what to outsiders appears to be a solidarity community, opposing constructions take place. In comparing several distinct Mexican American organizations, Benjamin Márquez noted crucial differences in how ethnic identity was constructed.

> Mexican Americans disagree over asserted identities because they are essentially contested concepts . . . that incorporate judgments about the causes and intensity of racial discrimination, the legitimacy of economic hierarchies and the value of Mexican cultural practices. . . . A variety of political identities can be formed by people who are

part of the same racial or ethnic group and share a similar economic status or cultural background. Ethnic and racial identities emerge from distinct visions of community life and politics. (Márquez 2003, 7)

Solidarity Communities in a Multicultural Society. Solidarity communities create a sense of togetherness based upon shared racial, religious, or linguistic characteristics. Today, though, the multicultural and multiethnic composition of an increasingly diverse society complicates matters. Larger cities, and even smaller places, are increasingly populated with a crosscutting array of those from different ethnic and language groups. Further, people labelled by outsiders as belonging to one solidarity group may themselves consider they belong to numerous, sometimes contending, subgroups—Asians divide into country of origin as do Spanish speakers, then divided further by social class and political history.

Efforts to create communities solely based on ethnic pride are antagonistic to a broader goal of creating a multiethnic, multiracial organization to combat shared problems. Pride in shared culture may result in denigrating those who are not part of the group, as in a multicultural community's effort to build solidarity within each group often plays upon negative stereotypes one group has of the other (Goode and Schneider 1994, 209–41).

Solidarity bonds can make issue organizing difficult. Socially conservative African American churches that unite those in an ethnic group find it hard to reach out to others on issues such as gay rights (hooks 1989, 123). The Catholic church-based Campaign for Human Development that has brought together people within solidarity communities to work for economic justice "will not consider projects or organizations which promote or support abortion, euthanasia, the death penalty, or any other affront to human life or dignity"—as defined by Catholic church doctrine (Fellner 1998, 21). In Hispanic communities, the traditional solidarity values conflict with feminist concerns. For Hispanic men, politics is separate from the personal, while for women the political and personal blend together (Hardy-Fanta 1993, 34).

Organizing in a multicultural community requires special understanding and talent, recognizing both the importance of building on the bonds that unite those within one solidarity group while recognizing the necessity of building bridges between different communities. We shall explore this crucial topic further in Chapter 15.

Building Culture within Issue Communities

Issue communities emerge among those who share a common **framing** of both the problem and the acceptable solutions and often in doing so end up creating bonds of solidarity that go beyond the immediate issue. Steven E. Brown, cofounder of the Institute on Disability Culture, observes:

> "People with disabilities have forged a group identity. We share a common history of oppression and a common bond of resilience. We generate art, music, literature, and

other expressions of our lives and our culture infused from our experience of disability. Most importantly, we are proud of ourselves as people with disabilities. We claim our disabilities with pride, as part our identity. We are who we are: We are people with disabilities." (Fleischer and Zames 2001, 203)

Such framings turn what some had considered problems into a shared culture of pride.

As with other cultural groups those in an issue community create icons of noted individuals and crucial events that define their shared cause. Present-day civil rights activists continue to honor Dr. Martin Luther King, Jr. or César Chaves. Housing activists respect and share the memory of Cushing Dolbeare, the founder of the National Low Income Housing Coalition, while treating the Community Reinvestment Act as a sacred cultural icon that must be preserved at all costs. The gay movement celebrates as part of its shared cultural history the Stonewall demonstrations, in which gay activists fought the police who taunted them because of their sexual orientation. In general, those in an issue community develop **shared narratives**, stories of who they are and why they do what they do, that are passed from one activist to another in ways that allow a culture of resistance to be sustained. Narratives can include pride in what others consider to be outrageous actions, as shown in the pride taken in some of the more flamboyant events of the sixties.

The very act of participating in direct actions strengthens the cultural identity of individuals within an issue community almost irrespective of the success of the actions (Nepstad 2004, 56). Sharon Kurtz describes how the clerical workers at Columbia University organized a union that had to cross race, class, and gender lines and in doing so created a shared culture that promoted economic justice through group activities of shared song, dance, and rapping. The emerging culture created a sense of unity as it "helped members feel they were on a moral crusade, part of a community and at the same time have a lot of fun" (Kurtz 2002, 99) while "the cross union and community support helped to create an empowering upbeat culture that drew together many traditions, labor, minority and women" (Kurtz 2002, 155).

Building on and Strengthening Social Capital as Part of Community

Social capital refers to the density and patterning of connections that enable people as well as institutions to work together and consists of "the resources embedded in social relations among persons and organizations that facilitate cooperation and collaboration in communities" (Committee for Economic Development 1995, 12). Social capital includes a willingness to share knowledge, help in handling ordinary matters of daily life, as well as the sharing of information about and connections to government, banks, or businesses (Putnam 1993; Temkin and Rohe 1998; Weil 2005, 226–27). In communities in which social capital is high a parent can leave a child with a neighbor, people help each other in finding jobs, doing repairs, and support one another during the life crises. Neighborhoods with more social capital are less likely to decline economically and "more likely to remain stable over time" (Temkin and Rohe 1998, 81, 84).

Social capital provides a base upon which organizing can be built as people who feel obligations to their neighbors are more likely to participate in community problem-solving (Lelieveldt 2004). In places with high social capital community institutions—churches, businesses, social clubs, political groups, nonprofits, schools, branches of local government—are considered as sources of help, support, and information. But more is needed to stimulate collective action, as people must also believe that others have a willingness to stand together for common interests, a concept that is termed **collective efficacy** (Gibson, Zhao, Lovrich, et al. 2002, 539; Sampson 2001, 95). Collective efficacy

> combines notions of trust and cohesion with shared expectations for intervening on behalf of commonly held goals such as keeping an eye on neighborhood children. Such efficacy . . . moves beyond the now widely used concept of "social capital" because it speaks not just to the tools at hand for people to be part of society, but also to their ability and willingness to take action. (Williams 2004, 7)

Even in the poorest and most crime ridden neighborhoods "collective efficacy . . . is linked to reduced violence" (Sampson, Raudenbusch, and Earls 1997) as people are willing to set up community crime patrols.

Social capital measures the potential of people being able to work together and help one another, while collective efficacy indicates the belief that such action will succeed. Both provide a way of looking at a community to measure strengths that go beyond material wealth. A community with industries that are owned by outsiders and that employ many who live elsewhere might have material assets but little social capital and little chance to control its own destiny. In contrast, a community in which people help one another, are linked through shared experience, kinship, or religion, or one in which the norms are those of cooperation might be rich in social capital, irrespective of its material wealth.

But how do activists try to turn social capital into a sense of collective efficacy? To begin, they look for the social and economic assets that are already in the community, rather than simply concentrate on the problems (Kretzman and McKnight 1993). Assets include the interpersonal connections between community members, the linkages between people and institutions, and the connections between the institutions themselves. Then based on these linkages, actions are begun to solve easier problems in ways that expand social capital. If there are no block associations, a block party can help neighbors get to know each other and pave the way for more organized activities. If there is no way for residents to follow neighborhood news, a few community members can write and distribute a newsletter. As people see that collective action both can solve problems and bring people closer together the willingness to join in other activities increases.

Projects that social change organizations introduce to expand economic development can increase both economic and social capital. For example,

> microenterprise programs are typically thought of as economic development strategies . . . the community development element—which involves connecting people to each other and to critical organizations—is often overlooked. . . . Microenterprise . . . programs (have) emphasis on relationship building. . . . (Servon 1998)

Microenterprises contribute directly to the creation of social capital by connecting people to each other and with community institutions, linking women with banks or with community colleges. Other strategies of engagement build social capital,

> such as community visioning strategies, role playing exercises, trust-building exercises and negotiation exercises, . . . Social events, such as street fairs and carnivals are also effective engagement strategies. In communities that contain social factions, we also need to design strategies carefully to bring factions together and assist them in finding common ground. These are the types of activities that are likely to build social capital and facilitate community change. (Rohe 2004, 162)

Mario Luis Small describes how a community institution, a tenants' association—Inquilinois Boricuas en Acción (IBA)—increased social capital by encouraging volunteer work.

> Although IBA is, above all, a human services-provision organization, it can also help sustain community participation, whether by providing rooms for brainstorming ideas . . . running programs, . . . helping publicize events in newsletters . . . or providing the institutional backing to formalize a budding activity. (Small 2004, 61)

By building on whatever social capital is found, organizers enable community members to identify with and take responsibility for the geographic area.

The implication of the social capital-collective efficacy approach to organizing is that actions that strengthen a geographic place can encourage individuals to better connect to one another. As Robert Sampson argues, "the general implication of my analysis is that there is an important role for policy in trying to change the dynamics of place rather than people" (Sampson 2001, 101). For instance, in the case of a Spanish-speaking neighborhood studied,

> having access to not only basic goods and services—such as health care, day care, grocers, grooming, and mail—but also those specific services targeted at Spanish-speaking and Latino groups—such as Spanish-speaking health care workers, Spanish religious services, and ethnic foods—means the residents had significantly fewer incentives to leave their neighborhood than others equally poor but resource-deprived neighborhoods (Small 2004, 181)

and then encourages people to work with one another. This bootstrapping of social capital takes place when it is government that sets up the institutions so long as the institutions are accountable to the citizens. In a study of both the Chicago's police review boards and the local community school boards, Fung learned that when the boards are responsive to the citizens the participants then form other "associations and engage with one another in ways that build social capital" (Fung 2004, 122).

Another way of expanding social capital is found in **Community Building Initiatives**. Advocates of Comprehensive Community Building Initiatives (CBI) (Kubisch 1996; Smock 1997; Stone 1996) set up a multipronged, multiorganizational, coordinated approach to building on and expanding community assets. Recognizing, for instance, that helping teenagers requires better schools, systems of mentoring, linkages to the job market, and recreational opportunities. Poor people need jobs, but they also need affordable housing, and are more likely than others to be deprived of adequate medical care.

CBI is built upon several premises, each of which is about strengthening local networks or expanding community assets in ways that increase social capital:

> Integrate community development and human service strategies
> Forge partnerships through collaboration
> Build on community strengths
> Start from local conditions
> Foster broad community participation
> Require racial equity
> Value cultural strengths
> Support families and children (www.ncbn.org/about/principle.htm)

Social capital expands as organizations work together, for instance when a housing group assists a job training service in finding employment for tenants. Further, the newly linked organizations expand social bridges by connecting those in the community with sister organizations throughout the nation.

Conclusion: Community Building for Collective Empowerment

Community provides a foundation for collective empowerment by providing the bonds that link individuals in ways that encourage an increase in the trust that can lead to a mutual sense of responsibility for one another (Lelieveldt 2004). Further, when people feel confidence in others, and often in themselves, they are willing to experiment with new ideas, verbalize different solutions, and daringly suggest that change is possible.

Community provides a safe locale for such experimentation. In the African American civil rights movement, for instance, the Highlander Center in the rural South provided a safe place for activists to talk and plan social change efforts, and, not so incidentally, allowed blacks and whites in the segregated South to socialize together. Similarly, a community of disability activists found safe grounds at Long Island University when:

> school officials made its Brooklyn campus accessible to people with disabilities in order to take advantage of the potential enrollment. . . . Soon the university served as a propitious breeding ground to nurture disability activists, generated by their physical proximity . . . and an activist milieu. . . . The energy unleashed by the gathering together in one place of a heretofore often disenfranchised group of people, coupled with the political upheaval of the 1960s, open up new possibilities. (Fleischer and Zames 2001, 73–74)

Feeling part of a community creates the solidarity that motivates collective action, while the social capital within a community provides some of the wherewithal to act. Organizing involves recognizing the ways in which people feel bound to one another and then building upon these connections to bring into being a social change organization.

CHAPTER

6

Empowering through Building Progressive Organizations

We live in a world of formal organizations. Organizations coordinate those working on a common goal or purpose—making a profit, reforming the banking system, cleaning up the block, bird watching. To activists, the very idea of an organization gives off mixed messages evoking the images of large businesses or irresponsive government agencies. Government bureaucracies are seen as creating endless paperwork with no one taking responsibility, while business organizations concentrate economic power in ways that threaten democracy.

Yet, *community action works through organizations*, though in this case progressive organizations that empower people, not control them. Progressive organizations concentrate resources and expertise to bring about capacity for positive change. An individual might rant and rave at an injustice; a social change organization employs people with the research skills to document injustice and the expertise to coordinate a mass protest. Activists learn about organizations as a tactic in structural jiu-jitsu, that is, turning a tool of the establishment into a weapon for ordinary people to fight back.

In this chapter we examine how progressive organizations enable individuals and communities to focus the resources and knowledge required to solve problems. We compare social change organizations with their mainstream cousins, describe how organizations can empower people, and then examine the ways in which social change organizations work to balance empowerment goals with being efficient and effective. In a later chapter we provide technical details of organizational administration.

How Progressive Organizations Structurally Compare with Their Mainstream Cousins

At first it might seem foolish to ask how progressive organizations differ from their mainstream counterparts: The twenty-person Alden Neighborhood Watch Association, led by a rotating chair, looks nothing like General Electric with hundreds of thousands of employees spread throughout the world, and governed by a top-down bureaucracy. The Bank of America, whose purpose is to make a profit through financial transactions acts in ways that dramatically contrast from ACORN, whose members picket the B of A. But boundaries do blur.

Organizational Goals

Conventional organizations are about maximizing economic profit or quickly carrying out the will of politicians. In doing so some goals might be suspect—selling shoddy products to the unaware or listening in to the conversations of political opponents. Other goals are laudable—a government agency that makes sure water is pure and safe or a for-profit developer who builds affordable homes. Retail organizations are about making a profit but do so by satisfying needs of the customers. There is nothing sinister about selling a warm coat at a profit to a willing customer.

The organizational goals of social change organizations differ from those of conventional organizations in two ways. First, they are *mission driven* rather than *profit driven*, where the mission is one of accomplishing some part of the broader progressive agenda, battling for social or economic equity, working to bring about a more harmonious world, or respecting the environment. Missions are about increasing social equity, not imposing social control, improving the life of the poor, not maximizing profit. Second, the goals that determine the organizational mission come about through a democratic process in which organizational members, not owners or politicians, collectively decide what should be done and why.

Legal and Bureaucratic Structures

Organizations are legally defined entities that take shape through charters that spell out their purpose and overall structure. With smaller, less formal organizations a simple statement of mission might suffice, but more permanent organizations will *incorporate*—that is, obtain a state-sanctioned charter that declares that the organization itself is now a legal entity and as an organization can enter into contracts or undertake programs or projects for which the organization itself, not the individual members, hold responsibility.

Organizations incorporate either as for-profits or nonprofits. *For-profit* means the organization is set up to return profits to individuals who invest capital and that ownership is either in the name of a single individual, a partnership, or through shares that are bought and sold as stocks. *Nonprofit* means that no member of the organization makes any personal profit over and above that of normal wages. Most nonprofits are "owned" by a board, frequently consisting of community members, who also are not allowed to personally profit. Social change organizations can incorporate as either 501(c)3 or 501(c)4 organizations. Both are nonprofit but 501(c)3 is set up in a very tax-advantaged way so those who contribute can receive tax deductions, but in turn are limited in political activity. 501(c)4 nonprofit organizations can be involved in politics but neither they nor their contributors receive tax advantages. A **foundation** is a nonprofit organization set up to distribute money, usually obtained from bequests from individuals, mostly to nonprofit organizations. Money must then be spent for a public or social purpose, including the work of social change organizations, though in practice most money is distributed to mainstream efforts in support of arts, museums, education, and medical research.

Nonprofit does not mean the organization loses money. A Community Development Corporation needs to break even, at the very least, on the homes it sells, while a community social service agency must have sufficient revenue to pay its staff. However, if a nonprofit social change organization makes a profit (for instance, a CDC introduces a successful store in a redeveloping neighborhood) the profit then has to be used consistent with the social change goals of the organization (for example, by providing a job training program for community members) and is not distributed to the members.

Almost but not all social change organizations are nonprofits, but for technical reasons some cannot be. For instance, many housing projects are done in partnerships with banks and corporations that for tax reasons must operate through a for-profit organization. In this case, the social change organization will form a for-profit subsidiary to set up the partnership, but in ways that all profits, if any, revert to the parent organization that then spends the money consistent with its overall mission. Or, another type of social change organization is a *cooperative* (whose structure we describe later on) that technically is a for-profit organization collectively owned by either its employees, if a business cooperative, or its tenants, if a residential cooperative. Profits in a housing cooperative either go back into the housing or are evenly shared by its members. In business cooperatives, profits are distributed to members, but in proportion to the number of hours worked, rather than as a return on capital invested.

For-profit does not necessarily mean being socially irresponsible. For-profit companies provide jobs, goods, and services in poor communities; for-profit housing developers build homes or shelters for lower income people. On the other hand, only a small percentage of nonprofits are about social change. Many do provide public services, supporting hospitals, museums, universities, and zoos, as well as providing conventional charitable work through the Red Cross, Salvation Army, or hundreds of nonprofits set up to battle diseases.

To accomplish their goals, organizations will set up internal structures. Most familiar are the top-down hierarchies of conventional firms and government agencies with clearly demarcated reporting structures, specialized divisions to handle specific tasks, and support divisions to provide backup assistance. Nonprofit social change organizations will often emulate such structures. A national advocacy organization will have policy divisions that keep track of congress and regulators or a section devoted to providing member services, while community organizations might divide into sections, one for organizing and activism, the other to do renewal projects.

Larger organizations set up **work teams** or **project teams** that draw expertise from the entire organization to focus on a specific problem. More militant direct action organizations often organize their membership into **affinity groups**, people with close relationships to one another, who act as peer groups to assure that proper tactics are followed, and if arrests occur support one another.

Nonprofits associate with one another through **coalitions**, groupings of organizations that join to work on a shared issue. Organizations advocating for the homeless, another building homes, a third providing legal services for tenants might form a coalition to support increased funding for affordable housing. When the coalition itself needs organizational permanence, member groups might set up a **coalitional organization**, a separate nonprofit whose purpose is to implement the shared goal of its diverse membership. Other times, separate social change organizations might share employees who come together in **working groups** to pool their knowledge in a particular problem area.

Some national social change organizations spin off local **branches** that carry out a uniform policy but do so in ways that accommodate local needs. These branches, though, are controlled by the national organization. In contrast, **affiliated** organizations tend to accept the same values, frequently communicate with one another, yet remain independent and choose actions on their own.

Governance and Decision Making

A major difference between conventional and social change organizations is in their governance structures, that is, in how decisions get made. In many conventional organizations decision making is strictly from the top, along explicit lines of command, and heaven help those who violate the hierarchy. In contrast, some social change organizations are governed under *participatory democracy* in which each member has a full say on all decisions, and actions are delayed until consensus is obtained. In cooperatives, by law, each member has an equal vote and a right to participate in setting overall goals, though in practice, many members do not choose to be involved.

In general, differences in governance between conventional and social change organizations are less extreme. Both are governed by a board usually elected by owners or, in nonprofits, by members, but in nonmembership organizations the board itself can decide who is on it and how they are chosen. Boards hire the senior officers of the organization who take on day-to-day responsibilities. Board members are actively involved in setting the direction of the organization and assuring that the direction is carried out. While boards are about setting general policies, in many nonprofits board members have a deep interest in the mission of the organization and themselves work on that mission.

Most nonprofit social change organizations try to govern themselves in a democratic way. Major decisions are taken at annual meetings in which each member has a vote. Boards are chosen through open elections, with positions being actively sought. For national social change organizations, boards tend to meet before annual conferences, usually have several other face-to-face meetings a year, and parts of the board meet as specialized committees—for public policy, membership, organizing meetings—often through frequent phone conferences.

Many social change organizations have rules in place mandating that the board must reflect the membership composition in terms of gender and ethnic distribution. A board of a housing advocacy organization will include low-income African American women living in public housing as well as economically better-off white men from housing finance organizations. For instance, the Dudley Street Neighborhood Initiative that works in an ethnically mixed neighborhood wanted to ensure its board reflect all constituencies both from different ethnic groups and from community institutions. To do this, the charter mandated a democratic election but reserved seats in the following way:

> 12 Community Members elected separately from black, Cape Verdean, Latino, and white constituencies
>
> 5 nonprofit agencies from Health and Human Services
>
> 2 community development corporations
>
> 2 small businesses
>
> 2 broader business community members
>
> 2 religious community members
>
> 2 nonprofits from an adjacent area
>
> 1 city official
>
> 1 state official
>
> 2 others chosen by the board to assure racial/ethnic/age/sex representation (Medoff and Sklar 1994, 58)

In neighborhood organizations staffed by professional organizers, great care is taken to balance responsibilities in setting overall policy between the organizers as staff members and other leaders of the social change group. As Warren describes for the IAF:

> top leaders and organizers structure all decision making within affiliates through informal, but highly systematic, consensual processes. . . . Before any meeting, leaders develop an action plan or proposal and consult with other relevant leaders to revise the plan and reach agreement. Meetings primarily ratify plans which have already been developed and then discuss implementation. The IAF justifies this approach as the most democratic and effective. . . . Christine Stephens put it, that "people operate, and ought to operate through leadership." (Warren 2001, 230)

Social change organizations also experiment with alternative governance structures, for example, by routinely rotating who is in a leadership position or only taking actions after full consensus has been achieved.

Workers, Employees, and Volunteers

In both conventional and social change organizations, managers or owners in smaller for-profit organizations coordinate the work of others, each trying to hire the best employees to accomplish required tasks. But important differences exist in employee relationships between conventional and social change organizations.

Social change organizations are about empowering individuals. So, in hiring, employees might favor those from the community who can grow into the job, rather than hiring those who already have the skills. Another difference is that in many economic and social production (ESP) organizations that provide social services, the border between client and employee blurs. Patients at a hospital do not become physicians. In contrast, abused women who seek help from a shelter are taught to help future victims. In progressive organizations many clients morph into activists and perhaps future employees of the organization.

In addition, much work in social change organizations is done by volunteers, rather than paid employees. Different incentives are required to motivate and coordinate volunteer workers than are needed for paid employees, a topic that we shall discuss in Chapter 11. In conventional charities, much of the work of volunteers is strictly controlled by paid employees, calling up and asking for contributions, for instance, by reading a prepared script. In contrast, social change organizations try to empower volunteers by having them work side-by-side with the paid professionals on the same task, each learning from the other.

How Social Change Organizations Empower and Build Capacity

Progressive organizations are the tools for accomplishing social change goals, in ways that bring about democratic empowerment. Empowerment comes about by focusing, coordinating, and motivating the energy of individuals; by showing those in the establishment that others are watching what they are doing; and through being the depository of the narratives of success that demonstrate that the effort is worthwhile. As entities with a permanent, usually paid, staff, organizations develop expertise to accomplish tasks and are able to react quickly to solve problems. Organizations store and share knowledge on what can be done and how, and by so doing build community capacity. Finally, progressive organizations can be structured to run in ways that preconfigure changes that are sought in the broader society.

Social Change Organizations as Tools for Empowerment

Organizations empower their membership and the communities they serve by battling the structures that enable big businesses and the rich to sustain their dominance.

Organizations Focus Power. Social change organizations concentrate their resources in people, expertise, energy, motivation, money, and time, to increase power to effect decisions. Organizations coordinate the actions of large numbers of people—and politicians pay attention—while the continuity of the organization shows those in positions of power that ordinary people are willing to stay the course. When those in power receive a complaint from an individual, it is often ignored. The same correspondence on the letterhead of an organization implies that there is clout behind the concern. Nowadays, social activists build on this perception of organizational power through such devices as *sign-on letters* in which one organization requests its sister groups sign on to a letter that details a problem and an expected solution, increasing the perception of those that receive the letter that many are concerned.

Organizations Provide Continuity. Confronted with worker or citizen demands, those in power delay responding, hoping that activists will lose interest and go away. Having an organization in place, especially one with a paid staff means that the interest in the issue will persist. Organizations have the time and staff to obtain evidence that a problem exists. They hire staff that can trace problems over the decades or investigate current situations, for instance, testing to see if discrimination in hiring or housing exists by sending out people of various ethnic, racial, and religious backgrounds to see who is helped and who is not. When those in power make promises, organizations stick around and can monitor whether these promises are kept. They can check whether grant funds were spent to house the poor, as the new policy provides, or find out how well an antipollution law is enforced. Organizations are around to publicize failures on the part of public authority, and once again mobilize people if promises are broken.

Organizations Can React Quickly. Problems can occur rapidly. Drug dealers might move into a neighborhood or conservative legislators could introduce amendments to gut existing social legislation. If each time such situations arose activists had to mobilize anew, the game would be over before it even started. Fortunately, established, progressive organizations scan the action environment, noting what has changed and respond quickly to prevent problems from getting out of hand. Those in the organization closely monitor city hall to make sure that decisions don't negatively affect the neighborhoods or set up a police liaison who can immediately call attention to drug traders in the tot lot.

Support organizations, such as the Center for Community Change, or the National Low Income Housing Coalition, maintain a permanent presence in Washington, D.C. When legislation is proposed that can affect members' interests, messages quickly go out mobilizing people to phone their elected officials.

Social Change Organizations as Tools for Capacity Building

Community capacity refers to the collective knowledge of the individuals within a community as well as the economic, material, social, and institutional resources available to focus on a problem. Organizations help build capacity for both individuals and for the broader communities that they represent.

Organizations Help Individuals Develop Personal Capacity. Social change organizations help individuals increase their own capacity. ESP organizations teach people business and job skills, how to cope with personal problems, to become financially literate, and to gain home ownership skills, among many other matters. Some organizations help individuals economically perhaps through training in business skills, while others help people overcome disabling problems—drug addiction, for instance—and gain the strength to build a new life. Leadership skills that organizations teach (public speaking, doing research, listening to others and acting on what one has heard) have an importance in life in general. Capacity that is gained by working with social change organizations becomes the antidote to both learned inefficacy and the self-blame that disempowers.

Organizations Build Capacity by Garnering Expertise and Information.
Setting up a facility to care for young children with AIDS requires more than compassion; service providers must follow numerous daycare regulations and have a wealth of medical knowledge. Advocates for the poor must master the complicated program requirements for each program and then work to make sure that the requirements for the separate programs mesh. For instance, activists in national organizations discovered that changes in welfare law would have made people presently housed ineligible for affordable housing programs and then successfully proposed a solution to the problem. Social change organizations hire people who are responsive to community members and who have the knowledge and expertise to effectively guide change.

Organizations become the depository of knowledge obtained through successful projects and actions, storing these experiences in the memories of their employees—the professional organizer, the president of a Community Development Corporation, or the executive director of a community-controlled social service agency—or in the documents and records that the organization maintains. How to pressure a bank to live up to the Community Reinvestment Act (CRA) is recorded in memos or in pamphlets produced by the organization. Promises made by businesses and politicians in response to community actions are recorded, vulnerabilities of targets are noted, and successful strategies are remembered.

Those in power try to avoid fixing problems by pretending they don't exist. Social change organizations gather the information that belie these excuses. Community development corporations document the deterioration of housing in the community, consumer organizations maintain data on product recalls, while economic justice organizations gather and publicize information on mortgage discrimination, predatory lending, and other such abuses. Fair Housing organizations document that in spite of decades of laws against discrimination, people of color, gays, and those with disabilities face more difficulty than others in being housed.

Capacity and Organizational Networks.   Social change organizations come together within networks in ways that expand community capacity. As Kristina Smock describes:

> By bringing together such a diverse array of institutions around a common vision, [community-building organizations] developed a *sense of collective identity* among institutions representing a wide range of social groups and institutional niches. As [one of the interviewees] put it "when you work on your job on a daily basis, you basically just see what's around you. . . . But working with the [community-building organization], you're able to hear the concerns of other organizations . . . so it kind of like lets you see the whole picture." (Smock 2003, 81)

Capacity expands as social change organizations link their efforts in a common mission.

These networks expand capacity by sharing knowledge about problems. For example, in Chicago predatory lenders, those who trick individuals into signing unfavorable mortgages and strip value from the homes, were victimizing individuals. Some victims ended up asking for help from community-based legal service agencies who worked with them on a case-by-case basis. At the same time, leaders in an NPA-affiliated neighborhood organization noted that people in their communities were losing titles to their homes. Fortunately, the NPA affiliate, the legal service agencies, as well as a policy organization that analyzes data on mortgage practices were members, along with other groups of Chicago's Community Reinvestment Coalition. At a coalition meeting the neighborhood organization and the legal service organizations shared their concerns; the policy shop indicated that it had hard financial data documenting what the others had observed. From this initial network meeting, a campaign was begun to change state laws to curtail predatory lenders and gain recompense for some victims.

Tensions That Occur in Building Empowered Organizations

Organizations are the tools for accomplishing goals and projecting power but can be beset with internal tensions that could weaken these efforts. Balance is needed between those characteristics that make social change organizations special—a desire to rock the boat and empower while doing so—and the conventional organizational concerns that provide the organizational wherewithal to undertake effective action. Let us examine tensions revolving around the role of leadership, those that come about in balancing democracy and hierarchy, and the problems caused by the need for financial support.

Leaders and Collective Organizational Power

Ideally it is the social change organization itself that is seen as representing collective power, not individual leaders. In practice, though, the image of a social organization often resides in the persona of the leader, especially when that leader was the person who founded the organization and spearheaded its initial successes.

An organization without a visible leader has difficulty gaining public attention. However, when an organization is led by dominant individuals, the broader public, and many whom the organization is supposed to empower, may attribute successes solely to this individual. Organizational members must stay alert lest charismatic leaders arrogate to themselves the policy decisions that should be made by the broader membership. Worse yet, some social change organizations "that purport to be open and democratic are in fact dominated by a self-perpetuating elite, the so-called 'iron law of oligarchy'" (Osterman 2002, 67) that even occurs in quite progressive organizations.

There are two ways in which the iron law of oligarchy could pay out in the context of the IAF. First, the full-time organizers may come to dominate, despite the doctrine that puts leaders at the core of the model. Second, even among leaders an established in-crowd might hold on to power, making it difficult for new leaders to emerge. (Osterman 2002, 69)

Still, organizations should not be so afraid of powerful leadership that they deny them needed powers. While bad leaders seek after their own glory, creative leadership is about showing both members and the public that change is possible and success is likely. Leaders coordinate complicated social action campaigns and are around to make adjustments to quickly respond to changing events. Someone must decide on the spot what to do if the police start arresting the demonstrators. While the overall goals of a community organization and its guiding philosophy of action (for instance, the choice of whether to use civil disobedience or not) must be decided through the democratic involvement of the membership, having a leader coordinate the details involves minimal loss of member control.

Creative leaders frame social and political issues to show that change is possible and in so doing transforming others by impressing on them the importance of assuming a collective responsibility. This comes about as

> followers feel trust, admiration, loyalty, and respect toward the leader, and they are motivated to do more than originally expected to do. A leader can transform followers by: (1) making them more aware of the importance of the task outcomes, (2) inducing them to transcend their own self interest for the sake of the organization . . . . Transformation leaders influence followers by arousing strong emotions and identification with the leader, but they may also transform followers by serving as a coach, teacher, and mentor. (Yukl 1989, 211)

The actions and words of the leaders can reinforce a democratic organizational culture, by encouraging involvement and by teaching people to respect each others' opinions (modified from Schein 1985).

However, to make sure that leaders do not overstep their bounds and threaten the democratic nature of the organization, progressive organizations make sure that overall policy is set by either an elected board or the overall membership. Another approach is to make sure leadership turns over. Osterman describes how the IAF tries to cope with this problem.

> As Ernie Cortes frequently comments "All organizing is reorganizing" and the IAF is vigilant about breaking up patterns that can cause problems. To avoid domination by a self perpetuating elite, the IAF constantly recruits new leadership. When new institutions join the organization, for example when a new congregation is signed up, new leaders naturally emerge. (Osterman 2002, 69–70)

Preconfiguring a Better Society

In the ways in which they are structured, social change organizations attempt to preconfigure in their own structuring the changes they want in the broader society, doing so in ways that do not interfere with effectiveness or efficiency. For instance, an important progressive goal is to eliminate discrimination based on ethnicity, gender, sexual orientation, or physical condition. In staffing, social change organizations demonstrate that a qualified black woman is every bit as good as a qualified white male, while neither being wheelchair bound, nor gay affects the competence in doing technical tasks.

Where the situation can be a bit more problematic is in balancing democratic processes with maintaining effective coordination within the organization. Efficient, hierarchical, bureaucratic structure can make democratic participation difficult, if not impossible, as top-down decisions might dominate. But the opposite extreme might not work either. For instance, some organizations such as the Students for a Democratic Society (SDS) avoided hierarchy and tried to carry out a full participatory democracy in which members deliberated about each issue as a group. But as a result, SDS ended up doing a lot of talking and taking very little action (Gitlin 1989; Miller 1987). Rather than promote pure democracy, loosely structured organizations end up with a "tyranny of structurelessness" in which there is the

> development of informal leaders—individuals who gained power due to media attention or personal characteristics. Such leaders were not chosen by the group and thus could not be removed by the group. (Iannello 1988, 4–5)

Such patterns are also undemocratic.

Much thought has to go into finding the right balance between bureaucratic efficiency and democratic involvement. Several approaches appear to work. In one, organizations start out with minimal structure, imposing rules only after they are shown to be absolutely needed. In another approach, the founding leaders of the organization work hard to create a democratic organizational culture that then becomes the persisting norm within the organization.

Let Structures Emerge to Mesh with Strategies. Rules and formal structures should be kept to a minimum except when the need for them becomes apparent. An organization that routinely undertakes complicated renewal projects requiring many interdependent technical steps, or one that needs tight coordination between legal and direct action tactics might have to set up a moderately strict hierarchy. By contrast, a counselor in a community run antisuicide hot line can't check out each emergency with a boss and doesn't have to coordinate his or her decisions with those of many other people. Bureaucratic procedures should be added only when absolutely necessary.

Beginning in a period of great ferment, an organization starts with a flexible structure and a handful of guiding procedures, with the expectation that rules will emerge that speak to the specific tasks to be accomplished. There are few routines and everything is discovery. But as the organization learns that certain solutions work, it builds routines to ensure that these solutions are in place. A daycare center need not reformulate its mission every month, so long as community members monitor the center to make sure that it is helping children grow emotionally, socially, and intellectually. However, as strategies and goals change, so should structure. A protest organization using the tactics of the 1960s in the political environment of the 2000s is likely to be ignored or laughed at; new structures that facilitate coalition building are required in the present day environment.

Fighting Formalization by Creating a Democratic Organizational Culture.
Initially, small organizations may be able to make decisions consensually, but as organizations age, some degree of bureaucratization sets in. Either specialists are hired or some staff and volunteers develop expertise that then separates them from others. In a housing organization someone must know the technical details of doing tax-credit deals, yet that person must remain responsive to community members who decide where the housing is to be and for whom. An advocacy organization needs a professional lobbyist on staff to track both legislation and what legislators are thinking, but the lobbyist should not be the one who determines which issue the organization will pursue. When possible such decisions should be made by the membership or in larger organizations by a representative policy committee.

The best protection against over bureaucratization is an organizational culture—the basic assumptions and beliefs of the organization—that values dissent and participation and that expects the membership to direct the organization (Schein 1985, 6). Democratic cultures come through the norms set by the initial members that are then perpetuated through the choice of successors. When leaders continue to listen to others with respect, convene group discussions, search for answers from any and all within the organization, not from just those at the top of the hierarchy, they communicate to staff and members alike that their opinions count and that the organization is owned by its members. In an organization with a democratic culture, staff and volunteers habitually question rules and oppose the tendency to set up a rigid hierarchy and are not frightened of their bosses. Members of democratic organizations assume that criticism of procedures is good, as long as it is not couched roughly or hurtfully (Rothschild and Whitt 1986, 84).

Many activist feminist organizations were initially structured in ways that reinforce a democratic organizational culture (Ferree and Yancey 1995) by working to minimize formal rules, reducing hierarchy, and concentrating authority in the whole group, rather than just the administrators or officers (Rothschild and Whitt 1986). Such organizations recognize that technical knowledge is required but rather than hire expertise, the ethos of the democratic-collectivist organization is to recognize "ability or expertise within the membership" (Iannello 1988, 21). Examples of successful democratic-collectivist organizations can be found among small worker-owned cooperatives, in small companies that produce organic foods, among community newspapers, and in smaller social service agencies.

Even larger, national social change organizations have found ways of reconciling a democratic culture with the more formal bureaucracy that size and geographic scope requires. The central organization has a clearly designated hierarchy with functional divisions and ranks. Yet, the main office is run with frequent consultations between all staff and intentionally scheduled face-to-face discussions over coffee or in meetings called to share what each has learned and how individual actions best fit into the broader picture. To encourage participation, an active board is chosen in ways that reflect the many different constituencies, and board members are kept informed before changes in course are undertaken. In addition, the organization seeks to keep its business transparent, answering questions when members call or e-write and widely sharing information on web pages, through e-mail and in open and frequently held conference calls. Democracy is preserved through the spotlight that such openness entails.

Gaining Funding without Losing Empowerment Goals

Social change organizations need money, whether to pay for ordinary daily expenses or the millions sometimes required to carry out larger renewal projects. But in receiving money from government, foundations, or businesses, organizations can be *co-opted*, that is end up adopting another's agenda as their own, a dangerous thing to do especially when the funder represents big business or government. Yet, to provide social services or build homes, capital is required. And even advocacy organizations end up taking money from the conventional sector. For example, ACORN has partnered with large national banks for funds to build affordable housing and many of the organizations set up to defend CRA receive some operating support from the larger banks. Care is required.

Co-optation can occur in subtle ways. For instance, to obtain certain federal money for housing, community groups are required to set up business-like subsidiaries. Doing so can displace empowerment goals with business value. Further, organizations that already have a businesslike structure while more likely to receive funding (DiMaggio and Powell 1991, 73; Meyer and Rowan 1991) tend to be less concerned with empowerment.

Values can subtly change. An accountant hired at the behest of a foundation may be reluctant to put money into risky ventures, while the community group may feel that is precisely what they are supposed to be doing. Those in the organization hired to keep track of money might want to view those being housed as merely rent-paying tenants, rather than community members being taught about housing in ways that are empowering. In general, organizations staffed by professionals have better opportunities obtaining funding but end up being less owned by community members as seen in the experience of women's shelters in which volunteers were replaced by professionals at the behest of the funding agencies (Schecter 1982, 107–108).

Organizational structures, especially those set up to please outsiders, carry with them values that can change the organization's mission and make it less participatory and empowering to the membership. Worse yet, some organizations become so focused on obtaining the funds needed to pay the staff now employed that they alter missions to chase the money. By doing so, their progressive agenda can be lost and rather than empowering others they end up as just one more organization hustling for the buck.

Organizational Transformations and Reconciling Contradictions

Social change organizations are live and dynamic and change over time—some accomplishing their goals, others being co-opted, while some, either lacking resources or failing in their missions, die. More often organizations evolve to mesh with a changing mission; in advocacy organizations volunteers are replaced by paid policy professionals, while in general organizations take on bureaucratic forms to match the action strategies they will use (Andrews and Edwards 2005).

Changes in structure, though, need not imply changes in tactics. Cheryl Hyde describes that even though feminist organizations did eventually move from a fully participatory group to take on conventional bureaucratic forms, yet with a prevailing organizational culture supporting democracy were able to maintain much of the enthusiasm of volunteer groups (Hyde 2000). Formalization can occur, yet still not affect goals and tactics. Daniel Cress argued that in the homeless shelter movement organizations that incorporated did not change their tactics to any significant degree (Cress 1997, 358).

In addition, social change organizations can be kept on track through both pressure and peer support with sister organizations. Leaders from empowered neighborhood organizations who serve on the board of a service or ESP affiliate monitor the sister organization to make sure that empowerment goals are not ignored. Fearing that community development corporations could lose their social change focus, the Massachusetts state trade association for these economic and social production organizations sponsored a program to fund neighborhood organizing and advocacy work run out of the CDCs (Greenberg 2004).

Over time some organizations do fade away or disintegrate, especially when members strongly disagree on their purposes. The Whittier Alliance in Minneapolis, a successful neighborhood-based organization for decades, died when the progressive staff and more conservative board disagreed about whether the group should fight for poor minorities or work to preserve the middle class character of the neighborhood (Rubin 2000). Organizational death can occur when the task exceeds the available technical or administrative capacity. A number of prominent community housing and economic development organizations folded, including Eastside Community Investment in Indianapolis, ESHAC in Milwaukee, and People's Housing in Chicago, when each tried to accomplish a vital community task that turned out not to be economically viable. In a study we did in the early nineties, we praised CANDO as the nation's leading local coalition supporting neighborhood-based economic development (Rubin 2000). Yet, in 2002 CANDO shut its doors. In part, it had run out of money, but more important it had failed to carefully track its political environment and lost its sense of mission. As Immergluck reported:

> CANDO's demise can be partially attributed to drifting away from its core mission, excessive program growth and dependence on city contracts. More importantly, CANDO neglected to build its members' own political capital . . . instead choosing to manage a number of narrow programmatic initiatives that did not build the power of

its members or the movement. . . . This, in turn made the organization more vulnerable to change in political climate and ultimately less valuable to its membership. (Immergluck 2005, 29)

Recognizing that social change organizations are always changing, activists try to make sure that empowerment and capacity building goals are not put aside. If organizations need to bring on professional staff, ask if that can be done by training those already in the organization or finding experts from the community itself. That failing, recruit professionals from other social change organizations who have already shown the commitment to empowerment ideals.

Try to avoid "mission drift," that is, a slow step-by-step movement away from the initial goals. Sometimes movement is necessary—as when a feminist advocacy organization evolves into a service provider because of the pressing need for a rape counselling center—but mission change should come about only after careful deliberation. Social change organizations must hold retreats (or at the very least large open discussions) in which board, staff, and members together reflect on whether the organization is still achieving its purpose and if not, whether it is time to change what it is about. Only after such reflections should change be brought about and then formalized through revamping the organization's mission statement, a consensual, arrived-at rendition of what the organization is about.

Conclusion

Organizations are tools for empowerment. But as a tool organizations must be controlled and monitored carefully so that when they lose their progressive focus or energy flags, the effort starts anew. Progressive social change organizations must accomplish the tasks at hand: pushing for policy changes, assuring rights, and renewing communities, among hundreds of tasks, but do so in ways that teach people skills that empower. To assure that organizations remain on the path to bring about empowerment as well as capacity building, activists must reflect on what the organization is doing and how, then when it is necessary to regroup and work to bring back the organization to its core mission. Just as organizing is a continuing process so is sustaining an organization in ways that remain true to empowerment ideals.

PART THREE

Problems, Programs, and Precedents

In this section we ask what is meant by a social problem, describe the ways in which social change organizations in the past responded to problems, and explain how to learn about current problems through participatory research. Chapter 7 explains that what constitutes a problem and a policy are both social constructs that reflect underlying ideologies and evolve over time. Chapter 8 traces the history of how social change organizations respond to ever-changing social problems, doing so as the political and economic environment alters, while pulling out lessons for present-day organizing. Chapter 9 provides the tools of participatory research that are used for learning about present-day problems.

CHAPTER
7 Social Problems and Public Policy

People organize to gain power to overcome shared *problems* either on their own or by pressuring government to adopt policies and programs that are meant to alleviate the problems. But what is meant by a social problem or a policy? At first blush, the answers seem simple enough: A social problem is a matter that bothers large numbers of people, while policies are descriptions of how government (or corporations, or any organization for that matter) plans to act. These are then carried out through ongoing programs. Government adopts a policy to alleviate poverty and sets up a program to provide food for people in need.

But matters are rarely this simple; first blushes are deceptive. What is considered a problem will differ from person to person. To many the war in Iraq is a problem of an abuse of power, but to others it is a solution to terrorism. The presence of immigrants, both documented and undocumented, is seen as a problematic violation of laws to some and to others an illustration of the ability of our country to attract people with energy. Similarly, policies are often not responses to problems, but instead can reflect underlying ideologies of what should be done almost irrespective of the actual situation at hand.

In this chapter we examine how both social problems and social policies are constructed by individuals in ways that serve particular interests or mesh with underlying political and social preferences. Seeing homelessness as stemming from laziness or substance abuse is quite a different matter than attributing it to a lack of affordable homes or too few decent-paying jobs. Each construction of the problem has quite different implications for policy. In the second half of the chapter we illustrate in practical terms how different framings of problems and policies have affected the ways in which government has responded to concerns about economic inequality and urban decline.

Understanding Social Problems as Contested Framings

What constitutes a problem and what actions are required emerge from people's framings of the issue, that is, from shared socially constructed understandings (Baylor

1996; Goffman 1974; Polletta 1998; Snow, Rochford Jr., Worden, et al. 1986). Framings are intentional efforts to define why problems occur, who is responsible, and what solutions are appropriate and possible. Do problems stem from personal factors or from broader economic and social inequalities, or some combination of the two? Do problems just happen or do they come about because some benefit at a cost to others? Those supporting the status quo argue that poverty will always be with us because of the sloth of some; activists reframe the issue to show that low wages and poverty are ways in which the rich stay rich by exploiting others. Those who oppose abortion frame the issue as protection of the unborn child. To them, abortion is murder. The solution is to ban abortions or terrorize abortionists so they won't kill fetuses. Those who support abortion rights frame the matter in terms of a woman's right to control her own reproductive system. For them, the issue is one of privacy and individual choice. Activism involves a competitive framing process in which each side tries to discredit the frame of the opponent (McCaffrey and Keys 2000).

Socially constructed frames affect how the "facts of the matter," the objective conditions, are understood. To us, 10 percent unemployment means the economy is failing, 50 people working in a small factory creates unsafe overcrowding, while a highway with 12,000 cars a day means danger for school children. But to others, 10 percent unemployment means people are too lazy to work, the overcrowded factory is an inevitable step on the path of business growth, while the busy highway is little more than a quick path to jobs and shopping.

Frames distort history. As of mid-2006 a vicious debate is underway on immigration policy, with some claiming that illegal migration from Mexico is out of control even though careful analysis shows that the percentage of those from Mexico working in the United States has not changed (Massey 2006).

Framings are intentionally constructed by victims, by the media, and by those in positions of power, often reflecting underlying social prejudices. For instance, battering was framed by those in positions of power as a private domestic problem whose cause was biological and hence almost inevitable so

> police did not arrest men who battered their wives, even when victims were in serious danger and directly asked officers to arrest . . . Activists in the battered women's movement saw failure to arrest as tacit support for battering. (Ferraro 1989, 61)

Battles over local housing policies are often framed in terms of who deserves public support and why (Sidney 2003). Conservative mayors explain that housing deteriorates because of irresponsible tenants and such homes provide a base for crime, so they suggest tearing down slums. Progressive mayors frame the same issue in terms of the neglect of landlords and the lack of neighborhood-based policing, and they set up loan programs to make repairs.

Framings affect the scope of solutions proposed. If an industrial plant is polluting a particular river, killing the fish and threatening water supplies, the problem can be defined as one of controlling effluent from this plant, or cleaning up this river, or it can be more broadly framed as lack of enforcement of laws due to public officials' fears of putting an economic burden on a major industry.

Interpretative understandings affect what people consider constitute success. The welfare reform measures introduced in 1996 (discussed below) are considered successful by those who define success as cutting the size of the welfare rolls; but for others, success is seen by what happens to those who are now no longer receiving aid. To complicate matters, most programs have multiple impacts, so judging their success or failure is far from simple. HOPE VI, for example, a program to tear down high-rise public housing and improve neighborhoods, has brought about many changes. Some focus on the fact that prior tenants have moved to areas with better homes and jobs, while others emphasize that those displaced have had to double in housing in other poor neighborhoods or have fallen off the radar entirely (Popkin, Katz, Cunningham, et al. 2004).

Framings are often communicated through *typifications*, a story, or set of examples, that encapsulate the matter. President Reagan, for instance, offered such a typification with a made-up image of a "welfare queen," a person stealing from the welfare system and driving a Cadillac, communicating the need to sharply reduce welfare to end fraud. Typifications vie with one another; for instance, the typification "the deserving poor" evokes an image of a disabled widow with young children, while the typification of "the undeserving poor" is that of an able-bodied young male more willing to sell dope than find a job and hence not worthy of public support. Typifications are used in ways that harm the vulnerable. For instance in the discussion of poverty, the typification "underclass" was introduced by scholars (Wilson 1987) as a sympathetic portrait of people who face numerous problems, often due to racism. But the conservative press and politicians appropriated this typification as a code word for negative racial stereotypes and used it as an excuse to reduce support for those in need (Gans 1995, 59).

Ideologies are more sophisticated framings that put forth a broad perspective of why society is the way it is along with a model of the way it ought to be. Ideologies shape which solutions are tried, for example, from the time of Franklin Roosevelt on through Lyndon Johnson a liberal ideology prevailed, promoting the idea that problems were socially caused and that government has an obligation to help those most in need. As such this ideology—this macroframing—legitimated building a broad social safety net. Those of conservative bent disagreed with this approach, putting forth a conservative ideological framing arguing that problems are caused through individual laziness and that government programs do little to help people. This ideology then was succinctly articulated through a politics of resentment pushed by right wing politicians, talk show hosts, and conservative think tanks and has been used as a justification for tearing down the social safety net (O'Connor 2004).

Social Problems: Structural or Personal?

The term **structural** refers to underlying, persisting economic, cultural, or political conditions that shape an action environment. The system of capitalism or the rules of democracy are structural elements. Pervasive religious beliefs are structural elements. Structural forces contrast with **personal attributes**—honesty, ambition, energy, intelligence. Supporters of the status quo frame problems as stemming from personal attributes, trying to deny that there is any structural basis, hence no need for reform. Progressive activists work to determine the structural causes of social problems and then organize to battle these underlying causes.

But care is needed as battles against broader structural problems can distract from here and now efforts. Should action focus against the cultural values that demean women as sexual objects or on the more immediate task of setting up rape crisis centers? Working to establish job training programs or helping individuals set up their businesses are ways of fighting poverty, but neither engages the larger underlying structural problems caused by globalization. Should activist organizations concentrate on the local job development efforts or is it better to join with other social organizations to combat the structures of dominance by big business? Decisions on whether to focus on immediate problems or to combat the underlying structures are never simple.

Further complicating the choice of strategies is the fact that personal and local factors do complicate the structural bases of problems. Structure limits the number of decent paying jobs, and homes are too expensive, but still some of the homeless are addicted to abusive substances, adding personal problems to structural concerns. Many of the problems young African American males face in seeking jobs are due to structural factors—the reduction of manufacturing positions and the lack of skills training in schools focused on minorities, as well as pervasive racism. Yet, studies show that people who have been abused by racism and lack quality education adopt personal behaviors that can worsen the situation—joining gangs, dropping out of school (Edelman, Holzer, and Offner 2006). While trying to battle the structural problems—a culture of racism, the move of businesses away from neighborhoods of color—progressive activists must also keep in mind that personal behaviors can worsen the situation, and also work to handle these issues, perhaps by establishing antigang efforts or counselling programs.

Problems and Agency

Progressive activists understand that structures do not simply spring into being out of nothing, but instead structures are made to happen because specific individuals or organizations, termed *agency*, benefit. The minimum wage is low not because of some invisible (structural) market force, but rather because companies profit. The impersonal market, a structure, might demand that those who are poor credit risks pay higher interest rates; but when activist researchers carefully examined predatory lending, they learned how, through lies and deceptions, predators cheated the poor, and high rates had nothing to do with a market structure (Karger 2005; Lord 2005; Squires 2004).

In responding to social problems, activists must ask why they occur, who benefits, and whether or not action campaigns should focus on the agency rather than the more immediate and visible symptoms. *Redlining*—the unwillingness to lend money in certain, primarily minority communities—initially came about as part of federal government rules that benefited the real estate profession. Government support of the massive highway construction starting in the fifties made easier the white-flight to suburbia while opening up a vast market for developers; massive tax cuts meant to appease the wealthy end up starving social programs. In each case, government working at the behest of business interests was the agency that exacerbated a problem.

Social Problems, Public Policies, and Organizing

Problems escalate. Jobs are outsourced, unions destroyed. The gap in income between the top 10 percent and the rest steadily increases. With public assistance greatly limited, many mothers with children have to take on low paying work, mostly without health insurance. Immigration worsens intergroup tensions, with xenophobic reactions against undocumented workers. Forty years after fair housing laws were passed, racial minorities and the disabled continue to face discrimination. People fear terrorism yet responses seem more to threaten civil liberties than to battle potential threats. Religious groups strive to impose their beliefs on those with different traditions. Fights over abortion or stem cell research raise the temperature of public discourse, as do battles over evolution or gay marriages. The No Child Left Behind laws have focused attention on inadequacies in education but provided scant funds to solve the problems. Medical costs escalate, yet tens of millions remain uninsured; people who used to look forward to retirement now fear that their pensions will disappear. Housing costs escalate. Climate change from global warming has become measurable. Downtowns flourish with new steel and glass office towers, often subsidized by the public sector, yet the homeless still sleep on the streets, while older neighborhoods continue to decline.

Available jobs, at least those that pay a living wage, are less available to those without a college education. Immigration has changed the ethnic composition of the nation with many of the poorest inner city neighborhoods heavily minority, including new immigrant groups. Racial and ethnic cleavages in big cities have increased, yet the political structure has failed to accommodate (Logan and Mollenkopf 2003). Some recent immigrants do not speak English, which accentuates cultural conflicts, while in many large cities, minorities end up battling each other.

Most of these problems exceed what organizations can solve on a local level. An organization might be able to house twenty people, but doing so does little to solve the problem of there being tens of millions underhoused, while small economic development projects do little to combat the harms of globalization. To handle broader problems, government intervention is required. Bringing this about requires activists to understand how public policies and programs come into being, or, more often than not, fail to do so.

Understanding Public Policies

Public policies reflect the choices and priorities of those in political positions as well as their preferred ways of responding to situations. *Programs* are the tools for carrying out policies and are usually administered by bureaucratic agencies. However, the connection between policies and programs is far from straightforward since "policy language is often vague and ambiguous when it comes to stipulating precisely what actions implementors should take in order to . . . achieve policy goals" (Yanow 1996, 129).

Policies emerge slowly, sometimes over many years if not decades, hammered out from compromises made between business, lobbying groups, nonprofits, as well as bureaucrats themselves (Kingdom 1995). As the ideology of those in power changes, programs are reshaped to mesh with current ideologies. A program to tear down high-rise public housing, a liberal effort to deconcentrate poverty, morphed into an effort to displace the poor and abandon public housing when ideological conservatives took over.

Policies can reflect unbending ideologies: Those who ideologically believe that government is a threat want to cut taxes and reduce services; racists (racism is a negative ideology) oppose civil rights programs irrespective of their need. To ideologues the causes of problems are rarely examined but are presupposed consistent with the underlying ideological beliefs. Conservative ideologies claim that tax cuts expand the economy even when evidence shows they mainly benefit only the top 10 percent. Claiming that the free market and self-help will solve most problems, those ideologically opposed to "big government" or "taxes" have managed to undo much of the social safety net (O'Connor 2004). Policies can emerge out of anger or resentment; for instance, economic fears are displaced upon newcomers and harsh immigration policies are put in place or social support programs are cut back on the belief that someone else is benefiting.

In addition, in our complicated federal form of government, there is rarely a consistent policy approach to any one issue with major differences seen in federal, state, and local policies. Policies that begin at the federal level usually allow sufficient scope so that states and localities are able to interpret them in distinct ways, leading to a plethora of possible contradictory responses to the same issue (Sidney 2003). For instance, policies that oppose predatory lending were initiated at the state and local level and are now being fought and weakened at the national level.

Policies to handle one problem can have unanticipated consequences in other areas. Antidrug policies led to massive arrests, causing crowding within the penal system, while imposing a permanent blot on the record of many young people of color. As those arrested for drug crimes finish their terms, they return to poor communities, adding to the local problems as the returnees lack both skills and background for conventional jobs. An unintended consequence of drug policies has been to increase the joblessness rate in poorer communities.

Present-Day Meta-Policies That Impact Organizing for Social Change

Actions taken also reflect what we term *meta-policies*. Meta-policies are framings about how to think about and respond to problems, almost irrespective of which problem is at hand. Meta-policies are how ideologies are put into practice. Meta-policies change over time, but today after a long period of conservative dominance, seven seem in place, each making it harder to battle for economic and social justice.

Social Agendas Dominate. Today social and cultural issues, as framed by conservative religious groups, define how issues are seen. Economic conservatives have discovered that by supporting the wedge issues of the religious right—opposing abortion and homosexuality, or supporting an increased role of religion in public life—they can gain support in their efforts to cut back public services or change the tax structure to benefit the rich (Frank 2004). Wedge social issues have made it far more difficult to gain support in the battle for economic justice agendas.

Strangling the Federal Government in a Bathtub. Conservatives actively promote shrinking the federal government, with extreme individuals such as Grover Norquist arguing for strangling the federal government and drowning it in a bathtub. One path to shrinking government is through tax cuts that have primarily benefited the top 1 percent of the households (Kamin and Shapiro 2004), since with less money available less can be spent on social programs. To worsen the situation, at the local level, tax limitation movements have reduced the money counties and cities can raise from their own sources, again shrinking resources for programs that help the poor.

To further carry out this policy of cutbacks, budget gimmicks are used. For instance, thirty-five years ago *block grants* were introduced by Uncle Sam to allow localities to more efficiently spend money. Block grants put together money from several similar programs into one big package and then allowed localities to decide which part of that package to spend the money on. At first glance, block grants made sense but in practice what has occurred is that by block granting money it has become easier for the federal government to shrink the overall amount allocated (Waller 2005, 8).

Other gambits lower funds for social programs. With the rob-Peter-to-pay-Paul approach when special programs are passed for extraordinary purposes (for example helping with Katrina relief), the money is taken from related but ongoing social programs, depleting funding for social programs elsewhere in the country. The George W. Bush administration set up what is called the Program Assessment Rating Tool (PART) that is supposed to measure the efficiency of federal programs. But it too is part of the strangulation strategy. When PART scores are low, officials argue that the economic, social, or housing welfare program should be cut back; but when they are high, no suggestions are made to increase funding (OMB Watch 2006).

Hollowing Out of Government. Hollowing out involves *devolving* responsibilities to the states for social services, economic development, or health programs, but doing so without providing the requisite financial support. In addition, hollowing out occurs as the delivery of public services are privatized (Karger and Stoesz 2002).

Most recently, privatization has involved funding faith-based organizations. The conservative supposition is that faith-based organizations can deliver services at less cost, ignoring that when they do so it is usually because they pay their staff too little.

In addition, concern is present that, while providing services, faith-based organizations will push for particular religious values, blurring the line between state and church, yet at the same time not have the capacity to deliver the social service (Kramer, Finegold, DeVita, et al. 2005).

Federal Inconsistency in Relating to the States: Devolution or Pre-emption.

Within our federal system public policies can originate at the local (city), state, or national level. Ideas on how to renew neighborhoods were initially tested in larger cities and then were imitated by the feds. With housing programs like HOME, or renewal efforts such as the Community Development Block Grant (CDBG), the federal government provides the funds but decisions on what projects to build are made locally, though in accordance with federal rules.

Unfortunately, in recent years, federalism is carried out in ways that is biased against those seeking progressive change (Golden 2005). Conservative officials do argue that decisions on social and redevelopment programs should be made locally, an approach that is consistent with beliefs held by many progressives. Yet funds for these social and redevelopment efforts are then not made available. Responsibility is devolved to the localities but the wherewithal to act is not provided.

Yet, at the same time, on regulatory and social issues, the federal government claims pre-emption, that is asserting that federal policy must prevail, but doing so only on matters in which the states seem to oppose the interests of either big business or conservative social groups. For example, in the battle against predatory lending or in efforts to provide standards for food safety, states have set up strong laws. But then financial institutions as well as manufacturers who oppose these laws convince their friends in the federal government first to pass weaker laws and then pre-empt (that is displace) the stronger state rules. Similarly, when states are seen as more liberal on gay rights or on marijuana, the federal government steps in, again claiming that these matters should be determined on a national, not local, level.

Devolution is used to cut back funding, while pre-emption comes about to protect business interests or to thwart progressive social agendas.

Regulatory Rule Making Weakens Policy Decisions.

In recent years, even when conservatives have been unable to rewrite laws, they make sure they are not strongly enforced by the regulatory agencies. Government agencies set up to protect natural areas are run by officials who advocate mining and forestry, while antipollution standards are ignored by those in charge of the Environmental Protection Agency. To combat low voter turnout among the poor and minorities, laws were enacted to allow individuals to register to vote at public assistance agencies. Yet, because of lack of administrative enforcement, few have registered (ACORN 2005). Bank regulatory agencies that are supposed to enforce the Community Reinvestment Act have chipped away at CRA through partially exempting smaller banks.

Courts Have Become Less Relevant in Interpreting Policy Matters.

Historically, courts were the place of last resort where activists could argue that policies were not being carried out or regulations were inconsistent with policy intent. But the role of the courts has lessened, at least for those concerned about progressive change.

Appointees for the courts are chosen from those who support big business and are less willing to listen to complaints about government neglect.

Extreme Partisanship. Elected officials often disagree on issues with, in recent decades, Republicans less likely than Democrats to support progressive causes. Yet on many issues the gap between parties could be bridged. For instance, while liberals and conservatives differed on how best to provide affordable housing, once enacted, housing programs had maintained bipartisan support.

This bipartisan accommodation has broken down, displaced by extreme partisanship. Rather than nibbling down the size of a social program, if that program had been introduced by one party, partisans from the other work to eliminate it in its entirety (O'Connor 2004). A few years ago, an innovative idea introduced by a member of one party could often garner bipartisan support, admittedly after each side made compromises. Nowadays, the mere fact that a Democrat has proposed an idea creates Republican opposition and vice versa.

Clusters of Problems

When facing a here-and-now problem, activists do not have the time, nor should they take the time, to stop and do extensive research on the problem's history or the policy responses engendered. Yet knowledge of policies and programs are important to guide current action. We suggest that activists should set time aside, perhaps between crises, to examine the history of the problems their organizations face and the policies government has adopted in response to these problems. In so doing, activists seek

- to obtain factual background on a particular problem so as to better understand its underlying structural causes
- to learn about how these problems have historically been framed
- to discover how one problem is or is not connected to another
- to recognize the political fact that while policies emerge in response to problems, the connection need not be immediate or direct

We will illustrate this type of analysis by examining two clusters of problems, the first concerning issues of economic inequality and the second matters of physical decay of neighborhoods and housing within neighborhoods. These are but examples and are not meant to privilege these problem clusters over other issues. Literally hundreds of issues are of equal import, ranging from battles against ethnic or racial prejudice, unfair treatment based on gender or sexual orientation, environmental degradation, or matters of war and peace, but space does not permit discussing each. We have chosen examples from the issue areas in which we are personally most active.

Problems of Economic Inequality and Poverty

In spite of an expanding economy, poverty persists as the gap in income between the rich and poor increases. People of color remain poorer than others, as do women,

especially divorced or unmarried women with children whose income is about 40 percent of the average. Further, "the employment and income picture has gotten worse
for people of color since 2000, eroding the progress made during the 1990s. For the
first time in 15 years, the average Latino household now has an income that is less
than two-thirds that of the average white household" (Leondar-Wright, Lui, Mota, et
al. 2005, 1).

Many people who work earn the minimum wage, lack health insurance, and
have to work more than one job. Goods sold in poor communities are often over-
priced, while economic predators target the working poor and the retired elderly with
overpriced payday loans and deceptive mortgage practices. Over 12 percent of the
population, that is more than 36 million Americans, try to survive with incomes below
the official, but quite inadequate, poverty level. In 2005 the official poverty level for a
single parent with two children was $15,375. Further, as scholars at the Economic
Policy Institute describe:

> Over the past few decades, the benefits of economic growth have flowed largely to
> those households at the top of income or wealth scales. . . . In 2000, the share of
> income held by the top 1% by income was the largest since the run-up to the Great
> Depression. . . . In 2000, almost half of all income (47.4%) went to the top fifth income
> class of families, while the poorest fifth received less than a tenth as much (4.3%). The
> top 5% of families received 20.8% of total income that year, more than the bottom
> 40% combined (14.1%). (Economic Policy Institute 2005)

Geographically poverty is least likely in the suburbs, most frequent in the central
cities, and most extreme among the poor living in farm areas and on reservations.

Income is vital for daily survival, but economic assets—that is, savings or equity
in a home, car, or business—are also important as they allow people to weather periods of unemployment or low income and medical emergencies. They also provide a
pool that can be borrowed against (for instance, by increasing a mortgage) to invest in
a business or pay for a college education. Poor people typically have little or no economic assets with the wealth of the top 1 percent matching all the wealth owned by
the entire bottom 95 percent. Black net worth is about 12 percent of white, while
median Hispanic net worth is zero (United for a Fair Economy 1999).

Poverty is associated with a wide variety of other problems. It can mean living
in a house that is cold in winter, hot in summer, often rat and roach infested, and
located in dangerous neighborhoods; it often means a poor diet, few doctor visits, and
higher frequency of disease. People from poor families on average have less formal
education than others, and may be prepared only for the industrial jobs that are rapidly disappearing. Children from poor families are more likely to drop out of school,
have children out of marriage, and get entangled with the legal system. Poverty does
not simply mean the lack of income, but implies a myriad of associated and reinforcing problems. Further, poverty extends far beyond those living on welfare with the
working poor earning wages that "do not lift them far enough from poverty to
improve their lives" (Shipler 2004, ix). The working poor, and nowadays many in the
middle class, are part of the contingent working force who have jobs but lack security.
In addition, many face the chances of being poor with a 40-year-old now having a 36

percent chance of spending a year with an income below the poverty level (Eckholm 2006).

While poor people are found throughout the nation, poverty is most visible and devastating when concentrated in inner city neighborhoods. These extremely poor areas of the city, often with poverty rates exceeding 40 percent, are described as hyper-ghettoes, tend to be populated by minorities, have many dilapidated or abandoned buildings, lack jobs, and have high rates of violent crime. Most middle-class residents have fled these areas, as have industries and the normal complement of commercial stores (Jargowsky 1997). The concentration of poverty causes problems to compound—the lack of jobs increases crime and the fear of crime discourages people from opening stores. However, in recent years the number of hyperghettoes has decreased with a higher proportion of the poor now in the suburbs (Kingsley and Pettit 2003); but now there is an increase in very poor suburban places (Swanstrom, Flack, and Dreier 2004).

Economic predation on the poor has increased. A large array of unscrupulous businesses—over-priced car dealers, rent-to-own furniture and appliance stores, deceptive credit card issuers—prey on those of marginal income (Karger 2005). Further, the poor are more likely to be victims of high-interest payday loans (with rates of over 400 percent a year), or of crooks offering deceptive mortgages that end up depriving people of the equity in their property (Squires 2004).

Policies Dealing with Economic Inequality and Poverty

Over the last seventy-five years, government has had an on-again off-again response to poverty and economic inequality. Programs to reduce poverty have included direct cash transfers, such as Social Security; social support programs such as the present-day Temporary Assistance to Needy Families (TANF), or heat assistance, or Medicaid; as well as tax rebates that provide money to the working poor. While states have had their own array of antipoverty and social service programs (Karger and Stoesz 2002; McNichol and Springer 2004), Uncle Sam is still the dominant provider of antipoverty funds, sponsoring Medicare, Food Stamps, Social Security, money for WIC (Women, Infants and Children), a nutrition program, housing, school meals, and the earned income tax credit, while paying for more than half of Medicaid and TANF (Coalition on Human Needs 2005). Our discussion concentrates on federal policies.

Even though much more remains to be done, the social safety net has helped make millions of Americans healthier and more economically secure (Center on Budget and Policy Priorities 2005). Yet, with conservatives now in power an effort is under way to unravel the social services safety net attacking programs such as Social Security that were set up as far back as the Great Depression of the 1930s, along with other antipoverty efforts. But many of these programs slowly faded away during the next two decades as poverty was increasingly ignored. But during the 1960s, poverty was rediscovered, in part because of the personal interests of Presidents Kennedy and Johnson, then made salient by actions of civil rights campaigners who pointed out that many people, particularly those of color, had not benefited from the boom of the fifties.

During this liberal interlude, the federal government put in place programs to battle poverty and to improve deteriorated neighborhoods, most as part of the War on Poverty administered by the federal Office of Economic Opportunity but run locally by Community Action Agencies. These programs included Head Start, to help children of poor families start school on an equal footing with their peers; the Job Corps, a training and employment program; and the Food Stamp Program. In addition, the federal government helped fund Community Development Corporations (CDCs) to carry out housing and community economic renewal. The legal services programs hired attorneys to help the poor to deal with their immediate legal problems, or to deal with government bureaucracies. The elderly benefited as Social Security payments were increased and health programs were established. In addition, President Johnson supported the Older Americans Act (OAA) which set up programs in support of the elderly. Though many of the War on Poverty programs failed to empower the program recipients, they did create a tradition of community participation and control that outlasted the federally funded Community Action Program. Remnants of these programs are present today, although they are targets of conservative politicians.

Policies adopted during the Nixon and Ford Republican administrations (1968–1976) weakened the community participation aspects of the War on Poverty programs, although funding was only marginally reduced. However, the Office of Economic Opportunity was abolished, eliminating many bureaucrats who were willing to shape programs in ways that helped the poor. The Nixon administration funded the Comprehensive Employment Training Act (CETA) as a jobs programs, but at best only a few were created. Ironically, given the conservative nature of the Nixon administration, CETA helped sustain social activism by allowing local governments to hire organizers who worked in community-based social service agencies.

The subsequent democratic administration of President Jimmy Carter (1976–1980) tried without much success to increase funding for programs that benefited the poor. Still, localities were allowed to use money from the Community Development Block Grant (initially a physical redevelopment program) for social service activities and social activists were appointed to federal positions. While programs under Carter encouraged public participation and targeted benefits to the poor, little efforts were made to increase budgets.

The overriding goal of the Reagan administration (1980–1988) was to reduce the costs of social service programs while convincing people that liberal social policies caused more problems than they cured (O'Connor 2004, 157–81). Building on a politics of social resentment that pushed the belief that the working were funding the lazy, President Reagan successfully framed a negative image of antipoverty programs by creating a typification of a (mythical) welfare queen who rode in a Cadillac and collected dozens of welfare checks. Program funds dropped. Even ignoring the effects of inflation, Aid to Families with Dependent Children (welfare) dropped 6 percent, food and nutrition assistance went up only 1.4 percent, while employment and training funds were halved (Weicher 1984).

To both obscure the size of these cuts and make future ones easier, conservatives starting with Nixon, and increasingly during the Reagan years and continuing on to the present day combined separate, earmarked federal grant programs into a single *block grant*, one for community development and later another for social services.

Prior to the invention of block grants, the federal government allocated money to states and cities in what were called *categorical grants*, that could only be used for specific, narrowly defined projects, such as repairing blighted houses. A block grant put together several related programs such as those for repairing blighted homes, sewer repair, and community redevelopment into one larger program. The total for the block grant was usually less than the sum of the individual categorical grants comprising it, but the locality could spend all of the grant on any of the allowed uses, rather than on programs that it might not need. However, this approach was not always beneficial to the poor. For instance, the Social Services Block Grant (SSBG) that included AFDC was redesigned, but the total for the block grant was only 70 percent of the amount spent on the categorical programs that it replaced and then was later reduced to 50 percent (U.S. Conference of Mayors 1986, 177–78).

President Clinton, a middle-of-the-road Democrat, was seen as a hope to save social programs. But with the conservative revolution in Congress, Clinton had little choice but to capitulate to pressures in instituting major reforms of the social welfare system (O'Connor 2004). This legislation dramatically changed the support system for the very poor.

> The Personal Responsibility Act . . . limits the time (to 5 years) that a family head can receive cash assistance under . . . Temporary Assistance to Needy Families (TANF) . . . . [H]alf of all single parents must be working. For two-parent families, at least one parent will have to be working in 90 percent of the assisted families. Work activities are tightly defined in the law. . . . The law requires unwed teen parents to live at home . . . . and to be in school in order to receive benefits . . . for immigrants, the law is especially strict (Nathan 1998, 4).

States are allowed broad discretion in implementing the law as long as their policies reduce welfare rolls. Recipients are no longer automatically Medicaid eligible, limits have been placed on the amount of food stamp money recipients can receive, and funding for child nutrition has been cut. States readily accepted the new responsibilities since at first the funds from the federal government exceeded the money states were then spending. Early on, with the economy robust, welfare rolls have contracted sharply, by 43 percent over four years. Of those, about two-thirds have found some kind of work, but the work was often low paying with wages hovering around the poverty level (Brauner and Lopest 1999).

States quickly discovered that many welfare recipients require a variety of supporting programs, including assistance with transportation, medical care, daycare, and family problems. Further, many who had been receiving federal housing subsidies found that now they were working they were no longer eligible, yet did not earn enough to pay for housing on their own. Overall, in its initial years:

> Welfare reform has dramatically reduced the numbers of welfare recipients . . . and just as dramatically increased the numbers of working poor families. It is as though, in a social policy version of the Invasion of the Body Snatchers, millions of families went to sleep one night as welfare recipients and woke the next morning as the working poor (Cutler 1999, 1)

Experiments began with other antipoverty efforts, most focused on helping those living in public housing projects. Overall these efforts to find jobs for public housing residents either by moving them to locations with more jobs available or helping with job training had mixed results. They seem to have some benefits but are far from solving the core problems (Turner and Rawlings 2005, 3).

By its sixth year (as we write) the George W. Bush era has required a nonstop fight by activists to prevent the shredding of the social safety net. Motivated by an unquestioned ideological belief that government is too big and that the poor abuse services, conservatives pushed for cuts in service and antipoverty programs while arguing that what aid is provided is best given through faith-based charities. There is a sad irony here, because research shows that the very antipoverty efforts Bush seeks to cut back such as Medicaid, Food Stamps, the Women, Infant and Children food supplement program, food stamps, and the Earned Income Tax Credit, as well as supplemental Social Security have all significantly reduced poverty (Center on Budget and Policy Priorities 2005).

Programs such as TANF, Food Stamps, or assistance in paying heating costs (and housing assistance programs that we discuss below) each year are threatened with severe reductions, as are other programs that provide security for the elderly. Smaller, more focused programs are also on the chopping block. For instance, PRIME, that helps small startup businesses, or the CDFI fund that provides money to community financial institutions are targeted for elimination. Much effort is spent by progressive activists just to keep program funding for major efforts such as TANF at an even keel, while making sure states use TANF money to provide the assistance, child care, and medical assistance that the working poor require. Some states work to provide such holistic packages, but in many places TANF is run in ways to reduce the welfare rolls as rapidly as possible, forcing people to be employed at low wages, and leaving mothers with small children with insufficient support (Golden 2005).

While forcing people into lower paying jobs, conservatives have steadfastly resisted attempts to increase the minimum wage, even just to keep up with inflation. Yet, at the same time, the Bush administration has gotten massive tax cuts whose gains are going to the top 10 percent and even a higher proportion to the top 1 percent (Kamin and Shapiro 2004, 3)

Activists are increasingly paying attention to what states can do to help the poor. Efforts are in place to establish state antipoverty programs such as EITC to make up for federal gaps (McNichol and Springer 2004) but the amount of money available is far too small. Still, social change organizations have successfully campaigned for state minimum wages that exceed the paltry federal level and have convinced many local governments to assure that all public sector employees and those employed by companies receiving public sector contracts or incentives receive a living wage.

Problems of Neighborhood Decline and Affordable Housing

A core belief of progressive activism is that people have a fundamental right to live in clean, affordable housing, within safe neighborhoods with a well-maintained social and physical infrastructure. Unfortunately, for tens of millions of individuals, disproportionately those of color, this is not the case. Housing in many neighborhoods is often ill-maintained, overcrowded, and has costs far too high for the inferior quality received, while homes that are accessible to those with special needs are lacking.

Housing problems are severe throughout the country, but are particularly problematic in older, inner city neighborhoods that have economically declined. Manufacturing jobs left the older cities for suburban locations (and nowadays abroad) reducing both the tax base and encouraging the better off to move. White-flight accelerated the decline and was facilitated by government policies of paying for new highways while providing support for mortgages in newer suburban homes.

Raw racism, and racism's more subtle economic manifestations, accelerated the decline. Capital is needed to sustain both housing and infrastructure, yet with full concurrence of the federal government, banks (as well as real estate brokers) *redlined*, that is intentionally denying inner city neighborhoods mortgage loans and investment capital. Efforts to eliminate blight often added to problems of poor neighborhoods. So-called renewal programs tore down single room occupancy housing for the poor, as well as older, dilapidated rental buildings, and factories and often replaced them with upscale shopping, middle class condominiums, and office buildings for middle class jobs, as well as entertainment centers such as sports parks. Improvement programs tended to focus on downtown; an activist group discovered that in Chicago the two downtown wards received as much money for infrastructure repair as the other forty-eight wards combined.

Recognizing that cities do need middle class inhabitants, many city governments encourage gentrification. With gentrification, older neighborhoods are recycled to provide elegant housing for wealthier people. Gentrification forces poor people from their homes and—since gentrifying areas often are adjacent to the few remaining inner-city manufacturing districts—away from their jobs as upscale housing displaces smaller industrial firms. Gentrification magnifies the loss of industrial jobs for those with low incomes while reducing the stock of affordable housing.

Housing problems extend far beyond the inner city, as high rents and escalating purchase costs affect lower income people and increasingly those of middle income, irrespective of where they live. Further, people with special needs, the wheelchair-bound, for instance, and the elderly, more generally, have difficulty finding homes that are accessible. Worse yet, even with Fair Housing laws being on the books for forty years, discrimination still occurs against minority group members as well as people with large families, with rentals difficult to find and those who seek to purchase homes far more likely to have to pay exorbitant sub-prime rates (ACORN Fair Housing 2005). Finally, predatory lenders, unscrupulous firms who deceive homeowners into signing loan documents at outrageous rates, prey most often on minorities and the elderly.

Affordability of housing remains a core problem. More than thirty million households are considered shelter-poor, spending far too much of their income on housing (Stone 2006); to afford a typical two-bedroom apartment requires a wage of $15.78 while "extremely low income households, with incomes equal to or lower than 30% of the local Area Median Income (AMI), . . . have virtually no affordable housing options in the private market" (Pelletiere, Wardrip, and Crowley 2006). In addition, "14.3 million households, or one in seven, spend more than half their incomes on housing" (Joint Center for Housing Studies 2005).

Urban Renewal and Housing Policies

Federal urban renewal and housing policies have dramatically changed over the last forty-five years, with a marked decline in support in the last few years (Dolbeare, Saraf, and Crowley 2004). The earlier federal government urban renewal programs, mostly started after World War II, were about clearing out slums but did so in ways that displaced large numbers of poor people, especially African Americans. New housing was built, using federal financing, but the subsidies to the middle and upper classes for housing, such as the mortgage interest deduction, far outstripped those provided to house the poor. For instance, between 1949 and 1960, the total cost of public housing units constructed was matched by the average federal subsidy provided in a single year to the middle class (Struyk, Turner, and Ueno 1988, 62).

As part of the War on Poverty in the sixties, President Lyndon Johnson initiated the Model Cities program that combined urban redevelopment efforts and social service programs. However, the impact of Model Cities was greatly attenuated as Congress insisted that the small amount of money made available be shared by a large number of cities. Initial requirements for citizen participation in the Model Cities efforts encouraged the growth of community organizations; but mayors resenting their loss of power successfully demanded that laws be changed in their favor. During this period, cities gained some clout when in 1965 the Cabinet level Department of Housing and Urban Development was created, and legislation passed to set up Community Development Corporations—socially responsible nonprofits that engage in home building and business development efforts. Some efforts were made to combat the pervasive racial discrimination in the housing market when Congress in 1968 passed Fair Housing legislation.

During the 1960s, government itself built about 27,000 public housing units each year, but then stopped and instead set up a variety of indirect programs to subsidize the private sector to construct affordable housing. These efforts often backfired, with many homes shoddily built or not fully repaired, then aggressively marketed to people who, with incomes inadequate to pay the mortgages or maintain the properties, often defaulted. Worse yet, unscrupulous real estate brokers played upon racial fears to encourage white families to sell their homes to speculators who in turn sold them to poor African American families who lacked the income to maintain the property, both creating slums and encouraging "white flight" (Levine and Harmon 1992).

Major changes in federal policy occurred in the Nixon-Ford years with the passage of the Housing and Community Development Act that set up the Community

Development Block Grant (CDBG) program by merging categorical grants for street repairs, sewer construction, housing construction and rehabilitation, urban planning, certain specified community services, the preservation of historic buildings, and economic development work. Cities receiving CDBG grants were required to set up citizen advisory groups, but these citizen groups often had very little say and early on some local governments spent the money on projects that benefited wealthier citizens. However, because of the persistent efforts of community organizations, CDBG increasingly has been recognized by city governments as money meant for the poor and poor communities and activist organizations have gained an effective say in how funds are spent (Rich 1993; Sanders 1997).

The Section 8 Housing Program introduced during the Nixon years dramatically changed how the federal government funded lower income housing. Rather than building homes, Section 8 provides vouchers to (a fraction of) those who need affordable housing who then can use these vouchers to rent HUD-approved housing on the free market, with the voucher covering the rental costs that exceed a given percentage (initially 25 percent, now 30 percent) of the tenant's income. Another provision in Section 8 provided subsidies for builders who constructed apartment buildings in which a given percentage of the units were made available as part of the Section 8 program.

During the Ford administration the Home Mortgage Disclosure Act of 1975 was passed requiring banks to publicize by geographic area where mortgage loans were made and providing data that could document illegal redlining. In 1977, after further pressure from activists, the government passed the Community Reinvestment Act (CRA) that permits banking supervisors to sanction banks that are not loaning money in or otherwise serving poor communities.

During the Carter years, HUD officials more aggressively fought efforts by white suburbs to exclude minorities, responding to the 1976 Supreme Court ruling in the Gautreaux case that mandated, because of past discrimination, government must now provide Section 8 housing certificates to house the urban poor in suburban areas. Studies of Gautreaux and similar programs have found that relocated families get superior education and obtain better jobs. Carter helped social change activists by appointing people sympathetic to the community movement to ranking HUD positions while providing funds to neighborhood organizations to monitor CDBG to make sure money was spent to directly benefit poor individuals.

After the election of Ronald Reagan as president, the climate for housing and community development soured. Social service programs were cut back and federal money for affordable housing simply dried up. CDBG declined to half its peak size, while little attention was paid to whether CDBG money was actually spent on the poor. The Section 8 program was changed so that people now had to contribute 30 percent of their income. Homelessness increased and though the administration wanted to ignore the problem, Congress in response to activist lobbying passed the McKinney Act in 1987 that provided some support for housing the homeless.

As an alternative to federal housing programs, and at the urging of a coalition of community groups, banks, and builders, in 1986 Congress passed the Low Income Housing Tax Credit (LIHTC). LIHTC is a complicated program, but to simplify, it allocates tax credits that allow wealthier corporations tax benefits if they invest in affordable housing projects. Some activists complained that LIHTC is "feeding the sparrows by feeding the horses" (Hartman 1992), but overall LIHTC has provided billions and is now a mainstay of funding for affordable housing, although not for the very lowest income groups.

In 1990 during the first Bush presidency, Congress passed the National Affordable Housing Act, putting together what was left of many federal housing programs into a lump sum payment to localities, while reinstating the requirement that 70 percent of CDBG money go to low and moderate income communities. Other provisions encouraged local governments to improve public housing (the HOPE program) while setting up subsidies to help the poor own their own homes (the HOME program). The Affordable Housing Act mandated that at least 15 percent of housing funds be set aside for projects developed by nonprofit, community-based organizations.

For those concerned about housing and community renewal programs, the Clinton years became a terrifying roller coaster ride. Clinton, while sympathetic to the urban poor, was not willing to fight hard for the programs. His appointees at HUD were active supporters of community causes, but the Republican dominated Congress strongly opposed programs for the poor. Pressures to balance the budget encouraged Congress to reduce social services, housing, and urban renewal programs, while trying unsuccessfully to abolish HUD. Congress weakened fair-housing legislation and under the guise of banking modernization, seriously weakened the Community Reinvestment Act. The Community Development Block Grant survived as a tool for urban renewal and helped pay for hundreds of thousands of housing units, but the same amount of money had to be spread over more cities, reducing its impact. The major Clinton innovation to help urban areas was the Empowerment Zone Program, in which $100,000,000 in grants (over ten years) were provided to a handful of cities that successfully competed for the money while some other cities designated as Enterprise Zones received smaller grants.

In late 1998, federal housing efforts dramatically changed with the passage of the Quality Housing and Work Responsibility Act (HOPE VI) that encouraged local Public Housing Agencies to tear down older derelict projects and provide those displaced with Section 8 vouchers. In addition, funds were to pay for comprehensive planning and social service efforts in areas surrounding public housing. While the destruction of crumbling units sounded like a good idea, some feared that destroying public housing projects located near the central business districts would encourage gentrification. Further, there were not enough Section 8 vouchers (or landlords willing to accept Section 8 tenants) to house the individuals who were displaced. Matters were complicated by the uncertain fate of Section 8, especially on what became known as the expiring use permits problem. In previous years, Section 8 helped developers build apartments on the condition that the apartments remain affordable for a contractually determined number of years. Once those years passed, the owner was allowed to do as he or she wished with the building.

We are writing during the sixth year of the George W. Bush administration which has been a near disaster. As part of slicing back the social safety net, urban renewal and, in particular, housing programs have been targeted for reduction and some for elimination. Efforts have been made to reduce the CDBG budget and to move the entire program from HUD to the Department of Commerce where it would languish. Programs to fund both community economic development and community financial institutions were zeroed out but were later restored through congressional action. Attempts to end HUD were on the agenda, funding for HOME was threatened, and HOPE VI received no support. Administrative budgets of public housing authorities were reduced. Money for Section 8 was threatened each year and since "early 2004, voucher assistance for more than 100,000 families has been lost" and administrative rules put in place that further limit how they can be used (Sard and Rice 2006). No extra help has been provided for reducing homelessness, while at the local levels, being homeless is increasingly treated as a crime rather than as a social need (The National Coalition for the Homeless and The National Law Center on Homelessness & Poverty 2006).

These cutbacks are unfortunate because evidence increasingly shows that housing and renewal programs can work. HOPE VI efforts to repair neighborhoods with deteriorating public housing projects, while far from perfect, have helped overall (Popkin, Katz, Cunningham, et al. 2004); community development corporations have brought about important and positive changes in neighborhoods in which they work (Galster, Levy, Sawyer, et al. 2005); the low income housing tax credit has encouraged thousands upon thousands of homes to be built, and a federally chartered commission has encouraged even more efforts at providing affordable housing (Millennial Housing Commission 2002).

Conclusions and Implications for Organizing Work

We have presented how social problems are understood, ways in which policies come about, and then traced out the recent history of two important policy areas. Space limited our presentation to the two issue areas with which we are most familiar, so activists working with other issues should read the abundant policy literature that speaks to their own work.

We have not covered how policies and programs emerge at the state and local level because of lack of space. In summary though, many principles remain the same—the importance of ideology, the overlapping of issues, and constant change as political regimes come and go. But three major differences should be noted: First, that while local level policies often mirror what is occurring nationally, local policies reflect the different cities and cultures. Second, local agendas tend to fill up with only one or two issues, so many concerns are ignored for some time, leading to far less continuity in programs and policies. Third, certain issues—land development, industrial and commercial attraction, and sprawl—are high on the agendas of states, and cities and towns while often not being even a blip at the federal level.

What lessons can activists take from our discussion? To begin, while people of each generation feel they are discovering problems anew, most issues in fact are longstanding, with all the historic baggage that they entail. Second, problems are understood as they are framed, irrespective of the facts of the matter. Battles over programs are battles over images, framings, and perceptions. Don't believe for a minute that the facts will speak for themselves with either the public or with elected officials. Next, programs set up by government ostensibly to solve problems can make matters worse, as occurred with early efforts to help fund housing that ended up contributing to neighborhood decline.

Another lesson is on the complexity and irrationality of the public policy system, in which a lack of connection exists between problem, policy, and program. We'd like to think that when a problem is examined, solutions particular to that problem present themselves. In practice, nothing like this occurs; instead, problems are evaluated in terms of broader, ideologically shaped understandings. Similarly, solutions often reflect what we have termed meta-policies, tools to be applied almost irrespective of the situation.

Public policies fluctuate. Vital laws such as the Community Reinvestment Act are constantly in danger of being eroded or terminated. Affirmative action has been weakened. Even constitutional issues like the separation of church and state are continually contested. To effectively design campaigns, activists must understand the source and background of different social programs.

Still, the successes of past organizing efforts have improved the environment for present day efforts. Thousands of community development groups now provide affordable homes for hundreds of thousands of poor families. More people of color are in positions of responsibility than ever before. Women have many more opportunities in sports, education, and jobs than a generation ago. A generation ago, raw racism was (in certain social sectors) acceptable and the intentional and overt subordination of women was a common practice. Now racism and sexism, while still real, are no longer normative. Further, activists have learned that as problems are linked so should efforts to solve them; rather than working issue by issue, activists now join with others in ongoing coalitions, many of which fight multiple problems. Organizing is about teaching community members the power of working together and then having the wisdom to recognize that the same principle holds for the activist organizations themselves.

CHAPTER

8 Intersecting Histories

Community Organizing, Issue Mobilization, and Social Movements

The previous chapter sketched out government response (or lack of response) to social problems. In this chapter, we trace the brief history of how activists have responded to problems in different eras to show how lessons from the past shape present-day actions.

History teaches that the battle against big business and unresponsive government has been an uphill fight but one in which, when faced with long odds and with slim beginnings, social activists can win. David can beat Goliath because he has in the past. But we also learn to be patient yet persistent as past movements faced lean days in which little was accomplished. Organizers can look back and see that other organizations overcame threats—their members jailed, jobs taken away, their demonstrations broken up by violence. Slow times need not mean the death of hope as bad times are turned to good purpose when activists understand they are part of a shared history of solidarity, pride, and success. Still, history makes quite clear that some problems persist, especially those of oppression based on race, class, gender, and sexuality.

History provides lessons on what tactics and strategies have been tried and to what end. The now-legendary antics of organizer Saul Alinksy teach us what can be accomplished by disruptive humor while the nonviolence of Dr. Martin Luther King, Jr. makes clear that unarmed people can face billy clubs and fire hoses and win actual victories. But activists are forewarned that short-term concessions made by opponents are not really victories without laws that back them up and without having an organization to assure that promises are kept.

Past failures, too, teach present-day organizers. The women's movement lost the fight for the Equal Rights Amendment in part because of dissensus among activists who were divided by class and ethnicity. History illustrates how social change organizations have crashed and died when they overextended themselves financially; dedication and concern are vital, but bills also have to be paid.

In short, history sensitizes us to the problems and possibilities of change, provides concrete advice for present-day action, and sustains our action with the hope and pride that comes from learning of past successes. The history of social change is far too complicated to narrate in a single chapter. We can, though, pay attention to core historic themes whose impact is still felt.

A Brief Overview of the History of Social Activism and the Neighborhood Movement

The history of organizing for social change brings together three separate streams—one of neighborhood activism, another of issue and identity organizing, and a third of broader social movements. Sometimes issues in each stream are separate, with neighborhood groups battling local crime, or those involved in issue organizing, working for peace. But often local actions, issue organizing, and social movements come together, as for instance when those involved in the civil rights movement saw how social injustices impacted local communities and fought not only for broader civil rights legislation but to end environmental racism (polluting industries mostly locate in areas of cities in which poor minorities live).

History shows how activism ebbs and flows, creating "waves of protest" (Freeman and Johnson 1999). Periods of quiescence alternate with eras of near-revolutionary action. The quiet acceptance of the status quo during the Eisenhower years were followed by the sixties—a decade of endless questioning of the social and economic structure. Activism responds to what (for the lack of a better phrase) can be termed the *climate of the times*: Is it a time of fear as was present during the repression of the Palmer Era or the McCarthy Era, or are people so hungry and ill-housed as they were during the Great Depression that actions occur because people have little to lose?

To some extent, the transition from quiescence to activism comes about through systematic organizing, but some external trigger is needed. Broad-based discontent against the injustices blacks faced had been stewing for many years, but were given focus through courageous sit-down actions and bus boycotts. Gay activists had been railing against the discrimination they faced for years, but the movement was invigorated when a handful battled back at a local gay bar against police-sponsored gay bashing. A serious crime, or an auto accident at an unprotected intersection, or the threat by government to tear homes down to build an expressway or expand a sports arena has triggered neighborhood action.

Since space does not permit examining the broad history of social action, let's focus on what has occurred at the neighborhood level and then see the impact of broader issue-based organizing during years of ferment.

A Brief History of Neighborhood Organizing

Building on the work of Robert Fisher (Fisher 1994; 2005) we divide the history of neighborhood organizing into eight separate periods. The first period occurred during the Progressive[1] era, approximately from 1895 to 1920, during which activists

---

[1]The label the progressive era uses the same word—*progressive*—as we do to describe our approach to social action. The progressive era was about reform; progressive organizing is about effecting more fundamental structural changes.

tried to bring about reforms of overcrowded housing and bad water supplies while at the same time trying to impose middle-class values on new immigrants groups. A more radical approach took place during the Great Depression, followed by a period of conservative complaisance after World War II and through the Eisenhower administration.

In the 1960s, activism was reinvigorated with major battles against poverty and sexism, occurring during an era of broader upheavals against racism and the War in Vietnam. The seventies were a period in which past gains were solidified while during the Reagan-dominated 1980s, a backlash occurred. During the Clinton period, a sophisticated, professional neighborhood and social change movement developed to go head-to-head against conservative forces, but by the Bush era social change activists were once again on the defensive.

Research Bureau and Social Welfare Neighborhood Organizing. Research bureau and social welfare organizing were paternalistic efforts of an upper class to help the poor. Change efforts were initiated in various research bureaus that documented the extent and severity of problems, especially those facing immigrant communities, assuming once evidence was available, government would be forced by moral compulsion to fix what was wrong. At the same time, social welfare organizers tried to combat overcrowding and poor sanitation that new immigrants faced in urban communities. Upper status women working out of settlement houses like Hull House taught immigrants English, how to prepare American foods, and otherwise sought to help the new immigrants blend into middle class life. Individuals were indeed helped, but there were few efforts at empowerment or building pride and solidarity among the various ethnic groups (Fabricant and Fisher 2002) with the exception of the International Institute which was about neighborhood organizing that celebrated ethnic traditions (Betten and Austin 1990, 57).

The most radical organizing scheme of the era was the Cincinnati Social Unit Plan (1918–20) that tried to combine empowerment work with the amelioration of social problems. With this approach, activists, mostly middle class, set up Social Units in poor areas to be run democratically by a policy council formed of block workers from the neighborhood. However, even the small successes of this approach aroused opposition among professionals who feared the Social Unit actions would harm the rich, the mayor who labelled the whole effort as Bolshevik, and the business people who feared that cooperative buying by community members would cut into profits. Lacking deep community support, the movement faded away (Betten and Austin 1990, 35–53).

Organizing in the African American community took place separate from that in white neighborhoods. Activists such as Ida B. Wells-Barnett fought against lynchings, helped set up women's clubs for social services, and agitated against unfair treatment of African Americans, while other organizers such as Lugenia Burns Hope set up neighborhood service organizations to improve health and education and to agitate (unsuccessfully) for better employment opportunities for African Americans. As a result of these efforts, "in cities throughout the North and South, African Americans established hospitals, clinics, schools, kindergartens, Y's, homes for single working

women, day nurseries, orphanages, mutual benefit societies . . . and old folks' homes
. . . [often] supported and controlled by the African American community" (O'Donnell 1995, 15). Though several of the organizations had working class leaders, most of
the leadership came from better off African Americans.

For neighborhood organizing, the progressive era displayed mixed themes of
working to help the poor, yet at the same time reinforcing the economic, social, and
racial status quo. In addition, little effort was made to set up empowered community
organizations.

Radical Neighborhood Organizing.   The relative prosperity of the 1920s ended
abruptly with the economic crash that led to a Great Depression that lasted over a
decade. At its nadir, over a third of the working population was unemployed, yet no
one initially assumed responsibility for the poor. During this period of national
trauma, three forms of neighborhood organizing developed. The Communist Party
organized unemployed workers while radical social workers encouraged militant
actions in the neighborhoods. In a third thrust, the modern version of neighborhood
organizing began when Saul Alinsky set up neighborhood-based organizations in
which community members agitated for social and economic reforms.

Capitalizing on Depression-era fears, the Communist Party organized unemployed workers, directed sit-ins at relief offices, defended tenants evicted from apartments, and worked within black communities to promote interracial cooperation. The
party established neighborhood workers' councils that demanded economic relief
from government, but gradually de-emphasized neighborhood action as it organized
against fascism during Hitler's rise to power.

In response to this pressure from the left, and in reaction to the suffering of the
American public, the Roosevelt administration created the New Deal, an evolving and
overlapping assortment of federal programs, that became the base of the modern welfare state. Relief programs for businesses, farmers, and ultimately the unemployed followed one another. Social Security, Aid to Families with Dependent Children, and
capital projects to stimulate economic growth were initiated. As part of the New Deal,
the number of social workers rose dramatically (Ehrenreich 1985, 85–102). A radical
faction of social workers, the Rank and File Movement, moved from providing services to undertaking community organizing work (Wenocur and Reisch 1989,
189–207). Rank and File activists considered that both they and their clients had to
fight oppression together, along class lines (Wagner 1989). However, the Rank and
File lost much of its organizing momentum as social workers were increasingly
absorbed by the expansion of New Deal social welfare programs (Wenocur and Reisch
1989, 197–99).

Little influence on neighborhood organizing remains from the Communist
Party or the efforts of the Rank and File Movement. In contrast, the work of Saul
Alinsky still has a direct impact on present day neighborhood work and social action
in general (Horwitt 1989; Reitzes and Reitzes 1987). Combining the perspective that
social problems have a community basis with the militant tactics used in labor organizing, Saul Alinsky set up problem-focused, nonideological community-based organizations.

His approach was to gather together existing local organizations in a coalition that then together engaged in direct action campaigns to resolve immediate problems facing community members. The initial Alinsky group, the Back of the Yards Neighborhood Council, was set up in the densely populated, under-serviced area surrounding the stockyards in Chicago (Slayton 1986). The neighborhood was already in ferment from left-wing labor activists who were working to fight the awful working conditions at the meat-packing plants. Alinsky persuaded Catholic clergy, who feared the ideological left, that they should help form an indigenous, nonideological organization to solve economic and social problems. In 1939 Alinsky was able to persuade numerous church-based organizations and social and ethnic clubs in the Back of the Yards neighborhood to come together and form a neighborhood council.

Through participatory processes, the council determined to focus on problems such as the lack of employment opportunities and the deteriorating housing conditions and did so by using dramatic and confrontational tactics (for instance, having numbers of poor people deposit on the lawns of politicians garbage from neighborhoods with infrequent pickup and in this way forcing an increase in garbage collection). Similar efforts were used to gain stop signs or set up local health stations. While the short-run goal was to solve the immediate problems, the longer-run goal was to build a permanent organization that could keep up pressure on government and businesses. Day-to-day work of the organization was carried out by a professionally trained organizer who was an employee of the neighborhood coalition.

Post–World War II Conservative Organizing. From 1945 to 1960 the United States experienced dramatic economic growth and rapid suburbanization, yet remained socially and politically conservative. National attention was focused on the Cold War, with problems of poverty and racism either ignored or bulldozed away.

While liberal issue-oriented social movement organizations were alive and Alinksy groups continued to protest, most local organizing was about preserving the status quo, as seen in the proliferation of conservative neighborhood improvement associations. As Fisher argues "the association serves to protect property values and community homogeneity by opposing commercial development and excluding members of lower classes and racial minorities" (Fisher 1984, 73). To carry out their exclusionary work, these associations relied on restrictive covenants that forbade sales to specified minorities. After the Supreme Court ruled such covenants illegal, neighborhood associations switched tactics, pressuring suburban governments to adopt zoning and building codes that made houses too expensive for the poor (Danielson 1976).

The Drama of the 1960s. From 1960 to the early 1970s, the nation was in ferment, with hundreds of thousands participating in both community organizing and broader social movements. "Nothing was sacred, everything was challenged" and people were considering "disturbing questions" such as whether America was racist, imperialist, or sexist (Anderson 1995, i). Issues raised by the counter-culture—drugs, freer sexual behavior, changes in dress—blurred into concerns with peace, environmentalism, racism, and sexism. Students, feminists, and civil rights workers all engaged in overlapping battles. During this period the "old left" with its moribund European labor-oriented, socialist views was replaced by a "new left," vibrant with American ideals of promoting social justice. Issues of national concerns were seen locally, with neighborhood organizations pushing for racial justice or in self-help groups that reflected national themes such as the liberation of women. The federal government was both the devil and the angel, the devil that waited too long to respond to problems, and the angel that funded community work and passed laws that helped foster broader social change.

The courageous actions of civil rights workers in the South provided the most dramatic impetus to change—as seen in the Montgomery bus boycott, the sit-ins to desegregate public facilities, and, later, the voter-registration drives that succeeded but at the cost of having both black and white organizers murdered. Activists in the Southern Christian Leadership Conference (SCLC), the Congress of Racial Equality (CORE), the Student Non-Violent Coordinating Committee (SNCC), and hundreds of local people (Payne 1995) confronted southern racism head-on. After much strife, Congress passed the civil rights and voting rights bills that provided the basis for subsequent social justice work. Fair housing and open access legislation were also approved.

As the civil rights movement moved north, minorities became active in protesting against horrible living conditions. A new round of actions was stimulated by the assassination of Dr. Martin Luther King, Jr. Partly in response to such protests and partly to carry out the unfulfilled promises of President Kennedy, the Johnson administration supported a series of community-based social welfare programs.

The federal government funded "War on Poverty," implemented a Model Cities program, and established the Office of Economic Opportunity (OEO) that became the institutional scaffolding for programs to aid the poor. Money was made available for affordable housing programs, Headstart helped poor preschoolers build skills, while food stamp programs helped feed the hungry. Federally funded Community Action Agencies (CAA) set up a permanent presence in localities to carry out social programs, while Community Development Corporations received government funds to build homes, create shopping areas, and provide jobs in areas of deep poverty. Concurrently, federal dollars supported community health care and mental health agencies. While large by historic standards, overall funding was still modest.

Regulations required city officials to work with neighborhood organizations on setting priorities. Meanwhile, Community Action Agencies hired neighborhood organizers to work with the poor; the federal VISTA Program (Volunteers in Service to America) engaged volunteers, many of whom later became professional organizers; and the federal Legal Services Corporation employed attorneys funded to speak for the poor. For a while it seemed that community groups, supported by Community Action Agencies and Legal Services attorneys, would have an effective say in directing programs to alleviate poverty.

Concurrently, hundreds of smaller neighborhood organizations emerged as people in neighborhoods inspired by these public efforts themselves got together. Initially such community activism emerged within African American communities, but organizing quickly spread to other groups. Long-festering grievances among Chicanos first turned into direct confrontations and then demand for community control (Chavez 1998). In larger cities, such as New York, neighborhood organizations battled to gain a say in running the school system and demanded better employment and job training opportunities, while throughout the nation activists opposed construction of federal highways that destroyed inner-city communities.

Protest groups carried out numerous direct actions. Through confrontations, Alinsky organizations such as FIGHT in Rochester, New York, successfully demanded jobs for poor minorities, while former civil rights organizers formed the National Welfare Rights Organization (NWRO) and used sit-ins and marches to bolster their demands for more resources for the dependent poor. In the west, César Chaves merged issues of ethnicity, civil rights, and labor in forming a farm workers union and then through picketing, hunger strikes, and ultimately a nationwide boycott of grape products, the union improved the working conditions of farm laborers. Native Americans publicized historic wrongs, reminding the country that their land had been taken from them by force and deceit, leaving them in poverty. An Asian American movement began to stir when working class Asians fought displacement from transient hotels in big cities in California (Wei 1993, 22–23).

Organizations moved from protests to physically redeveloping their neighborhoods. Among hundreds of community rebuilding efforts, The Woodlawn Organization (TWO), an Alinsky direct-action group, began providing services and undertaking physical renewal projects. In the west, Hispanic activist groups moved from direct action to setting up economic development corporations such as the East Los Angeles Community Union to provide jobs and stores for the poor (Chavez 1998). Throughout the country Community Development Corporations began building affordable homes in poor neighborhoods.

The agitation of the sixties began over issues of poverty and racial injustice, but motivated actions on other concerns. On campuses, college students protested the rules and traditions that treated them as children and demanded educational reform. Student activists in SDS (Students for a Democratic Society) worked in the South as part of the civil rights movement and later organized in northern cities and in Appalachia, helping to build democratic self-help programs among the poor.

During the sixties, the women's rights movement, which had been relatively dormant for years, was resurrected, demanding equal job opportunities, abortion rights, and a constitutional amendment guaranteeing women equal rights under the law. However, factions within the women's movement, between gay and straight women and between those of different social classes, weakened the efforts (Ryan 1992). Gay activists came out of the closet after the dramatic confrontation between gays and the police at the Stonewall Inn in New York City in which the oppressed physically fought back. The environmental movement became more radical and more broad based with environmental organizations such as the Clamshell Alliance and the Abalone Alliance now willing to use direct actions (Gottlieb 1993). Most dramatically, activists protested the Vietnam War. First those from the peace movement, then the larger student population, and finally a cross section of the American public took to the streets, asking why we were fighting halfway across the world, when problems remained unsolved at home.

With this constant questioning of the status quo, a threatened establishment fought back. Protesters were portrayed as long-haired hippies in need of a bath, not messengers pointing out problems. Mayors who resented citizen control regained say over antipoverty funds. Although laws were on the books guaranteeing voting and civil rights, enforcement was sporadic. Under the guise of helping cities, the federal Law Enforcement Assistance Administration helped local police suppress social protests. State and federal officials spied on protesters, both those engaged in antiwar efforts and those fighting for civil rights such as Dr. Martin Luther King, Jr. (Branch 1998).

By the end of the decade some activist groups were in trouble. Many Alinsky-style organizations fell apart once the organizer left. White college students in the Students for a Democratic Society never overcame the class and racial gaps between them and the minority communities in which they worked and SDS disappeared. Within many organizations women were exploited as second-class citizens, and racial tensions between black, white, brown, and red weakened efforts to secure civil rights. Many activists became disillusioned and dropped out (Gitlin 1989, 424).

Still, much was accomplished and the era of the sixties providing a lasting legacy for today. As Terry Anderson reflects:

> activists succeeded in bringing about a sea change, a different America. . . . The first wave asked about the rights of black citizens, the rights of students, about their obligation to fight a distant and undeclared war. They provoked the nation to look in the mirror. The second wave expanded the issues to include all minorities and women . . . , liberation and empowerment have become threads in the nation's multicultural social and political fabric. . . . By confronting the status quo, activists inspired a debate that since has taken place in Congress, courts, city halls, board room, streets, and even bedrooms. The debate involves the political and the personal, and it asks the central question of this democracy: What is the meaning of "America"? (Anderson 1995, 423).

The Nixon and Carter Eras.   Even though federal programs were rolled back during the Nixon and Carter years, many of the gains of the sixties were maintained, with funds still available for community-based housing and economic development efforts. Activist groups that had engaged in protest during the sixties now refocused their efforts to build homes and create jobs in poor neighborhoods. In addition, numerous Community Development Corporations (CDCs) expanded efforts to create affordable housing and some began economic development projects (Peirce and Steinbach 1987). Realizing now that they could not act alone, activists set up an array of national progressive technical assistance organizations such as the Center for Community Change.

Broad-based neighborhood organizing continued, with notable successes among Hispanic populations in the Southwest, especially in Texas. Many organizations concerned about social, gender, and economic issues moved from organizing people to providing the needed services themselves, though were concerned that if in doing so they would weaken efforts for structural change. Women's groups pressed for job and economic equality, sought federal support for the Equal Rights Amendment, and set up local organizations that helped victims of rape and spouse abuse, while others concentrated on maintaining access to safe abortions. Gay activists, mostly living in the more left-wing communities, sought to end de facto housing and job discrimination against homosexuals, while groups of seniors continued efforts to end age-based discrimination. A crucial victory for neighborhood activists came as a result of the work of the National People's Action that convinced Congress to pass the Community Reinvestment Act (CRA) that gave neighborhood housing and redevelopment groups a new tool with which to battle bank-sponsored redlining by requiring reinvestments in poor neighborhoods. Finally, broader issues of economic justice became part of the agenda for social equality. As Dr. Martin Luther King, Jr. observed, it "made no sense to be able to sit down and order a hamburger if you could not afford one" (Delgado 1986, 18).

The Reagan-Bush Backlash. Conservatives, as well as the religious right, had been organizing since the mid-sixties starting with an unsuccessful effort to support Barry Goldwater for president. By 1980 their efforts paid off with the election of Ronald Reagan whose agenda was to undo the major accomplishments of the prior twenty years. The gains of women and minorities in the workplace were particularly galling to conservatives, who attempted to rescind affirmative action and return women to their traditional subservient roles (Faludi 1992). Budgets for social programs were reduced, federal housing efforts virtually dried up, and officials actively opposed to environmentalism were appointed to offices meant to monitor the environment. Federal officials spoke about the importance of self-help, but self-help implied a voluntarism of benevolent charities rather than empowerment. Neighborhood organizing took on a perverse face as wealthier individuals moved into gated communities, set up primarily to exclude the poor and those of color (Blakely and Snyder 1997).

Still, activism remained very much alive in more sophisticated forms that combined direct action and street campaigns with sustained lobbying efforts. Advocates for the disabled successfully lobbied Congress for passage of the Americans with Disabilities Act that mandated accommodation for those with disabilities. Community-based development groups, no longer routinely receiving money for housing, expanded their missions to include economic development work.

National coalitions as well as training and technical assistance organizations came into being. Each of the major networks, the Industrial Areas Foundation, ACORN, PICO, Gamaliel, DART, and NPA provided technical assistance and training to an emerging coterie of professional organizers. At annual meetings of national networks, activists talked with one another about how to cope during conservative times. Technical assistance organizations did background research to inform campaigns, for instance, pinpointing banks engaged in redlining or highlighting neighborhoods most impacted by globalization.

In many cities, neighborhood organizations and the coalitions they formed became part of the local political system. Cities with progressive elected officials devolved some decision-making functions to elected neighborhood groups, at times allowing a full veto on neighborhood projects (Berry, Portney, and Thomson 1993; Goetz and Sidney 1994; Medoff and Sklar 1994). In Texas neo-Alinsky groups were able to influence the public agenda both at the city level (Wilson 1997) as well as at the state level (Warren 2001).

Finally, political involvement became an accepted activist tactic. In Chicago, a coalition of neighborhood groups successfully campaigned for Harold Washington as the city's first African American and community-focused mayor. In many other cities, ethnic assertion was converted to political clout with neighborhood groups supporting African American, Hispanic, and Asian people in successful bids for public office. As Robert Fisher summarizes, organizers learned that

> a primary target for contemporary grassroots efforts must be a responsible public sector . . . effective community organizing requires a legitimate and accountable public sector and a zeitgeist, a spirit of the time, that encourages its citizens to be active in public life. (Fisher 1994, 175)

The Clinton Era.   With the election of William Clinton, a moderate Democrat who had as governor supported the community movement, activists anticipated better times. But unfortunately, the times remained conservative. Backlash activists of the previous decade continued their assault on social welfare programs and programs passed by Congress emphasized getting people off welfare into jobs (O'Connor 2004). Social change organizations remained on the defensive. New economic justice organizations such as the Kensington Welfare Rights Organization joined older networks to simultaneously work locally and nationally on shared issues. Other social change organizations came together to battle structural problems such as globalization that hurt working people. Federal support for affirmative action declined, while housing and neighborhood groups spent much effort to preserve the Community Reinvestment Act that remained under attack. While the activities of the community-based housing and development movement rapidly expanded, some feared that these organizations were now so focused on building homes and creating jobs that they neglected their mission of empowerment (Stoecker 1997).

Cross-issue coalitions and organizations emerged. Building coalitions between neighborhood groups representing people from different ethnic backgrounds became a priority, a process made more complicated by both legal and illegal immigration. Activism spread from older, inner city neighborhoods to suburbs, especially those to which immigrant and minority populations had moved. Suburban sprawl inspired slow growth and antigrowth movements, as well as smart growth efforts that united environmentalists concerned with preserving open space with inner-city activists who saw the redevelopment of the older neighborhoods as preserving land. Activists concerned about school reform joined with neighborhood groups to try to ensure that the poor and minority children received quality education (Shirley 2002).

Battling the Counter-Movement: The Bush Administration.   The George W. Bush administration supported by a conservative, congressional majority has created a hostile environment for social activism. Funding for the social and economic services has been cut and is threatened by further shrinkage; legislative actions restrict what nonprofits are allowed to do, for instance, limiting their right to register voters; while many worry that increased concern with national security is, in part, used as an excuse to spy on or discredit activist organizations. Business regulations have been reduced, forcing the poor to fend more for themselves against economic predators. Further, the underlying ideology of those in office is to reduce government's role and to rely more on charity and faith-based solutions to social problems.

The backlash started during the Reagan years is now well organized with a sustaining base among religious conservatives. Efforts continue to weaken affirmative action, to attack gay rights, or women's right to choose; conservatives organize to stop stem cell research; and an unholy, but politically powerful, alliance has come into being between religious fundamentalists and those who support extreme tax cuts. Even programs such as No Child Left Behind, whose rhetoric of equal, effective education cannot be faulted, has harmed school systems since the resources needed to carry it out are not available. Activist organizations fight to preserve Social Security and oppose cutbacks in housing programs, battle against harmful rules in welfare programs, or fight to stop pernicious actions that harm the environment.

Rather than simply remain on the defensive, some organizations have stepped up their actions. Gay rights groups moved from fighting to end discrimination to battles for gay marriages, that, unfortunately, have engendered a strong backlash. Dozens of immigrant rights organizations and ethnic organizations have come together to press for justice for both documented and undocumented migrants, while battling a xenophobic reaction. Activists have to step in when government fails. When government was slow to react to Hurricane Katrina, and then reacted in ways that ignored the poor, national neighborhood networks and their local affiliates from ACORN, PICO, the IAF and others were on the ground working and organizing the displaced poor.

Changes have taken place in how organizing is done. Closer relationships are in place between advocacy organizations staffed by graduate-level trained professionals, traditional social change networks, and neighborhood groups. Progressive think tanks document problems, pose options, then join with issue organizations to push for legislation. ACORN might work with a homeowner harmed by predatory lending, a progressive think tank will independently document the extent of predatory lending, and then a grand coalition of neighborhood groups, economic justice organizations, and advocacy professionals together lobby for legislation to end economic predation.

Issue organizing now more readily flows into neighborhood work. National issue organizations fight for economic justice, meanwhile the localities—neighborhood organizations following traditional models of local action—mobilize community members to push for living wages at the city level. Union organizing now is more than simply organizing where people work but has linked with efforts of neighborhood associations to work with immigrant groups. Community organizations network with national economic justice organizations in a shared battle for economic justice, opposing new Wal-Marts or demanding that cities stop give-away subsidies to wealthy mega-corporations. Coalition work brings together social production organizations and direct action groups. Meta-cross movement coalitions come into place to battle budget reductions and tax cuts for the rich.

Action organizations continue to rely upon traditional tactics, but modify them for the Internet age. With e-mail connections people can be mobilized almost instantly while information on campaign issues and emerging problems is readily shared. Tactical guides for action are readily available on-line both in full and in summary forms. Trade associations and staff of coalitions actively monitoring and lobbying for (or against) legislation share what they learn nationally through the web and by doing so mobilize a broad constituency to lobby on the issues.

In the past, most activist organizations paid little attention to mobilizing or registering voters, arguing that voting efforts distract from work on core issues. But nowadays many activists have rethought this issue, noting the harm of the extreme conservatives in office. Nowadays activist organizations work in (nonpartisan) voter registration drives—awkwardly termed voterization efforts—even if doing so takes time away from other matters.

Lessons from the History of Organizing for Social Change

From the discussion of the history of neighborhood organizing, supplemented by readings on the history of issue- and identity-based movements—civil rights, gay activism, feminism, disability rights, and economic justice, among others—we can extract a series of five lessons for present-day activism:

1. History provides the narratives, icons, and symbols that motivate present-day actions.
2. Social action strategies and tactics do accommodate to changing political and social climates.
3. In battles for economic and social justice progress is rarely steady.
4. Social change organizations do not work in isolation but rather are part of a broader field.
5. History points out the stresses and strains that activist organizations face.

History Provides the Narrative, Icons, and Symbols That Motivate Present-Day Actions

Through a series of iconic events, history narrates the possibility for successful change. The Seneca Falls women's rights conference in 1848 put forth a declaration of rights, including that all men and women are created equal, is treated as a core event by women activists. Dramatic confrontations—Greensboro, Birmingham, Montgomery, or Selma for the African American civil rights movements, Wounded Knee for the Native American, Stonewall Inn for gay activism, or Sproul Hall in the student protests, the grape boycott for farm organizers, or Seattle for those protesting globalization—have become symbols for present-day actions. Martin Luther King, Jr.'s jailing and César Chavez's fast still resonate among a wide variety of activists far beyond the civil rights movements. For many, the phrase, "that summer" (Dittmer 1994) evokes the Freedom Summer of 1964 in which black and white, male and female converged on Mississippi in a collective, public outcry for social justice.

At their annual meetings, neighborhood organizations share with old and new members alike what has been accomplished, pointing out with pride the park that is now the home of the neighborhood soccer team, or what is now a shelter for the homeless had been a dope house. In their newsletters, organizing networks rehearse past victories as preludes for present action. In 2005, ACORN sponsored a conference not only to reflect on where the organization had been and was going but to share the successes of the past with current activists.

Writings about history themselves become icons for that same history. Activists reflect upon Students for a Democratic Society's Port Huron Statement, Dr. King's "Letter from Birmingham Jail," and the various manifestos put out by ACORN, and now readily accessible on the Internet. Alinsky's two books *Reveille for Radicals* and *Rules for Radicals*, though somewhat dated, still represent a common lore shared by those involved in social change organizations.

History is encapsulated in heroes—dramatic, daring individuals—whose actions personified the courage to battle for change. A hero symbolizes the cause, focuses media attention, and motivates others to join in and provide exemplars that show what can be done by those willing to try. It is hard to think about the Women's Movement without recognizing Susan B. Anthony, or to talk about the civil rights movement without also talking about Dr. Martin Luther King, Jr. César Chavez came to represent the Hispanic farm workers in their effort to unionize; Lois Gibbs represented the battle against toxic wastes; Maggie Kuhn symbolized the empowerment movement for the elderly.

Still only seeing history as a parade of heroes is dangerous as it minimizes the importance of the thousands of ordinary people whose day-in day-out involvement is what makes social activism succeed (Dittmer 1994). It took more than a Dr. King to fill up the Birmingham jails and though Russell Means and Dennis Banks were central to the American Indian Movement, the seizure of Alcatraz or the standoffs at Wounded Knee were collective efforts (Nagel 1996).

Social Action Strategies and Tactics Do Accommodate to Changing Political and Social Climates

History teaches the importance of choosing issues and strategies to mesh with changing political and social climates. A campaign that would be inconceivable at one time may be successful at another time.

History shows that society varies in whether or not it is willing to even admit the extent of social injustice. For generations, many white people looked at segregated facilities, toilets for whites and toilets for blacks, drinking fountains for blacks and drinking fountains for whites, and did not cringe. More recently, whites would look at schools with mainly black students and fail to see sagging roofs, broken windows, sporadic heat in winter, and old textbooks. But at other times, society can see what it is shown. The sight of poverty in Appalachia pricked the conscience of a president and through him the conscience of the country. The image of black children being marched off to jail during the civil rights era mobilized a nation and gave impetus to a social revolution. Ideologies and broad approaches change over time.

Models change over time. In separate eras, feminist movements respond quite differently to tensions from race, class, or sexuality (Reger 2005; Roth 2004). The settlement house movement, one of the progenitors of neighborhood organizing, has passed through several incarnations, with long periods of quiescence, alternating with serious community-building efforts (Fabricant and Fisher 2002). In its early days under Alinsky the IAF was considered only as a radical, direct action organization; nowadays, while IAF affiliates are still willing to be confrontational, they are more likely to partner with government and work to reach accommodation. While ACORN still maintains its militant approach, it increasingly is willing to join with more staid organizations in housing development work.

Actions and issues vary depending on place. A gay pride parade might work in New York City, but might increase opposition to gays in small rural towns. A rally to support the right to bear arms would have more positive effect in states where original settlers and later farmers routinely shot "varmints" that threatened their livestock than it would in neighborhoods where gang warfare often catches school children in the crossfire.

Local climates, though, can dramatically change. Under former mayor Richard J. Daley Chicago's government itself attacked civil rights activists; a generation later under Mayor Washington, leaders and staff from neighborhood groups were appointed to public office and the city funded activist community groups. After Mayor Washington's death, the city returned to a more conservative business-oriented model, but the rampant racism of the past had been reduced, and poor neighborhoods received some, albeit not yet a proportionate, share of redevelopment money. Local climates affect actions taken, as shown in a study of federal housing and community reinvestment policies in which tactics in cities dramatically differed even when advocating for the same federally mandated programs (Sidney 2003).

In Battles for Economic and Social Justice Progress Is Rarely Steady

From history we learn that considerable progress has been made in empowering neighborhoods and in bringing about social reforms. Unions are legal. Laws require reasonable accommodation to people with disabilities. Minority group members register and vote, have access to better jobs than in the past, and are subject to fewer racist encounters. CDCs build affordable homes, and abortion is still legal, despite a determined opposition. Tenant organizations are common. Discrimination against women and minorities in business organizations is now illegal, and antigay discrimination is declining. But history shows that we still have a long way to go to build a society that is both socially and economically just.

Further, it appears that after taking four steps forward we end up pushed back three, as problems reappear under a new guise. After an era of rapid progress, efforts to promote civil rights declined (McAdam 1999). Recent waves of immigrants have stimulated fear and prejudice, resulting in situations in which rights are denied not only to illegal aliens but also to legal ones. Political pressure has been brought to eliminate bilingualism and promote English as the only language. Courts have become increasingly conservative and less likely to defend civil liberties. Backlash has occurred against gains made by women and gays. For years, activist groups worked to get affordable housing as an accepted part of the political agenda and succeeded, only to see a concerted effort during the Bush administration to cut back funding.

Most losses occur because of conservative backlash. But activists themselves can shoulder some of the blame. The very victories achieved end up lowering enthusiasm to fight and decrease involvement. Further, activists end up not fully sharing the narratives of success so that those that benefit in later years are ignorant of past struggles and do not recognize that the battle is sometimes unfinished.

Social Change Organizations Do Not Work in Isolation But Rather Are Part of a Broader Field

Activists are not alone. Organizers teach one another, person to person, keeping traditions alive while those in one organization learn from another. Tactics are tried out in one setting and when successful emulated elsewhere. Civil disobedience made popular by civil rights activists quickly spread to other movements. Consciousness raising, introduced by feminist organizations, is now a model for how people share experiences and concerns with one another. The broad lessons of welfare and civil rights organizing are incorporated in organizing networks such as ACORN.

When one movement flags, another might inspire it to come back. Women activists have had a proud history of their own but seemed quiescent until being energized by the activism of the sixties. Most present-day movements are in many ways inspired by African American activism. The cauldron of activity in the sixties brought together activists from a variety of movements, each teaching and learning from one another: counter-culturalists influenced civil rights workers, civil rights activists set a model for those involved in antiwar work, while the environmental movement which took on a more aggressive stance has learned from others the value of direct action (Anderson 1995). More recently, those who oppose globalization have emulated tactics introduced by fighters for gay civil rights (Shepard and Hayduk 2002).

History Points Out the Stresses and Strains That Activist Organizations Face

History also points out persisting tensions that weaken present-day activism. Class and race have always made organizing more difficult on issues that cross groups. For instance, the feminist organizations dominated by upper class white women are seen as excluding African Americans or those from the working class. The history of gay activism points out that in spite of shared oppression because of their sexuality, gay men and gay women are often divided by issues of gender.

History makes clear the persistent divide between those who want to bring about radical change to the economic or social structure and those content with incremental improvement. The NAACP tried to slowly undo a racist system through working through the courts, while the Southern Christian Leadership Conference, the Congress of Racial Equality, and the Southern Nonviolent Coordinating Committee in their direct attacks on Jim Crow laws felt that anything short of radically changing the rules would be insufficient. Some economic justice organizations push for a major overhaul in the economy with wealth being shared, while others are about enabling people, especially the poor and those from minority groups, to get their piece of the action.

Questions of the tradeoff between means and end are everpresent. For instance, when is violence, or at least the threat of violence acceptable? The icons of the civil rights era preached and followed nonviolence, but other advocates of civil rights were willing to threaten confrontations and on occasion, even gunplay. At times militancy works, but more often than not, extreme militancy leads to a backlash, destroying gains that have been made.

Conclusions

History sets a context for present-day actions while providing both lessons and warnings on what can be done. History shows that while progressive changes have sometimes been slow in coming, progress has been real. History provide heroes, both those whom we know by name and the anonymous heroes who marched and rallied and filled the jails in protest, who provide inspiration to those involved today. History emphasizes that patience, persistence, and understanding are vital to achieving long-term success.

In the next chapter we focus on learning about present-day problems, but in doing so keep in mind that current issues have historic roots. Knowing how government has or has not responded and what activist organizations have done in the past helps shape present-day campaigns.

CHAPTER 9

Learning about Personal, Community, and Social Needs through Action Research

Social action research involves a systematic effort to gather, analyze, and interpret information that describes problems and suggests solutions. Such research is based upon *data gathering and analysis techniques* that adhere to high scientific standards. The term *action* means data are gathered and analyzed for the purpose of solving a problem. *Participatory action research* (*PAR*) goes one step further as PAR is conducted by the very people who are affected by the problem and will work to bring about a solution.

Participatory Action Research empowers by linking the knowledge of problems to the actions taken. Through social action research, organizational activists *stay attuned* to problems. Papers point out pressing difficulties, memos prepared by national support organizations detail emerging problems. The National Low Income Housing Coalition's weekly *Memo to Member* details changes in housing policy: OMB Watch narrates how changes in federal policy affect nonprofits, while the Center on Budget and Policy Priorities circulates data-rich analyses of how changes in the budget affect social action. PAR researchers examine a neighborhood impacted by toxic waste to document the number of school days children have to miss to visit doctors with complaints in breathing, nausea, or skin rashes (Sen 2003, 119).

But how these problems are understood depends on their framing. Do people even recognize that payday lending is a scam that hurts the working poor? Is affordable housing seen as a place that harbors gangs rather than as shelter for working families? Having facts and figures is important—knowing that interest rates at payday lenders can approach 400 percent, or learning that a person needs to earn $15 an hour or more to afford ordinary housing—but such data will do little good if people believe that payday lenders are simply a convenience, and that there is plenty of housing available for anyone who works.

Through action research, organizations assess the overall strengths and problems of a geographic or social community. Researchers physically examine the neighborhood to see what assets it has to offer as well as the problems that it faces. How much crime? What about job loss, housing deterioration? Is the neighborhood threatened by gentrification or the deterioration of its infrastructure? Are Latinos treated only as illegal immigrants? Activists then use the data obtained, for instance, to pressure government to undertake cleanup and renewal programs (Shlay and Whitman 2004) or to vigorously prosecute slum lords or shut down dope houses. Researchers using the *asset-based community development* approach ascertain the strengths of the community (Kretzman and McKnight 1993; McKnight and Kretzman 2005), discovering what services, resources, or agencies are already in place (Hardscastle, Wenocur, and Powers 1997, 152–95). Through a *SWOT* analysis model (*s*trengths, *w*eaknesses, *o*pportunities, and *t*hreats) researchers systematically note both positive and negative community attributes (Stoecker 2005, 98).

Research is undertaken to obtain information on the immediate issue of concern to the action organization to determine how much of a problem exists, whom it affects, and where and when. What is the average wage rate? Why is it so low? What groups receive the most, which the least? What can be done and who needs to be persuaded? If pressure is to be brought, action research is focused to learn about the target, how it works, who owns it, how big it is, and what its weaknesses or vulnerabilities are. For instance, Inner City Press collects detailed data on where and to whom banks lend, while other organizations document the workings of predatory lenders, each providing data on which to base economic justice campaigns (www.innercitypress.org/). Understanding the motivations of politicians is increased by carefully studying their voting records at the same time a list of campaign contributors is examined.

Finally, research is about finding solutions. Why reinvent the wheel when a web search, a post to an e-list, or an examination of the website of a support organization will readily produce a model that can be emulated?

Social Implications of Action Research

Action research builds empowered capacity. As people discover that they are not alone, that many others are ill-housed, underemployed, and have faced sexual harassment, the social nature of problems become clearer. Data from research enables people to change self-blame into social indignation.

Data Are Power

Banks claim they do loan less in communities of color because people of color are poor and are worse credit risks. Data refutes this claim as it shows that banks lend less often or at higher interest rates to people of color who have the same income and same credit status as dominant group members. Conservatives admit that women earn less, but then argue that it is because women work fewer hours and lack the same background as men. But this claim evaporates with data showing that women with the same background as men still earn less than do men. Arguments against having subsidized housing are hard to sustain, when hard data show that people need to earn over

$15 an hour just to afford rental housing, while new jobs that are being created pay less than $10 an hour. *Data speak in action campaigns.*

Research Builds Capacity

Learning to research builds *capacity* through the skills that people learn. Activists can easily find out about government policies and actions by going onto the web; much census data can be obtained through a click or two on-line. Most data-gathering techniques of observation, interviewing, and surveys, using available data can, with some instruction, be mastered with a modicum of effort gaining both information and the confidence that comes from learning a new skill. More sophisticated data gathering and analysis techniques do require graduate level training, but such expertise can be found in the larger social change organizations that employ data wonks who work in ways to empower others.

Going door-to-door to talk with people informally or to survey them on their concerns expands the capacity of the organization by becoming part of recruitment. The interviewer introduces himself or herself as a member of the action organization, solicits information using an appropriate research tool, and then when people ask, as they invariable do, what can be done about the problem, suggests joining the organization. When data on problems are publicized some people search ways of becoming active. For instance, research data on the harm of secondary smoke encouraged people to join organizations seeking to ban public smoking.

Research expands capacity through the partnerships set up between universities and activist organizations (Butterfield and Sosak 2004; Nyden, Figer, Shibley, et al. 1997; Wiewel and Knaap 2005). In such partnerships, professors can provide technical information on designing a study and do the more complicated statistical analyses, while the organization members focus on the core questions and provide much of the labor in gathering the data. Activists learn skills while those in the university rediscover their obligations to work for a better society.

The environmental disaster at Love Canal shows how such collaborative research can come about (Levine 1982). Not knowing that the Hooker Chemical Company had filled up the canal with noxious chemicals and covered it over, people purchased homes in the former industrial site. Eventually residents, noticing the high rate of health problems, joined together in the Love Canal Homeowners' Association and approached the government for help. Public agencies first denied there was a problem, then prepared technical reports that minimized the health risks. Frustrated with this indifference, members of the homeowners' association then partnered with university scientists to re-examine the official data and ended up documenting the extremely high rates of illness. With the data in hand, activists were able to pressure the government to declare an emergency and compensate homeowners so they could afford to move away.

Nowadays a conservatively dominated government, as well as businesses, recognize that information provides power and has acted to restrict access. For instance, banks are required to publicly release data on how loans are given out, but, to frustrate activists, released the data on printed forms rather than on computer-accessible spread sheets, dramatically increasing the costs of doing an analysis. Data on economic, social, and housing conditions are collected and disseminated by government agencies; information from the federal study (the American Community Survey) are mined by activists (and academics) to show the extent of problems. Conservatives have attempted to eliminate the collection of such data or at the very least its public release.

When government is reluctant to release information, citizens can call upon federal, state and local *Freedom of Information Acts*. Under FOIA, the government has to provide good reasons why information is not being released and if such reasons cannot be provided, make the information available. Often the very threat of using FOIA has encouraged the government to release reports and documents. Unfortunately, in recent years the government has been far less responsive, saying no with increasing frequency. For example, "in 2004 the Feds slapped down FOIA requests 22 percent more frequently than they did in 2000." (www.sfbg.com/40/23/cover_bush.html). In addition, the government has begun to charge outrageous fees for processing requested documents, putting such information beyond the financial reach of many activist organizations. The same pattern is now occurring in the states (Tanner 2006).

Undertaking Social Action Research

As *consumers* of social research, social activists use data obtained by others to suggest the extent of a problem. As *producers* of social research, activists themselves pose the questions, collect, and then analyze the data. In either case, social data must be credible or else it will misguide activist efforts or be used by the opposition to discredit the social action organization.

Social action data must be *accurate*, that is correct and consistent with what other researchers find. Data must have a *relevance* or *germaneness* to the specific problem. Data that show minority group members feel that they are discriminated against can be useful, but less so than material documenting specific incidents of minorities' paying more for goods and services or being denied housing. Finally, social action research must be *communicable* to others. The statistical significance of the F-score of a beta coefficient in a regression equation does not easily communicate, but its implications will when explained that the statistic shows that minority group members who have the same income, education, and family status as do nonminority group members are far less likely to get a prime-rate mortgage. What communicates depends upon the audience: government data nerds are most persuaded by hard data statistics, the press and the broader public by dramatic case studies.

Social action research must be *timely*. When public officials propose changes, activist researchers need to be able to evaluate the implications of these changes before the changes are put in place. Most small social change organizations cannot work so fast, but national support organizations, such as the Center on Budget and Policy Priorities employ researchers who specialize in topical areas, keep data handy, and in a matter of days can figure out the implications of the proposed policy changes.

To become an expert in research does require training, and today many support organizations do employ graduate trained researchers who are concerned about social change. But the basic principles of social research are not all that hard to grasp and knowing these can be empowering.

The Overall Flow of a Research Project[1]

Action research flows through several stages from posing the initial question to disseminating the findings. Depending upon the questions, different data-gathering techniques might be used. For instance, to learn how well different ethnic groups get along might entail examining if bars, restaurants, and other entertainment venues are ethnically mixed—an observational approach. To find out how many people in a community have visited a payday lender, or the length of their commute to work, requires doing a survey.

Working Out the Overall Approach

Research begins with an overall question, perhaps asking why access to health care is limited in the community, or why so many people are declaring bankruptcy. There are endless possibilities. But how specific the initial question is can vary. With *exploratory research*, researchers feel that something is wrong but haven't quite put their finger on it. A neighborhood is obviously in decline, but no one knows the details. Exploratory research involves a broad reconnaissance mission to figure out what is going on overall.

With *explanatory research*, activists have an idea of what is happening and want to test that idea with more precision. African Americans tend to be housed in one area, Latinos in another, Asians in a third, and Caucasians in a fourth. Is this occurring because of intentional choice or because of steering? Women seem to be moving up the business hierarchy less rapidly than do men. Why? Do men and women differ on educational background, experience, hours spent at work?

A third approach is *evaluation research*. Evaluation research asks to what extent a program intended to solve a problem is working, and if not, why not. Are needy individuals being reached to receive heating assistance? Has the state funded organizations to help those returning from prison reduce recidivism rates?

Research Design

Design links the way in which you gather data to the way in which questions are asked and data obtained. *Surveys* are most appropriate for gaining short, precise answers from large numbers of people, while details and deeper understanding are best obtained through *focused interviewing*. In the design stage, you anticipate how the data are to be analyzed. If you want to generalize to a large number of people, you have to follow precise scientific sampling procedures for which professional help will probably be required. During design you figure out if you are focusing on a specific population—the homeless with children or perhaps examining all who are ill-housed.

[1]Based on Rubin 1983 and Rubin and Rubin 2005.

During design you make sure you are actually getting the data to answer the questions you intend. Asking people how satisfied they are with police services measures perceptions, while counting crimes or arrests provides what are termed objective measures. Which do you want? Either or both can be useful. Are you trying to learn if people feel their housing has enough space, or are you trying to measure the actual space of their housing? Sometimes perceptions are what you want, at other times, objective measures; in the design stage make sure you do not confuse the two.

Design anticipates what can go wrong with the research and tries to prevent these problems. You want to ensure what you are asking is validly measuring what you think it is. "*Validity* refers to whether or not the measure being used actually represents what you think it does" (Rubin 1983, 480). When you survey people about President Bush's housing policy, are you asking about President Bush, housing policy in general, or some combination of the two?

Demonstrating validity can be difficult. What does it mean if you observe that people from different racial/ethnic groups work together at their places of employment, but then notice that they socialize separately? Is that measuring intergroup tensions, racism, or is it a result of housing segregation? Should a valid measure of income of poor people include not only money that people earn from work but also funds from government programs such as EITC, or Section 8 housing? You have to know what you want to measure before you can work out valid indicators.

Design seeks to improve *reliability*—determining if answers are consistent when obtained by different people or asked in slightly different ways. If survey questions are asked to members of an identity group—African Americans, Asians, women, gays—and the answers differ depending on whether the interviewer is a member of that identity group, concerns about reliability are present.

Reliability can be improved through training those doing the research or doing it twice and checking. When entering figures into a computer, have separate people do it and compare what they have entered, and then examine discrepancies. The reliability of observations can be improved through training. A person skilled in the building trades can teach a book author how to more reliably note housing code violations.

Another part of design is figuring out whom the findings of the study describe. At public hearings, victims present narratives of racial oppression, being defrauded by unscrupulous lenders, or going hungry, but those in office want to know the typicality and extent of a problem. Horror stories collected through depth interviews illustrate how bad a problem can become—a disabled homeless mother with children—but are usually not typical of the problem. To show the extent and typicality of a problem, research data can be collected from an entire *population*, but doing so is expensive and time consuming. Instead, most research is done from a *sample*—an intentionally chosen set of people (or incidents).

Careful design works out methods of collecting information from a sample in ways that represent the larger number of people impacted by a problem. Sampling is done in different ways depending on the data-gathering procedures. Using random sampling procedures in choosing people to be surveyed, or in picking out case files from official records such as death certificates, it is possible to extrapolate answers to what the entire population thinks on the issue or what percentage of deaths are attributed to which causes with a known degree of accuracy (Rubin 1983, 131–62). Different sampling techniques are used in depth interview or observation studies to give confidence that what was seen or heard from a few most likely holds for the broader group (Rubin and Rubin 2005, 64–78).

Design is also about figuring out how extensive a study you can conduct with the financial and personnel resources at hand. While a large amount of funding does not necessarily mean doing better research; trying to do too much with too few resources is a waste. Five volunteers cannot carry out a communitywide survey. It is better for them to do depth interviews or run some focus groups.

Design also anticipates the ultimate audience for the research and plans accordingly. If the goal is to increase mobilization, depth interviews that elicit personnel narratives might be best as the findings will resonate with potential activists. In contrast, if the report is intended for a bureaucratic agency, seeking out hard numbers might be more appropriate, as bureaucrats are likely to dismiss narratives as mere anecdotes.

Data Gathering

The bulk of the time in research is spent in data gathering using the methods that we shall describe in the next section. In design the choice is made between which techniques or combination of techniques to use. Is it better to talk with a few people in depth or obtain a more superficial cross section of opinions? In practice, when time and resources permit, *triangulating research* (using multiple data-gathering approaches to the same problem) produces the most credible information.

Data Analysis

Data analysis is when you extract the meaning of the information. Analysis must be anticipated in the design of the research or else the appropriate data might be missed. If you are concerned with pay discrimination by ethnic, racial, gender, or age group, you would build into the initial questionnaire items on pay, career history, education, and of course the personal characteristics of the individual.

Data analysis techniques differ dramatically depending upon whether the material is *quantitative*—numeric—or *qualitative*—made up of observations and verbal responses (Rubin and Rubin 2005). Some analyses are quite direct: for example calculating the percentage of renters in a neighborhood. Often though, data analysis requires technical skills that are unlikely to be present in most smaller social change organizations, so when more sophisticated analyses are anticipated, it makes sense to enter into collaborative research partnerships with progressive universities or Policy Research Action Groups (Nyden, Figer, Shibley, et al. 1997).

Writing the Report and Disseminating the Results

Action research is about mobilizing people, pressuring targets, publicizing problems, and combating misinformation put out by opponents. The worst thing that can happen in action research is that the findings sit on a shelf unused. Reports need to be widely disseminated—the web allows doing so inexpensively—in understandable language that highlights both what was found and the implications for action.

Research Ethics

Action research must obtain information in an ethical manner. Ethics implies honesty with data so results cannot be distorted. If data seem suspect, even if it seems to support your cause, it should not be used.

Academic researchers argue that ethical research should do no harm to those being studied. Certainly no harm should be done to the people the organizations are trying to help. Wasting peoples' time is harmful, so if data are not potentially useful the research should not be done. Ethics requires that promises to preserve confidentiality must be kept.

But researching vulnerable populations poses special ethical concerns. To learn how to help people with severe personal problems can require deep, frank, and open interviews in which people discuss what has caused them problems. Such interviews can be quite stressful. Balance is needed in obtaining information but without emotionally harming people. Too often vulnerable populations are researched by students and professors for their own reports with little done to alleviate the problems that people face. Ethical action researchers make sure that what they learn will lead to actions that help those studied. Even here caution is required as documenting a problem to motivate action might backfire. Data that detail a social problem—high crime in a neighborhood, or frequency of being victims to consumer fraud—can be turned on its head and used by those who oppose progressive change to blame the victims for the situations they face.

We strongly feel that no harm should be done to a vulnerable population and that research can only be done with their consent. But what about the research on potential targets: Is it okay to use back-door methods to learn about internal policies of predatory lenders (or even conventional banks)? What about using secret documents, obtained from whistle blowers from chemical or pharmaceutical companies, that indicate that the companies were aware of the problems caused by their products? To us, it is less vital to obtain consent from corporate targets once indications exist that they are harming others and that they are unwilling to cooperate with the data gathering.

Data-Gathering Techniques

As both producers and consumers of research, community activists rely upon a wide variety of data-gathering techniques as shown in Table 9-1.

Action research can build on information that others have obtained, much of which is now available on the Internet; or researchers can observe what is happening and then later on interview people. Some interviews are conducted at great length and

TABLE 9.1   Data-Gathering Techniques for Action Research

Technique	Description
Available Data	Relies on information that others have collected, usually by an official government agency; skills involve knowing how to access the data and measure its quality
Survey Research	Using a standard instrument—a survey questionnaire—to obtain large amounts of comparable, numeric data from a carefully chosen sample population representative of a larger population
Experimentation	Research done by intentionally manipulating (changing) something (introducing anticrime programs in a community) and then comparing the consequences of the change on people or places receiving the change with those that did not
Observation and Participant Observation	Watching and noting what is occurring. With participant observation the observer is also part of what he or she is studying
Depth Interviewing	Extended one-on-one conversations focused on specific issues of concern to either the action organization or the community members
Focus Groups	A monitored open group discussion among selected community members on a topic chosen by the social action researchers
Community Network Analysis	Discovering the connections between individuals and organizations within a community

depth, seeking out both detail and individual experiences, while other interviews ask quicker questions to large numbers of people to obtain representative, numeric data on specific issues. With focus groups, researchers listen as several people hold a conversation on how they understand a problem or try to work out possible solutions; while with techniques such as network analysis, researchers discover the linkages between individuals and organizations.

In practice, most projects combine several different data gathering procedures. Suppose that a neighborhood organization is interested in documenting the fairness of police services. Observations can be made of both patrols and police-citizen interactions which are then supplemented by background surveys of community members to learn how the police are perceived. Answers then can be examined in light of the public records kept by the police on arrests and other incidents.

Different parts of a problem might require separate data-gathering techniques. Housing problems can be documented through observational research, supplemented by data obtained from housing courts. Data provided by banks to satisfy the Community Reinvestment Act will show whether or not reinvestment capital is made available to maintain housing quality while on-line data from HUD and the National Low Income Housing Coalition provide typical costs for housing.

No data-gathering technique is better or worse than any other. To find out deeper feelings and understand how people experience problems, depth interviewing—a *qualitative* approach—is the way to go; while if you want to figure out what percentage of those in a community have a problem or share a belief, a *quantitative* survey—numeric—is probably best.

Some practical considerations intervene in the choice of data-gathering method. Available data from a trusted source is usually worth searching for, as it is quicker and cheaper than gathering information yourself. Experiments are very expensive and time consuming and rarely are done by social change organizations; however, understanding them is important as many are done by the government. When it is possible to obtain data of equal quality, it makes most sense to choose the technique that involves organizational members in the process. Finally, those whom you are trying to persuade to use your data often prefer specific types of information. Bureaucrats in technical agencies tend to respond best to numeric evidence of the extent of problems, while case studies and first-hand testimonies are often more persuasive to organizational members and elected officials.

Using Available Data

In doing surveys, depth interviews, observations, experiments, and network analyses, researchers go out and obtain the *original raw data*. In contrast, *available data* are information collected by someone else, often an official governmental agency, that others then can use.

Available data are seen as official records that are maintained for legal purposes—how legislators voted, what bills are in front of Congress. Available data come from research that others have done; tens of thousands of census collectors count individuals, planners survey neighborhood residents, or regulators file reports about banks on their lending practices. Some available data are readily usable with little or no processing; to obtain reports on population size or ethnic composition you click onto the census bureau website, put in the location and, voilà! the information is there, at least as of the last census. Other available data might require processing: Police record where crimes took place, but to get a block by block picture might require grouping the crimes by address into the separate blocks.

Available data are made available by support organizations and much of it is on the web; the trick is to know where to look. The National Low Income Housing Coalition reports on housing costs, housing gaps, homeless, by locale, often by ethnicity and income. ACORN as well as NTIC have documented predatory lending practices, while the National Community Reinvestment Coalition has studies on the web that show how, through inflated appraisals of home values, poor and minority borrowers are harmed. Using electoral data that the Federal Electorate was mandated to collect, ACORN demonstrated that the effort to register voters at public assistance agencies was a "promise unkept" (ACORN 2005). The Economic Policy Institute documents the economic status of the American worker, while the Center on Budget and Policies Priorities puts out reports analyzing the implications of budgetary decisions for social programs. The Center on Budget and Policy Priorities (www.cbpp .org) breaks down the federal budget by issue areas and prepares reports on the implications for action. Think tanks like the Urban Institute and Brookings Institution provide backup reports on a wide array of social problems such as *Concentrated Poverty: A Change in Course* (Kingsley and Pettit 2003) that examined census data to systematically track social problems. National support organizations document incidents of predatory lending, racial and neighborhood discrimination in mortgage interest rates, or the fate of the homeless in different cities. Knowledgeplex (www.knowledgeplex .org) opens up a gateway to information on housing and community development while www.communityinvestmentnetwork.com will provide a wealth of available information on redevelopment issues.

Available data has several advantages. First, it is available, often at little or no cost, while collecting information on employment or health conditions on your own can cost thousands of dollars, if not millions, and might take years to do. No ongoing group of social activists (or for that matter few businesses or local governments) could pay the almost $200,000,000 cost of the Census Bureau's American Community Survey that examines social, economic, and housing conditions nationally. In addition, when presenting public officials with data their own agencies collected, public officials have little choice but to assume that it is correct.

Available data, though, are far from problem free. Often the precise information wanted is not available. Age of housing in a community can be found, but does age reflect its physical condition? Next, it is hard to judge the quality of available data. Reputable data collection organizations such as the Census Bureau or most national think tanks clearly explain how they collected information, their attempts to ensure reliability and validity, and the sampling procedures followed. But this might not always be the case as some available data are manipulated by organizations for their own internal purpose. Further, by political intent, government is collecting less and less data that reveal social problems and is less willing to voluntarily release what it has.

Still, reams of data are available from federal government agencies. Web gateways to federal statistics can be found at www.fedstats.gov or the various sites that Maria Roberts-DeGennnaro has documented of particular interest to community practitioners (Roberts-DeGennaro 2003). Individual agencies maintain informative sites, with the Department of Housing and Urban Development presenting available data on housing conditions as well as federal policies and actions on the elderly, the homeless, Native Americans, and the handicapped. HUD provides software (called Community 2020™) that enables users to access demographic data and housing information for small geographic areas. Statistical information can be obtained from HUD on public housing projects in specified geographic areas as well as projects funded with the Low Income Housing Tax Credit. The Department of Labor releases material on unemployment rates, while state employment offices prepare material on both new hires and unemployment for many locales. Such data must be examined with care since unemployment figures only include those who are currently unemployed and are looking for work and omit those who have simply given up. The Centers for

Disease Control and Prevention (CDC) in Atlanta monitors death rates by cause, while CDC data provide insights into environmental problems by documenting hot spots—areas of the country with unexpectedly high mortality.

General information on social, economic, and demographic data are found in the surveys and censuses done by or for the U.S. Census Bureau. Every ten years, the Bureau counts each individual in the country, obtains background data as well as more detailed information from a sample of the total population. In addition to the population census, the Census Bureau conducts a survey of housing conditions in major metropolitan areas every few years. For wealthier communities, census material is considered quite accurate, but in poorer and minority communities many individuals are missed, distorting the overall information. Of great importance is the ongoing American Community Survey that provides detailed information from a carefully drawn sample.

Population and housing data are released by census tracts, geographic areas that usually contain about 4,000 people. In larger cities, the Census Bureau tries to match the boundaries of the tracts to neighborhoods, at least as the city officials define neighborhoods. Data are not released on individuals, only on groups within areas, and if too few individuals of a given social background are found in any tract, that category is excluded from the published data.

Researchers can examine census data to learn about the poverty level, quality of housing, the amount of education people have, and other quality of life indicators. Comparisons of census data over time point out trends that can guide community work, such as the expanding number of female-headed households or the increasing likelihood that children will live in poor households. Census data also permit comparisons of wealth, unemployment, or living conditions by racial and ethnic groups as well as by geographic area over time.

For quick statistical descriptions on communities, researchers can electronically query the Web page of the Census Bureau. By clicking on a map, or by specifying census tracts, zip codes, or the names of places, the researcher is presented with a list of census variables, then checks off the ones for which information is required. To obtain more detailed information, community researchers can acquire census tapes or CD-ROMS with census data and do the data analysis themselves. For aggregate analysis at the tract level such research is possible, but the Census Bureau will not release raw data on individuals, so certain forms of analysis are difficult.

Public laws, another form of available data, are posted on the Internet by the Library of Congress (www.Thomas.loc.gov). Thomas enables researchers to do a quick search initiated by almost any appropriate set of keywords that describe policies or legislation, such as "housing" or "disabled" or "environment." The researcher will get summaries and text, if desired, for all laws passed in a specified term of Congress that contain the researcher's choice of keyword. Majority and minority parties often maintain separate websites, with their own interpretations of recent legislation. Thomas also offers links to federal agencies and state and local sites. Thomas lists all roll call votes for the current session, including how senators and representatives voted on an initial proposal, through all the amendments, to the final version. If a particular member of Congress introduced an amendment to completely gut a piece of legislation advocated by a community group or coalition, voted for the final version, and then claimed that he or she supported the legislation, the researchers can see through the charade. Advocacy organizations that want to know what a representative or senator said on the floor about the topic can look up the Congressional Record— just click on the box in the Thomas site—and enter into the search both the topic of concern and the legislator's name. What then appears is a list of the speeches made by that person that mention the topic.

Thomas has links to the House and Senate websites, which maintain information on committees and subcommittees and upcoming hearings, and suggest who to contact and about what. Some committees provide transcripts of selected hearings. By examining the hearings, an action organization can figure out where controversies are likely to occur and by seeing who testified and what they said, activists can determine potential allies and enemies on this issue. Powerful computer search engines allow researchers to find information quickly on specific topics of their concern, pulling out the relevant parts from hearing transcripts that may be 600 pages long.

Individual states vary in the quality of their on-line data sources—some match the federal government while others are still opaque. Several states have on-line legislative search engines similar to Thomas, while general news stories on state legislative actions can be found at www.stateline.org/. The gateways to state web pages tend to follow a similar format with Illinois being www.state.il.us/. Data on some local communities can be found at www.dataplace.org.

Local government offices keep records that are descriptive of communities, such as crime rates by location and type, traffic accidents by intersection, housing complaints against particular buildings, the location of road repair projects, as well as the emergency response time for police, fire, and ambulance. Other data maintained by city or county departments include land use by residential, commercial, and industrial categories, requests for zoning changes, and building permits.

Sometimes a target of a campaign might be a large company. Often data on the company can be found on the Internet (Mattera, 1999). Sites such as www.hoovers .com provide brief descriptions of firms, while for larger companies the federal Securities and Exchange Commission requires electronic filings that describe the owners of the company, major stockholders, and others who could be pressured. Increasingly Secretary of State's offices post background data on registered companies, while sites such as the one maintained by the Center for Responsive Politics (www.crp.org) provide information on which corporate political action companies have contributed to which politicians.

Gathering Data through Observations

Social research can build on the everyday skills of looking, listening, and talking. With this approach researchers gather information

> by *observing* and by *talking with and listening* to . . . people . . . in their ordinary settings . . . analyze what they have heard and seen, and then convey to others, in rich and realistic detail, the experiences and perspectives of those being studied. Naturalistic

researchers obtain data through *participant observation* and *qualitative interviewing*. (Rubin and Rubin 2005, 2)

Observational research involves observing what is going on, perhaps asking what it means. In participant observation, the activist researcher is part of the matter that he or she is studying, for instance, being a member of neighborhood watch. Observation research can put a human face on the issues, turning cold statistics—the city is sheltering 28 homeless people—into a portrait of a person with a disability sitting on the corner because she has no place to go.

Observations focus attention on problems. Observational researchers can go to the emergency room of the local hospital and document what happens. Disability advocates walk through a public building, noting what facilities are accessible to those in wheelchairs and what are not. Signs of blight can be noted—abandoned cars or bordered up buildings—as well as the conditions of homes, businesses, parks, and roadways. Broken windows or graffiti are usually a warning of trouble, as are gang insignias. Poor drainage will show up in flooded underpasses; sewer backups will be apparent through their stench. Through an observational tour, city researchers might note teenagers hanging around street corners or observe the spray-painted names of street gangs on the walls, or they may see people hurrying home at dusk, trying not to be caught out alone after dark. Attending a neighborhood meeting, an observational researcher hears people's complaints and listens to understand how community members interpret their world. Is it a world of hope and potential or one in which the people have given up? Are members of other ethnic groups blamed for problems or is the fault put on government?

Observations can note high food prices in markets or whether there is panhandling on the streets. Reading bulletin boards can hint at problems—people looking for odd jobs; frequent advertisements to sell household goods. If there are many day-labor employment offices in the community, that tells a story, while a lot of empty storefronts suggest a shrinking economy. The researcher can observe if the community is served by branch banks or only money exchanges, or over time note if the number of liquor stores and payday lending outfits is increasing.

Observational research can also document available resources. Are there service agencies for medical help, hospices, a van that transports the elderly to clinics or shopping? Are there special housing facilities for the old? Are there youth centers, and places for daycare for children and the dependent elderly? Is there a transportation hub? Are there organizations already in place that can help with organizing efforts? For instance, "researchers in one low income Chicago neighborhood found over 150 associations" varying from political clubs, to square dancers, to religious groups, to women's organizations, to alcoholics anonymous (Kretzman and McKnight 1993, 111).

Focused, Depth Interviews

In focused, depth interviews researchers talk with others about a limited range of topics, carefully listening to hear the meaning of what the others have to say and then explore in depth and detail the issues raised (Rubin and Rubin 2005).

Interviews can clarify observations as well as facts and figures that have been read about. Seeing patronage in a newly constructed mall in an otherwise deteriorated neighborhood suggests interviewing on how the mall was built, if there had been community involvement, and how people respond to the new facility. Depth interviews elicit rich, detailed accounts of events as well as individual feelings, experiences, and perceptions. They can provide sensitive stories about embarrassing encounters with police, frustration at the inability to use a restroom when wheelchair bound, or humiliation at a public meeting when bullied by those in office. People might talk about their fear of walking from public transportation to their apartments after dark, or their difficulty paying doctor bills, or how they were deceived by a predatory lender and had to sell their house. These individual narratives of suffering become the human face of social problems that must be solved.

Depth interviews are also the tool to use to figure out the who, what, and when of complicated problems. In a youth employment program, teenagers with the requisite skills are being sent off for job interviews, but few succeed. Why? The depth interviewer asks participating teenagers to describe what happened when they applied and learns from their narratives what these young people wore and figures out they did not know the proper dress. The researcher also discovers that when those doing the hiring asked pointed, personal questions, the teenagers acted in hurt or defensive ways. Such detailed knowledge enables the community agency to redesign its job training program, to include advice on dressing and how not to be offended by personal questions.

Why would people be foolish enough to go to high-priced payday lenders, or check cashing services, or furniture rental stores? That question puzzled some action researchers. From depth interviews of both victims and of owners of these exploitative services, researchers learned of the complicated interplay that occurs. The poor have been rejected by the mainstream financial sector and are not fully literate in financial matters, so are rudely handled by the mainstream. Yet when dealing with financial predators they are treated with respect and courtesy and so do not question the financial details (Karger 2005).

Learning how to conduct a depth interview takes practice, though for the most part it is about careful listening. A major skill is in letting interviewees know that what they say is of interest and that they should feel free to talk at length. To do so, interviewers rely on brief statements, such as "that's interesting" or "please continue." Interviewers solicit details with gentle probes or follow-up questions such as "then what happened?" Or, "you've described a bad incident with the landlord, have you had other such experiences?" Sometimes just looking interested is all that is required (Rubin and Rubin 2005).

The core part of the interview is then the *follow-up* question in which the researcher encourages the interviewee to explain in depth and detail issues that have been raised of concern to both. If an activist researcher asks a community member his or her opinion of city hall, and the answer is, "they are a bunch of s.o.b.'s," the interviewer still does not know what the issues are. Follow-up questions such as "have you had experience with city hall? If so, what was it like? What happened? Can you describe it to me?" are then asked to learn the details that reveal what is wrong and what should be done.

Depth interviewers gain a portrait of a community or an understanding of a problem through choosing to talk with a wide variety of people with different experiences. In general a variety of perspectives is required to best understand the situation. If people in the neighborhood are thinking about setting up a crime watch, researchers might interview victims of crimes, the police, and business owners and residents in the areas with the most crimes. In addition, interviews in similar neighborhoods that already have a crime watch will probably provide insights about what to do and what to avoid in setting up a similar program.

Focus Group Interviewing

Depth interviews provide rich, deep detailed data on a person-by-person level; survey interviews that we discuss below obtain standard answers to a wide array of questions from a larger group of respondents. Focus group interviews are an in-between approach, trying to obtain depth, but doing so from a larger number of people than can be interviewed one-by-one.

A focus group interview expands the logic of ordinary group conversations that occur in ordinary chit-chat as well as in consciousness-raising sessions in which the ideas of one person spark another's response. Focus groups try to recreate this small group exchange, but in doing so focus in on a topic that is chosen by the researcher rather than by the group members (Greenbaum 1998; Morgan 1988).

In setting up focus groups, activist researchers figure out who in the community would represent the variety of opinions on the topic and also be informed on the matter. If the goal is to learn about typical problems in the community, researchers might invite a wide array of individuals roughly matching the various demographic categories. If the information sought is ways of improving a daycare center, one focus group might be made up of parents whose children are attending, another might consist of parents who have decided not to use the service, and a third could be daycare providers.

To encourage people to talk, focus groups are kept small. Once a focus group has been assembled and has had some time to socialize over coffee, the moderator introduces the topic and, if needed, makes a few comments to get the conversation going. What needs improvement in the neighborhood? Are women treated with respect in this organization? What changes are needed in the shopping area? Early in the session, participants may be asked to jot down a few ideas and then speak briefly on them without others responding. This is done to assure that everyone's ideas are on the table. Once this initial round is over, people are encouraged to talk about their feelings, experiences, and ideas on the matter at hand, each taking turns speaking, but following no particular order. The stories and experiences told by one person often jog the memories of others who are then able to narrate occurrences that they probably would not have thought of otherwise.

When a topic seems to have been exhausted, the moderator might suggest moving on or perhaps terminating the discussion. He or she can summarize the conversation, and ask if that is a good description of how people feel or if it leaves some important theme out. If necessary, a moderator might toss out a different slant to stimulate further conversation: "Seems like everyone wants new affordable housing in the neighborhood. Does it matter if the housing is rental or owner occupied?" If the conversation seems to be getting too raucous, the moderator tries to calm it down.

The discussion, usually an hour or so long, is videotaped or tape recorded for later analysis that can reveal both what the overall sentiments were as well as make important interactions apparent. Are there tensions between people from different ethnic groups, between genders or those based on political or social beliefs? In one instance, a focus group was held among community activists to work out ideas for an application for federal housing assistance. All agreed on the importance of getting more housing, but in the focus group they strongly disagreed about how to define the eligibility level for those receiving housing assistance. Some wanted the funds to go only to help individuals in extreme distress while others wanted money to help working-class people buy small homes to stabilize the economically declining community. The exchanges in the focus group discussions brought these divisions to light and enabled the members to then concentrate on ways of working out differences.

Survey Interviewing

In a survey, a set of uniform questions, usually with standardized categories for answers, is asked of a large number of respondents. Surveys are probably best done as part of a collaborative research project with academics or think tanks writing questions. Choosing a sample and carrying out the statistical analysis requires experience and formal training.

The purpose of a survey is to determine overall sentiment, the percentage facing a particular problem, or the division of those satisfied or dissatisfied with a particular service. In its massive American Community Survey the Census Bureau learns about economic, social, and housing conditions nationwide, while a smaller community organization might survey its members to gain a sense of what the organizational priorities should be. Sometimes organizations rather than individuals are the respondents to a survey, for instance, to find out which funding sources housing organizations use or to tally the accomplishments of community development groups.

When survey respondents are chosen through a scientific sampling procedure, answers from a modest number of people can be generalized to a larger number with a specified degree of accuracy. However, survey answers lack the depth and detail of focused interviews and require people to react to questions posed by the researcher rather than articulate their own perspectives.

Background surveys seek out overall information about a community and its residents. Researchers can learn such things as the satisfaction of people with their housing, public transportation, the impression of their neighborhood, images of different ethnic groups or community services, or jobs people hold. A *needs assessment* survey focuses on problems that people face and resources that are missing. *Satisfaction* determines the extent to which people are content with a service they've received. *Outcome* surveys ask organizations about their accomplishments, how much they have produced, or how many people have been served, and might try to ascertain at what cost, while *evaluation surveys* document how well specific programs or projects are carried out.

Survey Questions.   In preparing survey questions keep in mind the following hints:

1. Questions must make sense and appear important to the respondent. Questions should be relevant to the situation people face and not be on some distant concern. A researcher would ask housing cooperative members about housing conditions, but probably shouldn't pose questions about issues of war and peace.

2. Keep survey instruments as short as possible by only including questions that provide information that is needed by the action organization. If working on setting up a daycare facility for the elderly, questions on the number of elderly in each household or the medical coverage they have would be relevant while general opinions about Medicare would probably be of little use.

3. Word questions carefully with language that is simple, direct, and familiar to the respondents. Avoid using technical terms or government jargon. Do not ask about "a unit" when you want to know about an apartment or a home. The wording of questions should be pretested with people similar to those being studied before the questionnaire is used.

4. Avoid questions that are loaded or double barreled. A loaded question virtually forces a given answer, for example, how can someone say no to "Do you oppose dumping of toxic chemicals?" A double-barreled question asks two items in one question, such as "Do you want to tear down existing housing and build a home for the elderly?" People who want to keep the old housing in place but still support housing for the elderly cannot answer that question in a meaningful way.

5. Keep the answer categories fairly simple, and make sure each category is distinct. With opinion questions, standard categories such as "strongly agree," "agree," "neutral," "disagree," and "strongly disagree" or "very satisfied" . . . "very dissatisfied" are easily understood. Make sure all possible answer categories are covered, including, if necessary, a category called "other" or "no opinion."

Sometimes a needs assessment survey asks people to order the importance of problems such as lack of shopping, crime, or the inconvenience of mass transportation. If using a ranking, don't try to compare more than three or four items at one time and make sure that the comparisons are between similar items. People might have concerns about cost-of-living increases and also be worried about whether they will get enough heat in their apartment building, but asking whether it is more important to have affordable housing or to end a war is really comparing apples and fish.

6. Be cautious about using open-ended questions on a survey that allows the respondent to say whatever he or she chooses. Open-ended answers on surveys confuse more than they illuminate, as people vary in the clarity, scope, and depth of what they say. If researchers want to explore issues and learn what people think in detail, they are advised to use a depth interview, not a survey.

Sampling. The goal of surveys is to find out how common an attitude or experience is and among which groups: What percentage of people are angry enough to work against the mayor? How long does it take the average person to get to work and what percentage of people use public transportation? To answer these questions would seem to require talking to far more people than the organization has time or money to survey. However, if people are chosen using scientific sampling procedures, answers from a smaller number can be generalized to the entire community with a known degree of confidence.

Scientific sampling requires following exact procedures in choosing survey respondents. While the technicalities can be complicated, and probably should be done as part of collaborative research, so long as three basic principles are followed, the results will tend to be accurate (Rubin 1983, 131–62).

First, researchers precisely specify the broader group whose opinions, concerns, or factual descriptions are of interest—the overall population. If the researchers want to know what problems adults in the neighborhood feel are important, the population might be all people over eighteen who live in the neighborhood. In this case, a couple living with two college-aged children would count as four people. If on the other hand, the organization is interested in measuring the extent of housing blight, each dwelling place is treated as one member of the population (of housing units) no matter whether it is empty or three families are sharing it.

Once the population is specified, the researcher prepares a way of uniquely identifying each member of the population. For some populations, such as voters, lists are available, while in residential surveys lists of addresses can be used. Sometimes, appropriate lists are not available. In this case, researchers must avoid just grabbing anything that looks like a list, because doing so can distort the results. For example, using a sign-up sheet for those who attended a city-sponsored neighborhood planning session as a proxy list for community members would end up choosing only the most active.

If a researcher randomly chooses people (or organizations) from the lists, the answers that these people provide can be mathematically extended to the whole population described by the list. Random does not mean hopping and skipping down the list any old way, but rather using a statistical procedure so that each person on the list has an equal chance of being chosen, but no one knows in advance who will be picked.

There are a few catches. People must be willing to answer the questions in a truthful manner. Further, if large numbers of listed people cannot be found, or many simply refuse to answer, the sample might not really be random. If only the most angry or most active people answer while the others refuse, a totally distorted view of the community could result.

Social Experiments

In ordinary language, to experiment means to try something new. In social research, experiments involve a bit more. First in an experiment something is intentionally changed, that is *treated* or *manipulated*, in ways that are supposed to bring about an *outcome*. For example, introducing a job training program, an income supplement to help families with children, or a recycling program are all illustrations of experimental treatments, while an increase in employment, improvement of the health of children, or reduction in waste sent to the landfill are outcomes.

Second, in an experiment some individuals (or communities or organizations) receive the treatment, and are termed the *experimental group*, while others, the *control*, do not. Comparisons are made between those in the experimental group and the control group to see if the treatment affects the outcome. In more sophisticated experiments, different combinations or amounts of a treatment are given to different experimental groups, for instance, providing job training programs of different lengths, or providing both extra money and a counselling program.

Finally, in full-fledged experiments, individuals (communities or organizations) are randomly assigned to different treatments or to the control group. That way, the different social characteristics of those receiving the treatment are more or less evenly divided between the treatments. In the best of experiments, people do not know which treatment group they are in.

With the very important exception of a type of experimentation called *testing*, most social action organizations do not conduct full-fledged experiments as they are expensive and very time consuming. Still the experiments government or foundations run provide important information for social change work. For example, with *individual development accounts* people in job training programs or school are given matching dollars for money that they save to pay for education, buy a house, or start a business; the outcome being the amount saved. Experiments test what happens when the amount of money matched is varied or whether those in the program are receiving counselling (Sherraden, Johnson, Clancy, et al. 2000).

The Department of Housing and Urban Development felt that moving people out of crowded public housing in poorer neighborhoods to smaller apartments in better off areas would solve both the problems in the housing and allow people who move to better themselves economically. To test this idea, the agency ran three separate experiments. In one, comparisons were made of the economic success between public housing tenants who received certificates allowing them to live anywhere and those that remained in the public housing. In another, public housing tenants were offered different amounts of training for jobs. The third compared individuals who received varying assistance in getting to and from the jobs. Each experimental manipulation increased the income levels of those in the experimental group (Turner and Rawlings 2005).

A type of social experimentation that both activist groups and governmental agencies use is termed *testing*. Testing takes place when a government agency or an action organization suspects individuals are being illegally discriminated against because of their social background or personal conditions. While a true experiment cannot be set up (people cannot be randomly assigned racial or gender characteristics), an approximation is arranged in which individuals with or without the characteristic, but alike in all other ways, seek to receive a service.

To test if racial discrimination occurs in access to housing, black and white testers with identical (made up) job histories, finances, housing experiences, etc., seek to rent an apartment; more often than not African Americans are refused more than whites. Testing was used to demonstrate how individuals with mental, visual, hearing, and mobility disabilities were discriminated against in their search for housing (Turner, Herbig, Kaye, et al. 2005), while the activist feminist group Nine to Five used testing in the workplace to document gender discrimination in job placement efforts by temporary employment agencies showing that better jobs were mainly made available only to men (Sen 2003, 125).

Of all the data-gathering techniques, testing most closely links social research to social action.

Social and Organizational Network Analysis

To discover linkages between people and organizations, activist researchers undertake social network analyses—that is asking who knows whom, what resources are exchanged, who contacts whom and similar matters. Network analysis can document how easily young people are connected to employment opportunities or how readily a message or request for support will spread. It can describe how tightly community members as well as activists are linked. Are the networks of those who know one another at work, those who are connected by politics, and those who are linked through community participation overlap? Are the networks of those involved in one political or social issue connected; for instance, are those who are linked together to battle for daycare also networked to people working to preserve the environment or defend civil liberties? Are organizations sponsored by one church linked to those sponsored by another; do service agencies connected to advocacy organizations work on the same problem? Are there groupings of organizations, termed *organization sets*, whose actions are mutually interdependent?

Data Analysis and Presentation

Research findings must be presented in a clear and understandable way so that the research leads to action. Doing so requires careful *data analysis* to pull out the meaning and then *strategic presentations* to share the information with activists, policy makers and the broader public.

At its simplest, data analysis of quantitative data might involve counting the number of people with a problem while more sophisticated analysis can require mastery of advanced statistics. The simplest qualitative analysis involves little more than selecting typical cases, testimonies of individuals facing a problem, or the stories of individuals who have benefited from a program—a former TANF mother who, because of a community program is now an owner of a small, thriving business. More sophisticated qualitative analyses examine interviews and observations seeking to pull out underlying and shared themes—whether people have a sense of hope or what frustration with government bureaucracy means (Rubin and Rubin 2005). For the most part, data analysis should be done in partnership with progressive research jobs or academics.

While the details of doing data analysis are beyond the scope of this book certain principles are important to keep in mind. Data analysis must be done so as to convince others—both allies and targets—that the analysis is accurate. Opponents will look over your results and point out weaknesses; better to find and correct them yourself. Anticipate arguments that can be made against the conclusions of your data and see if these arguments hold. Suppose data clearly show that banks lend less in poor, especially minority communities. Banks will argue that is no big deal because poorer people are worse credit risks and unfortunately minorities tend to be poorer. Examine this claim: compare lending records of banks to people of different ethnic backgrounds but with similar financial standing, or compare white and black neighborhoods with similar economies.

Publicize the findings in ways that suggest action. First make sure audiences understand what the findings imply. Translate sophisticated quantitative analyses into understandable yet accurate language by having those who prepared the technical report work with people skilled in public relations to work out the common sense meanings of the data. If you are trying to convince people that problems differ by race, ethnicity, or gender, make sure the results are broken down by these social categories. Show the need for action by presenting sharp contrasts in the data, assuming that such contrasts are there. For example, in the Hospital Accountability Project, activists showed marked differences in reinvestment made by the same hospital chain in white and black areas in Chicago, demonstrating medical redlining (Hospital Accountability Project 2004).

When presenting numeric data, assume that people (especially elected officials) won't read a table; instead prepare graphs or pictures that make the findings obvious. Include *executive summaries* that highlight both what was found and the action implications. Today with computers and programs such as PowerPoint, visually exciting displays of data can be prepared. Even in statistical analyses, try to include case studies of real people, projects, or communities that add flesh and bone to the numbers. Use maps to show the extent and location of problems, especially when dealing with elected public officials who think in terms of voting districts.

If possible come up with simple indices that communicate problems in a concise but memorable way. Housing activists, for instance, communicate costs of housing through the housing wage—the amount a person has to earn per hour to afford a typical two bedroom home. When you show that the housing wage is $18 an hour, people quickly understand that many workers do not earn that much.

Title reports in ways that catch attention—for instance, *Up Against the Wall: Housing Affordability for Renters* (Treskon and Pelletiere 2005) or in ways that suggest a problem such as *Credit Unions: True to their Mission?* (NCRC) or *Losing Ground in the Best of Times* (Nelson, Treskon, and Pelletiere 2004). Make the titles dramatic and catchy but still informative—*Greed: An In-depth Study of the Debt Collection Practices, Interest Rates, and Customer Base of a Major Illinois Payday Lender* (Monsignor John Egan Campaign for Payday Loan Reform 2004).

When releasing a report, aim to maximize the publicity. First set up a buzz; hint through public lists, or informal conversations to reporters, that the research is forthcoming and the results startling. Then release the report to organization members to start spreading the findings. Then turn the way the report is released into an important event, by holding a press conference, preferably at a location that illustrates the problem documented, or perhaps have a special session at a conference and invite the press. Better yet, work with supportive politicians and present the report at a governmental hearing that the press is covering. Finally, place the report on a website, in three forms, a press release, an executive summary, and a PDF file of the entire report.

Whether talking to the organization's own membership or making presentations to public officials, research reports should not just present what was found but also the implications for action. For instance:

Conclusion of Report on Health Care in Southside
To improve the health conditions in Southside where research shows 15% of the children show below-normal growth patterns resulting from protein deficiency, Southside Community Organization strongly advocates that the city finance a combination daycare and food cooperative paid for using money from the Social Services Block Grant.

Conclusion of a Report on Housing Conditions in Northside
Our community survey showed that 60% of the housing in Northside is owner occupied by working people with modest incomes. Two-thirds of this property needs repair. Northside Community Redevelopment organization will establish a revolving loan program for home repair. Startup funds have been promised by Conglomerate Bank that has also promised to double the home repair money lent in Northside.

Conclusion

Community research is part of the broader organizing process. Doing the research can involve many organization members while the findings themselves can create the anger that moves people to action. Research helps guide campaigns, pointing out the issues that mobilize people, the vulnerabilities of the targets, and what changes can be made. Research provides background for policy advocacy. In all cases, though, effective research must be accurate, focused on the problem at hand, and directly connected to proposed actions.

PART FOUR

Building Capacity to Initiate Collective Action

Capacity involves both the confidence to try as well as the administrative, political, social, and economic knowledge to succeed. This section presents ways in which capacity can be built. Chapter 10 describes the catalysts for the social action, the leaders, professional organizers, and issue activists who motivate others to join the effort. To have the capacity to guide change, social change organizations must be effectively run. Chapter 11 provides an introduction to administration for nonprofit social change organizations. Capacity also expands as activists share ideas, hopes, and aspirations while learning from one another the technical skills to accomplish their shared goals. Many of these efforts are accomplished in a wide variety of meetings that are discussed in Chapter 12.

Capacity building skills need not be re-invented for each organization or each endeavor. Instead, they can be learned from a wide array of support organizations that have become the depository of shared knowledge and experiences and that work to teach others what is known and what resources are available, while helping social change organizations learn from one another. Chapter 13 describes these support organizations.

10 Activists, Organizers, and Social Change Professionals

Social change work is catalyzed by activists and organizers, as well as social change professionals. An **activist** is a person who voluntarily contributes extensive amounts of time, energy, and money to solving problems. **Organizers** are "the salaried staff of social action organizations" (Mondros and Wilson 1994, 7), who work to solve problems by motivating others to join in the battle. As Edward Chambers, the head of the Industrial Areas Foundation (IAF), describes:

> Organizing means an endless search for talent, passion, vision, and the ability to relate to other people. Organizers . . . push [people] to make a world they can believe in, not accepting things as they are, but pushing for things as they could be. . . . Organizers teach engagement in public life as a means to moral meaning. (Chambers 2003, 107)

As a paid employee, an organizer is one type of **social change professional** who works for organizations whose mission is to alleviate social problems by empowering others. In addition to being organizers, social change professionals work in community development organizations and are employed as policy analysts who gather, analyze, and disseminate information. Some are lobbyists for progressive causes, along with employees of coalitions, progressive trade associations, and liberal think tanks.

Organizers and social change professionals approach their work with a wide array of methods. Two generations ago, the activist Stokely Charmichael shook up the system with his public cries for "Black Power" that were seen as a threat to businesses and government alike. At the opposite extreme another organizer, Mike Eichler, quietly worked behind the scenes to set up local organizations to work with business and government in a common effort to restore neighborhoods. For some, such as Shel Trapp, the tools of the trade are the flamboyant, public actions that loudly call attention to a problem. For instance, in a fight for the rights of the wheelchair bound:

> we hit the American Federation of Transport Associations, which was refusing to recommend that city public transit agencies install lifts on buses. They were having a

fancy dinner at a restaurant. . . . We blocked the driveway, the only road in, then discovered that the AFTA folks were getting off the bus on the other side and scaling a steep, fifty-foot-high hill. We had women in gowns and guys in suits literally crawling up the hill. [We had] folks in [wheel]chairs at the top of the hill. So, when the officials on the way to their dinner celebration got to the top, they had two choices: go back or climb over the wheelchairs. It was one of many actions that helped people with power to understand how people in chairs felt when they were physically unable to get where they wanted to go. (Trapp n.d., 72)

In contrast, Josh Silver, a former street-level organizer and now a social change professional working for the National Community Reinvestment Coalition (NCRC), uses data as power. As a policy analyst, Silver prepares statistical reports (and their nontechnical summaries) that members of NCRC then deliver to congressional offices in Washington, D.C., as part of a broader, orchestrated lobbying campaign.

A Variety of Social Change Professionals

Street-level organizers work to mobilize people within a geographic area, as do many *community organizers* who also might work with identity organizations. *Issue organizers* coordinate activists working on a specific issue—access for the disabled, equal rights for minorities, housing for the homeless, preserving the environment, reducing armaments, defending civil rights, or pressuring for affordable housing or economic justice, among dozens of others. *Policy analysts* track both data on problems and legislative and regulatory actions meant to respond to these problems, while *equity planners* garner data that speaks for neighborhoods of need.

Historically, *union organizing* was separate from community organizing, as it focused on places of work rather than communities. But today, union organizing and street-level activism have grown closer as neighborhood organizers hired by progressive unions work to stem the loss of working class jobs (Simmons 1994) or focus on issues that immigrant groups face both at home and at places of work (Needleman 1998).

Institutional organizers work for the social service agencies, often funded by mainstream charities or the public sector, to help abused women, the mentally disabled, and the homeless; improve community health, or provide job training. But their work goes beyond that of ordinary social service employees. Institutional organizers are about mobilizing those they first meet as clients to become activists in battling the problems they face.

Developmental activists are employees of organizations such as Community Development Corporations (CDCs) that build affordable homes, create jobs, and provide shopping within poor neighborhoods. As skilled technicians, developmental activists find capital to build homes or orchestrate their physical construction, and then as organizers, they seek to mobilize those who benefit to join in community actions, such as joining anticrime patrols. As part of a community rebuilding program a development activist might help single mothers become certified daycare providers. Then they do their work in houses that the CDC helped build, (Rubin 2000a).

Social change advocates who work for support organizations provide backup assistance for other organizations. For instance, those working for the Woodstock Institute in Chicago, the Center for Community Change in Washington, D.C., or the Center on Budget and Policy Priorities closely follow and document legislative and regulatory issues and gather data on problems. The data then are provided to direct action organizations that use them to pressure government. In addition, the social change advocates themselves will lobby government and regulatory agencies.

During their careers social change professionals move in and out of a wide variety of these different positions. For instance, Ivory Perry at different times was a volunteer activist, issue organizer, street-level organizer and even for a short period an institutional organizer for a governmental agency. As an activist, Perry faced personal brutality in the civil rights struggle. As an organizer in St. Louis he went door-to-door to organize people to fight poverty and to combat unjust landlords. And then as an institutional organizer he obtained information that became part of the battle against lead-based paint (Lipsitz 1995). Heather Booth began her work as a civil rights and women's organizer, then started a training academy while doing work in environmental organizing as well (Booth 1994, 8). John Taylor, whose career began as a developmental activist in Somerville, Massachusetts, now runs the NCRC which battles banks as they try to weaken the Community Reinvestment Act; while Kevin Jackson, whose work began as a street-level organizer, now heads the Chicago Rehab Network. As a teenager, John Barros was employed as a youth organizer for the Dudley Street Neighborhood Initiative, then contributed as a board member, and today is the executive director of this empowering community organization (Dudley Street Neighborhood Initiative 2005).

Why and How Do a Variety of People Become Activists and Organizers?

A job advertisement for a professional organizer could easily read as follows:

Help Wanted: Organizer
Willing to work long and inconvenient hours at less pay than could be earned elsewhere. Must have the patience of Job and a hide thick enough to withstand constant criticism and slow progress. Must be willing to accept the blame for failures. Must not try to claim personal credit for successes. Must be willing to learn new skills while helping others discover how to work together in organizations that bring about social change. Good communication and analytical skills desirable. Being able to articulate a vision of the future and having an empathetic personality a plus.

Social change professionals, organizers, and activists are often swimming upstream doing battle against an existing, powerful establishment that more often than not prevails. Social change work requires sacrifice in one's personal life, staying away from family, physical dangers, and setting priorities that others might not understand. One friend, a progressive policy analyst, took time out from his honeymoon to do data crunching needed by those in his organization.

Why do it? Why even try? No simple answer can be found, as the decision to become involved is often personal. Some begin their work in their neighborhood, fearing the harm of a proposed incinerator, by knocking on doors. Lois Gibbs, who became nationally known as an environmental activist, noticed numerous illnesses in her community and slowly figured out that the diseases were caused by chemical pollution left by the Hooker Chemical Company and started organizing to protect her family. Other personal experiences motivate people to become active when they experience racism, sexism, or homophobia first hand. Appalled by the poverty that she and her neighbors faced as well as how those in the establishment demeaned poor people is what motivated Linda Stout to begin her organizing career (Stout 1996).

Some activists are moved by what they learned in school about social injustice or what they see working as interns in poor communities. Dr. Martin Luther King, Jr., was called upon simply because he was a young and energetic preacher whom others trusted, who spoke eloquently, and who had reflected on moral issues of social justice. Shel Trapp, a leader in the National People's Action (NPA), had a "nice, safe job as a minister" when he heard Tom Gaudette, a radical organizer and follower of Alinsky, lash out at the indifference of the clergy. "With some arrogance and a tone of fear, I called Gaudette for an interview. He offered me the job of organizer and I jumped at the chance" (Trapp n.d., 15).

We would suggest that people become social change professionals as a result of four reinforcing elements: a personal, sensitizing experience, a cognitive understanding that indicates action is possible; a reinforcing involvement in social change actions; and focus, direction, and training through linkages to the social change infrastructure.

A Personal, Sensitizing Experience

Some people experience a "click event," a moment of self awareness during which he or she recognizes a problem. For those from disadvantaged groups, such sensitizing experiences occur daily—the slights caused through pervasive racism, insulting homophobic humor, sexual predation, the inability of the wheelchair bound to get from place to place. Linda Stout, an Appalachian white woman and later founder of a major peace organizing project describes these episodic experiences: Being demeaned in school because she was a poor girl, an experience at work when her bosses "were laughing about the fact that a black family had . . . been harassed by their white neighbors . . . " (Stout 1996, 28) or later on witnessing the police beating up on a black man (Stout 1996, 31). Students from middle-class households, when volunteering or interning in poor neighborhoods, have a click experience from the unfairness of what they now see—that was our own introduction to activism. A woman or a minority who is passed over for a promotion for a less qualified white male is quickly made aware of structural unfairness.

Fear as well as outrage can motivate. James Jasper labels these motivating personal experiences as "moral shocks" that

> are often the first step toward recruitment into social movements, when an unexpected event or piece of information raises such a sense of outrage in a person that she

becomes inclined toward political action . . . the triggers may be highly publicized events such as a nuclear accident or personal experiences such as the death of a child. They may be sudden, like an accident or public announcement, or they may unfold gradually over time, as in the gradual realization by Love Canal's residents that they were living over a toxic waste dump. (Jasper 1997, 106)

A Cognitive Understanding That Indicates Action Is Possible

Personal experiences are not enough, as individuals can interpret what they have seen in ways that reinforce their own sense of disempowerment. Why demand racial justice when the police will simply beat you up? To be willing to act, a personal, cognitive understanding of the problem is required, an understanding Ernie Cortes, the organizer of the Texas IAF, described as *cold anger* (Rogers 1990). Individuals must learn that the problem goes beyond themselves: Many like myself are poor, because a few are rich and laws are set up in ways that preserve their wealth irrespective of the harm to others.

Future activists must believe in the possibility of change, perhaps by studying history that makes clear that change does come about but only after people like themselves are willing to put their bodies on the line, or at the very least, spend endless hours working. This discovery leads to a moral commitment that then becomes a core part of the activist's self-identity (Teske 1997, 93–138) that links the personal with the political. For those involved in faith-based organizing, this moral obligation emerges from personal self-reflection on the meaning of their faith. As Richard Wood learned in his study of faith-based organizing:

> leaders expressed . . . as the primary motivations for being involved: as "following Jesus" in "holding the authorities accountable . . . "; as "answering God's call to build the Kingdom"; as . . . "walking the walk just like we talk the talk." (Wood 2002, 71)

A Reinforcing Involvement in Social Change Actions

Seeing and being appalled by injustice is a start, but it is not enough unless there is an understanding that fighting back does bring results. Such discoveries are made perhaps by a tentative sticking of a foot in the water. An individual might join in as one of thousands at a peace demonstration, or an assembly to reassert racial justice or gender equality. Or it might involve working with a few dozen neighbors in a program to clean up the block or successfully petition the city council for a traffic light. For a student not yet ready to commit, this stage often involves signing up for an internship in a social action organization. While but tentative steps, future social change activists discover that they are not alone but are fighting with and for others who have shared beliefs, needs, and problems.

This involvement expands on an emotional level to create an **activist identity**—high valuation of *doing something* about what they see as the problems of our society and world (Teske 1997, 97–98), while implying a moral obligation to be involved. Slowly but surely the emerging activist moves from passive involvement in rallies, to perhaps speaking at a rally, or canvassing—going door to door to encourage others to become involved.

> For some activists, their involvement served to develop emotions that allowed them to do things that they previous had felt unable or unwilling to do. For example, many activists spoke of an increased personal confidence, a new willingness to speak in public forums, a greater desire to follow public affairs, a greater introspectiveness, a greater attentiveness to various social ills and evils that they had previously ignored, and most generically an ability to grow as a person. (Teske 1997, 122)

In addition, activism is reinforced as people see their participation help them grow as individuals, as a female Mexican American activist described on joining the organization:

> I was a submissive housewife . . . But once we came here to this organization, we all learned something . . . I got my liberation after being suppressed for 15 years. (Louie 2001, 21)

Focus, Direction, and Training through Linkages to the Social Change Infrastructure

The earlier stages in the making of a social change professional are those of self-discovery and personal awareness. But a desire to make change, a responsibility to do so, and a recognition that change is possible are not enough to become a professional social change activist. Knowledge about what to do and how to do it are needed. In this last stage, the future organizer or committed activist becomes linked to others in the social change infrastructure and a sense of belonging to a cause develops. As Todd Gitlin described for the sixties:

> The real badge of belonging . . . it was joy that came from the sense of movement. Not the herd instinct—we were, each of us too strong-willed for that—but vitality and conviviality together, a feeling of overcoming drift in favor of mastery. It was comradeship—the feeling of trust. (Gitlin 2003, 21)

Being linked to others who care reinforces the decision to become active.

Further, belonging opens up an array of information about resources, tactics, and history as well as understanding the political environment that become the skills for action. Future social change professionals meet others more experienced than themselves, who provide mentoring, advice, a sense of direction, and, most important, encourage jumping in the water of activism, not just dabbling their toes. Linda Stout describes her transition from activist to organizer as one of discovering a new language:

> I met a women who was a full-time organizer. I asked her how she got paid to be an organizer and explained that I wanted that type of job. She said that I had to raise the money and that it was very difficult. That I would have to write "proposals" and raise

the money from "foundations." I didn't know what a foundation was. (Stout 1996, 42)

For others, training comes about through an apprenticeship with a more experienced person, learning hands on what to do. Shel Trapp, later one of the nation's leading organizers and teachers of activism, recalled his first day with Tom Gaudette, an organizer who trained with Saul Alinksy:

My first day in the office, Gaudette drove me around the streets of Austin. Although usually very vocal, he didn't say a word the whole ride. Back at the office he asked me, "What did you see?" Not knowing what I was supposed to see, I was very confused and thought, there goes the job. He waited a few seconds and screamed, "Did you see all the For Sale signs?" Austin was a racially changing community. "Did you see the bad building at the corner of Quincy and Lavergne?" His questions came like bullets out of a machine gun. My training had begun. (Trapp n.d., 15)

More formal training programs are available through institutes run by the organizing networks, through social work schools, as well as special programs offered for economic and social development professionals.

The Tasks of Organizers and Social Change Professionals

But what exactly do organizers and other social change professionals do? Alinksy portrayed the work of organizers with a rhetorical flourish:

It is the job of building broad, deep Peoples' Organizations which are all-inclusive of both the people and their many organizations. It is the job of uniting through a common interest which far transcends individual differences, all the institutions and agencies representative of the people. It is the job of building a People's Organization so that people will have faith in themselves and in their fellow men [sic]. It is the job of educating our people so they will be informed to the point of being able to exercise an intelligent critical choice as to what is true and what is false. (Alinsky 1969, 202)

This vision still holds, but how is it accomplished? What skills and training are required? How are these skills obtained? From whom and where?

The work of social change professionals varies from the exciting and scary to the downright boring. Direct action organizers who challenge the system through leading demonstrations or civil disobedience experience excitement or even terror in their work as even ordinary demonstrations are fraught with the potential for violence. Ed Chambers describes the tensions in a racially charged battle with Kodak:

We arrived . . . at 7 a.m. on the morning of the stockholders meeting . . . a totally non-violent, disciplined, orderly group of over 1,000 black congregation folk coming to protest at Kodak's annual meeting. . . . When the stockholders meeting began, our church folks remained outside, while Minister Florence, with nine other leaders, Saul

> Alinsky, and me, marched into the meeting . . . After three minutes, Minister Florence took the floor microphone and interrupted . . . "Mr. Chairman, Mr. Chairman, will Kodak honor the agreement it signed with FIGHT?" The chairman replied, "No." Minister Florence announced that Kodak had one hour to reconsider. Then we turned and walked out with national TV and other members of the media following us. We were cat-called with ugly racial epithets all the way up the aisle. (Chambers 2003, 97)

To bring this exciting event off required days of working out routine details, arranging transportation for thousands, orchestrating media coverage, and ensuring that the large group of people remained calm and orderly.

Organizers spend endless hours knocking on hundreds of doors, handing out flyers, chatting with people, only to discover few are willing to show up to a meeting. Fund raising is continuous. For an institutional organizer, setting up a homeless shelter can be exciting, but then there are endless details—making sure there is enough food or figuring out what to do if someone is disruptive. Direct action is glorious but someone has to check that the sound systems are in place, follow up with letters to politicians, or pay bills for transportation. Civil rights organizers are portrayed in leading daring sit-ins. But much more time was spent on mundane but equally important work—canvassing house-to-house or encouraging people to try to register to vote (Payne 1995, 244 ff). Bob Zellner, one of the early Student Nonviolent Coordinating Committee (SNCC) organizers,

> once compared organizing to a juggling act—how many plates can you keep spinning at once? Organizers had to be morale boosters, teachers, welfare agents, transportation coordinators, canvassers, public speakers, negotiators, lawyers, all the while communicating with people ranging from illiterate sharecroppers to well-off professionals and while enduring harassment from the agents of the law and listening with one ear for the threats of violence. Exciting days and major victories are rare. Progress is a few dollars raised, a few more people coming to pay poll tax. (Payne 1995, 246)

A typical day for street level organizer Gabriel Gonzales began by scanning the newspapers for stories about his neighborhood. While he was checking that thousands of flyers announcing a community meeting had been distributed, he was interrupted by a call from a city council member. Rather than answering this official's questions, he told the city official to call an elected board member of the organization (and then picked up the phone and quickly warned his board member). Gonzales spent the afternoon planning a community-wide meeting with the board members, then returned to the phone to talk with allies about a joint campaign to expand a social service agency. He took some time to teach interns how to strategize for a direct action against a public office and then spent a frustrating hour trying to locate a key for the hall for the evening meeting. The day ended with a community-wide workshop discussing what to do about overcrowded public schools.

An economic development professional, Bob Brehm was equally busy, having spent much of his morning calling both foundations and banks to ask when the promised money for a supermarket type of project would arrive. He was quite tired from working late the previous evening with the board members of an apartment cooperative on how to battle encroaching gentrifiers. Late morning he went to another bank to negotiate the terms for a loan for an affordable housing project his CDC was sponsoring. He had to keep reminding himself to be on his best behavior and not give in to his fatigue and tell off the bankers for neglecting the community, as he felt like doing. That afternoon was spent physically hammering shelving in a facility being constructed to house community entrepreneurs, a project Brehm's organization had initiated.

Both Brehm and Gonzales usually work in blue jeans; in contrast Josh Silver, Vice President for Research and Policy for the National Community Reinvestment Coalition routinely wears a tie and jacket. Josh had begun his activism as a transportation organizer, was educated as a policy analyst, and now spends his time in gathering, analyzing, and disseminating data on economic injustice. That morning, he had arrived early to work to brief his boss who was going to testify to a congressional committee on how banks were ignoring parts of the Community Reinvestment Act (CRA). Afterward, Josh strolled over to a regulatory agency to learn what plans the regulators might have for revisions in the CRA and then set aside an hour to work on data analysis that he and his interns were preparing on how well credit unions serve the poor. Early and mid-afternoon were tied up with a conference call with NCRC activists throughout the country who shared ideas on how to oppose a merger of two large banks that would reduce branches in poor communities. Late afternoon, Josh was questioned by the press officer for NCRC on the meaning of the statistics in a technical report; the press person thought the report could get national coverage if rephrased in ordinary language. Tired, Josh headed home, but couldn't resist turning on his e-mail and checking activist lists to see if any trouble was brewing.

The job advertisements for social change professionals that nowadays appear on-line show both the variety of jobs and the needed skills. One advertisement follows:

Senior Community Organizer:
IMPACT Silver Spring seeks a motivated and committed individual with at least five years of community organizing experience, to continue building two key programs: Community Empowerment, a nine month leadership training experience, and Lasting IMPACT, a mutual support network for graduates of the program. This position requires a demonstrated history of successfully working to empower others, a combination of strong program management and human development skills, and a passionate commitment to building effective multicultural communities. Strong interpersonal and creative problem-solving skills necessary. Ability to work in a team setting with other staff, community volunteers and consultant facilitators is a must, as well as the ability to maintain a flexible work schedule, including nights and some weekends. Bilingual language skills helpful.
Salary range: $35,000 to $45,000, commensurate with experience.
Please see full job description, attached or posted on www.idealist.com.

Activist Organizer:
The role of the Activist Organizer is to build organization in low and moderate-income communities around health care and other issues. House by house, family by family, organizers hear from community residents about their health care issues and

the solutions they would propose. They work with community residents to hold meetings, do research on key issues, and develop campaign strategies to get these issues addressed. The ACORN Activist Organizer's job is to work for the membership of ACORN, helping them build the power they need to win on the issues that are most important to them and their communities. . . .

Responsibilities:
- Recruit members.
- Identify pressing social issues.
- Develop leaders.
- Organize meetings, rallies, protests, press conferences, marches, etc.
- And run campaigns.

Requirements:
- Applicants should be committed to economic justice, social change, and working with diverse neighborhoods.
- Office Work/Field Work (Any Field Work Requiring Transportation is Compensated)
- Some College or College Degree.
- Ability to Work with People from Various Cultural and Economic Backgrounds.

We Offer:
- Paid Training
- Advancement/Travel Opportunities
- Excellent Benefits/Full Health Coverage
- Compensation starting at $25,000

Other advertisements mention skills such as "good at working with and motivating people"; "competent with word processing software"; "fluent in Spanish and English"; "able to prepare an operating budget"; "successful fund raiser"; "knowledgeable about public/private sector funding programs"; and "experienced in nonprofit management."

Advertisements for other types of social change professionals emphasize different skills. The Center for Community Change that helps organize local groups and provides technical assistance advertised for a health organizer:

Wanted: a Health Care Team Leader
Principal Responsibilities:
- Lead a staff team that will design and implement a long-term strategy to increase the voice and impact of lower income communities in the health care debate.
- Develop and maintain relationships with community-based organizations, organizing networks, national policy groups, and resource providers.
- Manage the health care project work plan and budget.
- Prepare monthly reports and other progress assessments.
- Participate in the performance evaluation of team members.

- Work in partnership with the CCC Development Department to market the project to funders and donors.
- Attend Organizing Unit staff meetings; team leader meetings; and CCC staff meetings.
- Participate in other organizational projects and teams as assigned by the Lead Organizer or the Deputy Executive Director for Organizing.
- Maintain an appropriate balance between the strategy of the health care team, the goals of the Organizing Unit, and the broader mission of the Center for Community Change.
- This position reports to the Deputy of Operations in the Organizing Unit.

Development organizers, often labeled *executive directors*, require a different background, one in fund-raising, project administration, and financial management. An institutional organizer, working at a shelter, might need skills in counseling; a social change professional working in a community economic development organization has to be able to prepare spreadsheets, understand interest rates, and be able to quickly switch from talking about social injustice with foundation people to leveraged investments with bankers—radicals with business suits.

The jack-of-all-trades is the street-level community organizer who is partly an agitator, administrator, propagandist, bookkeeper, solicitor of funds, assuager of hurt feelings, public speaker, back room negotiator, and, in many cases, general handy person. In the morning, an organizer might listen to the problems of community members, in the afternoon desperately try to reconcile the expenses of the organization with an uncertain funding base, while at night canvass to increase the membership. Organizers must know how to run meetings and conferences, understand litigation, read research, and deal with the press, among many other skills. In addition, organizers are about maintaining personal relations, building unity in communities, calming hurt egos when tensions are high, bridging differences between committed volunteers, and reassuring members when failures occur.

Organizers have to understand what others have to say and then, based on what they hear, figure out which issues are really important and will motivate members. Are people really concerned about that stop sign, or is the complaint a way of saying that nobody cares about the neighborhood? Such empathetic hearing skills are especially vital in working in multicultural environments and in those in which gendered concerns are central (Bradshaw, Soifer, and Guttierrez 1994). Organizers learn that people from separate cultural and ethnic groups, as well as different genders convey information in distinct ways so that an organizer may have to become a **cultural broker** who not only understands what people from different backgrounds are trying to get across, but can communicate these insights to others.

Overall social change professionals take on four complementary roles. As **catalysts**, they mobilize others; as **teachers** they help people gain confidence and capacity. As a **linking person**, social change professionals connect community members and action organizations, obtain information and resources from the outside, while at the same time themselves *symbolize* to others what is at stake. Finally, as **implementors** they work to make sure organizational goals are carried out.

Social Change Professionals as Catalysts

Catalysts stimulate and empower others to act and show hope that change is possible. In doing so, though, organizers try to follow what Ernesto Cortes of the IAF describes as the Iron Rule:

> there's an Iron Rule in organizing. It is a little different from the Golden Rule. The Iron Rule says: Never, ever, do for people what they can do for themselves. And, it is a very difficult rule to follow. (Rogers 1990, 15)

The iron rule is about releasing the energy already present among the local leaders. Civil rights organizers explained "in many cases, [the organizers in] SNCC did not so much develop leadership as remove barriers, so that leadership that was already there might emerge" (Payne 1995, 194). A development activist shared this perspective with us:

> We think of ourselves as catalysts and in the true sense of the word, a catalyst doesn't get used up in the reaction. . . . [if our effort] doesn't ignite activism and ignite a sense among people about what can be done when people work collectively and struggle for what is needed, then we've done little.

Social Change Professionals as Teachers

Social change professionals are teachers in the Freirean sense (Bell, Gaventa, and Peters 1990; Freire 1970), that is, teachers who empower others by showing them the possibilities of what can be done (Freire 1970, 72). In this role, social change professionals guide others in a gentle and nonauthoritarian manner, encouraging them to examine their own experiences and from this reflection work out possible actions: "When you asked the banker for a loan, what happened?" "If we showed up as a group outside of the polluting plant what do you think might happen?"

Organizers are not teachers who stand in front of a classroom spouting off or pouring predigested facts and figures into passive students' heads. Teaching is dialogical, not top-down, with discussions carried out in ways that encourage each person to air his or her own opinions and share his or her own experiences and then move toward actions. Organizers teach through example, both to show possibilities of success and to lay out a variety of options that others have tried.

Like the best teachers, organizers encourage people to follow up their own ideas even if these are not the ideas the organizers would have chosen. Technical matters are directly taught—how to contact politicians, to lobby with them, deal with the press, prepare and implement a budget—but only after those in the group recognize the need to learn them. The goal is to put tools into easy reach rather than having the organizer do the tasks for the group. If success occurs, people feel empowered, while if failures happen, the organizer is there to make sure the thrown rider gets back on the bicycle and tries again.

Teaching is about learning from one another and discovering shared problems and shared solutions. It is also about learning democracy and equality, as teaching is done in ways that the opinions and experiences of others are respected and conversations are low key, allowing consensus to emerge.

Leadership Development.   The catalyst and teaching role of the social change professionals come together in *leadership development* efforts. Social change professionals are well aware that they cannot and should not do it alone and so they work to find local leaders, individuals who are deeply respected by others and who care enough about issues to set aside much of their personal time to work for broader concerns. Leadership development then involves four stages—identification, confidence building, mutual sharing, and technical training.

First, those leaders whom others respect are found and efforts begun to build their confidence by both figuratively and literally walking with them. Social change professionals help local leaders recognize that "yes they do know what to do" and then the belief "yes, it can be done." At times, this means tossing the local leaders into the water to show them that they can swim—by handing them a microphone at a rally, or having them speak for the group when negotiating with funders, or following up their ideas for an action.

The last stage of leadership development occurs only after the potential leader has developed some self-confidence. At that time, the local leader is invited to attend technical training on matters that are unlikely to emerge from their own experience—how one creates a video to increase the chances of its appearing on TV, or ways of filling out a grant application, or the importance of the internal rate of return in getting funding for a low-income housing tax credit project, or the nuts and bolts of running a demonstration. Such technical training involves a more formal process of teaching with the knowledgeable expert talking with those who are less informed. But even in these more formal settings, the expert listens respectfully to the local leader knowing full well that the true expert is the local leader who will put the technical information to use.

Values, Theories, Ideologies, and Models.   As teachers, social change professionals should not try to impose their ideological beliefs on community members. Yet, social change professionals must be aware of their values and implicit ideologies and keep in mind, as Fisher has stated, "organizing must create a more consciously ideological practice" (Fisher and Kling 1994, 228). Doing so can come about by encouraging reflections on why certain actions are needed and how best to carry them out.

Once the membership or at least the organization's leaders have begun to think about the goals of organizing, the social change professional can then initiate discussion on how well the organization's approaches mesh with the broader goals of progressive work. For example, are women's ideas given less respectful attention when planning for community actions, and if so does this indicate an underlying sexism? What steps has the organization taken to ensure that decisions are made by the whole group, rather than a narrow group of activists?

While organizers should not impose a set of values on the organizations with which they work, part of their responsibility is to help people discover from their own experiences their own values and implicit ideologies. In doing so they are acting as teachers and encouraging both themselves and other activists to understand the world through the lens of an *organic intellectual*.

Organic Intellectuals.   By reflecting on what they have seen and then refining the ideas through dialogic discussions, social change professionals and activists work out an organic theory that explains what should be done, what has worked, and why. Through these *"educational projects*, [that are] carried out *with* the oppressed in the process of organizing them" (Freire 1970, 70), activists become what the Marxist intellectual Antonio Gramsci described as organic intellectuals. An

> organic intellectual [is] a manipulator of signs and symbols, an educator and an agitator rationally translating the needs and aspirations of [the] community into effective action. . . . In order to succeed, organic intellectuals rely on collective memory—shared experiences and perceptions about the past that legitimate action in the present—and on social learning—experiences with contestation in the present that transform values and goals for the future. (Lipsitz 1988, 228)

The understanding of organic intellectuals grows from contact with the oppressed, not from distant academic theories, as a developmental activist explained to Herbert Rubin: "I didn't get [this knowledge] out of no book, I got it out of the streets. I got [what] was a real problem, I listened to the people, I was there holding their hands. I know what the problems are."

From their daily encounters, organic intellectuals gain the substantive knowledge that will motivate people to join in the fight as they collectively reflect on what has happened and what implications it has for future action.

Social Change Professionals as Linking People

A major task of social change professionals is to be a linking person who represents the organization to others while at the same time gaining from others the information and resources that the organization relies upon. When organizers attend conferences, they bring back new program ideas and knowledge on what actions work. Policy advocates and activist researchers scan technical reports, news, and books for information that can guide activism. What new regulations or bills are pending that affect the organization? What do studies now show about how housing costs affect those in poverty?

Linkage, however, is a two-way process. Just as the outside world needs to be understood by those in the social change organization, those in the outside world need to know what social change organization is about. Such interpretations come through the press releases and through careful framing of the actions that we describe in later chapters. In addition, though, by acting as *symbolic leaders*, social change activists put forth an image of what the organization is about to the broader public.

Symbolic leaders shape and frame how people understand the issues at hand. Their voices carry to both those engaged in the struggle and to those in positions of power. As a symbolic leader, Martin Luther King, Jr., voiced the sufferings of African

Americans in a moving and eloquent language, as in his "I Have a Dream" speech, has become part of American cultural lore. Lesser known organizers communicate a similar important symbolic message motivating those in the organization. For instance, when Mrs. Fannie Lou Hamer, an organizer in the rural South spoke:

> Immediately, an electric atmosphere suffused the entire church. Men and women alike began to stand up, to call out her name, and to urge her on . . . She went on to speak about the moral evil of racism itself and the grievous harm it was doing to the souls of white people in Mississippi . . . She did not do so in accusation, but with a kind of redemptive reconciliation, articulating a vision of justice that embraced everyone. She ended up leading the assembly in chorus after chorus of a rousing old Negro spiritual . . . When she finished, the entire assembly was deeply shaken emotionally. People crowded around her to promise they would join the struggle. (conversation with Robert Jackall reported in Payne 1995, 242)

Further through their actions as well as their words, symbolic leaders shape the definition of both problems and their solutions. César Chavez became a symbolic leader of poor farm workers through his acceptance of arrest and in his hunger strikes. Dr. Martin Luther King, Jr., exemplified a belief in pacifism by accepting incarceration in a dignified manner, and in so doing, redefined jailing as a matter of pride rather than humiliation (Branch 1988). Symbolic leaders shape a political language that communicates the need for change. They collect the humiliation and disempowerment of the oppressed and transform these stories into motivation for collective action. In general,

> *Symbolic leaders give voice and image where there was noise; they define humiliation as a collective experience and transform that experience into political energy for change.*

Since symbolic leaders can be seen as embodiments of the values of the organization, they must reflect on their own behavior and values to ensure that the image they communicate is appropriate. Organizers have to live their values in a visible way, which means that those values have to be deeply and sincerely felt. Organizers must not forget they are always on display, which means even in their leisure time they have to avoid behaviors that can cast disrepute on the causes for which they speak.

Social Change Professionals as Implementors

Implementation means carrying out action to accomplish a goal. Organizers act as *facilitators* to implement routine actions: making sure that halls are rented for mass meetings, double-checking the schedules of politicians to ensure that when the membership arrives the politicians will be present. They take the time to figure out how to fill out loan applications for home repairs and mortgages and then teach others how to do so. Facilitators keep abreast of news stories, read technical publications about community projects, and follow the vagaries of local politics. In addition, as implementors, social change professionals become administrators handling day-to-day decisions in how services are provided, managing personnel, coordinating volunteers with paid employees, keeping books, and numerous other tasks.

Acting as implementor might make it appear that the social change professional is violating the iron rule. However, common sense indicates that community members with full time jobs and families, cannot spend their days running a program. Professional lobbying can't be done only by volunteers, since lobbyists have to be "on the hill" or "under the dome" when the legislators are in session. As implementor, the social change professional often is *doing for* rather than *doing with* or *catalyzing* others to do for themselves. Does doing such work empower community members?

Sometimes not. When social change professionals think of themselves as housing developers (albeit socially responsible ones) or social service administrators, they belie the core philosophy of empowerment. However, this need not be the case as being an implementor can be consistent with bringing about empowerment *so long as the social change professional takes careful direction from those he or she serves.*

Direction doesn't mean asking how to build to code, or prescribing the right medicines in a community health clinic. It does mean asking community members, and following the community consensus, on whether the CDC is about providing rental homes, starter homes for low income people, or slightly more expensive homes so police, fire, nurses, and teachers can afford to buy. It means that the social change lobbyist prepares a set of talking points on a legislation issue, then walks to the hill with the community member. But it is the community member himself or herself who talks with the elected official by merging ideas from the talking points with first-hand experience and knowledge.

Learning to be a Social Change Professional

Many paths are followed in learning the skills of a social change professional. We hope that studying a book like this one is one path, but recognize that many others are just as good. For many, learning takes place experientially as people teach themselves what works and what does not—sometimes a slow and painful process. As Ed Chambers describes:

> Organizing in the 1950s and '60s was a low-paid, hair-shirt existence with long hours, heavy-drinking, and a *machismo* style with its attendant bad habits. Then, as now, organizers learned by their own and other people's mistakes. In the early days, we had no training for leaders and a have-gun-will-travel approach for organizers. (Chambers 2003, 100)

Today systematic approaches are available to teach skills, though many still begin with the school of hard knocks that is then refined by the array of books, online sites, training sessions, and conferences that are found that provide technical information. Other social change professionals learn their craft by apprenticing with an established organizer, developer, or advocate or as interns in agencies. Many of the city-wide, state, and national advocacy networks seek out eager interns who will work for low wages and, in turn, be taught a craft. Like many national organizations, the National Low Income Housing Coalition works with interns, some of whom it later employs, but does so after testing them by throwing them right into ongoing campaigns.

Organizer training academies that are associated with the various organizing models provide more formal instruction. The Center for Community Change trains those working in very low-income communities, while the Center for Third World Organizing runs programs to help people of color and to promote multicultural organizing. The Consensus Organizing Institute teaches how community groups can work with government and businesses while the National Training and Information Center (NTIC), associated with the National People's Action, instructs on the direct action techniques as does the training program set up by the Industrial Areas Foundation.

Instruction can range from short, focused courses that teach a technical procedure, to a more philosophical approach that explores what social activism is all about. Some programs combine both. IAF training concentrates on relationship building and goes far beyond teaching technical skills, although these are important. Training involves

> how to make clear to yourself your self-interest; how to be an initiator rather than a reactor; how to listen to and affirm other people; how to distinguish between leaders and followers; how to identify and proposition current and potential leaders; how to run a meeting; how to hold members of your own networks accountable; how to hold other leaders accountable; how to raise money; how to analyze institutions (both your own and those you're up against) how to negotiate with other decision-makers; how to run an action; how to run an evaluation of an action; how to pick issues so that you're not running into the biggest issues at the start; how to plan issue campaigns; how to develop realistic schedules; how to view and accept tensions; how to live and grow with a *process* of dealing with issues rather than with the particular issue or task; and how to invite in new institutions and develop allies. (Warren 2001, 227 quoting Chambers 1978, 21)

Some training academies concentrate on working with local leaders rather than professional staff. Programs differ on their emphasis on being confrontational or working to build consensus, though focus changes over time. Initially, the IAF encouraged organizers to carry out the Alinsky model of direct confrontation, albeit tempered by humor. Today, IAF's approach has been toned down to emphasize the importance of building on shared values while being more willing to compromise with those in power (Fisher 1994, 192–96). By contrast ACORN is still committed to a "radical ideology and confrontational tactics" and trains its organizers accordingly (Fisher 1994, 197).

Numerous organizers have taken the five-day courses offered by the Midwest Academy at a cost of about $800. During a five-day course the work balances technical concerns—of recruitment of members, issue selection, investigative research, and grass-roots fund-raising, much of it taken from the Academy's own handbook (Bobo, Max, and Kendall 2001)—with general background instruction on the purposes of community organizing, the dynamics of power, and coalition building. Much time is spent on learning about the importance of story telling as an organizing technique (www.midwestacademy.com/page8.html). In contrast, at training institutes for consensus organizers, set up by Michael Eichler, activists are taught how to unite community groups, businesses, and government to participate in programs to physically renew poor communities.

Those involved in economic and social production work attend other programs, though many of these are meant for mid-career professionals needing to expand their skills. For instance, social change professionals in community economic development might undertake course work at the School of Community Economic Development at Southern New Hampshire University or the more focused programs sponsored by the Pratt Institute Center for Community and Economic Development. Many developmental activists participate in formal programs presented at the Development Training Institute that balance classroom training with hands-on work on community renewal projects.

Some activists only have time for brief instruction. Fortunately, specialized training programs can be obtained at conferences as well as through on-line courses. For instance, the National Community Capital Association offers ongoing seminars in the intricacies of program and organizational management for professionals running community loan funds. The Enterprise Foundation and the Neighborhood Reinvestment Corporation present seminars on the multitude of tasks developmental activists must learn, varying from overall understanding of community renewal work to very specific technical financial courses needed to sustain affordable housing. They are offered in ways that can lead to certification in specialized technical areas (www.nw.org/network/training/courses/default.asp).

Information can be obtained on-line from Knowledge Plex, an informative website sponsored by the Fannie Mae Foundation. Training academies such as the Center for Community Change place many how-to pamphlets on-line, for example *A Guide for Education Organizing*, that shows how to build on the techniques of community activism to improve local education. Social change professionals also teach one another through on-line dialogues that occur on lists sponsored by trade associations or are set up by volunteers. For example, activists on the list sponsored by the Association for Economic Opportunity, a micro-enterprise trade association, have explored issues on how to handle interest on loans to those of the Islamic Faith, while a wide variety of strategic information on direct action tactics are periodically presented on the Comm-Org list, a discussion group of practitioners and academics run out of the University of Wisconsin at http://comm-org.wisc.edu.

Academic Instruction for Social Change Activists

Specialized training programs for social change activists build on cumulative practical insights. But these programs are often limited in time, so of necessity focus on the here and now. More extended curriculum in universities allow for grounding social change work within its larger economic, political, and social contexts, while at the same time allowing students to contrast a variety of models. For instance, a well-known course at Harvard taught by organizer, now professor, Marshall Gans interweaves theoretical and experiential education seamlessly. It includes extensive readings from such intellectual and philosophical leaders as Plato, de Tocqueville . . . and such community organizing pioneers as Alinsky, Ross, Chavez, and Wiley. Gans involves students in devising and launching organizing campaigns around issues the students select as they work with existing groups or create new ones to pursue systemic change. Recent field experiences including organizing residents of subsidized housing, organizing non-unionized university employees and launching a campaign to reverse current Presbyterian church policy concerning the ordination of gays and lesbians. (Mott 2005, 26)

Academic programs are housed in a wide variety of disciplines: social work, planning, urban studies, sociology, and schools of planning, among others (Brophy and Shabecof 2001, 194–230; Mott 2005). Even training in the law has proven useful, especially for social change professionals involved in Fair Housing Programs, civil rights, enforcement of environment regulations, or the ADA, ending gender or sexual discrimination and similar matters.

The most extensive university training in organizing can be found in schools of social work with curricula that span matters from social planning, in which community members collectively suggest what should be done to improve their neighborhoods, to street-level organizing work. Much of the instruction emphasizes the importance of working with people from a wide array of ethnic, cultural, religious, and gender groupings (Bankhead and Erlich 2005; Hyde 2005).

Social Change Work as a Career

Before committing to a career in social change, future activists have to balance the downside of such a career with its rewards.

The Downside of Social Change Work

Social change work involves long hours at salaries, that while livable, are far less than those for comparable private sector work. Further, for those who choose social change work, it becomes an all-consuming vocation, not just a nine-to-five job. Days might be spent pressuring government and businesses with nights set aside for recruiting members. One economic justice activist we know sends out his e-mail commentaries at 3 a.m. We asked why and he explained that it was his only free time for doing so. Problems, when they occur, often require immediate response before the opposition solidifies. As paid employees, social change professionals work long hours for their organization, and then as activists, themselves participate in events sponsored by other social change groups.

In social change work, occasional victories must provide the morale that makes up for frequent losses. Efforts seem Sysiphean as opponents find new ways of advantaging themselves, and persuading officials must begin anew each time new officeholders are elected. Activists recognize that the goal is to change unjust underlying structures, yet much of the work involves fire-fights in response to immediate problems.

In confrontations social change professionals are often outgunned by equally competent individuals working for the opposition. A coalition leader described to us a story typifying this problem. She (a physically small female) was on her way to a congressional hearing, wearing ordinary business clothes and found herself alone in an elevator with half a dozen Brooks-Brothers-dressed male lobbyists for the opposition going to the same meeting. How does one person feel when up against a highly bank rolled cadre?

Burnout is a problem, as discouragement sets in, and either emotional concerns or a variety of physical symptoms set in. To moderate the impact of burnout, social change professionals build into their work time for reflection to remind themselves of the importance of what they are doing. Others make sure to add to their projects— some humor in a protest, satirical skits at a meeting, or singing and dancing at an ethnic festival or block party.

The best antidote to burnout is a successful campaign or project that empowers both members and the community. Winning a battle energizes, boosting the morale not only of organizational members but of the organizer himself or herself. Seeing the homeless housed, or the downtrodden speak with confidence admonishing those in power, or uniting people from a wide variety of cultural and ethnic backgrounds to overcome shared problems are the successes that help conquer burnout. Such victories need to be celebrated. As one developmental organizer told us,

> After every project you must celebrate because you've built yourself up and up and up and all of a sudden when it's done you think, . . . and that's why you have to celebrate it. You have to force yourself into celebrating and saying, "We did a good job." . . . You've got to celebrate. You gotta celebrate every little victory. It's mandatory.

Conference calls and electronic lists enable people to share victories with one another. Knowing that the fight has been won in St. Louis helps motivate the battle in Buffalo.

The Upside of Being a Social Change Professional

> Most social change professionals find their work personally rewarding and satisfying. Organizers are sustained in their jobs by their commitment to the ideals of organizing and by a sense of efficacy in pursuing these ideals. In addition, Chicago organizers are sustained by the more mundane advantages of the job—the joy of "wins," the variety of tasks and skills the job demands, and autonomy and flexibility of determining how to get the job done. (O'Donnell 1995, 8)

Other studies show that pride in bringing about social change remains an important motivator (Sherkat and Block 1997).

We have met individuals who have left the world of banking, of the church, and of the corporate nine-to-five rat race, for the satisfaction of social activism. Social change professionals recognize that they are helping others, moving society, albeit slowly, in a progressive direction, and all the while having fun. They take visible pride when high government officials or bank directors have to stop what they are doing and listen to what ordinary people feel. Working with a homeless and jobless person and then providing a shelter, as well as job training, while at the same time pressuring government to make funds available to help those most in need is as rewarding work as it gets.

But even the daily routine can be fun and rewarding. A social change professional might counsel a victim of predatory lenders, working with other professionals to help the individual reduce her losses, then join with others in a direct action to pressure government to make illegal such economic predation. Just matching wits with those in power can be satisfying. One individual, a street-level organizer and now a developmental activist, described his feelings when negotiating with bankers for projects that benefit poor neighborhoods.

> There's a side of me that loves that shit, cause I could mess with these guys. And I can understand them. I have a mind that works on the math . . . I can sit with Fannie Mae and negotiate them and stuff and I can understand the legal documents in a reasonable amount of time so that you don't get lost with just lawyers controlling it.

Conclusion: Social Change Work as Both a Calling and a Profession

We have described how people become activists by building on the fire in their heart for change and then learning a wide array of practical skills to accomplish their tasks. Activism is both a calling, a dedication to helping others, and a recognition that when faced with social problems we all have a responsibility to act. It is also a proud profession, one with skills and practices learned from others, and one dedicated to bringing about a better society by helping others battle economic and social injustice.

CHAPTER
11 Creating Capacity through Effective Organizational Administration

Progressive organizations focus the energy of large numbers of people on a common task, garner expertise, and sustain an effort over a long period of time. But social change organizations are not magical entities that succeed because their members have high ideals and enthusiasm. Without the knowledge of how to administer a social change organization, little will be accomplished.

There are however no simple set of administrative rules for social change organizations as their structures and purposes vary greatly, from a volunteer neighborhood group with no officers, funded out of pocket, to larger Community Development Corporations (CDCs) that in structure look very much like capitalist businesses. Still, effectively running social change organizations requires understanding ways of

- defining mission
- structuring the organization
- choosing personnel
- managing personnel, tasks, and workflow
- gaining and sustaining funding
- fiscal management
- engaging the environment
- planning and evaluation

Whole courses are taught on each of these separate topics. Here we will provide a sketch of what each entails, emphasizing those aspects that are most important for building capacity within social change organizations.

Defining the Mission

Social change organizations are *mission driven*, not *profit driven*. A mission might be to give voice to a neighborhood, or to house the homeless, or to fight for speech rights, or to preserve the Community Reinvestment Act (CRA), or to restore quality and affordable shopping. Early on, those who set up an organization agree on its purpose, its mission, sometimes just orally, but sooner or later put it into writing. A small startup voluntary organization with which Herb Rubin works has as its mission:

> The DeKalb County Housing Action Coalition (DCHAC) advocates for quality, accessible housing for families and individuals with a variety of income levels and needs.

The mission statement of the National Community Reinvestment Coalition (NCRC), a national organization with a multimillion dollar budget and staff of over two dozen

> is to increase fair & equal access to credit, capital, and banking services/products because discrimination is illegal, unjust, and detrimental to the economic growth and well-being of our society. NCRC seeks to support and provide long-term solutions which include providing tools to building community and individual net worth. (www.ncrc.org/whoweare/index.php)

Mission statements evolve as organizational members better understand what must be accomplished to achieve shared goals. An organization whose initial mission was to lobby for funds for housing, over time might change its mission to build homes. To make sure the organization's mission reflects what it is now about, organization members and leaders should periodically convene retreats (see below) to reflect on the matter.

Structuring the Organization

Structure refers to the legal form of an organization; whether or not it has separate sections for each task, or the ways in which board, staff, and volunteers relate to one another. Does the organization require a membership department, public relations section, or a congressional liaison? What types of decisions should the President or Executive Director be allowed to make, and which decisions should require working with a committee or obtaining board approval?

The core principle in establishing a structure is to allow it to emerge slowly. Structure should never be imposed from the get-go simply to imitate another organization. Too cumbersome a structure can turn off organizational members and slow down actions, but too little can create disorder. No one approach is always necessarily right or wrong. The question to be continually asking is: does the current structure enable the organization to accomplish its goals and do so in a way that empowers?

An early decision about structure is whether or not to *incorporate as a not-for-profit corporation*. If the organization plans to be around for a while, it makes sense, as incorporation turns the organization into a legal person that can own, buy, and sell property, contract debt, sign contracts, and receive and spend money, rather than each being the responsibility of individual members. Incorporation is a relatively simple and inexpensive process and is usually handled by a state government at the office of the Secretary of State. In the application, the group describes its purposes, provides an address, notes the names of the Board of Directors and officers, and chooses a unique name. Sometimes incorporation papers also specify bylaws—the rules to be followed in running the organization.

Once incorporated, most community and social production groups are eligible to apply for a tax-exempt status under Section 501(c)(3) of the Internal Revenue Code. However, nonprofits that are primarily involved in political work and undertake substantial amounts of lobbying are not eligible for 501(c)(3) designation. Usually it takes a while for the IRS to approve the 501(c)(3) status, but startup organizations can find a temporary home as part of another nonprofit that has received the 501(c)3 designation, perhaps as a project of a local church. Such tax exempt organizations do not have to pay federal taxes on income collected for the approved charitable or social purchases, while donors can receive a tax break when they contribute. Further, many private foundations restrict their giving to tax exempt organizations while professionals such as lawyers and accountants are ethically obligated to provide some pro bono (free) services to not-for-profit organizations. There is an important catch: a 501(c)(3) organization is not allowed to spend a substantial amount of its time in direct efforts to influence legislation, but it is easy enough to set up a sister organization that focuses on political work.

As an organization grows or as its tasks expand, the next question is whether to set up a formal structure with separate sections, each responsible for specific tasks. Organizations interested in fair housing issues probably need a legal staff; those constantly involved in outreach efforts might want to have a public relations section. If owning property is a goal, a division that manages the property is needed. To survive over the long run, someone needs to do fund raising, membership recruitment and similar matters, again suggesting sections within the organization.

An important question is how much to structure an organization around *functions* and how much around *specific projects* or campaigns. A function is a task like accounting, fund raising, publicity, or research that is done almost no matter what the project or campaign, while a project or a campaign is an effort to accomplish a specific goal such as defending immigrants' rights or building a community supermarket. If the organization is set up by projects, each project team can be separately funded, but there might be unnecessary overlap (i.e., each housing project does not require its own accountant). On the other hand if all work is done by functional experts, no one develops the in-depth knowledge about a particular project.

As organizations grow and take on multiple tasks, new sections are added, perhaps with one concentrating on organizing community members, another on building homes, a third on managing rental property, and a fourth on running a job training program. Or a 501(c)3 that wants to actively lobby might want to spin off an affiliated group to do the lobbying. Social production organizations often partner with for-profits to build homes or set up community enterprises (see Chapter 20). By law, these partnerships must be for-profit businesses in which the nonprofit becomes a stockholder. While setting up subsidiaries can be complicated, doing so has advantages. For instance, neighborhood groups might attempt risky projects—renting to the very poor or helping to establish micro-enterprises—that can lose money but if these risky projects are done within a subsidiary organization, the parent organization can still survive even if the business goes under.

As structural complexity increases, the time and energy required for coordination can get out of hand. In these situations, an organization should spin off separate affiliated organizations to handle specific tasks. Neighborhood organizations might spin off a community development corporation to focus on home building, while the neighborhood group concentrates on neighborhood organizing and direct action campaigns.

Personnel

In the smallest neighborhood organizations, personnel are all volunteers, responsibilities are assigned on a case-by-case basis, and decisions are made by the collectivity. At the other extreme, in large national organizations as well as community economic and social production organizations, much of the personnel structure parallels that of conventional firms—a board of directors in charge, a chief executive officer, vice-presidents and division heads.

In all incorporated organizations, the Board of Directors is legally responsible for the organization. Depending on state laws and the wording of the incorporation papers, boards adopt the goals of the organization, hire and fire the chief officers, and sometimes have a say on other personnel matters. The board approves the organization's budget and is the legal signatory for most contracts, though, at times, this authority can be delegated.

Boards in smaller neighborhood types of organizations are more like committees of the local leadership set up to determine overall policy and hire a professional organizer who runs the organization on a daily basis. Either the membership as a whole or the board itself will elect from the membership a President who becomes the public face of the organization, working closely with the organizer. The boards of economic and social production organizations also set overall policy and hire a professional to run the organization, handling budgets and staffing matters while suggesting projects to the board. In social service organizations, this professional is often called an Executive Director, while in Community Development Corporations, the title President is used to show the community that a CDC is a business, albeit a community-controlled one.

Major differences in personnel do occur between social change and more conventional organizations. First, the position of organizer itself has no real analogy in conventional firms. Next, unlike business firms or government offices, social change organizations "employ" large numbers of volunteers and so have to work out ways of balancing the responsibilities of the unpaid volunteer activists with those of the paid CEO and professional staff. Encouraging participation among volunteers, yet ensuring that staff expertise is not ignored, is a core challenge of personnel management in social change organizations.

Another common position in social change organizations is that of *interns*, short-term employees, usually college or graduate students, often not paid, though sometimes receiving a living stipend. Individuals train as organizers by interning, a modern-day apprenticeship, but interns do take on major responsibilities as many are involved in doing background research work using data on social problems while others orchestrate action campaigns or coordinate lobbying efforts. Activist organizations will capitalize upon the enthusiasm and college training of their interns, assigning them to front line work.

Leadership Tensions

Personnel problems need to be recognized even in progressive organizations. For instance, many social change organizations are the creation of a single, dedicated individual, or perhaps a small group of activists. Yet, for effective long-term functioning, the organization has to pull away from this dependence upon the initial leader or leaders.

The publicity that charismatic leaders receive makes the public aware of the issues on which the organization works. However, when an organization is led by dominant individuals, the public may attribute successes solely to the personality of this individual. Still, charismatic leaders are important. Through the force of their personalities and their courage, these creative leaders frame social and political issues in ways that gain attention and transform the membership by impressing on them the importance of assuming a collective responsibility. This comes about as

> followers feel trust, admiration, loyalty, and respect toward the leader, and they are motivated to do more than originally expected to do. A leader can transform followers by: (1) making them more aware of the importance of the task outcomes, (2) inducing them to transcend their own self interest for the sake of the organization . . . Transformation leaders influence followers by arousing strong emotions and identification with the leader, but they may also transform followers by serving as a coach, teacher, and mentor. (Yukl 1989, 211)

Leaders coordinate complicated social action campaigns and take responsibility for sequencing what is done and making the adjustments needed to quickly respond to changing events. Someone must decide on the spot what to do if the police unexpectedly start arresting the demonstrators. In social production organizations, leaders have the drive and reputation that enable them to better convince funders to pay for a project that the membership wants rather than simply carry out the funders' agenda.

But when leaders who become CEOs treat their organizations as personal fiefdoms, failure is almost certain, when the founding leader steps aside. Care must be taken early on to assure a smooth leadership succession and to set up structures, perhaps through full membership meetings, in which the leader is made accountable to the larger group.

Boards of Directors

The Board of Directors are the governors of an organization and are legally responsible for what it does. Selection of board members must be done with care to preserve a democratic culture and should fairly reflect the membership of the organization or the constituencies it serves, especially in balancing its ethnic and gender composition. Yet, in economic and social production organizations that require funds to build complicated projects, having upper status professionals on the board can be advantageous, as they bring expertise as well as assurance to foundations that the projects will be managed well. Balance is once again required between expertise and democratic involvement.

Efforts should be in place to ensure the board represents people from different social, economic, political, and ethnic constituency groups. As one approach, the Board of the Dudley Street Neighborhood Initiative mandated representation from each ethnic group in the community. A national advocacy organization whose current board includes street activists, CDC directors, fair housing advocates, and even an academic, put out a notice for new board members suggesting that they satisfy the following criteria:

> Power and Influence (movers and shakers, widely known)
>
> Geography (currently underrepresented on the board, see our website for current members)
>
> Dedication to Economic Justice
>
> Gender (we are seeking more women)
>
> Time to Serve
>
> Past engagement with (the social change organization)

Board members must agree with the purposes of the organization. They must be prepared to ask staff difficult questions to make sure that the organization stays on target and is effective in its undertakings. In addition, in looking for board members, the following questions should be kept in mind:

1. Is the person really interested in the organization and willing to spend time to help?
2. Does the person have some skill or resource that is badly needed by the organization? Skills might be technical ones such as accounting or the law, but they also might involve the ability to network with community members.
3. Might there be a possible conflict of interest? Housing development organizations might think twice before inviting the head of a construction firm on the board, if that firm will be seeking work from the group.
4. Will the proposed board member help lend legitimacy and visibility to the organization? Political notables and successful business people often provide outsiders with a comfort level with the organization but care is needed lest such individuals try to take over the group. Established clergy from neighborhood churches can provide legitimacy with less fear of co-optation.
5. Are some board members personally familiar with the tasks to be accomplished? Tenants' organizations often choose tenants as members of their boards, while advocates for those with disabilities make sure people with those disabilities are on the board.

6. Are there members on the board to represent gender, racial, ethnic, geographic, or interest groups in the community? Some organizations reserve a few seats for constituency groups.
7. Are members willing to engage in out-of-the-box thinking? In these conservative political times, boards of several action organizations have shown a daring willingness to allow the organizations they supervise to become more active politically.

Nonprofit boards are rarely paid, even though the members have great responsibilities and involvement can require trips away from home and overnight stays. At the very least, organizations should have ways of paying the out-of-pocket expenses of board members, though those from corporations or foundations in turn should not accept the money.

It is one thing to think about the criteria for choosing individual board members, another to think how these people might work together. In less successful boards, the diversity of membership increases conflict and misunderstanding (Daley and Angulo 1994, 175). But if everyone thinks the same way, major problems may be missed, and new solutions may be overlooked. Good boards develop a dynamic in which people play off each other's strengths and complement one another's knowledge.

Staff, particularly Presidents or Executive Directors, might prefer a captured board, that is, a group of people who go along with what the staff recommends. While having curmudgeons on the board is no fun, having sheep does not serve the organization well. An active board should ask hard-nosed questions on projects, on how money is being spent and force the staff to look beyond day-to-day problems to make sure the organization stays on mission.

Personnel Management

Personnel management is about how those higher up in an organization work with employees, volunteers, and board members. In social change organizations, personnel management should be done so as to empower, avoid strict hierarchical decision making, and work out ways of amicably settling differences. With care in hiring to make sure that people share the ideological goals of the organization, supervision can be reduced to a minimum. For instance, organizations such as cooperatives, in which staff feel they are the owners, require fewer supervisors than other organizations (Jackall 1984b).

Quality training programs reduce the need for supervision while improving organizational output. Supervisors need to be cautious to make sure that when they provide advice they do so in ways that avoid demeaning people. Evaluation should entail public praise, especially the sort that lets people know they are contributing toward organizational goals, rather than blame people for failures.

When highly motivated people work together on controversial tasks, conflict is almost inevitable. People quarrel about who will get limited resources, disagree about priorities and may resent others whom they think are not carrying out their share of the work. In neighborhood organizations, conflicts can be exacerbated by underlying racial, ethnic, or religious tensions. When quarrels do occur over substance, someone with good mediation skills can help, talking to both sides, and trying to find a position that will be acceptable to everyone. If staff know how limited the budget is, they might not squabble over funds they know are not there.

Larger organizations with a division structure can experience tension between those working on separate tasks. Sections in the organization that do physical renewal projects employ people with very different world views than those who do direct action organizing. The former use up the largest amount of money, yet organizers often wonder if social production work is really the way to bring about needed change. Such situations are handled through developing complementary tasks, having advocates fight for funds for housing, and organizers setting up tenants and owners associations, while the Economic and Social Production (ESP) people work to build the projects. Another bridging mechanism involves setting up *project teams* in which staff members from different divisions work together on a particular project.

Working with volunteers can be problematic, as volunteers come and go, while organizations require constant steady efforts. A solution, often tried, is to assign volunteers to less central tasks in which one person can easily substitute for another, but unfortunately, doing so does little to empower the volunteer. Another response is to assign volunteers to less complicated tasks but ones that clearly contribute to the broader goal. For example, having volunteers collect signatures on letters that are then presented to officials is both straightforward yet empowering.

Interns are increasingly a valuable resource for social change organizations. Unlike volunteers who work part time over a long period of time, interns are full time employees, though for a designated period of time. In the past, some organizations treated interns as free labor to do boring work—a waste of both time and resources. Today, the better-managed social change groups treat interns in the same way they would handle new employees: assigning meaningful tasks—often those related to their college training—but making sure the work is done in close association with a mentor. In national organizations, interns are often used to co-author technical reports on the problems that the organization combats, doing so along with the organization's professional research staff.

Fund-Raising

While smaller neighborhood organizations can survive on contributions or member dues, most organizations need to obtain other funds. But fund-raising is difficult and takes time away from campaigns or projects. Further, in seeking funds, organizations might face a *mission drift* in which the organization ends up carrying out the agendas of the funder rather than its own. To raise money requires an overall strategy on what is needed, who can provide it, and, most important, how to obtain the money in ways that support, not distort, the organization's own mission.

Types of Money

All money is not the same. It is possible for an organization to have millions put aside for a housing project yet not enough in its checking account to pay the light bill. Dues and unrestricted contributions can be used for almost any organizational purpose while using money obtained to do job training to pay for a neighborhood organizer is illegal.

Money can differ in terms of its proposed use. *Operating funds*—also known as organizational *overhead*—are for ordinary, continuing daily expenses (salaries of staff, rent, light, heat, postage, and insurance). *Project funds* pay for the costs of a specific service or activity such as providing counseling, heat assistance, or the capital expenses for housing. But matters are more complicated. Project money often includes some funds for overhead, and permanent employees of an organization can be paid from a project budget if they are working on that project. To further complicate matters, established organizations often undertake several projects at once—perhaps building affordable apartments, setting up a supermarket, and providing job training, with each project funded from a separate project grant. In such situations, the organization has to *segregate* the money for the separate projects, not using the job training fund, for instance, to pave the parking lot of the supermarket.

Capital funds are meant for one-time expenses of items that will last a long time, such as an automobile or purchasing the building in which the organization resides. Usually organizations save for capital purchases and in doing so must resist the temptation of dipping into capital funds to pay for ordinary, operating expenses. *Seed money* are funds provided by foundations or government to begin a project, for instance to buy the land for housing, before all the money is in hand for doing the entire project.

Government and foundations are reluctant to pay for core operating expenses. First, such expenses never end, and second, government or foundation officials have nothing to show their bosses, politicians, or foundation board what was accomplished. While obtaining project money is always competitive, doing so is easier than obtaining operating funds, since a physical project provides bragging rights to supportive politicians or foundation officials.

Money is received in different ways. *Contributions* are gifts usually from individuals and at times from corporations; *dues* are what members pay to join, sometimes with an escalating scale, with poorer individuals paying less. *In-kind* contributions are gifts, usually of material items, but sometimes of personnel, to help the organization. A corporation might provide an in-kind gift of a computer system or an older vehicle, while a church might donate its services of to help set up the organization. Funds from *contracts* are received when the organization signs a legal document promising to provide a service or undertake a task, paid for by government, or at times by business. A *grant* is a sum of money given by foundations, or government, and occasionally by a rich individual, to accomplish a specific task, though at times it can be used for general overhead or even the salaries of the organizers. Contracts and grants overlap, but contracts tend to specify more how the task is to be done than do most grants which often indicate the ends to be achieved. *Loans and mortgages* are borrowed funds often secured by physical property. *Generated revenues* are monies the organization earns on its own, from rents from homes, or profits made from *enterprises*, for instance, stores, owned by the organizations.

Dues and contributions are the most flexible of funds and can be used for almost any organizational purposes. Contracts are the least flexible, and how they are to be used is carefully spelled out in writing. Grants are closer to contracts, though at times grants are made by progressive foundations that are for general operating costs, allowing great flexibility in their use.

Concerns about Fund-Raising

Fund-raising can create problems that need to be anticipated. Organizations that ought to be allies might compete for the same pot, while fund raising in general takes time away from accomplishing an organizational mission. Further, in the search for funds *mission drift* takes place in which the organization alters what it does depending on what it is that government or the foundations are willing to support. Fund-raising is about raising money to accomplish the mission your organization is set up to do, not just chasing the money. Organizations that go from grant to grant changing their work to satisfy what funders are willing to pay for do not bring about sustained change.

Co-optation is an ever-present danger. In the search for funds the social action organization pulls its punches. For example, economic justice organizations solicit and receive funds from banks, even though some banks are the very causes of the problems the social change groups are battling. These organizations have to ask themselves: if they can take money from a bank for a housing project or to support a financial literacy program, can they still be able to protest against the bank if it is not complying with CRA regulations? One approach is to seek out money from a variety of sources, so that no one funder can dominate the social change organization.

Both mission drift and co-optation can occur in subtle ways. For example, funders often decide which organizations to support on the basis of whether an organization is staffed in ways that make the granter feel comfortable (DiMaggio and Powell 1991, 73; Meyer and Rowan 1991). A funder might require that a community group hire an accountant, a person trained to push for efficiency as well as caution, who might object to some of the riskier projects required to help those in need. Or funders might insist on having only a professional staff. For example, battered women's shelters were initially staffed by trained volunteers but funders forced the hiring of professional counseling staff as a condition of providing grants (Schecter 1982, 107–08).

Getting the Money

Funding sources include (synthesized from Flanagan 1982; Klein 1996; Seltzer, Klein, and Barg 2001):

    membership dues

    money obtained by canvassing communities

    personal contributions from community members, wealthy people, and board members

    fund raisers, special events

    private companies including banks

    labor unions

religious groups

community charities and federated fund-raising organizations

support organizations such as organizing or financial intermediaries

government

foundations

profits from owned enterprises

Obtaining the money is an ongoing activity of the social change organization that requires mastering a whole set of administrative skills from record keeping to learning how to write a grant proposal.

Much of fund-raising is a personal enterprise, a one-on-one encounter in which the organization's needs are described and money requested. In neighborhoods being organized, *canvassers* go door-to-door, talking about issues and asking individuals one by one to join the organization and pay a membership fee. In seeking contracts, bureaucratic staff or politicians often are aware of the organization and have impressions of its capabilities. Banks seem impersonal but in practice loans are issued by a banking officer with whom the organization might have worked out a previous relationship. Foundations are not some impersonal machines but rather are staffed by *program officers* who take learning about the capabilities of applicant organizations as part of their jobs and themselves have ideas on what projects to try. How personal factors can affect fund raising can be seen in the story told to Herbert Rubin by an activist seeking funds for a startup neighborhood improvement organization:

> We were operating voluntary, had a free office over there. I was living on love. And, we couldn't get funded. I would go to all kinds of funding sources, . . . I wrote proposal after proposal, no one would touch us. We didn't fit in social service. We didn't fit in housing. We wanted to do a shopping center. . . .
>
> Got turned down by all of them. . . . Finally, I remember it was December. I was extremely pregnant, I was trudging around taking buses, I looked just pitiful . . . I mean being pitifully pregnant is the best fund raising technique but I can't do that every year . . . I remember I went to the [major community foundation] and they are known to be innovative and they take risks. . . . And, I told him my story and he asked me all kinds of questions. And, I said, "I don't know." We were so dumb. And, I was honest, I don't know but we will figure it out. And, they agreed to give me a $10,000 start up grant.

Personally interacting with program officers, government funders, and those who make decisions in banks and businesses is important as doing so enables them to assess your capability, enthusiasm for the task, and learn that your organization can do what it promises to do.

Obtaining Funds from Members.   *Membership dues* are the most flexible form of money usually coming with no strings attached but taking a lot of time to raise as money must be obtained person-by-person. Still this type of fund-raising is empowering as canvassers get to meet individuals, learn about their problems, and work with community members on ideas for solutions and, as activists say, "fund-raising is organizing" (O'Donnell, Becket, and Rudd 2005, 15). A *canvasser* is a member of the organization, often on its staff, who goes door-to-door to describe the organization, talk about shared problems, solicit funds, and sign up new members. Dues are set at a level that members can afford, though often there are special categories for individuals who have more disposable money.

In canvassing, activists wear something identifying their organization, show up at reasonable times, and, when possible, send out a note saying that they will be coming around. Once greeted at the door, the canvasser presents his or her name, the organization's name, its purpose, its accomplishments, the nature of the problem the organization is now confronting, and how the person being canvassed can help, especially by joining and paying dues.

For national organizations raising money from members must be done by telephone or through mailings, or, increasingly, through the Internet. Appeals made to current members and contributors should begin with thanks for past support as well as some indication of what the organization has accomplished. Then future work should be explained by focusing on an issue that has gotten media attention. For people already members of the organization, the e-mail or snail mail or telephone solicitation also will contain requests to take some political action, such as contacting a congress person or sending an enclosed card demanding that a company stop polluting. Many people will not give out credit card numbers, so phone solicitors coordinate their work with mailers who quickly send out a clearly labelled pledge card and postage-paid return envelope. E-mail appeals are often linked to a website that provides useful information for those who care about the issue at hand, providing information and reinforcing commitment to the cause.

Personal contributions above and beyond dues payments are also sought. Board members are often asked to contribute or request contributions from friends and business associates. Knowing how to ask is important, and standard fund-raising books provide a wealth of ideas. For instance:

1. People give to people. Ask in person.
2. The best people you can ask for money are those who already have given money. Keep complete records of your donors.
3. People cannot respond unless you tell them what you want. Always ask for a specific amount or item. Be enthusiastic, optimistic, and bold. You get what you ask for.
4. People who ask for money become better givers. People who give money become better askers.
5. People want to back a winner. Be proud of your organization, what you do, and how you do it. Success breeds success!
6. More people mean more money and more funds. Find a job for every volunteer. Make it more fun to be on the inside and participating than on the outside and looking in.
7. People want recognition. Send thank-you notes! (Flanagan 1982, 170–71)

Skilled fund-raisers know why people contribute—because they agree with what the organization is doing, they care about the community, they feel better about themselves, and perhaps want their name to be recognized as a concerned person (Seltzer, Klein, and Barg 2001, 159–61).

Special Events as Fund Raising.   Another way of obtaining funds is through sponsoring *special events*, such as fairs, art festivals, pot luck paid dinners, and concerts (especially when the entertainers volunteer their services). As these events require tremendous effort on the part of organization members diverting work away from the organization's core mission, we feel that they should only be held when the event is directly connected to mission. A wildlife preservation organization can collect fees for leading canoe tours down a lonely river, both making money and showing others the wonders that are being protected. For neighborhood organizations special events—a street fair containing ethnic foods, booths with art, jewelry, or clothes made by community members, and ethnic music—can symbolize the cultural richness and integration within the community and both raise funds and strengthen local bonds.

In-Kind Support.   Requesting in-kind support from local businesses, religious groups, and labor unions is another way of obtaining revenue. Businesses can donate functioning but older office equipment and businesses, religious groups, and unions often have space in their building they are willing to share. Some organizations will allow their employees to work for a nonprofit while still receiving pay from the home organization.

Raising Funds from Enterprises.   Some social change organizations set up their own profit-making enterprises hoping money can be earned to pay for core expenses, activism, and social services. Doing so, however, is a mixed bag (Seltzer, Klein, and Barg 2001, 341). At times, enterprises do pay off. For instance, New Communities Corporation, a CDC in Newark, N.J., earned thousands of dollars in profits from its partnership with PathMark Supermarkets from a jointly owned store. But later on when other profit-making ventures failed, New Communities lost millions of dollars. Studies describe how social activist groups have made money from landscaping services, running malls, sponsoring industries that refurbish goods, setting up community restaurants, and similar smaller ventures. The best enterprises are linked to the organizational mission, for example, an organization training people for jobs can then hire them as employees of businesses it owns (Shore 2003).

But ventures run by social change organizations are risky and can distract from the organization's core mission (Seltzer, Klein, and Barg 2001, 343). Projects fail and if the activity appeared to be profitable, a private sector firm probably would have already been doing it. Previously, successful neighborhood organizations such as ESCHAC in Milwaukee and CDCs such as ECI in Indianapolis lost so much money in commercial endeavors that they had to fold.

Our advice is as follows. If the mission of the organization is to provide a service or to do economic renewal in a neighborhood it might want to try to make a profit with ventures that fit into the core mission. Linking a job training program to a business owned by the social change organization or selling produce grown by a community food cooperative complements the mission of the organization. But to choose to start a venture simply to make a profit is likely to distract from the mission and probably not make any money.

Foundation Grants, Government Contracts, and Grants. Foundations and government grants are the major sources for larger chunks of money. We briefly described foundations in Chapter 6 as nonprofit, set up to hand out money for charitable purposes; we will discuss their structure further in Chapter 13. Over the years major general purpose foundations such as the Ford Foundation, Rockefeller, the John D. and Catherine T. MacArthur Foundation, Aspen, and Annie Casey, among others, have provided money for social services, less often for community renewal, and on occasion, for advocacy and direct action organizations. A few billionaires such as George Soros, acting through a personal foundation, have supported activist social change organizations. For smaller social change organizations or those most focused on neighborhoods, community-based public foundations (Cohen 2004b) do provide support, for instance, the Liberty Hill Foundation has been a patron of social activists in Los Angeles.

> [T]he Living Wage campaign in Los Angeles . . . would not have happened without the seed grant support from Liberty Hill; the creation of the $100 million housing trust fund in Los Angeles with support from Liberty Hill to core housing activists, the successes in labor organizing . . . the success of the Los Angeles Alliance for a New Economy . . . and many more. (Cohen 2004b, 27)

In Chicago the Wood Foundation has supported progressive, activist organizing efforts (O'Donnell, Becket, and Rudd 2005). Unfortunately, such efforts are still small compared to the amounts foundations spend in support of cultural events or the funds conservative foundations provide to those who battle against progressive change (Cohen 2004a).

Foundations are most likely to support visible physical projects, or social services in which the number of clientele served can be counted, and least likely to support general operating costs. Money is most likely for demonstration grants provided to well-known and successful social change organizations that are willing to work on projects that fit into the designated programs of the foundations; the hardest money to get is operating support for startup groups. Fortunately, foundations do provide money for general organizing purposes, with about two-thirds of organizing being paid for through such grants, though the sums are small compared to the needs (O'Donnell, Becket, and Rudd 2005).

Unfortunately, operating funds are hard to obtain and foundations are reluctant to support social mobilization work. As Rick Cohen indicates, community development funding at best accounts for 4 percent of grant making, and civil rights and social action maybe 2 percent, while in recent years operating support from foundations has dropped from 18 percent to 7 percent of the budgets of progressive organizations (National Neighborhood Coalition 2005). To increase the chances of obtaining money, some activists have set up their own fund-raising entities that collect money and distribute it to social change groups. There are almost 200 such alternative funds that distribute several hundred million dollars to progressive causes.

Foundation support for projects rarely is provided for a long enough period of time, allowing perhaps three years or less for solving problems that have developed over many decades. Reports issued by the National Center for Responsive Philanthropy point out that foundations tend to set the agendas that local organizations end up following, though occasionally foundations will be responsive to ideas put forth by community advisory boards. Rick Cohen argues social change and community groups should pressure foundations to increase funding for advocacy efforts (National Neighborhood Coalition 2005).

Literally hundreds of grant and contract programs are available from Uncle Sam. Some are housed in obvious places: the Department of Housing and Urban Development funds housing and urban renewal programs, the Department of Education funds school efforts, or even the Department of Justice funds neighborhood watch programs or programs to help returnees from prison, and community service money comes from the Department of Health, Education, and Welfare. But more esoteric programs exist, for instance, the Treasury has complicated tax provisions that allow community organizations that work with businesses to indirectly obtain money for housing or economic development programs.

Though most government money is for specific physical projects or for providing a contractual service, some is available for general operating support of community organizations. For instance, a Community Development Block Grant can be used for the operating expenses of community groups that have a neighborhood focus. For example, Minneapolis has used CDBG funds in each of its officially designated neighborhoods to set up community-based planning organizations. In Chicago, starting with the progressive Mayor Washington, numerous neighborhood organizations were designated as delegate organizations, receiving money for undertaking city services but also being allowed to use the money for general overhead expenses. Unlike some foundations that allow very little money for organizational overhead, government programs do recognize the need to pay for overhead, though strictly limit the amounts through predetermined formulas.

Government and foundation grants are obtained by first learning what funds are available and seeing if the purposes mesh with what the organization wants to do. If so, then the next stage is an informal inquiry to talk with program officers, people who handle the applications, to make sure your organization really understands what it is they are seeking. Then a formal procedure begins in which an application is filled out (often taking weeks and weeks of work), submitted, and then reviewed by a board that ranks the requests received. Getting contracts is a bit different with a more focused application in which the organization answers what is known as a *Request for Proposal* (*RFP*) in which the organization describes how it will provide the service and its capacity for doing so.

Understanding how to get money from government is far from simple, in fact it is sometimes quite Byzantine, hence the frequent use of grant writers to prepare an application. Some government money comes directly from Uncle Sam, other money from the state, and some from cities or counties; often, though, state and local grants are pass-through funds from programs paid for by Uncle Sam. To further complicate matters, some money comes as grants—that is, the money is used for a task or project chosen by the social change organization though from a government program that supports that type of task; while other funds are allocated as *contracts*—agencies negotiate with government (sometimes after a bidding process) to provide the service the government wants. At times, when social change action organizations become government contractors they are little more than extensions of the government, providing a useful service, but rarely being about empowerment. Governmental contracts are issued on a competitive basis, but with the competition often based on a fairly rigid formula. So agencies with longer histories and better balance sheets serving the very poor are more likely to get a contract, for instance for heating assistance, than a newer group working with a slightly wealthier population.

Several ideas need to be kept in mind when seeking out either foundation or government grants. Both foundation program officers and government officials have rather fixed ideas on what they would like to fund, sometimes quite specifically stating these in a program announcement. At a federal level, it is pretty hard to persuade individuals to change priorities. With foundations, activists can talk with program officers and in these conversations communicate what should be funded. In both cases, it makes most sense before formally applying for a grant to figure out what might be acceptable. Phone calls, or even visits to the granting agencies by appointment, are fine. Or, take advantage of the publicity that government funders or foundations put out in which they describe successful proposals.

Keep in mind that competitive federal grants, in particular, are scored on many different criteria, with the highest scoring proposals winning. Usually the major category with the most points is on the ideas for what your organization plans to do. But many other scoring categories can be included—the poverty of the neighborhood you serve, whether or not your organization has staff with certain expertise, among many other items. It's possible to have a clever idea and the wrong demographics, or a clever idea and not include enough background material in an application and therefore not be funded.

Grant seeking and writing is complicated and time consuming. Below we describe how to find some information on your own, but having an expert do the work might be a better approach. Larger social change organizations employ full-time grant writers, while consultants can be hired by other organizations. These people keep on top of what is being funded at the present time, know the key phrases to use in the application, and are careful not to skip parts of the application.

Requesting Grants from Foundations.   To learn more about foundation funding, consult the web pages of the individual foundations and explore information published by the Foundation Center (www.fdncenter.org). This center puts outs lists of foundations, their objectives, how much money they have, and how to make contact with them. The Grantsmanship Center publishes the Grantsmanship Center News which provides information on deadlines, how to manage grants, and ways of applying.

In applying, remember foundations don't want to bother with irrelevant applications, so they are forthright in their descriptions of what they will fund and will answer in a phone call or in a brief letter if a project is relevant, or you can learn what they fund by visiting a foundation's web page where more likely than not they will describe the projects they are now funding. Wise applicants pay close attention to documents put out by the foundation explaining their purposes before wording a proposal, but close attention is required because what foundations are willing to fund changes frequently.

After checking to see if the foundation is receptive, the organization prepares a formal written proposal, perhaps with support from a consultant. The proposal explains the problem faced, how the organizational effort will solve the matter, how much it will cost, and precisely the ways in which the money will be spent. In addition, proposals describe the capacity of the organization to handle such a project. Prior success in getting grants and carrying out projects is one way of demonstrating capacity.

In writing a proposal, try to take the perspective of the program officers who initially review proposals and then have to convince the boards of the foundations of the proposal's merits. Program officers want to encourage innovative ideas and are usually not afraid of efforts to bring about community change. But they have to sell their ideas to a board, often consisting of upper status people, who are more conservative than they. If the idea can be framed in such a way that it makes the program officer's job easier, it is more likely to be funded.

While there is no surefire way of getting funded, some of the following advice should help:

Preface the proposal with a brief overview of the project's goals, its budget, and procedures for evaluation.

Early in the proposal, clearly discuss the objectives and the plans for achieving these objectives. Funders look for innovative plans. Don't go off the wall with some flight of imagination, but do have a clever twist that will gain attention. A utopian housing scheme in the inner city might be discarded immediately, but proposals that house poor people who have physical disabilities in apartments that have an additional room for their care givers might be treated more seriously.

Provide evidence documenting the problem, but make sure that the evidence speaks to the immediate issues at hand. Funders get bored reading endless statistics showing certain neighborhoods are poor.

Funders are looking for evidence that the organization can actually accomplish what it proposes, so the application has to include a description of the staff, what the organization has achieved, and who has benefited. Take a few sentences to show how prior experiences relate to the present proposal. Having picketed city hall is not appropriate experience for managing a large housing rehabilitation grant, but rehabbing several small buildings might be.

Be precise in the project budget, carefully justifying how resources will be spent, and indicating whether the requested grant funds will be combined with money from other sources. If the foundation or governmental agency accepts the ideas and believes that the organization has the capacity to implement them, the budget becomes the central focus of their evaluation. Too big a budget will make them nervous about the percentage of their funds going to one organization. Too small a budget and they will worry about whether those proposing the activity understand the realities of doing the work.

Describe the contributions of equipment, labor, and cash that the community and members of the organization will provide. Where appropriate, show that work is already underway and has been already successful. Sweat equity—the voluntary contribution of community members' labor—is an important indicator to funders that people are involved. A proposal has a better chance of getting funded if some costs are being covered by other agencies. Describe how the organization will evaluate the project, as evaluations reflect good management and show a determination to improve.

Finally, and especially for innovative projects, indicate how what is learned will be shared with other community groups. With standard projects—a rehabbed house, or a daycare center—funders know what to expect and are satisfied if so many people are housed per dollar, or so many children are cared for at a reasonable price. But innovative ideas may be complicated and costly and are more easily justified as demonstrations, so work out the kinks, and then teach others how to do them. To assure funders they will get this additional advantage, it is useful to build in a dissemination plan that may include sending out reports to other organizations doing similar work, or presentations at conferences, or special workshops.

On occasion, a proposal is presented orally to a panel or the board of a foundation or corporation. In such personal presentations, describe the idea briefly. Even if the organization has submitted a written proposal, assume that the panel has not yet had the time to read it. If board or panel members are interested in the proposal, they will ask questions that will help them justify funding it.

Don't get discouraged if you are turned down, as few organizations get funded every time. Fortunately, foundations and government agencies usually provide feedback on grant requests. Pay attention to these comments when rewriting the proposal. Also keep in mind that there are many agencies and foundations to apply to, so if the idea is sound, just keep rewriting it and sending it out again.

Professional Fiscal Practices

No matter how money is obtained, it is important that it be wisely managed. While the fiscal practices described here may not sound like the heart of social change work, they are vital for keeping an organization alive. Good financial management has immediate payoffs. Organizations that have cash in hand don't have to borrow and appear efficient and honest to potential donors, lenders, and to their own membership. In addition, sound fiscal practices such as audits—legal verification by accountants on how money was spent—are required both by funders and often by the law.

Budgeting and Accounting

The heart of good financial management is a two-step process of budgeting and accounting. Budgeting links revenues to plans for projects and accounting demonstrates that money was spent appropriately and wisely.

A budget is a statement that estimates future revenues and expenditures while describing the allocation of money between tasks. Budgets reflect the reality of actions and of projects and have to be built up step-by-step from details of what is being planned. How many staff members at what cost will the work take? How much will rent be? What are the total costs of running the office—for furniture, computers, printers, photocopy machines, or postage meters? What will the land cost for the housing? the construction? Once capital costs are calculated, what will the long-run operating costs be?

Budgeting for personnel should be realistic and sensitive. Professional organizers and staff members of nonprofits deserve medical coverage and should receive contributions to their retirement. But a social change organization has to balance the number of personnel with the funds available. Hire too many and funds run out; too few and work doesn't get done.

In addition to costs for planned projects and personnel, all organizations need to budget for contingencies—emergencies that are hard to predict such as broken equipment or unexpected lapses in funding. In addition, budgeted funds should be put aside as seed money to help jump start future projects. Before a foundation will provide money, the organization may have to demonstrate the feasibility of an idea, by doing a market survey, for example, or demonstrating the extent of the underserved population, or hiring a consultant to evaluate the project's feasibility.

Budgets are calculated in terms of service levels or cost packages. Some costs go up in a straight, linear way. Suppose it costs $1,000 to de-lead an apartment; for each grand of money one apartment can be done. But other activities can only be done as a total package and either you have the money for them or you don't. It is hard to rehabilitate half a building and leave the rest to the rats. Many projects go up in a linear way until a threshold has been reached. With a kitchen in place, the cost of providing extra hot meals depends only on whether there is a little more money for the food, but when a space limit is reached, the organization would need a whole new kitchen to serve any additional meals, with a large increase in costs implied in such an endeavor.

Core to budgeting is making sure that revenues and expenditures are in balance, that is, acting in a fiscally conservative way. The most fiscally conservative approach is to make sure that fixed, re-occurring expenditures are kept below income that the organization is virtually certain to obtain. While a wise approach, doing so might prevent taking vital actions when problems become urgent, for instance if a sudden job loss rapidly increases the number of homeless. Social change organizations have a moral obligation to try to alleviate misery, even if the funds are not immediately at hand. Does it really matter if you have saved your organization and failed at its mission?

Accounting and Cost Control

A bookkeeping system should be started as soon as the organization is set up.

Bookkeeping is simply a way of documenting money received and spent. For a small, informal community group, recording and keeping check stubs might be sufficient. For groups running several programs at once, a more complicated system is required that carefully tracks dollars, reporting on when they came in and where they went, making sure that funds for different projects are kept separate, and that money is on hand prior to the time it must be spent.

Careful accounting allows the organization to figure out where money can be saved. A social change organization can compare its overall expenses to similar organizations and then examine areas in which expenses seem high. Similar cost controls can be applied in projects the organization runs. If heating costs in a home for the elderly seem too high, perhaps it's time to see if it is worth investing in better insulation.

Risk Management

Community organizations, especially those working with volunteers, must be prepared for financial risks that can occur because of accidents, malevolence, or lawsuits. Anticipating such costs is termed *risk management*, a matter handled by purchasing insurance.

What type of insurance to get depends on the mission, though in most cases a general umbrella policy should be obtained to handle unforeseen circumstances. Almost all organizations need routine fire, theft, and liability insurance. Special insurance is required for vehicles used in providing a service such as taking the elderly shopping. For organizations providing support for the abused, health services, or child care, professional malpractice insurance is a must. If some members of the organization handle large amounts of money, they should be bonded. Bonding is a guarantee that if someone runs off with the organization's money, the insurance company will make up the loss. All projects are insured for the property and possible liability.

Insurance can be expensive, especially for small organizations. Fortunately, professional associations of community organizations now offer group rates, somewhat lowering the costs.

Organizational Planning

Planning involves working out what you are going to do, when, and how, while *evaluation* asks if you have succeeded and why or why not. Planning is an iterative process, that is, organizations set up plans, attempt to achieve them, then sit back, figure out what went right or wrong, and then set up new plans.

Once an organization is under way, a structure in place and perhaps a campaign or project attempted, the time has come for staff, members, board, and volunteers to step back and ask what they actually plan to do by working out a *strategic plan*, that is, an explicit, written statement of what the organization intends to do, why, and how. Strategic planning includes careful examination of and often a reformulation of the mission statement for the organization.

The first pass at strategic planning should come after an initial shakedown period in which those in the organization test the possibilities of achieving their initial goals against the reality of practice. Strategic plans are not meant to last forever, probably no more than five years. Periodically, they need to be revised, and if and when an organization seems adrift, projects are failing, staff are quitting, or membership is in decline, it is time to work out another plan.

Strategic plans state the overall broader goals to be accomplished, expanding upon the mission statement. *Goals* are general statements: improving the housing in the community or helping immigrant labor. *Objectives* are more precise indications of what these goals entail—building 100 units of affordable rental housing, and developing 60 units of energy-efficient single family privately owned homes, or setting up a bilingual law clinic, or a job service that protects non-English-speaking individuals from discrimination. Objectives should be measurable so that later on you can see how well they have been achieved.

Strategic planning can be done both in-house—that is, by the organization staff and members—and with the help of a professional planning organization. At board and staff retreats or at membership or committee meetings in larger organizations people brainstorm on what they want the organization to do while reflecting on past successes and failures and examining hard data on what has been accomplished and what has failed. These planning discussions are often held at *retreats* at locations away from the normal place of work and with only one task at hand, talking about the plan.

The resulting ideas are then put into writing in a succinct form, with the overall mission spelled out, goals specified, perhaps in bold print, and then objectives placed as numbered items under each of the separate goals. Once in written form, the document should be circulated to the broader membership, to people and communities served, as well as to the full staff and board for comments. If necessary, an anonymous procedure should be in place to receive comments, but better yet, open meetings with give and take should be set up to dialogue on the issues. Before adoption, either the board, or board-staff, or board-staff-volunteers-members should have a retreat to hash out the final document.

At times, strategic plans seem to disappear onto dusty shelves never to be seen again, at least until the next planning takes place. But if the planning process were done correctly with full inclusion of a wide variety of stakeholders, the planning process itself should secure sufficient buy-in to the overall approach so that literally following the plan step-by-step is of less importance.

Conclusion

In this chapter we presented an overview of organizational administration and highly recommend that those planning social change careers explore these matters in more detail. Effective and efficient organizational administration builds capacity for carrying out campaigns and projects and can be accomplished in ways that empower both organizational members and the communities the organizations serve.

CHAPTER
12 Expanding Capacity through Empowering, Participatory Meetings

Meetings are about expanding collective involvement in social change work. Information shared at meetings increases the competence of people to act. Mobilization meetings help change personal indignation into a willingness to fight together, while providing information on the skills and techniques needed for the battle. Some meetings, rallies, for instance, are themselves an integral part of an action campaign; other meetings, those held at conferences or at annual membership gatherings, create a sense of we-ness by celebrating shared success. More specialized meetings build capacity by presenting knowledge on techniques. Finally, at decision-making meetings organization members and leaders come together to work out action strategies.

Table 12-1 summarizes a variety of meetings that together expand organizational capacity. Before examining the specific meetings in more detail, let us point out principles of carrying out successful meetings that enable participants to reach good decisions, come up with an array of ideas, and learn from each other.

Encouraging Involvement in Meetings by Creating a Flavor of Success

How do good and bad meetings differ? Bad meetings are long and boring. Nothing is accomplished. They are often chaotic and decisions are made even when information is not at hand. Bad meetings alienate people and create a sense of the impossible: How can we defeat them if we can't even run a simple meeting?

Good meetings are exhilarating. They flow from issue to issue in a fast-paced, logical progression and move toward accomplishing goals, whether setting up a community daycare center or leading a protest against a Fortune 500 company. A skilled chairperson ensures democratic participation by following a meaningful agenda set up in advance and enforcing rules that encourage participation. People who attend good meetings feel that they own the outcomes and have a responsibility for carrying them out. Good meetings create an increased sense of unity and possibility: How can anyone stand in our way when we are so strong together?

TABLE 12.1   Types of Meetings

Membership and Beyond	
Full Membership Meeting	A gathering of all organization members to examine what the organization has accomplished, problems the organization faces, and actions to be taken.
Conferences	A gathering, usually held on an annual basis, to share information on topics of shared concern
Plenaries (at Conferences)	A meeting of all those attending the conference to hear about the most pressing problems or to celebrate successes
Mass Assemblies—Rallies, Demonstrations	A display of organizational power in which activists gather together to publicly display concerns (described in Chapter 17)
Training and Instruction	
Training Workshops	A small meeting to provide specialized training either on a peer-to-peer basis or from a (hired) expert
Conference Breakout Sessions	Smaller sessions held at conferences during which peer-to-peer instruction is presented
Decision Making	
Full Membership Meeting	Official decisions—the choice of officers or on major policy changes—are taken up at full membership meetings
Action Committees, Policy Committees	Smaller, working committees that work out what to do about specific issues; decisions often require approval of the membership or of the board
Board of Directors Meeting	Meetings of the governing board of an organization, during which legally binding, authoritative actions can be taken on organizational policy, staff, funding, and other matters
Retreats	A meeting usually of board members, sometimes including senior staff, for open discussion on problematic issues. Often held at a setting away from the normal office of the organization
Interorganizational Sit-Downs	
Strategic Planning and Coordination	Discussion sessions between lead activists in different organizations to share experiences and to determine if coordinated actions should be planned
Cross Sector Partnership Meetings	More formal meetings between organizational activists and foundation, government, or business partners to discuss specific projects

Preparation is required for meetings. Advanced notice of meetings is vital. Better yet, meetings should be held at regularly scheduled times. For local organizations, membership meetings are announced door-to-door, by leafletting a community, mailings, e-notices, through newsletters, and through press releases for radio stations or local newspapers, making it clear that everyone is invited to attend. National meetings are announced through mailings and electronically and are usually held at the same time each year.

Attendance is affected by numerous details. Is the location for the meeting one that will attract individuals from different groups in the neighborhood without turning off others? Some people might be uncomfortable meeting at the Catholic church, while others might feel out of place at the Hispanic Center. Organizational headquarters are usually fine for smaller workshops and decision meetings among activists, but headquarters are too small for membership meetings.

Locations for national meetings require much thought. Some cities are more expensive than others but have amenities that might encourage people to attend. If the purpose of the meeting is to show off what local groups have accomplished, rotating the site between cities is the way to go. But if lobbying is part of the goal, the meeting must be held in either the state or the national capital.

Physical matters are important. If a room is too small, people feel uncomfortable, but if the room is too large and looks empty, it appears that no one cared enough to come. Light furniture is useful, both for setting up and adding more chairs if additional people come to a membership meeting, while in training sessions movable furniture enables people to break up into smaller groups to practice what is being taught. Those setting up the meetings must be able to see flip charts and blackboards. Equipment for PowerPoint and video presentations must be available, as well as food and restrooms. Microphones must be placed throughout the room so that participants can ask questions. For small meetings, having a single table everyone can sit around adds to the feeling of solidarity. If possible, choose a round table without an obvious head position. People who sit opposite one another may act antagonistic, so encourage those who might disagree to sit next to one another.

While it is easier to see and hear the speakers if they are on a raised platform, such an arrangement suggests hierarchy. Instead, if the meeting room has a raised platform, meeting organizers might want to put the podium to one side, and seat part of the audience on the platform. At the initial community meeting of the Dudley Street Neighborhood Initiative, those providing grant funds sat on a platform above the membership and few from the audience seemed involved. The whole flavor of the meeting changed when a community activist grabbed a microphone and turned her back to those on the platform to address the membership.

In bilingual or multilingual communities, it is best if the speakers present their ideas in several languages, alternating which language is presented first. It doesn't matter if the speaker is not terribly skilled in one of the languages; effort counts, and the effort is a mark of respect. Sometimes, however, translators are needed. People from a single language group should sit near one another and have an interpreter in their midst, or better yet have earphones that broadcast a concurrent translation.

If the meeting is going to last for a while, the schedule should include time for sociability. Start off with coffee and a little bit of pleasant chatter. Have frequent breaks, and make sure coffee is available. If possible, try to arrange for people to have the opportunity to eat together sometime during the meeting; don't let everyone go off on their own for lunch; and try not to let people go off together in cliques. Informal mealtime conversations can defuse potential antagonisms.

National meetings almost always have formal workshops and planned periods of sociability. People who have not yet met are encouraged to share a meal. Workshops are interspersed with tours to see what other organizations have accomplished. Sessions can be held in buildings that host organizations have rebuilt, creating an opportunity to meet casually; while driving to the building in a bus provides an opportunity to talk and learn from others. Receptions are set up for late in the day so that people have a chance to socialize and make network connections.

Balancing Openness with Formal Rules

Meetings, especially those of the full membership, can be complicated affairs; so while it is important to maintain a tone of informality, it is also necessary to maintain order and direction. In larger meetings with invited speakers, rules for questions and answers are set up in advance. At membership meetings at which anyone is allowed to speak, microphones should be strategically placed, so that those wishing to comment can line up behind each microphone. Time limits should be placed on presentations, with a moderator there to gently remind people to be brief.

In small workshops, whether training sessions or breakout sessions at conferences, speakers should be clear about whether they will take questions while they speak or if they prefer questions at the end. Planning or decision meetings usually have a chair who can encourage conversation while maintaining order. A person speaks and then finishes, and, rather than having the next person jump right in, people face the chair who nods toward the next speaker. When disagreement is apparent, the chair should try to alternately call on those whose perspectives differ.

When more formality is required, agendas, bylaws, and rules of procedure come into play. Agendas spell out in advance what topics are to be covered. Bylaws and rules of procedure are about regulating who can talk, when, and on what topic. Bylaws promote democratic participation by specifying how often certain types of meetings take place, who can vote and stand for office, and the minimum number of people who must be in attendance for decisions to be made. Procedural rules describe how discussions are to take place, providing a sense of order and fairness in allowing all sides to be presented. The goal is to prevent a few determined souls from dominating the discussion. What types of procedural rules and how strictly bylaws are imposed will vary from organization to organization. The fewer the bylaws the better, so long as those in place ensure fair representation and the inclusion of less dominant members in discussions. Still it makes sense to work out in advance who should be on committees and how committee members are chosen. By lot? Election? By constituency or ethnic group?

At meetings, issues must be fully discussed, different sides aired, and some accommodation reached. But if a very small group feels strongly that its opinions must prevail and disrupts discussion, making every meeting tense, this factionalism will eventually destroy the organization. To reduce the tyranny of a small minority, bylaws might specify a minimum number of members that must be present before business can take place—a quorum—and set that number larger than the size of factional groups. Another bylaw that can reduce unnecessary conflict is the one that allows only final votes on issues that have been included on the agenda that was circulated early on.

Agendas should be widely publicized but have on them only a limited number of items, since slogging through a long list is demoralizing. Agenda items should be linked to actions and not just declarations of intent. Condemning the lack of bilingual education is not enough; instead the items should demand that the school district give special help to students from non-English-speaking homes. Putting new items on the agenda during the meeting for discussion at that same meeting is problematic, because members don't have a chance to think about the issues. Only in real emergencies should organizational leaders add items at the last moment, and then they must include a full explanation of why the rush.

Bylaws, formal meeting rules, and carefully worked out agendas reduce the chance of meetings being so contentious that members don't get a chance to discuss things or fully listen to each other's arguments. Often bylaws are adopted from standard publications such as *Robert's Rules of Order*, though most organizations simplify these detailed rules. For instance, *Robert's Rules* specifies that unless recognized by the chair, people should not speak, except to clarify procedures. Discussions are limited to the content of the motions, with the chair working to ensure that what is said is germane to the topic at hand. In the absence of rules of procedure, it makes sense to follow Robert's Rules, but it is better to work out your own rules that make the membership most comfortable.

To ensure that other matters can be raised, many meetings leave time for expressing general grievances, usually after the formal items on the agenda have been discussed. During these gripe sessions, few limits are placed and the conversation can move from topic to topic. When important issues are raised, the chair should assign it to a committee for further thought, encourage people to meet informally on the topic, and then bring it back to the next meeting as an item on the agenda.

Another crucial set of rules speaks to how final decisions are made, whether through formal voting or consensus discussions. In formal voting, a certain percentage, usually a majority, needs to agree on an issue. For major issues, votes might require a two-thirds majority to pass. In an alternative system—*consensus decision making*—everyone has to agree, more or less, to the proposition on the table before it can pass.

Consensus decision making empowers everyone since anyone can veto a decision. In the full consensus decision-making procedure rather than taking votes, individuals try to persuade each other by explaining their reasoning and then reformulating the proposition until everyone can agree with it. While sounding democratic, consensus decision making can often exclude the less aggressive or allow a very small minority to disrupt a group, leading to no decision being taken at all. As observers have argued:

Consensus voting, where people discuss an issue until a formulation is reached with which everyone agrees is . . . both elitist and undemocratic. It is elitist because consensus meetings can go on for hours—hours that working people and parents do not have. It is undemocratic because it assumes that disagreement is a sign of group weakness rather than actual strength. (Burghardt 1982b, 54)

Fortunately, consensus decision making can be modified to reduce many of its drawbacks. One approach is to allow discussion to continue until almost everyone agrees. Then those who still are not satisfied are asked if "they can live with the decision that the others want." If they say, "yes," the discussion is then ended. Another way is to put a time limit on the discussion and then if no consensus is achieved, use some other procedure such as turning the decision over to a smaller committee.

Meetings with Large-Scale Involvement

Both membership meetings and conferences bring large numbers of people together to reinforce a collective sense of purpose, to handle major issues that require member support, and to rally the troops in action campaigns, while also proving a setting in which peer-to-peer training can occur.

Membership Meetings

General membership meetings (sometimes known as annual meetings or, in neighborhood organizations, community conferences) enable the entire membership to learn what the organization has accomplished, focus attention on crucial, pressing issues, elect officers, and set overall organizational policy. Membership meetings are a chance to show off to the members, potential recruits, and the press what the organization has accomplished.

At the initial membership meetings, participants work out the goals of the new organization and choose temporary officers. Leaders from the community, often those who called the initial meeting, and professional organizers introduce themselves and discuss the problems that motivate setting up the organization. At both initial and subsequent membership meetings, organizers need to be sure to get the names, addresses, and phone numbers of people who attend. Recruitment literature should be made available. It is also important to collect dues, both to receive the money and to reinforce people's commitment to the organization.

At all membership meetings the role of the chair is important. Initially, the chair might be the professional organizer, but as soon as possible an elected leader should take over. This person must have good speaking skills, a touch of humor, and an ability to both inform while arousing emotions. In our multilingual and multicultural society, language skills are a plus. The chair needs to show vision and, by sharing narratives of success, indicate that goals can be accomplished. Speeches should be dramatic, vividly recounting recent battles and earlier victories of the organization, so that those who are new begin to share past experiences.

In established organizations, membership meetings are a time for celebrating victories, discussing progress and the difficulties faced while handling routine business such as elections and the presentation of financial reports. Volunteers are sought for standing committees, new staff introduced, information on how funds are obtained, and what alliances with other social change groups have been formed.

Many organizations are built up of smaller groups—block associations for neighborhood organizations, regional groups for national economic and social production organizations, or state and local coalitions as part of a national coalition organization. Time should be set aside at the membership meeting so those in the separate groups or coalitions can share with others what they have accomplished.

Conferences

Conferences are scheduled meetings meant to accomplish multiple tasks, ranging from technical training and planning campaigns to celebrations of the victories. On occasion, a local organization will arrange for a conference, but for the most part conferences are set up by activist networks, or by the support organizations described in the next chapter. National coalitional organizations will usually hold their regular membership meeting as part of a conference; support organizations will embed training sessions to be held concurrent with the conference.

Conferences contain a wide array of events. At *plenaries*—meetings of the whole—movement notables discuss important successes, or the leader or policy staff describes pressing action to take on legislative or regulatory matters. Some plenaries are about honoring speakers—a politician who has helped the organization or reporters or writers whose work positively framed the movement. *Breakout sessions* (also called workshops or panels) focus on specialized matters with topics varying from how to use a spreadsheet to the current status of proposed legislation, or from doing community analysis to the nuts and bolts of funding economic development projects. Most conferences include awards ceremonies to highlight the exemplars of the field as well as ample opportunities for networking at receptions or at shared meals. Conferences of more activist organizations schedule time for political work—conferences set up by ACORN or NPA usually include a *hit* on the office of a ranking official, while more sedate groups will schedule lobbying visits to Capitol Hill. The board of the organization as well as many of the organization's committees will hold their meetings on the days right before or after the main conference.

Conferences, especially those involving lower-income people, are complicated events requiring much planning and can be expensive. Successful conferences are held at the same time each year so attendees know to schedule them. Organizations set up conference committees and often a local host committee that works with staff (and sometimes paid professional conference coordinators) to handle the thousands of details such as negotiating with hotels about rates, arranging for food, and contacting airlines for special rates. Since the goal of many social change organizations is to empower poorer people, efforts are taken to find the funds to help pay the expenses of lower-income people who want to attend, while general subsidies for the conference are sought from foundation grants, businesses, or banks.

Conferences that develop a reputation for providing informative sessions and exciting speakers draw attendees year after year. Exciting can depend upon the particular conference—an in-your-face activist is exciting by being involved in a direct action while for CRA activists having a bank regulator speak is an attraction. To further encourage people to attend, conference organizers will often package side trips, some recreational, but many relevant to social change work—visiting exciting renewal projects accomplished by members, for instance. In addition, receptions and time prior to hearing speakers during meals is set aside for informal networking, while larger conferences might include amusing events such as a roast, or a session mocking the opponents of the cause.

Successful conferences are integrated around a theme, which usually evokes a current policy problem that becomes a guide for the speeches presented at plenaries. Topics of breakout sessions usually cover a wide range of matters and attempt to balance out technical topics—funding a project or understanding new government regulations with concerns on policy problems; lack of enforcement of CRA or what to do about the re-entry problem of those returning from prisons to poor communities—as well as some sessions about organizational development such as fund-raising. Some workshops are set up to teach the novice, but if attendance is to be maintained, other sessions must be more specialized to interest the more experienced. Larger thematic panels with guest speakers are set up to cover topics of broader interest—the role of foundations in supporting social change, for instance.

Conferences are also about celebration of victories and successes. Awards that highlight successes are presented during the membership meetings or a celebratory meal. Increasingly, at conferences of one organization, sister organizations are praised for their work, and often leaders of sister groups will attend and speak to show that the separate organizations are part of a broader movement.

Conferences are empowering. The narratives of success shared during speeches show the possibilities for change while joining together in lobbying or motivating those involved. Even plenaries can be shaped in ways that empower. For example, at conferences sponsored by NCRC, a coalition of economic justice, fair housing, and CRA advocates, *interactive plenaries* are scheduled. In these sessions, notables whose opinions differ on issues of import to the membership are on the stage at the same time. For example, bankers, bank regulators, and community activists who oppose the indifference of banks are seated next to one another. Microphones are set up and audience members toss questions at the panelists, almost always eliciting a wide variety of contending perspectives. Organizing a session in this way reverses power relations, putting those in the audience clearly in charge.

Instructional Meetings and Sessions

Through a variety of instructional meetings and training sessions (as well as in the schools and training academies discussed in other chapters), social change activists build capacity by mastering the technical and political skills from fund-raising, to housing management, to orchestrating direct actions. The details of instructional meetings differ depending on the subject matter. Learning how to eliminate hazardous materials (a common problem in redeveloping inner city properties) might be presented on an contaminated site in a hands-on manner. Learning how to plan a budget takes place in a small room, where people sit with computer-generated spreadsheets and collectively watch how the numbers change.

In general, there are many commonalities in how empowering training sessions should and can be run. Instructional sessions should be involving for the individuals, rather than being a passive exercise. Formal lectures, where people just sit in the audience and listen, should be kept to a minimum. Instead, models that follow the philosophy of the pedagogy of the oppressed (Freire 1970) break down the border between student and teacher, as both teacher and student share with each other their experiences and the knowledge on what actions will work. After brief discussions on general principles, teaching sessions then break up into smaller workshops that can practice the matter at hand. Sessions should include both watching someone do the task and then having those learning also do it themselves.

The instructor should know more about the subject than those who come to learn, yet not make others feel either ignorant or incompetent. At training sessions make sure the speakers are those who have actually accomplished the task being explained—built a shopping center, ran an antiredlining protest, been audited or arrested, applied for a grant—and were successful. The instructor must indicate that there is nothing he or she has done that others cannot also do. "Five years ago I was sitting where you are now." "Here's how it works, I did it, you can do it, try it now," ought to be the basic message communicated.

A blurb for a training session offered in the Chicago area illustrates the hands-on purpose of many training modules, taught by individuals with actual experience in the matter, but from different perspectives.

Tools for Development without Displacement: Neighborhoods in the Shadows of Universities - March 7 - 8, 2006
Date(s): March 7 - 8, 2006
Faculty: John Barros (Dudley Street Neighborhood Initiative) David Perry (Great Cities Institute, University of Illinois at Chicago) Joe Hoereth (Great Cities Institute, University of Illinois at Chicago) Dwan Packnett (Trinity Plus One Consultants) Sean Allen (Rochester Area Foundation, Mayo Clinic) Samantha Dekoven (Metropolitan Planning Council) Kathy Ryg (State Representative) Stacy Young (Office of the Mayor in Chicago) Lillie Jernigan (Neighborhood Housing Services) Joel Bookman (LISC) Michelle Colins (Shore Bank)
Location: Summit Executive Center, 205 North Michigan Avenue

This workshop will explore critical roles that community based organizations (CBOs) play in partnering with large urban employers such as universities, in securing, developing and delivering employer assisted housing (EAH) in the context of community development and planning. The workshop will focus on opportunities and challenges for CBOs working in the "shadows" of large urban universities. Using practically relevant case studies, interaction with experienced CBO peers, local and state officials, funders. (e-mail from Housing Action Illinois March 02, 2006)

To communicate technical material without being intimidating, trainers prepare folders that link written backup for what is being said that those in the audience can refer to later on. If the first speaker is talking about legal constraints on door-to-door solicitations, the first tab in the folder might contain a copy of the state laws on solicitation of funds.

In general, trainers have four responsibilities: they should build skills, integrate values with the skills taught, help set realistic goals for those learning new material, and generate enthusiasm for the topic at hand.

Build Skills.   At the training session, have people practice. Don't let people leave until they have shown that they can use the knowledge they gained. People learning to do a community analysis, for instance, can practice using demographic data on the neighborhood or can take a walking tour to document neighborhood problems.

Another approach is to role play that both teaches but can also be funny or dramatic. One community member can represent advocates for clean air and back a polluting business owner into a legal jam; or one of the trainees can make a plea for funding that presents graphically what drug rehab means to addicts with kids.

Integrate Values with Skills.   Technical skills should be integrated with the underlying values or philosophies of progressive change. For instance, in teaching about civil disobedience, people learn how to accept arrest passively or how to act as a dead weight when the police cart them out of a building. But these skills are meaningful only when the philosophy of nonviolence is understood. Training teaches people not only how to piece together resources to restore a strip of stores in a poor neighborhood, but also why it is important to keep money in a community and recirculate wealth.

Be Realistic.   Instructors should be realistic in what they teach people, for example, not exaggerating the chances of getting a competitive grant. They should let those who are learning know how often people will slam doors in their faces or make false promises to attend neighborhood meetings. Those teaching how to recruit members should encourage action, but also warn the future canvassers that door-knocking in some neighborhoods can be dangerous and that it is better if people do it in pairs.

Build Enthusiasm.   It is possible to be realistic and build enthusiasm at the same time. Ten people might refuse to join the organization, but when one more does, it is a victory. Big business does have an inside track, but activist groups do prevail. Excitement is catching. A well-told story makes the trainees feel like they are there, builds hope and enthusiasm, and in doing so reinforces the feeling that "Yes, we can do this, and now we know how."

Focused Decision-Making Meetings

In democratic organizations, major policies must reflect the priorities and preferences of the membership. Mission statements should be ratified through a membership vote. But broad membership meetings are too cumbersome a forum to allow detailed, interactive discussion on many issues. Instead, such concerns are delegated to a smaller decision-making body—the board of directors of the organization, or other times to special committees of the membership set up to work on policy matters, or perhaps plan for particular projects or actions. Mechanisms should be in place to ensure that these smaller decision-making committees reflect in their composition the diversity in the broader membership, both in terms of ethnicity and gender as well as in their preferences for different approaches.

In general, small decision-making committees are appropriate when

- either bylaws or governmental rules require that actions be taken by a responsible body
- time is needed to carefully consider detailed (and often technical) facts (and figures), for example balancing out budgetary priorities, or examining the action strategies in response to complicated legislative or regulatory actions
- time is needed for give and take on deeply held values on which members could disagree
- a forum is required to allow people to spark off one another—brainstorm—to work out new ideas
- time is needed to work out the broader direction of an organization, perhaps by preparing a *strategic plan*

Effective Structuring of Decision-Making and Idea-Generating Meetings

Effective decision-making groups are structured to encourage creative problem solving, maintain democratic involvement, and prevent people from being too intimidated to express their real opinions. Preparation facilitates good decision making.

To begin, decision-making committees should be kept fairly small, usually with no more than a dozen participating. Backup material such as financial statements, or perhaps physical layouts of rally sites, or drafts of regulatory proposals should be in committee members' hands long before the meeting. When Boards of Directors meet, staff members should be available to answer technical questions while specialized committees should have the relevant staff person present, for example a committee working on the organization's image might want the public relations staff person to attend. In many cases, having an Internet-connected computer is helpful so that participants can access data. In brainstorming types of sessions, such as occur at retreats, flipcharts and magic markers are a must, unless the room is wired so that ideas can be placed on a shared computer page.

In general, to make people feel comfortable and encourage them to participate,

- Keep committees small. It is better to form several subcommittees than have one large one where some are too intimidated to talk.
- Arrange the physical setting in ways that symbolize equality. Sitting at a circular table is less formal than sitting at a conference table with a head.

■ Follow a pre-arranged agenda. Everyone's time is valued, there is little mean-dering over the different topics.

■ Don't try to accomplish everything in one meeting. Time should be allowed for people to get to know each other and take on specific roles before the group feels comfortable enough to make difficult decisions.

■ Share history through narratives and stories. Shared history creates trust among members and gives them common examples to draw on.

■ Leave time for informal conversations. Such exchanges enable people to get to know each other and increase their willingness to listen to each other.

■ Assign responsibility for carrying out the group's decisions. It is frustrating to call another meeting to continue working on a problem and find out that the previous decisions have not yet been carried out. (Adapted from Jones, Barn-lund, and Haiman 1980; Kowitz and Knutson 1980)

To help meetings flow from topic to topic, set up an agenda and distribute it in advance. Here are several recommendations for arranging an agenda.

■ Place routine business or announcements first. Read brief reports, if there are any.

■ Place the most important decisions (or most controversial topics) about fifteen to twenty minutes after the start. People tend to be most alert at this point.

■ Limit the number of difficult or controversial items to be handled at any one meeting. Estimate the time to be spent on each item. When people see that a discussion is supposed to last no more than half an hour, they will try to reach a decision in that time.

■ Wrap up a meeting with noncontroversial items such as authorizing the pay-ment of routine bills.

Agendas are intended to guide meetings so that progress can be made and time is not wasted on minor matters. But agendas should not become so rigid that they restrict the number and variety of clever ideas that are brought forth.

Meetings require a chair, someone to convene them, call on people, try to ensure that the time spent on different issues on the agenda is balanced, and that the meeting does progress. Chairs must assert sufficient control so that discussion does proceed, yet not so much control that ideas are not brought forth. Sometimes the chair is determined through the bylaws, so that the chair of the Board of Directors will run a board meeting, or the President, lead organizer, or the Executive Director a staff meeting. In less formal meetings, to make sure a chair does not dominate, the traveling chair model can be used. With this model

the person who is talking is responsible for calling on the next participant. She or he speaks and then calls on someone else who has indicated a desire to contribute. The process shares the responsibility and power of recognizing speakers . . . and generally increases participation, commitment, and involvement. (Avery, Auvine, Streibel et al. 1981)

Another approach, especially when the goal is to get a wide variety of opinions, is to have a facilitator, often a paid person from outside the organization, to guide the committee meeting. Facilitators encourage participation in several different ways:

- They emphasize what people have said by repeating the key ideas that have been raised.
- They encourage people to take turns in talking rather than allow a few to dominate the conversation.
- They show respect for all ideas, even those that at first appear to be silly.
- When people don't complete their thoughts, the facilitator probes for further details, but otherwise does not contribute his or her own thoughts.
- The facilitator works to gently keep the discussion on target, often by repeating the core questions at intervals or when the discussion seems to be wandering.
- The facilitator keeps people on their own schedules by reminding them when they agreed to stop.
- After a while people seem to run out of ideas. Facilitators know that decision-making groups get a second wind and encourage people to stick at the task a while longer. (Adapted from Kaner, with Lindd, Toldi et al. 1996)

Facilitators do not contribute to the substance of the discussion and do not have a vote.

Those running meetings have to recognize that conflict will occur and successful decisions often come about through reconciling these differences. Still conflict can get out of hand and become all-consuming. Sometimes to calm the waters all that is needed is to call a break so that people can relax. Or when two people radically disagree, the chair or the committee can call on others to move the discussion along (adapted from Kaner, with Lindd, Toldi, et al. 1996, 114–19). As long as conflicts are not based on personalities or on core values that guide the organization, fully articulated disagreements can get people actively involved and act as a safety valve for frustrations (Jones, Barnlund, and Haiman 1980, 153–53). Committees that know how to handle conflicts usually produce better decisions, generate more alternative solutions, create more interesting meetings, and force members to be specific about the information needed to resolve problems (Kowitz and Knutson 1980, 171–75).

Discussion leaders handle conflict differently depending on the matter under dispute (Jones, Barnlund, and Haiman 1980, 146–47). Individuals might disagree on assertions, that is, untested statements of personal preference or belief. These assertions may reflect unresolved feelings about race, ethnicity, gender, or people in certain occupational positions. Such statements can derail a discussion or an effort to make a decision. One approach to handling this sort of conflict is for the discussion leader to particularize.

For example, if Mr. Jones asserts, "It is impossible to work with bankers," the discussion leader might ask, "Do you think you can work with Ms. Smith?" (Ms. Smith is a community banker that has helped fund the group before). "Of course, I can. Ms. Smith is an exception, not like those folks from downtown." Such an agreement can resolve the immediate conflict, without speaking to the broader question of whether or not bankers can be trusted.

Individuals might disagree on the logic of an argument. Sometimes further explication of the facts or spelling out the logic in more detail resolves the difficulty. For instance, a leader of a community-run social service agency might take a position against financing a shelter for abused women. Spelled out, the reasoning is that in this middle-class community few women would need or ask for these services and the shelter might attract people from elsewhere. When others point out the number of police calls made by abused women in their community, the person who objected to the proposal is likely to back off.

Sometimes it is the evidence itself that people disagree on. For example, a group member might argue, "We can't target Exxon to clean up the river, it will cost too much, and one industry will never pay that amount." In this case the conflict can be bridged by finding out the actual cleanup expenses involved and learning the history of cases in which environmental groups pressured industries to pay for problems businesses created.

The most difficult conflicts to resolve are those on values, that is, fundamental beliefs. These beliefs may be about the goals, what equality means, for example, or about the means, such as whether violence is ever justified. People may come together initially because they are disempowered in a similar way—because of the color of their skin, their gender, or the coincidence of living together in a neglected neighborhood. But once together they discover they differ in values. In such circumstances, as has occurred in the civil rights era, among feminists, and environmentalists, different groups spin off, agreeing on the need to solve core problems of racism, gender inequality, or environmental deterioration, but having to work separately because they disagree about what actions are appropriate.

Conflicts can disrupt committee meetings, turning what should be productive discussion into bickering and backbiting. But too much agreement and consensus can also be harmful, leading to decisions that can harm the organization. People become enthused through working with others of a like mind: "We're finally together, we're going to rebuild the neighborhood or teach those chauvinist pigs that women are not decorations." When people work together in groups that are highly motivated and get along well, they reinforce each other's ideas, get caught up in the enthusiasm of the moment, and become so concerned with being part of the group that bad ideas are no longer challenged. Irving Janis called this phenomenon *groupthink* (Janis 1982, 9).

Groupthink can easily occur within action organizations. People come together because they care deeply about some issues, demonize their opposition, and feel that right is on their side. Seeing others with similar beliefs, activists may feel invincible and have no need to check out the feasibility of the committee's plans. Or they may be so fearful of falling out among themselves that they apply strong pressure on anyone who dissents, resulting in an inability to evaluate their own proposals (Janis 1982, 174–75).

The result of groupthink may be unwise decisions, failed campaigns, and loss of support. If decision makers feel invulnerable, they may underestimate the strength of opponents. Or they may be so convinced of the rightness of what they are doing that they forget to build support for the project and are blindsided by opposition. To prevent groupthink, decision-making committees should be forced to gain the concurrence of those outside of the committee before acting and in doing so revisit the strengths and weaknesses of their own arguments.

Table 12-2 illustrates the balancing act that is required to bring about effective committees.

Stimulating a Wide Variety of Ideas

Sometimes decisions are relatively straightforward: authorizing paying a bill, for instance. But more often the problems confronting decision-making committees are truly perplexing. How does one reduce pervasive, lingering pockets of poverty? Will a partnership with a bank compromise the ability of the organization to do direct action? Not only must answers be found, but the answers must be those that the members of the organization can accept and for which the organization has sufficient resources to carry out.

TABLE 12.2 Decision-Making Groups Require Balance in How They Discuss Issues

Structure

With too much structure, talking is inhibited because people are afraid of making a procedural error.	With too little structure, people defer to either the more aggressive or the high status people and fear to talk.

Leadership

Too strong a leadership makes group members afraid to contribute.	Too weak a leadership and the discussion wanders and loses focus.

Cohesion

With too much emphasis on cohesion, people defer to the majority opinion, irrespective of what they individually think.	With too little cohesion, people are afraid to present their ideas.

Conflict

Constant conflict disrupts meetings, leads to leadership fights, and makes it harder to reach a decision that people will actually follow.	Without conflict, ideas go untested.

Decision-making meetings must be conducted in such a way that people feel comfortable suggesting a wide variety of ideas and be willing to accept honest and open discussion of their feasibility. Doing so requires both skills on the part of the discussion leaders, as well as knowledge about various techniques to encourage innovative, perhaps controversial, ideas to be suggested.

The discussion leader sets the tone for the committee. Discussion leaders don't yell at those who get excited or out of hand, but rather gently ask them to tone down the discussion. Continued courtesy in the face of rudeness points out to people the need to respect each other's ideas, while discouraging disruptive personality conflicts. Disagreements are recast as shared issues, not as personality matters. Say, "Mary and Tom have a problem coordinating their work schedules," not "Tom is never around when Mary needs to consult with him" (Avery, Auvine, Streibel, et al. 1981). Discussion leaders call on individuals who have not spoken to elicit all sides of an issue; a skillful chair will know who might want to disagree but has not yet done so. A discussion leader might ask a speaker to explain further what was meant. "I understand the first part of what you said, but I'm not sure what you think we ought to do after meeting with the alderperson."

Even in the most effective, harmonious groups, ideas come forth slowly. A good idea may have to simmer for a while until it has been refined and gradually becomes group property and not simply an individual's pet scheme. The first time the idea comes up, it may meet with criticism, and be tabled, or even die. If it has considerable appeal, it will come back again later, in somewhat modified form, to handle prior criticism. "The same basic solution may go through a number of such transformations before it is accepted" (Jones, Barnlund, and Haiman 1980, 166). Social psychologists term this process of letting an idea simmer *decision-modification*—encouraging the recycling of ideas until they become group property.

> A wide variety of techniques can be used to solicit ideas. One way is through brainstorming, a procedure wherein members are encouraged to suggest any idea about the problem that comes to mind. The ideas are written on a blackboard or flip chart, and no positive or negative evaluation of the ideas is permitted, including scowls, groans, signs or gestures. (Yukl 1989, 289)

The excitement generated encourages people to jump in with additional thoughts.

A variant of brainstorming is called round-robin (Moore 1987) in which somebody suggests an idea and puts it down on a pad. The pad is circulated, and everyone is required to add or cross out a statement to build on the original ideas. A more lively variant of this process is a structured go-around (Kaner, with Lindd, Toldi, et al. 1996, 80) in which, depending on the variation chosen, (1) people sit in a circle and the person clockwise to the speaker speaks next; (2) the speaker tosses a bean bag (or some such thing) and the person who catches it must contribute an idea. The goal is to free people from the embarrassment of choosing to talk since the way the game is set up, they have no choice.

With nominal group techniques people jot down their ideas on slips of paper that are shuffled before the ideas are placed on the board, without any names being attached. Once the initial set of ideas has been collected, the leader or facilitator tries to get each participant to discuss the strengths and weaknesses of the individual ideas. Better yet, the group as a whole might suggest how separate ideas can be combined into a stronger approach.

Sometimes in discussions people get excited and jump in, not letting others speak, intimidating those with less confidence or lower social status. A skillful discussion leader can normally restore order with a few polite words. Another approach that encourages critical discussion while preserving order is to use a talking stick. An object, such as a stick, is placed in the middle of the room. People agree to talk only when they are holding the talking stick. When they finish talking, they place the stick back in the middle where the next person then picks it up.

Committee members can come up with some terrific ideas using these techniques, but the process should not stop when the first good idea is surfaced. It needs to be evaluated, to see if it would work, or what its shortcomings might be. To do this, each group should select one or more *devil's advocates* whose role is to look for weaknesses and report back to the group, before any action is taken (Yukl 1989, 225). This approach allows people to put forth clever ideas in a spontaneous manner, but gives the group a chance to reflect before going off half-cocked.

Interorganizational Committee Meetings

One of the more difficult meetings to orchestrate are those involving several different organizations that need to work out an agreement. Community economic and social production organizations might meet with government, foundations, or private businesses to negotiate funding for a project. Sister action organizations meet to see if they should work on a single campaign together. In Chapter 18 we will describe how negotiations in such meetings occur. Here we will examine some of the logistical concerns in arranging interorganizational meetings.

Meetings should be arranged so as not to threaten any of the participating organizations. For instance, having one organization or another chair the meeting might be considered a threat, as others then feel less equal, so a convening organization is termed a "host." It's even better if the host is an organization that is really not part of the discussion but is simply facilitating it for others. The host handles logistical details, finds a room, provides refreshments. Meeting sites can move from the offices of one organization to another or better meetings can be held at a neutral spot, a conference room at a hotel, or one owned by an organization not immediately involved.

Conclusion

To some, meetings might seem a waste of time, talk rather than action, but this is not the case as in democratic organizations meetings are where members assert control, set agendas, and reflect upon what they have accomplished. Some meetings are celebratory—sharing the glory of successes and reinforcing the idea that change is possible. Others focus on technical matters, learning skills from one another and in doing so building capacity for further actions. Meetings help build solidarity among both those already in the organization and by reaching out to those in other organizations to build a shared agenda.

CHAPTER

13 Building Capacity by Working with the Support Sector

Empowerment is about developing the capacity to bring about change. Often capacity comes about through experiential learning. But why reinvent the wheel when there are numerous **support organizations** and **support networks** that can provide technical assistance, information, training, and, at times, financial resources to bring about progressive change. From support organizations activists can learn the skills of street-level organizing or master accounting techniques, study civil disobedience, be taught how to measure dioxin, prepare news releases, or discover which banks are redlining.

In this chapter we shall describe the variety of support organizations and the assistance they provide to those engaged in social change work. Later, in Chapter 19, we examine the direct action work that support organizations themselves orchestrate.

A Wide Array of Support Organizations and Support Networks

Support organizations come in many sizes and shapes—some distribute information or set up peer-to-peer helping networks. Activists can go on-line and look for information on websites maintained by support organizations or join peer-to-peer mailing lists and ask for help on specific problems ranging from how to set up Spanish language accounting programs for micro-enterprises to what a newly released governmental statistic implies for social action. Some support organizations provide financial assistance; networks offer training programs for organizers, while national intermediaries send out expert consultants to help with economic and social production work.

To get the flavor of what is available, let us examine the variety of support organizations, grouping them in terms of who set them up and for what purposes.

Support Organizations Mostly Maintained by Front-Line Activists Themselves

Many support organizations were initially established by social activists themselves and are still maintained by those activists. As described in Chapter 3, **institutional**

networks bring together organizations that share a similar philosophy. Each institutional network maintains a formal headquarters office and offers ongoing, technical support as well as training programs. Several of these institutional networks are described below.

IAF	The Industrial Areas Foundation offers training to individual organizers and when invited into communities by churches and local organizations will do the initial mobilizing and organizational building work itself.
ACORN	The Association of Community Organizing for Reform Now offers training in confrontational, political approaches; organizes communities from scratch; and provides technical assistance in areas such as housing renewal. It produces data papers on social problems and maintains national level lobbyists.
DART	Direct Action and Research Training is a southern-based network that offers training and technical assistance to members.
GAMALIEL	Gamaliel trains and provides advice to grassroots organizations, mostly faith-based groups in the Midwest.
PICO	The Pacific Institute for Community Organizations offers guidance and training to West Coast and Midwest organizations in its network.
NPA	National People's Action began as a national coalition of neighborhood groups battling redlining. Through a loose network of self-selected affiliates, it works to link local issues affecting neighborhoods to national policies, teaching how to undertake actions, and, through its affiliate NTIC, offers training and technical support in campaigns.
NCLR	National Council of La Raza, a constituency-based Hispanic organization, provides technical assistance to its affiliates while trying to build a consensus on policy recommendations.

Less formal **peer-to-peer networks** are in place facilitating the sharing of information. The National Organizers' Alliance brings together social change activists from different issue areas to exchange experiences, while participants on the computer list COMM-ORG and the associated website http://comm-org.wisc.edu/ have brought into being on-going, informal, continuing dialogue among community organizers, progressive economic and social service providers, as well as academics.

Activist coalitions are organizations that formalize what usually begin as informal meetings between activists working on the same problems. Neighborhood organizers might meet at lunch to discuss how to persuade the new alderperson to pay attention to community problems; over coffee and donuts, developmental activists puzzle out the newest vagaries of federal financing. Eventually, from these casual conversations a coalition is set in place, coordinated voluntarily, or perhaps with very small staff. A city-wide affordable housing coalition set up in this way then monitors how localities spend housing funds and pressure to increase programs in support of affordable homes.

Recognizing that housing is a national issue, activists throughout the nation came together to set up the National Low Income Housing Coalition that coordinates works to preserve and increase housing for those of modest means, while in a parallel effort those concerned about the fate of the CRA established the National Community Reinvestment Coalition to monitor the act. The Coalition of Human Needs came into being as activists in a variety of areas noted that a coordinated voice that went beyond concerns for individual programs was needed to speak for the economically less well off.

For organizations involved in social and economic production work **trade associations** provide backup support, teach technical skills, and coordinate lobbying efforts for resources for ESP work. The Association for Economic Opportunity (AEO) speaks for organizations involved in micro-enterprises, monitoring federal small business programs and providing training in business matters, while the National Community Capital Association (NCCA) helps community-based and community-centered financial organizations by running seminars on the intricacies of micro-banking. As with activist coalitions, boards of trade associations are chosen from the leadership of member organizations.

Independent, Progressive Technical Assistance and Financial Support Organizations

The next grouping of support organizations are independent technical assistance providers, foundations, and research shops that, while set up to help those doing social change work, are legally independent of the organizations they help and rarely are membership organizations. Still employees of these support organizations are often hired from direct action and ESP organizations and almost all set up an advisory board of front-line social change workers.

Core to this sector are **social change intermediaries**. For example, the Washington-based Center for Community Change (CCC) (from Rubin 2000a and on-line information from CCC) provides training and information to other social change organizations. CCC publications have explored topics ranging from fundraising, economic development tools, media relationships, and federal housing programs, as well as philosophies of direct action. The Washington staff of CCC monitors government programs on poverty and housing and lobbying and electronically circulates alerts to those in its network as well as to broader mailing lists.

As an intermediary, CCC helped set up many local direct action and social production organizations by first obtaining grants from foundations and then using this money to provide free technical assistance to startup organizations. However, CCC is careful in choosing those whom it helps. As a CCC organizer told us,

> we're particularly focused on very low income organizations mostly led by people of color . . . Cause it really is an organization that believes in grass roots of empowerment

and skills transformation. In addition, CCC works primarily with organizations whose boards are made up of community members on their boards.

CCC's staff itself advocates for programs to support low-income housing, has worked in antihunger efforts, and in general is a fighter to expand programs to alleviate poverty. In the past CCC has been at the forefront of efforts to maintain the Community Reinvestment Act, but nowadays its mission has moved away from housing. Its two major recent efforts were to work with local organizations to help shape federal legislation impacting welfare laws, while also orchestrating a national voters' registration drive.

Over the years the CCC has developed trust among many other organizations and as such can host meetings bringing together diverse (and sometimes rival) groups. CCC has become the home for ongoing national projects that involve a variety of local organizations in a coordinated effort. The CCC houses the Surface Transportation network that coordinates numerous environmental, economic justice, and transportation organizations to press for affordable public transit, while its long-running Housing Trust Project has assisted hundreds of localities to set up housing trust funds and dedicated income streams to subsidize affordable housing.

National **financial intermediaries** such as LISC, Enterprise, and the Neighborhood Works, along with city-wide intermediaries such as Neighborhood Progress Inc. in Cleveland (McDermott 2004), package funding for economic, housing, and social development projects undertaken by ESP organizations. Financial intermediaries solicit funds from banks, corporations, and foundations that help ESP organizations in their work, while at the same time assisting ESP organizations to design projects that appeal to outsider funders and investors (Liou and Stroh 1998; Rubin 2000a). In addition, intermediaries provide technical assistance to ESP organizations and conduct training conferences for them. Enterprise, a housing intermediary, works in poor communities in programs that link housing with social service efforts, while LISC coordinates residential renewal efforts with commercial development in a variety of cities. In addition, Neighborhood Reinvestment Corporation, a federally sponsored intermediary, aids hundreds of local Neighborhood Housing Services that in turn repair and build homes in poor communities. At the local level, in Cleveland, for instance, the Cleveland Housing Network helps package funds for renewal projects while working as a partner with neighborhood groups on site selection and in guiding the physical reconstruction of buildings (Rubin 2000a).

Information can be power, though most activists do not have the time, and many lack the skills, to go through reams of statistical, legislative, or bureaucratic information to compile data. Fortunately, several major organizations do **policy research** focused on social problems. The Woodstock Institute analyzes community reinvestment data along with other information on banks and credit unions to determine how well financial institutions serve the poor. At the federal level, the Center on Budget and Policy Priorities compiles budgetary information and then works out the implications of federal budgetary decisions on social programs, posting what it finds on the Internet in language that makes clear what much of the federal numeric gobbledygook tries to hide. The Economic Policy Institute reports on the ways in which structural economic changes impact lower-income people, while the National Center for Responsive Philanthropy analyzes foundation data, noting how little of this untaxed money serves the poor. Meanwhile, OMB Watch documents the broader policy environment of the federal government, noting in particular decisions that impact the nonprofit sector.

Advocacy coalitions, trade associations, and intermediaries send out newsletters that summarize their policy research as well as maintain websites that post current studies and policy information. Intermediaries also sponsor informative journals such as *Bright Ideas* that disseminate new approaches to housing renewal work, while the National Housing Institute publishes the bimonthly *Shelterforce*, now available online, which keeps people up-to-date on changes in the housing field. The Fannie Mae Foundation sponsors Knowledge Plex, an on-line data bank for economic and housing development issues, and periodically sets up training sessions as web casts. The Institute for Community Economics provides information on how to set up land trusts, Ruckus advises on confrontational tactics, while the Community Media Workshop explains how to improve press relations. Corporation for Enterprise Development (CFED) provides general help with those involved in micro-enterprise work while various organizations offer legal assistance to battle issues of poverty, racial discrimination, fair housing, or women's rights.

In addition to the intermediaries, numerous technical assistance organizations provide hands-on assistance to local organizations engaged in building homes or restoring local economies. Community Builders in Boston works with CDCs, helping them prepare cost estimates, hire contractors, or supervise physical construction. South Shore Advisory Services advises on establishing incubators, running community businesses, and has helped CDCs that faced financial problems do workouts. The Center for Urban Economic Development at the University of Illinois—Chicago researches the economics of community projects, while organizations like the Property Management Research Center helps teach groups how to manage property. The Consortium for Housing and Assets Management assists organizations in managing the capital assets accumulated by owning affordable housing.

Another way of gaining technical assistance is to hire **consultants**, individuals who work for a fee on designated tasks ranging from preparing bylaws, writing grants, teaching how to remove asbestos, or just about any matter. Consultants have worked step-by-step with community organizations as they set up their first affordable housing projects or advised on the nitty-gritty details involved in developing supermarkets in poor neighborhoods. **Lobbyists** are a special type of consultant who are paid to help organizations persuade elected and regulatory officials. Several lobbying firms such as Rapoza Inc. specialize in the concerns of progressive nonprofits.

Foundations

Foundations are nonprofit organizations established by wealthy families, or sometimes from community contributions, for a charitable purpose, as defined by the Internal Revenue Code. Religious networks also set up organizations that behave very much like foundations, such as the Catholic Campaign for Human Development.

Foundation policies are usually specified in a charter as interpreted by a Board of Directors and carried out by hired professional program officers. As numerous reports from the National Center for Responsive Philanthropy indicate, only a very small percentage of foundation funds go to social change causes, with most going to medical research, arts, and higher education.

Some foundations, though, fund community and social change work. Ford has provided startup money for organizations that battle poverty, work to preserve the environment, and fight for ethnic social justice, as well as grants for community-controlled renewal activities. Annie Casey focuses on helping organizations that work with children but in doing so recognizes that supportive communities are part of the ways in which children are helped. Lily has funded religious groups working for economic justice. The Pew Foundation and the Mott Foundation have programs to support micro-enterprises. McArthur funds community policy shops that research government and has helped provide money to religious leaders working in organizations that rebuild social capital in devastated neighborhoods. Smaller community foundations also have supported renewal and economic production work (Lowe 2004). Banks and gigantic federally chartered agencies that purchase mortgages at times spin off their own foundations that provide funds in support of the affordable housing movement as well as sponsor conferences and training sessions at which developmental activists learn more about their craft.

In addition some foundations undertake *social justice philanthropy* (Cohen 2005b). For instance, the Haymarket Foundation in Boston supports organizations involved in direct action while other progressive foundations are part of the National Network of Grantmakers whose purpose is to

> increase financial and other resources to groups committed to social and economic justice . . . eliminate discrimination and oppression based on age, class, disability, ethnicity, gender, race, religion, and sexual orientation . . . promote the significance and vitality of the grassroots community in the broader movement for systemic progressive social change. (Shuman 1998)

Foundations will specify in which area they will fund programs. A few years back the progressive Mott Foundation helped fund "intermediate support organizations" that included the Center for Community Change, Community Training and Assistance Center, Mississippi Action for Community Education, the National Council of La Raza, the National Training and Information Center, as well as the Seventh Generation Fund for Indian Development. In turn, each of these support organizations provided technical assistance to local organizations. For instance, the Community Training and Assistance Center worked with tenants' groups in public housing to help them build the capacity to take back the community from disruptive elements, while the national Council of La Raza helped set up a Community Development Corporation in neglected neighborhoods near San Juan (Betzold 1998).

Unfortunately, the attention span of many of the liberal foundations seems limited, with their being unwilling to provide the long-term funding social change efforts require. In contrast, seventy-nine conservative foundations are more steadfast in pushing their agendas, for instance, by providing sustained funding to conservative think tanks such as the Heritage Foundation that battle progressive change (Cohen 2004a; 2005a).

Other Support Organizations

Many other organizations also provide financial and technical support. Religious groups help social change organizations, with money for the IAF, for instance, coming from the Campaign for Human Development. Individual churches, synagogues, and mosques often allow community groups the use of their facilities, and sometimes encourage religious leaders to spend time working on community issues while being paid by the religious group.

Information provided by *think tanks*—research organizations that are usually independent of universities—such as the Brookings Institution or the Urban Institute, speak to many issues of concern to social change activists. Specialized centers associated with universities such as the Joint Center for Housing Studies at Harvard that authors the annual report on the *State of the Nation's Housing* or the Great Cities Institute at the University of Illinois, or dozens of urban research and social welfare research centers provide information for social activism. Activists do not have to keep on top of each since specialists working in trade associations and advocacy coalitions monitor these centers and share relevant findings with activists on electronic lists. Some universities help social change organizations through partnering in participatory research projects (Nyden, Figer, Shibley, et al. 1997; Stoecker 1998; 2005). Universities have collaborated in efforts to bring about smart growth (Wiewel and Knaap 2005) and partnerships—some successful, some not—have occurred in urban renewal programs (Gilderbloom and Mullins 2005).

Capacity Building through Working with Support Organizations

The infrastructure of support helps build capacity for social change by providing information on what is possible while teaching techniques to bring projects to fruition. But gaining support can come with a cost in time, money, or even organizational independence. Let's examine the types of help that are available and how to access the help, while noting possible problems that can occur in doing so.

Activist Socialization and Technical Training

Socialization is about learning the norms and values of a field, while technical training involves mastering specific skills. At conferences and conventions and through training opportunities, support organizations help to socialize activists and help them gain important technical skills.

Conferences and Conventions. Trade associations, activist coalitions, intermediaries, and at times foundations, as well as activist organizing networks sponsor conferences that allow activists and their supporters to share information, seek out technical help and create supportive networks. At conferences, participants discuss the values that guide their work and in doing so agree on a shared meaning of their social change organizations. Conferences are focusing events that help create a social movement. (Rubin 2000b, 35)

At conferences, activists meet and learn from one another, set up and reinforce helping networks, share narratives of success while strengthening each other's resolve to continue the battle. Community and economic development conferences include several plenary sessions examining the overall direction of the movement and about three dozen panels on technical matters, such as how to finance commercial real estate or form micro-enterprises. Some workshops focus on emerging tools of the trade— electronic communications, or techniques for applying for an Office of Community Services grant, the major source of federal money for community economic development. Representatives of funders and technical assistance providers teach about how to package funds or explain the intricacies of reselling loans. At breakfast round tables, conferees chat informally about their experiences (Rubin 2000b).

At *plenaries*, leaders of the support organizations, notables in the field, and invited guests ranging from famous activists to politicians talk about past victories and current problems. While at *panels* (or breakout sessions) smaller groups of people come together to explore a specific matter. For instance, breakout sessions at the meetings of the National Low Income Housing Coalition examine the technicalities of new housing legislation or ways of working with tenants' organizations. The best-attended panels are those on emerging issues—changes in federal funding policies, or how to use the Internet for activism, or getting discussions up to speed on the spread of predatory lending. *Site visits* are part of the teaching during which participants visit successful projects and learn how they came about. Seeing a new supermarket with quality goods built within a city's worst neighborhood teaches visitors what it is possible to do.

Conferences of activist networks such as ACORN or NPA almost always include a direct action—a protest at a bank or at the offices of a politician or bureaucrat. Trade associations and activist coalitions schedule *lobbying days* to coincide with their conferences during which activists meet with their elected representative and then later on at the conference share with one another how the politicians responded to the issues.

In contrast to the wide array of topics covered at conferences, some organizations periodically sponsor *summits*, gatherings that focus on a single issue. For example, the National Technical Information Center has sponsored summits to examine how to change the Community Reinvestment Act to cope with the rapid evolution of the financial system. The National Low Income Housing Coalition convened a wide array of organizations in the housing field to work out ideas on how to improve the administration of the Section 8 voucher program.

Technical Training.   In Chapter 11 we described the organizer training programs run by activist networks as well as the degree-granting programs at Southern New Hampshire University for developmental activists. Other training is also available.

The Development Training Institutes offers a Development Leadership Program with twenty-six days of training, including a hands-on introduction to community renewal work, as well as specialized classes on economic, development, and organizational skill. To help community development organizations build capacity, a consortium of support organizations led by the Enterprise and LISC set up the National Community Development Initiative to teach technical skills in project development, while helping community groups form partnerships with government and business to complete these projects (Walker 2002). Each year the National Community Capital Association offers a training conference on the technical matters needed to run a community development financial organization. Neighborhood Works holds training seminars in different locations throughout the country in ways that set up a series of linked and cumulative courses on home building as well as economic development techniques. Instructors are national experts and are carefully monitored to make sure their modules fit together. Individuals who are able to attend multiple meetings each time take more advanced courses and ultimately end up with a certificate.

Self-help technical training is available on-line from KnowledgePlex, maintained by the Fannie Mae Foundation. The on-line ACORN Living Wage Center web page provides technical information on how to campaign for a living wage, while the website of the National Housing Trust Fund Campaign, at www.nhtf.org provides specific background on trust funds. The Welfare Law Center has set up web pages containing information on welfare reform, including court cases. Tenant activists in New York set up web pages with suggestions on how action organizations could now cope with the changing housing code in New York City, while three housing intermediaries have on-line technical reports describing step-by-step ways of combating predatory lending (Baker 2003).

Publications abound. The Center for Community Change makes material ranging from instructions on how to organize to improve action, guides for influencing public policy, ways to link community and job organizations, to a recent report of fund-raising for nonprofit organizations—*Promising Practices in Revenue Generation for Community Organizing* (O'Donnell, Becket, and Rudd 2005). The Alliance for Justice publishes easily understood rules on lobbying for nonprofits while the Center for Neighborhood Technology prepares reports on brownfield redevelopment, tying together environmental cleanup techniques with job creation in the inner city.

Increasingly, technical training is provided through web casts. For instance, coalitions of support organizations using web casts shared information on how nonprofits could work with government agencies in relief efforts for Hurricane Katrina. Organizations such as LISC maintain on-line documents that provide backup material for web broadcast training seminars. In early 2006 the National Housing Law project and the Center on Budget and Policy Priorities jointly sponsored a training teleconference on the new rules of funding housing vouchers.

Support organizations also provide hands-on technical assistance. State level coalition organizations such as Housing Action Illinois send out personnel to help local housing coalitions set up boards, develop mission statements, and work out plans of actions. When the newly formed Dudley Street Neighborhood Initiative required technical assistance to bridge the tensions in its politically and ethnically diverse community, it hired the Community Training and Technical Center (CTAC) to help in the effort. For many years, the Center for Community Change would send out its professionals to help groups of low-income activists build effective organizations. Sometimes foundations sponsor peer-to-peer training by paying for *peer matches* that are "structured opportunities for teams of people . . . who are working on a similar issue to exchange experiences and practical knowledge toward resolving a particular challenge that has been identified in advance" (Building Social and Economic Support Networks, 2004, 35).

The Diffusion of Information

Social change organizations require a lot of backup information that most don't have time to find or analyze themselves. Processing census and housing data takes technical staff that local organizations can't afford to hire, while just staying on top of changing rules and regulations is a full-time job. Fortunately, trade associations, activist coalitions, and other support organizations compile information and diffuse it through computer lists, newsletters, and action alerts. Support organizations such as NCRC sponsor an electronic news clipping service, in this case tracing out change in the banking industry that impacts CRA and economic justice more broadly. Such information becomes the power that fuels action.

Action Alerts.   Support organizations stay on top of the ever-changing policy environment. When an issue has an immediacy and quick response is required—to oppose a harmful bill, persuade faltering legislators to keep their promise, or encourage people to write a lobbying letter—action alerts are distributed. An alert will briefly describe the problem, provide a link to a website where more detail can be found, and suggest what actions should be taken. Alerts will usually include a script for what should be said when making a call or a sample letter. Those receiving alerts are requested to repost them on other lists.

Both the Center on Budget and Policy Priorities and the Woodstock Institute distribute alerts that are often combined with technical analyses of the problem. For example, after Illinois passed some strong regulations against unscrupulous payday lenders and the lenders found technical ways of avoiding the intent of the law, Woodstock issued an eight page *Reinvestment Alert* apprising activists of the loopholes, providing backup data, and suggesting actions on how to modify the regulations (Feltner and Williams 2004).

Conference Calls.   Both trade associations and support coalition organizations sponsor conference calls that allow activists throughout the nation to coordinate their work and to learn important backup information from the policy analysts and governmental liaisons who work for the support organizations. For instance, in the aftermath of Hurricane Katrina as victims were being displaced by FEMA, a coalition of over a dozen support organizations ranging from activist organizations to funding intermediaries (Memo to Members, NLHIC 12-26-05) sponsored a series of conference calls that resulted in initiating a major court suit to help the victims.

Peer-to-Peer Communications.   Much technical information is spread by word of mouth, peer-to-peer, at coffee breaks during conferences, through personal calls, or on computer lists sponsored by support organizations. Illinois activists concerned about housing set up Housing.Net as a network through which to electronically share both what was happening in housing in the state and how to pressure the legislature. One trade association sponsored lists such as those maintained by the Association for Economic Opportunity (AEO). Participants ask about technical problems—ways of funding non-English-speaking entrepreneurs, for instance, or what computer software is most helpful for nonprofits. Posts on the list sponsored by the National Community Reinvestment Coalition focus on emerging policy problems or more specifically sharing information on banks that are about to merge.

COMM-ORG is a list run out of the University of Wisconsin that links over 1,000 social change activists from academics, to street-level organizers, to those involved in economic and social production work. Job opportunities are circulated, information on publications and meetings are widely spread, as well as reports on emerging social problems. In addition the list circulates news releases sent out by PICO or ACORN, as well as announcements on training programs. The list owner maintains a website (http://comm-org.wisc.edu) that stores much backup information needed for activism. COMM-ORG encourages discussions on matters on which activists might disagree—on the balance between confrontational and development approaches, how much formal training, versus experiential, as well as pressing matters facing organizers, for instance, how to respond to the arrest of student interns involved in environmental activism.

Periodic Publications.   Support organizations circulate their own publications that describe both the work they and their affiliated organizations have done and the policy changes while presenting summaries of more technical reports in action-focused language. The variety of these reports can be seen in the three types of publications put out for those involved in housing and community renewal work; similar material is available for other issue areas.

Shelterforce is published bimonthly, focuses on housing policy and community renewal issues, and is available on-line, by subscription, and as a benefit of membership in some national coalitions. A typical issue might discuss some projects accomplished by housing and community renewal organizations, list forthcoming meetings and training announcements of newly available technical reports, have a book review, and note job changes made by housing activists. Each issue includes four or five more extended, descriptive articles ranging from an analysis of gentrification, to fundraising, to building and maintaining alternative types of housing. *Shelterforce* articles, usually written by activists themselves, explore controversial matters, for instance, asking why many social change organizations in minority communities are not directed by minority group members.

Bright Ideas is a quarterly publication, paid for by the government-funded intermediary Neighborhood Works. Each hundred-page issue provides information about what local Neighborhood Housing Service organizations have accomplished, self-laudation of NW's own work, and announcements of innovative approaches to urban renewal and housing development. The remainder has technical articles usually written by activists on how to accomplish projects, perhaps by setting up business partnerships, or even more specific pieces on the nitty-gritty of improved construction techniques for building affordable quality homes.

The third set of publications are more academic in tone, each published quarterly, sponsored by the Fannie Mae Foundation. Articles in the *Journal of Housing Research* are written in an academic style with scientific prose and often rely upon advanced statistics. The thrust is on the social implications of housing, for instance, how housing quality affects crime. Another Fannie Mae Foundation journal *Housing Policy Debate*, is quite academic, with an abundance of statistical tables and scientific sounding prose. It focuses on the consequences of government policies on housing, residents of housing, and community renewal.

Our experience is that *Shelterforce* is widely read, *Bright Lights* is mainly noted by those in the Neighborhood Works network, while the Fannie Mae publications primarily have an academic and think tank audience. Far more widely read are the various *newsletters* put out by support organizations, some on a quarterly basis, others weekly, and others on an as-needed basis, and nowadays circulated electronically. Hundreds of these reports are available, but we will only describe a few. For instance, NCRC's quarterly newsletter and ACORN's semimonthly one have similar content describing major national projects of each group, accomplishments of members, and, when appropriate, happenings at the annual conferences sponsored by each group. Each article mentions a contact for further information.

Policy updates within specific issue areas—housing, transportation, immigration, welfare, etc.—can be obtained from the Center for Community Change or the Center on Budget and Policy Priorities. Both organizations also publicize technical papers prepared by their staff on a variety of issue areas, with the paper linking research findings to the actions that can be taken. As activists concerned about housing, we find the National Low Income Housing Coalition's *Memo to Members* incredibly valuable as it provides timely updates on federal legislation, not just on housing, but also on social welfare issues more generally. Crises receive detailed coverage—for instance, the on-again off-again rebuilding efforts associated with Hurricane Katrina, or on the continuing threats to Section 8 housing vouchers. HUD policies and programs are examined and actions that affect CRA are described. NLIHC staff peruse many technical publications on housing and social welfare matters and provide succinct understandable summaries, as well as web links to the full reports. Of course, the memo also contains a plug for NLIHC's annual meeting.

Policy, Program, and Problem Analyses

Analyzing an ever-changing policy environment requires both the expertise and the time that most local social change organizations lack, while gathering and analyzing data on social problems is best done by specialists. Fortunately research organizations such as Brookings, the Urban Institute, and the Center on Budget and Policy Priorities work full time at data and policy analysis, while trade associations and coalition organizations employ policy and legislative staffs that work on the more specific information needed by their membership.

Such data directly impact actions. The NLIHC's annual report on housing affordability, for example, is immediately incorporated in campaigns run by local housing activists. In ongoing battles with banks, activist organizations rely upon analyses of mortgage data by Woodstock or NCRC to show when banks are redlining and then pressure those banks to guarantee reinvestment. Analyses of real estate taxes prepared by the Chicago Rehab Network led to changes in how apartments were assessed that aided those involved in providing affordable housing.

Policy Analysis of Government Programs. Support organizations provide information on changing government programs along with an analysis of what such changes imply for social change. *OMB Watch* makes available a biweekly newsletter that describes issues on the federal budget, as well as other matters that affect nonprofits' ability to lobby. The Center on Budget and Policy Priorities constantly monitors the federal budget, examining both the implications of proposed changes on social programs while producing more detailed policy papers in specialized areas such as housing. Though liberal in its orientation, the data produced by CBPP is considered top flight and is relied upon even by those of differing political persuasions. Further, CBPP staff more directly impacts legislation by working closely with legislative staff, providing data and showing policy implications that the rushed legislative staff might miss. The Economic Policy Institute produces both statistical analyses and policy reports on income and wages while advocacy think tanks such as Good Jobs First provide backup material on how state and local governments end up subsidizing big businesses at a cost to the poor.

More in-depth studies come from both the Brookings Institution and the Urban Institute that examine major issues and then release monograph-length analyses, for example examining the impact of HOPE VI or the implications of TANF reform. In *State of the Dream*, United for Fair Economy describes the failure of Bush's ownership society to improve the economic lot of the poor; National Low Income Housing Coalition's *Changing Priorities* provides detailed data on the systematic, steady reduction in federal government support for housing.

These longer reports provide backup information that sets the broader context for campaigns. More immediate action is engendered by the briefer reports that detail proposed program changes that can affect those social changes organizations serve. For instance, when the Bush administration pushed for changes in the housing voucher programs, the National Low Income Housing Coalition, the Poverty and Race Research and Action Council as well as the CBPP all issued reports detailing the harm the changes would cause. Similarly, when a conservative bank regulator argued for reducing CRA requirements on small banks, the National Community Reinvestment Coalition quickly prepared and circulated a brief piece showing the overall negative impact of the proposed changes, along with a state-by-state breakdown that could more readily be shared with elected officials.

Briefs are also issued to rebut claims made by opponents. For instance, in one case, a bill was being considered that had one provision that would have provided funds for affordable housing. Opponents smeared the bill claiming that the provision was doing little more than setting up a slush fund for nonprofits, a blatantly false accusation. In response to this slander, the NLIHC released on its extensive e-mail list a three-page point-by-point rebuttal that local organizations could present to their elected officials.

Problem Documentation.   Local organizations need to have hard data to convince politicians, bureaucrats, and the press of the legitimacy of their concerns; such data are readily available in reports prepared by national support organizations. For example, *The State of Working America*, published biannually by the Economic Policy Institute, gathers and summarizes information on wages, poverty, and unemployment that economic justice organizations rely upon in their daily work. NCRC produces data on bank reinvestment policies both in the aggregate and locally, showing that both banks and credit unions fail in their missions to serve the poor. In Chicago, the Metropolitan Chicago Information Center statistically documented that supermarkets were scarce in poor and minority neighborhoods.

Elected officials are most interested in problems that affect their own constituents, so support organizations try to break down data by electoral areas, or at least by geography. For instance, the National Low Income Housing Coalition prepares an annual report on housing affordability entitled *Out of Reach* that documents housing costs by geographic area. It succinctly summarizes findings in terms of a "housing wage," the amount a person would have to earn per hour to afford a typical two-bedroom apartment for each of the nation's geographic areas and in doing so provides powerful, targeted information on housing affordability that can be directly incorporated in local campaigns.

Solutions Are Possible.   On websites and in periodic reports, support organizations detail program successes providing information that others can emulate. Both academic books (Reynolds 2002) and ACORN document how to conduct living wage campaigns as illustrated by the hundreds of successes that have already occurred. In periodic newsletters as well as in the longer *Home Sweet Home*, the Center for Community Change details how to set up housing trust funds modeling advice on those trust funds that are already in place. Other reports caution on what to avoid; for instance, analyses, sponsored by the Aspen Foundation, show that both micro-enterprise programs as well as efforts to set up individual development accounts do not always work.

To continue to receive support, social change organizations must show foundations and government that they have accomplished much. National housing intermediaries keep and publicize careful records of the number of homes built by the organizations while over the years the National Congress for Community Economic Development has produced a report on the number of homes built, jobs created, square footage renovated, and other similar statistics by community development corporations. The Association for Economic Opportunity does likewise for organizations working on micro-enterprises, while the trade group, the National Community

Capital Association, documents the accomplishments of various community development financial institutions.

Technical Assistance from Support Organizations and Consultants

Technical assistance (often called TA) refers to the myriad of ways in which support organizations and consultants provide hands-on help. TA is available from the staffs of coalitions and trade associations, sometimes for a fee, while individual consultants, again for a fee, provide case-by-case assistance on individual projects. When dealing in the legislative arena, assistance is sought from lobbyists who have expertise in contacting and persuading public officials. Several lobbyist firms are in place that specialize in working with nonprofits and social change organizations. At times, local organizations will request technical assistance for a project they have initiated on their own. Other times, though, the support organizations themselves will push for a particular approach, develop technical expertise itself in the matter and then offer assistance to local groups carrying out the projects suggested by the support organizations. Usually this occurs with economic development projects, for instance, with national efforts to encourage local organizations to work with franchises.

Working with Consultants. There are thousands of paid consultants who, for a fee, will provide assistance. Some consultants work on their own, others in established firms, while many are themselves successful activists who, either as part of their organization's mission or to supplement their income, assist other social change groups. Why repeat mistakes when a consultant from a sister organization can share his or her experiences? For instance, ESP organizations that want to build shopping centers in poor communities can learn how by consulting with the founder of the Kansas City Community Development Corporation who has brought on-line several such projects.

Consultants help train board members, prepare budgets for projects, write grant proposals, advise on press releases, or teach how to effectively maintain renewed apartment buildings. Campaigns to initiate housing trust funds are often gotten off the ground by following the advice of the national expert consultant from the Center for Community Change, who has worked on dozens and dozens of such efforts.

In working with a consultant, the trick is to ensure that the consultant empowers the organization rather than do its work for it. A grant writer has the expertise to structure the budget of a proposal in a way that will increase the chance of a project being funded. Little in the way of empowerment is lost if a budgeted item is put under category A rather than B or if the consultant writes up the proposal using jargon that appeals to the funders. However, much may be lost if the consultant chooses the idea for the proposal. Leading consultants understand the need to help build the capacity of community groups and not dictate their agendas. As one consultant described,

> We did [name's] . . . proposals . . . but those are [name's] ideas. Those are all his, we don't force anything else . . . the CDC has to be able to generate the idea. We can tell them what makes more sense as far as funding goes and then we work with them . . .

We work with their staff in generating it and we have to be sure that the CDC can follow on and deliver. Because if they can't, the money is lost. If the money is lost, it works against us. I mean you get a reputation of turning in those great proposals but no delivery. (interview with Herbert Rubin)

When hiring an independent consultant check to see if he or she has worked with other social change organizations, then make a few phone calls to make sure the other organization was satisfied. Second, be as clear as you can up front in telling consultants what their roles are to be and put it in writing. When choosing a consultant keep in mind that few activities can be carried out in a cookie-cutter manner, that is by simply applying what was learned elsewhere to the current situation; that's not the way to go. If a consultant comes in with a model that he or she wants to immediately impose without being aware of the local contingencies, you might want to steer clear of this person.

Consultants need to be paid. However, the money need not come out the organization's budget as foundations provide grants to coalitions, trade associations, or intermediaries to hire the consultants that community groups use. Some support organizations such as the CCC seek out their own grants to fund consultants they employ to work with the community movement. Similarly, LISC and Enterprise will fund consultants to help neighborhood economic and social production organizations. National membership organizations establish peer-to-peer consultant systems in which those from more experienced groups are paid to advise the less experienced.

Project Partnerships as Technical Assistance.   Support organizations work as partners with local groups on a variety of projects. Housing and economic development intermediaries will send in either their own staff or paid consultants to help local organizations on projects such as building a shopping mall. On a larger scale, national intermediaries, working in a complicated partnership involving intermediaries, government agencies, and foundations, set up the National Community Development Initiative, a multicity capacity building effort that provided funds for local organizations doing renewal projects as well as technical assistance and training of the staff of neighborhood redevelopment organizations (Walker 2002). Some developmental activists are cautious in dealing with national intermediaries as these resource-rich organizations can dominate local groups (Rubin 2000a).

At times, local organizations set up their own technical assistance providers that have the expertise, yet still are more amenable to community demands. For instance, in Cleveland, neighborhood developers established the Cleveland Housing Network (CHN). In this case

the separate community-based development organizations determine what properties to repair, while choosing future tenant-owners from their neighborhoods. CHN handles overhead matters, for instance, obtaining the tax credits, taking title to derelict property from the city, and sending out experts in evaluating building conditions . . . The CHN negotiates with banks . . . The network structure allows the partnering CBDOs to maintain both independence and a large semblance of control in the projects, while at the same time gaining needed technical support. (Rubin 2000a, 197)

Foundations such as ASPEN set up special programs to encourage micro-enterprise development, then will fund centers that develop expertise in the matter, and encourage local organizations to work with these centers as partners.

Employees of the national level networks such as ACORN, IAF, NTIC, PICO work directly with neighborhood groups on direct action campaigns. While, prior to the 2004 elections, the CCC worked with dozens of local organizations teaching them how to legally register voters. Coalitions such as the NCRC, as well as activist groups such as ACORN, have set up training programs for affiliated local organizations to train trainers that work for these local groups to teach their community members financial literacy skills.

Universities sometimes partner with social change organizations but care is needed in such relationships since urban universities themselves are often the ones causing some of the problems by displacing the urban poor (Gilderbloom and Mullins 2005). Progressive academics do work with nonprofits and poor neighborhoods to teach local organizations how to do evaluations, set up service centers, and work out broader redevelopment plans (Butterfield and Sosak 2004; Gilderbloom and Mullins 2005; Nyden, Figer, Shibley, et al. 1997; Wiewel and Knaap 2005). In an effort in Philadelphia, an activist organization partnered with a progressive research center from Temple University, gathered data to document the need for a citywide improvement plan and then successfully pressured for its implementation (Research for Democracy 2001).

Care is needed in partnerships to make sure both parties gain. Do not enter into these partnerships unless it is fairly certain the community group will then learn from the relationship how to do similar work itself. Also make sure that the partnership activity is one that the local organization would have done on its own, if it had the resources, not simply something imposed by the partner. Finally, the local organization should receive credit for the success of the project.

Support Organizations Spread the Message

Support organizations learn of new, often innovative approaches to social change, examine the approaches in more detail and, when appropriate, work to spread the idea. For example, several innovative CDCs had set up partnership projects with grocery chains to develop supermarkets in poor communities. Building on these documented successes, intermediaries put together a national program to encourage supermarket development. The Aspen Foundation became aware of some successful micro-enterprise programs, contracted for research to learn more about them, then disseminated the results while helping set up centers that provided technical assistance to organizations working to set up micro-enterprise programs.

Local housing advocates can be thwarted in their efforts because many in the public consider affordable housing simply to mean the crime-ridden high-rise public housing projects that exist in some large cities. In response to this perceptual problem, support organizations first in Minnesota and later in Illinois worked with media experts to set up a media campaign to communicate to the broader public that most occupants of affordable homes were working people—public safety officers, nurses, and teachers—who simply could not pay full housing prices on their salaries.

Finally, support organizations, especially coalitions, coordinate, and at times initiate national level advocacy campaigns ranging from battles to outlaw predatory interest rates and to push for a national housing trust fund, to defensive efforts to defend the community reinvestment act. In doing so, they are spreading the message for economic justice. We shall discuss these campaigns in Chapter 19.

Conclusion

Organizing is about building a community of activism. Support organizations and networks are part of the social capital on which local organizations can draw to gain the capacity, skills, and knowledge, and at times, financial resources, for the daily battle. We have described the variety of ways that support organizations help local groups, while pointing out some pitfalls that must be avoided in working with these larger, better-funded entities.

PART FIVE

Compelling Change through Social Mobilization

In social mobilization efforts, large numbers of people come together to pressure government and business. The tactics followed vary from quietly working with congressional staff to in-your-face confrontations. In Chapter 14, we provide an overview philosophy of social mobilization campaigns that empower but do not demean. In Chapter 15 we discuss how to gain the numbers needed for effective social actions through various efforts at mobilization.

Chapter 16 shows how lobbying, serving on boards and commissions, and working through the electoral process can bring about change in both elected and regulatory governmental bodies. When political and administrative engagement fails, confrontations that publicize an issue and bring forceful pressure are the next step. In Chapter 17, we examine a wide variety of confrontational tactics ranging from quiet vigils to massive rallies to civil disobedience. Chapter 18 describes three tools used in both political and confrontational actions—litigation, media campaigns, and negotiations.

Individual social change organizations often lack the strength to force change, so to gain power they come together within social action coalitions. Chapter 19 describes the pros and cons of working with coalitions, as well as narrates illustrative campaigns that have been carried out by local and, more recently, national and international advocacy coalitions.

CHAPTER
14

An Overview to Social Mobilization Campaigns

Through social mobilization campaigns organizations contend with authorities to change policies and procedures that limit life opportunities. Social mobilization efforts might focus on an immediate objective, such as convincing city council to put in a stop sign at a dangerous intersection, or involve a long-lasting campaign to end an unjust war. In general, in social mobilization campaigns activists

> **DEFINE** or **FRAME** a problem, **DOCUMENT** its extent, **PROPOSE** the desired change, **TARGET** those who can effect a solution, use **DIRECT PRESSURES** on the target to accept the changes, and then work to **ENSURE IMPLEMENTATION** of what is promised.

A **campaign** is a planned, coordinated, and extended effort to compel an opponent to concede to the demands of the social action organization. Campaigns follow long-term **strategies** that anticipate the goals to be achieved, whom to pressure, what tactics are acceptable, and what constitutes success. **Tactics** are the specific actions taken—lobbying, phone calls, and sit-ins, on up to sabotage. **Targets** refer to individuals or organizations whose behaviors or policies social change organizations want to change.

An **action** means carrying out a specific tactic against a defined target, for instance, by showing up en masse at city hall to demand an explanation why no fines have been levied against landlords whose buildings are fire-traps. Actions are chosen to match the vulnerabilities of the target as well the willingness of organization members to participate. A **hit** is a face-to-face confrontation with a target, for instance, surrounding the home of a cabinet secretary and demanding to speak with the individual.

With **civic** and **administrative engagement tactics**—lobbying, petitioning, working with bureaucrats, serving on public committees—organization members play by the rules set by the establishment. Engagement tactics imply that the system itself is working, but that it needs prodding. **Legal tactics**—law suits, court appearances, and restraining orders—are used when the targets have failed to abide by their own rules. With **direct actions** people take things into their own hands—"direct action [being] the wide range of do-it-yourself forms of people-power that allow communities and movements to assert their power to make change themselves" (Solnit 2004, xvii). Direct actions are those that take the shortest route toward realization of the ends desired. . . . A simple example might help to clarify. If a group of tenants is having a problem with a landlord refusing to make needed repairs, they can respond in several ways. They could take the landlord to court. They could get the housing and health inspectors to issue violations and pressure the landlord to make repairs. Or they could withhold rent from the landlord and use the money withheld to pay for the repairs. Along the same vein, they might picket the landlord's nice suburban home and leaflet all of his neighbors with information on how he treats people. The first two options put responsibility for getting something done in the hands of a government agency or law enforcement official. The latter courses of action keep tenants in control of what happens. (Knoche 2004, 307)

Direct actions need not be confrontational, for instance, an economic and social production organization takes matters into its own hands when it builds homes rather than relying on government to do so. More often, though, direct action is carried out through **confrontations** (sit-ins, pickets, marches, and other in-your-face actions) because people feel that they will not prevail unless old rules are violated and new ones promulgated. Confrontations are the social explosions that yell, "Pay attention! There is a problem here! And, if you don't find a solution, we will make our own."

Tactics change as organizations gain power. For instance, Communities Organized for Public Services (COPS) initially used direct action campaigns to demand federal money to repair Mexican American neighborhoods devastated by floods (Sanders 1997; Sekul 1983). Early on, when the city manager refused to release needed funds, "a delegation of COPS people, led by president Carmen Badillo, paid [the city manager] a visit in his office. They demanded with TV cameras present that the [city manager] meet with them" (Sekul 1983, 181–82). Today COPS, while still willing to be confrontational, more often only has to lobby to get its way as this group is considered an important and accepted voice of the community (Warren 2001).

Campaigns put together a variety of reinforcing tactics. Efforts to improve education might involve picketing school boards for more resources while at the same time partnering with teachers to help them reach out to minority students (Center for Community Change 2005). Campaigns to stop predatory lenders combine disruptive picketing of pay-lending stores, street theater—people dressing up as sharks and marching around the offices of big banks that fund payday lenders,—while at the same time lobbying supportive legislators to craft bills to outlaw usurious interest rates and ensure full disclosure on mortgages.

Campaigns can be national in scope. For instance, national organizations such as the Universal Living Wage Campaign encouraged city and state organizations throughout the nation to pressure for living wages, triggered by a major action:

September 6th, (Labor Day plus 1) Living Wage Warriors from across the nation will join fellow advocates and display our banners on specially selected, highly visible, rush hour traffic bridges . . . The banner we fly will read "Bridge the ECONOMIC GAP with a Living Wage" (www.universallivingwage.org/).

Antiwar organizations coordinate their protests. For example,

> On Wednesday, August 17, hundreds of thousands of supporters gathered at 1,627 vigils in all 50 states and the District of Columbia . . . From Alaska to Florida, Maine to Mississippi, Oregon to South Carolina and New York to Texas—we gathered together to acknowledge the sacrifices made by Cindy Sheehan, her son, Casey and the more than 1,800 brave American men and women who have given their lives in Iraq—and their moms and families. (www.political.moveon.org/cindyvigils/pics.html)

Care is needed that the fun of doing an action does not distract from the reasons the actions are necessary. In the fervor of an accountability session—when elected officials are forced to answer questions in a public forum—it is easy to forget that the goal is to solve a problem not discomfort a politician. In subsequent chapters we will examine the techniques of social mobilization. In this chapter let us examine the underlying motivations and broader goals of social mobilization campaigns.

Power and Social Mobilization Campaigns

Campaigns come about to gain power—the ability to affect decisions that shape social outcomes. For the establishment, power comes from the control of wealth and physical force. For activists, numbers and enthusiasm are two sources of power, backed up by the ability to undertake political, legal, or confrontational actions. Progressive activists recognize the importance of understanding what power entails.

> Organizers tend to have a rather straightforward approach to power. They want power. They want the people with whom they work to have power. And they want to build power organizations. They see power as essentially neutral. It can be used in the service of justice or abused in the services of evil . . . Organizers see power as what is needed to get things done. (Jacobsen 2001, 38)

Power does not mean dominance over others, but instead the ability to accomplish a goal.

Power can emerge from the shaping of ideas, determining how issues are framed. A person who points a gun at you has power over you, but only for that moment; but one who convinces you that his or her ideas about the distribution of wealth is fair, or that those in charge should be has an intellectual dominance that sustains more permanent control. Social mobilization campaigns are about creating both physical or material power while changing shared understandings so that the gains made persist. The struggle for power is in part convincing others that you are right.

Power Emerges through the Mastery of Social Mobilization Tactics

Social action organizations gain power by documenting and publicizing the extent of a problem. City council members are less likely to tolerate apartments with rodents and vermin once the problem has been shown on television. Power comes from embarrassing the opposition. Showing that a company that profits from sales to minorities has few executives from minority groups might create pressure for change. Why buy from someone who won't hire you? Power comes from the ability to delay the actions of opponents. Banks feel they have to merge or lose out in the competitive market. But mergers require approval of public authorities and community groups can hold up the merger by arguing to public authorities that banks ignore poor neighborhoods. Power can come from threats and disruption. The massive protests in Seattle during meetings of the World Trade Organization made apparent that those who oppose globalization would bring the system to a halt (Cockburn, St. Clair, and Sekula 2000). Still, disruption is a two-edged sword. If an organization ties up traffic on freeways in Los Angeles to protest inadequate public transit, the group demonstrates power but infuriates hundreds of thousands of people, weakening rather than strengthening the cause.

The prime source of power for action organizations is their ability to mobilize people in large numbers. If one family pays the rent late, the slumlord may be irritated, but unconcerned, because that family can be evicted. But if many families band together and intentionally withhold rent until the landlord fixes the plumbing, that same slumlord is financially threatened. Individually the *colonias* in Texas were unable to improve the education of their children, but united they were able to pressure the state to do so (Shirley 2002). If the organization represents a large number of constituents, politicians will show up to an accountability session. But how many is enough depends on the issue.

> Twenty seniors meeting with a powerful politician about the cost of prescription drugs is an action. Eight parents pressing the local school principal to improve pedestrian safety around the local schools is an action. Three thousand leaders meeting with the Mayor of Baltimore demanding that the city pay living wages is an action. (Gecan 2002, 51)

Power expands as the establishment sees how many are united. For example, in metropolitan Chicago

> The United Power for Action and Justice organization, rather than working in a section of the city, or even the whole city of Chicago, . . . set out to build the largest metropolitan citizens organization ever attempted to that point by bringing city and suburbs together under one big tent

and in so doing brought together thousands of leaders

> from religious, labor, and civic institutions . . . That assembly included blacks, whites, Latinos, and Asians; Christians, Jews and Muslims; city residents and suburbanites; members of faith-based institutions, secular folk, and labor union members. (Chambers 2003, 113–14)

Power requires building networks and coalitions that unite organizations that are skilled in a wide variety of political and direct action tactics. National level activists lobby federal regulators to forbid banks from funding predatory lenders, state activists work with legislators to change laws on allowable interest rates, while local groups march around the offices of the predatory lenders.

Power Expands by the Appropriate Choice of Issues

If actions are going to achieve more fundamental changes, they need to be cast in terms of the larger issues. Power is increased when people understand that their personal concerns speak to broader issues of social and economic justice. A system that allows people to work full time and yet not reach the poverty level, or one in which government provides the wealthy low taxes while the poor lack medical care is unjust, and showing this motivates people to join in. But to build power, campaigns must depend on what people personally know and feel. Individuals might not know how federal policies that support globalization keep wages low, but they do know they are poorly paid and that their bosses are often abusive. Broader issues of capitalist control are linked to the immediate discontents with work. Campaigns gain strength by evoking broader principles and concerns but do so in ways that link to personal concerns.

Many activists feel that to expand power "the issue must be winnable" (Sen 2003, 51 quoting Bobo, Max, and Kendall 2001). We certainly don't suggest running quixotic campaigns—believing a local sit-in will cause world peace. Still, major issues are rarely winnable in the short run. Instead we would argue that power expands by choosing smaller issues that can be won, but that do speak to larger concerns. Picketing to shut own a local drug house is a step in revitalizing a neighborhood, a process that could take years to bring about. Demanding a living wage is a step toward bringing about a more equitable economy.

Power Emerges through Understanding the Opponents and by Their Understanding You

Power is more effectively focused after understanding the strengths and weaknesses of the targets and opponents.

1. Can the target grant the demands made? Has the organization picked the right target—the state level government, rather than the national level, or the corporate offices of a company rather than those of a branch? Targets of campaigns must be able to effect a solution.
2. What is the power base of the opponent and which parts of that base are most vulnerable? Is the strength of the opponent based on corporate wealth, a strong client base, or only on a razor-thin electoral victory? Does a company need a favorable decision by a regulator or is it vulnerable to bad publicity at the time of stockholders' meetings?
3. How willing and able are the opponents to strike back? Has the city arrested people during demonstrations, or have they kept the police away for fear of provoking a violent confrontation? Can the targets weaken the campaign by pressuring employees to fire activists?

4. What sort of support do your opponents have and can this support be also targeted? When elected officials depend upon the business community, pressuring business might be the way to persuade government. (It is also useful to know when your targets are so trapped by their supporters that it is nearly impossible for them to concede. Activists in support of gay rights might try to pressure politicians, only to discover that even moderate Republicans can do little because they fear opposition in the primaries from the antigay, religious right.)

5. How much knowledge do your opponents have of your organization? If it has won previous battles, make sure new opponents are aware. (But keep in mind that opponents can learn about an organization's weaknesses. Rent strikes fail if landlords figure out which tenants can be bought off. When action organizations are labelled by the larger public as being extreme or "un-American," opponents can get away with calling in the police or using physical force.)

6. For what tactics are the opponents prepared and for which are they most vulnerable? A heavily bankrolled company can withstand an economic boycott, while landlords with vast holdings might be impervious to rent strikes. Government agencies or schools that have large, open, and insecure buildings might be vulnerable to sit-ins. (It is vital to remember that nowadays government and big businesses themselves study activist groups and have worked out ways of "managing activism" [Deegan 2001]. Most larger companies, schools, and businesses have standard procedures when picketing or demonstrations occur. If that is the case, cleverness is called for, perhaps by adding a mocking humor to what people expect to be an acrimonious confrontation.)

7. Can arguments be made that evoke the moral values that your opponents supposedly espouse? If, for instance, pharmaceutical companies claim their work is about keeping people healthy, point out that they are keeping drug prices high and are depriving people of care. If government argues that it is responsive to the will of the people, accept these pronouncements as if they were true and insist upon a public hearing.

8. Are the targets vulnerable to political jiujitsu? That is, can the action organization flip what the opponents do so that actions hurt them more than you? For instance, when opponents bring in overwhelming police force, passive resistance can make their brutality appear immoral.

9. Keep in mind action organizations have no permanent opponents, but, equally, they have no permanent friends. A city that has allowed slumlords to flourish can be pressured to provide grant money for action organizations to do housing inspections. Power comes about by picking a target, yet trying not to do so in ways that permanently alienate a potential ally in a later issue.

Power Emerges as Issues Are Framed in Ways That Legitimate Social Mobilization

Keep in mind that often force is counterproductive as the establishment controls the police and big businesses can move or shut down companies, while some disruptions become the center of attention distracting from the problems themselves. People might condemn the sit-in at the hospital because it inconveniences them and ignore the problems with inadequate medical care. Perceptions count.

Activist organizations need to convince people that the issues raised are important and that fault for the problem stems from a societal failing. In addition, activist organizations must convince the public that the tactics chosen are appropriate for the problems faced. Power increases when action organizations are able to **frame** issues to show that their cause is right and that people have an obligation to dissent. Frames define how issues are to be understood and become the ideological and conceptual lenses that "interpret, define and give meaning to social and cultural phenomenon" (Baylor 1996, 242 from Goffman 1974).

Are people who receive welfare lazy cheats or are they primarily seen as mothers with hungry children?

Is the factory a place that provides jobs or a source of environmental pollution?

Are stockpiled nuclear weapons a defense against tyranny or means of mass destruction?

Frames are manipulated by those in power, for instance, labelling those who want economic change as "communists" or those who object to an imposition of a religious agenda on others as "Godless." Dorothy Day, the Christian activist, describes

> When I feed the hungry they call me a saint. When I ask why people are hungry, they call me a Communist. (quoted in Jacobsen 2001, 42)

Frames reflect social prejudices. In the aftermath of Hurricane Katrina, in which much of New Orleans was destroyed, pictures of African Americans taking stuff from abandoned stores were labelled as "looting" while when Caucasians were shown doing the same the label used was "finding food" (http://dvorak.org/blog/images/katrina/).

Power comes from being able to frame an issue to show a social problem, not an individual one, and that collective action is an appropriate response. AIDS is not a punishment to gays, but a disease requiring public investment. Powerful frames show that an *injustice* is occurring, that solutions proposed are just, and that there exists an agency, a means, for bringing about the solution (Gamson 1992).

Frames need to appeal to both the broader public and those being mobilized. One way of doing so is through what is termed *rights talk* that links immediate, individual situations to broader principles and in doing so "rights became a lens through which to map and critique the gaps between reality and law, and between law and a broader vision of justice" (Gordon 2005, 153). Frames can link the broader issue to the personal. Shel Trapp illustrates how a "cancer" or "disease" framing emerged.

> Once I was doing a session with a group that was fighting the building of an incinerator in their community that was going to be used to burn medical and toxic waste . . . One person had done a lot of research and knew the names and amounts of all the toxins that would be released . . . As she was explaining all these terrible sounding things with huge names, people eyes began to glaze over . . . Finally someone asked "Do all of the things that you mention cause cancer?" . . . I suggested passing out a flier in the community saying, "Right now your chances of getting cancer are one in a hundred. If

the plant goes in, your chances will be twenty in a hundred. Do you want to be one of nineteen who will get cancer if this plant is built? If not, come to the meeting. (Trapp 1976, 112)

Through astute framings, action organizations combat false images and convince the public of the justice of the cause. For example, people with disabilities had been portrayed as helpless charity cases but activists in the disabilities movement reframed the issue as one about justice, equal access, and opportunity, not one of social kindness (Shapiro 1993). Effective framings convince the broader public that difficulties people face are problems worth battling, not minor complaints. Sexual harassment (or even stalking) was initially portrayed as boys being boys, and not until women were able to reframe the issue as one of structural sexism were their complaints seen as legitimate.

Action organizations work to construct interpretive frames that challenge underlying arguments that preserve the status quo. Society accepts the argument that the rich deserve to be rich and get tax breaks because wealthy people risk their money and create jobs for others. This framing ignores the fact that workers take risks with their health—more precious than money—when they handle pesticides or chemicals or work on scaffolding or in tunnels. Action organizations must persuade even their own members that the free market is not always right (or even free) and that social concerns are valuable as economic profit. Does a business always have a right to move if in doing so it destroys a neighborhood?

Framings change to accommodate the specific situations that activists face. For instance in campaigns held by Puerto Rican activists in different parts of New York City:

In Williamsburg . . . the political power of the Hasidim encouraged Puerto Rican activists to use an anticolonial frame. This frame linked local struggles around housing, AIDS, and drug abuse to the independence and anticolonial struggles of Puerto Rico . . . by targeting the Hasidim as colonialists . . . In the South Bronx, where Puerto Rican activists challenged a machine controlled by a Puerto Rican boss, activists used an antisystem frame; attacking the political system itself, and political parties, and politicians associated with the system. (Schneider 1997, 241)

Power increases as frames communicate to potential activists that there is a possibility of change. Those in power frame situations to communicate that things are the way they are because of some underlying, almost natural, economic or social laws. In contrast, activists frame issues to show that problems are caused by someone who benefits (slumlords get rich while people live in hovels) and argue that there are ways of changing the situation (having government enforce laws on housing standards).

Battling negative framings is also vital. Opponents understand that the public, informed only by an established press, sees the world through frames that disparage direct actions, for instance, communicating that the lack of decorum shown in a demonstration means that the action organization is too antisystem to deserve support. In a campaign to demand recompense for historic injustices, for instance, Native American activists physically took over symbolically important sites (places at which treaties had been negotiated that were later violated by the U.S. government). Little was accomplished, though, because the media concentrated on the militant tactics and ignored the underlying issues of land stolen from Native Americans (Baylor 1996).

Unfortunately, those involved in social actions too often disagree about how problems should be framed. Because of different historic experiences (i.e., minorities having faced forced abortions and sterilizations), how issues of choice in the abortion debate are framed differs from one ethnic group to another, making formal alliances that much more difficult. More generally, those supporting separate models of action, as described in Chapter 3, might hold contradictory framing with "each model of community organizing [having] its own collective action frame, shaped by a distinctive theory of change" (Smock 2003, 152). For example, in battling a drug house

> because the organizations . . . involved had very different theories of change, . . . [they] ended up framing and interpreting their problems in very different ways. CAPS, a civic organization defined . . . the situation as a technical problem stemming from the police's lack of sufficient information. In contrast, WON, a power-based organization framed . . . [the] situation as one of police accountability. . . . these distinctions in the organizations' interpretations . . . resulted in different strategies for solving the problems. (Smock 2003, 150–51)

Framings that make sense to activists do not always persuade the broader public. For instance, in the gay movement,

> New York City activists consistently privileged strategies that challenged dominant cultural values over those that would maximize the likelihood of policy success. By refusing to hold private hearings with the Human Rights Commission, activists increased the scope of conflict. Rather than allaying the fears of legislators and the public by reassuring them of the incremental nature of the policy reform activists exacerbated those fears by having transvestites testify at public hearings. (Bernstein 1997, 546)

It was more important for those in the movement to frame the issue to emphasize their culture than to win the immediate issues.

Images and framings are shaped by what appears in the media. The fight against predatory lending got a huge boost when network television secretly recorded discussions among lenders glorying in cheating people out of their savings. Recently Housing Minnesota and Housing Illinois ran advertising campaigns for affordable housing that emphasized that affordability means that nurses, teachers, and fire personnel can live in communities, working to disabuse the public of the idea that affordability means slum housing. When asked about the effectiveness of such campaigns, the organizer orchestrating them described

> There is significant change in people who say after they see the ads; they do not think affordable housing has such drawbacks to it. It goes from like 44% who say pre ads, yeah there are a lot of drawbacks with affordable housing, right, and after the ads it is in the 20's. So you have a full 15% change which is significant. (interview with Herbert Rubin)

Symbols as Controlled Framing.   Frames can be communicated in terms of symbols that provide people with simplified explanations of the problem as well as the possibility of solutions. A symbol is a word, phrase, image, icon, or person that stands for deeper, more complicated ideas. For example, public officials may argue that inner-city problems are due to "drug pushers." "Drug pusher" is a symbol suggesting an individual with no morals, an object of legitimate hate, best taken care of by putting the scum in jail. The cause of urban poverty is attributed to failed moral values with the implied solution of "law and order." By contrast, a neighborhood action organization will symbolize the cause of urban poverty in terms of the footloose firms that have abandoned communities, implying that an economic solution is required. An action organization might portray its campaign as one of "redressing grievances," a term that echoes the demands of the colonists in the Declaration of Independence (a positive symbol); at the same time the targets of the protest may label the demonstrators as disorderly and lawless. Those who opposed feminists called them bra burners, which became a symbol of people without respect for social proprieties. Feminists labelled their movement "women's liberation" suggesting a positive linkage to the civil rights movement.

Several strategies help in choosing effective symbols:

Symbols Create a Sense of Organizational Unity.   Action organizations need to symbolize the we-ness of those in the organization as well as their linkage to the broader community. Activist groups that press for neighborhood improvement might symbolize their cause with a picture of an attractive streetscape. Keep in mind, though, what works well within the group may sound threatening to the outsider, as occurred with verbal symbols, such as Black Power, that encouraged pride among some activists but was seen as a broader threat by others.

Come Up with Catchy Typifications.   Campaign symbols should typify the problem in an easily communicable fashion. The pro-choice and pro-life movements both created such powerful symbols with the coat-hanger and the partially formed fetus. Pictures of the cooling towers of nuclear reactors communicate the dangers of nuclear technology. Recently those opposing Wal-Mart ran a contest for a catchy slogan with people voting for the slogan "Wal-Mart: Killing Local Businesses One Main Street at a Time" (http://action.ourfuture.org). Songs and their titles (e.g., "We Shall Overcome") create powerful symbols, especially as the lyrics of protest songs often provide "diagnoses of what is wrong with the present order of things . . ." (Lewis, 1987, 169–70).

The Actions Themselves Can Become Symbols.   For example, to protest apartheid in South Africa and, more recently, to protest homelessness, students have constructed—and briefly live in—shantytowns on the lawns of universities. The shantytowns are easy to portray in the media, represent the problem, and become personalized symbols of the issues (Fordham 1986). Images of civil rights workers facing police dogs shows the nature of oppression as the image directly illustrates the problem. When

Greenpeace surrounds nuclear navy vessels with its small dinghies, the image is of David taking on Goliath and hopefully the public will root for David.

Personalize Symbols. Those in power try to symbolize social problems in terms of unworthy individuals. Opponents of affirmative action promote the symbol of an incompetent minority doctor or a woman promoted to boss with no experience. Such symbolizations are hard to counter since they are more readily understood than explanations of structural unemployment or institutional racism.

In response, action organizations create counter symbols that evoke appealing human scale images. One such powerful symbol is that of the victim, the blameless individual whose difficulties are so clearly caused by something for which he or she is clearly not responsible. A sick child becomes the symbol of toxic waste; a surgically mutilated house pet symbolizes the victims of medical experimentation run wild. During the Vietnam War era, peace activists were handed a dramatic symbol of the victim when television cameras recorded the agony of a young Vietnamese girl covered with burning napalm, running screaming down the street.

A symbol that is somewhat trickier to use is that of the enemy, "identifiable persons or stereotypes of persons to whom evil traits, intentions or attentions can be attributed" (Edelman 1988, 87). Alinsky's classic advice, "pick the target, freeze it, personalize it, and polarize it" (Alinsky 1971, 128), became a way of focusing attention on a problem in terms of an enemy that people can recognize. The Vietnam War became President Johnson's war; Sheriff Bull Connor, who turned the dogs loose on civil rights protesters, symbolized the racist South. On the other hand, symbolizing a problem in terms of an individual distracts from the social causes.

Create Symbols of Success No Matter What. In many campaigns, what is a victory or a defeat is not all that clear as "beliefs about success and failure are among the most arbitrary of political constructions and perhaps the least likely to be recognized as arbitrary" (Edelman 1988, 43). Even the jailing or death of organizational activists can be interpreted as a victory if it creates a martyr for the cause. When immediate objectives of a campaign have not been accomplished, symbolize the victory in terms of the steps already taken against the odds. For instance, Mansbridge concludes after describing the defeat of the Equal Rights Amendment (ERA): "Because the ratification campaign raised consciousness, helped women organize politically, and stimulated legislative and judicial action, that campaign was worth the effort put into it" (Mansbridge 1986, 188).

To summarize, one way in which action organizations get their issues on the public agenda is through the thoughtful use of symbols which then become the language of public discourse. At the beginning of a campaign, it is important to use symbols to justify taking public actions. During the campaign, it is vital to develop symbols that focus attention on core parts of the problem that also create sympathy for the organization and its cause—the undernourished child sewing clothes in a sweat shop. Toward the end of the campaign, the organization has to symbolize the progress made and the victories achieved to keep up morale among its members and to demonstrate that change is possible.

Power Is Imbalanced and Targets Can and Do Strike Back

Targets of social action do fight back, often with force, working to discredit the action organization as only representing a handful of malcontents. People in power stall, deny the legitimacy of demands, demean the protesters, refuse to take up the issue, or make promises and then ignore them. Banks will promise to spend more money in poor neighborhoods, then fail to do so. For instance, in Los Angeles, after a multi-year-long campaign, Los Angeles officials promised large sums to start a Housing Trust Fund and, in subsequent years, simply did not come through.

Government may investigate the organization and seize its books, records, and mailing lists, looking for financial irregularities to try to taint the protest group with scandal. Individual activists may be pressured to stop or face losing their jobs, eviction from their apartments, or blackballing—refusal to hire them anywhere. Right-wing talk radio hosts demean any who battle the status quo.

Protesters have to be prepared for the possibility of physical repression. Goon Squads were used against labor organizers, tactical police against war protesters, and southern law enforcement personnel assisted local hooligans in beating up civil rights workers. During the sixties, police raided homes of African American militants and killed them. Repression against African American and Native American militants included "eavesdropping, bogus mail, black propaganda operations, disinformation, harassment arrests, infiltration, snitch-jacketing—creating suspicion—through the spreading of rumors, manufacturing of evidence—that bona fide organization members . . . are FBI/police informers—, fabrication of evidence and even assassination" (Churchill and Wall 1988). The FBI and state level police spied on protesters, planted stories to discredit leaders such as Martin Luther King, Jr., and delayed enforcing laws that would have protected civil rights protesters (Branch 1998).

More recently in Seattle, protesters against globalization were attacked with clubs and tear gas as a police force ran amok, while during a sit-in at the capitol building in Nashville, Tennessee, the governor ordered that no food or water be allowed in. In this era of concern about terrorism, surveillance—both physical and through prying into personal records—is turned to stymie legitimate social dissent (Stanley and Steinhardt 2003). For example,

> The ACLU has denounced a classified FBI intelligence memorandum . . . which gives police detailed instructions on how to target and monitor lawful political demonstrations under the rubric of fighting terrorism. . . . Of particular concern is one section warning law enforcement about protesters' use of videotaping as an "intimidation" technique. (ACLU Online 2003)

Another tactic is for the police to arrest activist leaders prior to a scheduled demonstration and hold them until it is too late for them to act (Crespo 2002, 70).

Progressive movements are opposed by counter-movements. The right-to-life movement vigorously battles the gains of pro-choice activists; after affirmative action enabled women and minorities to have fairer access to jobs, contracts, and educational opportunities, a strong counter-movement grew up to oppose this leveling. A generation ago, conservative foundations decided to sponsor right-wing researchers whose work provides the ideological backbone for the backlash against progressive change. As part of the backlash,

> conservative funders have become much more organized, collaborative, and aggressive in their funding of policy research and advocacy, focusing resources on a few large, ideologically focused think tanks, including the American Enterprise Institute, the Heritage Foundation, the Cato Institute, and the Center for Strategic and International Studies. While liberal foundations fund hundreds of highly specialized groups on a plethora of issues . . . conservatives appear to have focused resources on groups with strong Washington connections to policy makers. Increasingly, they are also replicating this strategy at the state level. (Immergluck 2004, 15)

Describing the problems faced by gay organizations, Tina Fetner points out

> counter movement participants may attempt to create or overturn legislation. They may pressure a corporation, police department or elected representatives to take a proposed course of action. They may engage in cultural crusades to alter values and shared meanings. (Fetner 2001, 413)

Pro-gun groups, antichoice organizations, and those who oppose taxes have organized effective national campaigns. Backlash succeeds when activists let their attention drift. For years, in a poor Minneapolis neighborhood progressives working through a neighborhood association had brought about a supply of affordable housing. More conservative elements organized, encouraged their supporters to show up at the annual election meeting of the neighborhood group, and took over the organization and promptly destroyed the affordable housing programs (Goetz and Sidney 1994; Rubin 2000a).

Conservatives work hard to take over government and once in power work to roll back the clock. After successful voting registration campaigns took place in Ohio and in Florida, elected officials started enforcing petty regulations—on the weight of the paper on which the registrations were submitted, for example, to harass those seeking to register the poor. In Chapter 7, we described the ways in which those in the Bush administration have sought and often succeeded in tearing down gains of the last generation. In Louisiana activists worked through a law clinic to combat environmental pollution impacting the poor until those in office issued orders forbidding any public law clinic from engaging in class-action environmental suits (Chase 2005).

Conservative groups working through Representative Daniel Istook (R. Oklahoma) introduced legislation to forbid any organization receiving federal support from using federal money or other money that it raises to lobby public officials. So far this legislation has failed to pass (in part, because it would hurt such mainstream groups as the American Red Cross) but it represents an attempt to silence those who oppose the status quo. But different approaches are now in use as

> Government agencies and officials and conservative allies are increasingly targeting nonprofit organizations for their free speech activities, as OMB Watch documents . . .

Retaliatory action against government grantees that engage in controversial policy discussions or active advocacy that includes points of view different from the administration, regardless of how well those views are supported by science. (OMB Watch 2004)

When faced with a backlash, progressive activists have little choice but to fight to preserve past gains. To fail to fight is to concede the field to the backlash, but efforts spent in protecting past gains take time away from work on current issues.

Understanding the Environment in Which Social Mobilization Campaigns Occur

Strategies for action campaigns differ over time and place depending upon changes in the broader political and social environments. How to pressure for affordable housing is quite different in an upscale, suburban, Republican community than in an older, Democratic city. Working to improve family leave policy is a very different matter in a corporation with a gender balance up and down the hierarchy than in one with all male executives and women holding lower paid, impermanent positions. Strategies are also affected by the presence or absence of other social change organizations. In communities that have a rich variety of social change organizations, such as Chicago, for instance, coordination is often a must in planning successful campaigns, both to obtain allies and make sure those on the same side are not giving out contradictory messages.

Activists need to pay close attention to the **political opportunity structure**, that is, the receptivity of those in office to their demands (Tarrow 1994). A radical demonstration that would have been acceptable in the sixties in Berkeley, California, will cause only anger and backlash if carried out in present-day suburban America. In conservative times, civil disobedience is treated as an illegitimate affront to society that can be violently repressed. Economic issues—housing costs, job insecurity, the growing inequality of income—might be the primary concern of the action organization, but if the political discourse focuses on wedge social issues—public prayer, minority rights, gay marriage—gaining attention for the economic issues can prove difficult.

Keeping Up Morale over the Long Run

Sometimes social mobilization campaigns take so long that activists get discouraged and drop out (Gitlin 1989, 424). This loss of morale is most apparent in fights that persist over several generations, such as those for civil rights, gender equality, increased worker control, and a more equitable distribution of income. What does an organization do to cope with the loss of morale during long-run campaigns?

One response is to break up the broader campaign into smaller efforts for which a quick and reinforcing victory is possible. Working toward a neighborhood park can be the first step in reclaiming an entire community. When people get discouraged, spend some time together reviewing the history of successful movements. Examine how long they took to bring about important changes. Remind those who seem discouraged that the basic rights that they now assume came about only after a long struggle in which defeats were frequent. For instance, federal recognition of the right to unionize only dates back half a century, and took two generations to bring about. The United States is only two generations removed from legalized racial discrimination. The young women of today are the third generation who have legal access to birth control. A generation ago most gays were still in the closet, while those with disabilities were often treated as charity cases. Some of these campaigns still have a way to go, but improvement has been marked.

Activists should understand that there will be times in which action seems to stop. Keep in mind that if success were easy, the struggle would not be necessary. As Todd Gitlin describes in his reflections on the unfinished revolution of the sixties: "'It was not granted you to complete the task,' said Rabbi Tarfon nineteen hundred years ago, 'and yet you may not give it up'" (Gitlin 1989, 438).

Reflect upon Progressive Values during Social Mobilization Campaigns

Campaigns must demonstrate the values underlying the democratic, progressive model. In the nitty-gritty of hard ball lobbying or in the harsh mockery of street theater it is too easy to forget that campaigns are not simply about gaining immediate victories but instead are steps on the path toward building a "world as it should be" (Chambers 2003, 25). Campaigns should not demean others—for instance by calling opponents "rednecks" and in doing so demeaning people by class and ethnicity. Tactics should be chosen to empower those involved, even if doing so might at first pass seem the slower route. While going through the legal system is sometimes the only choice, doing so involves only a handful of participants and is less empowering than a broad-based lobbying effort.

Choose Tactics That Are Considered Legitimate and Appropriate

For campaigns to succeed in the short run, while remaining true to core values of progressive organizing, both organizational members and the broader public have to accept that the tactics used are appropriate. But what is considered appropriate changes over time and can differ by locale. Studies in Europe document the changing fashion for direct action tactics, some in a positive way, as large-scale demonstrations that had been associated with an anarchist past are no longer seen as a revolutionary threat (Rucht 1998).

In choosing tactics, a rule of thumb is that the more extreme the problem, the more accepting the public is of a militant tactic. Kidnapping a business executive to protest the dumping of toxic waste might have appeal but would rarely be seen as legitimate. Few neighborhood associations would conduct a violent demonstration to convince the city council to provide an additional stop sign; on the other hand, peaceful petitions to racist voting registrars in the South, at best, got a scornful dismissal, so more vigorous and confrontational efforts were required and were considered appropriate. However, "some socially unacceptable forms of protest will gain attention precisely because they are socially unacceptable" (Crozat 1998, 59). For instance, ACT-UP protests involved displays of sexuality that were meant to shock but did succeed in bringing attention to the horrors of AIDS that many were denying. When men undressed in public to protest the exploitation of women, it made clear the need to battle underlying sexism. Shocking tactics battle the attempts to deny the existence of a problem.

Means and Ends

Whether a tactic is viewed as legitimate depends in part on whether the means used can be reconciled with the ends sought. For some—though not us—the ends may justify the means. Thus radical environmentalists are willing to put spikes in trees, ruining them for lumber, but creating a risk of injury of lumberjacks, legitimating that this dangerous tactic is the only way of saving the forest. For others, the ends never justifies the means. If something is wrong, it is always wrong, regardless of the circumstances.

But as Saul Alinsky described, what might not be legitimate in one situation might be appropriate and moral in another. Alinsky was particularly concerned that the opponents would demand that a community group be forced to meet unrealistic ethical standards and in doing so be rendered impotent. Alinsky offered the following reflections in balancing ends and means:

1. One's concerns with the ethics of means and ends varies inversely with one's personal interest in the issue.
2. The judgment of the ethics of means is dependent upon the political position of those sitting in judgment.
3. In war the end justifies almost any means.
4. Judgment must be made in the context of the times in which the action occurred and not from any other chronological vantage point.
5. Concern with ethics increases with the number of means available and vice versa.
6. The less important the end to be desired, the more one can afford to engage in ethical evaluation of means.
7. Generally, success or failure is a mighty determinant of ethics.
8. The morality of means depends upon whether the means is being employed at a time of imminent defeat or imminent victory.
9. Any effective means is automatically judged by the opposition as being unethical.
10. You do what you can with what you have and clothe it with moral garments. (Alinsky 1971, 24–27)

Balancing means and ends can be difficult. It is wrong for leaders of a protest organization to deceive their members about planned illegal actions, but if the members know and agree, are illegal actions then appropriate? How the law is broken affects the legitimacy of the action. Is a break-in to obtain documents that seriously compromise a target (a planning report that shows that a company knew that the pollutant would cause cancer) worth the violation of law? Sitting in and being arrested in a bank lobby to symbolize the bank's unwillingness to provide loans in the community is clearly a political protest, and may gain public sympathy. Robbing the bank, even if the money is given to the poor, will not.

When violating laws, even unjust laws, people must be willing to accept arrests, as being arrested demonstrates commitment. Activists who risk their lives for the cause, by blocking factory entrances to protest the production of weapons or chaining themselves to bulldozers, accept known risk in ways that, because of the courage shown, often resonates in a positive way with the public. Laws can, perhaps should be, violated when the intent is to demonstrate the injustice of that same law. So when black and white civil rights workers entered restaurants together, shared drinking fountains, and shared seats on public transportation, they violated Southern Jim Crow laws to show how wrong the laws were.

Ultimately, as Martin Luther King, Jr., argued, ends are present in the means (Branch 1988, 871) and to accept without questioning that the means justifies the ends assumes the purpose of the mobilization is to solve an immediate problem, irrespective of whether or not it is a step to bringing about a better society. Activists have to be concerned about whether, to achieve a limited victory, they adopt the morality of the enemy, and in doing so lose the larger battle.

Violence and Ideological Nonviolence. Probably the most difficult question of means and end is determining when violence is appropriate, if ever, and what constitutes violence. This question is far from theoretical as violence has been present in labor organizing, antiwar efforts, and in battles over choice. Civil rights workers were beaten and shot, and many died. The Students for a Democratic Society grew out of pacifistic movements, yet the Weather Faction of SDS advocated sabotage as a way of stopping the war in Vietnam. In the civil rights movement, the nonviolent leadership of Martin Luther King, Jr., contrasts sharply with the militancy and violent self-defense in the philosophies of Malcolm X or "Rap" Brown.

We do not advocate intentionally seeking violent encounters as there is a fundamental contradiction between using violence and the respect for human dignity and autonomy that underlies the progressive ideology. As César Chavez argued:

> If we had used violence we would have won contracts a long time ago but they would-n't have been lasting because we wouldn't have won respect. Wages are not the main issue in the strike . . . No what is at stake is human dignity. If a man [sic] is not accorded respect, he cannot respect himself and if he does not respect himself, he cannot demand it. (Chavez quoted in Ecklein 1984, 15)

Yet, the potential for violence is present in many community actions in which angry words easily can turn into fights. Protesters may goad police, trying to elicit an overreaction that will make the police look bad, or police may provoke protesters. As Shel Trapp points out, one can be confrontational yet not violent:

> Actions are confrontational but they aren't violent. No one gets hurt at a demonstration. To my knowledge NPA never hurt another person or destroyed any property. The leaders of NPA are committed to non-violence . . . When you decide to go for violence as a way to create change, you are not better than a gangbanger doing a drive-by shooting, or Adolph Hitler. Violence brings on more violence. (Trapp n.d., 87)

Many social activists preach a policy of *active nonviolence* or *civil disobedience* that "requires a willingness to take risk and bear suffering without retaliation that on a most fundamental level, becomes the way through which people discover their social power" (Irwin and Faison 1984, 2). The devoted practitioners of nonviolence refuse to fight back when provoked, passively accepting abuse and going limp when being arrested.

Nonviolence can turn brute power against itself, a form of political jiu-jitsu. Society has fairly strong norms against anyone hitting or shooting an unarmed person. Nonviolence can persuade by creating a moral image for those in the action organization while making it clear how much the power the opponents have depends on repressive force. But nonviolence is more than passively sitting there.

> Nonviolent action is *active*—it involves activity in the collective pursuit of social or political objectives—and it is *non-violent*—it does not involve physical force or the threat of physical force against human beings. . . .
>   Non-violent action is *not* inaction . . . it is *not* submissiveness, it is *not* the avoidance of conflict, and it is *not* passive resistance. (Schock 2003, 705)

As expressed by Martin Luther King, Jr.:

1. Nonviolence is a way of life for courageous people
2. Nonviolence seeks to win friendship and understanding
3. Nonviolence seeks to defeat injustice, not people
4. Nonviolence holds that suffering can educate and transform
5. Nonviolence chooses love instead of hate
6. The believer in nonviolence has a deep faith in the future

Conclusions: Strategic Planning and Action Campaigns

Effective campaigns begin by formulating a strategy that addresses the overall purpose of the effort by balancing out the work to solve immediate problems with actions to bring about broader changes. Strategy goes beyond working on both the immediate and longer range problems to answer other concerns. Will the actions encourage new members to join the organization? How will it impact the current membership? Will the proposed actions brand the organization as one that is disruptive or as one that is perhaps overly accommodative and how will that image affect future actions? Is the issue important on its own merits or is it primarily a means for the organization to gain recognition and get a place at the decisional table?

Strategies evolve as campaigns progress so make sure time is set aside to re-evaluate while a campaign is going on. During these times ask: are the initial issues still appropriate or should the concerns be broadened (from homelessness to the over-all shortage of affordable housing), or perhaps narrowed (from the lack of funding of education, to the problems in the neighborhood school)? Also reflect if the approaches are consistent with the purposes of the organization and how the organization is perceived: Is the organization gaining a reputation as a concerned citizens' group or are the members seen as wild-eyed quasi-terrorists? Has the organization now become a player in the political game, one to be consulted and respected, or is it an intermittent participant mostly to be ignored? Are participants feeling successful and empowered? Has the campaign enabled community leaders to emerge, and if so, what role do they now play? What tactics have been mastered that will stand in good stead in the next campaign? Have alliances of people's organizations been formed and strengthened?

Strategies are carried out through a wide variety of tactics ranging from quiet petitioning to confrontational demonstrations. In practice, most campaigns involve a combination of approaches, a balance between working within the system as well as disruption. In the next several chapters, after discussing how to mobilize people to join in campaigns, we detail several families of direct action tactics.

CHAPTER
15

Mobilizing Individuals and Groups

Mobilization occurs when people who face similar problems come together to fight back in an organized way. But degrees of involvement differ from passively supporting a cause to having the cause become the driving force of one's life. Let us examine what mobilization can entail, why in a world of social injustice many are not mobilized, and then explore how organizers and activists seek to mobilize others.

Understanding Mobilization

Mobilization has occurred when people recognize they share a problem with others and that they must act together on the matter. Mobilization can begin when individuals recognize a problem, perhaps through *click* events (click as when a light turns on) that

> spring from "practical" matters which cause fear and anger in people's lives, such as parents' horror when they find out that their children have been drinking water polluted by toxic chemicals. (Krauss 1988, 260)

Or, recognition might come about after a conversation with an organizer, during which an individual recognizes that his or her fear of going out at night is a rational response to the drug traffic in the neighborhood, not some personal failing. Mobilization continues as people learn that others face the same problem and expands as people come together in an action organization that battles for change.

Mobilization Builds upon Pre-Existing Needs and Grievances

Mobilization often begins in response to what is both immediate and personal, perhaps to obtain a **personal material benefit**—better daycare, a job, health care, or an affordable mortgage. But mobilization based on satisfying immediate, material needs lacks staying power as shown in the history of the Massachusetts Welfare Rights Organization (NWRO).

NWRO organizers were able to promise welfare recipients that if they participated in welfare rights activities, they would soon be rewarded by supplementary welfare grants . . . many of the general membership gained enough confidence to make demands of the welfare office personnel without belonging to a group, others soon found that after a few major supplementary welfare checks had been won, there was little more that the group could continue to offer them. Thus all components in the welfare rights movement—members, organizers, and leaders—began to lose interest in maintaining the local affiliates and the groups began to fade away. (Bailis 1974, 3)

A more lasting mobilization occurs when people understand that they systematically are victims of a persisting oppression from, for instance, racism, sexism, or homophobia. They learn through a **trigger event** (McCarthy and Zald 1987)—a dramatic and public happening—that the problem they feel on a personal level has broader social causes. Organizers build on this trigger event to gel the preexisting, free-floating personal discontent into an organized and focused social change effort.

People feel problems on a personal level—coal miners know that their lungs are clogged, African Americans face discrimination, and those who suffer from a disability confront the obstacles society places in their path each day. What a trigger event does is highlight the societal nature of the problem so dramatically that both victims and the larger population can no longer deny its existence or importance and are moved from feeling the grievance individually to trying to do something about it collectively. In the civil rights era, southern African Americans were well aware of their oppression, but feared taking action. A trigger event occurred when young African Americans boldly sat down at lunch counters reserved for whites, provoking violence against themselves but by doing so making private grievances public. Individuals with black lung disease in the coal industry and brown lung in the textile industry knew their own suffering but took little action until physicians funded by the United Church of Christ and the (Catholic) Campaign for Human Development came to town and made public that company doctors had been lying about the health of the workers.

Professional organizers build on trigger events to mobilize individuals by showing that the immediate, personal problems faced are part of a broader structural problem that the trigger event has made visible. Doing so links personal grievances to the broader social concerns while showing that joining a social change organization is a way of seeking out a solution.

Mobilization by Believing in a Common Issue or Sharing an Identity

When people have a **shared understanding of an issue** or when they feel a **shared identity with a group** they are more willing to fight on that issue or to defend the interests of the group with which they identify. These **solidarity incentives** mobilize people in several ways. First those who identify with a group recognize that as a member of the group they have an obligation to support the broader community, even if only because as a member, they too will eventually benefit. "If the highway goes through here, the Armenian [Greek, Turkish . . .] Church will be unable to keep its social program. Kids, such as mine, my nieces and nephew, will find it harder to keep up the traditions. Perhaps I should join the Stop the Highway Organization."

People mobilize based on a shared identity as they see others like themselves benefit even if they themselves as individuals are not immediately impacted. Older women might march to support abortion rights, even though they are unlikely to need abortions themselves. Instead they are acting on an identity with all women—their daughters, nieces, friends, and acquaintances. Further, those in an identity group recognize that they share multiple concerns and help with others on one concern will encourage others to help with issues of more personal import. A wheelchair-bound person supports those with hearing disabilities, and vice versa, both recognizing that their shared cause is about creating a more humane and accessible society.

Once people feel part of an identity or solidarity group, they can be mobilized for shared issues, but membership in a solidarity group cannot be presupposed. According to the literature on new social movements (NSM) shared identities are not static, but instead involve an ongoing process of negotiation that is often shaped by underlying concerns of race and social class (Buechler 1995; Johnson and Castengera 1994; Larana, Johnston, Hank, et al. 1994). Africans who have recently immigrated to the United States, those of African heritage who lived in the Caribbean, and African Americans who are descendants of slaves brought to this continent centuries ago might be identified by others as black, but do they identify as a solidarity community?

What constitutes an identity or solidarity group is **constructed** and mobilization is based upon those who share agreement on what characteristics constitute the shared identity. For instance, black, Chicana, and white feminists responded so differently to issues of race and class that no one identity grouping as a feminist emerged (Roth 2004). Gays and lesbians might organize separately, if gender, along with homosexuality, is core to defining the identity, but might come together if identity is based entirely on sexual orientation. The organization "Queer Nation" successfully communicated that the oppression that both gays and lesbians separately face stems from the broader problem of homophobia, thus uniting men and women in the same campaign.

Identities can be constructed in ways that expand solidarity groups, increasing the numbers who come together. For instance, an Asian activist identity emerged when people of Chinese, Japanese, and Filipino descent, among others, interpreted the problems they faced as stemming from prejudices against Asians, not because of their separate national origins (Wei 1993). Similarly, after much discourse, the separate, but politically weak, cultural group that inhabited North America prior to European settlement determined they would be more effective in fighting a common oppression if they accepted a shared identity as "Native Americans" or "Indians" (Nagel 1996).

Identification with a solidarity community is not enough if such an identification implies inaction. For example, not so many years ago, the identity of "disabled" implied being helpless and incompetent. With this negative identity, many individuals with impairments sought to disassociate themselves from those who shared the same disabilities, and little action occurred (Scotch 1988, 161). But organizers worked to redefine what disability entailed so as to encourage collective action as:

> a redefinition of disability was required—one that treated disability as a label for a group of people who had the potential for political action and who were unfairly excluded from mainstream social institutions on the basis of their physical or mental impairments. (Scotch 1988, 163)

Now, seeing one's identity in a positive way, a disabilities movement came about that was able to push for the passage of the Americans with Disabilities Act and to advocate for broader sensitivity toward the needs of those with disabilities, while at the same time increasing the sense of pride for the accomplishments of those who were wheelchair bound or who have hearing or visual difficulties (Fleischer and Zames 2001).

Degrees of Involvement

Identifying with a group is a vital step in mobilization, but more is required as people must take the next step to identify themselves as *activists* (Nepstad 2004, 56). The movement to an activist identity occurs in several stages and can end up with different levels of involvement.

There are those who won't get involved at all—the **apathetics**. Many others—the **passive participants**—can be mobilized but in a limited way, contributing a little money, signing a letter, occasionally showing up at a meeting or a rally. **Foot soldiers** are people who will work hard on an issue—show up at meetings, prepare food or put out chairs, hand out flyers, draw posters, push a broom in a cleanup effort, go door-to-door to distribute information, sign letters—but rarely take on a leadership position. **Issue activists** are more deeply involved and themselves might start up a social change effort. Issue activists willingly spend much of their free time working on the matters and often act as **volunteer organizers** who encourage others to join. **Local leaders** are well known and respected individuals in their communities who help shape how others think about issues and if mobilized on an issue themselves become volunteer organizers. Finally, there are **professional issue and community organizers** and **progressive economic development and social service organizers** who work full time on social change matters, are paid for doing so, and then often continue the work on their own time (greatly modified from Milbrath 1977).

Mobilization Bootstraps but Participation Might not be Sustained

Successful mobilization efforts **bootstrap**, that is, involvement begins with a toe in the water but after victories occur involvement increases. A successful effort by a neighborhood association to chase drug pushers from one park encourages other community members to join in future work to take back the streets. Bootstrapping occurs as trust builds even from coming together in ordinary daily activities. In a study of public housing, researchers found that

> In the course of watching a neighbor's children . . . a relationship might develop that will in time lead to discussion of topics, including the social and health issues . . . It may also lead neighbors to work together to solve neighborhood problems and provide the impetus for contacting an elected official . . . neighboring becomes a way to establish and test the limits of trust and goodwill. When those limits have been established, residents are perhaps more willing to share their concerns about the neighborhood and their ideas about how to improve it. This is the essence of mobilization. (Bolland and McCallum 2002, 64)

Joining together in one effort, showing up at city hall for a hearing, for instance, encourages people to become even more committed to the cause, even when the initial efforts are only marginally successful (Speer and Hughey 1995), as an *emergent solidarity* develops among the activists (Fantasia 1988, 88).

But successful bootstrapping requires continued involvement, not just promises, as the willingness to participate declines as the effort and risk increases. For instance, far more people express support for an issue than are willing to demonstrate or even sign a petition, as shown in a study of peace demonstrations in Europe against the deployment of nuclear missiles. In a survey 74 percent of the people who were affected by the deployment of nuclear missiles opposed their placement. Eighty percent of those expressing opposition were contacted by activists who were setting up demonstrations. Even so, only one of six promised to show up and, worse yet, only one out of twenty-five actually did (Klandermans and Oegema 1987).

Later investigation sought out why people were unwilling to be involved even when they supported the issue. *The most important reason was that they had not been personally contacted by an organizer to encourage them to stay involved.* In addition, many people who said they opposed the missiles were only marginally opposed, did not want to disagree with the government officials who supported the deployment of the missiles, and were involved in peer and friendship groups that did not agree with the protest (Oegema and Klanderman 1994). Personal persuasion can increase involvement, but the effectiveness of contact can be diminished if the social networks in which people are involved offer a message opposite to that given by organizers.

Political Participation and Social Apathy: Should It Discourage Trying?

Mobilization is the antidote to the systemic forms of disempowerment discussed in Chapter 4—fear, learned inefficacy, the organization of consent, and the system bias. Unfortunately, many remain apathetic especially when dealing with political issues (Eliasoph 1998). People limit their activities to what is immediate to themselves and assume fixing underlying problems is not possible, rationalizing that authorities know what they are doing and that a complaint to those in power is the best that can be done to fix a problem (Eliasoph 1998, 59). Further they argue that involvement in politics is a "waste of time" (Eliasoph 1998, 129) and claim that activists should be ignored because they are primarily "puffing themselves up" (i.e., involved in an ego trip) (Eliasoph 1998, 135).

Political apathy (or is it fear or resignation?) can be seen in the low participation level in the ordinary act of casting a vote in Table 15-1.

These figures show that overall participation is not all that high and, worse yet, indicate those who are poorest are least likely to be politically engaged. Other data on who participates indicate that the well educated are politically more involved than the poorly educated; majority-group members are more active than are minority-group members; the wealthy participate more than the poor; and people in professional occupations participate more than blue-collar workers (Smith, Reddy, and Baldwin 1980; Steggert 1975). In addition, the participation rate of homeowners in 2000 was twice that of renters (84.7 percent vs. 43.8 percent) (National Low Income Housing Coalition 2004).

At first, these findings appear disheartening for those working with the poor or minorities. But other research offers more hope. To begin, voting is not the only act of political participation. About 8 percent of the population is involved in some community organization (defined broadly), about 14 percent have made contact with government officials, 30 percent work with others on local problems, and only a handful—3 percent—claim that they would participate in public demonstrations (Milbrath 1977, 18–19). Further, if people are interested in a particular local problem, they may participate irrespective of their educational or economic background (Wandersman 1981, 37).

Other predictors of participation also provide some optimism about the potential to mobilize people. People with stronger organizational linkages are more likely to become active, as models of social capital would suggest. For examples, studies of Latino/Latina communities in which participation overall is quite low, show that women, who are far more "embedded in (and more aware of their embeddedness in) social relations than are men," are more likely to form participatory and politically active social networks than are the men (Hardy-Fanta 1993, 24). Even being a client of a neighborhood service organization, one form of community integration, increases involvement in other local organizations (Thomas 1986).

TABLE 15.1 U.S. Census Bureau Data on Voter Registration and Participation in 2000

Income	% Registered	% Voting of Those Registered
Below $5,000	53.1	34.2
$5,000–$9,999	57.1	40.6
$10,000–$14,999	58.6	44.3
$15,000–$24,999	65.0	51.3
$25,000–$34,999	69.0	57.3
$35,000–$49,999	72.3	61.9
$50,000–$74,999	77.9	68.7
Over $75,000	82.1	74.9

Source: National Low Income Housing Coalition 2004

Identifying with almost any local group increases the willingness to become involved, while those who feel that a collectivity to which they belong is politically efficacious are even more likely to join in with others in political actions (Yeich and Levine 1994). Those who live in cooperative apartment buildings, and feel that other co-owners are active, more readily join collective activities (Saegert and Winkel 1996). Strong cultural or ethnic identification also increases political involvement. For instance, even though African Americans are less politically active than Caucasians, African Americans who emphasize their black identity are as politically involved as are whites. Identifying with a group increases participation (Milbrath 1977, 57).

People who have frequent contact with street-level government officials, especially positive contact, are more likely to become involved (Lawless and Fox 2001, 363). In "fact, confidence in social service workers bolstered an 'average' respondent's probability of being a voter by more than 19% and the probability of being a political participant by as much as 20%" (Lawless and Fox 2001, 373). The opposite finding held with the police; those who had bad experiences with the police were more likely to become involved (Lawless and Fox 2001, 376). People who have strong interpersonal linkages within their neighborhoods but are highly dissatisfied with city services are very likely to join in collective activities (Crenson 1980), while those who are involved in programs that mandate some form of civic participation, such as Head Start, are more likely to be involved politically (Soss 2005, 303).

Studies verify that political participation, both in voting or in participating on public boards, is lower among the poor than the wealthy—not because of indifference, but because of a feeling that their efforts don't matter. When efforts are shown to count, participation goes up. In his study of citizen participation in Chicago's community school boards and police advisory boards, Archon Fung noted that while participation is higher in wealthier neighborhoods, in poorer neighborhoods people are actively involved when they feel their actions count (Fung 2004, 101). A study of a public housing project showed that people who felt angry in general, felt their actions would count, and were socially connected to others were likely to be politically involved. Interestingly, the grievances felt need not be specific but rather simply feeling anger increased people's willing to be mobilized (Conway and Hachen 2005, 46).

Lessons from Studies on Participation That Guide Mobilization Efforts

What lessons can be drawn from this background material? First, moving people from inactivity to social action is difficult, though identifying with a solidarity group increases the chances of involvement as does self-interest. Perception counts. Individuals must believe that it is permissible to fight back and that efforts are not in vain and that solutions are possible. Involvement can differ in both intensity and duration from one-time passive support to dedicating one's whole life to the issue. With those already concerned about an issue, mobilization might be as simple as letting them know an event has been planned. On the other side, it can take years to build and then mobilize a national membership organization.

Still, activists should not expect everyone to join, even those that agree with the issues. Further, those who do sign up need continual reinforcement, because the opposition will be trying to discourage them from continuing to participate. But once involved in collective action an *encumbrance* occurs (Ogilvie 2004), that is, people develop a continuing and reinforcing sense of obligation to the community or the organization to which they have now become part.

Mobilization is much more than simply getting people to join an organization or even show up at an action. It involves an intellectual engagement, an understanding that what is being fought is both the broader structure of unjust power and a mindset pushed by those in power to convince people that they lack the capacity to fight back or even the need to do so. Mobilization is about wanting to join the fray and understanding why one must do so.

Mobilization Tactics and Processes

Mobilization is not a one-time matter. It continues through action campaigns as successes encourage those who have been involved to redouble their efforts while encouraging additional people to join up. This self-sustaining mobilization is what keeps activists, local leaders, and professional organizers involved and willing to continue the battle. The bigger challenge is then in moving those who are at present inactive, perhaps unaware of a problem or the possibility of a solution, to join the fight.

A wide variety of techniques are followed, some doing little more than sending out announcements. Most effective though are approaches that are based upon *relationship building*. **Canvassing** occurs when volunteer and professional organizers personally reach out to convince others to join in the cause. With **network activation**, organizers encourage those whom they know to reach out to their friends, neighbors, and acquaintances to join. Activists work with **established community institutions**— churches, social groups, political clubs, smaller block associations—and urge leaders of these in-place organizations to encourage their members to be involved. For the most part, canvassing, network activation, and mobilizing established community institutions are primarily about recruiting foot soldiers to an ongoing cause. **House meetings** and various forms of **consciousness raising** are also about recruiting foot soldiers but then become an important step in mobilizing issue activists.

Canvassing

Canvassing happens when either a volunteer or professional organizer goes door-to-door to meet people, hear what they have to say, and to introduce themselves and the social action organization. New organizers are often assigned to canvassing work, in part to test their mettle, and in part so they can learn first-hand about problems people face. Canvassing is important because

> Person-to-person contacts build organizations where people feel equally valued. When someone takes the trouble to visit to you and talk with you about his or her

organization, it means something, especially when you know that the person is not being paid to hustle you. (Kahn 1982, 110)

Interactions differ depending upon the purpose of the canvass. At times, a canvass is little more than a membership drive, where the organizer explains the purposes of the activist group but is mainly focused on soliciting a contribution or signing a person up as a member. Some canvassing is primarily about spreading information on an event and encouraging people to attend. Though important, these more passive forms of canvassing do little to empower.

But canvassing can also provide a time to listen as community members express what is bothering them. Sometimes people are just waiting for an opportunity to complain and the organizer provides that opportunity. Canvassers will hear about the personal aspects of larger problems. Individuals don't talk about income distributions; they worry whether they earn enough. People don't think about urban planning, but they care if the traffic is increasing on streets that their kids have to cross. In organizing, "As one activist put it, 'At the local level, you organize around dog shit, stop signs, whatever people are talking about'" (Cassidy 1980, 72).

But care is needed to make sure that real communication occurs. If a canvasser starts out the conversation by asking, "Is dirty drinking water a problem for you?" and the resident answers, "Yes, but . . . " and the canvasser says to himself or herself, "Aha, dirty water is a problem," a wrong conclusion might be drawn. The person could be bothered by the water, but won't take action on this issue, since there was something more important he or she wanted to say but didn't get a chance.

During a conversation held while canvassing, several things are accomplished, sometimes simultaneously:

- an organizer introduces himself or herself and suggests general concerns that might affect the overall community;
- the organizer encourages the people being canvassed to talk about the problems they feel strongly about;
- the organizer briefly describes the community organization, suggesting how that organization can help overcome the problems mentioned;
- the organizer encourages the person to join the organization and to show up for its meetings.

In the initial canvass, the organizer balances listening to what bothers people with letting people know what the organization can accomplish. For instance,

> **ORGANIZER:** Hello, I'm Herb Rubin a neighbor who is working for SDA— the Southside DeKalb Association. You've probably heard of the work we've done in pressuring city hall to pay more attention to the neighborhoods, especially the flood and sewer problems, as the city rapidly grows.
>
> **NEIGHBOR:** Yes.
>
> **ORGANIZER:** Well, we're trying to get some people together who are worried about how all the new housing might cause more flood problems. Are you concerned about problems of rapid growth?

> NEIGHBOR: Yes, but my house doesn't flood. I'm bothered by the increased traffic with all the new stores and traffic signals. I also worry about whether the growth will increase our taxes.
>
> ORGANIZER: That's interesting. In particular what about the traffic or taxes bothers you . . .

The organizer then listens to what the person expresses, and indicates how others are also concerned about similar problems. The organizer would then indicate that the SDA is working on these problems, and suggest that the person might want to sign up and attend a meeting. Assuming that SDA has prepared a flyer describing the organization and indicating when and where the next meeting will be held, the flyer is handed out.

Once such conversations are begun, it is sometimes difficult to get people to stop; they have found a sympathetic ear and want to pour out their frustrations. Skillful canvassers learn to listen and then draw the conversation to a close by showing how by working together neighbors can solve the problems they share.

When canvassing is being done by organizations that already focus on specific issues—for example, tenants' rights in a neighborhood owned by absentee slumlords—during the initial comments the organizer should concentrate on these issues, though still listen to other matters raised. He or she specifies that the organization has been set up to help tenants get better services for their rent dollars. The organizer encourages the potential recruit to talk about problems with housing (in the services received, in dealing with the landlord, and other similar matters). When the person wants to talk about other issues—lack of jobs, poor neighborhood schools—the canvasser has to perform a juggling act, empathizing with the expressed concerns, while at the same time steering the conversation back to the problems of housing and tenant-landlord relationships.

Difficulties can occur. In many neighborhoods it is hard to get people to open the door and talk; others are too tired or busy and some are simply afraid to open doors to strangers. Canvassers who show up night after night in the same community will find that people begin to recognize them and will open the doors and chat. Some organizers simply hang around the neighborhood, perhaps playing pickup ball with teenagers, or talking with people in public places. Another problem in getting people to participate is that they fear sticking out, of being first. To handle such concerns, meet with local leaders before beginning the canvass, and, assuming they are willing, include their names in brochures and conversations.

During canvassing, activists will hear excuses for noninvolvement that they recognize might not be real. For instance, a person might say "I am too busy to spend an evening a month at organization meetings" when in fact the real reason is he or she is afraid of being criticized by a boss. People may say they don't think a crime patrol will work, but they may mean that they don't want to get involved with the police under any circumstances. To handle such situations, "learn to search out the rationalizations, treat them as rationalizations, and break through" (Alinsky 1971, 112).

Organizers do so by listening to the reasons people give for not being involved and try to hear the undertones and then work to overcome unexpressed fears. For instance, people in the Edgewater neighborhood in Chicago did not want to participate in an anticrime organization for fear of having to show up in court. Hearing these fears, the organization set up a system in which community members went together when one was to testify in court (Marciniak 1981). At times, people are silent on issues because they do not want to embarrass themselves. Until newspaper and television accounts appeared that described predatory lenders (people who rip off homeowners through overpriced and deceptive mortgages) many victims simply kept silent, out of shame of being defrauded, and never raised the issues with organizers.

One-On-Ones

During canvassing a relationship between the potential recruit and the organizer is begun that can lead to deeper, longer one-on-one conversations that are another way of mobilizing people. For instance, "in bringing the United Power organization to birth in metropolitan Chicago from 1995 to 1997, the organizers and initial leaders conducted 9,000 to 9,500 relational meetings over two years" (Chambers 2003, 48). Further continuing one-on-one meetings later on reinforces mobilization both by making sure that members maintain a linkage to the action organization and that the organization itself is continuing to follow the path chosen by its community.

With this approach

> the crucial work . . . occurs through a process of face-to-face meetings between one committee member or staff organizer and an individual member . . . Such one-on-one meetings typically last about a half hour, and are simply conversations—but conversations rather different than most Americans are used to, in that participants are encouraged to seek what really motivates the other person, what they care deeply about and thus establish a relationship built on more than causal chat. (Wood 2002, 35)

The conversations empower by helping people verbalize what is bothering them and discovering that solutions are possible. In turn, organizers discover who among present and potential members has the ability and drive to become an organizational leader (Wood 2002, 35–36). As the faith-based organizer Dennis Jacobsen describes:

> The one-on-one interview is the building block of an organization. In the initial stages of developing a congregation-based community organization, hundreds of people are trained to conduct thousands of one-on-ones . . . On one level a one-on-one is as natural as a conversation over a backyard fence . . . On another level it is skillful, artful, intentional and focused. The one-on-one is a means of initiating or building a relationship. The primary (and usually only) agenda of a one-on-one is to get to know the other person . . . It is a conversation in which we come to understand what is important to another person, what motivates him or her, what is his or her passion. (Jacobsen 2001, 59)

Further, as Edward Chambers, the head of the IAF describes:

> A solid relational meeting brings up stories that reveal people's deepest commitments and the experiences that give rise to them. In fact, the most important thing that hap-

pens in good relational meetings is the telling of stories that open a window into the passions that animate people to act. (Chambers 2003, 45)

But gaining the trust for the initial one-on-one conversation can be difficult; why confide in a stranger? To encourage openness, contacts are made based on a common membership in a trusted group, most likely a church, synagogue, or mosque, in which the religious leaders support the organizing efforts (Wood 2002, 165).

House Meetings

A house meeting is little more than people getting together at someone's home to informally discuss problems. House meetings can end up as consciousness-raising sessions in which people first learn they share a problem, discover that the problem is socially caused, and then search for ways to collectively fight back.

Meetings are scheduled at the homes of volunteers, who are asked to invite friends. Only a few are invited to keep people from being embarrassed about saying what is on their minds in front of a large group. At the meetings, organizers try to encourage people to express their concerns, then together think about the reasons they all face the same problems. As people recognize that they share the same problems, organizers describe how the problems can be overcome by working together.

César Chavez, the farm-worker activist, organized primarily through house meetings.

> César opened with a few introductory remarks and then, suddenly leaning forward as though about to confide some marvelous secret, asked softly if they had heard of the new organization he was building in the valley—the Farm Workers Association. None of them had, of course, nor was he all that familiar with it himself, having just that day decided on the name. But the words held magic, because heads came straining forward.
>
> He sat in silence, letting the suspense mount before he went on. It is a movement, he said, in which farm workers could struggle to free themselves from the injustice of the job, the government, and life in general. There was no ready-made plan, he assured them. This was one of the reasons he was meeting with them and other workers—to gradually put together ideas based upon what they wanted, along with some of his own. He then passed around some self-addressed three-by-five cards with the lines on the back for the name and address of the worker, and for what the worker considered a just hourly wage.
>
> The idea was an instant hit. Always before, one worker said, others had decided what he deserved. Now he, himself, was being consulted. "It's like letting us vote," he said, "on what we think." . . .
>
> César called for more questions and other issues were raised—the use of Mexican braceros who took the jobs away from local people, the many times they had been cheated by labor contractors, the lack of toilets and clean, cold water in the fields . . . . They could have gone on all night, but César cut in, explaining that when the workers had their own Association, many of these things would be changed. They would be able to stand up to the growers, he told them, and demand an end to the injustices they had been suffering for so many years. (Levy 1975, xxi–xxii)

A house meeting provides protection for individuals so disempowered that they are afraid of openly defying their oppressors and meeting alone with an organizer. For instance, during civil rights campaigns in the South, African Americans who were more financially secure than others, especially those who held federal jobs, hosted house meetings at which racial oppression and the desire for voting rights could be discussed while hiding from the employers of others attending (Payne 1995).

A similar approach was used in mobilizing ill-paid immigrant workers in the garment industry, though meetings were not held in their homes. Because of the resistance of management, union organizers were unable to meet with potential members at places of work, while workers were afraid to be seen talking with the organizers even in their homes. Instead labor unions worked with community agencies to set up a place that provided social as well as legal services to the workers and the families. These sites became the locations where discussions similar to those that take place at house meetings occurred (Gordon 2005; Needleman 1998).

Network Activation

Networks are the links between people who know each other socially, as kin, or through work, and through which aid, information, and support flow. Research on mobilization has shown that

> Starting with social networks, being connected to others will make it easier to ask others to join some form of collective action . . . Levels of non electoral political participation are higher for people who are connected to others to a greater extent particularly when these others are neighbors. Next, the impact of trust on neighborhood-oriented forms of participation derives from the expectation of reciprocity. Trust . . . makes people more willing to contribute to the quality of the neighborhood when they are confident that others will take their turn as well. (Lelieveldt 2004, 536)

Further, those in social networks develop similar understandings of issues and more closely identify with those who are willing to become involved (Passy 2001, 176,181). For instance, people already linked together in a helping network—to provide assistance in times of financial trouble or grief, to aid the elderly, or to assist those with disabilities—have already defined themselves as potential activists on these issues. Initially the Gay Alliances in San Francisco were built up along networks (Castells 1983), while in the civil rights era in the South, organizers who were referred to people had to travel along social networks lest they end up talking with the wrong people and getting shot at, beat up, or killed (Payne 1995). In addition, even when people believe in a cause they will not become active unless they are closely connected to others in their social networks who also support the cause (McAdam and Paulsen 1993). If my friends and relatives say its okay to join, it is okay.

To organize within networks, activists seek out and talk with opinion leaders who are central to a network, but in doing so keep in mind that opinion leaders are effective because they reflect the sentiments of others to whom they are linked, and not because people passively follow them. Further, within one network, opinion leaders differ depending on the issue. A person who can mobilize support for a social justice campaign might not be the same individual whose help is needed to activate people in a housing project. The organizer focuses attention on these individuals, explains to them the issues at hand, and encourages them to spread the word. Network organizing at its best encourages those already recruited to bring in their friends and neighbors, an especially effective approach when the community appears to be threatened (Small 2004, 179).

How this is done can be seen in Lawrence, Massachusetts, where activists "built a network of 900 members, over 400 of whom are active on a monthly basis" (Traynor and Andors 2005, 9). This network organizing began by reaching out to individuals who were involved in English as a Second Language training, as well as those who were part of an Individual Development Accounts program (an incentive program that helps people build up a small nest egg) then built on the networks of these individuals. "For example, several of the women participating in our IDA program have become hosts for Neighborhood Circles, reaching out to others on their block or their personal networks" (Traynor and Andors 2005, 10).

Mobilizing through Established Community Institutions

Another way to mobilize people is to unite the membership of already established community institutions. At times, as is often the case in IAF organizing, it is the established institutions themselves—the local churches, synagogues and mosques, social service organizations, and perhaps block groups—who set up the organization and will then invite in a professional organizer (Chambers 2003, 64). With this approach the base of an organization is already in place, with individual members already united. The early Alinsky organizations were built this way, starting with individual congregations and then spinning off a federated organization that spoke for the broader community. At its best, mobilization was relatively quick as people already were members of their congregations and trusted one another, while the clergy acted to link people between the separate institutions.

But building a new community group based upon existing organizations has its difficulties. Just because a religious group or any other established community institution sees the need for community work and can mobilize its own members does not mean that they will work together within the larger federated organization. In response to this problem, Ernie Cortes in Texas

> created a hybrid organizational form. Its members were institutions, that is, churches. But the organization was not a coalition, composed of institutional representations. Its leadership was drawn more broadly from the membership of those institutions and leaders operated together in a single organization . . . [the] structure allowed member parishes and neighborhood leaders to take actions for the needs of their own particular neighborhoods at the same time as the organization could also act with a single will, as something more than the sum of its parts. (Warren 2001, 52)

In IAF organizing in Texas, separate action organizations were initially built based on African American churches and those emerging from Hispanic churches.

Over the years each brought about important changes in their respective neighbor-hoods and eventually joined together in a citywide group (Warren 2001, 66). Mobilizing through established institutions is more akin to building a coalition than forming a single group.

Techniques for Building Empowered Mobilization

Mobilization involves much more than getting someone to join an organization or encouraging participation in an action. These are only first steps toward **empowered mobilization** that comes when people understand that they are not alone in facing problems, that these problems are socially caused, and that together they can and must fight back. Empowered mobilization is about "eliminat[ing] barriers to participation through setting agendas and defining issues" and "shap[ing] belief systems, ideologies or shared consciousness" in ways that enable people to understand how their actions may succeed in bringing about change (Speer and Hughey 1996, 178).

But how does this understanding come about? Several approaches to mobiliza-tion—consciousness-raising sessions, study circles, or popular education—are set up so people reflect on the ways in which they are disempowered and through such reflection work out the reasons they must join together.

With **consciousness raising**, a technique popularized by feminist activists, individuals come together to share feelings and experiences and in doing so work out a "new awareness of self in relation to all society" (Lee 2001, 35). Consciousness-raising sessions usually raise incidents that create discomfort, others follow with sim-ilar stories, and hopefully a "click" will occur as the individuals recognize they face a common problem. A woman in the technology department is passed over for a pro-motion and is perturbed but accepts the matter. Another in advertising experiences the same, ditto for a person in sales. At lunch, over coffee, these employees talk about what they feel and what has happened and together discover that each has been dis-empowered in a similar, patronizing way, first being praised for doing good work, receiving a pat on the back, but then not being promoted. Collectively those in the group recognize that they as women are being shunted aside with praise rather than promotion. As a final step the participants join together to orchestrate a social mobi-lization campaign to change company policy.

> *Study circles*
> are dialogue groups that bring together community members to address public con-cerns . . . a study circles is 'a simple and powerful process for democratic discussion and community problem-solving. In these small-group, face-to-face settings, citizens address public concerns, bringing the wisdom of ordinary people to bear on complex issues. Cooperation and participation are emphasized so that the group can capitalize on the experience of all its members. (Gutierrez, Lewis, Nagda, et al. 2005, 351, quot-ing from Campbell 1998, 15)

Both consciousness raising and study circles in many ways extend ideas sug-gested by Paulo Freire (Bell, Gaventa, and Peters 1990; Freire 1970; 1980) on how to mobilize for change through **popular education** or **dialogic learning**. With the popular education approach, a teacher or a local leader, who in effect becomes the organizer, convenes people from oppressed groups to examine their shared problems. Then, as described

> In Freire's model, popular educators bring groups of people together to reflect on *generative themes*, that is high-priority community concerns such as job losses or environmental degradation. This process of using questions to reflect on generative themes sparks grassroots groups' active involvement in using their everyday experiences to understand more critically the political, economic, and social systems in which group members live. Freire called this the process of *conscientization*, or the development of critical consciousness. As they develop critical consciousness, group members are able to break through their lack of self-confidence, their apathy, and their action to plan and carry out collective action to improve their communities. Thus, there is a cycle of reflection using questions to reflect on key community issues and the larger systems in which these issues are embedded, alternating with taking collective action to improve the community. Freire used the term *praxis* to describe this . . . cycle of reflection and actions. (Castelloe and Gamble 2005, 264)

Each of these approaches toward empowered mobilization assumes that people understand their own world and need not be taught by experts. Each also teaches to move beyond mere recognition of a problem to the empowered mobilization required for action. As Paulo Freire argues:

> it is only when the oppressed find the oppressor out and become involved in the organized struggle for their liberation that they begin to believe in themselves. This discovery cannot be purely intellectual but must involve action; nor can it be limited to mere activism, but must include serious reflection: only then will it be a praxis. (Freire 1970, 52)

Reflection encourages social mobilization that is followed by more reflection on why what was done either worked or failed to bring about change.

The following suggestions might help to encourage the discussions that lead to empowered mobilization.

Build on Naturally Occurring Groups. Dialogic groups are most successful when the participants are already networked socially, through religious groups, sharing a workplace or through similar pre-existing bonds. Consciousness-raising groups might begin with friends swapping stories after work or school, while popular education groups emerge out of efforts to provide technical training to people who work with one another or live close together.

Narratives and Stories. Discussions in these groups are meant to be concrete and specific, to build upon the narrative of the life experiences of those involved. Knowledge grows as people recognize that the personal is really the political and that the political can grow out of personal involvement.

Role of Social Activist and Organizer. It is most empowering when those who take on a leadership role emerge from the discussion group itself. Often, though, paid organizers (or with popular education models, teachers) convene the group. When this is the case, for effective empowerment work, the professional activist must make sure he or she does not dominate the meeting. Instead, the organizer or the teacher must act as a catalyst for others and a facilitator for conversation. Then through *active listening* (Pilisuk, McAllister, Rothman, et al. 2005) the organizer pulls out the ideas suggested by the group member. Rather than stating principles or conclusions or adding "expert" information, the activist asks questions to the group of why things seem to happen, searching out not only elaboration of the experiences, but asking about what these experiences mean about what those in the group have in common. When narratives have been completed, the organizer does encourage action by asking why the problems described are occurring. The answers imply the actions that can be taken.

In one area, the professional might have to play a larger role. Oppressed groups are often oppressed because they lack technical knowledge on how to begin political or confrontational actions. If this is the case, the activist might share his or her own experiences, not as an expert, but as one who has been there before, to show how political and protest actions come about.

Reinforcing and Strengthening Commitment

Individuals might join an organization or participate in a campaign because of a here-and-now concern that motivates them to be active—perhaps a person needs to pressure for more accessible daycare or perhaps is angry about a foolish foreign policy decision. But mobilization cannot be a one-shot affair. Wars aren't stopped by a single protest march. Neighborhood improvement programs can run on for decades. A challenge for orchestrating effective social action campaigns is working out ways of sustaining mobilization over the long run, creating a mobilization cycle in which the very involvement in action increases commitment to participate even more.

Sustaining Mobilization through Active Involvement in an Organization. Involvement in the organization reinforces mobilization because of the satisfaction of shaping the direction that the organization takes (Jenkins and Perrow 1977; Knoke and Wood 1981; Kweit and Kweit 1981). Even involvement in routine tasks increases commitment so long as the tasks are not tedious. Making a reasonable number of phone calls to coordinate people in an action, or writing about a successful sit-in in a newsletter increases commitment to both the organization and to future campaigns.

Commitment can be reinforced through integrating rituals into campaigns, by sharing victory celebrations, collectively mocking the enemy, or sharing song and dances as seen in actions taken by those in environmental organizations; for example, when those in the Abalone Alliance danced and sang as they protested the development of nuclear reactors (Jasper 1997, 193). Rituals increase a sense of identity with the group as collective rites remind participants of their basic moral commitments, stir up strong emotions and reinforce a sense of solidarity with the group a "we-ness." *Rituals are symbolic embodiments at salient times and places of the beliefs of the group.* (Jasper 1997, 184)

Reinforcing Mobilization through the Fun of the Confrontational Actions. Commitment to future action increases when actions are amusing, visibly irritate those in power, and build camaraderie. Participating in street theater is fun, yet politically dramatic. For instance, to demonstrate how unscrupulous individuals defraud people through predatory loans, organization members dress up as sharks that circle their unknowing prey, doing so in front of the companies that offer such loans.

Robert Cassidy details what has now become a classical illustration of how fun can be effective and can increase the commitment of individuals to doing future actions.

> When we started the anti redlining battle the bank president told us that the bank didn't make loans in our area because it was a slum . . . Needless to say, people got mad about that. But what could they do? We had only $36,000 in deposits in that bank . . . We tried picketing. Nothing. We kept picketing. No results. They just ignored us and went on with business.
>
> Then one of our ladies said, "Let's have a bank-in!" We said, "Great idea!" Then asked, "What the hell's a bank-in?"
>
> The next day, we had our bank-in. We put five of our people at each of the windows. They would each withdraw a dollar. Then they'd deposit a dollar. Then they'd ask for change. We even tied up the drive-in windows. And we sent in a racially mixed couple to get a loan.
>
> Then Josephine . . . dropped two dollars in pennies on the floor. All the guards came rushing over to pick the money up. She thanked them, and dropped the coins again. Finally, the bank president came running out of the office asking what we wanted. We told him we wanted a meeting with the bank's board of directors that afternoon at two o'clock. "But all the directors live in the suburbs!" he bellowed. "Right," we said, "that's the problem—they live in the suburbs and won't make loans in the city."
>
> Well, we got our meeting, and we got a $4 million loan commitment, a review of all previously turned-down loans and a $1,000 contribution to the community organization. (Cassidy 1980, 80–81)

Victories Reinforce Mobilization. Since being part of a victorious team increases commitment to future action, what constitutes a victory should be broadly defined. Having a large number of people show up at a demonstration is a victory, the number who join in lobbying is a victory, having a politician come to a meeting is a victory. National advocacy groups encourage members to write to regulators, and consider it a victory when more letters are sent by members than by oppositional groups.

In protest organizations, each time the enemy is discomforted can be defined as a victory. Alinsky advised organizers to "personalize the issue" that is, identify the problems with a politician, banker, an interfering judge, or bureaucrat. That way, the organization can work on a series of easily accomplished actions, such as picketing the person's home or distributing fliers that show the errors of the target's ways. Each such action provides a short-term victory that keeps people engaged.

Still, organizations need not succeed on every issue. Any loyalist of a losing baseball team that sometimes beats the league leader demonstrates this principle. Fortunately intermittent reinforcement—that is, an occasional success—is sufficient to keep many members active.

Mobilization in a Multicultural Society

People mobilize to protect their own ethnic or cultural heritage, to preserve customs particular to their group, perhaps to argue for resources for their neighborhoods, or to battle prejudices and discrimination against their group. Doing so is well and good when an issue affects a particular solidarity group, but can create problems when people from different backgrounds must unite in shared battles, usually for economic justice (Maly 2005).

Mobilizing efforts that cross the lines between solidarity groups can prove problematic, as often the groups lack understanding of one another, or are perhaps rivals. Appeals to shared histories will rarely work: Masada would communicate little to a non-Jewish group, 10/10 resonates with those of Chinese origin, while religious rituals familiar to one group would seem strange indeed to another. Groups differ in how gender is understood, who talks with whom, about what, and the extent to which religion can be a basis for mobilizing. Dress, body posture, whether to quietly talk about a problem or shout it out will differ from group to group. Cultural sensitivity and awareness is required for organizing within particular solidarity groups.

Even ethnic identity alters over the years. For instance, whether or not members of particular Asian groups identify as "Asian" fluctuates over time (Okamoto 2003). Further, among a variety of Asian American groups "how strongly an individual identifies as an ethnic is not an accurate predictor of whether or not that individual will actively engage in single-ethnic or pan-Asian organizations" (Võ 2004, 222). But instead, a two-step understanding is required in which, to mobilize a person, he or she has to see the issue as first relating to his particular ethnic group—Chinese, Thai, Korean, etc.—then at the same time understand that the issues affect a broader Asian community (Võ 2004, 222–28).

What to do?

One approach is to examine each cultural group carefully for common concerns that do unite them such as shared worries that the public schools are neglecting their children (Rivera and Erlich 1995). A shared external problem can unite. For instance, in the Uptown area of Chicago, different solidarity groups lived nearby one another, but rarely worked together until gentrification began and affordable housing and displacement affected all groups. In response, in

> building a successful multi-ethnic, mixed-economic community, [the Organization of the Northeast] worked with residents of several buildings . . . to publicize and ease res-

> idential displacement . . . ONE coordinated tenant association actions in all the build-
> ings, created lines of communication between buildings, and cooperated with other
> community organizations and institutions. . . . ONE decided to organize all tenant
> groups together to fight on the larger policy issue of affordable housing. (Maly 2005,
> 83)

Though the separate buildings were from areas dominated by those from separate ethnic groups, the economic campaign mobilized the entire multicultural community.

Understanding that leads to common action is increased by inviting people to multicultural events that become opportunities to mobilize (Horton 1995). A major way of mobilizing organizing across solidarity communities is to make apparent that all face the same issue. Shared battles against stereotypes unite as occurred among those with separate backgrounds—Chinese, Thai, Vietnamese, Laotian, Japanese— when all were being negatively stereotyped by individuals bigoted against all Asians (Võ 2004). Campaigns to expand multicultural education or improve the schools, advocacy of public support for neighborhood (ethnic) businesses, or efforts to protect new immigrants from sweatshop working conditions are issues that attract participation from a variety of ethnic and religious groups.

A joint effort to battle racism can mobilize individuals in separate solidarity groups while at the same time set up the foundation for broader antiracism campaigns (Anner 1996, 166–67). In these efforts when "conscious attention is paid to educating members about each other's traditions and promoting open discussion of race among participants, cross-racial organizing can address racism" (Warren 2001, 153). For example, the predominantly Latino Texas IAF network "invited a series of prominent black intellectuals and scholars to the seminars . . . held bi-monthly for . . . organizers" (Warren 2001, 129). The very effort to bridge cultural misunderstandings itself becomes a technique for mobilization.

In multiethnic communities, meetings are structured in ways that encourage those from different groups to be involved. First in setting up the broad-scope organization make sure that all ethnic, religious, racial, or other groupings have members in leadership positions. Make sure meetings of the multicultural group rotate between neighborhoods dominated by the different ethnic groups. Try to have as speakers those who are multilingual and make sure interpreters are present. To show respect, organizers should not give priority to one language, such as English. But keep in mind that multicultural organizing is about getting people to work together on shared issues, not about blurring away the differences between the separate cultural groups. For instance,

> the multiracial organizations formed by the IAF are not integrationist. In fact, the
> institutional organizing approach is meant to respect the traditions of each racial com-
> munity, allowing these communities a degree of autonomy and initiative, while at the
> same time promoting common efforts. . . . The purpose of building broad-based
> organizations is to bring communities with different traditions and interests together,
> not so they become the same, but so that they learn to support each other and to find
> common ground for action. (Warren 2001, 153)

Conclusion

Before campaigns can begin people must recognize that they not only share a problem but that by working together can bring about a solution. Moving from passivity to a willingness to become involved in a social mobilization campaign takes time and patience and will not succeed overnight. In this chapter, we have explored why people are reluctant to participate, suggested motivations for joining in, and illustrated different ways in which people are recruited for activism. Once mobilized people are ready to participate in efforts at political and administrative engagement as well as in confrontational actions. Once involved in such actions the commitment to further effort is increased.

16 Influencing the Public Sector

Civic and Administrative Engagement

Through social confrontations activists call attention to problems that those in power choose to ignore or are unwilling to resolve. But resolution of issues requires changes in public policy, through influencing elected and bureaucratic officials. To do so effectively, activists must understand the structure of government, the ways in which policies do or do not come about, and then master a variety of techniques for civic and administrative engagement. With *political lobbying* or *petitioning*, activists provide information meant to influence political decisions and once decisions are made rely on *administrative pressure* to influence how bureaucrats carry them out. *Electoral participation* involves working to elect candidates who support progressive ideas, while with initiatives and referendum, people work to enact laws themselves. Finally, citizens serve on *civic boards* and from these positions can influence local government.

Are such efforts to work within the system worthwhile when the wealthy and the business community have far more resources to devote to the effort and in recent years have tried to limit public input into the political process (Berry and Arons 2003, 146 ff)? The answer is a qualified Yes. Research evidence indicates that progressive voices, when organized, are heard, especially on the federal level (Berry 1999; Berry and Arons 2003). Though the battle is hard fought and even when victories have been won, continual action is needed to preserve what has been gained.

Understanding Governmental Structures and Policy Making

In the United States, "government" refers to a mixture of agencies and elected bodies at the federal, state, and local levels. Well over 80,000 distinct units of government are found including the federal government, states, counties, municipalities, towns and townships, and special districts that can be responsible for anything from schools to abating mosquitoes. Most, but not all, levels of government are divided into executive and administrative parts that run and coordinate programs and bureaucratic agencies: a legislature that determines what programs to adopt and how to fund them and the judiciary to make sure laws are followed and that decisions made are consistent with fundamental constitutional provisions.

Which agency or which institutional actor is responsible for what decisions is not always clear. Policy at the federal level can originate in Congress or in the executive branch, be modified by the Office of Management and Budget, acting for the President, or by Congress in its various committees or as a whole. Once approved by Congress and signed by the President into law, decisions are carried out by administrative agencies that work out rules and procedures to carry out legislative policies. Which rules are adopted and how they are interpreted can change in response to presidential or congressional pressure. If legal cases are brought, eventually the Supreme Court can declare a law unconstitutional, forcing it to be dropped. In the states, power is diffused between governors, legislators, the courts, and administrators. In most states, the governor is the most powerful actor, but agency bureaucrats can make end runs around the governor, and legislators may have the power to bargain in ways that set policy. At the state level too, courts can overturn legislative or executive decisions.

Laws are passed by elected officials—politicians—who are subject to voter will, serve fixed terms, but need not have any special technical competence for the position. At the federal and state level, the heads of most bureaucratic agencies are appointees who serve at the pleasure of either the executive or legislative body. Local governments often appoint professional managers who are chosen for their technical competence, yet serve at the will of the executive or council (depending on the locale).

The heads of public sector agencies are frequently political appointees, though many are chosen because of their technical knowledge. Most employees within administrative agencies have the requisite technical competence for their jobs either from schooling or explicit on-the-job training. Public services are provided by well over ten million public sector employees—bureaucrats—ranging from police, social workers, bank regulators, and housing administrators, to nuclear scientists. Bureaucrats can be removed for cause, though those with civil service protection serve under many different politicians.

At the federal level, most administrative agencies are grouped together in cabinet level departments, with a few agencies independent. Each of the cabinet departments has an overall focus, although some agencies end up in a department for political rather than organizational reasons. The Department of Housing and Urban Development carries out housing and urban renewal programs, the Department of Labor is concerned with unemployment and training programs, the Agriculture Department with forestry, farms, and food production and inspection, while most social service programs are run out of the Department of Health and Human Services. The Treasury handles expenditures and taxes, but nowadays is of increasing import to social change activists, as many programs are indirectly funded through tax incentives. Both independent agencies and cabinet departments are supervised by congressional committees. Responsibilities of the committees have changed over time; in the past the same committee supervised HUD and the Veterans Administration; nowadays HUD is paired with Transportation.

Among many independent federal agencies are the Environmental Protection Agency, the Equal Employment Opportunity Commission, as well as agencies that supervise banks. Independent agencies are generally harder for social change groups to influence directly. Independent agencies have analogues at the state level with utility commissions or building authorities that borrow money for public construction.

Most state governments are structured like the federal government, with an executive branch that supervises numerous administrative agencies, two legislative houses (with Nebraska as an exception with just one) and a judiciary. Most governors have more control over the state budget than does the President over the federal budget and most governors can more easily control the actions of administrative agencies than would be possible at the federal level. Agency directors and reporting structures change fairly often, making it difficult to figure out who has the governor's ear, or more generally, who has the power to grant an organization's demands. Only rarely do local community groups pressure the federal or state government by themselves, instead most action is done as part of a broader coalition or orchestrated through a state or national advocacy organization. Many state and national advocacy organizations have fully professional staff and are successful at both administrative and legislative lobbying (Berry 1999).

Local governments differ widely in their powers and structures, though fortunately along a limited number of dimensions. A *broad-scope* local government can be responsible for a wide array of local services, including police, fire, sanitation, zoning, social services, community development, job training, education, and parks and recreation, perhaps even economic assistance, while a narrow-scope government might control only the police and zoning. In most places counties have narrow powers, so cities are a more important target for social change organizations, but in rapidly growing areas, counties do vie with municipalities in importance (Teaford 1997).

Generally, local governments have only those responsibilities specifically delegated to them by the states. Some states grant cities what is called *home-rule powers* that allow the locality to provide a wide variety of services and have independent taxing powers without asking for state approval. But often other constraints are in place to limit tax increases to population growth or to inflation and as such restrict what services can be provided.

General-purpose local governments are run by an elected council that decides on overall policies and an elected executive (mayor, village president, or county board chairperson) who makes recommendations and supervises implementation. In the council-manager form of government, the council and mayor appoint a professional administrator to supervise the administrative departments. In the mayor-council form, the elected mayor takes on the responsibilities of chief administrator. In a strong-mayor form of government, mayors have primary power over the budget, appoint the heads of city departments as well as the members of citizen advisory boards, and often have a veto over legislation the council passes. In weak-mayor cities, the mayor is just one member of the council with some additional ceremonial responsibilities. The commission form is a less common structure in which individuals are elected to a governing commission with each commissioner also being a department head of an agency.

Most people are aware of general purpose local governments, as mayors appear on television and are blamed or praised for what happens in their cities. Residents are less aware of special purpose governments, often termed districts, that do just one task. The best-known special purpose government is a school district, but there are others, such as fire protection districts, sanitary districts, drainage districts, mosquito abatement districts, park districts, and recreation districts. In some locales, bridges and highways are the responsibility of special districts, while some locales have redevelopment authorities, with powers to borrow money, buy real estate, and help fund renewal projects. Residential neighborhoods and business areas can set up their own special service districts to collect taxes from the area to provide services beyond those that the city makes available. Some special-purpose governments are run by an elected board, though many are headed by political appointees.

Public Sector Cultures

Governments differ in both form and structure and—over time in their cultures, that is, a set of shared beliefs—on how those in the public sector should act. One cultural distinction is between reformed and unreformed city governments. Historically, unreformed cities were dominated by political machines that bought support from new immigrants with jobs and food. Most such political machines have disappeared, but in some cities, even in smaller towns with an established "old-boy" system, organized groups more or less have become a machine and are still able to elect and re-elect the same officials. In reformed cities, the political culture makes it hard to use public resources to buy votes because council members as individuals lack control over funding decisions and the mayor does not have power independent of the council. In these cities, day-to-day administration is carried out by a professionally trained city manager who is responsible for running the city in a fiscally prudent and managerial efficient way.

Political scientists and urbanists have expanded the view of local culture using what they term an *urban regime* approach. An urban regime "refers to (a) the public officials and private interests that function together as allies in the city's governing coalition and (b) the nature of the policy agenda pursued by this coalition" (Imbroscio 1997, 6). The regime perspective describes that governmental actions are influenced by both public discourse (official input from citizen advisory groups) and through informal, social contacts between favored constituents and elected officials. In most cities, business interests dominate the urban regime but in some places progressive regimes link the concerns of community-based organizations to those in government (Imbroscio 1997, 97–38).

The best-known progressive regimes came about when politicians such as Harold Washington in Chicago were elected with the support of community and social change organizations. In the Washington administration, important government positions were staffed by community activists, previously hidden city records became public, funding dramatically increased for both economic development and social services in neighborhoods of need, and community groups themselves were funded to provide public services. With a progressive culture in place, neighborhood and social change activists have ready access to bureaucrats and elected officials (Clavel and Wiewell 1991).

The Policy Process

Social action organizations try to shape the policy agenda, but doing so is difficult because what is in the policy agenda depends upon a complicated mix. As Kingdom argues,

> we conceive of three process streams flowing through the system—streams of problems, policies and politics. They are largely independent of one another, and each develops according to its own dynamics and rules. (Kingdom 1995, 19)

How problems are understood, what solutions are considered acceptable, and who is in power changes over time. The trick is to get ideas into the policy cauldron, framed in ways consistent with the organization's social change goals and then find reasons politicians need to support these ideas. At times, this means linking up your issue to totally different but politically popular concerns, a tactic called "getting on the train that is leaving the station."

In undertaking policy work, activists become part of a *policy community*, that is, those organizations and individuals who on a particular issue stay informed and participate on a daily basis on the matter. Policy communities bring together legislative staff, some elected officials, a variety of bureaucrats from different agencies, and those seeking to influence outcomes, both from progressive organizations and those representing the status quo. Policy communities cross administrative borders. For instance, housing issues will involve participants from HUD, from Treasury, bank regulators, researchers from the left and the right, housing advocates for the poor as well as for businesses, and those from the banking and development community, among many others. Individuals in a policy community know one another, meet at hearings, talk and negotiate in private, and recognize that they will be interacting over the long term so some semblance of honesty and openness occurs, even among those whose views sharply differ.

In this setting activists try to affect the policy process

- to get on the agenda with issues framed in ways that support the cause;
- to work out a variety of acceptable options;
- to communicate to those in office what options are desired;
- to pressure those individuals to adopt the ideas proposed by the social change organization; and
- to make sure that the new policies are actually carried out.

Framing Issues and Establishing Policy Alternatives. The first step is to set the public *agenda*, "the list of subjects or problems to which governmental officials, and people outside of government closely associated with those officials, are paying some serious attention at any given time" (Kingdom 1995, 3). One way is through public actions taken by organizations, for instance, by holding a demonstration or rally to make an issue salient. Newspaper stories or scandals or natural disasters place an issue on the public agenda. Issues get on the agenda as a result of reports issued by think tanks, and occasionally by academics, documenting a problem. These reports are then strategically circulated both to the press and to the appropriate bureaucratic agencies. Persistence is required. For years, the disabilities movement had pushed for attention for their concerns to little avail, until by chance a supportive set of officials happened to be on the appropriate legislative committees and were able to put what eventually became the Americans with Disabilities Act on the agenda (Fleischer and Zames 2001). At times, agenda setting seems almost a matter of luck as there is an

> extraordinary looseness of the information system. Ideas, rumors, bits of information, studies, lobbyists' pleadings—all of these float around the system without any hard-and-fast communication channels. Subordinates cannot control that flow of information because their bosses have many others from whom they hear—lobbies, academics, media, each other, and their own experience and ideas. (Kingdom 1995, 77)

In getting an item on the public agenda, great care is required in how the matter is framed. Getting drugs on the agenda, but framed as a problem of inadequate police vigilance, could result in crackdowns against minorities, not programs of economic repair. At times, an issue is best framed in narrow terms—stopping unscrupulous lenders from cheating the elderly out of their homes resonates across political parties, rather than framing the issue into terms of broader concerns with regulating banks. Other times, a broader framing is best, for instance, talking about how particular policies or actions will promote "civil rights" or "economic justice." For example, trying to get a discussion of building a transit line in a poor, minority community onto the policy agenda might work best if framed as a civil rights issue.

Further, the ways in which an issue is cast might depend on whether it is the attention of politicians or bureaucrats that is being sought. Attention of politicians is easier to get if the problem is framed in ways that the politicians will get credit with constituency groups for providing resources to solve the matter. Bureaucrats respond best to problems that are framed so as to increase the power and role of their agency.

Points of Discretion, Points of Power.   Next, to affect the policy agenda locate those who have the power, funds, or discretion to make the decisions sought. At times this is obvious; you contact a public works department about fixing potholes. But for major changes in laws or policy, legislative action is required and here power is diffused and found in many locations.

At the federal level, laws require action on the part of the Senate and the House, as well as presidential approval. But real power usually lies at the legislative committee or subcommittee level, for instance, housing policy is now discussed by the standing committee on housing and transportation, while some social policies actually are determined by committees dealing with taxes. When committee members support a policy proposal, they assign committee staff—experts in writing laws—to do background work and draft the legislation. Working with these staffers is vital in shaping a bill. Once progress has been made, public hearings are scheduled, though rarely are the hearings about obtaining new information. Instead, they allow advocates and opponents to have their say, often in ways that back the perspectives of the legislators (or their staff) on the committee. Assuming the legislation is still alive after the hearings, the committee holds a markup session during which final drafting is done. In complex legislation where more than one committee has jurisdiction, a bill may go from one committee to another, and from one set of hearings to another. Once approved by the committee(s), the bill is forwarded to the floor of the legislative chamber for an up or down vote.

Sometimes the Senate accepts a bill written in the House or vice versa, but often two bills are wending their way through the separate legislative bodies. If both houses pass different versions of the bill, it is sent to a conference of legislators from each house who work out a compromise. In the past, only minor changes were made, but more recently, conference committees have begun to change the bills dramatically, often in ways that weaken what progressive activists want. After both the House and the Senate have passed identical bills, the proposal then goes to the White House for the president to sign or veto.

Even if the legislation passes, the work of the action organization is not through. For a new program to be effective it must be funded, and to obtain funding, at the federal level, requires an entirely separate legislative process. In each house, there is a budget committee which establishes overall ceilings on spending for a series of related programs, such as for housing or the environment, and then within this limit subcommittees appropriate money for the separate program. Because each subcommittee is working within an assigned spending ceiling, if committee members raise the appropriation for one program, they have to lower something else in their jurisdiction. Money spent on housing the elderly might mean less for housing poor families. Close attention is required.

As legislation goes through committees and between houses or branches of government, changes can be made, now improving the situation, now making it worse. Devastating amendments may be proposed, and defeated or passed, only to be dropped again in conference. Sometimes legislation is dropped one year, only to be picked up again the next. Significant bills normally run into opposition as opponents introduce amendments that will weaken the proposal or render it inoperable, or, worse yet, offer a bill of their own. Social activists have to follow the progress of the bill intently, ready to react, mobilize support, lobby, or make a new proposal at a moment's notice.

State level processes differ from place to place. In some locales, the two houses may have joint committees and hold only one hearing while financing may occur at the same time as does program design. Social change organizations and their coalitions have to delineate the process in each state in which they plan to campaign for legislation or budget.

At the local level, the process tends to be simpler. Social action organizations can ask the mayor or manager to introduce their proposal to the council, or a friendly council member can present the measure. In addition, bureaucratic staff can be approached on ideas on how to accomplish a particular policy; rather than doing an end run around the police, ask the chief how to step up neighborhood patrols. Often city level issues are decided on a case-by-case basis, with broader underlying concerns never broached. A bill might provide a neighborhood with a park, but the council will avoid the broader question of how much open space is required.

But to bring all this off requires patience and staying power as well agreement among progressive organizations on exactly what is wanted. For example, before Congress passed legislation that funded affordable housing, a wide variety of community housing organizations—varying from those who work comfortably with bankers to those who have protested the same bankers—negotiated and agreed among themselves what they would present to Congress. Congress heard a united voice and that voice prevailed over opposition. In Illinois recently, legislative supporters of housing programs insisted that the dozens of action organizations agree on a handful of issues they could all support. When this was done, several of the bills passed that had been languishing for a while.

Rule Making and Implementation.   The passage of legislation is far from the end of the policy process. Once bills become laws, bureaucratic agencies are responsible for carrying them out, not always in ways that were anticipated. Sometimes it is easy to figure out how the law is being implemented. If the city council has passed a bill authorizing a new traffic light, activists can go out and see if the light has been installed. If an increase in minority or female hiring was mandated, organization members can look at new hires to see if the target figure was achieved. Sometimes, though, tracking implementation is far more difficult.

Often legislation specifies general principles without spelling out how the policy should be carried out, for instance, not detailing formulas for allocating money. In these circumstances, bureaucratic agencies are required to set up rules that are consistent with legislative intent but the details of these rules can dramatically influence the impact of the program or policy. For example, in programs designed to benefit poor people, agencies have to specify how poverty is to be measured, a controversial technical issue.

Federal bureaucratic agencies and some state agencies must announce in advance what rules they are considering. At the federal level, these announcements are made in the Federal Register while under the Administrative Procedures Act, federal agencies must solicit commentaries on proposed rules. Activist groups try to provide commentaries that support their issues (Bingham, Nabatchi, and O'Leary 2005, 550 ff). In addition, action organizations must make sure that the stated rules are actually followed. During the Reagan administration people who held offices at HUD opposed affordable housing and were so negligent in following the program rules that nonprofit housing developers were unable to get funds that Congress had intended.

Regulatory agencies require especially close supervision as such agencies are often understaffed and make decisions by working closely with the very businesses they are supposedly regulating. In the George W. Bush administration agency heads were appointed who opposed the very regulations the agencies were supposed to enforce. A lobbyist for chemical companies was appointed to a high position in the EPA while banking regulators were chosen who wanted to gut the Community Reinvestment Act.

The national government often assigns responsibilities (and sometimes provides funding) to the 50 states for implementing federal programs. Among hundreds of programs, welfare and job training programs are now state responsibilities (with certain federal controls). As a result of such decentralization, 50 state-level policies may replace one national guideline and state-level activism has become increasingly important.

Policy, Regulatory, Advocacy Systems Are Always in Flux.   Policies are rarely just a here-and-now matter but instead reflect long histories; meanwhile actions taken in one policy arena might be little more than spillovers from another. In addition, many issues of import to social activists—housing, civil rights, welfare policy, environment, transportation, open access—blur together. A housing bill can affect where transportation is needed, while concerns with civil rights underlie almost any issue involving poor communities.

To further complicate matters, laws passed at the federal level (sometimes the state) are implemented in quite different ways locally depending upon how local bureaucrats or politicians understand the issues. In some areas, for instance, federal Fair Housing Laws, meant to ensure that individuals are not excluded from housing because of race, religion, or gender, and the federal Community Reinvestment Act that requires banks to reinvest in poor communities were vigorously enforced in some, and in others virtually ignored (Immergluck 2004; Sidney 2003). Drawing lessons from the CRA and Fair Housing experience, Sidney concludes that:

- National policies are constraints, not straight jackets
- Advocates can think about how and whether policies foster or undermine their coalitions
- It may take both federal requirements and local pressure to move fair housing and community reinvestment up on local government agendas. Thus, a combination of local and national advocacy is important
- Recognize the value of legitimacy that arises from government partnerships
- Choose allies not only based on shared interests or goals but also based on complementary political skills and resources (Sidney 2003, 152–54)

The implication of such complexities is that social change organizations have to work hard to coordinate their efforts. One approach is to set up national advocacy groups such as the National Community Reinvestment Coalition that bring together national, state, and local organizations all concerned about CRA. Another tactic involves coordinating the actions taken by confrontational organizations with those that focus on policy matters by working out when the policy agency lobbies and when the direct action agency protests.

Tactics for Civil and Regulatory Engagement

We shall discuss four broad but overlapping sets of tactics for handling civil and regulatory engagements—political lobbying, administrative engagement, electoral involvement, and civic board and committee services. Which of these four approaches makes most sense differs over time and by place. When political supporters are in office, serving on civic boards might be worth the time as ideas will be given credence by friends already in office; with the opposition in charge civic boards are just a waste of effort. Administrative engagement can be slow and cumbersome with bureaucrats wanting to cross each "t" and dot each "i" and feeling no pressure to accommodate. But with supporters in elected offices, bureaucrats are more likely to pay attention. Involvement in the political or bureaucratic process, or service on civil boards, means working closely with those in power, risking co-optation, that is, ending up agreeing with those in office. Yet, at the same time close work can lend credence to the ideas of social change organizations.

Tactics should be examined for their effectiveness, but also in terms of how well the approach meshes with work to empower organizational membership. If people don't have the time or money to travel downstate to lobby, perhaps they could write a letter to a politician or click on an automatic electronic site to do so. Without full-time employees, negotiating on a bureaucratic rule can prove problematic, as discussions continue over many months and require having facts and figures at one's fingertips. Other times, the purpose is to gain publicity. In this case, bureaucratic encounters might not be the way to go as the press is unlikely to pay much attention to a wording change in section 6, paragraph 3. In contrast, cleverly orchestrating lobbying appearances at public hearings—for instance, presenting a young working couple who cannot get insurance for their child at a hearing on expanding medical care—can often garner front page coverage.

In practice, all four approaches are relied upon, often simultaneously, to set the agenda for the same issue.

Political Lobbying

Lobbying is about communicating to those in office how members of an organization feel about a particular issue while providing background information that supports the organization's case. Lobbying strengthens the backbone of officials already on your side letting them know how many people care about the issue. Lobbying efforts vary from having people just sign a petition or click on an e-mail letter, to showing up to testify at a hearing, on up to spending hour after hour working with legislative staff providing technical data and, with luck, helping to write the actual legislation. *Lobbying takes place with a quiet voice that gains power because of its informed persistence.*

Some lobbying matters are accomplished fairly quickly: neighbors show up to a city council meeting to object to a waste site opening up, prevail, and the issue is gone. But most matters on which organizations will lobby are not decided once and for all as the issues are visited and revisited. This being the case, to keep on top of matters, effective neighborhood organizations make sure some of its members attend all city council meetings and major committee meetings. To monitor issues continuously and to increase power, at a state and national level, social action organizations band together to form advocacy coalitions (Sabatier and Jenkins-Smith 1993) that hire staff to monitor the issues of concern to the coalition's membership. For instance, for over a decade now several dozen national organizations, along with thousands of local organizations, have coordinated their lobbying for a trust fund for affordable housing, an idea that goes up and down depending upon those in office. Meanwhile, the advocacy coalition, the Coalition of Human Needs, with a membership of dozens of organizations, keeps track of social service issues that benefit the nation's poorest.

Skilled lobbyists provide politicians with ideas on how to satisfy what at first might appear to be contradictory demands. For instance, housing lobbyists pressured Congress for money to fund affordable housing at a time when corporate interests were pressing for lower taxes. Lobbyists for housing groups came up with the idea of having a special tax credit that would allow rich companies that invested in affordable housing projects to be able to substantially reduce their tax bills. This idea allowed legislators to satisfy what at first appeared to be irreconcilable differences, between business and the poor.

Effective lobbyists suggest where funds can be found for policy initiatives. After examining a city's finances, a neighborhood organization might argue that the city can refund an expiring bond at a lower rate of interest and use the difference to repair neighborhood schools. Activists lobbying for neighborhood organizations have taught city officials how to use block grants for innovative projects that benefit the neighborhoods while not increasing local taxes. Recently at the federal level, social change activists suggested using profits made by the private mortgage agencies that the government sponsors, Fannie Mae and Freddie Mac, to fund affordable housing programs.

Over time, lobbyists gain credibility with politicians and their staff by providing reliable information. A lobbyist who has been following an issue for years knows what has been tried before, what was rejected and why, and what suggestions are likely to garner support now. Further, the continued presence of a lobbyist makes it clear to the elected officials that the issues will not go away. On the other, an organization that comes in at the last moment with its ideas and tries a gung ho lobbying effort will probably have little impact, no matter the quality of the ideas. One of the reasons given for the failure of the Equal Rights Amendment (ERA) to gain the needed 38 states for constitutional ratification was that many feminist organizations that were lobbying showed little staying power relying on "intense one-time activity, and little follow-through" (Mansbridge 1986, 158).

As we write, we are in the sixth year of a conservative antiprogressive federal administration that is not receptive to progressive concern while lobbyists for the rich, big business, antienvironmentalists, and those for a conservative social agenda have the ear of elected officials. Yet lobbying remains a must, both to push for the important causes, and to show politicians that progressive activists are watching and have a voice that must be heard. The advice on what to do provided by the Center for Community Change of a decade ago, during previous conservative times, holds even more strongly today:

Carefully pick your issues
Prioritize issues and make sure those chosen are vital to the organization and are those with which organization members are familiar.

Make a commitment to it and assign responsibility
Make sure someone is in charge to follow up on the issue.

Recognize that there's been a sea change in who has power
When conservative Republicans chair important committees, activist groups need to build new relationships.

Don't assume that an ideological difference is insurmountable
Even conservatives are willing to work with organizations that show a strong reliance on self-help.

Examine your language
With conservatives in office, militant language does not work as well as framing issues in ways that appeal to the right. Label the poor as workers not sponges and talk about everyone's desire to own property.

Expand your horizons
Lobbying coalitions can unite together street activists and social service providers in a common effort.

Don't let one "no" stop you
When ignored, you can make some noise through direct action, but in any case, don't give up.

Never stop having your members educate the people in power
Encourage calls from community members and on local issues have people make frequent visits to those in office.

Use the media both to educate and pressure legislators
While talking with legislators make sure to provide background stories to the press.

Be willing to confront and express outrage
Lobbying does tone down confrontations, but when necessary express anger, perhaps in a dramatic way.

Be prepared for a long struggle
Few issues are resolved in one-time approaches to politicians; decades of education and pressure may be required. (excerpted from Center for Community Change 1996, 17–20 with the illustrations rewritten)

In lobbying, certain core rules hold whether working at the local, state, or federal level: Have someone physically present, be honest, be polite, but be assertive. Other rules differ depending upon what level of government is being lobbied—getting people to show up at a city council meeting is far easier than paying for transportation and possibly hotels to lobby at the state or federal level. Also the focus on lobbying will differ as bills in state and national levels differ dramatically from local ordinances. At the local level, issues tend to be separate—an antismoking ordinance, a living wage law, or an inclusionary housing proposal will appear in front of the council each by itself. At the state and national level, major bills tend to package provisions that speak to a wide variety of causes, only some of which are relevant to the social change organizations.

Let's examine some of the lobbying tactics at the federal and local levels, while keeping in mind that lobbying at the state level is a blend of each.

Information Sharing as the Core Tactic of Lobbying. Lobby is about sharing information, not coercing. In dealing with friendly public officials, activists assemble the detailed information political supporters need to defend their (and your) positions. For instance, advocates for the Community Reinvestment Act provide supportive officials with the facts and figures on the benefits that have come about through community reinvestment.

Presenting facts in a politically astute way is what lobbying is about. For instance, in lobbying against an ill-thought-out redevelopment project, find out how many people will be displaced from their homes and how many small businesses will be destroyed, while using engineering studies to show the problems with the proposed new traffic patterns. When presenting the data, have the facts and figures in written documents, then put a human face on the matter, perhaps by orchestrating testimony of people who had been displaced by similar projects and had no choice but to share small apartments with their relatives.

It is crucial that the facts presented are correct, even if they slightly weaken the case. When possible use official federal government data to make a case, from the agencies described in Chapter 9. The information provided by these official sources has been so persuasive in the past in highlighting problems, that conservatives now in office have established rules making it harder to access these facts and figures.

At the local level, data collected by county or city departments can turn into lobbying ammunition in support of neighborhood improvement programs. Engineering departments do traffic counts that document the need for traffic signals and stop signs, community development departments keep records on the number of households below the poverty line and the number of dilapidated buildings, the county clerk has evidence on the number of houses being rapidly sold in one area (which can be an indication of block busting), and police departments typically keep data on the amount, type, and location of crime. Activists should not assume that because local government departments produced it that elected officials are aware of it.

Often opponents distort information, so in preparing to lobby, obtain data that inoculates politicians against such misleading arguments. Banks had argued for years that they did not discriminate against African Americans, simply that African Americans were poorer than others and poorer people received fewer loans. Official reports written by the Federal Reserve Board showed that what the banks were saying was wrong: Even when income and other background factors were the same, African Americans still were less likely to receive loans. Similarly, companies that received contracts from cities vociferously argued that living wage ordinances would bankrupt them. These arguments were weakened once a few cities had adopted such ordinances and evidence was at hand to demonstrate that the policies helped workers and caused no harm to their employers.

Creating a Supportive Environment for Lobbying through Media Campaigns. Lobbying can be more effective if there is "buzz" about the issue in advance that can be created through orchestrating a letter to the editor campaign or perhaps releasing a technical report that speaks to the issue and holding a major press conference to do so. Some organizations have orchestrated television campaigns, for instance, to combat the prejudices against affordable housing, organizations produced TV spots that show that ordinary working people—nurses, construction workers, public servants, police, and fire—often cannot afford to purchase their own homes. We shall return to this topic in Chapter 18.

Letter Writing and Internet Contact.   Face-to-face communication is the most powerful way of communicating a complicated policy idea. But lobbying is also about showing that large numbers of people support the idea and that these people can be mobilized. Through letter writing campaigns—both by snail mail and electronic means, faxes and Internet responses—organizations demonstrate the extent of support for the organization's cause. Some organizations do much of their lobbying work electronically, for instance MoveOn "has become a more or less permanent online advocacy group, with . . . supporting campaign finance reform and other causes" (Schwartz 2002, 89) having generated on occasions literally hundreds of thousands of advocacy letters. Many activist groups maintain lists of those who have volunteered to write or call public officials and can activate these lists quickly.

Effective letters indicate that the writer is aware of what the official has already done on the issue, while providing suggestions on future actions. A person can write about the general lack of enforcement of fair housing laws, using statistics from a form letter that the organization circulates to its membership, and then add on her own experience, as a minority member, of being turned away when a non-minority friend with the same income was able to rent the desired apartment. Personal letters that provide anecdotes are probably the most effective form of mail communication.

To make letter writing easy, organizations share sample letters at meetings, in printed or electronic newsletters, and also on web pages. Commercial services such as Capwiz allow for easy customization and tracking of the letters. With Capwiz, a member or supporter of an organization logs onto a website, identifies himself or herself by address, the Capwiz program locates the appropriate elected officials, and then helps the person to send a form letter, or modify and then send a form letter, all the while copying the sponsoring organization on the actions.

Increasingly, electronically circulated sign-on letters have become a tool for lobbying. With a sign-on letter, organizations send copies of policy statements to potential supporters, asking people to sign their names and organizational affiliation and pass on the letter to other similar groups. At the end, the letter returns to the initiating organization that then presents it to the appropriate officials. Especially when time horizons are short (such as when opponents have convinced someone to change a bill during a markup session) electronic media are an important way to get supporters to lobby legislators.

No one knows for sure how effective electronic communications are in persuading officials. Some officials are not electronically skilled, while others consider electronic lobbying as just a sophisticated form letter. A decade ago studies concluded that e-mail was less effective than other forms of communication (Wilcox 1998, 96), but since the anthrax scares in congress, many legislators now prefer receiving either faxes or electronic communications.

When writing to a national office don't always expect a response, though electronic letters now do receive automated replies. If you are a constituent, make sure the letter includes that fact as it will more likely generate a reply. Copying a lobbying letter to the local press is also a way of increasing its impact, especially in smaller cities where many such letters are published.

Petitions. Letters are usually written and signed by an individual. Petitions are requests that many people sign that are then handed in to an elected official or a bureaucratic agency by a representative of the campaign. The content of the petitions can vary from requests to adopt policies or to stop specific actions, on up to legal documents required as part of an initiative campaign (see page 312). Almost anyone can sign a petition, but if the petition involves putting something on the ballot the signatures must be from registered voters.

Signatures can be collected by going door-to-door, or through *tabling* in which representatives of the activist group set up a table, at a public square, or at a festival, or even at a rally and request that individuals sign. More technically savvy activist groups are able to get signups for petitions through interactive websites.

A **sign-on letter** is a type of petition but one whose signatories represent organizations who agree to support the specific cause. Signatures are usually obtained through passing the letter through the activist networks often linked on on-line lists.

Personal Contact with Elected Officials and Their Staff. Public officials and their senior staff are often overwhelmed with the large numbers of contentious issues. Making them notice your issue is often the purpose for lobbying and is best accomplished through face-to-face contact, during which give and take is possible. In all except the largest cities, setting up an appointment with council members requires little more than a phone call and determining a mutually convenient time.

However, for federal legislators, state legislators in larger states, and, in larger cities, council members, personal meetings are not all that easy to arrange. Some established social change organizations, especially those that can turn out the vote, are able to arrange a personal meeting with senior elected officials, but many are not.

Busy elected officials employ staff members who are more readily accessible, who often know more about specific issues than do most elected officials, can situate the particular concerns of your organization within the broader political context, and are willing to listen and dialogue on the issues. In many cases, the staff members who work directly for the elected officials are trusted almost as alter egos, and are the ones who actually draft the legislation.

Senators and federal Representatives are in their home districts part of the year and during that time appointments with either the official or their staff are somewhat easier to make, but staff members who work on your issues might not be there, as many of these are D.C.-based. State elected officials are probably best met in their home district, but if contact is needed with staff of the legislative committees a trip to the state capital is required.

A particular effective form of personal lobbying is to invite politicians to visit projects your organization has done. Lobbying for more money for community health care is easier once the official has seen how efficient and well managed and busy the present facility is. Also when media opportunities are provided that link the politician to a successful project, he or she is more likely to appear.

Many state and national coalitions and trade associations set up lobbying days that coincide with their annual meetings in Washington, D.C. (or state capitals). Prior to the conferences, legislative experts employed by the national organizations work with activists from different legislative districts to set up meetings with elected officials and their staff and then before the meetings provide the activists with information packages that explain the core issues that can be then dropped of at legislators' offices. Similarly, "some groups, such as the Sierra Club, have a membership lobbying corps, which comes to Washington when key bills are under consideration to lobby members and their staffs" (Wilcox 1998, 97), while other groups keep phone networks of local organizations that can lobby on specific issues when elected officials are home in their districts.

Certain norms are followed during lobbying sessions. To begin, these meetings are not battles, or allowed to end up as argumentative debates, but rather are intended to provide reasoned presentation, an exchange of information and mutual listening. In this way, lobbying is quite different than the hard-nosed negotiations that occur with elected officials during direct action campaigns.

Courtesy is a must, as is careful preparation. Elected officials and staff have limited time, so be prompt. Have your arguments carefully worked out and have written material at hand that explains technical details along with a bulleted summary of what actions are needed. Assume general awareness of your topic (staff probably have glanced at the material you sent in advance; elected officials are unlikely to have done so) but assume ignorance of the details. Present matters succinctly and make sure you point out what action is being requested. Arguing on the importance of supporting employment training for low income people is fine and good but do not forget to strongly state that voting for House Bill 1234 is the way to bring about such training.

Personal lobbying requires very good listening skills to learn from the silences, the facial expressions and the questions being asked, the perspective of those being lobbied. When a politician or staffer interrupts and asks for details, you of course provide, but note that the very fact that they ask is a hint that support might be given on that part of the matter. Revamp your argument accordingly. Our experience with federal staff is that they politely listen but when you touch upon an area in which your interests and theirs overlap, they begin to take notes; that's when to elaborate. Listen closely when the person being lobbied explains constraints they face. Sometimes all they are doing is politely putting you off, but as often as not, they are suggesting to you which parts of your ideas are politically feasible to pursue.

Public Hearings with Elected Officials or Appointed Political Commissions.   At public hearings, social change organizations (and their opponents) present their arguments in an official forum to elected officials and regulatory bodies. A wide variety of issues come up at such hearings—discussions of budgets, zoning issues, ways of allocating money from federal programs, and other matters. Often the hearings are meant to gather information for proposed legislative and regulatory changes. Hearings are often recorded and frequently receive press coverage.

Hearings are formal occasions, with rules and procedures often set by law, and pervasive expectation that participants will respect the process. At the federal level (and usually at the state level) an invitation is required for a person to testify so the trick is to get on the witness list. In Congress, both majority and minority staff get to choose who testifies, though the hearing itself is orchestrated by the majority party. Organizations that have their representatives in Washington are more likely to be called to hearings, in part because these people are available quickly. Further, over time certain organizations gain the reputation as "spokes people" for a cause and in that guise are likely to receive an invitation. Even if an organization is not invited to testify usually it is allowed to submit written testimony as part of the official record. National organizations that are invited to speak will often ask for input from other like-minded groups and include these ideas in the prepared testimony.

Except in the largest cities, local public hearings are quite open affairs at which the city council will allow almost anyone who signs up to address the body, though time limits are usually imposed. To communicate their full message, social change organizations will help those testifying coordinate their statements to cover all important points. Testimony at a public hearing is addressed to the chair, or the committee as a whole, and not to those in the audience, though savvy presenters learn how to communicate to both. Direct give and take between presenters is rarely allowed—an environmentalist cannot fight with a spokesperson from the utilities—but instead questions are posed to the chair in the hope that the committee itself will then pose these questions to the opponents.

At the federal level (and usually the state) testimonies are carefully worked out in advance (sometimes with the cooperation of supportive bureaucrats). Brief testimonies are best with longer arguments and backup data put in the written copy that is placed in the record. Most testimonies include a thank you for being allowed to speak, a brief description of the organization, emphasizing both its concern about the topic and indicating how many members it represents. Testimonies should quickly hone in on the immediate issue, link case study and personal evidence with background data, and emphasize the positive consequences of what is being requested both in general and on those individuals from the electoral districts of those hearing the testimony.

At the local level, public hearings are also held at city commissions, before the issue reaches the city council, allowing subsequent testimonies to be modified to answer questions posed by opponents earlier on. At such hearings, make sure your supporters attend, let those running the meeting know how many in the audience are on your side, perhaps by asking people to stand, but confine the oral presentations to a handful of the better speakers. Boring those conducting the hearing through repeating the same ideas again and again is not the way to go. In preparing presentations, especially on contentious issues, officials at a local level are often amenable to compromise solutions. If your group has such a solution in mind and can live with it, suggest the idea during your testimony.

Your supporters should be in attendance, but also (usually) should behave in a respectful way. Social change organizations might want to carry out demonstrations, rallies, and other direct actions concurrent with the hearings, but the events should be separated, as elected officials resent having meetings disrupted. Politicians recognize the intensity of opinion implied by a demonstration outside city hall or on the steps of the capitol and do not need the same to occur at the hearing.

Since the norms of how to behave at public meetings differ from place to place, attend a few meetings and observe what is expected. Does the speaker address the council, (usually the case) or are you allowed to address the audience? Do those making presentations use the formal titles of elected officials or personal names? How do witnesses dress? Pay attention to the mannerisms of lawyers and business lobbyists. They recognize that while the immediate issue is important, so is maintaining long-term access to the legislative body.

Experienced activists know their presentation time will be limited so they work out carefully what they will say beforehand. Larger organizations and coalitions usually try to have their best speakers present an overall summary and then have others provide the details, alternating between backup data on the topic, how crowded schools are, with personal stories of what time a child has to leave home and when the child returns home. When the arguments require statistical data (or, when pictures speak louder than words) attractive charts or graphs should be posted or handed to the council members. Statistical material should not be read out loud, it is boring and hard to follow.

Dramatic presentations can be effective as long as they make a clear point. For example, a legislator who worked with activists for the disabled described a presentation at a state legislative hearing on economic assistance to the disabled:

> we brought out a fellow who has cerebral palsy . . . I mean he could talk but you couldn't understand him. He had an interpreter . . . [who] would tell you what he was saying. You saw somebody who definitely was unemployable. Instead he owns a business now that employs 11 people . . . It's a small newspaper, community newspaper . . . And he is an entrepreneur. . . . We brought him in to testify and once people saw that. I mean their mouths dropped. No one said a word against him in both houses.

The legislation passed, in part, because people learned that those with disabilities can work and be productive.

At public sessions, opponents may fight vigorously for their side of the issue. The trick is to avoid direct confrontations, but at the same time not allow opponents or legislators that favor the opponents' side to twist your words. If an official bases a question on facts you know aren't correct, simply cite the source of your correct facts. You don't want to make him or her lose face in a hearing, but you do want to show that those facts are wrong. Present the correction, calmly and forthrightly, setting aside your emotions (Alderson and Sentman 1979, 282).

When someone asks a hostile question, try to treat it with respect, but state that you want to correct the misunderstandings. Suppose an alderperson harshly questions a representative of a spouse-abuse center. "Those women in the shelter can't be from our community, they must be coming from neighborhood towns. Spouse abuse is what happens to poor people, when the men are out of work." A respectful and informative response could be, "Economic stress is certainly a cause of violence, as the alderperson indicates, but there are other causes. Spousal abuse happens at all economic levels and more than 70% of those in the center have local addresses."

Refuting arguments that opponents might make is difficult because public hearings are not debates. But if your organization knows enough about the arguments of opponents it can include refutations in its presentations. Suppose a neighborhood organization is trying to stop a developer who wants city permission to build a large housing complex that would destroy open space. Spokespeople for the environmental group can:

1. **Disagree with the evidence presented.** The developer will describe the amount of green space to be left when the project is completed. Environmentalists point out most of that space will be in small front yards, not in parks and open areas that everyone can use.
2. **Point out inconsistencies in the arguments.** The developer describes how easily the city can accommodate the small increase in population, while describing how much more money the city will get in taxes. You argue that either growth is moderate or the gain in taxes is moderate. The developer can't have it both ways.
3. **Challenge the assumptions in the arguments.** The developer argues that traffic congestion will not be a problem. After examining his backup information you learn that he assumes only one car per family, while modern developments average 2.2 cars.
4. **Challenge the priorities within the arguments.** The developer argues that housing is needed since people want to move to the suburbs. Environmentalists argue that the reason people move to the suburbs is to get open space, and if the proposed development goes in, congestion will replace that open space.
5. **Challenge the track record of the opponent.** The spokespeople for the environmental organization present pictures of other projects built by the developer, showing that they result in high density and crowding. (modified from Alderson and Sentman 1979, 236–239)

Markup Sessions.   During a markup session, legislators (and their staff) literally sit around a table and negotiate on the details of a bill, what it is meant to accomplish, or, if money is on the table, specify how it can be used. Influencing markup sessions requires a hands-on presence, so the task is usually done by professionals from Washington-based (or state capital-based) organizations who are personally acquainted with staff. Activists do offer technical suggestions and when a contentious issue is on the floor, might contact their organization's members from the districts of the legislators working on the markup to push their legislator to accept the preferred wording.

Pressuring Administrative Agencies

After laws are passed or programs funded, rules on how to carry them out are left to various bureaucratic and administrative agencies. Rules and changes in rules can be quite technical matters, yet of real import. Recently CRA activists deluged the bank regulators with letters opposing a rule that would change the definition of a small bank (that has less CRA responsibilities) from a bank worth a quarter of a billion dollars to one worth over a billion. This rule, which unfortunately was adopted, allows thousands of banks to reduce their investments in poor communities. Rule changes and lack of enforcement can be harmful. With conservatives in office, environmental rules are less strictly enforced. For example, at the end of 2005, the EPA proposed changes that would allow companies to increase the pollution they released yet not have to report on their actions (www.ombwatch .org/pdfs/TRI_Report.pdf). CRA is the law of the land, but the ways in which banks are judged for obeying this law, what are considered appropriate investments and what not, depend upon regulatory decisions.

Activists understand that bureaucratic and regulatory agencies have discretion and work out ways of pressuring agencies. The simplest approach to pressuring regulatory agencies is by making a complaint. Responsive bureaucratic agencies will collect complaints and, when numerous ones appear on the same matter, might initiate their own investigation. But complaints too often are ignored until outside publicity makes them salient. For instance, banking regulators were aware of the large number of mortgage scams and the fraud from payday lenders but took no steps until activists brought the matter to the attention of the media. Other times pressure is brought indirectly through lobbying an elected official who in turn calls an agency to strongly suggest what actions it should take. Whether this works or not depends on the power of the politician, how vulnerable the agency is to decisions the politician effects, and if the politician's party is or is not in power.

Another approach to gaining bureaucratic attention is by preparing and releasing a technical report on the items for which the agency is responsible, for instance, a report on how many homeless are on the streets, the over-enrollment in a school, or the ways in which minorities are deceived by mortgage lenders (ACORN Fair Housing 2005). In an effort to push for enforcement of rules, disability advocates mapped walkways or lack of the same in public buildings to show that public agencies were not in compliance with the ADA and then released the report at a press conference, more or less forcing the agency to pay attention.

When agencies propose changes in rules, input is vital. Periodically HUD will modify CDBG rules or the formula for how Section 8 certificates are allocated, while state and national banking regulatory agencies issue rules on how to enforce CRA. In these circumstances, activists orchestrate mass letter-writing campaigns to suggest what rules are appropriate and, when hearings are held, offer testimony. On occasion, changes are worked out by the agency as a compromise between the different sides by forcing opponents to talk with one another and "once the interest groups agree on a rule, the agency issues it as a government policy" (Berry and Arons 2003, 38). The trick is to make sure those who support progressive change are at the table when such *negotiated regulations* are worked out.

Participation in Candidate Elections

Studies show that when progressive officials are in office, community and social change organizations benefit. Pierre Clavel argues that

> progressive governments did make a difference. [They provided] support for neighborhood organizations and pressured local administrations to depart from the traditional hierarchical models of government. (Clavel 1986, 233)

Further, with activists in office, governments are more likely to fund *advocacy and equity planners* who work with neighborhood groups and speak for the poor. Mayors Flynn of Boston, Goldschmidt of Portland, and Washington of Chicago all emerged from the neighborhood movement, and once in positions of power were open to community concerns, supported programs that helped neighborhood causes, and appointed people to office who were active in the community movement. In smaller cities, such as Santa Monica, California or the multi-cultural Monterey, California (Horton 1995) neighborhood organizations worked to get their slates in office to bring about specific changes, in the former, rent control, and in the latter, increased sensitivity to the needs of the different cultural groups (such as having multilingual signs). In general, minorities seem better able to protect social and economic gains when representatives from their groups serve as the elected officials (Browning and Marshal 1997). At the national level progressive politicians such as Rep. Bernie Sanders (VT), Rep. Jan Schakowsky (IL) or now retired Senator Mikulski (MD) all were experienced in local social change activities and once in national office steadfastly supported progressive causes.

The question is not whether social change organizations should work with supportive politicians, but how much effort should be put in to electing them or whether activists themselves should run for a political position. Historically, as part of civil rights organizing, action organizations have set up alternative political parties. The Freedom Democratic Party in Mississippi ran many of the local activists in the voting rights movement for office. In Chicago, Jesse Jackson's run for the presidency helped build up the Rainbow Coalition that in turn mobilized large numbers of voters who then worked for other community causes. Numerous activists dropped their organizing work to join the mayoral campaign of community activist Matt Gonzales in San Francisco (Carlsson 2004).

At first blush working for an activist candidate, or better yet as an activist running for office, would appear to be the pinnacle of empowerment. But caution is required. First, nonprofits cannot directly support candidates for office lest they lose important tax advantages. Backing an activist against an incumbent can permanently alienate the incumbent—not so bad if the person always opposes your issues anyway, but problematic if the person can be swayed to your side. Next, assuming the activist wins, it can be a mixed blessing. Serving in public office creates responsibilities, as office holders have legal and moral responsibilities for more people than those that backed them during the election. Activists in office tend to become separated from ordinary members of social change groups, might absorb a go-along-to-get-along mentality, and may be increasingly reluctant to press for the more radical alternatives as they seek support for re-election. Finally the time required to run an electoral campaign is so great that little else gets accomplished, while "even committed activists eventually grow weary of putting their energies into progressive races that are clearly doomed from the start" (Ashkenaz 1986, 17).

For the most part, activists have opposed electoral participation. However, as a result of the pronounced unfriendliness of the Bush administration to progressive causes, many activists now feel it important to work to ensure that progressive candidates win. Prior to the 2004 election many national social change organizations including ACORN, the Center for Community Change, along with hundreds of state and local activist organizations set up a voter registration campaign—the Get Out the Vote Campaign (GOTV)—to register voters in poor neighborhoods. To stay within the law, activist groups could not discriminate on whom they registered or endorse candidates, but of course assumed that the poor and neglected minorities were more likely to vote for the progressive candidate. Many were registered and voting participation was up substantially in poorer neighborhoods:

> Project Vote breaks all records and the numbers say it all: 1,123,270 low- and moderate-income African American and Latino voters registered in 26 states and 102 metro areas; 8,713,553 GOTV voter contacts; 1,000 lawn signs, 25,000 window signs, 1.6 million flyers, 1.3 million doorhangers distributed; 500,000 mobilized in 2000, 2,293,579 mobilized in 2004; 50% higher increase in voter turnout than the national average increase over 2000; 90% of Project Vote canvassers hired from the communities of color in which they worked; face-to-face visits + 3 live reminder calls = 50% higher voter turnout than the national average. (From: "Dave Leland" <pvnatasst@acorn.org> To: <newsletter@projectvote.org> Subject: Project Vote 2004 Executive Summary Date: Friday, March 18, 2005 1:27 PM)

Ballot Measures and Recall Elections

Another way in which organizations (of both the left and right) are politically involved is through recall elections and ballot measures such as referenda and initiatives (material on referendum and initiative extracted and paraphrased from IRI www.iandrinstitute.org/ unless otherwise cited). Recall elections are about collecting signatures to force a vote on whether or not a sitting politician should be removed from office. While the recall of a California governor and his replacement by Arnold Schwarzenegger garnered a lot of publicity, recalls are rare and tend not to engage the interest of progressive social change organizations.

Both initiatives and referendum are about placing policy questions directly on the ballot so citizens can vote yes or no on the specific issue. With popular referendum people collect signatures and then can vote for or against bills already enacted by the legislature, while with a legislative referendum the legislature proposes a bill that then requires citizen approval. With initiatives, citizens collect signatures to get a policy proposal onto the ballot that then is either approved or denied by the electorate.

In the entire century in which initiatives have been legal only 2,000 have been proposed and 800 passed (Waters 2000)—more frequently in California than in other states. Proposition 13 that passed in California dramatically limited local tax revenue, affecting the ability of both the state and cities to provide funds for social and educational services. In 1998, referenda and initiatives were held opposing affirmative action, the legalization of marijuana for medical use, animal rights, gender equality, legalization of gambling, and cigarette taxes (Verhovek 1998). Other issues that recently appeared are on the legality of physician-assisted suicide as well as concerns with bilingual education. Tax limits are a perennial favorite and, if passed, leave the government short of money for social programs.

Community groups have sponsored local referenda to stop block busting in racially changing neighborhoods (Scheiber 1987), and social movement organizations have set up votes to oppose nuclear power and weapons (Zisk 1989). In 2004 major ballot issues of concern to activists included matters on marijuana, stem cell research, illegal immigration, employee provided health insurance, clean energy, and special sales taxes for education (Seven Worth Watching, 2004). One ballot initiative sponsored by ACORN was successful in Florida even though the state was supporting less progressive political candidates:

> On November 2, ACORN and Floridians for All won a raise for working families in Florida when over 71% of Florida voters approved a ballot measure, Amendment 5, to raise the state's minimum wage by $1 above the federal level, with annual indexing to inflation. Florida is the first Southern state to raise its minimum wage above the federally mandated level. The wage increase . . . affect an estimated 850,000 Floridians, providing a full-time minimum wage worker with an additional $2,000 in annual income. ACORN collected nearly one million signatures to get the minimum wage proposal on the ballot. (ACORN 2004 annual report)

Social change organizations must be ready to fight against backlash referenda. For instance, in 1998 in California, legislation was proposed through a referendum that would forbid any money deducted from employees' checks to be used for any political purpose, unless the employees explicitly approved of each case. Progressive organizations fought this referendum and prevailed (Bass 1998).

Progressive organizations have little choice but to work to combat harmful initiatives that promote racial or ethnic discrimination, those that discriminate against gays, as well as tax limitations that reduce funds for social programs. On the other hand, conducting a statewide initiative campaign even on an important issue can be so time consuming that an organization ends up doing little else (Dresang and Gosling 1989, 180). Another concern about proposing ballot measures is that they have to be phased so that they can be answered with either a yes or no. Such wording oversimplifies complicated issues as people do not have simple feelings about immigration or abortion but the wording of the questions might force people to the extremes when in fact, few prefer it.

Community Boards and Commissions

Citizens volunteer to serve on a wide array of community and neighborhood boards including official city commissions, such as planning or zoning; federally mandated citizen boards, for instance, those that recommend how to spend Community Development Block Grant dollars; and occasional ad hoc task forces. Sometimes local governments decentralize decision making to the neighborhood level and establish neighborhood commissions that under progressive governments actually have some say over local decisions.

Whether to participate in these voluntary boards and commissions depends upon the powers granted to them. Both environmental organizations and those concerned about neighborhood preservation and repair might seek out seats on planning commissions or zoning boards, as each have an impact on what is being built. But being involved in neighborhood planning efforts is a judgment call as the reports that such bodies produce are often tossed on the shelf and ignored (Chaskin 2005, 408).

Just labelling a board "participatory" or "community-based" does not mean that it is worthwhile for community organizations to participate. Older studies are somewhat cynical about how democratically empowering such boards might be as most are run by a self-perpetuating local elite and allow for very little effective involvement by ordinary citizens (Cnaan 1991). Other scholars worry that rather than empower, community boards end up pitting neighborhood against neighborhood. As described in New York City:

> with a shrinking pie, a division of the city into separate community boards tended to place neighborhood interests in competition with each other. Neighborhoods were divided from each other, not united, by the arrangement. (Marcuse 1988, 281)

More recent research, though, is more optimistic. One national study examined cities in which there was high participation in community boards and discovered that in effective boards, citizens who demanded the right to be involved often were and in addition received money to accomplish their tasks (Berry, Portney, and Thomson 1993, 48–51). Community members have joined local school boards that then put into place progressive educational and social reform (Shirley 2002). In Chicago, citizens on local police boards have a real say over police policies while members of local school councils who developed increased control were able to appoint principals and have some say over the budget (Fung 2004).

In Boston, the Dudley Street Neighborhood Initiative itself prepared the redevelopment plan for its community that the city adopted, then was given significant say into zoning decisions, and actually had the right of "eminent domain," that is, it can exercise the city's power to forceably purchase land needed to improve the community (Medoff and Sklar 1994; Tulloss 1995). In Minneapolis, a series of Neighborhood Revitalization Boards have an effective say in allocating redevelopment funds and strong powers on zoning matters and have major input on which city projects are built where (Nickel 1995). Cities that have set up Housing Trust Funds, ways of funding affordable housing, often have neighborhood activists serve on the boards that allocate the money. For boards to be empowered though, cooperation is still required from officials. For instance, in Dayton, Ohio, citizens from separate neighborhoods are members of Priority Boards that have effective say in shaping the city's budget but first are taught how to do so by city officials.

Before advising members to get involved in neighborhood boards, an action organization might want to ensure that participation is not a waste of time. Are the decisions made binding, rather than being merely recommendations? Are the stakes high enough to be worth the time? Having a say on a city budget or zoning is probably worth the effort, but being on the advisory board of a planning effort can often turn out to be a waste of everyone's time if the plan is tossed aside. Are democratic procedures followed in choosing who is going to be on the board? Appointed boards often easily are co-opted as part of the political system, while elected boards might stimulate community involvement.

Constraints on Political Participation

Progressive activists who become engaged in political and administrative actions face numerous constraints. Most commissions and committees are unpaid and meet at hours that are inconvenient for working class people. Writing letters or even clicking on e-mail letters is easy enough, but working people can rarely do so during working hours, while representatives or big businesses are ordered to do so by their bosses. In advertising political ideas, progressives are outgunned as

> "Businesses can buy disproportionately large amounts of advertising, and this may skew political speech and therefore public policy. The imbalance in legislative issue advertising targeting those who live and work in Washington means that policy makers may be repeatedly exposed to uncorrected and one-sided claims." (Two reports show influence of business lobbying spending, 2003)

In running for office, activists face being demeaned by being accused by conservatives in office as being somehow un-American for speaking for peace, free speech, or civil rights. Recent efforts to register voters, especially among poor and minority groups, have been successful, but in turn caused a backlash. In Ohio in 2004, for instance, insufficient voting machines were available in poorer areas causing long lines and discouraging voters. Proposals also have been made to require official photo IDs to allow voting, knowing full well the poor, elderly, and minorities are less likely to have such cards.

Explicit efforts have been made by those in office to limit the political speech of nonprofit organizations. Advocates for reproductive rights or for AIDS victims have been strongly pressured to be silent and when the Bush Administration tried to reduce Head Start funding, organizations that contacted political officials were threatened with a cutoff of money, while the IRS has increasingly audited nonprofits that advocated for their own issues (Bass, Guinane, and Turner 2003). In October 2005, a bill was on the house floor to use money from the profits of government-sponsored housing enterprises to help pay for affordable housing; so far so good. But a rider to that bill was offered that mandated that no nonprofit agency that has worked to register voters, offered criticisms of those running for office, or even referred to federal issues within two months of an election or is closely associated with an organization that did be allowed to receive any of the funds. For-profit organizations are under no such constraints (various e-mails NLHIC October 2005). Nonprofits fear audits for political work and evidence exists that those in office will use such audits to intimidate activist organizations that they oppose (Berry and Arons 2003, 72–85).

Internal Revenue Service Code limits organizations incorporated as 501(c)3 nonprofits in the amount of lobbying they can undertake, as spelled out in the Lobbying Disclosure Act of 1995. Those that incorporate as 501(c)4 organizations can undertake political activity but are not eligible for many tax advantages. In practice, many nonprofits will simply set up an affiliated 501(c)4 organization for political work. 501(c)3s nonprofits that employ at least one person who spends at least 20 percent of his or her time in lobbying, or that spend $20,000 semiannually on lobbying must register as lobbying groups.

Fortunately, the provisions are not all that strict and apply only to the federal level. Many activities do not count against the limits, for instance, educating people about an issue, or doing technical analysis or studies are permissible. Distributing nonpartisan information on issues, providing testimony at the request of the legislature, or defending the organization from attacks by opponents are *not* considered lobbying. As the legislation stands, it allows for as much effort as most groups are able to undertake, with the main problem being the need for detailed recordkeeping. In addition, organizations that fill out a simple form and take what is known as a 501(h) election can maintain their nonprofit status and lobby so long as the money spent on lobbying is below a certain (generous) and specified amount that differs according to the size of the organization (Alliance for Justice 2001). Unfortunately, many in the nonprofit world, either intimidated by those who try to stop them from lobbying or by not understanding the laws, unnecessarily limit their own lobbying efforts (Berry and Arons 2003, 42).

Conclusion

We have described conventional ways to influence both the political and regulatory systems, arguing that using them makes sense as a first pass. But when political access is blocked, or issues ignored, more aggressive actions are needed as described in the next chapter. These more confrontational actions create a base of political power that then allows the social change organization to be more effective in its use of the more conventional tactics for influencing politicians and bureaucrats.

CHAPTER
17 Compelling Change through Power Tactics

In this chapter we present an array of power tactics through which activist organizations vigorously pressure for change, or as the leaders in the Dudley Street neighborhood of Boston state "the squeaky wheel gets the oil . . . so we squeak" (Medoff and Sklar 1994, 84–85). Massive demonstrations helped end the war in Vietnam; daring sit-ins, boycotts, and civil disobedience brought down state-sanctioned discrimination, while peaceful picketing has shamed the police to pay attention and do something about the local dope trade.

Power tactics can be humorous, ridiculing the hypocrisy of big business or the lies of politicians through mockery. In contrast, other actions gain power by their quiet dignity as when people kneel down together along with clergy in a silent prayer vigil to pray to ask that the police step in and end gang warfare. Demonstrations show their power through the numbers involved, and the implicit threat of disruption, while boycotts target a business's bottom line. Teach-ins and public assemblies involve constitutionally protected speech rights (though the establishment at times forgets), while other tactics—directly sabotaging polluting factories—are blatantly illegal. With civil disobedience, activists violate a law, but do so peacefully to show that something is seriously wrong and must be changed. Table 17-1 summarizes the variety of power tactics.

All power tactics loudly call attention to problems and shout out that a solution must be found. A few people might pass the homeless sleeping in parks and doorways, but millions see pictures on the six o'clock news of the shantytowns set up on the capitol lawn to protest the poverty that leads to homelessness. By shutting down Seattle for a day, demonstrations against the World Trade Organization called attention to how globalization has hurt the poor to benefit large companies (Cockburn, St. Clair, and Sekula 2000). Disruptions led by ACT-UP made visible government's neglect of the AIDS epidemic; confrontations inspired by the Justices for Janitors Campaign (McCarthy and McPhail 1998) publicized persisting economic discrimination against those working in less desirable jobs. Power tactics battle the invisibility of injustice often by doing

> flamboyant things: Initiating traffic blockades . . . ; chaining themselves to buildings of targets . . . and to the White House fence, disrupting network television broadcasts . . . occupying legislators' offices . . . and the U.S. Capitol (where thousands of blood-stained pennies were scattered); setting off stink bombs in the U.S. Congress . . .

TABLE 17.1   Families of Power Tactics

Family *Specific Tactic*	Description
Educational	**Framing a contentious issue through the presentation of background information that suggests what actions need to be taken**
Public Documentation	Circulating technical reports as ammunition to motivate other power tactics
Testing	Showing that there is a problem by running test cases, for instance, having black and white families that are similar economically apply for housing to see if there is discrimination
Teach-Ins and Community Education	A teach-in occurs in a public assembly, during which individuals present background material on an issue to refute the ideological and substantive myths those in power use to justify not resolving the problem. Community education programs are similar but done in smaller groups in churches, neighborhood meetings, and similar places.
Cool Media Events	Colorful stunts, often carried out as mini-plays termed sociodrama that call attention to a problem to embarrass those responsible to take corrective actions. At times, activists try to turn ordinary press conferences into cool media events.
Moral Protests	**Dramatizing an issue through personal sacrifice or devotion**
Vigils	A quiet gathering of a group that builds upon religious symbols to shame those in power into making changes
Fasts (or hunger strikes)	Focusing attention on an issue by refusing to eat until demands are met
Jailings	After being arrested not posting bail in order to symbolize the injustice (and at times tie up the legal system)
Power Displays	**Large gatherings that call attention to a problem by creating the potential for disruption and communicate a threat if solutions are not found**
Rallies and Public Demonstrations	Gatherings addressed by activist speakers that call attention to a problem, motivate others to join in the action while publicizing that large numbers demand action be taken. Usually held in a large public space.
Marches and Caravans	Activists march together (or drive together) while carrying placards describing both the problem and the demands for solution. The march route usually passes by locations controlled by the target.
Direct Confrontations	**Displaying power that comes from large numbers of people who either disrupt and targets or create substantial economic costs on the targets**
Face-to-face Confrontations	Organized individuals collectively and directly confront the target

Family *Specific Tactic*	Description
Intense Complaint Tactics	Orchestrated campaigns in which complaints are made to those in power in a public way
Accountability Sessions	Prearranged meetings between public officials and organization members in which officials are pressured to explain why changes have not been made or to promise what they are doing to solve a problem
Picketing	A march around a building or space controlled by the target, replete with signs describing the problem, the target's role in creating the problem, and the demands for solution
Sit-ins	Physically occupying an office, building, or territory controlled by the target until demands are met; sit-ins might block traffic or construction equipment if the goal is to stop an unwanted building project
Dramatic Hits	Hits are any of a variety of specific loud, often raucous, face-to-face confrontations with targets, varying from yelling at a public official at his or her home or office, to shouting out demands at a company's annual meeting
Economic Confrontations	***Orchestrating economic might to pressure targets***
Boycotts	Arranging for large numbers of people to not buy a particular product or patronize a specific company
Labor Strikes	Pressuring an employer by denying labor
Rent Strikes	Pressuring a landlord by denying rent
Sabotage	***Destruction of property or other physical damage intended to directly stop the behavior that is the object of the protest; almost always involves illegal actions and subjects those involved to arrest***

illegally distributing hypodermic needles to drug addicts . . . and even covering Senator Jesse Helms' house with a giant replica of a condom. (McCarthy and McPhail 1998, 102–03)

Such actions force responses from targets by making them fear continual disruption, a fear that gains credibility as activists literally put their bodies on the line.

Power tactics catch the public eye, scaring the targets while rallying newcomers to the cause as they see the bravery of the early activists—civil rights and antiwar protesters who faced death when surrounded by hostile opponents. Yet, power tactics are not enough to resolve issues. Boycotting a redlining bank does not magically make money appear to reinvest in poor communities, unless the bank changes its policies or Uncle Sam more vigorously enforces the CRA. Power tactics are part of a broader campaign that links the flamboyance of demonstrations, rallies, and vigils with political actions that ensure that promised changes actually come into being.

Shared Characteristics of Power and Confrontational Approaches to Social Change

When conventional political approaches fail, more militant tactics are required, but that does not mean that an organization should immediately stage a demonstration, do a sit-in, sabotage the offender, or boycott its products. Questions need to be asked on whether power tactics really are appropriate, which ones work best for the specific organization, and then to make sure that power tactics, if used, will have an impact.

Questions on the Use of Power Tactics

Before engaging in a confrontational campaign several questions should be answered: Are power tactics the correct strategic choice? To what extent does the use of power tactics create an appropriate framing of the issue? and, finally, Are the tactics chosen consistent with both progressive values and the moral concerns of those in your organization?

Is the Action Strategically Appropriate?   When communication has broken down, and abuses persist, militancy is required, but wise activists still question if power tactics are the way to go. We were having a conversation with a friend, a leader of a national social change organization, about whether he would agree with those in his organization who wanted to conduct a militant street demonstration against a government bank regulator. This individual made us rethink the idea by asking us:

> What makes such actions a great idea? Is it because of any of the following:
>
> - People get energized
> - People get some press
> - It's a bonding experience
> - It has an impact
>
> You'll probably get agreement from me that the first three indeed are accurate, but on the final and most important point; having an impact . . . two years ago we did a press conference (stimulated by [the militant activists], attacking [the head of the regulatory organization] and his policies . . . he only became more vigilant in his commitment to undermining CRA. Perhaps one could argue that he got even more personal in his commitment to undermine and attack CRA.
>
> As an old street fighter, let me offer some advice. If you're on the way for a fight you'd better have a plan to win something. Fights have a way of energizing both sides of the aisle. If we could have adequate numbers that would tie up the streets, shut down the office and maybe even have a few folks willing to get arrested over this, maybe then we could get some of the press we need to have an impact.
>
> Political action ought to have a purpose, a goal that is even remotely attainable, otherwise we expend a lot of energy for naught, that may be expended more judiciously and effectively.

As our friend suggested, activists must ask if militant tactics are going to be effective. Power actions should be attention getting and communicate a clear message, but they should not be undertaken simply to be in the limelight. If there is much publicity but little followup, organization members will end up demoralized. Public relations are important. Tactics must be seen as appropriate to the cause. Conducting a demonstration before asking the opponent to seriously talk can backfire; acting militantly once the door has been slammed in your face is a different matter. Sabotaging equipment may slow down the construction of a highway, but it also risks hurting construction workers and turning the public against the cause.

Action organizations are caught in an interesting bind: Tactics chosen must be strong enough to be compelling and outrageous enough to attract attention, yet be acceptable enough not to alienate potential supporters. Violent and disruptive tactics are considered acceptable only in very serious situations. As Gamson has argued over history, "unruly groups, those that use violence, strikes, and other constraints, have better than average success" (Gamson 1997, 364), but these groups were successful because the situations they faced were deemed serious enough to warrant confrontations.

Effective power tactics are carefully integrated within a broader campaign strategy. Activists don't simply do street theater to show that many jobs are at poverty level wages, without at the same time working with politicians to press for living wage ordinances (Luce 2002; Osterman 2002, 150–55). Further, effective campaigns need to be sustained and sustaining direct actions over long periods of time can be difficult. Those who oppose globalization were able to mobilize thousands to go to Seattle in street protests, but involvement in later protests on the same matter in Washington, D.C. were far less impressive, weakening the entire effort (Cockburn, St. Clair, and Sekula 2000).

Does the Action Appropriately Frame the Broader Issue?

Effective power tactics frame issues to simultaneously show the severity of the problem, the importance of achieving a solution, while making it clear that there was no other way other than using a power tactic to call attention to the problem. The tactic itself should symbolize the issue.

A symbolic protest of throwing money into the trading pits on Wall Street attracted attention and symbolized greed; blocking a public health facility caught the public's eye and called attention to lack of care for AIDS victims. Activists symbolized poverty by setting up shanty housing in public squares, or the dangers of nuclear energy by having people lie down as if dead next to a nuclear reactor site. Those protesting predatory lenders dress up in shark suits to illustrate the vicious nature of the unfair loans. To symbolize the unfair way in which the federal budget is allocated, activists portrayed how little money went to poor people in a media event involving bringing out an eleven-foot budget pie (out of ice cream) and then cutting out the tiny slice that went to those in need. The Kensington Welfare Rights Organization set up mock tribunals to make the case that the U.S. government was guilty of human rights violations because of the way the poor are treated. Large groups of antiwar people have held silent vigils around army bases, as if to mourn the (future) dead.

The knowledge that a nonviolent protester is putting his or her life in danger itself becomes a powerful symbol of a movement. Environmentalists who sail into weapon test zones are risking their lives to make apparent the danger of nuclear weapons to wildlife and people. Preservationists have chained themselves to trees to block development; if the trees were to be cut down the activists would be torn apart. A dramatic turning point occurred in the civil rights campaign in Birmingham, Alabama, when the children began to march putting themselves in danger, and in doing so symbolizing the depth of their and their parents' commitment:

> Reporters saw things they had never seen before. George Wall, a tough-looking police captain, confronted a group of thirty-eight elementary-school children and did his best to cajole or intimidate them into leaving the lines, but they all said they knew what they were doing. Asked her age as she climbed into a paddy wagon, a tiny girl called out that she was six. (Branch 1988, 757)

Protests that are meant as media events must communicate the actual matter in dispute. During a campaign for a living wage, activists had thousands mail in paper plates during the Thanksgiving season to city council members "symbolizing the struggle to feed a family on poverty wages" (Reynolds 2002, 161). Gay activists made apparent the extent of the AIDS epidemic by constructing a giant quilt on the Mall in Washington, D.C. in which each portion represented a victim. Ruckus designed a set of playing cards on which a picture was placed of individuals who were profiteering from the war economy. In protesting against Liberty Loans, a predatory lender, ACORN used a mockup of the Statue of Liberty as a central icon for the problem, punning on both the company's name and the freedom of which it was depriving its victims.

Is the Action Consistent with the Values of the Organization Members and the Broader Public?

In choosing a confrontational approach, activists must make sure the actions are consistent with their own values. *"Tactics are rarely, if ever, neutral means about which protesters do not care. Tactics represent important routines, emotionally and morally salient in these people's lives"* (Jasper 1997, 237). Of equal importance, tactics must appeal to the values of the broader public. Tactics that are seen as proportionate to the problem are more readily accepted. People accept that battles against racism justify more extreme responses than the absence of a stop sign. But here understandings can clash. Dedicated animal rights activists feel it is moral and just to release lab animals; those less involved might see the protesters as doing little more than breaking and entering and harming vital medical research.

One way of appealing to the broader public is to build upon traditions that have been accepted from previous campaigns. In the civil rights era, Freedom Rides, in which courageous activists thwarted segregation, at times at the cost of their lives, were initially controversial but came to symbolize bravery in opposition to oppression. Building on this understanding,

> In the fall of 2003, ACORN members played an active role in the historic Immigrant Workers Freedom Ride. 15 ACORN members from Seattle, San Jose, Los Angeles, St.

Paul, MN, Chicago, Orlando and Phoenix rode the Freedom Ride buses, while ACORN members in Little Rock, Phoenix, Chicago, Columbus, New York, Minneapolis, Orlando, New Orleans and other cities participated in kick-off and welcoming events. At the Ride's final event, a 100,000 person rally in Queens, New York, ACORN president Maude Hurd spoke along with other civil rights leaders. (ACORN annual report 2004)

How societal perception and activist morality are connected can be seen in the traditions of civil disobedience, made most famous through the actions of Dr. Martin Luther King, Jr. (Schock 2003; Tracy 2002). With civil disobedience, activists intentionally but pacifistically violate what they consider to be unjust laws or social norms, doing so with willingness to accept arrest. Participants require the courage to undergo arrest, and to chance the taunts and brutality of opposition, often including the police, without fighting back. Civil disobedience communicates several messages. By putting bodies on the line, activists communicate that they deeply care about the issue yet at the same time respect the rules sufficiently to accept arrest. Their actions imply that those in power will change, not because of force, but because it is the moral thing to do.

Actions Have Implications for the Organization

Power tactics affect both the image of the action organization and its ability to conduct future work. Successful actions enhance the power of the organization making it a player in influencing political decisions. Mobilizing hundreds of thousands of individuals at a mass rally or picketing city hall and convincing officials to more diligently battle the scourge of drugs all create an image of a powerful can-do organization. Such power builds upon itself, as the next time simply threatening to act might be sufficient.

Tactics are effective because they hint at greater power, encouraging the use of bluffs and threats. Alinsky once got the city of Chicago to concede a point by threatening to have organization members occupy each bathroom stall at the airport; but they never had to carry out the threat. As Alinsky argued, "Power is not only what you have but what the enemy thinks you have" (Alinsky 1971, 127–30). The potential for disruption may be more effective than disruption itself. Politicians might work with an organization to prevent a mob scene in the council chambers, but if an actual demonstration occurs, they may use the police to quell the uprising to show who is in charge.

Demonstrating power through confrontational tactics can increase the size and dedication of an organization's membership. Further involvement in power tactics increase commitment upping what people are willing to do (Kurtz 2002, 4). People reason that "I am not just a supporter of equal rights for women but I have marched with my sisters and brothers in the Equal Rights Organizations and now am willing to do more."

Involvement expands when actions get the results that show the efforts are worthwhile (Alinsky 1971, 127–30). Early in an organization's life, power tactics focus on concrete issues—clear causes—those that are possible to win often by targeting specific individuals (Sen 2003, 51). For instance, fighting a corporation like the telephone company can seem futile, but putting pressure on an executive in the company, an individual with a name, a house, and a reputation in the community seems more doable. As Alinsky argued, "Pick the target, freeze it, personalize it, and polarize it" (Alinsky 1971, 127–30).

Pragmatic Concerns

In planning a demonstration, rally, sit-in, sociodrama, or any of the dozens of power approaches, activists have to pay attention to many pragmatic matters, ranging from negotiating with the police about arrests, to the visibility of signs on television, down to making sure there are adequate sanitation facilities at a rally. But broader concerns also must be kept in mind—knowing how to multiply impact through combining power approaches, mastering tactical jiujitsu, and preparing for when the opposition strikes back. Power tactics don't just happen but instead require careful training before they can be carried off.

Combining and Magnifying Power Tactics.   Power tactics cascade. A teach-in inspires people to participate in a mass rally. When a few dedicated individuals conduct a hunger strike or other moral campaign, the broader membership becomes more willing to join a rally. Marches gain attention for the cause that in turn force political leaders to meet with the organization. Power tactics multiply the effectiveness of conventional politics, for instance when organizational leaders, bolstered by the concurrent mass demonstrations occurring on the streets, quietly lobby in the chambers of power.

With better communications facilitated by both the Internet and cell phones, the power of actions can multiply by having them take place in different locations at the same time. For instance, in *Days of Action*, orchestrated by national organizations, a march or rally is held in Washington, D.C., while local organizations simultaneously hold rallies in their home towns. The take back the night campaigns, vigils in which people light candles and march around their blocks in protest of gangs and crime, are often orchestrated on a national level, creating a crescendo of publicity.

Tactical Jiujitsu.   Rather than relying on his or her own physical strength, a jiujitsu expert will cleverly use the power of the opponent. When a large person charges, the jiujitsu expert captures the opponent's momentum and uses it to flip him or her over. Tactical jiujitsu works in a similar way, by demonstrating the unfairness of those in power, for instance, when those in a civil disobedience campaign, especially children and those in clerical garb, are seen being led away by large and armed police. Passive resistance makes the establishment appear to be a forceful bully, flipping its strength into a weakness.

Other times tactical jiujitsu involves being patient until the targets make a mistake. Perhaps the opposition will deny activists the right to speak in a public forum which leads to court suits; the threat to freedom of speech magnifies whatever issue was being fought. On our college campus, an action organization was gaining little attention in its effort to protest Nike's use of sweatshops but was patient in its effort.

After a while a foolish campus administrator, in violation of university rules, stopped the group from putting up posters, which until that time few even noticed. The fight over free speech gave the action organization far more publicity about the sweatshop labor than did the initial campaign. Protests in Seattle in 1999 against the World Trade Organization provoked massive police action, including the beating and arrest of a reporter trying to show his press credentials. Because of the publicity the police violence generated, the public learned that the demonstration was occurring and about the issues involved.

Tactical jiujitsu can be about mocking the rules of the establishment. For instance, during the Vietnam War, the draft board intimidated protesters by calling them up to serve. In response, activists clogged up the bureaucratic procedure by following draft board rules in minute detail. As Gene Sharp described:

> We want everyone to take this law so seriously that they inform their board of every single change, even if they're over age or have already completed their service. This means wives, mothers, and friends as well. They should submit documents attesting to any change in the status of the registrant. The Selective Service just cannot stand up administratively to absolute obedience to the draft laws. (Sharp 1973b, 417)

Training, Preparation, and Coordination. Often the difference between a disorderly riot that creates a bad image for the social change organization and an effective demonstration that gains public support is day after day of careful preparation. Virtually all organizer training academies provide how-to-do information on effective power tactics, while the former Greenpeace activists now working for Ruckus teach people about how to carry off the more flamboyant stunts—for instance, climbing buildings and unfurling very long signs supporting the cause. In setting up protests, action teams work closely together to ensure that the planned details are carried out (Warren 2001, 115).

Civil disobedience, especially nonviolent resistance, requires days of training: It takes discipline, a trained discipline, to quietly sit there while being either verbally or physically provoked by opponents or the police. Unfortunately, few people can stand a beating without wanting to fight back. During the Montgomery Bus Boycotts, action organizations conducted training schools in nonviolence and only people trained and experienced in nonviolence were allowed to become Freedom Riders (Branch 1988, 438). Even after selecting the people most likely to be able to resist provocation, it is wise to make sure that those with the greatest experience are scattered throughout the assembled group, ready to intervene if, in the heat of the moment, tempers flare.

Even if an organization has trained individuals to be nonviolent, the police do not always cooperate and will look for any excuse to beat up on peaceful protesters, or to clear the streets by arresting everyone in sight. As part of preparation, action organizations should encourage neutral parties to be present and observe what happens, and be prepared to testify in court to help the protesters get a fair hearing.

Training and preparation helps on less dramatic matters. Ensuring food for sit-ins and sufficient sanitary facilities for large demonstrations, working sound systems and projectors for teach-ins, and making sure the press is there and understands what you are doing are all important. In addition, when civil disobedience is planned or even when the purpose is to assemble large groups, organizations might negotiate with the police to establish public order management systems (McCarthy and McPhail 1998, 104) agreeing on what rules will be followed.

Practical details need to be planned. If a group is planning to take over a floor of a building for a sit-in, leaders of the event need to be sure they can get participants into the building, have access to rest rooms and water, can feed those involved, and can communicate with the press, police, and emergency services. Prior to when the Dudley Street Neighborhood Initiative picketed to shut down illegal garbage sites:

> leaflets had been dropped at hundreds of homes; follow-up home calls had been made during the previous two nights; several city officials had been invited to attend and had confirmed; hundreds of "Don't Dump on Us" buttons had been produced in three languages; rides, child care, refreshments, and translations had all been arranged. (Medoff and Sklar 1994, 71)

But sometimes things are missed. In one embarrassing case, activists planned to occupy a federal educational agency to demand a meeting with the director to discuss the neglect of schools in poor communities. The activists rushed the building expecting to find token opposition (and even sympathy) among the targets, only to be met with strong police opposition. In its planning, the organization had missed that a government intelligence agency shared the premises with the educational bureaucracy.

As part of the initial planning for confrontations, event organizers should sit in a room together and game out what could possibly happen and plan how to react. What should the organization do if the police start hitting protesters? Plan for every situation. Activists must have communication gear and batteries or electricity with which to power equipment if coordination is needed between separate parts of a large group.

In planning a rally, march, or demonstration, teach participants to respond quickly to signals from marshals: when to advance, retreat, sit down where they are, or quiet down. Targets are impressed when a large unruly crowd suddenly becomes silent at the mere suggestion of the leaders. Making sure that happens requires practice. Training can include instruction on how to breathe (for a while) when under tear gas assault, or how to deal with arrest. Everyone should have change to call the organization's lawyer, access to bail money, and have nothing in their pockets that can be construed as a weapon, not even a nail file. Participants need to be sure they are not carrying any drugs, or anything that could be mistaken for illegal drugs.

Applying Power Tactics

As seen in Table 17.1, power tactics vary greatly but each are about accomplishing three ends:

1. Widely publicizing an issue to frame both the cause and solution consonant with the goals of the action organization;

2. Increasing the commitment of activists while mobilizing others to join in the collective efforts;
3. Forcing those in power a step closer to accepting the solution wanted by the action organization.

Tactics also need to be evaluated in terms of their appeal to the organization's membership and the capacity of the organization to successfully carry them out. First time activists, mildly upset about a policy, aren't going to join in a hunger fast, while a small organization is unlikely to have the resources to bring off a major demonstration on the Mall in Washington, D.C.

We have grouped the power tactics into four broad families, roughly in order of how confrontational they appear to be. *Educational tactics* dramatically publicize that a problem exists, *moral protests* gain support through showing commitment, *power displays* create disruption and force an issue through creating a threat, while *direct confrontations* immediately create visible problems for an opponent while at the same time publicizing the issue more broadly.

Most campaigns sequence a variety of tactics, with a teach-in, for example, being a prelude to a rally that then leads to picketing. The signs carried in marches and while picketing more aggressively communicate the same message that is presented in quieter ways through educational campaigns.

Educational Campaigns

Educational campaigns spotlight issues by providing factual information so that festering problems cannot be ignored. As the leadership of the National Community Reinvestment Coalition argues "information is power" while in general "the information capacity of the liberal groups was a key to their status and influence" (Berry and Arons 2003, 129).

Public Documentation.   Documentation involves collecting information for policy work but in ways that make sure that neither the public nor officials can ignore what was learned. For instance, in Chicago, a coalition of neighborhood groups documented how much money the city spent on capital projects, such as roads, sewers, and transit facilities, in different parts of the city, and discovered that most neighborhoods in contrast to downtown were short-changed; with the evidence in hand they successfully demanded that the mayor set up fairer allocations (Rubin 2000a). Public Interest Research Groups document when stores are selling spoiled meat and corporations are selling faulty and dangerous products, and then present such data to regulatory agencies, while at the same time publicizing the findings through the press.

The facts of the matter can be shared in ways that garner publicity. For instance,

> Toronto ACORN members organized a "Cockroach Derby" and a Code Enforcement Tour to draw attention to poor living conditions in two large apartment complexes . . . ACORN members showed their City Council representative . . . and code enforcement team . . . some of the most egregious issues in the buildings, including mold, giant holes in the walls and cockroaches crawling out of phones and in people's beds.

> To highlight in particular the major pest infestation issues in the apartments, ACORN members held a Cockroach Derby where residents competed to see who could round up the most cockroaches from their apartments. (ACORN News Letter Nov. 18, 2004)

Testing.   Testing shows through public, first-hand experiences, that agencies are not enforcing their own rules. To test for discrimination in housing, individuals with identical family and economic backgrounds but from different ethnic groups go out to look for housing to see if there are differences to whom apartments are rented, homes sold, or mortgages offered. Testing has also been used to see about access to affordable mortgages, whether blacks or whites are treated the same in bars, and other similar comparisons. In most cases persistent racism is documented. Testing data are then presented to the agencies to insist on better enforcement of laws against racial discrimination.

Testing can be done in a more confrontational manner when it is apparent that regulatory agencies are indifferent to problems. For instance, after government inspectors ignored poor quality food in local stores, the action organization set up its own inspection forms, called the police to warn them what was going to happen, entered the supermarket, and took down information on problems with the food and the high prices charged. Store managers were panicked and many immediately signed a form indicating that quality would improve (Gecan 2002, 67–68).

Teach-Ins.   Teach-ins and community education programs blend mobilization with confrontation by providing information on problems to belie the propaganda put out by those in power. Political education extends the effort by showing how more immediate problems people face, such as high prices for food, stem from broader structural factors, the power of the food processing industry, for instance (Sen 2003, 166–82).

During a teach-in, people with first-hand knowledge share what they know, contrasting their information with the official sources. For instance, teach-ins on Vietnam that were led by academics who had been doing research on Southeast Asia and had solid information to report put to shame the hemming and hawing of the government employees who showed up to defend the war-time policies.

Skillfully orchestrated teach-ins and community education programs are a type of jiujitsu in which opponents can be trapped into discrediting themselves. For instance,

> anti nuclear activists have sometimes sponsored debates with representatives of the nuclear power industry . . . Many groups report that industry or government representatives are often so ill-informed or deceptive that they discredit themselves. An official of Dow Chemical, for example, testified at a California public hearing on [a pesticide] that despite animal research showing testicular damage from the pesticide, it had not occurred to Dow that it might also harm human male reproductive ability. (Freudenberg 1984, 139)

Effective teach-ins and community education programs are meant to immediately link to other power tactics, for example encouraging attendees to join in a subsequent demonstration.

Cool Media Events.   Cool media events become the sound-bites of educational campaigns, though caution is needed lest the "coolness" of the event distract from the underlying message. Cool media events range from mock press conferences that satirize those in power, sociodrama—small plays that visually portray a problem—to "stunts" that are colorful enough to catch media attention. For instance, activists in the antipredatory lending and antipay lending movement might dress up as sharks (i.e., loan sharks) and march outside of the offices of the exploitative lenders, after forewarning the press about the event.

Media events can backfire. As a cool media event, gay activists held massive marches, only to find that the press focused not on the message about discrimination but on showy cross dressers. An "outing," in which gay activists reveal that key establishment figures are homosexuals, catches media attention, portrays the hypocrisy of those in power, but can cause a backlash because the tactic violates personal privacy.

Media events should symbolize the problem in ways that are either poignant or humorous. If people cry along with the group, as they might with a sociodrama portraying AIDS' deaths, or laugh, as they did with Alinsky's bathroom take-overs, there is a reasonable chance the message is communicated. Better yet, make sure the cool media event literally portrays the problem. For instance, Food and Medicine illustrated widespread unemployment by setting up an unemployment line "which stretched a long block in downtown Bangor and gained statewide public attention. [followed by] the "Cemetery of Jobs" action, where we made 75 signs and arranged them cemetery style in the front lawn of a closed factory" (Food and Medicine website).

The symbolism of cool media events must be clear:

1. Protesting the lack of rat-control measures in poor neighborhoods in Washington, D.C., activist Julius Hobson threatened to trap large numbers of rats and release them in Georgetown, a posh residential area. He then drove through Georgetown with cages of rats atop his car to make the threat more dramatic.

2. To demonstrate the hazards of radiation escaping from nuclear power plants, Californians released 2,000 helium-filled balloons at a power plant site with the attached message: As easily as this balloon reached you, so could the radiation from Diablo Canyon Nuclear Power Plant if the plant goes into operation (1–2 from Alderson and Sentman 1979, 214–15).

3. In reaction to the firing of a secretary for not making coffee for her boss, Women Employed arrived en masse (followed by TV camera) to a Chicago law firm. While the camera whirled, they taught the lawyers how to make coffee (Boyte 1980, 111).

4. When a representative of *Playboy* was speaking on the campus of Grinnel College, both male and female students publicly took off their clothes to protest the portrayal of women in the magazine (Deckard 1983, 339).

5. "In Yellowstone National Park . . . [environmental activists] dressed in bear suits to protest a new hotel smack in the middle of traditional grizzly bear feeding

ground. When asked to leave, several members checked into the hotel and ordered berries from room service" (Savage 1986, 36).

6. After being ignored by Housing Secretary Jack Kemp, who had made promises to help them, the activist housing group ONE "sent a singing telegraph to one of Kemp's representative (sic) who was addressing a public meeting in Boston." Just as the representative [was] about to speak, the telegraph was delivered by a person dressed up as a chicken who sang "Jack the Giant Windbag" to the tune of "Puff the Magic Dragon" (Nyden and Adams 1996, 19).

7. To symbolize how large cars waste energy, activists in Paris deflated the tires of SUVs parked in rich neighborhoods (Rotella 2005).

8. To show the complicity of big banks in funding unscrupulous lenders "community groups will follow a money trail of oversized dollar bill footprints leading from the Wells Fargo Bank . . . to a nearby Money Mart. There, a giant check for $55 million will be presented—the amount that Wells Fargo funds Money Mart to make 460% interest rate loans" (Press release California Reinvestment Coalition 4-25-2005).

9. Concerned about the new gun laws in Florida that allow easy access, gun control groups set up booths at rest stops on highways tourists use and at airports and handed out brochures warning about the dangers of being shot (Goodnough 2005).

10. Needing to catch media attention in Washington, D.C. "About 500 members of the Association of Community Organizations for Reform Now showed up at the American Financial Services Association's building last week blowing whistles, jeering, and holding aloft a giant inflatable shark—the Loan Shark of the Year Award (American Banker Monday, March 31, 2003).

United for a Fair Economy (UFE) specializes in producing cool media events that catch public attention on issues of economic injustice such as seen in the following sociodrama held in Boston Harbor:

> Rep. Dick Armey was in Boston to promote regressive flat tax and sales tax proposals. But we're ready for him. As he was about to dump the tax code in the harbor a plastic dingy boat suddenly appeared with two protesters from UFE dressed as a working family complete with a baby doll and a sign that read "Working Family Lifeboat." At the same time members of the "Rich People's Liberation Front" started shouting for him to "Sink 'em with the Sales Tax" etc. When Armey dropped the tax code, he overturned the dingy, forcing the working family to swim to shore. We stole the show. (reported on comm-org 4/16/98)

The Activist Cookbook: Creative Actions for a Fair Economy (United for a Fair Economy 1997) details a wide variety of creative cool media events. Some of these actions involve clever design of posters—a Sun Maid Raisins' poster with a skeleton rather than the healthy woman on it to symbolize death from herbicides—and street or guerrilla theater in which activists take over a public forum and perform skits that symbolize the problems at hand:

1. When conservatives were to end a dinner by carving up a 17 foot pie (that symbolized that everyone gets a share), activists dressed as rich business people jumped into the pie shouting out "it's all for me."
2. Activists dressed as government and business people got into bed with each other and rolled the bed into the halls of a legislature to symbolize the tight connections between government and business. (United for a Fair Economy 1997, 1, 10, 12, 32)

Media events can mock official actions. In response to the Bush administration's printing playing cards with the pictures of those they wanted to arrest in Iraq, the Ruckus society printed a deck of cards with pictures of those it labelled "war profiteers."

Cool media events are best staged when the press is already present. So at the Republican National Convention that was swarming with the press, numerous cool media events were held.

> In one event . . . , several members of Act Up blocked traffic, naked, on Eighth Avenue in front of Madison Square Garden, the convention site, to protest the Bush administration's record on AIDS. . . . members of a group called Operation Sibyl rappelled down the front of the Plaza Hotel to drape its facade with a giant anti-Bush banner. The banner displayed on the hotel had two arrows pointing in opposite directions, one bearing the word truth, the other the word Bush. (Cardwell 2004)

In 2005 pro-labor activists working with a limited budget prepared a DVD portraying how Wal-Mart profited at the cost of its employees. Both the DVD and the way it was released became cool media events. Rather than have a theatrical release, the film "will premiere at an astonishing 6,000+ homes, churches, family businesses, schools, living rooms, community centers, and parking lots across the country—a true people's premiere." (e-mail Robert L. Borosage, Campaign for America's Future Nov. 8, 2005). Using a website, individuals could find out the closest place at which the video would be shown. The presentation of the message was the action.

Moral Protests

In contrast to the humorous tone of the cool media events, moral demonstrations—voluntary jailing, fasts, and vigils—are somber actions, often taking place in Houses of Worship, to symbolize the moral nature of the cause. In a moral crusade, especially one that follows the tenets of nonviolence, participants put themselves in danger. People can die during hunger strikes, be beat up in jail, and harmed during vigils. To block construction, environmentalists fasten themselves to trees, risking their lives if bulldozers knock down the trees. The danger to the participants is what creates the power of moral demonstrations.

A *vigil* is a moral demonstration in which protesters show up at a location where the problem is taking place—a drug "shooting gallery" or the headquarters of a company that exploits child labor—and by their quiet presence call attention to the issues—usually by praying. Vigils have been held outside of jails where civil rights workers were incarcerated; the Dudley Street Neighborhood Initiative conducted a vigil outside of a park that dope pushers had taken over; while in Chicago, Bethel New Life led a prayer vigil at a hospital site to prevent its closing. PICO organized a simultaneous prayer vigil across the country and outside the offices of 20 senators and 40 congress people to press for faster relief to those hurt by Hurricane Katrina (from: "PICO National Network" <gwhitman@piconetwork.org>).

Many vigils build upon religious symbolism, especially shared prayer. For example, a PICO organization

> won support from the Mayor of East Palo Alto for a redevelopment project that would create a new supermarket, affordable housing and a pre-employment training center on vacant land. In March 150 people gathered for a prayer service . . . PIA in East Palo Alto held a clergy led prayer service and action in front of city hall and across the street from a four-acre vacant lot where residents envision getting a supermarket built along with affordable housing and a pre-employment training center built for their community . . . the Mayor attended the prayer circle and agreed to work with the clergy of PIA. (Pico Web page 4-19-2005)

Chapters of Amnesty International hold vigils in winter passing lit candles from one person to another to symbolize that in the dark there is still hope (Hart 2001, 154). Candlelight civil rights vigils were held on Martin Luther King, Jr.'s, birthday, to protest the police slaying of an unarmed African American in Cincinnati (ACORN web page).

While rare in the United States, hunger strikes have been effective as moral protests. For instance, during rougher moments in the effort to unionize farm workers, César Chavez, a community and labor organizer, fasted.

> (Chavez) set up a monastic cell, with a small cot and a few religious articles. Soon hundreds of farm-worker families began appearing . . . to show their support for Chavez and to attend the daily mass with him. A huge tent-city, with thousands of farm workers, sprang up . . . There was a tremendous outpouring of emotion during the masses . . . the fast became an important means of unifying farm workers and educating them about the importance of the strike and boycott. (Castillo and Garcia 1995, 85–86)

Chavez's fast communicated to the outside world the seriousness of the workers' plight and created fear among the opponent lest Chavez were to die.

Being jailed is often part of a moral protest especially when those arrested refuse to post bail. For instance, as part of the civil rights campaign in Birmingham, Dr. Martin Luther King, Jr., was arrested and jailed. Numerous individuals (including opponents) offered to pay his bail, but as a part of a moral demonstration he refused to accept. The enemy was discomforted while allies in government were motivated to take action lest King be harmed. While in jail, Dr. King wrote and smuggled out his eloquent "Letter from Birmingham Jail" that explained the moral basis of the civil rights movement.

Power Displays

For many, rallies, demonstrations, marches, and caravans typify what social action campaigns are about—large numbers of people come together, led by dynamic individuals who shout out slogans, exhort actions, while describing problems and demanding solutions. Messages are presented in speeches, on placards, banners, t-shirts, hats, and sometimes written on the bodies of the participants themselves.

Through power displays people vote with their bodies, demonstrating a democracy in the streets (Miller 1987). At times, a million or so might participate, although far smaller numbers are more common. The impact stems from the numbers involved, as well as the implicit threat of visible, rising discontent. Further, bringing off a demonstration or a march requires an incredible amount of work, showing that the activist organization is a force to be reckoned with.

The message from power displays must be carefully considered, as by their scope they address multiple audiences who do not hear the same message. Actions—endless pep rally sloganeering, for instance, that can motivate those who believe in the cause and are already involved—might turn off new participants. What the media shares with others is hard to control and can communicate a different impression than the organizers had intended. A well reasoned though enthusiastic speech on economic injustice is loudly applauded by the participants, but rather than report its content, the media highlights the disruptive actions of a few.

Rallies and Demonstrations.   In rallies and public demonstrations, the organization (or coalitions of like-minded organizations) arrange large numbers of people to appear at one time and at one spot. Rallies and public demonstrations show the opposition that a groundswell of opposition exists, provide information to both activists and the press, and recruit individuals for more focused actions. As Trapp argues, "demonstrations are the result of injustice, and reflect anger at injustice" and "demonstrations show power" (Trapp n.d., 89).

Speakers should make strong enthusiastic statements that inspire activists and prepare for further action, but these statements have to be constructed to communicate well in the mass media. The message, not the demonstration itself, should become the focus. The news should lead off with "people displaced by the new highway demand safe housing" not "police curtail unruly mob."

The history of social activism provides many examples of effective public demonstrations. The 1963 March on Washington for Civil Rights is legendary for Dr. King's "I Have a Dream" speech, as well as for the size and excitement of the huge crowd. The whole nation (including the President and Vice President) were exposed to the power of King's oratory. Another huge rally took place to support maintaining abortion rights when the Supreme Court seemed to be weakening those rights. Small rallies can also be effective, especially when integrated within a long-running campaign. Campus groups in the United States have demonstrated against Nike and other clothing manufacturers who exploit child labor in manufacturing their products.

Larger rallies and demonstrations are often orchestrated by coalitions of organizations, each with a complementary message. At a Missouri rally in support of affordable housing, fifty-one organizations sponsored the event with representatives from fifteen of them speaking. All advocated for more resources for housing, while separate groups spoke for the homeless, those with disabilities, maintaining federal subsidies, and housing for the elderly.

At rallies, speakers engage those in the audience, asking for a show of hands and inviting boisterous responses such as cheers, applause, amens, or shouted encouragements. Speeches portray the problem or concern and outline the solutions. At a rally sponsored by the South Bronx Churches, an IAF affiliate was working to gain control over land as well as the financing to build affordable housing on the site. Speakers "dripping with contempt" and "pound[ing] home a class-driven analysis" contrasted the more affordable, better quality single family homes that the IAF wanted to build with smaller condos that the city was willing to provide. People were then asked to join in the ongoing political battle (Rooney 1995, 141–49).

While few organizers plan huge national rallies, the chances are good that a more modest rally will end up as part of a local campaign. Such events require considerable attention to detail. The following are some guidelines (modified from Burghardt 1982; Cassidy 1980; Gecan 2002; Midwest Academy various dates; Trapp n.d.):

1. Get permission to use the rally site. In public places permits are required but at times officials will deny the permit. This denial then can become an issue itself. As part of the arrangement make sure police are informed of the event.

   When possible, choose a site that signifies the issue. For instance, many rallies addressing Congress are held on the Mall in Washington, D.C. Public spaces in front of state capital buildings are also a favored site. In response to efforts to tear down public housing without providing alternatives, organizations held rallies on lots adjacent to the buildings about to be torn down.

2. Look over the rally site. If it's a wide plaza, make sure cameras will be located in places that make the group appear larger. Place loudspeakers so everyone can hear. If the rally is taking place inside a building, make sure people can get in. If the rally is being held in a public forum controlled by the opposition, plant somebody inside just in case the opposition tries to lock the door.

3. Widely publicize the event, but in doing so slightly underestimate the size of the expected turnout. If activists estimate that 100 people will be there, announce that 75 will show up, and try to get a space that will hold 70 to 100. Don't underestimate by too much, though, lest supporters be discouraged and not show.

4. Do the leg work to ensure that people will turn out. Don't rely on mass advertising alone. If it is a neighborhood rally, leaflet each home a day or two in advance. Maintain a telephone network of supporters and call them; have supportive clergy announce the event in church. With e-mail it is now possible to quickly notify members of a more impromptu rally, when for instance, a politician appears at the last moment.

   Make sure that events are held at convenient times. For larger rallies that are often held away from people's homes, arrange for transportation and make sure adequate time is provided for the trip. Use the time in traveling to encourage people to get to know each other, share stories about the problems they face, and talk about how to behave during the event. When mobilizing faith-based groups, schedule rallies after church services and then have buses available at the churches to transport people.

5. Work out in advance what will happen at the rally. The time to come up with creative ideas is while planning the event, not in front of the mass media.

6. Arrange for crowd control. Make sure enough bathrooms and drinking water are available. Encourage people to listen respectfully to speakers, to feel free to show enthusiasm but to do so in ways that reflect positively on the group. For large rallies, marshals should be placed strategically throughout the group to watch for excessively boisterous participants, or plants from the enemy, and to coordinate action, such as a safe retreat.

7. Try to start on time; this is easier to do with indoor events held in church auditoriums, for example, than with massive outdoor demonstrations.

8. At the event make sure there are flyers that explain the purpose and the concerns. Also make sure that information is available at the rally site for those who want to join the organization.

9. Music can be an important part of a rally. Protest songs give off the core message of the organization, while singing together helps unify people. A band playing on the podium quickly gets the attention of people and can help maintain focus if the crowd becomes restless.

10. Try to make sure that speeches, messages on signs, and other communications are readily available to the mass media. When possible coordinate the content of the speeches so that they do not sound repetitious. If the highlight of the rally is a flag burning and that is the image the group wants to communicate, make sure the media know where to point their camera. If the goal is to communicate factual details—mortgage discrimination, for instance—make sure that the media receives a fact sheet. Assign an articulate spokesperson to work with the media.

11. Try to arrange speeches in ways that balance those meant to intimidate opponents with those that stir up supporters. In dress and mannerisms present a "cooler"—less disruptive—image than the content of the messages might indicate. A neatly dressed speaker can get away with a militant speech without appearing so threatening that the message is ignored. Clergy, especially those from churches that encourage oratorical skill, make especially fine speakers.

   Paint slogans or complaints neatly to encourage them to be photographed, but if threats—even mild ones—are part of the rally, try not to put them in easily photographable formats. Targets will hear the threats anyway, so why chance alienating others?

   Rallies are a good time to carry out imaginative media events. A musical chairs game in which each chair represents a missing job and someone gets left out at the end might symbolize a shrinking economy. A mock funeral, for example, burying an effigy of "affirmative action" after the state stops enforcing it, makes the point clearly, yet maintains the culturally accepted solemnity of a funeral.

12. Plan the end of the rally. Organizers should not leave large numbers of inflamed people milling around. Police raids can occur after the speeches are

over. Troublemakers may prey on chatting groups of demonstrators, trying to start a violent episode. One way to end the rally is to march out together singing solidarity songs.

Marches and Caravans.   A march is a moving demonstration, while a caravan is a motorized march that passes by locations that symbolize the problem—an office building housing legislators who have not passed a required bill, or the headquarters of a business that continues to pollute. March themes are shown in banners and signs, and in accompanying press releases. A participant described an antiwar march in Los Angeles involving 10,000 people:

> What a multi-cultural event! American Indians in full traditional garb, Indians from India and surrounding areas in full garb; black, white; Asian, Hispanic; people wearing cowboy hats, baseball hats and Middle Eastern Scarves, etc. Nuns were present, the event was sponsored in part by the interfaith community (Catholics, Protestants, Jewish, Hindus and Muslims). . . .
>   We marched for more than a mile to the Ronald Reagan Federal building, the outside of which became filled with pro-peace people. During the march, we were singing songs (We Shall Overcome; Imagine), chanting chants, holding signs (e.g., healthcare, not warfare), talking and hanging out. People on the streets were cheering us on, as were people who stuck their heads out of windows. (Michael Francis Johnston; comurb_r21@email.rutgers.edu' Date: 01/11/2003)

Caravans can last over many days and, with luck and preparation, gain press coverage all along the path. For instance, the Kensington Welfare Rights Union organized national marches and caravans to publicize the plight of the welfare and working poor. Signs communicated the campaign message, "Housing is a Human Right"; "Poverty is not a Crime"; "End Poverty Not Welfare." The demonstrators also ask for support: "Honk for Justice" (Orland 1998). While the multisection caravan started in different cities, the separate groups came together at two important symbolic sites, the Mall in Washington, D.C., and Wall Street.

The very way a march is orchestrated can symbolize issues. To preserve abortion rights, three generations of women marched together, symbolizing persisting concerns that unified them. During the civil rights era, Freedom Riders rode in integrated buses through the segregated South, symbolizing the brutality of the opposition (as some buses were destroyed) and the courageous dedication of the protesters (Payne 1995, 107 ff). To show that segregation was not simply a southern problem, Dr. Martin Luther King, Jr., led marches in Chicago and nearby Cicero where participants were taunted and stoned. ACORN led a seventeen-day multicity caravan attacking predatory lenders, marching by the sites of the lenders, and then, while in each city, setting up free tax preparation services to contrast with the ripoffs sponsored by the predators (ACORN newsletter April 8, 2005). After having its concerns about affordable housing ignored, the IAF affiliate Micah arranged a march that ended with a direct confrontation at the mayor's house. Signs were carried describing housing as a civil right, clergy in full religious garb joined in, while great care was given about who would speak with what message once the target site was reached (Hart 2001,

88–91).

A number of steps can help assure a successful march. First obtain a permit, carefully work out the routes, make sure transportation is available and let the press and police have some idea of what is going to happen. Signs must succinctly convey the message. Marches are intended to be nonviolent acts of speech, so trained monitors must be there to calm down a fracas if one occurs. In recent years, people terming themselves the Black Bloc covered their faces and bodies in black garb and joined in marches, and by doing so threatened violence. Such groups are frankly anarchistic—"interested in nothing less than the total destruction of capitalism, the state, and the creation of a classless, stateless society to replace it" (Barricada 2002, 63) and their presence can distract from the core message of the protest.

Direct Confrontations

A direct confrontation zeros in on the immediate target with an explicit attempt to inconvenience the target, while at the same time making the larger public aware of the harm the target has caused. Demonstrations, rallies, marches, and caravans can focus in on the target by being held adjacent to the building of an offending company or government agency, but direct confrontations carry this to the next level. Picketers surround a business or government office responsible for the problem; sit-ins occupy property owned by the target. Intense complaint tactics and accountability sessions put regulatory or political officials physically on the spot. Economic confrontations, boycotts, and strikes are financially punitive. Hits are an extension of cool media events, with more intensity and less humor.

Before rallies, demonstrations, or picketing occurs, activists usually obtain permits from public officials; in contrast, the power and effectiveness of hits (as well as sit-ins) come from there being a surprise, often bordering on the illegal. However, because of their raucous confrontational nature, great care is needed in planning to make sure they do not get out of control. The goal is to pressure a target, perhaps through intimidation, but not to bring about a disorderly mob scene. When actions are illegal, activists need to be prepared to be arrested, preferably having undertaken prior training in civil disobedience.

Face-to-Face Confrontation: Intense Complaint Tactics. Complaints are about violations of building or safety codes, speeding on residential streets, or police who ignore illegal drug sales in public parks. Often politicians or bureaucrats respond to complaints made by a phone call or by filing out a form, but too often they are ignored. In this case, the organization brings together many people who are complaining, perhaps through a petition drive and then presents the petition to those in power in ways that make the point dramatically. For instance, a state legislature and governor had been cutting back funding for affordable housing and ignoring the complaints on the matter. In response, action organizations held

> first annual neighborhood fax-in. . . . We found out that there were two fax machines in the [state] house; two in the Senate and one in the governor's office. And we inundated those SOB's. We sent out so many faxes . . . We get a phone call . . . "the gov-

ernor just called, the governor's office just called and they're listening . . . knock it off!!" and . . . it had only been two hours and we said "well gee you know, we're really not capable of doing that. We've turned them all loose." (Rubin 2000a).

Fax-ins can tie up the bureaucratic office or business sponsoring a project the social action group opposes, as can mass e-mailing campaigns to one e-mail account.

Intense complaint campaigns blur into *days of action*. During a day of action, large numbers will show up at an official office to present their complaints and demand immediate solutions. For instance,

> ACORN members in the Sunset Heights neighborhood are fighting the attempted reopening of a toxic plant . . . ACORN members coordinated a day of action. In El Paso, ACORN members marched into the Texas Commission on Environmental Quality (TCEQ) and won an on-the-spot meeting with the head of the local TCEQ office where they demanded that TCEQ meet with ACORN regularly to discuss ASARCO's permit application. . . . El Paso ACORN members then marched to the El Paso EPA office and won a meeting with the local manager. (Acorn newsletter February 11 2005)

Face-to-Face Confrontations: Accountability Sessions.
Accountability sessions are set up to make sure that elected or bureaucratic officials take responsibility for promises they make. For instance, an IAF organization will invite politicians to attend meetings, and politicians accept because of the known ability of IAF to get out the vote. Once at the meeting, the politician is seated by himself or herself on a stage and members of the organization ask questions. Waffling and evasion are not allowed. Unless clearcut yeses or noes are given, the audience heckles the official. Similar tactics are used to pressure bureaucratic officials. A PICO affiliate, Compassion Outreach Ministries, organized a large community meeting to complain about the physical neglect of a neighborhood. They invited code enforcement officials, showed them pictures of debris and junk cars and obtained then and there a promise from the officials to have the mess cleaned up (PICO web page Copeland Community to be Cleaned Up Affiliated Congregations to Improve our Neighborhoods 02-18-2005).

Hits (see below) are combined with an accountability session when activists show up at a legislative or city council meeting to press officials to keep their promises. For example, Texas state representatives had promised to support reform in a health package, but opponents delayed the measure. When members of the Texas IAF were in Austin and noted what was happening:

> Members of the TIAF organizations flooded the capitol dome, yelling, charging, and effectively blocking the major exits. A group of Hispanic legislators went to the Governor's Office, accompanied by Ernie Cortes [the staff organizer] and leaders of the TIAF organization, to demand an immediate special session . . . under all these pressures, the governor had no choice but to call a special session to begin the following day. (Wong 1997, 112)

When legislation decisions are being made behind closed doors, activists show up and demand accountability. For instance, when state legislators tried to renege on promises on housing, a coalition of housing activists in Illinois stood in the anterooms behind where the legislature was meeting chanting slogans and shamed those who promised help into action. After Hurricane Katrina, hundreds of displaced victims organized by ACORN corralled FEMA officials asking why promised assistance was so slow in coming (Turner 2005) while the Houston affiliate of the IAF compelled local relief officials to appear at an accountability session set up by displaced individuals who demanded control over where they were to be housed and questioned how relief funds had been spent (Blumenthal 2005).

Direct actions are sometimes needed to set up an accountability session. When we asked one organizer how his neighborhood group managed to get Federal Education Secretary Riley to a meeting to talk about desperately needed school construction, he responded, "when we were in Washington, I paid a visit to Riley's office, along with six hundred of my close friends." He elaborated, explaining that as part of a Neighborhood People's Action conference in Washington, D.C., ten busloads of people showed up at the Department of Education's office building, then stormed the offices and demanded of a guard that Riley be informed that a meeting was wanted. Riley was out of town, but the number two in the department quickly set up a session.

Face-to-Face Confrontations: Picketing.   Picketing is a more aggressive form of marching, meant less to publicize a problem than to embarrass and inconvenience opponents. With picketing, activists choose a site of importance to the opponents, such as a nuclear plant or a sweatshop, or the office of an offending loan agency and march around the site, expressing their grievance through signs and with chanted slogans. With *informational picketing*, activists march but do not block entrances or exits, allowing customers and workers to come and go. With more aggressive picketing, that sometimes violates laws against trespassing, activists surround a site, march around its entrances and exits, and while not physically stopping someone from passing try to make it socially awkward for people to cross the picket line.

To oppose redlining, protesters have picketed banks to inconvenience customers and embarrass the managers. People from the Dudley Street neighborhood picketed illegal dump sites, blocking garbage vehicles and forcing the city to shut down these health hazards. Daring individuals from neighborhoods beset with drug problems have picketed the open-air "drug supermarkets," sometimes also picketing the homes of suburban customers of the dope dealers. Protesters have surrounded nuclear reactor sites while members of the Love Canal Homeowners Association, in their fight against toxic waste, picketed the governor of New York and later President Carter. In the Vietnam War era, activists picketed military draft boards and recruitment offices, while today, the home offices of manufacturers that exploit labor are the subjects of informational picketing. Through a combination of picketing and cool media events, ACT-UP, the AIDS Coalition to Unleash Power, gained publicity for AIDS victims and changed government policies.

Picketing can be done in ways to embarrass public officials. For example, as part of its convention in Milwaukee where many welfare reform experiments were taking place, ACORN activists engaged in picketing.

> The target . . . Wisconsin Governor Tommy Thompson, the architect of W-2 [the state's welfare to work program] who was attending a $250-a-plate dinner celebrating the opening of Milwaukee's new $200 million convention center. As guests in tuxedos and evening gowns made their way down the red carpet to the entrance, picketers marched alongside them chanting "Hey, hey, ho, ho, W-2 has got to go." (www.igc.apc.prog/community/reports/acornrep908.1998.contemt./html)

Planning pickets must be done carefully. Where should the picketing occur? Seriously inconveniencing a bank that won't make loans in the neighborhood sends a direct message. Picketers should have precise demands—paying people legal wages, letting loan applicants who are eligible for less expensive loans know that's the case, having a bank provide funds for a community project. As part of the picketing, activists demand that a person in authority discuss the demands then and there.

Be cautious. Picketing that inconveniences an uninformed public might create sympathy for the target. People who want to buy milk at the supermarket on their way home from work might not be sympathetic to picketers' demands that the store buy fruit only from farms that reduce the use of pesticides. If counter-picketing occurs, make sure distracting confrontations do not take place by training volunteers not to respond to taunts or provocations. Some cities restrict the types of materials that can be used for picket signs to prevent them from turning into weapons. Find out these laws and obey them. Finally, the organization needs to make preparations to handle arrests and be prepared if the picketed company threatens a lawsuit.

Face-to-Face Confrontations: Sit-Ins.   Sit-ins inconvenience the opponent by taking over offices or shutting down highways, lunch counters, lobbies, or public places. Advocates for the homeless have encamped in public parks and outside government buildings, demanding that the public sector pay attention to their plight (Wright 1997). Native Americans have seized small military facilities, demanding that the land be converted to an Indian cultural center (Nagel 1996, 165). When targeted organizations are more or less sympathetic to activists, sit-ins can blur into a form of cool media event. For instance, students concerned about exploited labor in the clothing industry have taken over university offices and held knit-ins to pressure schools not to allow university logos to be used on products made by exploited laborers (Van der Werf 1999, a39).

Sit-ins must visibly symbolize the problem. African Americans who refused to move from lunch counters until they were served symbolized the injustice and humiliation of segregation. When state laws abrogated the fishing rights of Native Americans (that were guaranteed by treaties), activists staged a fish-in, an active form of a sit-in, catching fish (illegally, according to state law) and doing so in full sight of the game warden (Sharp 1973, 318). Squatting is an extreme form of sit-in; activists take over property by literally sitting in. Squatting should only be done when the symbolic message is clear, for instance, squatting in homes that the government owns but has abandoned, while people still lack shelter in the same community.

The equivalent of sit-ins can be found that do not involve trespass. For example, when employees are upset with their own organizations, they employ a tactic called *working to the rule*, during which participants precisely follow each procedure so that the whole workflow slows down. In a campaign to improve salaries and facilities, doctors at Boston City Hospital held a heal-in. They admitted every patient that could possibly benefit from hospital care and then provided the best medical service possible. The facility was soon overcrowded, and serious negotiation with the hospital administration began (Sharp 1973b, 394).

Sit-ins require careful preparation. First, some knowledge of how the target is likely to respond is important. Will the police be called in to arrest the participants or will the target try to maintain a good public image by supplying food and water? Second, check out the site carefully. Who controls the water and from where? Where are the bathrooms? Can the police sneak in through a back door? Will those arrested be carried out through a door that the media cannot see? Are participants prepared to tolerate long periods of boredom? Do people have sleeping bags? Make sure people who need medicine have it with them, and, if arrest is possible, make sure that participants have bail arranged and don't have anything incriminating on their persons. If arrest is not wanted, see if there are escape routes. Plan to use the time sitting-in to share information or experiences about the problem at hand, especially if the media are present.

Further, since the goal of a sit-in is to force some immediate concessions, members of the action organization must be available to negotiate with the target. Details on how to plan for such negotiations will be presented in the next chapter. Just make sure that there is careful coordination between the timing of sit-ins and that of the negotiations. Giving up the sit-in too early weakens the leverage of the action organization; too late, and the organization gets labelled as more interested in the glory of the action than in resolving problems.

Face-to-Face Confrontations: Hits. Activists use the word "hit" or "action" to describe almost any confrontational power approach, and for the most part doing so causes no confusion. But for us, hits share some special characteristics.

- Hits are dramatic, disruptive, and emphasize the threat posed by large numbers of angry individuals.
- Hits focus on individuals as targets in ways that are embarrassing and personally annoying.
- Hits are kept secret (except from cooperative media) and appear to be spontaneous, although in practice are carefully orchestrated.
- Hits are meant to be media events to start off a longer run campaign through dramatically putting the spotlight on an issue.
- Since hits are disruptive and borderline illegal, the organization must be ready to show that those in authority have ignored requests or made it nearly impossible for the voices of ordinary people to be heard.
- The threat of a hit is often as effective as actually carrying it out.
- Successful hits become the lore of an organization. Hits become a recruitment tool for the organization by showing both the power and the fun of collective confrontational actions.

Hits occur when government has ignored people's concerns and those in the organization disrupt a public meeting. For example,

> more than 300 Providence, RI, ACORN members, Providence Teachers Union members, and other community members took over a School Board meeting where the board was scheduled to vote on a proposal to lay off 102 school district employees . . . ACORN members quickly filled the room and chanted until the School Board agreed to move the meeting to a larger venue. . . . ACORN members testified for an hour about the harmful impact the proposed layoffs would have in their children's already struggling schools. (ACORN web page)

Such a hit called attention to the issue, forced those in power to pay attention, and, in this case at least, led to negotiations on the issue.

When companies are the targets, activists hit their annual meetings or target the CEO. Since entry to annual meetings requires a person to be a stockholder, members of activist groups might purchase a few shares. A recent hit made it clear that financial institutions cared little about environmental damages so long as profits were to be made.

> Environmental activists demonstrated again Tuesday outside Wells Fargo & Co.'s annual meeting.
> The Rainforest Action Network used giant puppets—one showing Wells CEO Dick Kovacevich dressed as a cowboy riding a stagecoach—and banners to call attention to Wells' dealings with companies that the group says have poor environmental and human rights records . . .
> In the days before the annual meeting, environmentalists in the San Francisco Bay Area put up posters reading "Wells Fargo: Lootin' and Pollutin' Since 1852." (From: NCRC News <ncrcnews@ncrc.org> Date: 04/28/2006)

Even fast food restaurants have been subject to hits by those caring about the humane treatment of animals. For example, PETA (People for the Ethical Treatment of Animals) orchestrated a

> "weekend of action" that will kick off with a noisy protest at a local KFC restaurant and feature a giant, crippled "chicken" crossing the road and protesters carrying signs that read, "KFC Tortures Chickens." The barrage will continue with a visit to the headquarters of KFC's parent company, Yum! Brands; canvassing of top executives' neighborhoods; and PETA's "Kentucky Fried Truth Truck," which is equipped with huge screens and will cruise the streets of Louisville showing graphic footage of what happens to chickens raised and killed for KFC. (Press Release PETA November 2, 2005)

Government officials are hit personally when they ignore requests. For instance, members of an economic justice organization, concerned about how bank regulators simply ignored 4,000 negative comments on proposed rule changes showed up in the [regulator's] lobby to express some sarcastic get-well wishes for Mr. Gilleran and his colleagues, whom they said must have been feeling ill when they made their decision (American Banker March 21, 2005).

A legendary hit never took place, as the threat was sufficient. The new HUD secretary Jack Kemp had been ignoring requests to meet with National Peoples' Action and refused to show up at the NPA conference. NPA threatened to "hit" Kemp at his home, where he was planning a wedding reception for his daughters who were both being married on the same day. Kemp felt threatened. The organization then compromised a bit and agreed upon meeting with the Secretary in his office (Trapp n.d., 85).

Economic Confrontations: Boycotts. In a boycott, people refuse to purchase from a company or buy a particular product. Consumer groups have sponsored boycotts to protest price increases, ethnic groups have organized tourism and convention boycotts of cities that discriminate, while feminist organizations have tried to set up boycotts of states that refused to pass the Equal Rights Amendment. Environmentalists have organized boycotts of tuna caught in ways that endanger dolphins, while Greenpeace tried to organize a boycott of all products from nations that refused to stop whaling.

If the membership and supporters of an action organization are numerous enough, a boycott can have a financial impact on the target. When the African American community boycotted stores in smaller and middle-sized southern cities, the economic loss was sufficient to convince the small merchants to hire black sales staff and be more courteous in selling to African Americans. But usually the number of people actively involved in the action organization is too small, so allies are needed, as occurred in the national boycott of "scab grapes" set up as part of the campaign led by César Chavez to organize farm labor.

By law, a store itself cannot be legally boycotted as part of a boycott against a particular product. However, it is legal, as a primary boycott, to encourage people not to buy a particular product. But it is possible to get around such limitations. For instance, during the grape boycott supporters conducted a

> "shop-in" . . . A respectable-looking housewife entered the store, filled her basket and then suddenly discovered that these were scab grapes. She demanded to see the manager. How could he put scab grapes on the shelves when some farm worker's children were starving? The drama became the center of attention. With the eyes of the checkers and customers riveted on the front of the store, the housewife lectured the grocer and then triumphantly marched from the store with children in tow (Jenkins 1985, 168–69).

Companies that are concerned about their reputation are particularly vulnerable to well-publicized boycotts. For example, the action organization INFACT orchestrated an international boycott against Nestles for marketing baby formula in poor countries because the formula was less healthy than breast feeding. The direct economic impact was minor compared to the negative publicity that implied that a company that sells baby food was not concerned about the health of babies.

Nowadays a variant of a boycott can be found in the campaigns against Wal-Mart—the nation's largest company that refuses to unionize, pays low salaries, and displaces small businesses. The WakeUp Wal-Mart campaign has multiple parts, some following a boycott strategy. One approach is to organize community members to not allow Wal-Marts to open in their cities; that is, boycott the chain entirely, for instance, by pressuring a city council not to allow land to be rezoned for big box stores. Meanwhile support is increased by publicizing the firm's bad practices through the screening of the movie "Wal-Mart: The High Cost of Low Prices" (www .wakeupwalmart.com/community/strategy.html).

Economic Confrontations: Labor Actions and Strikes.   A strike is an economic confrontation during which workers deprive employers of their labor. Strikers have to believe the economic sacrifice of not working is worth the effort. During the strike, workers march around the building, or at least its entrances, carrying placards that succinctly indicate the problems they face or what they see as a solution.

In recent decades the number of workers organized through strikes has dramatically shrunk, both because of worker fear and a changing economy. Government has been less supportive of unions, while the larger manufacturers in which many union members were employed have downsized and outsourced manufacturing abroad. Many workers fear (justifiably) that if they organize, or even mention the possibility of a strike, their plants might close and work will be sent abroad.

One exception is that of service workers, such as janitorial workers, some office staff, those who provide home daycare, and medical employees (Kurtz 2002; Tait 2005), as these jobs cannot be easily outsourced. Many of these service jobs tend to pay low and lack health care for workers, while many employees are minorities, often immigrants, both legal and illegal. But service workers are widely scattered. Home daycare providers, for instance, work alone, and are difficult to organize. Problems are compounded as workers come from competing ethnic groups while often are not fluent in English. Further, many service workers are employed by specialty firms, such as janitorial services, that are subcontractors of a larger firm— a Wal-Mart for instance. So while Wal-Mart is actually paying the bills, those who strike are employed by a smaller service company. Who to target can be problematic.

In response, organizing among service workers ends up being part of a broader neighborhood and ethnic organizing effort. Strikes are planned and recruitment takes place at community centers (Tait 2005, 117). Strikes are set up in ways to show the hypocrisy of the employers. For example, workers picketed the building housing the American Medical Association with signs saying that the janitorial staff receives both low pay and has no health benefits while an antibiotic treatment would cost an entire day's salary (www.seiu82.org.).

Economic Confrontations: Rent and Tenants' Strikes.   In a tenants' strike, renters whose building has poor maintenance or lacks heat band together and refuse to pay rent until the landlord has solved the problems. On occasion, a sympathetic city government might help the tenants by stepping up code enforcement, but for the most part tenants are on their own. Tenants' strikes usually focus on unscrupulous landlords, but public housing authorities can also be targeted, as much of public housing is poorly maintained.

Tenants' strikes are difficult to pull off. Unlike picketing or public demonstrations that are constitutionally protected rights, in many states tenants are not allowed to withhold rent, no matter what. Fortunately, they can in other states so long as the rent money is to be set aside in an escrow account that is held by a third party until the dispute is resolved. In some places, the tenants' organization can withdraw money from the escrow account to make repairs in the building if the landlord does not make them.

Convincing people to participate in a tenants' strike can prove difficult, because renters are afraid they will be evicted. During rent strikes, landlords often try to destroy tenant solidarity by pressuring or bribing a few to break ranks with co-strikers. Several counter strategies are used. In one

> organizers promoted what they called the "rent slowdown" . . . a strategy in which all tenants held back their rents until the middle of the month, when the tenant leader handed them all to the landlord at the same time. It was an eloquent demonstration of tenant solidarity, and therefore, also a warning to the landlord, who often responded to tenant grievances at this point. For the tenants, it was in fact an organizational and emotional preparation for a strike should the landlord ignore the warning. (Lawson 1986, 227–28)

Organizers of tenants' strikes try to meet frequently with participants, usually in group sessions, to bolster resolve. Another way of creating group solidarity is for tenants' groups from different housing complexes to schedule rolling rent strikes. With this approach, only selected landlords are struck, but tenants in the allied groups support and encourage those striking. Doing so can pit landlord against landlord, rather than tenant against tenant.

Sabotage and Monkey Wrenching

Sabotage involves the intentional destruction of property to bring a halt to what the target is doing. For instance, animal rights activists have released research animals from medical research labs, freed captive fur-bearing animals, or tossed blood on fur coats. During the Vietnam War era, the Weather Faction broke from the Students for a Democratic Society to engage in sabotage. Road Rage in England publicizes ways of physically destroying road construction equipment to stop highways, while carefully detailing how to mob the police to avoid arrests.

We oppose sabotage on ethical grounds. Physical destruction of property while chancing harming human life is simply inconsistent with the moral underpinnings of progressive activism. Pragmatically, the use of sabotage virtually guarantees that a social change organization will be labelled as a terrorist group with both the legal and image problems that such a label evokes.

Some justify minor acts of sabotage, though again we disagree. For instance, letting air out of car tires rather than burning a vehicle, or, as occurred during the period of the Vietnam War, throwing blood on draft board records, does not hurt people.

Monkey wrenching (Russell 1987) lies on the border between symbolic and violent protest. For instance, to protest over-fishing, a flotilla of small fishing boats in

Canada surrounded larger ships, literally stopping commerce. Another monkey wrenching tactic is to deface signs and billboards to present a case—antismoking slogans written over pictures of the Marlboro man, for instance. Opponents of lumbering that denudes mountains sometimes put spikes in trees, which destroys the trees' economic value as lumber. If lumberjacks hit the spikes, they can get seriously injured. In general, we oppose such tactics because of their potential for harm and seriously wonder if these actions really do bring about economic and political change.

Conclusions and Concerns about Confrontational Actions

We have described an array of confrontational tactics. Confrontations must receive broad attention, present the organization's case, and be carried out in ways that while assertive remain ethical. Confrontations strengthen bonds among activists as they join together in both a daring and fun event and learn that they are not powerless against big businesses or entrenched politicians.

But there are downsides. Confrontational approach can be quite risky, and their benefits might not always outweigh their costs. To paraphrase Shakespeare, activists must make sure that confrontations are not merely sound and fury, signifying nothing. Are they merely showmanship that might feel good but accomplish little? César Chavez, who gained fame from moral demonstrations, picketing, and protest marches, still emphasized that

> a movement with some lasting organization is a lot less dramatic than a movement with a lot of demonstrations and a lot of marches and so forth. The more dramatic organization does catch attention quicker. Over the long haul, however, it's a lot more difficult to keep together because you're not building solid. (Chavez 1984, 28)

Those in power have standard ways of responding to confrontational actions, sometimes by conceding in the short run and then ignoring promises, and other times by playing the public relations game and successfully labelling activists as disruptive malcontents. Confrontations can and do backfire. Are demonstrators getting beat up and arrested? Are legislators passing restrictive laws making protests more difficult and repression easier? Do confrontations motivate opponents to work with those in office to undo prior progressive changes?

The most important concern about confrontation tactics is whether they lead to long-term solutions. Faced with the threat of a sit-in or ongoing demonstrations, an opponent might concede for the moment, only to then renege later on or propose a variety of pseudo-solutions that do little to solve the underlying problem. Is establishing a Human Relations Committee sufficient to solve fundamental problems of racism or sexism or merely a ploy to quiet things down? Activists in Appalachia managed to shut down strip mines and enforce reclamation laws using confrontational actions, but strip mining persisted because the opposition had better staying power. As an organizer explained:

it is clear that we did not give enough thought to how direct action would translate into a movement capable of mobilizing a lot of people . . . Some of us were influenced by romantic slogans and the notions of armed struggle which were part of the anti-war movement of the late 1960s. We did not appreciate the long, slow work that fundamental social change requires. (Bingham 1986, 28–29)

That lesson is even more apparent today, as conservatives in office continue to roll back the gains of the last two generations.

To summarize, confrontational approaches can be stimulating, intimidate the opposition, entice organizational members and supporters to join, while dramatically calling attention to problems. Yet, the possibility of violence and the threat that the enemy will strike back should create caution among those contemplating confrontational tactics. The drama of the actions should not distract from their fundamental purpose of forcing changes upon recalcitrant opponents. Community and social action organizations must look beyond the immediate actions to make sure that what is accomplished in the short run remains through better laws and the enforcement of agreements. Successful confrontational campaigns must lead to long-lasting institutional solutions.

CHAPTER
18

Tools for Strengthening Social Mobilization Campaigns

Lawyers and Litigation, Publicity and the Mass Media, Negotiations

In this chapter we examine three tools used in both influencing the public sector and in confrontational campaigns. Through litigation the courts are evoked, publicity efforts frame how the public views the issues, while skillful negotiations are vital to ensure that promises are carried out.

Lawyers and Litigation

Litigation is undertaken to force officials and businesses to uphold the law, carry out regulations or to end the violation of constitutional rights. Activist lawyers sue banks for failure to comply with the CRA (Lee 2003; Relman 2003), or for permitting predatory lending tactics. Housing courts can mandate that landlords treat their tenants fairly or set up ways to mediate landlord-tenant disputes (Jaquay 2005). The law is evoked to ensure that laws already on the books, such as the Americans with Disabilities Act (Fleischer and Zames 2001), or gender neutrality of job ads (Pedriana 2004) are followed. Speech rights are defended by civil liberties lawyers. Lawyers represent immigrant workers against sweatshop employers who violate labor laws (Gordon 2005). Legal service attorneys who help individual clients are often the first to note broader abuses and then inform social action organizations about these problems.

Forms of Legal Actions

Legal action might require little more than requesting that an attorney send an official looking note reminding government or business that appropriate regulations are not being followed, and that the next step might be to seek an *injunction* or *file a lawsuit*. Injunctions are court orders to stop possibly harmful actions until additional facts are gathered. A city might be enjoined not to distribute block grant money until it can show that federal rules for fair allocation of the funds have been followed.

Suits are filed to right a wrong, to claim compensation for harm done, or to make a party live up to an agreement. *Performance suits* force a party to carry out a contract already signed while *procedural suits* are intended to force a government agency, regulatory body, or in some circumstances, a business, to follow their own rules. For instance, activists have sued the Food and Drug Administration when it appeared to be excessively slow in approving new medicines, such as those that combat AIDS. *Substantive suits* or *torts* are intended to gain compensation for harm done, as when people get hurt from defective products.

Sometimes what is sought is a *consent decree* in which an agency or business agrees to an action suggested by a court, although without admitting fault. For instance, activists felt that the Los Angeles Transit Authority was discriminating by providing rapid transit to wealthier areas but only sporadic bus service to poorer neighborhoods. The Bus Riders' Union sued

> to force the MTA [Metropolitan Transit Authority] to deliver quality transit services to the poor and people of color. It forced the MTA to sit down with the BRU and negotiate. What emerged was a consent decree that ordered the MTA to stop discriminating against its bus riders and to correct the bus-rail service disparities it knowingly created. (Mann 2004, 46)

Sometimes harm to an individual is so small that bringing suit would be prohibitively expensive. In such cases, *class action suits* occur in which many smaller complaints are combined. Most are for defective consumer products, but class action suits have been successful in bringing about more equitable funding for education (Banach, Hamilton, and Perri 2003) or getting compensation for victims of fraudulent lending practices. Unfortunately, businesses have convinced government to make it harder to bring class action suits. Legal service attorneys can no longer do so, while more generally lawyers now have to get permission in writing from *all* of the clients before suing, a difficult task if people are scattered throughout the country.

Suits are useful in another way, as once they are filed lawyers can use *discovery motions* to require documents germane to a case to be made available. For instance, using discovery, environmental organizations located internal reports of the Department of Interior that showed that public water was being sold at far below market costs to large-scale commercial farmers, while other discovery motions have brought to light internal personnel records of companies that show patterns of gender- or race-based discrimination.

Difficulties with Legal Actions

The legal weapon is a two-sided one, especially since big business and government employ well-paid and skilled lawyers. Countersuits are frequent, putting action organizations on the defensive, for instance when action organizations run boycotts and companies sue asking for damages from lost business. Protesters can be ordered by the courts to stay away from sites they want to picket. Action organizations have lost suits to be allowed to picket or even hand out information at private shopping centers and in malls, while activists who oppose military recruiting in high schools and seek to present information on alternative careers have lost out in court rulings.

Losses can set back the broader progressive agenda. For example "On March 25, 2003, the U.S. Supreme Court ruled 9–0 in favor of an Ohio suburb . . . [that] the predominately white Cuyahoga Falls, Ohio, did not violate the Constitution's due process and equal protection clauses by allowing voters to initiate a referendum to block a low-income housing development" (Engdahl 2003). Courts have ruled that private citizens (and by extension social change organizations) might not have individual rights to sue if federal programs are not being carried out according to the rules that only the states have these rights (Pear 2005). Subpoena powers have been used to quash dissent by allowing the FBI to obtain records from universities that show who is involved in antiwar protests (Foley 2004).

Businesses now file SLAPPs (Strategic Lawsuits Against Public Participation) meant to silence activists by suing for damages if protests delay development projects. While SLAPPs rarely succeed, fighting them is expensive (www .thefirstamendment.org/aboutfap.html). Fortunately, states are beginning to recognize that SLAPPs are just intended as intimidation to stop dissent and are adopting regulations to protect citizens against this form of harassment (Jones 2005, 11).

Legal venues can be changed and when they are, doing so often advantages the powerful. For instance, the federal government has been less vigilant than states in suing banks that seem to be violating the Fair Lending Act. As a result, Attorneys General, especially Spitzer of New York, working with activist groups, have taken up the burden. But recently, the A.G. was sued in federal court and banks were "granted an injunction prohibiting Spitzer from suing them under the Fair Housing Act" (Matthew Lee [at] innercitypress.org <mlee@innercitypress.org>), moving the cases to the far less friendly federal level.

Another difficulty with legal actions is that they necessitate hiring expensive professionals whose very involvement can disempower activists. In addition, the way the legal system works often precludes involvement by working people.

> [T]rials are held during the day, which often precludes attendance by workers. The litigation time line is not controlled by members and can be lengthy. The role that members can play is extremely limited, so a litigation project does not facilitate leadership development . . . , which means it is difficult to build the power of the organization. (Gaventa, Smith, and Willingham 1990, 115)

Fortunately, social change organizations have figured out ways of using the legal system while empowering the members. Members do research to help the case by, for instance, tracking down ownership of derelict housing properties so their attorneys know whom to sue. ACORN encourages tenants to serve legal papers on derelict landlords (McCreight 1984, 183). Another approach is to directly connect the legal moves of the lawyers to the direct actions of the membership. For instance,

On Monday, June 28, ACORN filed a national lawsuit against Wells Fargo in San Francisco County Superior Court. The suit charges the company with a broad range of unfair and deceptive lending practices. . . . On the day the lawsuit was filed, more than 2,000 ACORN members marched from City Hall through the streets of Los Angeles to the Wells Fargo Building downtown to personally deliver the suit to Wells (ACORN marches on Wells Fargo, files lawsuit, 2004).

Further, lawyers of the left do use legal issues as an organizing tactic. For instance, Jennifer Gordon, an attorney, set up the WorkPlace Project to provide legal assistance to individual workers (mostly immigrants) who were forced to work long hours in sweatshops or as domestics without overtime, or whose wages simply were not paid. Next, she set up programs to show each of the workers their legal rights and hired a professional organizer who mobilized the workers to insist on these rights. Eventually, this led to a successful campaign to compel the State of New York to enforce labor laws (Gordon 2005).

To summarize, legal tactics are varied and often effective, though slow and expensive. Despite major outlays, some legal tactics fail in court. The need to win the case may give attorneys disproportionate say over how the case will be brought, threatening the sense of empowerment of members. Yet, by working out partnerships in which activists do participate, litigation can be empowering, but usually only within a broader campaign.

Obtaining Publicity

For social change organizations, publicity campaigns accomplish much.

Provide the Organization's Framing for the Problem. Publicity efforts are "frame contests" (Ryan 1991, 75–90) through which activist organizations simultaneously communicate that problems stem from broader structural forces while proposed solutions are consistent with widely shared values (Center for Community Change 1997).

Frames are often communicated through *typifications* (Best 1995)—dramatic and readily understood examples of victims of the problem—a child with a disease that is not treated because of inadequate medical services, or by illustrations of success—an older woman whose home has been saved from a predatory lender.

Disseminate Information to Both Supporters and the Broader Public. Publicity campaigns are about sharing the facts of the matter—the low wages paid by Wal-Mart, or the sharp cutbacks in funding for housing—in ways that show that action is required.

Encourage Mobilization and Recruitment. Well publicized successes are a major tool in recruiting both supporters to the cause and new members to the organization.

One form of using the media to recruit is to encourage people to view movies that support community organizing. Among our personal favorites are the *Milagro*

Bean Field War, about a poor Mexican American community organizing to preserve land against a recreational developer; *Building Hope*, a documentary about the Dudley Street Neighborhood Initiative; *Norma Rae*, on a union organizing effort in the South; as well as dozens of documentaries on individual campaigns, such as organizing efforts against Wal-Mart.

Keep an Issue on the Front Burner.   Both elected officials and the broader public have limited attention spans. Through *media advocacy efforts* (Wallack 2005) action organizations make sure that continuing attention is paid to the issues.

Target Opponents.   Publicity focuses attention on those who either cause a problem or, at the very least, have been unwilling to work toward a solution. Media messages change the passive voice (housing conditions are poor) to the active one (Mr. Jones, a slumlord, refuses to repair the apartments he owns).

Claim Credit for Success in Ways that Brand the Organization.   Organizations that win are better able to attract new members and in future campaigns more easily pressure politicians or business. Publicizing successes is important: An environmental group might boast about a bird coming off the endangered species list, or an economic justice organization for putting a predatory lender out of business.

Through such credit claiming, organizations gain reputations as being skilled and effective in particular areas and are *branded* (as in "brand-name") as capable of accomplishing specific tasks. For instance, ACORN is known for orchestrating multicity demonstrations on economic justice, or the Center on Budget and Policy Priorities is branded as the source for trustworthy technical analyses.

Publicity is about getting out your message. But first you must determine which audience should be the target. Is it worth the extensive effort to gain the attention of the national audience or is access to a community cable station or a neighborhood paper sufficient? How broad is the target for the message? On wedge issues it might be the entire public, but at times the target is more focused. Thom Clark of the Community Media Workshop convinced activists in Chicago to design an entire media campaign to get the attention of one person, Chicago's mayor (Center for Community Change 1997, 31).

Working with the Mass Media

Though many journalists are concerned with social issues, newspapers and television are money-making operations that depend on business advertisers and access to established politicians, so they do not push for a social change message on their own. Worse yet, dominant radio talk shows and major networks such as Fox News tend to oppose progressive causes.

Fortunately, there are sympathetic local media. ACORN, for example, has a close association with a radio station that tapes programs that can be rebroadcast elsewhere. In Chicago, the Media Workshop lists dozens of sympathetic, albeit often small, media outlets, and a message initially placed can be picked up by the larger, mass media (www.newstips.org/interior.php?section=Resources). Further, while the community press might not be all that sympathetic to social change causes, community papers need news to fill space and a social change organization can provide that news (Moss 2002).

Getting media attention and ensuring the stories are accurate can be problematic. Protests are only selectively covered and then only when the issue being protested is already one of broader concern (Oliver and Maney 2000), while it can literally take years of persistent work to gain coverage for organizations concerned with local social problems (Ryan, Anastario, and Jeffreys 2005). Controlling how a message is communicated is difficult. A message intended to show the power of the action organization—portraying a successful sit-in—might end up portraying the activists as a disorderly mob. Rather than focusing on the placards in a demonstration that detail the problem, the press focuses on the rowdiness.

Messages have both *texts* (the literal content) and *subtexts* (what people also take out of what they see and hear that later can obscure the intended message). Antiwar protesters carry informative placards detailing unnecessary deaths with the plea for peace their literal message—the text. But the observer picks up the subtext of the casual dress of the activists, or perhaps that people are marching while others are working—both discrediting subtexts.

Publicity efforts are affected by practical constraints. Mass media need to make a profit, so an attractive story that can be covered at less expense—a demonstration held next to city hall—is more likely to get space than a more expensive story taking place in a distant neighborhood. One approach is to tag the community organization's events onto activities that the media are covering anyway, such as a major press conference or a national political convention. Making life easier for the press helps gain coverage.

Learn to time stories to fit into media rhythms. An anti-drunk driving campaign is more likely to get attention on New Year's Eve or on Prom Night when the press is concerned about drunk driving. Stories released on a Friday are more likely to be covered in the paper, but less likely to be read. An early morning action can make the evening news, but an evening event, at best, will not get reported until the next day. An event scheduled too close to a media deadline will get ignored; why should reporters kill themselves to make a deadline when other stories are available?

Media hunger for stories varies over time. A war, disaster, or political scandal might absorb all reporters and dominate headlines, but during a lull, community groups can more easily gain access. When much is happening, talk shows might not want to interview people from a local organization, but later on when other stories are scarce, they might want to do so. Persistence and willingness to appear at the drop of a hat can gain the organization greater visibility.

Fortunately, events can be staged to provide the excitement that the media wants. The cool media events described in the last chapter are built around communicating a message in the lively fashion that makes for good visual presentation. Activist organizations will schedule *days*, such as Earth Day, or *weeks*, such as Affordable Housing Week, during which so many different media events are held that by their frequency and repetition some are actually covered.

In addition, the media world is very competitive. Making a story attractive enough for one outlet to cover virtually forces others to pay attention. A central purpose of the cool media events, the moral demonstrations, and the large-scale marches is to create events of such interest that the media have no choice but to cover them. Even issuing a technical report can be done in ways that gain media appeal. In one instance, an environmental organization wanted to disseminate a technical report on how strip mining in the Cumberland Mountains destroyed the land near a beautiful waterfall. The group created a media event by designing a huge banner—100 feet long and weighing 200 pounds—and hanging it over the waterfall—a dramatic and difficult task. The waterfall and banner provided an eye-catching backdrop for a scheduled press conference and did lure in the media (Center for Community Change 1997, 36).

Gaining Attention with the Newsworthy Story.   The bottom line in gaining media attention is having a newsworthy story that will sell papers and create a television audience. The Center for Community Change offers 12 rules used by the media to judge whether a story is newsworthy:

1. Is it timely?
2. Is it new?
3. Is there conflict?
4. Does it involve a scandal?
5. Is it visual?
6. Does it involve prominent players or famous faces?
7. Is there broad and passionate support?
8. Is it possible?
9. Is it credible?
10. Is there human interest? a good story?
11. Is there paradox, irony, hypocrisy, or the unexpected?
12. Is it meaningful to readers or viewers? (Center for Community Change 1997, 44–48)

The need to make a story interesting can make it hard to communicate facts or figures, but fortunately there are several ways of doing so. First, customize the language to match what reporters for a specific paper, or even a section of a paper, will understand—a reporter for the *American Banker* will understand CRA data while one working for a press service probably will not. Second, release the report at a press conference that humanizes the technical material, for instance, having people at the conference who are victims of a problem and can be interviewed. A report documenting that a community needs $48 million in mortgage money doesn't explain what a housing shortage entails as well as testimony from families sharing an overcrowded apartment. Use diagrams and charts that turn numbers into visual images.

Working with Reporters.   Success in publicity efforts involves maintaining good relations with the press. Press relations are ongoing, not one shot, one-time activities.

Invite reporters to visit your office, provide them with background, and always answer their questions, even if doing so might reveal some weaknesses. Reporters respect such frankness and will be more ready to listen when their support is really needed. When you run across a story of interest, even if it is not germane to your organization, inform the press. Major national housing and economic justice organizations receive good coverage in *The New York Times*, in part because their leaders have worked out ready access to members of the paper's editorial board.

In the crunch of a campaign, reporters need reliable information quickly. Assign personnel to a media team that can meet with reporters and provide material quickly. Designate a Press Information Officer (PIO) who is on call 24 hours a day (Kleyman 1974). Make sure that the Press Information Officer has made contact with reporters long before the action begins, perhaps by inviting them out for coffee or lunch to describe what the organization is about. Prepare and keep a standard press kit, with background on your organization, the list of its successes and media contacts; have pictures and videos readily available.

Be honest. If a reporter catches a deception, the group loses credibility. If an organization routinely gives reporters good stories that they can run with, the reporters will be back. Stories should be balanced and easy to check out. Reporters want to be seen as unbiased professionals, not flacks for a community organization.

Releasing Your News to the Mainstream Media. For events you want covered provide the press with plenty of advance notice and let reporters know what it is your organization is planning to do. (You want to share such information only with trusted reporters if you are going to do something marginally legal.) Help the press, especially television; set up their cameras in places that you know will have the most action. Prepare a press release describing the action. Such news releases (and increasingly news videos) can be hand-delivered to papers or television stations.

If a social action organization has hard news to release, it can hold a press conference. In planning a press conference first inform the local papers, television, and the wire services of the time of the conference. Have the PIOs phone their friends at the local stations and papers, send personalized letters, and then follow up with a reminder. Organization members should show up at the press conference; their fervor will communicate the importance of the issue to the reporters.

If the organization is releasing statistical data, take the time to prepare attractive graphics, using computer software that is now readily available. Explain the meaning of data using dramatic personal illustrations. A child with a disease caused by toxic waste can be present at the news conference to humanize the figures on how much pollution factories are releasing. If the news conference has been called to publicize a project or demonstration, the organization can provide copies of a video for TV, or, for newspapers, 8-by-10 glossy photographs.

All the reporters who attend the conference should receive the media package with the press release, graphics, photos, and videotapes. Leftover packets should be sent to media people who were not there. Besides the news editor, the editor of the Homes page might be interested in the plight of a displaced family, while real estate or business editors pay attention to campaigns to pressure banks and businesses to reinvest in poor communities. Business editors are also interested in community-based housing and commercial projects.

If preparing a video, leave time for editing and retakes. A certain homemade quality adds credibility, but the video has to be good enough to broadcast. Press releases should look professional, be neat, with correct grammar and spelling, and with space between lines so they can be edited. Sentences and paragraphs should be short. The closer the news release comes to a style that newspapers and broadcasters use, the more likely the release is to be quoted.

Press releases should answer the questions: Who? What? When? Where? Why? and How? Below we have included a press release on a confrontational campaign that was circulated on the Internet (www.npa-us.org/04immrights.htm).

Press Releases for NPA—National People's Action—Fighting for Our Neighborhoods
810 Milwaukee Ave
Chicago, IL 60622
Email us: npa@npa-us.org

FOR IMMEDIATE RELEASE
Contact: Emily Severson
April 2, 2004
(312) 243-3038

**Community Leaders Visit Karl Rove's Home,
Demand White House Support the DREAM Act—Washington, DC:**

Hundreds of grassroots leaders representing National People's Action (NPA) paid a visit to the home of President Bush's Senior Policy Adviser Karl Rove on Sunday, March 28, 2004 because he refused to meet with them to discuss the rights of immigrant youth.

NPA and immigrant rights' leaders want the White House to support the Development, Relief, and Education for Alien Minors Act (DREAM Act). It would grant access to in-state tuition for children of immigrants whose families have been in the county at least five years.

"We paid our way to come to Washington D.C. to talk to Rove, and he wouldn't listen," said Tomasa Fonseca, an educator from Marshalltown, IA. "So we came to his house to ask him to support the dreams of our youth."

It is estimated that 50,000–65,000 undocumented students graduate from high school in the U.S. each year. Upon graduation these youth cannot work legally, nor can they qualify for in-state tuition at universities because they aren't considered residents.

Recently, the Bush administration came out in support of a guest worker plan, which would allow immigrant workers temporary residency for a maximum of six years. NPA leaders believe that Bush's plan will divide hard working immigrant families. The DREAM Act, on the other hand, is an example of positive immigration reform that would give immigrant youth the opportunity to realize the American Dream by becoming workers, tax payers and positive community leaders.

"We are here today to send a strong message to the Bush administration," said Emira Palacios, NPA Co-Chairperson. "We are telling them that if they want the Hispanic vote, they must give us the DREAM Act!"

National People's Action is a 33-year-old multi-racial/ethnic, inter-generational non-partisan coalition of hundreds of local community organizations that volunteer their time to make communities throughout the U.S. safer, healthier and more stable environments.

NPA was founded by Gale Cincotta in 1972. With her leadership, NPA spear-headed efforts to pass the Community Reinvestment Act (CRA) and the Home Mortgage Disclosure Act (HMDA). CRA is credited with investing over $1 trillion dollars in low/moderate income neighborhoods and families.

Note the funnel writing style. The core event, the hook for the story, is reported first. More details are given later. Background on the organization is provided. The hope is the press will use the story as written, but if it has to be cut, the earlier parts alone present a coherent message. While reporters will sometimes dig for a story, if they are approaching deadline, they may use the news release without much change. In case reporters want more details, make sure the release has the name and phone number of a contact person whom they can reach easily and who can provide additional information.

Besides using press releases, activists can use public service messages on radio to announce meetings or major events or write letters to the editor of newspapers. Letters might be shortened, but often are printed as submitted. Web sites of activist organizations provide proto-typical letters that can be sent, while sophisticated web engines (available on some organization's websites) quickly identify papers by local zip code allowing electronic submission of a letter to multiple papers within a zip code.

Letters should be brief, focus on the core issue, and be made personal. Writing should be straightforward (sarcasm or satire rarely works). Directly attacking opponents can create an argumentative tone that can turn off readers. Larger papers often run op eds, thoughtful commentaries written by advocates of particular views, in which organization members can explain current events as seen by the organization. For example, gay rights groups can write about the murder of a gay soldier as an illustration of the failure of the government's "don't ask, don't tell" policy, or a gun control group can write about the mass shootings in public schools as a reason to curtail the availability of automatic weapons. National campaigns now prepare sample op ed pieces that can be rewritten by local organizations and then sent off to the community press.

Controlling Your Own Publicity

Social change organizations work to shape the publicity they receive by carefully planning out how the press will portray what happened. Media-wise organizations understand that having a radical speaker who challenges authority by using the f-word will create a very different image than having an ordained clergy lead a prayer vigil. Still by relying on the mass media, social change organizations allow others to filter their message.

With the advent of the Internet, the availability of inexpensive digital recording devices, and the ease of distributing DVDs, action organizations themselves can better control their media campaigns and can learn how to do so from progressive media workshops such as Community Media Workshop in Chicago (www.newstips.org/index.php). Messages can be placed on bumper stickers, in displays in libraries, on wall posters, or printed on T-shirts and badges. Cleverly designed logos both brand an organization and help spread its message, for instance, using the peace sign, or a picture of an animal being rescued. Neighborhood organizations can set up displays in store-front offices, community centers, or city hall showing successes in turning deteriorated buildings into decent housing or garbage-strewn lots into vest-pocket parks.

Newsletters can be easily set up on desktop computers and should be routinely sent out to community members. National organizations maintain e-lists of those who want to receive their newsletters that are then filled with stories and dramatic pictures and that are often recirculated on lists of sister organizations. Pamphlets can be prepared and sent out on (snail) mail lists. For instance, the SEIU working with ACORN prepared a colorful informative pamphlet on how hospitals in poor neighborhoods are less likely to be up-to-date than those in wealthier places.

Alerts that mobilize supporters to make phone calls or show up at city hall or at a rally are sent out by e-mail, while organizations now maintain their own web pages. The web page maintained by the Kensington Welfare Rights Organization, for instance, describes the background of the group, details its campaigns, presents a diary of individuals who work closely with the organization while linking to press releases, books, and films about the organization, and at times has included an online radio interview with leaders of the organization.

Nowadays action organizations set up BLOGs in which members and supporters discuss issues and plan out strategies. At their best, BLOGs become the electronic equivalent of a community meeting, enabling people to share ideas. BLOGS are mainly visited by those already active in a cause, but Internet search engines pick up the content of BLOGS and circulate messages far more broadly. Activists now share narratives of success through PODCASTS, files that download to computers, ipods, and similar devices that can share the daily adventures in organizing.

Activist-controlled media become central to the broader campaign. To encourage states and cities to set up housing trust fund organizations first in Minnesota and then in Illinois designed a media campaign. Focus group studies showed that most people thought affordable housing meant gangs and crime. To counter this image the organizations prepared videos that portrayed that teachers, nurses, police, and other workers could not afford current housing prices, while the steady rise in costs would force children to move away from their home communities. Surveys showed that viewers changed their beliefs to become more supportive of legislation favoring affordable housing (Rehab/HAI web pages).

In the Wake Up Wal-Mart Campaign, SEIU and ACORN heavily relied on media presentations by sending out frequent e-mail notifications of actions, constructing websites filled with facts and figures on abuse, and recruiting people through electronic signups. The coalition helped design a video called "Wal-Mart: The High Cost of Low Prices." that detailed how low prices came on the sweaty backs of exploited workers. Six thousand copies of the video were produced and sent to volunteers, who signed up electronically then invited friends and neighbors to see this damning film on its opening day. This innovative use of media itself became a story that others in the press disseminated.

Negotiations

On occasion, a confrontation will lead to an immediate improvement of the situation. But that's not all that common. Instead, situations are resolved through extended negotiations (Goodpaster 1997; Susskind and Cruikshank 1987).

Planning Negotiations

In planning negotiations, keep in mind three broad principles:

1. Negotiations can occur concurrent with lobbying and confrontational actions. Talking with the target while sitting in at an office, or demonstrating on the street is more customary than not. Negotiations are an extension of action, not a separate stage.
2. Skill is required in negotiations as what appears to have been won through actions can easily be lost through inept negotiations.
3. Successful negotiations end with a verifiable *program for implementation*, a way of carrying out what has been promised that the action organization can monitor.

Negotiations Are a Continuation of Lobbying. The borderline between lobbying—providing information to elected officials and staff—and negotiating on the content of a particular bill can blur. Successful negotiations build on a history of having provided elected officials and staff, through lobbying, with credible information that supports your cause so that they trust what you are requesting.

Keep in mind though, that when negotiations occur as part of a lobbying effort, politicians often find themselves in the middle. Is housing the disabled more or less important than sheltering the homeless? Effective negotiations recognize the constraints placed upon elected officials who answer to multiple constituencies.

Complexity of the Issues. On some issues like pressuring to get a company to set up a daycare center, negotiations can stay focused on the immediate matter. But in the political realm, this often is not the case, with the issues that affect your organization often being little more than a sidebar to a broader matter. For instance, housing activists have been negotiating for a national trust fund for over a decade. As we write, this issue, vital to the housing community, is but a small concern in broader discussions of how government is to regulate the trillion dollar mortgage industry.

Side Negotiations. Negotiations are rarely just dyadic discussions between one organization and politicians or bureaucrats. Not only do action organizations have to persuade elected officials, but also must keep their own members happy, and, if part of a coalition, the other organizations in that coalition. Before bargaining with elected officials, a coalition has to first reach a consensus among its members. Few things hurt political negotiations more than allies presenting different demands during the same negotiation session.

At times, when working with elected officials who do have the final say, the politicians will themselves step out of the way and try to force the action organization and its opponents to work out a compromise. So, for instance, a neighborhood might have older rooming homes that housing activist organizations want to convert to affordable single-resident-occupancy buildings, while the local homeowners association would want them torn down and replaced by single family homes. While the city council does have the final say on such matters, often the council will indicate that it will ratify any reasonable deal worked out between the homeowners association and the housing action group.

Negotiating Strategies

Negotiations come about only after the opponents are made to understand through persistent power tactics that they are better off talking and reaching an agreement, or as Shel Trapp says, negotiations are "where the bacon is" (Trapp n.d., 91). But the game begins anew when negotiations start. An inexperienced negotiator might accept unenforceable agreements, or, perhaps, the organization is tricked as the opponents take a slice-and-divide approach in which minor concessions are made while the larger problem remains unresolved. Politicians may pretend to negotiate but then water down any concessions promised. To avoid these and other problems, preparations are required.

Negotiations Are about Power and the Perceptions of Power.   Successful negotiations come about after the organization has demonstrated that it has power, even if only the power to disrupt. Both sides do better when each understands that the other has some power since

> the greater the total amount of power in a relationship, the greater the use of conciliatory tactics . . . an unequal power relationship fosters more use of hostile tactics and less use of conciliatory tactics than an equal power relationship. (Lawler 1992, 17)

Mutual respect, in part based on fear but in part based on understanding the other, leads to a better outcome.

Understand the Political/Social Factors That Affect the Opponent.   A liberal church that has neglected to set up child care for its employees is far easier to negotiate with than a sweatshop factory. You can push the church with vigor, it has no place to go; sweatshops often disappear overnight. A politician who had a razor thin victory in the last election is more willing to bargain than one who opposes your group and who has not had any substantial opposition in years. Before beginning negotiations, research the background of your opponent and the constraints that the opponent faces.

In Planning Negotiations Think beyond the Immediate Problem at Hand.
Solving the immediate issue is important, but negotiators should not lose track of the underlying social and economic structures that created the situation. Short run solutions might leave long run problems in place. Convincing a university not to allow its logo to be used on clothing made with sweat labor helps, but, better yet, if the action organization persuades the university to set up a permanent policy not to purchase from firms that have a history of treating their employees badly. Forcing the city to preserve an affordable apartment building is a victory, but it would be even better to negotiate the right of the community groups to make land use decisions that affect their neighborhoods.

Have Specific Demands in Mind. Without having specific demands neither you nor your opponent know where to begin. As Trapp argues,

> We do not want generalities. We want specifics. That is why we usually frame the demands in a "yes" or "no" manner. Often we even set up a chart with the demands listed and a big "yes" or "no" behind each demand, which the leader checks off as the enemy gives an answer. (Trapp n.d., 94)

Activists learn where the opponents are most vulnerable and focus demands there. After years of facing police oppression and economic deprivation, activists in Cincinnati began a boycott and listed eight pages of detailed demands, yet still recognized the evolving nature of the negotiations.

> To resolve the issue we must collectively find meaningful solutions to the problems identified in the demands that would allow various factions to come together to build and grow our community in such a way that benefits all citizens. (Cincinnati Boycott Council 2003, p. A)

Demands might come from the strategic plans that guided the initial campaign, such as seen in the guiding principles of the ACORN initiated negotiations with the public sector to help those displaced by Hurricane Katrina.

1. Respect and a voice—Our voices need to be at the center of developing and implementing relief and reconstruction programs.
2. Right of return—The people of New Orleans will not be kept out by deliberate attempts to change the makeup of the city, or by neglect, which gives the richer and more powerful first access to choices and resources.
3. The means to take care of ourselves and our families—Survivors need help with housing, health care, income from unemployment, and assistance for those who've helped us.
4. Rebuilding the right way—Reconstruction should include good and affordable housing, living wage jobs, and good schools for our children.
5. Recovering together—The hurricane should not be used as an excuse to cut health care and food assistance programs that help families across the country.

6. Accountability and honesty—An independent investigation is necessary so we can understand what went wrong and how to protect ourselves in the future (ACORN Katrina Survivors Association, 2005).

Negotiators Speak for Constituencies, Not Simply Themselves.   Individuals who meet frequently develop a rapport that increases trust and allows each to better comprehend the others' arguments, so that having only a handful involved in the actual negotiations is important (Susskind and Cruikshank 1987). However, these same negotiators must keep in mind that even if they end up agreeing with those from the other side, they do not have the final say. An agreement that does not satisfy the larger group represented simply won't fly.

Negotiations Often Involve Multiple Players on Each Side.   Negotiation can involve multiple partners on each side. A coalition of housing groups, CDCs, neighborhood organizations, and advocates for the homeless might be on one side, trying to pressure government to provide more housing subsidies. Should the coalition stick together at all costs? Can separate deals be made that benefit individual members of the coalition, at little harm to others? Will opponents offer concessions to selected members of the coalition hoping to break up the alliance? Leaders of action organization who are partnering should spend time with each other to work out these concerns, to agree on their demands and at what point they will consider the negotiations completed or impossible.

In Picking the Negotiating Team, Choose People with Complementary Skills.   Who is quickest on his or her feet? Who can tactfully sum up a situation, appear conciliatory to the opposition, yet not concede on fundamental issues? Who has the facts and figures at his or her fingertips and can catch the opponents' deceptions? Is there someone whom the opponents trust? If the negotiations drag on for a while, who has the patience and humor to help everyone keep their cool and stay at the bargaining table?

Before a negotiating session, negotiators plan an overall strategy examining what they have already accomplished from the direct actions. Have businesses been financially pressured? Do public figures want to reduce the embarrassment they face in the press? Then as part of this strategizing, negotiators figure out how the opponents might behave during bargaining. Are public officials limited in their scope of action by promises made to other groups; is the scope of action of director of a branch of a large company curtailed by a stubborn home office?

With these issues in mind, the negotiating team then simulates—games out—the negotiations. Divide the team into two and have one group pretend to be the opponents and try to imagine what the opponents might offer and what concerns or constraints they may be operating under.

Make sure your negotiators have mastered the facts. If the problem is lack of expenditures in poor neighborhoods, double check that the negotiators know the size of the city's infrastructure budget and where funds have been spent in the past. In efforts to end gender or ethnic discrimination, make sure the team knows how many men and women from which ethnic groups work at different levels.

Most important, those on the negotiating team must work out in advance how much they can concede and still gain a victory. Most campaigns do have room to maneuver. An organization arguing for a fairer allocation of government contracts to minority groups might initially demand that contracts be let in rough proportion to the population of the various groups. If African Americans constitute 13 percent of the local population, negotiators might demand that 13 percent of the contracts go to African American-owned firms. In fact, negotiators might be willing to accept an allocation of contracts in proportion to the number of minority firms; negotiators can back off the original demand and still bring about improvement.

Keep in mind that concessions extracted during negotiations should be expressed in specific and verifiable terms, not as vague, unenforceable promises. Activists who negotiate with banks about community reinvestment demand exact figures on how much money will be put back into the neighborhood and how quickly, whether new bank branches will be opened, and how many business loans and mortgages will be offered.

The Mechanics of Confrontational Negotiating Sessions

Preliminary agreements are needed on the mechanics of the negotiating sessions, especially when the two sides to negotiations have a history of mistrust (Cormick 1989). On whose turf will the sessions be held, or is a neutral setting required? How many from each side can show up for the sessions? Are the negotiators from the other side able to make concessions or are they simply flunkies who are unable to say "yes"?

Will there be neutral third parties and, if so, how will they be chosen? Will recordings be allowed? Will the press be kept informed, and if so, how often and by whom? Will negotiators be required to keep all discussions confidential, even from their own organization members, to permit the participants to try out off-the-wall ideas without fear of embarrassment? How long will the meetings last?

One activist described how neighborhood groups created a set of such procedures that helped them in negotiations with bankers.

> We met with those guys and we all, our poor community people, and they had their guys and we set the agenda: Does it mean that there will be no smoking or no breaks every five minutes (chuckles) . . . There is only one break during the morning. Only one lunch break, only thirty minutes, you know, if anybody wants to call a break to chat about a piece of the agreement, they're only allowed five minutes. No smoking. We knew all the executives there smoke . . . You know a bunch of poor community people got together . . . they were getting upset because they were used to having their secretary bring them coffee and all of that. We said, none of that. Only persons allowed in this room are the people invited to this meeting. No phone calls, no phones in the room. We met from like eight-thirty in the morning to five-thirty, six in the evening. So that was a long meeting for those top, number one executives. (Chicago activist interviewed by Herbert Rubin)

The negotiations ended with the community groups receiving a written guarantee for tens of millions of dollars of affordable housing.

During negotiations the goal is to discuss issues, not people. Little will be accomplished if either side is responding to personal animosities (Pruitt and Carnevale 1993, 151). To bypass personal animosities, each side might appoint as principal negotiator an individual who was not a central figure in the campaign leading up to the negotiations. The Mayor and the President of the Community Group might not be speaking to one another, but the chosen negotiators begin with no personal animosities. To improve relations further, skillful negotiators chat with each other during breaks and try to discover the common interests. Still, just because people like one another doesn't mean they will reach agreement, but if bargainers think opponents are incarnations of evil, no one will listen or respond in good faith.

Negotiations can run on, be fatiguing, and appear to be accomplishing little. To keep the negotiations going, each side must see some short-term progress, even if that progress is more symbolic than real. Professional negotiators advise making some minor concessions to keep discussions alive. For instance, if bargaining between environmentalists, public officials, and developers on how much land to reserve for park space has stalled, environmentalists might concede that open space next to a mall is not required. Both sides recognize that little is really being granted, as the land near the mall is too expensive for public authorities to buy for a park, but the willingness to make the concessions communicates that we can talk and encourages the other side to be less stubborn.

Sometimes negotiations are merely a ploy by the opponent to make an action organization cease its pressure tactics. Opponents may posture and make speeches, without listening to the action organization's proposals. If this is occurring, it is probably time to leave. Sometimes, though, both sides are delaying because they don't know how to reach a resolution. If this seems to be the case, set a firm deadline by which time the negotiations must be concluded. As such deadlines approach, people tend to be more willing to make concessions.

Negotiating tactics involve a delicate balance between having a fixed goal in mind and being able to concede some points without giving up crucial issues, while being flexible enough to respond to unanticipated ideas from the opponent. Research suggests that firmness usually pays off (Pruitt 1981, 74), but also recognizes that social change organizations will have to concede something, even if just to preserve the face of the opponent. If concessions are made too quickly, your side may be seen as weak, but if they are made too slowly, the opponent may also get stubborn (Pruitt 1981, 20). However, if opponents bring in an unanticipated offer, take a break and caucus to think it over. For instance,

> Let's say that we're members of a tenants' organization negotiating with the landlord over a rent increase. The landlord has announced a 20 percent increase. In our planning sessions . . . we agreed that we would accept no increase but that we would actually be willing to accept $7\frac{1}{2}$ percent . . . The landlord comes up with a totally different sort of suggestion . . . he will agree to no rent increase but that instead of a month-by-month rental, there should be year-long leases with a one-month security deposit for damages. This is a possibility that we had not thought of. Rather than trying to think

this through in front of the landlord, the thing to do is to call for a "caucus." This means we take a break to discuss the new offer. (Kahn 1982, 164–65)

Opponents who fear that confrontations will resume have an incentive to come up with mutually acceptable agreements. So examine their proposals carefully and do not automatically reject them. Numerous ways can be found to structure offers that encourage opponents to work toward what your side wants (Goodpaster 1997, 33–50). One is to split the difference, finding a position halfway between the initial stance of the community organization and the counteroffer of the target. With "salami" tactics, an issue is broken into parts to enable the opponent to make smaller (and less threatening) concessions, until, piece by piece, the entire issue is resolved. A quite different approach is to link issues together into one package that has something in it for everyone.

Some tactics can inadvertently terminate the discussion and so should be used with care. One approach when concessions are not forthcoming is to escalate demands rather than seek a compromise (and then hope that the initial position is reconsidered with the respect that it deserved). Another is to threaten to walk out.

Negotiators worry about how honest to be with the opponent. Lying might help in the short run, but if the lies are discovered, the organization loses the credibility it needs for continued discussions. Short of outright falsehoods, there are a variety of forms of mild deception that are common in bargaining, for example, asking for more than the group really needs or understating the amount of flexibility that the negotiator actually has. Gambits such as shifting attention, not fully answering questions, or avoiding questions by asking another question are accepted tactics (Goodpaster 1997, 51–61). Negotiators often bluff, threaten to do something that they don't really intend to do, as part of the bargaining.

The goal of negotiations is to reach an agreement that both sides accept as just. Skillful negotiators look for a mutually prominent alternative that

> must stand out in both parties' thinking either because it embodies some standard of fairness or reasonableness or because it enjoys perceptual "uniqueness, simplicity, precedent or some rationale that make [it] qualitatively different from the continuum of possible alternatives." (Schelling 1960, 70)

Environmental activists who want to protect land that harbors an intact and rare ecosystem may get into seemingly irresolvable disputes with developers who don't want to give up the property. One possible mutually prominent alternative might involve a land swap, in which the developer gets to keep the original land, but donates a large tract with similar characteristics farther from the city.

Conclusion

In this chapter, we have described tools that are used in both conventional and confrontational campaigns. Through the legal system activists pressure those in power to live up to their own rules, while the threat of legal action can force negotiations.

Campaigns are affected by how people understand issues, so learning how to work with the media in ways that your message gets out is an important part of activism. Finally, opponents usually do not just surrender and say "we will give you what you want" but instead campaigns must be concluded through sustained negotiations.

CHAPTER
19

Social Action
Magnifying Power through Coalitions

Successful political and confrontational campaigns are frequently carried out by several organizations working as a coalition (Roberts-DeGennaro 1997). Unions join with neighborhood groups to sustain jobs in a community (Nissen 1995; Simmons 1994) while environmental activists form coalitions with ethnic identity organizations to stop pollution in poor, minority communities. Housing activists and economic justice organizations work together to preserve the Community Reinvestment Act. Living wage campaigns are orchestrated by coalitions of poor people's unions and neighborhood groups, as well as national networks such as ACORN (Reynolds and Kern 2004; Tait 2005). Women's organizations that represent those of different ethnicity or social class come together in larger coalitions to battle rape and spouse abuse (Bevacqua 2001).

Some coalitions bring together organizations whose styles of action are similar but draw from distinct memberships. For instance, Ruckus, with its origin in the environmental movement,

> is teaming up with Jobs with Justice and ACORN to bring you a National Quarantine of Wal-Mart. On Friday, June 2, during Wal-Mart's annual shareholders meeting, thousands of concerned citizens dressed in hazmat suits, and armed with yellow caution tape, will be putting Wal-Mart sites across the country under "quarantine." (The Ruckus Society <action@ruckus.org> Date: 05/09/2006)

Coalitions bring together complementary strengths, uniting those adept at confrontations—the "tree shakers"—with those more skilled at implementing projects—the "jam makers" (Peirce and Steinbach 1990). During the height of the civil rights movement organizations that differed greatly in their willingness to be confrontational joined umbrella coalitions such as the Council of Federated Organizations (COFO) and as a coalition fought against racist local governments (Payne 1995). In the fight for the Equal Rights Amendment:

> One organization within the [coalition] movement would attract a more conservative membership, another a more radical one. Internally, this decentralization let members of each group feel more comfortable with one another. Externally, the division of labor

> made possible a "Mutt and Jeff" . . . act, in which the more conservative organization could tell relevant power holders that if certain concessions were not forthcoming it could not hold back the radicals much longer. (Mansbridge 1986, 194)

In local housing coalitions

> the combined strategy of different actors in the housing movement seems to be a (perhaps unplanned) version of "good cop, bad cop" in which one or more groups engage in highly visible acts of protest to publicize housing problems, while other groups work in a more cooperative mode with local officials to exact and implement policy changes. (Goetz 1993, 71)

Today diverse groups are in coalitions set up to protest the war in Iraq (Meyer and Corrigall-Brown 2005).

Coalitions enable those on the same side but differing slightly on what to do to work out a common agenda before facing a target. As such

> coalitions are arguably the central method for aggregating the viewpoints of organized interests in American politics. They serve as institutional mediators reconciling potentially disparate policy positions, in effect "predigesting" policy proposals before they are served to the legislature. (Hula 1999, 7)

Some coalitions are small, temporary, local, and focused. Two small organizations from adjacent neighborhoods join forces to save a transportation hub that serves both neighborhoods and then go their own ways. Other coalitions are large, permanent, national in scope, and themselves evolve as agendas change. For example, the Coalition of Human Needs was

> founded in 1981 by organizations concerned about President Reagan's proposals to consolidate targeted federal funding for human needs programs into block grants, the Coalition has since expanded its work into other issue areas. The Coalition promotes adequate funding for human needs programs, progressive tax policies and other federal measures to address the needs of low-income and other vulnerable populations. (www.chn.org/about/index.html)

All in all, coalitions are central to battles for social change. In this chapter, we describe a variety of coalition structures, examine what they can accomplish, and then point out the difficulties in sustaining them. We conclude the chapter with illustrations of successful social mobilization campaigns orchestrated by coalitions.

The Variety of Coalitions

Coalitions come in many shapes and forms. We are active in the DeKalb County Housing Action Coalition that is little more than a talking group of social service and housing providers with no officers, offices, or other organizational appurtenance. At the other extreme, major national coalitions such as the National Community Reinvestment Coalition set up to defend the CRA employ several dozen staff, maintain offices, conduct training programs, run conferences and campaigns, actively serve a large membership, and recruit new coalition members.

Coalitions start in response to an immediate threat that concurrently impacts separate constituencies. Some coalitions are transient; of the 37 major organizations that joined early on in the Win Without War Coalition (opposing the Iraq invasion), two years later, in 2003, only 11 were still active, most having found new issues with which to be involved (Meyer and Corrigall-Brown 2005, 341–42). But if successful in its initial effort, a coalition might expand to take on a more proactive agenda (Hula 1999, 45). For instance, NCRC, established as a desperate effort to save the Community Reinvestment Act from being gutted by conservatives, succeeded, and a decade later now brings together organizations to work on many separate economic justice issues.

The term *coalition* refers to coordinated action involving two or more organizations, while the phrase *coalition support organization* describes a formal organization established to coordinate the work of other organizations that themselves constitute a coalition. *Alliance* describes organizations that work together on a single focused task. *Networks* are those that share information and stimulate action on a focused task. The Transportation Equity Network has in it dozens of organizations that battle to ensure access to transportation for the poor while together lobbying to convince Uncle Sam that money for transportation is spent to fund public transit. *Response networks* link organizations that are willing to act individually but at the same time on specific issues. *Round tables* or *working groups* come about when separate organizations want to share information on a common problem, though are more comfortable working by themselves in solving the issue.

Member organizations in a coalition differ in how active they are willing to be. Core members contribute funds and volunteer staff time. Supporters join in actions and perhaps provide some money. Peripheral members care about the issues but have very little time to spend on a particular issue (Kaufman 2001, 23), and sometimes do little more than sign petitions or allow their names to be used on letter heads (Meyer and Corrigall-Brown 2005, 330).

Increasingly, coalitions are set up as part of a *nested, hierarchical structure*. Local organizations come together in a citywide coalition then the city coalitions unite in a state coalition that in turn joins with other state coalitions in a national organization. A citywide housing coalition might pressure a city to spend CDBG money for housing, the state coalition might fight for a state-funded housing trust fund, while the national organization monitors Congress and HUD and lobbies to preserve Section 8 programs, among many other tasks.

Coalitions are frequently governed by steering committees elected from the membership, usually with each of the most active organizations having a seat. The more progressive coalitions insist that the steering committees be demographically balanced and represent the individual constituencies served. So a housing coalition tries to ensure that not only housing developers are on the board, but so are people who need supportive housing, the homeless, as well as those living in public housing.

Advantages of Being within a Coalition

Coalition actions enable organizations to build on each other's strengths. Just as organizations empower people, coalitions empower organizations.

Creating Power through Numbers

Coalitions expand the number of people involved in an action, as a dozen groups bring 50 members each to a demonstration. When testifying to the legislature, representatives of coalitions brag about the size of their membership. For example, at a congressional hearing, an activist from an economic justice coalition began courteously introducing herself but making sure the Congress people understood that she was speaking for hundreds of organizations throughout the country.

> Chairmen Ney and Bachus, and Ranking Minority Members Waters and Sanders and Representatives Miller and Watt, it is an honor to be here today as the voice for over 600 community organizations from across the country that comprises the National Community Reinvestment Coalition. NCRC is the nation's economic justice trade association dedicated to increasing access to credit and capital for minority and working class families. Our member organizations represent communities from your congressional districts. Organizations such as the Coalition of Neighborhoods in Ohio, the Community Action Partnership of North Alabama, the Community Action Committee of the Lehigh Valley in Pennsylvania, and finally the North Carolina Fair Housing Center where I am the executive director. (www.ncrc.org)

National coalitions have members in many different electoral districts allowing simultaneous contact with representatives by their own constituents on the same issue.

When those in power can strike back, coalitions can buffer individual organizations from retaliation. Housing organizations sometimes have to protest the same banks or government agencies that fund them and appear to be biting the very hand that feeds them. To handle this awkward situation, a coalition director described:

> there is a strategy you're finding more, especially with this [more conservative city] administration in office. People are creating [pause], I tend to call them shell coalitions. And, a shell coalition stands up and say [shouts] "Mayor so and so." And, so you [the mayor] get mad at that coalition and mad at that staff person executive director of the coalition. (Rubin 2000a)

In Chicago, the Neighborhood Capital Budget Group (NCBG) formed a shell coalition of housing advocates, economic developers, community developers, and neighborhood groups to protest that most development funds were going to the central business district and not to neighborhoods. During this campaign, employees of the shell coalition, who were not requesting funds, led the more aggressive actions and were the spokespeople, allowing the housing organizations to avoid offending the people who provided financial support. Shell coalitions protect their members from retaliation by creating a buffer between those who need the money and those who are pressuring government for the funds.

Coalitions can work out a coherent set of demands that supportive politicians appreciate. When a dozen organizations all on the same side of an issue approach a political body, they might have a dozen different proposals and supporters do not know which to support, while opponents will use the differences to squelch them all. But as members of a coalition, the organizations can more readily work out a joint proposal.

Coalitions combine the distinct skills and knowledge of the separate member organizations. For example, a coalition that forced the First National Bank in Chicago to enter into a neighborhood reinvestment agreement was made up of

> Gale Cincotta . . . leader of the original redlining fight . . . Mary Nelson was executive director of Bethel New Life, one of the most productive community development corporations in Chicago struggling to develop low-income housing in . . . one of Chicago's poorest communities. Jim Capraro, executive director of Greater Southwest Development Corporation, was a national pioneer in commercial and industrial revitalization. The combination of perspectives that included community organizing, low-income housing development, and commercial and industrial revitalization was key to shaping an agreement. (Pogge 1992, 137)

In Cleveland, the Environmental Health Watch organization documented pervasive lead poisoning in lower income housing and then, because it was in a coalition with Cleveland Tenants Organization, a recognized player in Cleveland politics, was able to pressure the city council to pass an ordinance to abate lead paint hazards (Scott 2005).

Increasing Power through Information Sharing

Just being in a coalition dramatically expands the information that the member organizations receive since

> coalitions are a lifeline of information, scuttlebutt, and rumors about developments in the policy process. Coalition partners may function as an early warning system for developing issues that a representative had not been following. (Hula 1999, 35)

For instance, the issue of predatory lending became apparent because of information shared by different members of a coalition. Neighborhood groups had noticed increases in foreclosures but did not know why; meanwhile legal and housing services were dealing with individual victims of predatory lending. These organizations were all part of a CRA coalition, chatted at meetings and in doing so were able to better understand what predatory lending was about. They then spun off a separate campaign to end this harmful practice.

Having a Say on Shared but Secondary Issues

Policy issues sometimes get ignored because while they are important to a lot of organizations, they are central to none. For instance, organizations expend much effort to push for budget increases for programs of direct concern to their members. Each recognize that the fight is harder when taxes are cut (and government revenue reduced) but none have the expertise on tax matters. A coalition support organization can develop this expertise and work on problems of concern to organizational members, but not of primary import to any one.

Advantages of the Coalition to the Member Organizations

Involvement in a coalition becomes a source of information of the variety of tactics to use, with in-your-face activists learning from policy shops the power of data, while more sedate types see what direct action can accomplish. Just by sharing experiences, organizations learn that what at first seems to be a narrow problem really is a symptom of a broader underlying structural injustice. For instance, in Milwaukee, after an arrested African American man died under suspicious circumstances, over five dozen groups came together, ranging from neighborhood associations to revolutionary African American organizations (Woliver 1993, 81). Discussions in this coalition, initially set up to obtain justice in this one case, enabled the organizations to better understand and then subsequently address the underlying structural racism that condoned the abuse of police power.

Advantages in Coalitions Guided by a Support Coalition Organization

Some coalitions are able to establish a *support coalition organization* that, as a separate organization itself, can hire staff to focus full time on the shared issues. The staff monitors legislation on the issues, examines data, and establishes ways to quickly notify member organizations that action is needed—a call to a legislator showing up in support for a local demonstration or endorsing a sign-on letter, a letter written by one organization that others in the coalition then endorse. Support coalition organizations sponsor conferences that bring member organizations together to learn new techniques, keep abreast of policy changes, and swap tales on what works and what fails.

Policy activists on the staff of the support organization work full time on the coalition issues. These individuals acquire expertise that enables them to help write legislation, prepare technical reports, work with legislative and bureaucratic staff and testify at hearings, all the while cultivating reporters to better understand the coalition members' perspective.

Assistance provided by a support coalition organization helps individual member organizations fight on local issues. Neighborhood action groups want to pressure banks to provide more mortgages or business loans, and banks will argue that they already do so, at least so far as making the loans is fiscally sound. If the local organization is a member of the NCRC, staff members of the support coalition organization will do the analysis for them to see if the banks are lending appropriately. Support organizations publish *fact books* that provide state or national data and then break it down into smaller geographic units that mesh with the needs of the member organizations. The NLIHC computes a housing wage—how much a worker has to earn to be able to afford a two-bedroom apartment (for each county in the country)—that local housing advocacy groups then use to document local problems.

Finally, a coalition organization can come in to a locality to buffer local members from retribution. In an Illinois city, a local housing group ran up against political opposition from city officials in an effort to preserve affordable housing in a part of the city where politicians wanted to build upscale homes. The local organization, though, was nervous in pushing the matter too far as it was dependent upon the politicians for its funding. Instead it asked a support organization from Chicago to intervene, and with pressure from the coalition organization, the federal spotlight was turned on the issue.

Establishing and Maintaining Coalitions

Establishing and maintaining coalitions can prove difficult. Organizational leaders might not have the time to participate, or rivalries between organization make coordination difficult.

Problems that Make It Hard to Set Up Coalitions and Alliances

Coalitions are difficult to maintain and can dissolve over philosophical differences. For instance, the COFO coalition fell apart as its members differed on whether or not to be engaged in electoral politics (Dittmer 1994, 338–62). Ethnic rivalries that divide neighborhoods can disrupt citywide coalitions when member organizations from different ethnic communities compete to obtain the increasingly limited money available. Social class can divide as occurred in a coalition of organizations working to help the homeless. Organizations dominated by the homeless felt they were treated as second class by their financially better-off allies (Wright 1997, 223). Tensions persist between economic and social production organizations and confrontational groups. A director of a coalition with members from both housing development and neighborhood activist groups described:

> I hear this everywhere I go around the country: God Damn developers. You don't come out when we picket. You don't come out when we have these press conferences. You don't come out and call the mayor a SOB. But when we go out and do it and shake the apple tree and some apples come down. You are the son of the bitches who get 80% of the apples and you didn't do any of the work. Damn it. Which is true. (Rubin 2000a)

Even when coalition members are in fundamental agreement on techniques, troubles can occur on peripheral issues. Jerold Starr details how organizations that each represented progressive causes came together in Pittsburgh to form the Alliance for Progressive Action, primarily focusing on economic matters but ending in a "conflict over whether to include reproductive rights in the statement of principles" (Starr 2001, 110).

Crossing racial boundaries is also difficult and no less so in the formation of coalitions (Betancur and Gills 2000; Leondar-Wright 2005). The problem worsens because of the lack of minority group members in leadership positions in powerful organizations,

> since the more traditional and powerful organizations in multiracial sites tended to have few minorities in professional positions while ethnic minorities staffed many of the less powerful organizations in the targeted neighborhoods. (Kadushin, Lindhold, Dan, et al. 2005, 262)

Ego problems weaken coalitions as each organization seeks to claim credit for the coalition's success. In one case we studied, a coalition of direct action organizations, developers, neighborhood groups, and progressive research shops successfully pushed for legislation against predatory lenders. The coalition, though, barely survived when a leader of a direct action organization in the coalition claimed in the newspaper that her group had accomplished the entire effort on its own.

Finally, maintaining a coalition entails a lot of administrative overhead. Keeping phone and snail and e-mail lists, making calls, setting up conference calls for national meetings, and keeping members informed takes time. One reason that support coalition organizations are set up is to handle such administrative overhead.

Setting Up and Sustaining Coalitions

No sure-fire way exists to effectively set up and sustain coalitions (Alexander 1995, 117–98). Sometimes when leaders of two neighborhood groups know each other well, a quick phone call might be sufficient to form a temporary coalition, for instance, to press the police to eliminate a drug house. Setting up a more permanent coalition is far harder, especially when it tries to unite a coalition of organizations that represent different constituencies. Uniting activists from organizations representing different movements, such as the labor, environmental, women's rights organizations that came together in the protests against the World Trade Organization, could stress a saint (Van Dyke 2003, 246).

Academic studies (summarized in Alexander 1995) indicate that coalitions are just one of many ways of bringing about coordination, so perhaps a formal coalition is not needed. Still, certain conditions do encourage coalition building: Coalitions are more likely to work if member organizations agree on ideology or share similar understandings of why problems occur. Coordination is better if organizations are led by those equally skilled in administration. Similarity in organizational cultures help while differences can be fatal. Organizations that make decisions by consensus are unlikely to easily work with groups that deferentially follow a charismatic leader, no matter how similar the organizations are in their goals. Frequency of routine contact between coalition members increases the likelihood of lasting coordination (Rogers, Whetten, and Associates 1982, 54–94). Coordination is more likely when leaders or professional organizers staffing the group know one another and have shared experiences (Galaskiewicz and Stein 1981).

Having a common enemy encourages coalition building as "alliances are most likely to form in response to political threats . . . and the prospects of legislative defeats" (Meyer and Corrigall-Brown 2005, 332) while "threats may be an important mobilizing condition" (Van Dyke 2003, 244) as those that have brought together unions and environmental groups learned (Rose 2000; 2004). Having powerful enemies, for example in the form of an antagonistic federal administration, inspires cross-movement coalition action (Van Dyke 2003, 244). Historically ideological competition within the women's movement has made it hard to maintain long-term coalitions (Roth 2004; Ryan 1992), but when core issues are at stake—the right to abortion, for instance—groups do come together. Nationally, in the early nineties, the Community Reinvestment Act was under severe threat, leading housing developers and their rival social change organizations to join and form the National Community Reinvestment Coalition. In Illinois, Chicago housing organizations and those downstate rivaled one another, yet when funding for housing was threatened overall, the rival organizations set up the State Housing Action Coalition, now Housing Action Illinois.

Coalitions emerge when activists from different organizations meet one another, especially in informal, neutral settings. Interpersonal compatibility counts as

> organizers approached the task [of coalition building] more from an interpersonal than an ideological perspective. Rather than seeking to build coalitions around issues that share certain principles or a common target, these organizers emphasized recruiting organizers who were practical and easy to work with . . . focus[ing] their strategy on long-term base building in which trust slowly was earned by helping with others' actions. (Starr 2001, 118)

Opportunities to meet at conferences, or just hang out together and share experiences (Bickel 2001; Kadushin, Lindhold, Dan, et al. 2005) help build a base for future coalition work. Before forming coalitions to battle against sweatshops, labor and community activists meet at Workers Centers (Tait 2005, 151) while in the homeless movement, soup kitchens become the meeting place for people from a diverse array of groups who formed the personal linkages that later facilitated formal cooperation (Wright 1997, 234). As activists move from job to job they end up in new networks that help facilitate subsequent coalition building (Hula 1999, 55).

Coalitions emerge when hosting organizations, themselves often a support organization, convene a meeting to discuss a specific issue and invite activists from a variety of organizations concerned about that issue to attend. For example, grant money funneled through the Surface Transportation Project paid for meetings that the Center for Community Change sponsored that resulted in the Transportation Equity Network coming into being. In an effort to push for a national housing trust fund, the NLIHC invited many different organizations to meet, ranging from moderate builders to radical social change organizations. At these early meetings, time was spent quibbling about small details, each from the separate organization's own agendas, on formulas for spending the proposed funds and little progress was made. Finally, attendees realized that almost any type of trust fund would be helpful and a coalition came into being focused on obtaining new federal money for housing without worrying about the details.

Cutting the Issue.   If issues are framed properly, even organizations that have seemingly contradictory goals can discover a common purpose. For example, those trying to create new blue-collar jobs have often been at loggerheads with environmentalists, whose push for a cleaner environment appears to reduce industries' ability to compete in an international market. Environmentalists reframed the issue as one of battling for the health of workers, especially those in minority communities, and were able to unite blue-collar neighborhood organizations with environmental groups in economic justice coalitions.

In general, to set up a coalition, organizers work to cut an issue in ways that encourage cooperation.

> Take the issue of public transportation. Senior citizen groups could support it because most seniors either don't drive or don't have the income to own cars . . . Unions might support it because it would mean additional jobs in construction and in operating an improved mass transit system. Women's organizations might support it if there were particular guarantees written into the program to assure safety at night . . . Minority organizations might support a plan which assured service between their neighborhoods and places where jobs were available. (Kahn 1982, 279)

Careful framing is a must in coalitions among multicultural constituencies. As a case in point, organizers had real difficulty in bridging the cultural gaps that divided organizations made up of members from different Southeast Asian countries. But activists saw a common framing in terms of the oppression of women since "the needs and constraints of most refugee women . . . were so similar that the bonds of commonality were firmly established and cultural distinctions seemed slight" (Bays 1998, 313). Similarly, the economic problems that divided Black from Hispanic neighborhoods in Oakland initially prevented the formation of a multicultural coalition until activists discovered that children in all the neighborhoods were being poisoned through lead-based paint and that health officials were ignoring the problem.

Campaigns Orchestrated by Support Coalition Organizations

Support coalition organizations themselves are able to coordinate campaigns or quickly put together *meta-coalitions*, coalitions of coalitions that then act on the issue. Recognizing the harm that a major tax cut would have on social programs, the Fair Taxes for All Coalition, a meta-coalition, brought together over one hundred members ranging from activist ACORN, many churches, labor, identity organizations, and economic justice groups among others.

Support coalitions are able to sustain long-run campaigns. In Illinois, the Monsignor Egan Campaign for Payday Loan Reform brought together hundreds of organizations ranging from the AARP, to CDCs, religious groups, some governmental agencies, and neighborhood organizations to orchestrate a five-year effort that led to state laws against the most rapacious aspects of payday lending. Over several decades, the Chicago Rehab Network, a citywide coalition organization that united housing activists, neighborhood groups, and CDCs, has successfully changed local laws to reduce the tax burden on affordable apartments while instituting mandatory inclusionary housing in city areas that are gentrifying. Similar coalition work at the state level, coordinated by Housing Action Illinois, brought about a dedicated funding source to support low income rental housing.

Illustrative Campaigns

To better understand how coalition support organizations orchestrate campaigns let us examine several examples and then extract principles that can guide future efforts.

Chicago CRA Coalition: Sustaining CRA Agreements (paraphrased from Bush and Immergluck 2003, 157–61). In response to a brief campaign by activist organizations in the early 1980s three major local Chicago banks agreed to a community reinvestment agreement. Over the years, the social change organizations who brought about this agreement joined with others to set up the Chicago CRA coalition that in the nineties had over one hundred local members. Using data supplied by the Woodstock Institute, a policy shop and the coordinator of the coalition, the group carefully monitored bank mergers to make sure that reinvestment agreements were still carried out by the successor and larger banks.

For the most part the coalition was successful. With the research shop, the Woodstock Coalition, as an active member, the coalition readily monitored whether or not the banks were living up to their agreements. Of equal import, banks were not able to selectively buy off coalition members because of the trust members had for one another due to their continuing work in the coalition. In particular,

> coalition members agreed that during a bank negotiation . . . they were not permitted to seek individual treatment for their own organizations. This prevented the divisive practice of coalition members seeking individual agreements from the bank. (Bush and Immergluck 2003, 161)

Los Angeles Housing Trust Fund Campaign (paraphrased from Breidenbach 2002) In 1998 activists in the Southern California Association of Non-Profit Housing (SCANPH), a regional housing coalition mostly made up of CDCs, agreed that a housing trust fund was a necessity in expensive Los Angeles. To bring this about the coalition expanded its membership to bring in labor, especially poor people's unions such as the SEIU, religious leaders, and tenant organizations and then later on organizations from the environmental, disabilities, immigrant, and economic justice movement. To get the tenants organizations aboard required changing the overall goal slightly as the tenants wanted trust fund money to be used for rent assistance while the CDCs were primarily concerned with funds for housing production. The campaign set as its target a $100 million fund, but left it open to the politicians on how the money was to be raised.

Over the multiyear campaign, tactics varied from confrontations, public lobbying, and political pressure during an election campaign to insider negotiations once a supportive candidate had won office. Media attention was garnered through demonstrations, when for example ACORN organized a rally with people marching and wearing T-shirts demanding the $100 million fund. In each year the campaign tied its effort to the release of the national report *Out of Reach* that dramatically documented L.A.'s affordability crisis. Next, to make sure the problem was understood, the coalition arranged tours for political candidates joined by religious leaders to visit slum housing and then compare what they saw to the quality, affordable housing built by nonprofits. The winning candidate for mayor, James Hahn, included the trust fund as one of his major priorities.

Once supporters were in office, the coalition approached both the mayor and the council to remind them of their promised support. ACORN led a march in support of affordable housing, while tenants' organization held Christmastime caroling sessions, singing songs that combined Christmas tunes with lyrics supportive of affordable housing. Other organizations lobbied privately and the mayor and council kept the promise, and three years after the campaign started the fund was on the books. Unfortunately, a few years later it appeared that Mayor Hahn was not fully keeping his word, proposing in his budget only a third of the promised amount, and then a large part of that being transferred money from HUD rather than new funds (Dreier 2005).

Ohio Trust Fund Campaign   (www.cohhio.org/newsletters/newsletters99/articles May.html). In 2001, the Coalition on Homelessness and Housing in Ohio, convinced the Ohio State legislature to set up a permanent, dedicated form of funding for a statewide affordable housing trust fund. The next effort was to find the money to put in the trust fund, with the coalition suggesting using fees on real estate transfers.

In this campaign, the coalition sought to carefully frame the issue to show that trust fund money that had been sporadically allocated in the past had been efficiently used throughout the state; now what was required was a stable source of funds. To get out this message, the coalition hired a Republican media adviser to handle the press campaign, focusing on swing legislative districts. In these districts, local housing organizations approached the editorial boards of the local media to get them on board, while at the same time getting testimonials sent to legislators from the local business community about successful projects. Finally, during conventions sponsored by COHHIO in the state capitol, advocates from all over the state descended on their representatives to argue face-to-face on the need for the stable funding source and were victorious. From beginning to end, this effort took but a year.

Illinois Anti-Predatory Lending Battle   (paraphrased from Bush and Immergluck 2003, 161–66 supplemented with original research). Predatory lenders charge outrageous interest rates or attach exorbitant fees onto mortgages. Coalitions in several states have battled these horrible practices with different degrees of success. In Illinois, activists who learned of these problems came together originally because they had already been working as part of the broader CRA Coalition. The coalition convinced the Federal Reserve Bank in Chicago to set up a task force consisting of

Woodstock, the Fair Housing Leadership Council, Chicago (activist) Neighborhood Housing Services, a legal assistance agency, and the National Technical Information Service that investigated the problem and then issued a technical report that called for strong legislation against predatory redlining. Opposition came about from the powerful trade association for the financial services industry that first opposed any changes and then suggested a bill that according to a Woodstock analysis would do little to solve the problem.

Woodstock notified several neighborhood organizations with whom it had worked to contact their legislators to oppose the weak regulations and they were withdrawn. The governor was personally persuaded to support a stronger proposal, regulations were put out, but the banking trade association once again tried to sabotage them. In response, Woodstock encouraged 120 groups—neighborhood organizations, religious, and even governmental groups—to write in letters of support. Task force members also met with the editorial boards of major papers that ended up endorsing the stronger regulations. Coalition activists contacted the three major banks in Chicago that had worked harmoniously with the CRA coalition over the years and these banks agreed, after certain minor technical concessions were made, to support the task force's ideas for stronger regulations. Finally, neighborhood organizations lobbied their representatives, with one—the Southwest Organization Project—orchestrating a campaign to send 10,000 postcards to their representative, the powerful Speaker of the House, who reversed his position and ended up supporting the stronger regulations that were then adopted.

National Coalition Efforts Supporting CRA and Economic Justice: NCRC. National coalitions, especially those coordinated by permanently staffed coalition support organizations, are almost always involved in campaigns. Two different approaches are seen in the actions of the National Community Reinvestment Coalition (NCRC) and, in the next section, the National Low Income Housing Coalition (NLIHC).

In the late 1980s opponents of the Community Reinvestment Act worked to gut this legislation. In response, major Washington, D.C.-based organizations got together and established the NCRC, a coalition organization whose initial task was to preserve CRA (Immergluck 2004, 174). NCRC was able to save CRA and afterward decided to set up a permanent organization to protect CRA and work for economic justice. Today, NCRC is a 500-plus-member organization with participants varying from housing developers to militant local action organizations.

Much of what NCRC does is help individual members learn about bank mergers, determine whether or not to oppose them, and if so, help prepare the data and testimonies presented to the regulators. In doing so, NCRC coordinates local organizations from different states to testify on mergers that nowadays spread nationally. Rarely are mergers prevented, but often, as part of the pressure, banks agree to CRA agreements that do benefit poor communities.

Much of NCRC's effort is defensive. When conservative opponents of CRA, such as Senator Gramm, argued that CRA was mainly a way of shaking banks down for money for nonprofits, NCRC provided data showing that only a minuscule percentage of money from CRA agreements went to fund nonprofits; the rest was for neighborhood investments (Immergluck 2004, 203). During the Bush administration conservative appointees to bank regulating agencies tried to seriously weaken CRA, loosening the rules that banks have to follow and virtually exempting smaller banks. NCRC has coordinated efforts to slow down this weakening of CRA.

NCRC and its members are also actively involved in economic justice issues, combating at the state and local level predatory lending and payday lending scams. Banks and some national regulators have claimed that states have no right to issue such laws and that they should be a federal prerogative. These banks push for federal pre-emption to replace stronger local laws with weaker federal regulations. NCRC and its members are involved in this ongoing battle opposing pre-emption or, that failing, ensuring that federal laws do have some teeth.

In its campaigns, NCRC follows a variety of complementary tactics. Many matters are primarily local, affecting only a handful of members. In these cases NCRC provides backup data while helping its members from different states coordinate their efforts against the national banks. NCRC makes available as a resource the public interest lawyers who are board members of NCRC who share their vast knowledge of the intricacies of banks with member organizations. A third approach is using phone or e-mail alerts to encourage NCRC members to show up at public hearings to offer testimony on bank mergers. This effort is supplemented by asking members to write commentaries to regulatory commissions, made easier by providing form letters on-line. NCRC will use its contacts with the staff of supportive legislators, whom NCRC officials visit regularly, to itself be invited to testify to Congress. When time is pressing the CEO of NCRC will himself testify, but when sufficient time is available, NCRC will fly in leaders of member organizations to share their experiences with elected officials.

As issues emerge in Washington, D.C., NCRC schedules conference calls among the policy committee members (calls that are open to all NCRC members) during which up-to-date news is shared and tactics planned. The content of the calls vary from discussing the minutiae of regulatory wording—which clauses to fight, which to accept—on up to broad strategic issues of whether or not to use direct actions or to rely mainly on more sedate lobbying. Much time at the annual conference is also spent on discussing policy issues as well as the necessary political background. The highlight of the national conference is a lobbying day during which NCRC members converge on offices of their elected officials, lobby, and then report back to the entire group, oftentimes bringing elected officials in to offer their support. For those organizations less experienced in Hill lobbying, NCRC staff will help with the logistics or even accompany members to the legislative offices.

National Coalition Efforts in Support of Affordable Housing.   The National Low Income Housing Coalition is a big-tent organization with members and the board ranging from militant activist organizations to churches, homeless advocates, and technical assistance organizations, to suit-and-tie national intermediaries. Beginning as a small one-person advocacy organization, the Coalition initially took on the task of circulating information to its members on changes in housing policy and over the years has grown to become a leading national advocate for housing matters. Technically the NLIHC is a coalition of state coalitions.

Like NCRC, NLIHC is engaged in a wide variety of issues. When HUD programs are threatened with cutbacks, NLIHC staff appear on the Hill, send out action alerts to its national membership, and on longer running issues orchestrate lobbying days to speak for the issues. NLIHC has become part of several meta-coalitions, one battling the large tax cuts that eventually will gut social programs, the other working to protect funding for Section 8 housing, while at the same time clearing up some of the unnecessary bureaucratic burdens associated with the program.

In response to the very unfavorable climate in the Bush administration for housing, the NLIHC has begun to act more aggressively. For instance, by chance in 2005, a day before NLIHC's national conference, HUD issued regulations that were extremely harmful to low-income public housing tenants. With full concurrence from its big-tent board, NLIHC staff asked the professional organizers on its board to orchestrate a full fledged march around the HUD building during the convention itself.

The major ongoing project of NLIHC is to create a National Housing Trust Fund as a source of federal money to fund construction of affordable homes and apartments for low- and very low-income individuals. The idea emerged several years ago after an informal get together of leaders of national groups, each of which had been involved in local campaigns to set up trust funds. A steering committee was set up, but initial progress was slow as the participating organizations differed in how any funds should be targeted and in the balance between rental and home ownership programs. As groups realized that any new program would be an improvement, the differences were glossed over and all joined in the larger effort to support any addition to the supply of dedicated money for affordable housing.

To administer what was anticipated to be a multiyear effort, a coordinating structure was put in place. Some of the organizations in the meta-coalition volunteered staff time and eventually NLIHC, using grant money, hired organizers to work on the matter full time. A policy group of Washington, D.C. organizations in the campaign meet frequently to discuss tactics, while a field group orchestrates lobbying from hundreds of local organizations. Various drafts of possible proposals were prepared by NLIHC, until Rep. Bernie Sanders of Vermont, who had set up a Housing Trust Fund when he was a city mayor, prepared a formal bill. During 2004, the campaign was able to persuade a near majority of the house to become co-sponsors of the bill but conservative opposition tied it up in committee and the matter died.

In 2005, an affordable housing provision was added to a proposed bill to reform Fannie Mae and Freddie Mac, government-sponsored enterprises that buy mortgages. The campaign supported this provision as a possible source of funding for affordable housing, but made it clear it would still lobby for the NHTF. Conservatives attempted to sabotage the provision in the GSE bill by adding an amendment that any organization that received funds could not do voter registration or be involved with any organization that did voter registration. The issue is pending.

The primary tactic of the NLIHC has been to build on nonstop grassroots lobbying that leads to constituent visits to congressional offices during the convention.

With a massive grassroots effort, the campaign has solicited endorsements from local organizations and public officials and as we write an incredible 5,000-plus housing, social service, religious, social change, and governmental organizations have signed on. The endorsements are broken down by legislative district and when NLIHC staff or members lobby on the Hill, they present to the representatives names of their own constituents who supported the bill. As we write, the campaign continues.

Advantages of Campaigns Orchestrated by Support Coalitions

Temporary, informal coalitions and alliances accomplish much and are to be encouraged. But longer term efforts are required since the opposition, whether big business, or an unresponsive government, has a permanence that can outlast transient coalitions.

To effectively fight for structural change, a coalition support organization is a virtual must. Coalition support organizations provide technical backup material. At the national level, NLHIC's *Out of Reach* documents data on housing costs in each metropolitan area (and is easily accessible on the web) and provides a talking piece for state and city housing advocacy groups as they fight for housing. The Chicago Rehab Coalition's *Affordable Housing Fact Book* provides similar data for metro Chicago, while its publications on housing preservation have enabled local organizations to save rental property from conversion to expensive condominiums. NCRC releases statistical data on banks increasing the bargaining power of the local member organizations that deal with the financial institutions, while providing summary reports on how well or poorly different financial institutions are meeting their reinvestment obligations. Staff of support coalitions closely monitor legislative bills and ferret out nearly hidden bureaucratic actions that could hurt the poor and then through national action initiate efforts to combat harmful changes.

Because of their permanence, support coalition organizations can simultaneously deal with firefighting—battling problems that emerge suddenly—while at the same time keeping an eye on the ball on the longer term issues. Of equal import, these organizations are able to see the broader social and political context in which issues are embedded—linking, for instance, the withdrawal of funds from human needs, housing, and redevelopment to the tax cuts for the rich. Larger support coalition organizations also provide an institutional memory, knowing for example how cuts to CDBG or Section 8 or food stamps were handled in years past, or being attuned to the array of tricks that opponents use.

Conclusion

Coalitions expand power and capacity, increasing the numbers involved and bringing together organizations with complementary perspectives and skills. While setting up and maintaining coalitions can prove troublesome, activists have little choice but to do so if they are to succeed in battles against entrenched power and wealth.

In the past, most coalitions were one-time groupings that focused on a single problem and then disappeared when the issue was resolved. Today support coalition organizations have become a tool to focus on issues over a sustained time, while providing backup resources that dramatically expand the capacity of member organizations to carry on the fight.

PART SIX

Implementing Change through the Community Economic Development and Social Production Approach

Social mobilization efforts are about changing the actions of government and business. In contrast, economic and social production organizations themselves directly bring about improvement by providing housing, creating employment, or enabling people to more readily access social and health services.

In Chapter 20 we discuss the philosophy of community economic and social production (ESP) work, provide examples of the wide variety of activities undertaken, and explore some of the problems that occur. Success in economic and social production work requires an array of managerial skills that are introduced in Chapter 21.

CHAPTER

20

An Introduction to the Community Economic and Social Production Model[1]

Changes in both the national and world economy have left poor people and poor neighborhoods in increasingly worst straits, impacting especially hard people of color (Leondar-Wright, Lui, Mota, et al. 2005). To battle economic decline, activists set up community-based economic and social production (CESP) organizations that follow a

> holistic approach we term humane capitalism [that] begins by redirecting conventional development to benefit poor neighborhoods. . . . Humane capitalism also can be accomplished through innovative techniques . . . Programs such as Individual Development Accounts . . . help families accumulate assets . . . while land trusts and cooperatives preserve and enhance community assets. Business incubators help would-be entrepreneurs find the economic and social resources to enter the market economy. Social service efforts improve the human capital needed for economic change . . . Advocacy groups work to bring about a humane capitalism through pressuring government to support set-aside jobs for the poor, fund guaranteed loan programs for community enterprises, redirect capital budgets for infrastructure repairs to poor communities, and provide contracts to firms that guarantee "living wages." (Rubin and Sherraden 2005, 475–76).

Community economic and social production organizations (CESPOs) undertake a wide variety of tasks. Some offer shelter to battered women, comfort the dying and their families in hospices, and partner with the police to combat neighborhood crime; others build, rent, or sell quality housing at reasonable cost. CESPOs battle drug addiction and gangs, set up health care clinics, and join in battles to improve school quality. They are involved in programs to reintegrate those released from prison into neighborhoods and work with those trying to reconstruct their lives after Hurricane Katrina. ESP organizations help welfare recipients learn skills and find jobs (Harrison and Weiss 1998). Individual Development Accounts help individuals

[1]Some material in this chapter has been modified from Rubin and Sherraden, 2005.

save for housing, education, or start-up businesses (Sherraden, Johnson, Clancy, et al. 2000); funding for micro-enterprises assists lower-income entrepreneurs (Sherraden, Sanders, and Sherraden 2004); worker centers bring together contingent laborers to battle for better job conditions (Tait 2005).

Economic and social production organizations work to recreate both the physical and social fabric of communities. CDCs build affordable homes and encourage commercial and business development. Community Development Finance Institutions provide capital to poor neighborhoods, cooperatives enable individuals to control their own housing, while municipal enterprises reduce the costs of utilities and Internet access (Aspen Institute 2005). CESP organizations pressure government to support locally owned firms, rather than subsidizing the Wal-Marts that destroy local stores (www.goodjobsfirst.org/). Affordable health care is made available in the poorest communities, while through sponsoring art and cultural events, CESP organizations strengthen community identity (Gunn 2004). When racial tension rears its ugly head, CESPOs teach tolerance and understanding.

CESPOs help coordinate efforts to rebuild whole neighborhoods, such as has taken place in large parts of the South Bronx in New York (Rooney 1995; Sahd 2004); or themselves create housing, jobs, and new stores as occurred in the deteriorated Dudley Street neighborhood in Boston (Medoff and Sklar 1994; Von Hoffman 2003); or in the declining neighborhoods in southwest Chicago (Capraro 2004).

Those involved in social production recognize that physical redevelopment, social services, and direct action are means to empower. People living in housing cooperatives are more socially and politically active than those renting homes (Briggs, Mueller with Mercer Sullivan 1997). Empowerment comes as hope is rekindled as new projects symbolize in a dramatic way the rebirth of a neighborhood (Von Hoffman 2003, 94). CESPOs catalyze the human spirit: After a community development organization built a mall in the impoverished Liberty City area of Miami, participants explained:

> "There is a real sense of pride in what has happened here," says Otis Pitts, the ex-cop who is Tacolcy's executive director. "It's not like people just coming to shop in a store. It's like they're coming to something that is a vital part of the community." Says a local merchant . . . "We don't just look good, we are good. Now everybody is committed to staying in the neighborhood. Why leave now? We sweated out the worst. Ain't nothing to do but look forward now." (Peirce and Steinbach 1987, 37)

Making visible investments in blocks that commercial businesses have abandoned counters the image of defeat. A developmental activist explained that a small mall built in a community that lacked shopping was as much about creating pride as it was about providing stores. This mall became a focus of pride because it was controlled by African Americans. People have something that they can say, "This is ours."

Economic and social production organizations provide material goods but in ways that increase **social equity** as well as **personal empowerment** by helping individuals gain dignity and pride. Dignity comes from holding a productive job that has a future, doing skilled work, and creating useful and healthful products. Pride increases as people own their own homes, perhaps through sweat-equity contributions in which their own labor builds the place in which they will dwell. As expressed by the Corporation for Economic Development, a support organization for CESPOs, the

> goal is to create a dynamic and inclusive economy where everyone has the opportunity to live in hope and with dignity. This means the opportunity to earn a family wage, run a business, own a home, or save for the future. An inclusive economy does not accept growing disparities in income and wealth. It . . . seeks not only to meet the demands of Wall Street, but also to promote equity and sustainability on Main Street. (CFED 1999, 7)

Community economic and social production organizations span the world of nonprofits, government, and the for-profit sector. But unlike for-profit firms, community economic and social production organizations face a *double-bottom line*. CESPOs must break even financially or else they go belly up. Yet, they are also about a social mission that has a financial cost—not just building homes, but building homes for lower income working people, or providing assisted housing for those with special needs, or not only sheltering the homeless but working to find out why they are unhoused and then trying to solve these problems. CESP projects, at one and the same time, contain a conventional cost that is market driven (building a home, or providing goods or service) and a social cost (helping lower income people understand home ownership or working to re-integrate those released from prison into the community or responding to cultural concerns).

As a social service provider CESPOs also work with government—providing assistance to those in need, doing so with public funds, and as such having to follow rules set up by the public sector (Salamon 1995; Smith and Lipsky 1993). In capital-intense projects—affordable housing programs, or refurbishing neighborhood shopping—CESPOs partner with the public sector for the grants required to lower costs. Yet at the same time CESPOs can find themselves opposing government policies—demanding that sprawl be stopped or that subsidies to Fortune 500 firms cease—or being part of an activist coalition pressuring a city to adopt a living wage or withdraw its funds from banks that discriminate against the poor.

Guiding Principles for Community Economic and Social Production Work[2]

While providing similar products to business, government, or charities, community economic and social production organizations do much more since they are "inspired by a *moral mission* to help the poor by fighting systemic economic injustice, recogniz-

---

[2]Expanded from Rubin & Sherraden (Rubin and Sherraden 2005, 476–77).

ing that just as poverty comes about through human neglect, intervention by human agency can reverse the process" (Rubin and Sherraden 2005, 476). ESP organizations are *mission driven*, that is, doing what they do because it is right, not simply to provide a profit. To stay in business, a CESP-sponsored supermarket must run in the black, but instead of looking for the most profitable site, the store is built in a neighborhood that firms have abandoned and in addition is set up to provide both training and employment to community members. Social production organizations that manage affordable housing also face social concerns that for-profit owners avoid:

> We don't see the point in developing affordable housing and then evicting somebody the first day they're past due on rent because they become unemployed. I mean we want to work with them to get a job and get their family back together . . . We don't see the point of doing affordable housing and then letting the gangs paint graffiti all over. . . . We want to rent to large families. It's more expensive to rent to large families. The kids tear the place up but that's why large families can't get apartments in this neighborhood so because they can't we are going to. (interview with Herbert Rubin)

Bottom line profits are lower because projects are about accomplishing a social mission.

Economic and social production organizations are part of a *holistic effort* at renewal. A community arts fair is about fun and sociability, but it also provides an opportunity for those from different ethnic groups to admire each other's talents. Commercial, housing, and job programs must be coordinated as a developmental activist told us, "there aren't going to be any bakeries here if there is no money to afford jelly rolls" (Rubin 1994). While it might be cheaper to build a home on a vacant lot, a CESPO will buy and refurbish a building that had been a dope house to improve the neighborhood. CESP organizations recognize that what is being repaired is an entire neighborhood (Von Hoffman 2003).

CESPOs recognize that social problems—dysfunctional families, or simply being in a one-parent household—aggravate job situations, perhaps by making it harder to get to work on time. Providing jobs is not enough if daycare is unavailable, or training individuals for work is no use if there is no public transportation to get to places of employment. A director of a project to teach women how to run their own businesses reported to us that "you pay as much attention to developing the business owner as you are paying to developing the business," for example, by teaching people how to maintain checking accounts. He continued stating that "our biggest success has been that we have been able to change people's attitude about themselves . . . Our biggest measure of success is how have we empowered people so they can take control" (interview with Herbert Rubin). *Community Development Corporations* (CDCs) are about empowering people. The founder of the Christian Community Development Association wrote

> The motto of community development in the 1960s could have been this: "Give people a fish and they'll eat for a day." The 1970s motto could have been: "Teach people to fish and they'll eat for a lifetime." . . . The 1990s (and beyond) approach to development needs to ask the question: "Who owns the pond?" (Perkins 1993, 119)

The answer given by CDCs is that it should either be the poor themselves or organizations responsive to the communities "for as a development activist argued 'if you own your own house, you are empowered' " (Rubin 2000a, 146).

Economic and social production work is about *empowering individuals and communities* by building capacity. Housing individuals in new homes but ignoring gang problems that trap people in these homes accomplishes little. Bethel, a CDC in Chicago, set up social service agencies in apartments it built and then taught community members to become service providers (Barry 1989). The New Communities Corporation in Newark constructed daycare centers for the children of those enrolled in job training programs, many of whom had been homeless and were now housed in apartments owned by the CDC. In an ethnically mixed neighborhood, a CDC turned an abandoned supermarket into a Mercado, providing space for low-income people to set up stalls and sell needed goods. When families have stable housing, either owning their own homes, or living in affordable rental properties, they are less likely to move and disrupt their children's education while their own self-esteem increases (Rohe and Stegman 1994a, b; Scanlon 1998).

Economic and social production organizations work to *preserve and expand financial and social assets* that help individuals escape from cycles of poverty. Assets involve knowledge that people have, capital for investment, and access to technical experts, as well as systems of peer-to-peer communication that enable people to learn from one another. A house is an asset that allows an individual to borrow money for education or to start up a business. Education is a personal asset while local quality schools increase community capacity. Profits become assets if they remain in the community as one developmental activist described:

> What we have is a community that exports more money than it imports. Part of what we are trying to do is to change that balance of payments. Over 53% of the community is rental despite being mostly single family. On Friday people export rent checks . . . . And, when people have to go outside of the community to buy goods and services which are no longer here that's gone in terms of exporting. What we really are trying to do over time is to change the balance of payments, to try to create wealth here in this community by importing dollars not exporting them. (Rubin 2000a)

A study in Miami showed that "it has been estimated that each $1,000 of goods or services sold . . . in the Cuban community generates $1,630 in total community earnings; the comparative figure in the Black community is only $1,140" (Bendick and Egan 1989).

Economic and social production organizations choose projects that *catalyze* other efforts. For instance, building new homes and the establishment of homeowner or tenants' associations increases voter turnout and helps reduce crime. Small grants that help homeowners improve property encourage others in the neighborhood to do the same. Rather than look for the least expensive site in a neighborhood, some CDCs will choose to refurbish the most derelict property to encourage others to improve less damaged sites.

As contract providers of social services, or owners or developers of property, economic and social production organizations understand bottom-lines, incorporation, and other appurtenances of capitalistic society. But these social change organizations *recognize that alternative non-capitalistic forms of organization with different value systems are also possible* and that economic projects should be evaluated not only in how much profit they earn but in terms of the social needs met. Better housing in a poor community is worth more than one in a wealthier area because the former helps alleviate a social problem. Municipal ownership can protect people from the decisions made by large absent companies and perhaps mitigate some of the effects of globalism. CESP organizations, while helping individuals set up profit making firms, promote both collective ownership and collective responsibility in ways "that improve the quality of life for those involved" (DeFilippis 2004, 35) and bring into question the dog-eat-dog competition of capitalism.

Organizational Forms and Community Economic and Social Production Work

Community-based economic and social production organizations often look and act much like conventional social service agencies or for-profit businesses. The PathMark Supermarket, in the poorest area of Newark, NJ, is set up as a partnership between a CDC and the supermarket chain is managed as a for-profit firm, while a nonprofit housing assistance agency appears very much the same as its government counterpart.

But to accomplish their tasks, many CESPOs take on organizational forms that differ from those found elsewhere in the mainstream economy. To begin, CDCs are a hybrid that structurally spans the for-profit and nonprofit worlds. CDCs harness the power and skills of capitalism to make investments in housing community businesses, while providing economic opportunities in neighborhoods in need. Yet, they incorporate as nonprofit 501(c)3s and as such are eligible to obtain grants from foundations and government. The Boards of CDCs are usually made up of community members and those CDCs that receive federal housing money must have boards with heavy representation from lower income community members. An estimated 4,600 CDCs are in place (National Congress for Community Economic Development 2006, 4).

CDCs focus on capital-intensive, physical development projects, such as housing, business incubators, or commercial strips, and can become stockholders or partners in commercial ventures, invest capital in projects, acquire debt, and maintain earnings from profits, so long as the earnings are used for community betterment. CDCs often partner with for-profit organizations in projects and because the nonprofit is a partial owner, foundations or government are willing to help pay for some project costs. CDCs do invest their own capital in projects and are at financial risk if the project does not pay off.

Other hybrid CESPOs are found. For example, *Community Development Financial Institutions* (CDFIs)—one of over 1,500 organizations—are set up to invest in communities of need. These community-focused financial institutions can receive federally insured deposits, issue mortgages and commercial loans, and today manage assets of over $14 billion (Aspen Institute 2005, 42–45). But unlike conventional banks, the mission of a development bank is to rebuild poor communities to benefit people already living there. The best-known development bank is the South Shore Bank that has helped renew parts of South Chicago. A *credit union*, a customer owned, nonprofit, savings and investment institution is a type of CDFI, as are various *community loan funds*, set up to funnel investment capital into community renewal projects, often by loaning to CDCs. Less common are Community Development Venture Capital groups that "promote use of the tools of venture capital to create jobs, entrepreneurial capacity and wealth to advance the livelihoods of low-income people and the economies of distressed communities" (www.cdvca.org/).

Another organizational type that spans the for-profit and nonprofit world is a *cooperative*. In *housing cooperatives*, tenants are the owners in common rather than a private landlord. In *producer* and *consumer cooperatives* workers control the business, rather than absentee stockholders. In most cooperatives, policy is set by an elected board. Workers in consumer cooperatives can accumulate ownership shares, depending on their work efforts and seniority, but only receive the cash value of these shares when they retire or leave the cooperative and cannot sell them before. In a cooperative, a worker or tenant owner has only one vote, regardless of the number of shares he or she owns. In cooperatives, human effort is the crucial investment; capital is a means for accomplishing collective goals, not the controlling element.

Some states allow the formation of *limited equity housing cooperatives* in which lower income people can invest a nominal down payment and then pay monthly charges that are enough to cover the mortgage and operating expenses for the cooperative, but do so as owners. The rest of the money for the down payment is often subsidized by charitable sources, church investments, or government. When people move, they get back their down payment (plus interest) but do not make a profit, even if the value of the building has increased. That way the building remains affordable for others. Today over 400,000 individuals are housed this way (DeFilippis 2004, 90).

Mutual Housing Associations are legal entities in which individuals own an organization that in turn owns housing, in which the individuals often live. A cooperative is a form of MHA, but MHAs can be larger scale corporations that build cooperatives or other forms of affordable housing. MHAs encourage democratic participation in both establishing and managing affordable housing.

CESPOs encourage alternative forms of ownership. In an *Employee Stock Ownership Plan* workers buy or earn stock in a for-profit firm that is managed to preserve worker jobs and to make sure that firms do not relocate out of their communities. In a *land trust*, ownership of the land under homes is separated from the ownership of the houses (www.iceclt.org) in ways meant to preserve affordability. A nonprofit owns the land that is leased to homeowners; when owners move they can profit from any improvement made, sometimes by a nominal inflation factor but other than that the cost of housing remains the same for future, lower-income homeowners. A land trust is governed by a board consisting of equal membership of the homeowners, nonresident community members, and public officials (DeFilippis 2004, 93). At present, there are 112 community land trusts underlying almost 6,000 homes (Aspen Institute 2005, 69).

Finally, some CESPs set up economic development *networks or coalitions* to accomplish their work. For instance, *Community Building Initiatives* are orchestrated by network organizations that coordinate efforts of a wide variety of advocacy, social production, neighborhood, and identity organizations, as well as government agencies, all working to renew one community (Stone 1996; Wright 1998).

Illustrations of Community Economic and Social Production Work

In this section we describe a variety of work done by economic and social production organizations, acting as

1. Advocates for progressive programs that build economic and social capacity
2. Neighborhood guardians
3. Providers of social and economic services
4. Housing developers
5. Economic developers
6. Guiding community building and preservation efforts

The categories blur into one another and there is no fixed rule on what form of CESP organization undertakes which actions.

Advocates for Progressive Programs that Expand Economic and Social Capacity

Economic and social production organizations act as advocates to pressure government to improve the economic well-being of the poor and poor communities. One approach is to encourage government to mandate local programs in which companies that receive contracts from city hall use local firms as suppliers (Williamson, Imbroscio, and Alperovitz 2003). In many cities, older working class factories are torn down, costing poorer people jobs, to provide space for gentrified housing. CESPOs pressure government to rezone cities in ways that preserve these manufacturing districts (Rubin 2000a). Other advocacy is in support of transit-oriented development (TODs) on which cities work with CESPOs to create stores and homes around newly upgraded transit stations.

Municipalities can be encouraged to own enterprises, for instance utilities—gas, electric, some phone, and increasingly Internet connection—in which costs are kept down for the citizens (DeFilippis 2004) while new jobs are created. For example, a municipal owned broadband network in Barbourville, Kentucky brought in 300 new local jobs (Aspen Institute 2005, 91–92). In cash-poor communities CESP organizations have helped set up sophisticated barter systems called local exchange trading systems (LETSs) (DeFilippis 2004, 118). An electrician, for example, might trade off wiring work for meat from a butcher. When goods or services aren't directly exchanged, people pay with a *time dollar*—an i.o.u. worth so many hours of labor that can later be exchanged for labor (www.timedollar.org/time_dollars_main.htm). At present, there are an estimated 100 LETSs in the United States (DeFilippis 2004, 119).

Locally owned businesses are hurt when behemoths such as Wal-Mart arrive so CESPOs along with action organizations work with government to dissuade big box stores from opening up. Another approach is to watch carefully when government provides business incentives to insist that a *Community Benefits Agreements* (CBA) is signed that contractually obligates businesses to provide jobs, goods, or services to those already in the community. CBAs might include *first source hiring* agreements that mandate that those from the neighborhood get priority in hiring, often from lists of individuals recommended (and trained) by the community organization itself (Gross, LeRoy, and Janis-Aparicio 2005; Purinton, Jilani, Arant, et al. 2003). For instance, ACORN negotiated a CBA with a firm doing a massive redevelopment effort in Brooklyn that ensures that the proposed commercial and sports complex would also include thousands of affordable apartments (Atlas 2005).

CESPOs also join with direct action organizations to pressure government to adopt progressive policies such as adopting *living wage programs* in which government will only contract with firms that pay their employees above the poverty level (Reynolds and Kern 2004). Another form of CESPO advocacy is to push for *Housing Trust Funds* that provide capital for affordable housing. In addition, CESPOs working with advocacy organizations argue for *inclusionary housing* programs that guarantee a certain percentage of new housing development will be affordable to lower income individuals. Payday lenders exploit the working poor through charging outrageous interest rates. In alliance with other social change groups, CESPOs pressure cities and states to cap interest rates and stop deceptive loan practices, while at the same time funding CESPOs that provide financial literacy programs.

Working with neighborhood groups, CESPOs advocate for better schools (Shirley 2002) or push for more parental participation (Fruchter 2001). For example in Chicago's Logan Square neighborhood such campaigns

> ha[ve] resulted . . . in the construction of five elementary school annexes and two middle schools [the Logan Square Neighborhood Associated] developed strong relationships with principals and teachers that led them to collaborate in the development of Parent Mentor program. . . . [that] has trained over 840 parents in leadership skills and brought them into classrooms where they provide extra social and academic help to children. (Gold and Simon 2003, 2)

Neighborhood Guardians

Working as neighborhood guardians, CESPOs expand people's pride in the community and work to strengthen community bonds. Pride increases as neighborhood organizations sponsor community festivals that build bonds between ethnic groups encouraging cultural sharing (Goode and Schneider 1994; Horton 1995). Another approach is to set up a community newspaper that becomes the shared voice of the neighborhood by publicizing successful projects and "boost[ing] the self-image of struggling communities that usually only receive major media attention for criminal activity" (Moss 2002, 13).

To learn about neighborhood needs, social production organizations routinely survey community conditions noting deterioration in streets, sidewalks, and housing and then share this information with government that is pressured to make repairs. The first effort of the Dudley Street Neighborhood Initiative involved a cleanup program in the parks done in partnership with the city (Medoff and Sklar 1994). In Philadelphia, neighborhood groups documented the location of abandoned cars and deteriorated homes and then pressured city hall to eliminate the blight (Research for Democracy 2001; Shlay and Whitman 2004). CESPOs themselves acquire and either demolish or repair abandoned buildings since such "properties, abandoned and neglected for years, are in gross disrepair, become magnets for criminal activity, and pose fire hazards. Surrounding properties lose value and are less likely to be maintained" (Ableidinger 2002, 9). Doing so catalyzes broader renewal efforts.

Providing Social and Economic Services

CESP organizations become social service providers helping individuals with problems varying from handling bereavement, obtaining medical care, fighting homelessness or unemployment to overcoming substance addiction. Some social service CESPOs aid victims of rape, spouse abuse, or those economically deceived by predatory lenders. For example,

> New Communities [in Newark, N.J.] . . . develop[ed] a wide range of social service programs which include job-training education programs; health care; day care; after school programs; a Hispanic Development Center that serves Newark's growing Latino community; . . . a nursing home, a medical day-care center for seniors; a visiting nurse service; a school of practical nursing . . . and a mental health service agency. (Aspen Institute 2005, 32)

At first pass, social services provided by governmental agencies or through religious organizations seem identical to those available through community economic and social production organizations. When acting as *contract provider* for government, CESPOs must follow the same rules as do public agencies and the question can be raised on whether or not a CESPO is really bringing about empowerment.

But CESPOs go beyond public agencies by encouraging easy access and working to accommodate those with special language or physical needs. Further, the professionals who work for CESPOs are taught ways of empowering those whom they help, perhaps by teaching those who begin as clients to become service providers themselves. Home health care programs enable the elderly to live with dignity in their own homes and avoid moving to institutional settings, help the individuals, stabilizing a neighborhood so old timers do not have to move, and provide local employment. For instance,

> [Cooperative Health Care Associates] . . . currently employs nearly seven hundred providers who move from home to home to deliver basic direct-care services to the

elderly, ill, or handicapped. What sets CHCA apart is a commitment to provide full-time work . . . Associates who have been with CHCA for three months can become worker-owners . . . and participate directly in its governance through involvement with a worker council. (Gunn 2004, 110)

CESP organizations provide alternatives to the expensive legal system. With *community mediation*, "disputing parties meet with trained mediators, who help them talk openly about their concerns and try to find solutions that will mutually benefit all involved" (Heisey 2004, 22), doing so without relying upon public authorities.

Most governmental social service agencies focus on a narrow, mandated task. CESPOs take a broader view about problems, recognizing that one issue is linked to another. Workplace centers set up by CESPOs provide gathering places for laborers, especially non-English speaking workers while allowing them to gain the trust in one another needed for union organizing efforts (Gordon 2005).

Through *community coordinated networks* separate social service agencies join together to help individuals facing multiple problems, perhaps working with those who are unhoused to find shelter while at the same time helping them battle a substance abuse problem. CESPOs link housing programs with social or economic services. For instance, as part of a large mixed income housing development, Inquilinois Boricuas En Accion in Boston developed a bilingual/bicultural child care service that supported mothers wanting to enter the workforce while at the same time encouraging the children to respect Puerto Rican culture and heritage (McKay and Lopez 1997, 42). In Grand Rapids, Michigan, a CESPO set up a service program to help street women, many of whom were prostitutes with substance abuse problems, and then built housing for them, in a mixed-use building that included a food kitchen/restaurant on the first floor that served many others in the community (Rubin 2000a). In *supportive housing projects*, CESPOs build homes for those with disabilities while providing space so that caregivers can also live with those they help.

CESPOs can respond to emerging community problems far faster than can government. For instance, people, especially those of color from poor communities, are more likely to be arrested and jailed than those from other places. That's bad enough. But after sentences have been served these individuals return to their neighborhoods with the baggage of having a jail record, with few job skills, and without a place to stay. Community economic and social production organizations have been at the forefront of the effort to handle these *re-entry* problems through providing housing and job training programs (Scally 2005).

CESPOs help with financial matters. In immigrant communities, workers remit earnings to their families back home, but for years had to do so through high cost services. CESPOs pressured banks and money remittance services to provide safe, less expensive ways of remitting funds. CESPOs help individuals not to be conned by teaching them to be financially literate (Birkenmaier and Tyuse 2005). CESPOs pressure banks to open branches in poorer neighborhoods so community members can avoid over-priced check cashing services and also to set up *lifeline checking*, low or no-cost checking services for those who can only maintain minimal balances. Finally, community groups have established *low income* (or community development, the names are used interchangeably) *credit unions*, cooperatively owned financial institutions that offer lending, checking, and saving services to their members at reasonable costs (Williams and McLenighan 2004).

Housing Development

New homes and new stores are the most visible projects done by community economic and social production organizations. Empty lots turn into single family homes, while a drug house is torn down and replaced by affordable rental apartments. Church affiliated groups, such as Habitat for Humanity, coordinate community members and volunteers to build homes; a neighborhood association or service organization might build a home or two but most often housing development is orchestrated by Community Development Corporations (CDCs) that package government and foundation grants with conventional mortgages to fund the efforts.

To make homes affordable, CESPOs package a wide array of subsidies. Using complicated forms of financing, for instance, the low income housing tax credit described in the next chapter, CESPOs can reduce the cost of building rental housing. Unfortunately, housing costs are so high that the tax credit alone is not enough so other aid is requested—free lots from the city, mortgage subsidies from the state, or buy-down mortgages from CRA responsive banks. In addition, many tenants still require Section 8 vouchers for the rent.

Another approach to cutting costs involves future owners helping to build their own homes and apartments, often supervised by trained contractors. This *sweat equity* allows future owners to substitute physical work for the cash down payment. For instance, in Boston, new owners of affordable cooperative apartments contributed 300 hours of sweat equity as their down payment (Medoff and Sklar 1994, 161). Another arrangement involves *lease-purchase* through which people rent homes owned by a CESPO, but each month a share of their rent counts toward the down payment of the home. Limited equity cooperatives and land-trusts also help keep homes affordable both for present and future owners.

Once constructed, rental housing must be managed, opening up a whole new world of complicated responsibilities for the CESPO. Because of tenant inexperience in living in quality housing, plus the personal problems that lower income people often face, maintenance costs for affordable housing are higher than comparable market homes (Rubin 2000a). Skilled managers must be employed, who understand that CESPOs are about affecting social change, not just collecting rents.

Housing development and social services efforts blend into one another. A CDC might build a project as transitional housing for the homeless then partner with a social service agency to provide a social service. CESPOs ally with organizations that support those with disabilities to design homes to meet special accessibility needs. Boards of housing cooperatives set up neighborhood watches for gang activity, or after school or summer educational programs, to both teach and occupy rambunctious teenagers while protecting property values.

Economic Developers

Home building programs increase neighborhood worth, encourage commercial ventures to open to supply the new residents, employ people in construction, and provide homeowners with an asset that can be accessed later on to pay for children's education or as capital for a new business. Housing programs are part of a broader effort to expand the local economy and improve the financial well-being of residents. Other such economic development efforts help individuals learn new job skills, start their own businesses, or work to sustain those businesses already in the community.

Economic development work requires capitalistic skills. In many commercial and business efforts a CDC must invest its own capital and failure can be quite costly, even leading to the organization's demise. When a CDC builds and tries to lease a mall, or invests in a grocery store or any commercial business, it enters the same dog-eat-dog competition of the capitalistic market. Meanwhile it also has to remember its social mission. Keeping this balancing act in mind, let's examine some community-based economic development programs.

CESPOs work with individuals to help them accumulate capital, develop financial skills, and learn to be entrepreneurs. One way is to setup up *Individual Development Accounts (IDAs)* in which the CESPO (using government or foundation grant money) works with an at-risk population to teach them to save by matching any money they save on their own.

> The goal is to enable families to accumulate assets for long-term personal and economic development, including education, job training, home ownership, small business (including microenterprise), and retirement. More than 350 community-based IDA programs are operating, and at least 100 more are in the planning stages . . . At the federal level, legislation for IDA demonstrations passed in 1998. . . . At the state level, 22 states have passed IDA legislation. . . . Welfare policy changes in 1996 included IDAs as state options, and 19 states now use TANF or welfare-to-work funds to offer IDAs to families with very low incomes . . . findings from a nationwide demonstration of IDAs suggest that the working poor can and do save when incentives and financial training are present. . . . (Rubin and Sherraden 2005, 481)

Success in IDA programs, though, requires intensive effort on the part of the CESPO to encourage participants both to save and learn about economic matters (Rohe, Gorham, and Querca 2005).

Another approach is to set up *job training programs*. For instance, New Communities Corporation in Newark "runs a Youth Automobile Training Center, which provides trainees who complete courses with guaranteed jobs offering $20,000 plus starting salaries" (Aspen Institute 2005, 32), while Bethel New Life CDC in Chicago has a training program moving people from welfare, to homemakers, to nurses' assistants to eventually being a registered nurse while an associated employment service helps place community members, many previously on welfare or released from prisons, in jobs in 60 cooperating businesses (Meyer, Blake, Caine, et al. 2000, 57–58).

Unlike the one-size-fits-all approach common in government training programs, successful community organizations customize their efforts. In the most effective models, community groups first contact potential employers and receive promises (even guarantees) of job placement for graduates who have mastered specific skills. The community groups then teach people the specified skills required. The success rate for such employment programs is high (Harrison and Weiss 1998). Some programs create their own businesses and train community members.

> New Communities Corporation (NCC) of Newark, New Jersey, manages apartments, restaurants, food preparation businesses, child care services, and health care facilities. At the same time, it contracts as a job trainer to prepare community health care workers, food workers, and others to work for NCC or find jobs in other firms. The goal is to provide job training that catalyzes other efforts; for instance, NCC restaurant trainees have built careers as independent caterers (Harrison and Weiss 1998, 80). In the Chicago area, for instance, Suburban Job Link provides van transportation for inner-city residents to reach suburban jobs (Giloth 1998, 56–57). . . . (Rubin and Sherraden 2005, 480–81)

Programs can lever job training to enterprise development. In Milwaukee, a program set up by Esperanza Unida to teach young people skills in car repair later expanded to an auto body shop, then to apartment rehabbing and an asbestos removal service, then a day-care service, all the while training community members as employees (Rubin 2000a, 15–18). Patricia Murphy and James Cunningham describe that to be successful training must be directly linked to available jobs, that in multicultural communities training must account for language differences, and that job training probably works best when positions can be found in firms that use progressive economic approaches (Murphy and Cunningham 2003, 295–302).

A variety of entrepreneurship training programs help individuals master the elementary business skills of doing a business plan, estimating expenses and income, and obtaining and handling credit. For instance, *microenterprises, kitchen capitalism* in Margaret Sherraden's terms (Sherraden, Sanders and Sherraden 2004), are startup firms that are

> either family run or sole proprietorships with few or no employees. [CESP] organizations provide microenterprises with business training, mentoring, technical assistance, and supportive social services. . . . , by 1997, there were 283 microenterprise assistance programs in the United States, assisting a total of 57,125 individuals in 24,145 businesses, including 6,300 startups. . . . (Rubin and Sherraden 2005, 478–79)

Microenterprises do not always succeed financially but still do provide "opportunity for personal growth and learning, flexibility for family responsibilities, empowerment, and a positive influence on children" (Rubin and Sherraden 2005, 479).

Other approaches might be through a *lending circle* in which people join with others, often friends, who need startup capital. To apply for a loan, each individual in the lending circle works out a business plan that members of the group and outside mentors approve and then the group collectively recommends who should receive the first loan. Members meet at fixed intervals and provide advice to each other on running the businesses. No new money is made available to group members unless those who have already borrowed have repaid their loans. In practice, the women in the lending circles provide help to each other with personal as well as business problems (Counts 1996).

Another approach involves *revolving loan funds* (Parzen and Kieschnick 1992). In this case, government agencies, foundations, and sometimes banks, to satisfy CRA requirements, make available a lump sum loan or grant to an economic and social production organization, that in turn lends the money to the new firms at below-market rates. Those in the CESPO personally know the individuals applying for the loans and can figure out which people are most likely to succeed, reducing the risk, while the CESPO receives money for overhead to absorb the costs of making the loans. As loans are paid back, the CESPO re-uses the money to make new loans.

In some parts of the country, larger amounts of capital can be obtained from *community development venture capital funds* that provide risk capital to businesses that benefit communities by locating plants and hiring people from lower income communities (www.cdvca.org/). Venture capital firms create jobs more efficiently than do conventional government programs—costing around $10,000 a job in contrast to the more normal $35,000 investment for government-aided small businesses (Aspen Institute 2005, 53).

CESPOs run *incubators* that offer inexpensive space for startup firms. In this case the CESPO acquires and refurbishes an abandoned commercial or industrial space that is then rented out at affordable rates to new firms. Many incubators have common facilities such as photocopying, faxes, and secretarial, legal, or accounting support that new firms need but might not be able to afford. Civic-minded businesspeople will often volunteer to mentor new businesses within an incubator facility. For instance, in New York City, the Greenpoint manufacturing and design center is a restored facility that now provides "home to sixty-five businesses, including antique restorers, glass blowers, sculptors, wood-carvers, and photographers" (Gunn 2004, 133). In general,

> Incubators have been successful in creating jobs that employ community members. For instance, the business center/incubator, the Brewery, created by the Jamaica Plain (Massachusetts) Neighborhood Development Corporation, brings jobs back into the neighborhood. A recent survey indicates that 20% of all employees live within five blocks of the Brewery, another 20% in the Jamaica Plain neighborhood, and another 40% in Boston; only 20% live outside city boundaries . . . Another example, the Appalachian Center for Economic Network (ACEnet), operates specialty food businesses using a community kitchen incubator that acts as a hub for networking as well as a place to produce and package products. (Rubin and Sherraden 2005, 479)

In another role, CESPOs instigate commercial renewal programs. In Chicago, the Greater Southwest Development Corporation joined with the Alinsky-style Southwest Organizing project to orchestrate in a poorer, multiethnic neighborhood an economic development effort from which "over $500 million has been invested in neighborhood development projects, which include industrial retention and development, commercial and retail growth, small business development and, of course housing" (Capraro 2004, 153).

CESPOs help firms that are part of the *alternative economy*—that is, companies that believe that maximizing bottom-line profits is less important than promoting social and economic equity. Producer cooperatives, in which the workers are also the owners and managers of a firm, exemplify this approach. The best-known case is found in the Basque region of Spain where the Mondragon cooperatives employ thousands of people, manufacture numerous products, and own and control their own banks (Whyte and Whyte 1988). Such cooperative business projects are less common in the United States, but there have been some successful ones. The Hoedad cooperative in Eugene, Oregon has employed over 300 members (Jackall 1984b) while in San Francisco, much of the scavenger business was run as a cooperative. Cooperative businesses range from those providing child care, to credit unions, to cooperatively owned electric utilities (Gunn 2004, 140–45). Cooperatives are more likely to have progressive labor policies and less likely to abandon a community because slightly greater profits are found elsewhere (Gunn 2004). Food cooperatives have been around for 3 generations or more (Gunn 2004, 70). Some food cooperatives are linked directly with producing farms, cutting out middle-person profits. Cooperatively owned neighborhood restaurants provide wholesome food and a place for community members to congregate, helping to establish a foundation for subsequent organizing efforts.

The most dramatic economic development actions taken by CESPOs occur when the organizations themselves become entrepreneurial developers. In such cases, the CESPOs take on the same risks of private firms (Aspen Institute 2005, 17). Over the last several decades, CESP organizations have created almost 800,000 jobs, while putting into play more than 126 million square feet of commercial or retail property (National Congress for Community Economic Development 2006, 13, 15). In Kansas City, the Linwood Shopping Center, built by a CDC, became the first inner city mall, replacing what had been a totally destroyed block, while in the same city new stores have been set up adjacent to a museum that celebrates both the birth of jazz and the Negro Baseball League. In Chicago, the Carroll-Fullerton incubator kept jobs in a community that businesses had fled; in Newark clean apartments, daycare centers, a new supermarket, and restaurants built by the New Communities Corporation provide a contrast to the surrounding decay.

By taking on the higher risks of the initial projects, CDCs make it easier for private businesses to follow at lower costs and with lower risks. In Milwaukee, Wisconsin, Esperanza Unida's auto repair and job training complex has taught hundreds of mechanics and, over time, has spun off day care services, housing, and commercial development, as well as an asbestos removal company (Rubin 2000a). In Chicago, a CDC started a recycling business that helped clean up neighborhoods and provided some profit, while training community members in handling the hazardous materials (Pellow 2002). In Los Angeles,

> Esperanza Community Housing cooperation . . . opened a large *mercado*, or market for low-income people to make and sell hand-made goods and services . . . Concerned Citizens of South Central Los Angeles operates its own businesses, On Time Printing

and Computer Center, where neighborhood residents learn and work at graphic design, layout, typesetting, copying and post script imaging . . . The Vermont-Slauson Economic Development Corporation . . . help(s) businesses . . . through a revolving loan fund and advice about capital, marketing, business plans, accounting and management . . . the organization opened a small business incubator with offices and services. (Von Hoffman 2003, 246)

Many of these businesses are triple winners—serving community needs, providing revenue to a nonprofit, while helping individuals (often special needs individuals) gain remunerative employment. For instance,

San Francisco's Golden Gate Community Inc. (GGCI) . . . operates three such social enterprises—a print shop, a restaurant serving organic and locally grown produce and bicycle repair shop. In addition, GGCI operates a safe house for homeless mothers and a Young Development Initiative Program . . . two-thirds of the enterprise's hires suffer from some form of mental health illness, half are at risk of homelessness, 22 percent are homeless and 29 percent had a criminal record . . . in 2002, 64% of the organization's gross revenue came from business income. (Aspen Institute 2005, 23–24)

In partnership with chain supermarkets, CDCs provide affordable, quality food and household goods in neighborhoods that have no supermarkets. In one case, doing so caused community members' grocery bills to drop 38 percent (Sullivan 1993, 125). With support from financial intermediaries "between 1995 and 2004, CDCs participated in a dozen and a half successful shopping center development ventures (Aspen Institute 2005, 34–35). Supermarket projects have ended up being profitable for both the CDC and the chains involved. Some projects, though, were controversial, as for instance the owners of a supermarket in Harlem came from an African American dominated CDC, while the smaller stores displaced were mainly owned by Latinos.

Guiding Community Building and Preservation Efforts

With community building and preservation efforts CESPOs proactively confront problems in a comprehensive way, sometimes working with local government. In Springfield, Massachusetts a network of social service and community agencies contracted with a progressive academic research shop to work with citizens and prepare an overall strategic plan to improve the educational, health, safety, and economic infrastructure in the community (Center for Reflective Community Practice 2003). Other efforts come about in response to major changes in government policy. For instance, under HOPE VI many large, high-rise public housing projects were to be demolished, with residents either rehoused in a rebuilt neighborhood or given Section 8 certificates to find housing elsewhere. Though the program has been at best a mixed success economically CESPOs when involved have worked to help people establish new homes and to rebuild the neighborhood (Popkin, Katz, Cunningham, et al. 2004). In a very successful partnership in Boston, the Dudley Street Neighborhood planned for community change and

> DSNI has overseen the development of 300 vacant lots into 225 new homes, play-grounds, gardens and community buildings. Working with government funds . . . the city and the CDCs continue to redevelop historic commercial blocks and lend money to help small businesses . . . the CDCs now focus on rehabilitating houses for one to four families. (Von Hoffman 2003, 107)

Similar redevelopment programs have been in place in the South Bronx in which several larger CDCs each coordinated holistic programs of neighborhood renewal (Sahd 2004) while smaller CDCs such as the Manna CDC in Washington D.C. with but 6 employees have been able to orchestrate neighborhood redevelopment work (Aspen Institute 2005, 36).

Based on the successes of individual CESPOs in stimulating broader renewal efforts, foundations, intermediaries, and governmental agencies decided to fund a series of comprehensive community building initiatives—CBIs (Chaskin, Brown, Venkatesh et al. 2001, 181–248; Meyer, Blake, Caine, et al. 2000; Murphy and Cunningham 2003, 43; Wright 1998). The smallest of these programs aided CDCs such as DSNI or Chicanos por la Causa that were already involved in multisector rebuilding efforts, while larger programs provided funds to coordinate social service agencies, CDCs, neighborhood groups, and, at times, direct action organizations to collectively work out ways of rebuilding neighborhoods. While each of the CBIs followed a distinct approach—the National Community Development Initiative was more concerned about physical redevelopment; the Casey Foundation initiatives focused on how improved community infrastructure strengthened families—all programs were meant to be holistic. As described:

> the first principle is that community development strategies need to address the inter-relationships among the social, physical and economic needs and opportunities within the neighborhood. This principle includes notions of *comprehensiveness* (addressing the full range of needs and circumstances) and *integration* (weaving together individual strategies that as a whole foster synergistic, sustainable change). The second principle is that neighborhood residents must participate actively and meaningfully in both planning and implementation, and organizational collaboration must be fostered among relevant institutions in both the public and private sector. (Chaskin, Brown, Venkatesh, et al. 2001, 182)

Concerns Raised by Community Economic and Social Production Work

Community economic and social production organizations do succeed in their work. Yet, activists, especially those involved in social mobilization, express concern, wondering if CESPOs are truly about empowerment or care about social transformation. It is hard to fault organizations that house the homeless, enable caregivers to live with the disabled, or build supermarkets in neighborhoods that lack shopping. Yet, questions are raised on whether providing homes or jobs or better social services simply alleviates problems while distracting from the broader need for structural change.

Our feeling is that both social mobilization and economic and social production are complementary and viable paths to bring about a more just and equitable society. Still we should examine some of the concerns expressed.

Organizational Mission, Form, and Staffing

Community economic and social production organizations interact frequently with both government and the for-profit sector and in doing so end up making structural accommodations that, at first glance, seem contradictory to social change work. To handle larger projects, CESPOS must hire those skilled in fiscal management, perhaps people with an MBA who pay more attention to spreadsheets than to organizing protests. Needing to run in the black, some CESPOs seek out those projects that are most likely to bring in a profit and in doing so "enter the world of community entrepreneurship" (Shuman and Fuller 2005, 9). Evidence exists that organizations can make a profit while doing social transformation work. For instance, Housing Works, a New York AIDs service agency, brings in over 85 percent of its service revenue from running revenue generating enterprises such as a used book store (Rouen 2003). But many worry that the time and effort spent in trying to make a profit distracts from social change work (Stoecker 2005b).

In general, can organizations that are financially dependent on those who represent the establishment still take independent actions? A study done in Pittsburgh suggests that when partnering with the city to obtain funds, neighborhood groups lose their community focus (Jezierski 1990). Developmental activists report "mission drift," the propensity of nonprofits to follow the priorities of the granting agency, as a director of one community-based economic development organization reflected:

> Housing seems to be the hot topic. Sometimes we get accused and maybe I accuse myself, of chasing grants. Don't look at your neighborhood to see what is important but find out what is hot and see how you can fit that into your neighborhood. (interview with Herbert Rubin)

Organizations comply with the funders because if they fail to do so, they will die. In Chicago, Voice of the People lost funding and eventually went out of business because it wanted to spend more time on social programs and less on housing than funders wished. In Minneapolis, the Whittier Alliance died, in part because it was far more aggressive in trying to provide housing for poor people of color than was acceptable in that city; and it lost out in funding. CANDO in Chicago, a supporter of CESPOs, alienated its funders, lost out on grants, and after a long history simply went out of business (Immergluck 2005b).

Empowerment and Professional Staffing

Running social production organizations requires expert knowledge. Keeping a spouse abuse center afloat requires skills in psychology and law, as well as fund raising; providing affordable housing requires understanding of finance, tax credits, and property management. But hiring those with this professional knowledge can weaken an empowerment mission. For instance, shelters for battered women were initially run by former victims who taught themselves how to help others. But as counselling professionals established "family violence" as a specialty area, they began to discredit and put down the volunteers who had been running the shelters.

> Shelters had to lay their claim to expertise in order to ward off competition from more traditional agencies and obtain funding . . . funding agencies, boards, and some staff advocated or demanded the hiring of professional directors or counseling staff in order to acquire the expertise needed to survive and help battered women. (Schecter 1982, 107–08)

Histories of CDCs show that many began with volunteer boards and staffs. But after a short time, most of the volunteers could no longer afford the time required and the organizations became more and more dependent on trained, professional staff (Rubin 2000a). Further, as

> the CDCs and the projects become more complex, time consuming, costly and hard to manage . . . This increasing complexity redirects ever more control to staff, who often live outside of the community and are more likely to emphasize the technical details of development over community empowerment. (Stoecker 1996, 14)

There are no simple solutions to the problems caused by the need for professional skills. For ongoing social production projects, pure volunteerism simply won't work. Volunteers don't have the time to spend months negotiating over complicated financial deals, and part-time inexperienced people should not be handling the finances of a community credit union.

One approach is to accept the need for permanent, professional staff, but then ensure that a strong supervisory board composed of community members is in place. Experts on the staff thus become the hired laborers whose job it is to achieve what the members of the organization want to do.

People and Places Dilemma

For a CDC to help a homeless person find both housing and employment, especially in a new firm set up by the CDC, seems to be win-win-win for the organization, the individual, and the neighborhood. But other efforts are more problematic. Helping an individual, especially one with a low income, gain job skills, is to the good. But what happens if the person gets a job in the suburbs? New businesses are all to the good, except when to set them up they require land clearance of homes of those already in the community, and hire commuters as workers.

Some CDC programs have had a perverse effect. To help improve the neighborhood, older derelict buildings are replaced by newer, quality affordable homes. Many of these neighborhoods, though, are ideally situated close to a growing central business district—that's what inner city means. With the CDCs taking the initial risk by building the newer homes, the neighborhood then becomes open for gentrified development (Higgins 2001). Care and balance are needed. Activists must set up special programs—demanding inclusionary housing, for instance, or making sure affordable housing is deeded so that it cannot be sold to gentrifiers (Newman and Wyly 2005).

Does Social Production Work Distract from Organizing?

Another question asked of those involved in CESPO work is the extent to which providing services and building projects distracts from organizing efforts. Is it better to pressure government to preserve the multibillion dollar affordable housing programs or to spend time building a limited number of affordable houses? Does the effort required in managing a small community medical service distract from the direct action campaigns and lobbying needed to pressure government to establish an equitable national health service?

When neighborhood organizations start to work on social production projects they may lose some of their militant edge. For instance, after a neighborhood advocacy organization started development work its "identity began to shift toward convergence with the conservative community" while "transformative populism within [the organization] ebbed" (Stoecker 1995, 121). Critics argue that CDC directors choose a "bottom-line business pragmatism" rather than working to promote "neighborhood controlled social change" and in doing so CDCs brush aside an "advocacy agenda" (Lenz 1988). Others fear that with efforts to set up partnerships with government, business, and community members in housing and economic development projects, the possibility for protest actions is decreased (Gittell and Vidal 1998). Further, as Shragge indicates, partnership programs are often about social control in which "governments have used their new collaborative relations . . . as a way to create the conditions to maintain harmony in a time of social deterioration" (Shragge 2003, 131).

Certainly social production is distinct from organizing and confrontational work; a person cannot manage an apartment complex and simultaneously march on the streets. Still, evidence is there that social production is compatible with direct action. Housing production organizations have joined with advocacy groups to pressure cities to set up housing trust funds, to attack banks that ignore the Community Reinvestment Act, and to pressure Uncle Sam to increase the money for affordable housing (Goetz 1993; 1996; Rubin 2000a). Legal aid clinics have become places where union and community organizers talk to individuals about the shared nature of problems faced (Gordon 2005, 198), though tensions between the individual nature of solving legal problems and the collective nature of community activist persists (Gordon 2005, 231–35). Social production organizations are cautious about joining advocacy efforts for fear of losing government money, but they do join, albeit indirectly through the advocacy coalitions described in Chapter 19.

In addition, social action organizations now do CESP work. Both the Industrial Areas Foundation and ACORN build homes, work to improve schools, and offer social and economic services—yet do so without forgetting the need for direct actions.

ACORN will conduct a sit-in at abandoned homes to demand that the homes be repaired while when IAF worked with the South Bronx Churches to build affordable homes, they relied on direct action tactics to persuade the city to cooperate (Rooney 1995). More militant unions seek out members at a community service center (Gordon 2005), while voter registration drives take place at housing and social service agencies. In general, individuals who benefit from social production projects tend to be more active in other activities that empower neighborhoods. For instance, people who live in housing cooperatives are more likely than most in the neighborhood to be involved in advocacy work (Briggs, Mueller, with Mercer Sullivan 1997).

It appears that the gap between organizing and social production work has narrowed although tensions remain. The bricks and mortar organizations require the additional resources that social action organizations have been able to pressure financial institutions and local and state government to provide. At the same time, social action organizations need CESPOs to translate the concessions won into actual homes and jobs. For instance, in Chicago, the Greater Southwest Development Corporation, an economic development group, works hand in glove with the Alinsky style activist Southwest Organizing Project to pressure government for resources for renewing the neighborhood (Capraro 2004). As the executive director of the GSDC, a person who began his career as an organizer for Neighborhood People's Action, describes "community organizing+community development=community transformation" (Capraro 2004).

Conclusion and Summary

We have presented an overall portrait of the community economic and social production mode and then provided illustrations of economic and social production endeavors showing both the successes and the tensions involved in the work that is done.

Still, community economic and social production organizations can do only so much. Without a change in underlying economic and political structures CESPOs can at best reduce some of the costs of unfettered capitalism. Political and confrontational tactics must complement the work of CESPOs to make sure that activists are not simply treating symptoms without curing the underlying disease. Still the effort of CESPOs to help people overcome the symptoms of poverty, neglect, and abandonment is well worthwhile.

21 Skills for Accomplishing Economic and Social Production Work

To successfully bring about economic and social production development activists master a variety of administrative and managerial skills. *Planning* is about determining which projects or services are appropriate and then working out step-by-step how to bring them to fruition. *Financing* describes obtaining money while *implementation* means carrying out hundreds of nitty gritty steps from finding a site, to making sure it is environmentally safe, to contracting and supervising physical construction. *Management and administration* are about handling the daily details—coordinating staff, hiring and firing people, making sure insurance is paid, filing reports on time, or checking that follow-through occurs with those served. Finally, *evaluation* asks if the goals of a project have been achieved, and if not, what changes are needed.

Planning

Planning takes place as developmental activists pro-actively work out what they want to accomplish, what steps are needed, and what problems to anticipate. Planning links broad social *goals* such as those of empowerment and economic justice to *objectives* (specific outcomes) to *tasks* (the actual steps taken to achieve the desired objectives).

Planning is also about sequencing the various objectives and tasks. If the objective is to keep a neighborhood economically viable, should the organization try to repair homes and build new and affordable housing first, or to concentrate on rebuilding the commercial strips? Planning helps clarify how solutions link to problems. Is shutting down a crackhouse enough or does the CESPO have to figure out why crack has invaded the neighborhood and work out broader solutions to this underlying problem?

Planning contrasts with *firefighting*—responding on a case-by-case basis. It might appear that firefighting is inevitable as organizations must react immediately when disaster happens as with Hurricane Katrina. But good planning reduces the need for firefighting since skilled organizations recognize that certain types of disasters are going to occur and have worked out contingency plans.

Planning empowers. By planning what is to be done, organizations communicate that they are on top of the matter and not simply responding to agendas set by others. Still, planning must be done with a realistic sense of what an organization can accomplish with the skills and resources at hand. It may make sense to try a neighborhood watch on a couple of blocks before extending it to the whole neighborhood. Plan to refurbish a six flat apartment building before attempting a combined shopping center and housing complex at the transit depot.

Planning and the Choice of Economic and Social Production Projects

Organizations are often set up to handle a specific, here-and-now problem. Victims of abuse, assault, and rape organize a Rape and Spouse Abuse Center, while a religious group appalled by the number of homeless set up a sheltering service. But other times organizations, especially those focusing on neighborhood problems, come into being because of an overall concern about a general deterioration or social malaise without having a specific project in mind. For these organizations, the initial planning effort is about choosing the overall scope of what to attempt to move from the present to a better future. During the initial planning, choices are made between hundreds of possible social service, physical construction, economic development, or community building projects. There are no hard and fast rules on which projects to pick, but overall, successful social production organizations seem to follow eight principles.

Projects Should Highlight the Core Missions.   Choose a project that makes the core mission apparent. A feminist organization that shelters abused women is doing good, but why not define the shelter project as part of a broader effort to have the police enforce domestic abuse laws, while teaching women in the shelter how to obtain economic independence? That way the shelter project clearly highlights the broader goal of women's empowerment.

Plan Projects that Fill Economic and Social Service Gaps.   Work on projects that provide goods and services that are lacking and fill an economic niche in the community. Supermarkets are needed if only mini-marts are present. Vacant lots but overcrowded apartments suggest a housing program, while teenagers hanging on the street suggest a job training program or perhaps partnership programs to improve the local schools.

Think Catalytically.   Choose projects whose outcomes are visible and that will trigger other actions by creating a sense of the possible. Sometimes taking on a difficult project first can catalyze others to work on less challenging but necessary tasks. As an example, a community-based development organization might buy a horribly deteriorated apartment building that is being used as a drug redistribution center and turn it into affordable housing. Tearing down a crackhouse or refurbishing a dilapidated building can encourage private investors to build homes or open up their own businesses since the eyesore has been removed.

Plan Symbolically. Social production projects should visibly communicate that change has begun. For instance, community art programs in which the young join with local artists to prepare wall murals, especially those that assert ethnic and community pride, symbolize hope for the future, especially when they replace gang graffiti. A new shopping area with lots of glass symbolizes the confidence of the community just as shattered windows and burned out apartments symbolize despair.

Plan with a Broader Scope. Think holistically. There is nothing wrong with planning a project that accomplishes a single important objective, especially as the organization's first major endeavor. But as organizations grow in capacity, they should take on more complex projects that accomplish both social and economic goals. Build homes, but why not use home building as a way to teach young people carpentry skills? Set up a daycare facility, but also train community people as certified daycare providers, giving them meaningful jobs, and all the while providing a service for other community members.

Plan Projects that Recycle Resources within the Community. Poor communities export money since people need food, medical care, clothes, and other necessities, but have to buy them elsewhere. Establishing supermarkets, clothing stores, and clinics that employ people from the community helps keep money in the neighborhood. Any business formed by community members that attracts outside money is a plus as is a home ownership program that stops the export of rent.

Plan So Projects Bootstrap. Success in one project can lead to the next. A shelter for the homeless requires a physical location that can then be used for job training for the unhoused. Construction projects can teach community members new skills. For example, if a building repair requires removing asbestos, rather than hiring an outside firm, send community members off to get the training and hire them. Refurbish a few apartment buildings and then leverage the success in doing so to obtain bank and government support for a larger housing project.

Plan for Empowerment. Projects should empower participants. Micro-enterprise programs provide people with technical skills that make them feel more competent and confident of their earning capacity, even if the initial businesses don't work. Spouse abuse shelters house the victims, but also empower by rebuilding shattered self-confidence.

Benefits and Costs

Another step in initial planning is to think about the overall benefits and costs of various ideas. A community-based housing organization might have to decide whether to build affordable apartments to house the very poorest, or to develop and build quality, single family homes to encourage working class people—police officers, firefighters, carpenters, plumbers—to remain in the neighborhood. Housing the poorest shelters children and provides adults with a permanent address from which to seek jobs, but might do little to encourage new jobs or stores to open up. Housing working-class people increases social capital and encourages new stores to open up, but it might provide an opening wedge for gentrification, harming the poor even more. Working out these tradeoffs is part of the early planning.

Specific benefit and cost questions include:

1. Is the project worth the effort overall? Even if the organization has the money and personnel, it might not be worthwhile to set up its own daycare center if a church group can do it instead.
2. Do alternative solutions produce more benefits at lower cost? Should a community group try to own a store, with all the management hassles that it might entail? Or is it better to try to attract private businesses, by providing parking, increasing safety, and job training for potential employees?
3. Who gets the benefits and who pays the costs? Programs to build new homes may improve the appearance of the neighborhood, but end up forcing out the poor as wealthier people purchase the homes.

In comparing costs and benefits, begin with the monetary ones, but then examine the value of opportunities foregone. For instance, the dollar costs of setting up and running a community daycare center include rent, personnel, insurance, and supplies. Monetary costs should also include the value of lost opportunities, in this case, what was not accomplished because the organization was working on the daycare center instead of a crime prevention program. The costs can then be compared to the value produced, for instance, the income people can now earn because they have a safe place to leave their children. Other monetary benefits include the tax payments that parents who are now employed can make, and the income earned by community members who work at the center.

Less tangible benefits and costs need to be included. For example, a project to clean up a park and chase away the gangs might be worth additional effort if it gets the attention of the mayor who will then be more willing to sponsor future work. On the other hand, a project that angers politicians by embarrassing them by calling attention to their failures might not be worth doing. Spending a bit more money to build homes in a conspicuous place in the neighborhood might be well worth it, if doing so symbolizes that the community is coming back. Think of the psychological and personal value to the elderly and their friends when a housing project for special needs elderly enable them to remain in their familiar community.

Caution though is needed in figuring out who benefits and who pays. Working with the city to help set up a new sports venue might benefit shop owners, souvenir sellers, restaurateurs, and ball park food vendors, but the stadium might bring a massive invasion of automobiles into residential neighborhoods. Pressure to increase the intensity of police patrols might make shop owners feel more secure but end up with humiliating stop-and-search routines of minority youths.

Comprehensive Community Planning

The communities in which CESPOs work confront multiple, interrelated problems. To respond to these a broader approach to planning—*comprehensive community plan-*

ning—is required. (This section inspired by Murphy and Cunningham 2003, 178–99). Comprehensive community planning involves a large-scale, multiorganizational effort that considers an entire set of needs within a specific geographic, while recognizing the close connection between social and economic issues. Fighting gangs through a crime watch is not enough unless work is done to find jobs or improve education; new affordable housing is all to the good, but if the community doesn't have decent public transportation many of those housed won't be able to get to work. With comprehensive community planning efforts, participants try to reach agreement on the broader goals, and then evaluate the separate projects undertaken by individual CESPOs along with government agencies and private firms, not only to see if the project is worthwhile but if the project fits into the larger effort.

Preparing a Comprehensive Community Plan. On occasion, a social change organization, such as the Dudley Street Neighborhood Initiative in Boston (Medoff and Sklar 1994) or even a city-wide activist group (Research for Democracy 2001) itself orchestrates a comprehensive planning process. Most often, though, an outside agency—usually a progressive foundation—is requested by local activists, social service, business, and governmental agencies to jump start the process. In the effort, all community organizations must participate—from very conservative groups, to those at the forefront of progressive social change, to action organizations, to those providing services, as well as to both elected and bureaucratic officials. To coordinate the work, a smaller planning committee is established that reports back to the governing board composed of representatives from all the agencies involved.

The comprehensive planning process involves several interrelated parts:

- working out the overall *vision*, the broader set of goals about what the community can and should become
- obtaining data on problems the community faces, assets it has, as well as general demographic, social, and business information
- reflecting on the problems in light of the shared vision, then working out objectives of what should be done
- planning for *implementation*, that is figuring out who will be responsible for achieving which objective
- determining which agency will handle a specific project

A vision statement is the overall set of goals on what the community should become. Too narrow a vision isn't enough—reducing crime is important but without describing what else will happen in the safer community it does not constitute a vision. Vision statements can emerge through *focus group discussions*—a wide variety of local stakeholders working out their sense of the future and then being tested in *charettes*, miniplays, that portray desired futures. Give-and-take sessions at public planning meetings are next during which people hash out differences in visions—between businesses and social change activists, or between those in separate ethnic groups. The goal is to build consensus.

Hard data drives the planning process building on information about the changing demography, crime, health conditions, and employment along with descriptions of the physical plant, transportation system, schools, churches, and other facilities.

Comprehensive planning involves an *assets assessment* (Kretzman and McKnight 1993) in which community members document the neighborhood's untapped resources in the skills of its residents, or the physical location nearby downtown, the presence of social service organizations, as well as the knowledge in the business community.

At this stage, the planning committee along with professional planners, if they have been hired, seek to bring together the overall vision, link it to the problems and resources of the community, and then work out a series of objectives for achieving the broader vision. Objectives are usually described sector by sector—those for housing development, for providing social services, economic change, recreational, political involvement, transportation, and the responsibility for accomplishing each task assigned to the agency or organization most familiar with the matter. The overall plan should then be submitted to the participants in the planning process for acceptance, tweaked a bit more and then written up and presented to the overall community for further discussion.

Now the hardest stage—implementation—carrying out what is suggested in the plan. Doing so requires both economic resources and the will of the agencies involved. Remember when plans are made and then ignored discouragement sets in. Our advice is that comprehensive planning should not be started unless prior to the effort there are credible promises that at least some of the ideas will be carried out. For instance, the Neighborhood Revitalization Program in Minneapolis that catalyzed separate comprehensive planning efforts had its own budget so was able to begin neighborhood projects, while public officials had promised that city agencies would spend funds to help work out the plans proposed by the neighborhoods.

Financing Projects and Services

Financing is about obtaining money. Though CESPOs can accomplish much through voluntary effort, people on neighborhood watches work for free, hospices rely in part upon contributed labor, and for some smaller projects such as furnishing a community room, donations from community members might be sufficient. But the costs of housing rehabilitations runs into tens or even hundreds of thousands of dollars an apartment; commercial projects cost even more, while paying salaries of qualified professionals requires a steady stream of funds.

Obtaining funds can be complicated. To begin, the funding environment for nonprofit organizations changes rapidly and often in unpredictable ways (Groenbjerg 1993). Government and foundation grant programs come and go, while what foundations support is ever changing, with developmental activists claiming that foundations change their minds about what is important every three years or so.

In addition, not all expenses are the same to funders. Getting money for the physical development costs of a conventional, charitable project, such as the construction of a soup kitchen, is comparatively simple, as the funders get to brag about the visible accomplishment. But community groups also need to pay for staff that locates the site and plans the project, as well as ordinary office expenses. Few foundations are willing to pay for these overhead expenses since there is no glory in doing so.

While financing is integral to implementing projects the fact that funding is available should not be the dominant motivation for starting a project. CESPOs are about accomplishing missions with the projects being the means to do so, not the end. Still, balance is needed in relating means and ends. At times, money is available for setting up supermarkets in poor neighborhoods; at other times for helping the working poor own franchises. Both help create jobs and provide services and as such are consistent with the mission of community economic development organizations. Running a drug rehabilitation program, even if funds were available, might not be. Similarly, adjusting the size of a project to mesh with available funds makes sense and rarely compromises the organization's core mission. For a housing organization, refurbishing 200 homes is better than repairing just fifty, but if money is available for just fifty, go for it.

More money is often needed for CESP projects than would be required by similar projects done by for-profit organizations. Building a home costs the same whether it is to be sold to gentrifying yuppies or to poor people in lease-purchase programs. But with a lease-purchase program, community groups have to find the funds to pay for teaching new homeowners about home maintenance, taxes, insurance, and financing. CDCs that are building affordable homes need not just obtain the mortgages to pay for the property, but need the money to pay for lawyers and accountants required to set up the tax credits that reduce the costs to the new owners. Housing projects and shopping centers built in neighborhoods with high crime rates have to pay for security costs that mainstream store owners avoid.

Funds differ. *Capital (or capital development) funds* cover the physical work and the money for land and building materials; while *operating funds* are those for running the service or project, for heat, light, taxes, or for paying staff. Before a project is undertaken, work is required to test out its feasibility, necessitating *pre-development expenses* for market research, paying architects, lawyers' fees to check on who owns what land—a problem that is most difficult in poor neighborhoods where land titles are often not clear—and money to test for environmental hazards among many other expenses.

Most commercial housing development and service projects lose money early on. Until occupied, apartments pay no rent, while commercial enterprises run in the red until a customer base is built. New stores or services must purchase equipment before any revenue comes in, while unoccupied homes or businesses have debts that need to be repaid. These early on expenses are termed *start up costs* that for a while are expected to exceed revenue, but over time revenue must exceed costs for project *sustainability*. *Earned income* describes any fees received for services, rent for housing, or profits made. Money received for managing the building of a project is termed a *developer's fee*, that can, though often does not, turn into a profit for the CESPO.

Subsidies are funds provided without expectation of being paid back by foundations, government, churches, charities, and sometimes by rich individuals or even banks under CRA pressure. A *capital subsidy* helps pay for the purchase price of a building or expensive piece of equipment, while an *operating subsidy* helps fund the daily costs of providing the service.

Great care is needed in how subsidies are spent. Unless explicitly authorized by the funder, subsidies for a specific project cannot be used to pay for overhead expenses of the CESPO, though, at times, funds are specified for overhead. In addition, subsidies for one project cannot be shifted without permission from the funder to another activity; money provided to reduce rents in a housing project cannot be used to fund a counselling service even for the individuals being housed. Keeping funds *segregated* is vital to stay in compliance with the grants, but can be complicated since many separate programs are often run by one CESPO. A CDC might house a previously unhoused person (and be able to do so because of having received capital subsidy for the building), work with the same individual to combat a personal problem (funded through a social service contract), and all the while work with the person in a job training program subsidized by a foundation grant.

Financing Projects through Social Enterprises.   As the amount of money available for subsidies from government decreases and foundations become less generous, CESPOs search for their own revenue sources. One way is to set up a for-profit business and then use the profits to pay for either organizing or providing services. CESPOs have set up a variety of for-profit firms ranging from community bakers, furniture manufacturing, catering, landscaping, running franchises in airports, and various forms of construction services (Shore 2003). CDCs have spun off for-profit construction firms, asbestos removal outfits, painters, and other crafts associated with home building. Anecdotal evidence exists of some of these efforts paying off, but making them work takes time and distracts from the core mission of the CESPO.

Anticipating Project Expenses

Before funding is sought, CESPOs estimate project costs. *Pro formas*—written statements of anticipated costs and revenue—are worked out along with the business plans that describe the product or services to be provided, anticipated revenue and expense streams, as well as narrative on why the idea will work. Nowadays these are presented on spreadsheets, allowing for easy adjustment as assumptions about the project are changed.

For the development of physical projects, the most obvious costs are for land, buildings, construction, and, in older neighborhoods, money for environmental remediation. Stores need stock, offices need machines and furniture. Depending on the business, specialized equipment or merchandise must be paid for. These material items are termed *hard costs*. In doing projects, there are also endless *soft costs*, fees that are paid or services rendered in acquiring, upgrading, or building property. Title searches are required, cash needed to pay interest on loans while building the property, as well as fees to consultants. Labor costs including salaries, money for training, and funds for fringes such as health insurance or retirement must also be carefully factored in. In housing projects, money for both routine maintenance and for a sinking fund to repair or replace furnaces, washing machines, roofs, and anything that can deteriorate over time must be put aside. Taxes have to be paid.

Paying for insurance is crucial. Projects require fire and theft insurance and liability coverage against accidents. If the community organization plans to take the elderly shopping, vehicle insurance and driver liability coverage are required. Organizations providing health, or any form of counselling services, should carry malpractice insurance. What if a counselor advised a woman to return to her husband after he had beaten her, and she followed the advice, only to be beaten again and hospitalized? The woman could sue for having been given bad advice.

Project expenses are also divided into fixed, lump-sum, and variable costs. Some capital purchases come in fixed sizes—a car will seat 4–6, a van 6–12 or so. Once you have purchased the vehicle, for instance, to transport people to hospitals outside the community, you have a fixed cost whether the vehicle is used to transport one, two, or twelve individuals. If you then have to transport thirteen individuals at the same time, another vehicle must be purchased, a lump-sum cost. Variable costs are for such items as fuel and maintenance that would depend upon how often equipment or a product is used. In an apartment complex, the mortgage and taxes are fixed costs, while utilities are variable costs.

Some costs are hard to estimate and are paid for as part of the general overhead or absorbed within the developer's fees. Unfortunately, most grants limit money for general overhead or the amount of a developer's fee for nonprofits to levels well below what are allowed for profit-making firms.

Raising Funds for Projects and Services

Depending upon the project, many sources of funds can be tapped. The most visible are government and foundation grants, though obtaining these is getting harder as funds shrink for social change and antipoverty efforts. To find out about federal grant programs, the *Catalogue of Federal Domestic Assistance* is helpful, or clicking on to the home pages of the relevant federal agencies. To find out what money is available from foundations, look in publications such as the *Grassroots Fundraising Journal* as well as on a variety of on-line resources.

Rarely is one source of funding sufficient, so developmental activists combine many separate sources, and seek to *leverage* what one source provides into convincing another to provide more funds. An Urban Institute report (Center for Public Finance and Housing 1994) noted that to fund affordable housing, community groups routinely work with seven major federal programs and also solicit state, local, and private sector contributions. Another study that focused on apartment housing projects run by neighborhood organizations concluded that the nonprofits "averaged 7.8 sources [of funding] per development." (Hebert, Heintz, Kay, et al. 1993, e-15)

Particularly hard to obtain is the money for overhead. A study showed overhead money for housing organizations in Chicago was obtained from the following sources:

Sales and Income	32.5%
Local Support	5.5%
United Way	0.7%
Government	20.8%
Foundations	13.3%
Corporations	9.7%
LISC	7.5%

(Pogge and Choca 1991, 12)

A developmental activist described how he leveraged LISC's support for a project into the large amount of capital he needed.

> You gotta go to all of these entities and sell your project . . . Usually LISC is the first group because they're the ones who give you the predevelopment money. So once you've got LISC money then you can go out and say, "LISC believes in this project, we want you in on this project."
>
> They've already put up some money so you sell that to the city, you sell it to HUD, you sell it to whomever. And as people begin to buy in then you've got more clout when you go to the next person so when you get a LISC grant, then you get a nationally competitive grant, then people begin to listen again. You see 'em saying, "well geez, these guys got a grant that's nationally competitive, it must be a good project."
>
> And then you go to the next group and say "ok I've got LISC, I've got [a federal grant] I need the city," and the city kicked in $200,000. Then you say "I got LISC, OCS, and the city, I go to the banks and say, hey I've got tax credits." (Rubin 2000a)

When paying for ongoing professional staff is needed to provide a social service, a *contract* is sought usually from a government agency. To obtain a contract, the CESPO must have the staff and experience to provide the service, be willing to follow the rules to set up the funder, while allowing itself to be both audited and evaluated. Periodically contracts are (or are not) renewed and organizations rebid for the contracts.

Physical development projects as well as startup businesses require large sums of money from banks, investors, foundations, intermediaries, and government. Most money is borrowed as a *mortgage*, a loan that is secured by the value of the physical property. Banks and insurance companies that provide mortgages want to earn a fair rate of interest and ensure that their capital is secure, but can be encouraged through CRA pressures to make such loans, sometimes at special rates. A city might be persuaded to donate the land or a house that it owns for back taxes, while foundations or charities might provide money that lowers the interest costs by depositing sums into a bank as a low interest *benevolent deposit* that is then loaned to the CESPO at a nominal rate.

Specific government programs—HOME, CDBG, HOPE VI, Section 202 Housing, programs for ending homelessness, or for supportive housing—all provide grant money for affordable housing. Similarly, money is available from the Office of Community Services, Economic Development Administration, the Small Business Administration. The Department of Agriculture will fund economic development work for some programs for projects in rural areas. These grant programs are extremely competitive, and in recent years the money allocated has precipitously dropped.

Other subsidies can be obtained from housing trust funds, again on a competitive basis. Trust Funds are monies specifically put aside for housing purposes that are automatically replenished, for instance, by a fee that is assessed when homes are bought or sold, or when paperwork is filed on real estate transactions. Usually the amount is quite small so other grants are required.

Capital projects are also funded through elaborate tax schemes that allow rich corporations to make money if they invest in projects that benefit the poor. In *low income housing tax credit projects*, CESPOs get a tax credit (a reduction in taxes) that they then sell to corporations for whatever the market will pay. This tax credit allows a corporation to reduce the taxes it will pay; the money the CESPO receives is used to lower the cost of a project. Unfortunately the amounts are insufficient to make housing affordable so other funds must be obtained. Some corporations are nervous about directly investing in nonprofit projects, so they do so through intermediaries.

With *land trusts* a nonprofit organization acquires the ownership of land. Housing is then built without having to pay the costs of the underlying land. In turn, though, the homes built on the land trust cannot be sold at a speculative profit. With *limited equity housing cooperatives*, government or foundations subsidize the mortgage costs, but again the individual cooperative owners are limited in what they gain when they sell.

Among the hardest money to obtain is the *risk capital* for business investments. Successful CDCs that have made money through developer's fees can recycle this money as investments in businesses while clever CDCs use grant money for training community members in ways that start community businesses. Rather than just training the individual, the CDC argues that setting up, say, an auto repair place will make for more realistic training (Rubin 2000a).

For large investments, capital is very hard to get though a limited number of sizable competitive grants are still available from the federal Office of Community Services. In the past, grants of up to half a million dollars from this source were used by CDCs as *equity investment* in inner-city shopping centers, or multiuse projects that combine housing with medical services or perhaps with grocery stores. Community Development Financial Institutions (CDFIs) will loan money, sometimes at below market rates, to economic development ventures in poor communities, while Community Development Venture Capital groups provide speculative equity capital.

Both CDFIs and CDVCs analyze projects with the same care as do conventional banks and venture capital groups; these are not charities. The difference is that CDFIs and CDVCs are set up to look for projects in communities that other investors ignore, often doing so in innovative ways. For example, in early 2006, a national consortium of CDFIs began a program to package mortgages from home buyers with less than perfect credit records (www.opportunityfinance.net).

Project Implementation: Development

Implementation refers to the myriad of steps undertaken in actually doing a project: securing financing, purchasing land, working with building contractors, negotiating with franchise venders, hiring and training employees, collecting rents, paying bills, leasing space, convincing neighborhood organizations of the appropriateness of the project, and on and endlessly on. *Development* refers to the steps as the physical project is built while *management and administration* describes how the daily work is carried out.

The details of implementation differ project by project. Supermarket development would involve conducting market research, finding a site, building the store, learning about the grocery trade, staffing, ensuring security, making sure parking is available, and encouraging people to shop there. Microenterprise programs involve locating people interested in starting their own business, helping them work out a business plan, assisting them in obtaining financing, setting up mentor relationships, and teaching bookkeeping. Implementing neighborhood watches requires training participants to ensure that they know what they are looking for, teaching what to do when problems are seen, setting up patrols, and obtaining communication equipment, while working with the police. Setting up a program to administer Individual Development Accounts involves getting the funding, deciding how much money is matched for every dollar the participants save, finding the participants, working with them in a financial literacy program, tracking them, and on and on and on.

Each project has unique aspects. One project we studied was delayed when a property owner wouldn't sell to those of a different ethnicity, requiring the intervention of a community identity organization. In another project a gender rebellion took place when women were excluded from a training program for mechanics. The CESPO quickly changed its approach. In another effort, a CESPO needed to work with gangs to stop gunfire pointed at a daycare center (the wall made an inviting target).

Both the initial development and the long-term management of projects undertaken by CESPOs are more complicated than efforts done by the for-profit sector. Rather than looking for upscale clientele or an established customer base, CESPOs carry out projects in neighborhoods that others have abandoned while working with the poor, the elderly, the unemployed, the handicapped, and people with little formal education. In these neighborhoods, crime rates are high while land is often a designated *brownfield*—having severe environmental problems. Because of these complexities, projects can take years before they come to fruition and during that time the initial financing can be lost.

Luring new businesses into the neighborhood is hard for the very reasons that businesses previously left—fear of crime, neglect by the public sector, and the perception (often quite wrong) that the poor neighborhoods are not good markets. A developmental activist described the problems in recruiting businesses for an inner-city incubator that his organization set up.

> When we go to talk to tenants [and say], "would you like to relocate to the [incubator]?" What are we telling them? We are telling them wouldn't you like to move into a high crime area in the inner city, in an old building with a developer who doesn't have enough capital to do all the repairs in an efficient way? (Rubin 2000a)

When working in neglected neighborhoods, physical construction often ends up being problematic. One activist described the problems that occurred in assembling a site for a community shopping center.

> Before the site was cleared, one Saturday night some winos were in the basement of one building. Torched it, burnt it, they pulled out a body Monday morning. So that,

there were so many things that went wrong. During construction people stole wood, they stole bricks, they harassed people. I was down there every night. Finally, we got the damn thing built.

Crime in a neighborhood increases insurance costs, and even when home costs are subsidized, individuals might still have trouble qualifying for a mortgage because of a checkered credit history. Property in the inner city often requires environmental remediation, repairing old homes or business sites necessitates removing lead paint and asbestos, replacing obsolete wiring with the cables needed for modern communication.

Projects aren't just plunked down full grown where and when the CESPO wants. Persuading people already in a community that a home for AIDS victims or work release prisoners, or transitional housing for people with mental illnesses will not destroy property values or threaten their personal security can prove daunting. Plus the CESPO itself questions whether it is right to impact poor neighborhoods with an endless stream of social service programs. Problems compound when social change organizations move from direct action to implementing development programs. As Bob Brehm points out, "A development project that strains an organization's capacity or siphons energy from its original focus can be worse than nothing at all. And a few houses cannot begin to address the need" (Brehm 2002, 16).

Still, CESPOs gamely work to implement complicated projects and often succeed.

Scheduling and Adaptation Development

Scheduling means laying out project steps in order, in advance, in ways that anticipate problems while adaptation implies midcourse corrections. Scheduling is pretty much a matter of common sense and experience. Land acquisition has to occur before construction can begin or a vehicle must be purchased and delivered before a program to transport the elderly to doctors can commence.

Once you know what the tasks are, and roughly in what order they should be done, it is often helpful to draw flowcharts that show when each task is supposed to start and how long it is supposed to last. Some tasks have to be done more or less at the same time, but before other sets of tasks. Table 22-1 provides an abbreviated version of the hundreds of steps involved in setting up an affordable housing project showing that financing, leasing, and physical development need to be coordinated.

Each of the steps listed can involve dozens of smaller tasks, from hiring carpenters and electricians to checking out what grants can be obtained. Later steps depend on the outcomes of earlier ones. If the pro formas—the spreadsheets on which costs and revenues are estimated—show that the rents will not cover the mortgage and operating costs, either rents have to be increased, or more effort required to find additional subsidies. Discoveries made when doing the physical construction, such as a defective sewer line or evidence of vandalism, increase costs. Communities might object when poor families are housed nearby, and then the organization has to decide whether to try to persuade neighbors, or to change the project to one that houses the

TABLE 21.1   Steps in Building an Affordable Housing Project

Property Development Tasks	Financing	Actions with Tenants and Community Members
Finding an appropriate property and having architectural and environmental assessment made	Obtaining funding to pay for site and property inspection	Determining the types of tenants wanted—families, homeless, special need populations
Acquiring the site, including doing title searches	Securing a subsidy from the local government, an intermediary, or a foundation to lower mortgage costs; seeing if trust fund money is available	Gain neighborhood support for the project, perhaps by offering to house those in the community most in need
Ensuring zoning compliance	Investigate special incentives such as historic tax credits that could encourage corporations to invest in the project	Locating tenants that have rent subsidies, for instance as owners of Section 8 certificates
Contracting for construction and rehabilitation, supervising the construction (this then breaks down into hundreds of smaller steps; each requiring government inspection)	Structure the deal in ways that enable banks and corporations to obtain the benefits of the Low Income Housing Tax Credit so they invest equity money	Check out the background of potential tenants. What is their credit history? Is there a history of crime? Are the people poor enough so that the building is eligible for the Low Income Housing Tax Credit?
Getting hookups for water, sewer, electricity from the appropriate agencies	Apply for Low Income Housing Tax Credit that the city or the state can allocate	Organize the tenants into a tenants' association
Gaining occupancy permits from government after the property is checked for safety, building codes, etc.	Locate a bank that will provide a mortgage, or evoke community reinvestment pressures to encourage the bank to be involved	
Set up a management team to collect rents, clean and maintain the building, and handle tenant problems	Calculate the total costs of running the property including the operating expenses and the repayment schedule for the mortgage	
	Calculate the rents needed and compare with the rents that can be reasonably expected. If the rents are not adequate, other subsidies have to be found to keep the property as affordable. Perhaps churches can be approached	

elderly poor. Scheduling makes clear the interdependence of tasks, determining when and where plans are required if failures occur.

More precisely in scheduling:

1. Divide up tasks into separable action steps. For example, break up a program to hold a community fair into the distinct steps of gaining permission to use a park, hiring security, arranging for cleanup, talking with other neighborhood associations on what they want to present, printing tickets, etc.
2. Examine tasks to see if something is missing to accomplish the overall project.
3. Examine the length of time to complete each task. It is especially important to know which tasks can be speeded up with more effort and which take a relatively fixed amount of time. A grant will or will not arrive on a given date—a task that cannot be hurried—whereas fifty people can clean up a park more quickly than can ten.
4. Note the interdependence among tasks. Legal title must be obtained to property before any physical work is done on it.
5. Prepare a chart, sometimes known as a Program Evaluation and Review Technique (PERT) chart, in which the timing and relationship among the tasks is laid out. The bottom line of the chart is marked with dates. Each task is represented by a line starting at its beginning date and continuing to when its conclusion is anticipated. The chart shows the interdependence of the tasks and points out potential bottlenecks.
6. The chart is examined for critical events, that is tasks that must be performed before the goal is reached. Not getting a permit for the park makes the fair illegal, while if the city tears down housing before it can be repaired, the plans for the organization's sweat-equity program will have to be terminated.
7. When roadblocks and delays are noted, resources are shifted to reduce the delays.

Partnering in Developing Projects

Many of the projects that community economic and social production organizations undertake require both expertise and capital that smaller CESPOs simply lack. To gain each, CESPOs will partner with private companies, government, intermediaries, or with other social change organizations. In partnerships, care is required to ensure that each partner knows what is expected, what tasks each is to perform, what costs are accrued, and how benefits or profits are to be divided.

Partnering with For-Profits. In partnering with for-profits, CESPOs bring a vision of the project, as well as access to grants that only nonprofits can receive. In turn the for-profit firm provides capital, technical expertise, and perhaps easier access to large loans. Responsibilities can be clearly divided; perhaps the for-profit will run and manage a new store, while the CESPO will handle the clearance and preparation of the site. Still, care is required in setting up legal structures that protect the interests of both partners, especially since nonprofits tend to be inexperienced in dealing with for-profits, while for-profits have difficulty in understanding what being mission driven, rather than profit-driven, entails (Chung 2004).

Some partnerships are informal, casual, more like a voluntary mentorship, often with a local businessperson who cares for the community, perhaps because he or she was raised in that area. Such people want to help community groups succeed. For instance,

> An African-American organization wanted to build a small office complex to rejuvenate a neighborhood, had access to grant money, but lacked the know-how. The developmental activist knew many business people including a well known commercial developer who had religious ties to the neighborhood.
>
> We told him we don't want you to develop this building for us and you walk away (as) a good deed and we don't benefit from the experience of having learned. What we want you to do is . . . assist us, so that we learn [emphasis], because we are doing this so that we can learn and we want to be in a position what we learn can be shared with the broader African-American community.
>
> And, this is what this guy said. "We'll do it." He said "The reason we'll do it is I don't feel that there is enough African-American participation in this city's development. And, we are not going to do it for you. We're going to do it with you and to the extent that you learn from us, then hopefully you will be in a position to do this your own self one day and help some other folk." (Rubin 2000a)

Such partnerships are mutually empowering.

Some partnerships are little more than legal arrangements. For example, many affordable housing projects are partially funded through the Low Income Housing Tax Credit, that by law requires a CESPO and investor to form a limited partnership. The private investor has to have sufficient confidence that the CESPO will follow the federal rules governing how tax credit money is spent but once the initial limited partnership has been negotiated, the private sector investor plays little role. Other partnerships are longer lasting, such as the one between New Community's Corporation (a CDC in Newark) with commercial firms, such as Path Mark Supermarkets or Dunkin' Donuts. In these partnerships, profit is fairly shared, stores are opened that benefit the poor community, and the CDC is actively involved in management. In addition, the CESPO might recommend (and train) community members to work in the firm.

On the downside, some types of partnerships must be avoided. There are unethical, for-profit firms that will pretend to partner with CESPOs, perhaps even pay them a fee for doing so, to obtain money from government programs. Similarly, some public sector efforts meant to assist the poor require that a certain portion of public funds be contracted to firms owned by the poor, women, or minorities. Unscrupulous for-profits pretend to partner with less experienced organizations while in reality just using the nonprofit as a front. Such situations should be avoided.

Partnering with the Public Sector.   Each time a community group receives a grant from a public agency, a partnership evolves in which the government as granting agent monitors that the money has been spent in a legal fashion. Compliance with HUD programs can entail obeying hundreds of pages of regulations. In such situations, partnerships are sort of one sided; the CESPO follows the regulations. A similar situation occurs when a CESPO is managing a social service contract for government.

Other times government, especially city governments, and the CESPO work hand in hand. Government might give land to a nonprofit for its project or use eminent domain to force slumlords to sell the land. In Boston, for instance, the city delegated its eminent domain powers, the right to force an owner to sell property, though at a fair price, to the Dudley Street Neighborhood Initiative. Government can help redevelopment projects work for the nonprofit by vigorously enforcing codes against derelict housing or by improving roads or water systems adjacent to commercial sites the CESPO is developing.

However, dealing with larger government bureaucracies can be a nightmare as government time cycles and the scheduling of nonprofits often run by very different clocks. In one case a developmental activist described, the CDC partnering with government was going to acquire and upgrade a city block on which to build a commercial strip. The CDC's plans were in place and had already received foundation funding. But then the city slowed the project, first condemning the wrong buildings, then misfiling the paper work. This delayed the project until after an election was held and all neighborhood projects were put on hold. With this further delay, the foundation withdrew support. Then the new city administration thought the land costs were too high and wanted to renegotiate the entire project, potentially delaying it another year. (Only after the CESPO threatened to embarrass the administration through a public demonstration was the logjam broken.)

In general, when partnering with government, enter the relationship gradually, and if a little bit works, try some more. Successful public-nonprofit partnerships emerge over time as city department heads realize that CESPOs with their experience in neighborhoods and in working with those in need are often far more efficient than more distant bureaucrats.

Partnering with Intermediaries. Intermediary organizations such as LISC, Enterprise, or Neighborhood Works help CESPOs find funding, package tax credit deals, and offer training. Through capacity-building efforts, such as the National Community Development Initiative, these intermediaries help CESPOs expand their ability to do projects, while as partners, intermediaries will hire expert consultants to work with local organizations. LISC, for example, will hire experts in supermarket development and work with a local CDC planning such a project. At times, though, local organizations fear that the intermediaries want to dominate what they do, finish a project, but not care whether the capacity of the CESPO has expanded (Rubin 2000a).

Partnering with Other CESPOs and Conventional Social Service Providers. A very effective partnership comes about when a less experienced CESPO works with a more experienced social change organization. In these peer-to-peer relationships, the newer CESPO determines what project is needed and then hires (sometimes with money foundations provide, other times as a pro bono consultant) experts from a sister organization to help implement it.

With another approach, a number of CESPOs partner and form what we term a *centralized task network organization* that handles shared technical tasks for all the nonprofit partners. For example, in Cleveland, community-based housing organizations set up the Cleveland Housing Network that hired specialists in handling tax credits, and staff who could do inspections to make sure refurbished homes meet building code standards and who could teach new homeowners and tenants skills. The smaller, neighborhood CESPOs determined which homes in their communities to refurbish and chose which individuals to house.

Finally, CESPOs partner with one another to set up social service networks to work with people with multiple problems such as the homeless who also suffer from substance dependence. Some of these networks link CESPOs with traditional social service providers, for example to help the homeless (Johnson and Castengera 1994) victims of environmental problems (Schopler 1994), AIDS victims (Mancoske and Hunzeker 1994); or to provide employment training, especially as part of welfare-to-work programs (Giloth 1998a; Harrison and Weiss 1998).

Project Implementation's Impact on the CESPO Itself

Project implementation might change the CESPO. At the extreme, working on larger projects can put the core organization at financial risk as dedicated activists find that the initial budget is not enough and are sorely tempted to find money elsewhere in the organization. Doing so is dangerous, it chances bankrupting the entire organization, and if funds are commingled can lead to legal sanctions.

Another danger occurs when the work on the project redefines the core mission of the organization without the activists intending this to occur. For instance, to complete the project expert staff are hired because of their technical skills rather than their fervor for social change. Such *mission drift* is not necessarily bad; transit-oriented development might be key to refurbishing the neighborhood, it's just not what the organization had been about, but it is too easy to drift and become just like a commercial developer forgetting that the goal is to empower others and help them build capacity.

Projects can also affect the broader image of the organization. Is the organization seen as that bunch of klutzes who tore down a building, never got the funds to build new housing, and now has created an empty lot that is used as an open air drug supermarket? Or, are these the folks who were able to bring back a quality supermarket so neighbors could walk and shop, rather than have to travel 4 miles?

Reputation counts. With foundations and government, an organization that has a reputation for bringing in projects on-budget and on-time and running them efficiently is far more likely to receive support for subsequent efforts, especially on the more complicated efforts that really do change the local economic structure.

Project Implementation: Management and Administration

A project has to be managed. Someone has to make sure that there is money to pay the bills, do the hiring, and ensure that the work is being done appropriately. Running a home for abused women means providing security, feeding people, doing laundry, finding legal support and medical backup on up to doing personal counselling, to say nothing about providing child care. At any time, problems can erupt, maybe a crisis in staffing, or a resident who becomes catatonic or a boyfriend who tracks down his victim.

More social production projects fail because of lack of good management than for any other reason, especially since management of social change projects is often more complex than that of for-profit work. For example, routine expenses are often higher in affordable rental housing property than in commercial projects since the buildings refurbished are often in worse shape to begin with. Running a social service organization that works with a multilingual clientele and hired multilingual staff creates managerial concerns with crosscultural communications. Those managing properties set up by community groups confront a "double bottom line" between their social missions and their need for economic survival (Bratt, Keyes, Schwartz, et al. 1994, 3). Developmental activists recognize

> We have to collect the rent. We're not a social service agency, per se, but in dealing with people [we] realize that there are a lot of folks who live in our units that have multiple problems. We've got babies having babies. . . . We've got people with very low education levels, people who are getting AFDC and towards the end of the month the food stamps run out. (Rubin 2000a)

Further, as landlords, developmental activists recognize that if they do not provide close supervision in buildings in rough neighborhoods that undesirables enter the building and destroy property. One activist explained what happened before management tightened up tenant screening:

> We started getting an average of 20 police calls a week to it. The management company was explicitly told to tighten screening like crazy, err on the side of being too conservative. . . . They screened like 200 people to get 11 units filled. . . . 20 cop calls a week. We got like 4 units that were averaging 5 domestic abuse calls to them a week.

Intense screening however, means that some people who desperately need the housing will be rejected and the community organization may be seen as authoritarian and rule bound.

Core to effective management is maintaining tight fiscal controls—watching where the dollars go and being concerned when outgo exceeds income. Enthusiasm in the development of a project can hide inadequate fiscal management. In Ohio, a CDC had set up a factory that repaired expensive industrial palettes. The project was exciting: it employed people from the area, rehabilitated an old, large, and unused building, cut costs for companies that purchased the palettes, and, in re-using material, was environmentally sound. But no one bothered to monitor the middle management who did not supervise the friends who were hired causing the operation to hemorrhage funds.

Being a nonprofit on a low budget, often obtained from grants, poses even more difficulties. To effectively run a project, employees must have the same (we feel better) skills than their counterparts in the private sector—in keeping financial records, preparing a pro forma, negotiating with vendors, repairing machines. Yet the private sector can pay much more than can most nonprofits. Keeping skilled staff can be problematic. Management must also be undertaken while at the same time foundation or government employees second guess decisions. For example, in a limited equity cooperative housing project, a board democratically chosen from the tenant-owners nominally is in charge, but outside funders will insist that the CESPO maintain title to the property and carefully manage the housing. Management then is reporting to two bosses with potentially two sets of objectives, a situation that is bound to lead to stress.

Management can be set up in ways that empower organization members. One approach is to have elected board members and community members evaluate both the projects and the staff. Another is to make sure the board has on it those who are receiving the service or at least have similar backgrounds to people being helped by the organization. Board and managers should interact frequently. The board needs to understand managerial problems—rents have to be collected or bills cannot be paid. The technical staff may need to be reminded that the bottom line is caring for people and improving the community, not simply running in the black.

Finally, empowerment ideals and managerial efficiency are best reconciled when those in administrative positions are themselves advocates of progressive social change. When possible, hire people who care about mission and then send them off for specialized training. Growing your own managers can be more costly and time consuming than hiring someone from the private sector with the requisite skills, but in the long run it seems to us it is better to ensure that the social change mission drives the administration and not the other way around.

Contract Administration and Contracting for Services

Community economic and social production organizations have to comply with contracts they receive and in turn often contract with others for services. When a social change organization administers a contract, the first rule is to make sure terms are consistent with the organizational goals—a contract with the city to do patrol as a form of crime prevention might be a Faustian bargain if it makes it harder for the organization to provide alternatives to help at risk youngsters. Contract administration means paying close attention to what expenses or actions are allowed by the contract and which are not. Can a contracted legal service organization go beyond helping individuals with legal problems and bring class action suits or undertake advocacy? Under current contracts most likely not, so other funds are needed for these activities. At the end of the contract period, the funding agency is going to want to know that its rules were followed and its objectives obtained so handling contracts implies keeping careful records.

Social change organizations themselves contract out for specialized services (to complicate matters as the money they use for doing so might in turn come from government or foundations that in turn monitor the contracts). Fortunately, many consultants and technical support firms provide services for nonprofits and community groups and recognize the importance of carrying out an empowerment agenda. Universities, especially those located in inner-city areas, maintain technical centers to work with community organizations while professionals, including lawyers and architects, can be hired on pro bono contracts—that is, work for free or at nominal costs for nonprofits.

When hiring consultants or technical assistance providers, it is vital to carefully spell out obligations in a legally binding contract and make sure to specify:

1. The scope, quantity, and quality of work expected.
2. The balance of responsibility between the contractor and the social change organization.
3. The time when the contract is to begin and when the contractor is to complete the work and submit the results.
4. An exact description of what the results are to be, including how the results are to be delivered to the organization.
5. The standards that must be followed in completing the contract. Spell out who judges whether these standards have been met and what happens when they are not met. Work out in advance who will reconcile disputes between the two parties.
6. The amount and timing of the payment. Some contractors want a down payment for materials. If moderate, such requests are reasonable. More often, the first payment may be made on the submission of the first deliverable—that is the first product done by the contractor—and the remainder may be paid as each step of the work is completed.
7. The conditions under which one or both parties can back out of the contract.

Care is needed in wording the contract since alterations can be expensive. Remember that contractors have schedules and other obligations and cannot always adjust if your organization changes its mind.

Evaluation and Monitoring of Economic and Social Production Work

Evaluation and monitoring build upon the research procedures described in Chapter 9 to determine how well a program or project is succeeding. Monitoring involves noting what is happening, perhaps on a daily basis, to be able to adjust actions in real time, while evaluation is to determine if at the end the program or project worked, why or why not, and what the overall impact was. To use a medical analogy, monitoring is the daily measurement of vital signs, while impact analysis shows if a treatment is effective.

More sophisticated social change organizations build in ongoing evaluation and monitoring of both their projects and the organizations themselves. For example, the community development corporation, Coastal Enterprises Inc.

(CEI) systematically started measuring and monitoring its program outcomes in the early 1990s in order to provide funders, policymakers and staff with a better understanding of the difference it was making in achieving its mission to help create economically and environmentally healthy communities in which all people, especially those with low incomes, can reach their full potential. (Coastal Enterprises Inc. 2006, preface)

But defining what is meant by outcome is far from simple. For CEI, impact means

"an outcome that would not happen but for CEI's intervention." Over the years, CEI realized that it was unlikely it could "prove" its impact since rigorous random assignment studies with control groups that are used to determine causal relationships to program outcomes were infeasible other than in exceptional circumstances. In reality, CEI "monitors outcomes" which occur after its program interventions. This enables CEI to look for anomalies and to question trends . . . CEI has searched for indicators and evidence that describe its impact. The process of inquiry, in itself, is valuable. (Coastal Enterprises Inc. 2006, preface)

In addition, social change organizations have to evaluate short-term gains while recognizing that they are but one step in the broader process of bringing about structural improvement (Coastal Enterprises Inc. 2006).

In general, evaluations ask about the impact of programs or projects on those who are the intended beneficiaries. Proper evaluations require agreement on what the objectives ought to be and how progress toward achieving them has occurred. If the objective in improving housing is to give people a secure base from which to find jobs, to give children the opportunity to attend the same school with the same classmates, and to stabilize the neighborhood, is the plan working? Do people who receive an IDA save more, and use the money to improve their education, housing, or employment? Do micro-enterprises move people into stable work situations? Has crime been lowered and are people more willing to deal with the police? How many women have been removed from abusive situations and of these how many have been placed in safer housing and have found employment?

Evaluations measure both primary and secondary impacts of programs and projects. For instance, one study evaluated the secondary effects of community-based housing on a neighborhood and found that in neighborhoods where community groups had built affordable housing people felt safer and were more willing to participate in community activities (Briggs, Mueller with Mercer Sullivan 1997). An evaluation of housing in New York City reinforced these findings, noting that people who lived in cooperatives were more likely to volunteer for collective efforts than those in regular apartments (Saegert and Winkel 1998). Impacts, though, can be negative. A program to improve housing can trigger gentrification, thereby displacing the very people that housing programs were meant to serve.

Impact evaluations ask, what were the goals of the program and were they achieved? It also asks who benefited from the program or project; it is almost always easier to run a successful project for the elderly than for families, to get jobs for experienced and educated workers, rather than inexperienced and uneducated workers, or to help successful rather than marginal businesses. Evaluations help point out the harder populations to serve.

Evaluations measure both objective outcomes and perceptions. Objective outcomes might be how much income has improved among those in a job training program. Perceptual or satisfaction measures tap people's opinions or feelings. For example, a question such as "Do you feel more secure in the neighborhood?" would be a satisfaction measure for a community crime watch program in contrast to the objective measures of crime rates. Neither objective nor satisfaction measures are necessarily better, but they should not be confused. If people feel safer, and because of feeling safer become more involved in community activities, that is to the good even if crime has not been reduced.

Evaluations enable funders as well as the CESPOs to see what works, and why, and then make alterations if the goals remain appropriate but the means of accomplishing them are not. For instance, evaluations showed that IDAs are more successful when those involved are monitored more closely and receive a higher match for every dollar they save (Sherraden, Johnson, Clancy, et al. 2000), suggesting how to run future programs.

Evaluations are also done to see the impact of a program on the community economic and social production organization itself. Has the program enabled the organization to expand, find crucial staff, and be better able to serve its community? Or has the demands of the program been such that the CESPO has dropped all other efforts and is doing little more than implementing the program task, ignoring other empowerment goals.

Program monitoring complements evaluation by following what is happening in real time to allow adjustments to be made answering such questions as:

How much service is being produced? How much money has the community credit union lent out with what return rate? How many women have been housed in the spouse abuse center, and of those, how many were able to restart their lives?

How many people are served and who are they? How many people come to the homeless shelter each night? Are they families or individuals? What is the income level of the people who participate in the lease-purchase program?

How do people in the social production organization spend their time and resources? Are workers in the housing organization spending full time responding to tenants' complaints, or are they able to find time to plan new projects?

Program monitoring helps an organization identify and shore up weaknesses. If only those who are relatively better off are buying the new homes built, perhaps the organization should try harder to reach out to the very poor. If abused women return again and again to the shelter, maybe different services are needed to bolster their self-confidence, or perhaps more practical matters need to be of concern—helping the women find alternative housing or to earn sufficient money so they're no longer dependent on the abusive partner. As part of program monitoring, the organization examines *efficiency measures* which indicate how much of an activity is being accomplished for how much cost. Community employment training is evaluated in terms of the money spent to train new employees for each permanent job.

Careful program monitoring distinguishes between effort and outcome. Effort indicates the energy, time, or amount of money spent by the organization to accomplish its goals: dollars put into rehabilitation or number of hours a day that an emergency hot line is available. Outcomes measure the changes brought about by the program: How much did the quality of housing improve as a result of the rehabilitation? Did the rate of illegal dope transactions decline in the area served by the hot line? Were fewer people cold in winter? People work hard on projects and want to be praised for their efforts, but hard work on activities that are poorly conceived or implemented is of little benefit to the community.

Conclusion

Social production projects provide a way for people to take control of declining economies and to overcome the disempowering consequences of personal problems. Such projects are part of the can-do spirit of community action that both accomplish a measurable task while reasserting human dignity.

Successes obtained in economic and social production projects show that mastering skills in social administration—in budgeting, in personnel management, in negotiations, in partnering with other organizations, or in preparing a spreadsheet—need not require withdrawal from a social change agenda. Instead it is through learning these technical matters that social production organizations renew hope and empower those in poor communities. Project development can provide a sense of the possible to those who have lost hope. Empowerment is not simply about feeling good, or making the establishment quake, but it is also about maintaining and sustaining projects that provide the wherewithal to do so.

EPILOGUE

Working toward a Progressive Society

Progressive social change is about defending the weak from the strong, gaining resources to reduce human hardship, and striving to promote an equitable society. It is about battling for economic and social justice, working to protect and enhance civil liberties, and respecting the environment.

We have described why progressive change is needed; examined the three pillars of organizing; presented the historic setting and policy environment that shape organizing; illustrated what has been accomplished through social activism; and presented an array of complementary tools for mobilizing individuals, building organizations, undertaking confrontational campaigns, and working on economic and social production projects. In this chapter we share our own personal reflections about progressive organizing.

Reflection and Organizing

Community and social change organizations provide the means to get from the troubled present to an empowered future. But activists need both time and place to reflect on what progress is being made, what seems effective, why failures have occurred, where innovations are needed, and, most important, to reinforce the confidence that the effort is worthwhile.

Reflection is about asking whether a social change organization has remained true to its mission, and, more deeply, whether or not that mission still holds. Activists reconsider the values of the organization, about where it is going, why, and if the actions being taken at present are getting them there. How militant should the organization be? To what extent should the organization work within the capitalist economy or try to set up alternatives? Is now the time to make a push for major structural changes or is it better to work on small improvements? Reflection points out contradictions between separate goals and indicates ways of reconciling them, while suggesting how to prepare for future activism.

But how do activists, scattered within a wide variety of organizations and working on many different issues, collectively reflect on what progressive activism is about? No single conversation is possible nor will suffice. Instead reflection is an ongoing, fragmented process that takes place when activists meet with one another at conferences, join together in shared actions, read and write for a common literature, or talk with one another on lists, and pass on traditions through training academies. Electronic lists such as COMM-ORG encourage such dialogue; reading and responding to quasi-biographical books such as Ed Chambers' *Roots for Radicals* (Chambers 2003) brings about reflection on which models are most suitable, while books such as Todd Gitlin's *Letters to a Young Activist* (Gitlin 2003) use the sixties as a mirror to reflect on present-day work. Recently the Ricanne Hadriane Initiative for Community Organizing sponsored a new journal, the *Journal of Community Power*, to encourage activists to examine the broader implications of their work, while in December 2005, to celebrate its thirty-fifth anniversary, ACORN held a conference, much of which was devoted to asking where the movement should go.

Finally, academics encourage reflection. Educational programs in schools of social work provide an opportunity, not simply to teach techniques but to question why we do what we do. Academic authors such as Harry Boyte, Eric Shragge, Randy Stoecker, Robert Fisher, and ourselves attempt in writings to pose questions about the future of progressive organizing.

Tensions and Reconciliations

We remain optimistic that progress to bring about a more just society is possible in spite of severe opposition from those in the establishment. Yet, we have noted major tensions that can paralyze social change efforts internally. Developmental activists ignore street-level organizers rather than work together to pressure government; proponents of confrontational actions barely speak to those who support consensus organizing. People from different ethnic-racial organizations fear one another to such an extent that they will not unite in a common battle for economic justice, while conversations across social class are strained at the very least. Let us examine major tensions that beset present-day social activists and organizers.

1. *Mobilizing by focusing on the individual or the collectivity.* How are the motivations for individual involvement reconciled with the communal spirit on which sustained activism depends?
2. *Interdependent problems and contradictory solutions.* Can the fact that solutions to one problem can exacerbate another be resolved?
3. *Faith and religion in organizing.* Faith provides a sustaining motivation for long-term battles, yet faith and religion can divide one group from another.
4. *The organization: means or end.* Organizations are the tools for conducting effective social change work, yet at times, sustaining the organization displaces social action.
5. *Balancing expertise and involvement within the organization.* Can technical expertise be harnessed in ways that empower others rather than making them dependent?

6. *Organizational partnerships: co-optation or empowerment.* Is it possible for those in social change organizations to partner with (or take funds from) those in the establishment without being co-opted?

Even more fundamental are two remaining concerns:

7. *Persisting tensions from race, class, gender, sexuality.* Just as the broader society is divided by race, class, and gender, so are those involved in social change work. Can these structural chasms be bridged?
8. *Social production, place-based organizing, social movement, or advocacy.* Different paths to social change work are followed. To what extent are these approaches antagonistic or complementary?

And finally, underlying many of these issues is the core question of what social activism is about:

9. *Is organizing about solving problems or changing the underlying structure.* Fundamentally, what should social activism be about?

The Individual or the Collectivity

Organizing people to solve personal problems is far easier than creating a sense of responsibility for the collectivity. People reject the idea of collective responsibility since our society values individualism while many quickly forget what it is they owe to the past activism. Today a young woman moving up the organizational hierarchy assumes her advancement has occurred because of her individual skills and contributions, forgetting that feminist activists had to campaign vigorously to open her path. We must bring back the idea that progressive gains for individuals come about only through collective progress.

Interdependent Problems

Organizing efforts can bog down when solutions to one problem seem to worsen another problem. Programs to upgrade homes in poor neighborhoods can so improve the community that richer people move in and displace the poor. In multiethnic communities, when one group organizes it is seen as a threat by others. To earn a living, native Alaskans, among the poorest people in the country, engage in extractive industries that are harmful to the environment. Nowadays some African American organizations oppose immigrants' rights groups, fearing that newly arrived workers will reduce employment opportunities.

These tensions are not always easy to resolve, especially in the short run. Poor people themselves have advocated to have toxic incinerators located in their communities, anticipating new jobs, and ignoring the severe environmental impacts. Either the polar bear's habitat should be preserved and Native Alaskans relocated to cities, or the Native Alaskans stay and polar bears starve. Either a job goes to a woman or minority, or to a white male. If a neighborhood is improved shouldn't the market determine who is able to live there? Recent evidence has shown that immigrant labor has slightly reduced the earning power of lower income workers.

Anticipating the problems, though, can reduce their impact. Experienced housing and neighborhood renewal organizations have worked out ways of battling gentrification. Repaired homes are sold to lower income people but with deed restrictions that do not allow them to be marketed to the rich. Environmental activists promote green industries, including recycling, that provide jobs without negatively impacting the environment. Eco-tourism in some areas helps people gain employment while protecting the fauna and flora.

Other times, what is called for is searching for the broader structural causes and then designing campaigns that confront these deeper causes. Immigrant labor is in demand because it will work at illegally low wages, often off the books, in working conditions that others simply would not accept. The solution here is in enforcement of labor laws and in ensuring that fair minimum wages are in place. When solutions to one problem seem to create another, both situations need to be recast to determine the underlying structural causes.

Faith-Based Organizing: Social and Economic Agendas in Conflict

Organizing has often been done with the help of faith-based organizations. People of the cloth, a Dr. Martin Luther King, Jr., or Reverend Jesse Jackson, were at the forefront of the civil rights movement; Ernesto Cortes motivates through biblical quotes; liberation theologists risk their lives to inspire people to fight for economic and social justice. Prayer is a tool in confrontation, a challenge to the targets to live up to their religious obligations. Social service missions of community groups are often an extension of the teachings and practices of faith-based institutions. Major organizing networks—IAF, PICO, Gamaliel—work through churches, synagogues, and mosques, recognizing that people who worship together already form a community. Progressive organizing has been driven by faith and has found a home in places of worship.

Yet, caution is required in organizing through faith as faith can divide as much as it can unite. The very bonds that unite co-religionists separate those of different beliefs, making it hard to form a broader movement. Further, on social issues of gay rights, abortion, the role of women in general, or even science versus theology, churches, even those that are progressive on economic matters, can be in the opposition. Conservative faiths might oppose gay rights and abortion, want to subordinate women, believe in biblical inerrancy, and oppose evolution, while joining with economically conservative politicians as part of a backlash movement (Phillips 2006).

For those focusing on local issues—reduction of crime, housing the homeless, home building or repair, advocating for parks or infrastructure repair, and perhaps, ensuring quality of schools—organizing with and through churches is still the way to go. Coalitions of churches have fought economic predators and worked against payday lenders. But in building a broader movement, one that focuses on wedge social issues, caution is advised in seeking out faith-based support.

Organization as Means or End

Without strong and effective organizations social change efforts would often be for naught. But there is a danger that sustaining organizations becomes the end in and of itself. Having a large membership provides clout, perhaps dues, but attracting members without ensuring that there is agreement on overall goals, or commitment to the broader issues, is not the way to go.

Organizations need money to stay alive. Yet, government or foundations are reluctant to pay for social change activity—the more radical, the less likely the funding. To what extent does changing a task to acquire funding constitute a sellout on the organization's mission? This question becomes more acute with organizations set up to do economic and social production work. Debate rages whether building homes or providing social services does anything to battle structural inequality or simply offers a palliative.

Expertise and Involvement

Increasingly technical expertise is required to run action campaigns, as well as social production efforts, but relying on experts distracts from mobilization and empowerment. Fortunately both are possible. Experts may not be needed for every task while shared expertise can be developed among organizational members.

The core way of balancing expertise with involvement is to make sure fundamental policies of the organization are made through informed membership votes. Experts can prepare background packages explaining what is at stake or providing alternative approaches, but the choice of where to go, how fast, and for what purpose remains a membership concern.

Autonomy or Dependent Partnerships

Partnering with government or the support sector can create a dependency that weakens the social change organization. Accepting funds from investors and government agencies might require following their conditions for the expenditure of those funds. Similarly, working in coalitions risks that other groups' agendas or values may determine what the individual organizations undertake.

Organizations, though, can build capacity through partnerships that have not yet become dependent. In coalition work, the trick is to ensure that the coalition's board is structured democratically so each participating group has an effective say. To buffer the pressure from funders, an organization must remain *mission driven* even if that means not getting a grant.

But when money is really needed funders do insist upon a say—after all it is their money. What to do? First, make sure the idea for the project or the service originated from the membership. Second, seek out support from several sources so that the organization can play off the objectives of the separate funders. Further, keep in mind that when social change organizations work through coalitions and trade associations they can shape the agendas of funders (Rubin 2000a).

Persisting Tensions from Race, Class, Gender, and Sexuality

Progressive activists battle societal inequalities that stem from the unjust hierarchies of people by race, ethnicity, gender, social or economic class, or sexuality. Unfortunately, these same inequalities can harm social change organizations themselves, often in complicated and unanticipated ways.

Stress comes about when organizations of people from one cultural group are run by individuals from another. Tensions can come about, based on ignorance or thoughtlessness, or a lack of ability to empathize with the other. Are fund-raisers, or celebrations, or parties set up in ways that assume that only heterosexual couples will attend? Are speaker systems in place to help those who hear less well, and are doors wide enough and ramps in place so the wheelchair-bound are not excluded? Do people with more formal education dominate discussions? Do minorities fully participate in organizational decisions?

Worse yet, the very bonding that those of a given ethnicity, class, gender, or sexuality have with one another creates divisions. Those who come together to battle for gender equality might find that black, white, brown, yellow, and red women see the issue in quite different ways. Feminist organizations have been torn apart by social class, as upper- and middle-class women have a different take on inequality than do poorer women. Gay organizations have broken asunder as the gendered concerns of lesbians and male homosexuals divide individuals more strongly than a shared gayness unites.

But what to do? First, do not deny that these tensions exist—feminists must recognize that all inequalities are not based on gender, while those who see the world through the lens of economic class must accept that people do not live by bread alone, that ethnic or gender identities can be of a higher priority than economic gains. Deal with these tensions explicitly, not as some underlying hidden matter. Don't pretend that just because everyone in the organization is a woman, that those who are black and white and brown might not have a different approach.

Organizing, Direct Action, Advocacy, or Economic and Social Production

Social mobilization is about getting people to join together for direct action—using pressure to force others to change their ways. Advocacy works through trained personnel that push a progressive agenda; and economic and social production actions are about providing goods, services, and social support. Unfortunately, supporters of each separate path squabble about what approach is best, with battles fierce and disruptive. Direct action organizers contend that social production organizations ignore "empowerment" and instead opt for "economic efficiency" and choose a "bottom-line business pragmatism" rather than work to promote "neighborhood controlled social change" and by doing so brush aside the possibility of structural change. Activists recognize the reality of what is being said. As a community developer shared with us,

> Organizing, well if I don't go out and talk to these people, today, I can talk to them next week. But, if I don't get this [financial] stuff in line for the development, it's not going to happen.

Community level organizers charge advocates with elitism when they work in a non-membership organization, yet seem willing to set the agendas for others.

Fortunately, bridges have been built. For instance, proponents of direct action and those of social production accept the need "to 'row the boat with two oars' increasing using these two strategies, and their related tactics, in complementary ways" (Callahan, Mayer, Palmer, et al. 1999). Many advocates work for larger coalitions whose membership combines activists involved in direct action, social production, and in advocacy. Studies show that even community-based development organizations are involved in organizing work (Center for Public Finance and Housing 1994). In fact, in Massachusetts the trade association for economic development organization is a principle sponsor for local level organizing. Research has shown that while developmental activists are often too busy to join in direct action, they support organizations so engaged (Rubin 2000a) and strongly believe that their work should be and is about structural social change (Dorius 2006).

We feel strongly that rhetoric that emphasizes the antagonisms between these separate paths for improving the lives of the poor and poor communities should be toned down. Each approach complements the other on the broader path to bring about progressive social change.

Problem-Solving or Structural Change

Organizing is about both problem solving and bringing about broader social change. Problem solving means fixing an immediate here and now matter while structural change focuses on revamping the set of beliefs, ideas, and political and economic institutions that allow inequalities based on race, ethnicity, class, gender, and sexuality to persist. Problem solving is usually considered to be a pragmatic approach, while most structural change work is guided by a more fundamental ideological belief that the system is not working and needs a serious overhaul. Some actions are clearly about problem solving; a call from the president of the local neighborhood association to city hall that gets a stop signed replaced, while the street demonstrations such as those in the militant protests against the World Trade Organization and globalization is meant as an attack of systemic economic inequality.

Tensions between problem-solving approaches and bringing about structural change persist with many fearing that in working to solve problems, broader questions are shunted aside. In reflexive writing, Harry Boyte has warned that activists must battle the tendency to concentrate too narrowly on the immediate and personal (problems) that are "detached from any enlarged political vision" (Boyte 1989, 12), while Fisher and Shragge lament how problem solving has "dulled the political edge of organizing and removed its passion for social change" (Fisher and Schragge 2000, 1). Instead, to them, organizing ought to be about "engaging in a wider struggle for social and economic justice" (Fisher and Schragge 2000, 8), and in so doing "build opposition, use confrontation in its diverse arsenal of strategies and tactics, . . . that begins at the local level and builds outward" (Fisher and Schragge 2000, 15).

Our tilt in this book has been toward efforts that are about structural change, but we strongly support accomplishing here-and-now projects. We question those who in the name of revolution demean developmental activists and social service providers, yet offer no alternatives in return, except vaguely formulated beliefs that the system must be changed. We feel that problem-solving efforts can be readily cast within the broader concerns of bringing about structural change. If what activists are doing is building a home that shelters, that's well and good, but not enough; if the home is meant as a tool toward empowerment through ownership and a fairer sharing of wealth, that's better. Winning in a confrontational campaign to stop a housing developer from destroying pristine land can be part of the broader struggle when it is made clear that the victory is about ordinary people gaining power, not just saving trees from destruction.

Activism is about battling the bigger issues, fighting for racial, sexual, and gender justice and working to reduce the extremes of economic and political inequality. But smaller victories and individual projects are part of this process so long as each effort is intentionally framed as a step toward the broader goal.

Where Do We Go from Here?

Social activism has created a persistent democratic culture that pushes for change and improvement. It does so by following a variety of complementary social action and social production models. Some changes are of a visible, material sense: quality homes where there had been derelict properties, better health care, more income for working people. Other changes are on how people see and understand the world—a belief that people are equal no matter their race, ethnicity, or sexuality, or of teaching people to have the confidence to speak out, not be afraid. Progressive activism is about changing the political structure to increase the voice of ordinary people; in part battling economic injustice, and in part ending inequalities based on race, gender, or sexuality. Progressive work involves respect for the natural environment and a belief negotiations beat violence whether in settling local disputes or disagreements between nations.

But what are the next steps? In the remaining pages of this book, we sketch some of the more pressing in-your-face issues facing those who want progressive change. We then conclude by arguing that solving these and other problems provide steps toward the broader, structural reform of society that can come about through building a broad-based, cross-issue progressive social movement.

More Immediate Issues

It is, of course, nearly impossible to anticipate what here-and-now concerns will confront progressive activists. Who could have predicted 9-11, the opposition to the war in Iraq, or the dramatic increase in the battle to preserve civil liberties and privacy?

Some issues persist. Racism, sexism, and homophobia continually must be battled, but now in more subtle forms than those that existed a generation ago. Racism is easy to recognize when crosses are burned or epithets shouted, but how does one distinguish racism in mortgage lending when those who refuse to lend say the decision is based on economics and offer as evidence that race and wealth are closely linked? Are those who oppose immigration reform battling an economic issue, concerned with the illegality of some immigrants so the concern is about law and order, or are they evoking a racist nativism against people of Latino descent?

Issues of economic inequality stay at the top of the agenda. As the wealth of the country expands it does so unevenly, with the rich getting richer, while the poor, and increasingly the middle class, falling further behind. Changes in the tax structure have deprived government of money required for social programs, while the lack of universal health care, combined with the instability in jobs, has left many working people both poorer and insecure. Actions to bring about living wages and just compensation become ever more important. Unions that had been irrelevant to social change work for generations are now strong allies, especially those who speak for people involved in service work. Globalization exports jobs while, as companies cross borders, pressuring them to be fair to labor becomes harder and harder.

With the rise of the religious right and the increasing influence of conservative talk show hosts, settled social issues have been re-opened. The support of family values becomes an excuse to question the status of women, while homophobia gains public legitimacy, and women's right to choose has morphed into issues of baby-killing. Social change organizations must accelerate their rearguard actions to protect past social gains.

Many problems stem from the profound demographic changes: the more established population ages while the newer groups are younger. The older groups are worried about the instability of retirement plans, the younger about the need to improve quality education, and both about the cost and quality of health care. Demographic change has further implications: Builders need to be pressured to construct accessible homes and offices, laws must be strengthened to prevent job discrimination against the elderly, and more hospice facilities are required.

To us, though, the crucial underlying issue is in battling an increasingly pervasive *politics of selfishness and greed*, a sense that there is no collective responsibility, that individualism is the only path. Privatization of retirement programs, the shredding of the social safety net, the unwillingness to set up a single payer health plan, the belief that to pay taxes benefits only others, all show a resurgence of selfish individualism. Selfishness and greed is seen in those that buy large cars and trucks, complain about gas prices, want to destroy the environment in the search for more fuel, refuse to fund mass transit, and deny the human causes of global warming. The immediate problem is how to bring back a sense of collectivity, convincing people that we are part of one broad community, rather than a collection of contending, self-centered individuals. That is the challenge for cultural reform.

Steps to Take

This book has been written to present the syncretic approach to social change that argues that social and economic production work, neighborhood organizing, direct action, and advocacy efforts are complementary to one another and together provide a multipronged approach to achieving a more just society. Together these approaches both empower individuals and help set up organizations to bring about change. Without a sense of empowerment people will not act, but without organizations in place they lack the capacity to do so.

But feeling empowered through shouting, yelling, and making those in high places cringe is not enough unless core changes are made. Scaring a banker into a meeting counts as does reaching an agreement to increase local investment. But each is but a step toward the broader goal of questioning why the financial system tilts toward the wealthy and big business, and then doing something about it. Shutting down a school board meeting when local demands are ignored demonstrates power. Gaining bilingual teachers and teachers' aides is a concrete step in helping the children of new groups learn and become part of the broader society. But asking why education is ill-funded, often warehouses the poor, and is split along class lines and then doing something about it is what structural change entails.

But the battle is also a fight over ideas, beliefs, or cultural understandings. Activists work to undo the cultural stereotype that people are personally to blame for problems they face by teaching others to understand how a biased economic and social structure creates many of the ills faced. The battle between individualism and shared responsibility, a belief that we should live in a community of inclusiveness, rather than being on our own is a core part of the ideational struggle for social activists. In doing this work we are, in Ernie Cortes' words, "reweaving the social fabric" (Cortes 1996). Doing so keeps alive both the hope that change is possible and the knowledge to do so. The sense that the personal is the political needs to be reinforced.

Possibilities are enhanced as we build toward a broader progressive movement. Rather than seeing the different social change models as rivaling one another, learn how they complement each other and build on that strength. Direct action and advocacy work bring about the pressure that makes available the resources required for social production work. Social production organizations provide a solid base in the community, a day in-day out contact. Bridging the gap between activists who focus on place, those on issue, or on identities remains vital.

A broader movement emerges as people understand how what initially appear as separate issues at their root are closely linked. Rather than just fighting crime or building homes or improving schools, activists now work to combine anticrime efforts and programs to upgrade the schools, seeing each as reflecting underlying inequalities. Those pushing for new jobs will also work on improved transportation and education or job training and daycare. Holistic approaches encourage activist groups to join together as issues of economic inequality and those of racial (or gender) justice blur into one another. Activists ask why those of a given color or gender almost always end up at the bottom of the economic heap. Recognition needs to be given that ethnic rivalries do exist but that to bring about core changes these rivalries must be bridged. Multiethnic and multicultural coalitions come about as the separate groups each understand that they all share the same economic and social problems.

In building a progressive movement, activist coalitions are vital. Within these coalitions, advocates, in-your-face direct action organizers, and development activists work together for a common cause. The movement expands as individuals who belong to several activist coalitions link these separate issue areas. A fair housing advocate in a coalition fighting for more housing will join organizations that defend the CRA, while also working with racial justice organizations. A transportation equity network brings together those who care about public transit-environmental activists, who join with numerous neighborhood organizations that in turn link a multitude of activists together. As activists working on different fronts come together, an increasing number recognize that progressive change extends beyond the immediate issues.

The energy and determination of those engaged in social change continue to grow. Lit by knowledge of past successes the path ahead is clear, though much remains to be done. Victories build on each other, providing hope for future progress, and teach us that social change evolves. As Todd Gitlin reminded us "movements are made not born" (Gitlin 2003, 26). Step-by-step we are building a cross-issue, multiethnic progressive movement willing to engage in the political process to challenge both unjust economic and social structures as well as the set of disempowering cultural beliefs to bring about a more just and equitable society.

Activism is about creating social change, action by action, project by project. This sense of progress gives people the energy to keep going, and we must keep going, as more needs to be done. We are hopeful but realistic, and accept the perspective of an activist organization that, on winning a crucial battle, declared:

Victory
"One Step Forward, One Mile to Go"

BIBLIOGRAPHY

Ableidinger, Amanda. "Target: Problem Properties: A CDC Targets Abandonment." *Shelterforce* xxiv (January/February 2002): 8–11.

ACLU Online. *FBI Targets Peaceful Protestors, PATRIOT Act Challenge*, 2003.

ACORN. "Ten Years Later: A Promise Unfulfilled: The National Voters Registration Act in Public Assistance Agencies, 1995–2005." Brooklyn, NY: ACORN, 2005.

———. "Acorn News," 2005—February.

"ACORN Katrina Survivors Association Will Unite Displaced Residents to Work for a Just Recovery." *ACORN News*, 18 October 2005.

"ACORN Marches on Wells Fargo, Files Lawsuit," 2004. www.acorn.org/index.php?id=8512.

ACORN Fair Housing. *The High Cost of Credit: Disparities in High-Priced Refinance Loans to Minority Homeowners in 125 American Cities*. Baltimore, MD: ACORN Fair Housing, 2005.

Alderson, George, and Everett Sentman. *How You Can Influence Congress: The Complete Handbook for the Citizen Lobbyist*. New York: E. P. Dutton, 1979.

Alexander, Ernest R. *How Organizations Act Together: Interorganizational Coordination in Theory and Practice*. Luxembourg: Gordon and Breach, 1995.

Alinsky, Saul D. *Reveille for Radicals*. New York: Random House, 1969.

———. *Rules for Radicals*. New York: Random House, 1971.

Alliance for Justice. *Worry-Free Lobbying for Nonprofits: How to Use the 501(h) Election to Maximize Effectiveness*. Washington, DC: Alliance for Justice, 2001.

Anderson, Terry. *The Movement and the Sixties: Protest in America from Greensboro to Wounded Knee*. New York: Oxford, 1995.

Andrews, Kenneth, and Bob Edwards. "The Organizational Structure of Local Environmentalism." *Mobilization* 10, no. 2 (June 2005): 213–34.

Anner, John. "Having the Tools at Hand: Building Successful Multicultural Social Justice Organizations." ed. John Anner. In *Beyond Identity Politics: Emerging Social Justice Movements in Communities of Color*, 163–66. Boston, MA: South End Press, 1996.

Ashkenaz, Judy. "Grassroots Organizing and the Democracy Party—the Vermont Rainbow Experience." *Monthly Review*, May 1986, 8–21.

Aspen Institute. *Building Wealth: The New Asset-Based Approach to Solving Social and Economic Problems*. Washington, DC: Aspen Institute, 2005.

Atlas, John. "In Red State Florida, Victory for the Working People." *Shelterforce* xxvii (January/February 2005A): 24–25; 27.

———. "The Battle in Brooklyn." *Shelterforce* xxvii (November/December 2005B): 12–15.

Avery, Michel, Brian Auvine, Barbara Streibel, and Lonnie Weiss. *Building United Judgment: A Handbook for Consensus Decision Making*. Madison, WI: The Center for Conflict Resolution, 1981.

Bachrach, Peter, and Morton S. Baratz. "Decisions and Non-Decisions: An Analytical Framework." *American Political Science Review* 57, no. 3 (1963): 632–42.

Bachrach, Peter, and Aryeh Botwinick. *Power and Empowerment: A Radical Theory of Participatory Democracy*. Philadelphia: Temple University Press, 1992.

Bailis, Lawrence. *Bread or Justice: Grassroots Organizing in the Welfare Rights Movement*. Lexington, MA: Lexington, 1974.

Baker, Christi. *A Practitioner's Guide to Combating Predatory Lending*. Washington, DC: Neighborhood Reinvestment Corporation; Local Initiatives Support Corporation Center for Home Ownership, 2003.

Banach, Mary, Deborah Hamilton, and Penelope Perri. "Class Action Lawsuits and Community Empowerment." *Journal of Community Practice* 11, no. 4 (2003): 81–100.

Bankhead, Teiahsha, and John L. Erlich. "Diverse Populations and Community Practice." In *The Handbook of Community Practice*, edited by Marie Weil, 59–83. Thousand Oaks, CA: Sage, 2005.

Barricada, Nicolas. "The Blac Bloc." In *Protest in the Land of Plenty: A View of Democracy from the Streets of America as we Enter the 21st Century*, edited by Al Crespo, 60–64. Miami, FL: Center Lane Press, 2002.

Barry, Patrick. *Rebuilding the Walls: A Nuts and Bolts Guide to the Community Development Methods of Bethel New Life, Inc. in Chicago*. Chicago: Bethel New Life, 1989.

Bass, Gary. "Lessons Learned from Proposition 226: Preparing the Nonprofit Sector." OMB Watch. www.ombwatch.orgl/ombwatch.html (1998).

Bass, Gary D., Kay Guinane, and Ryan Turner. "An

Attack on Nonprofit Speech: Death by a Thousand Cuts." OMB WATCH: Washington, DC, 2003.

Baylor, Tim. "Media Framing of Movement Protest: The Case of American Indian Protest." *Social Science Journal* 33, no. 3 (1996): 241–55.

Bays, Sharon. "Work, Politics, and Coalition Building: Hmong Women's Activism in a Central California Town." In *Community Activism and Feminist Politics: Organizing Across Race, Class, and Gender*, edited by Nancy A. Naples, 301–326. New York: Routledge, 1998.

Beck, Elizabeth, and Michael Eichler. "Consensus Organizing: A Practice Model for Community Building." *Journal of Community Practice* 8, no. 1 (2000): 87–102.

Bell, Brenda, John Gaventa, and John Peters, eds. *We Make the Road by Walking: Conversations on Education and Social Change Myles Horton and Paulo Freire*. Philadelphia: Temple University Press, 1990.

Bendick, Marc Jr., and Mary Lou Egan. "Linking Business Development and Community Development: Lessons from Four Cities." Prepared for presentation at the Community Development Research Center, Washington, DC, 1989.

Bernstein, Mary. "Celebration and Suppression: The Strategic Uses of Identity by the Lesbian and Gay Movement." *American Journal of Sociology* 103, no. 3 (November 1997): 531–65.

Berry, Jeffrey M. *The New Liberalism: The Rising Power of Citizen Groups*. Washington, DC: Brookings Institution, 1999.

Berry, Jeffrey M., Kent E. Portney, and Ken Thomson. *The Rebirth of Urban Democracy*. Washington, DC: Brookings Institution, 1993.

Berry, Jeffrey M., and David F. Arons. *A Voice for Nonprofits*. Washington, DC: Brookings Institution, 2003.

Best, Joel, ed. *Images of Issues: Typifying Contemporary Social Problems; Second Edition*. New York: Aldine de Gruyter, 1995.

Betancur, John J., and Douglas C. Gills. "The African-American and Latino Coalition Experience in Chicago Under Mayor Harold Washington." In *The Collaborative City: Opportunities and Struggles for Blacks and Latinos in U.S. Cities*, edited by John J. Betancur and Douglas C. Gills, 59–88. New York: Garland, 2000.

Betten, Neil, and Michael J. Austin, eds. *The Roots of Community Organizing, 1917–1939*. Philadelphia: Temple University Press, 1990.

Betzold, Michael. *Community the Vital Link: Intermediary Support Organizations: Connecting Communities with Resources for Improvement*. Midland, MI: The Mott Foundation, 1998.

Bevacqua, Maria. "Anti-Rape Coalitions: Radical, Liberal, Black, and White Feminists Challenging Boundaries." In *Forging Radical Alliances Across Differences*, edited by Jill M. Bystydzienski and Steven P. Schactt, 163–75. Boulder, CO: Rowman & Littlefield Publishers, 2001.

Bickel, Christopher. "Reasons to Resist: Coalition Building at Indiana University." In *Forging Radical Alliances Across Differences*, edited by Jill M. Bystydzienski and Steven P. Schactt, 207–19. Boulder, CO: Rowman & Littlefield Publishers, 2001.

Bingham, Gail. *Resolving Environmental Disputes: A Decade of Experience*. Washington, DC: The Conservation Foundation, 1986.

Bingham, Lisa Blogren, Tina Nabatchi, and Rosemary O'Leary. "The New Governance: Practices and Processes for Stakeholder and Citizen Participation in the Work of Government." *Public Administration Review* 65, no. 5 (October 2005): 647–658.

Birkenmaier, Julie, and Sabrina Watson Tyuse. "Affordable Financial Services and Credit for the Poor: The Foundations of Asset Building." *Journal of Community Practice* 13, no. 1 (2005): 69–86.

Blakely, Edward J., and Mary Gail Snyder. *Fortress America: Gated Communities in the United States*. Washington, DC and Cambridge, MA: The Brookings Institution and the Lincoln Institute of Land Policy, 1997.

Blumenthal, Ralph. "A Grass-Roots Group is Helping Hurricane Survivors Help Themselves." *The New York Times*, 2005, 31 October 2005, A11.

Bobo, Kimberley, Steve Max, Koba Kim, and Jackie Kendall. *Organizing for Social Change: Midwest Academy: Manual for Activists, 3rd Edition*. Santa Ana, CA: Seven Locks Press, 2001.

Bolland, John M., and Debra Moehle McCallum. "Neighboring and Community Mobilization in High-Poverty Inner-City Neighborhoods." *Urban Affairs Review* 38, no. 1 (2002): 42–69.

Booth, Heather. "Victories & Lessons." *The Neighborhood Works* 16, no. 6 (1993 January 1994): 8–12.

Boyd, Michelle. "Reconstructing Bronzeville: Racial Nostalgia and Neighborhood Redevelopment." *Journal of Urban Affairs* 22, no. 2 (2000): 107–22.

Boyte, Harry C. *The Backyard Revolution: Understanding the New Citizen Movement*. Philadelphia: Temple University Press, 1980.

———. *Commonwealth: A Return to Citizen Politics*. New York: The Free Press, 1989.

Bradshaw, Catherine, Steven Soifer, and Lorraine Guttierrez. "Toward a Hybrid Model for Effective Organizing in Communities of Color." *Journal of Community Practice* 1, no. 1 (1994): 25–42.

Branch, Taylor. *Parting the Waters: America in the King Years 1954–1963*. New York: Simon & Schuster, 1988.

———. *Pillar of Fire: America in the King Years 1963–65*. New York: Simon & Schuster, 1998.

Bratt, Rachel G., Lanley C. Keyes, Alex Schwartz, and Avis C. Vidal. *Confronting the Management Challenge: Affordable Housing in the Nonprofit Sector*. New York: Community Development Research Center: Graduate School of Management and Urban Policy: New School for Social Research, 1994.

Brauner, Sarah, and Pamela Lopest. "Where Are They Now? What States' Studies of People Who Left Welfare Tell Us." *Series A. No A-32* (1999). Washington, DC: The Urban Institute.

Brehm, Bob. "So You Want to be a Developer." *Shelterforce* xxiv (January/February 2002): 16–20.

Breidenbach, Jan. "LA Story." *Shelterforce* xxiv (March/April 2002): 12–15, 28.

Briggs, Xavier de Souza, Elizabeth J. Mueller, with Mercer Sullivan. *From Neighborhood to Community: Evidence on the Social Effects of Community Development*. New York: Community Development Research Center, New School for Social Research, 1997.

Brophy, Paul C., and Alice Shabecof. *A Guide to Careers in Community Development*. Washington, DC: Island Press, 2001.

Browning, Rufus, Dale Rogers, and Marshal Tabb. *Racial Politics in American Cities, Second Edition*. New York: Longman, 1997.

Buechler, Steven M. "New Social Movements Theories." *The Sociological Quarterly* 36, no. 3 (1995): 441–64.

"Building Social and Economic Support Networks." In *Building Social and Economic Support Networks with Time Dollars: A Making Connections Peer Technical Assistance Match Between Hartford, Connecticut, Portland, Maine and San Diego, California*. Washington, DC: Technical assistance resource center of the Annie E. Casey Foundation and the Center for the Study of Social Problems, 2004.

Burghardt, Steve. *Organizing for Community Action*. Beverly Hills: Sage, 1982a.

———. *The Other Side of Organizing: Resolving the Personal Dilemmas and Political Demands of Daily Practice*. Cambridge, MA: Schenkman Publishing, 1982b.

Bush, Malcolm, and Daniel Immergluck. "Research, Advocacy and Community Reinvestment." In *Organizing Access to Capital: Advocacy and the Democratization of Financial Institutions*, edited by Gregory Squires, 154–68. Philadelphia: Temple University Press, 2003.

Butterfield, Alice K., and Tracy M. Sosak. "University-Community Partnerships: An Introduction." *Journal of Community Practice* 12, no. 3/4 (2004): 1–11.

California Reinvestment Coalition, and Community Reinvestment Coalition of North Carolina. "Follow the Money: Press Advisory," 2005.

Callahan, Steve, Neil Mayer, Kris Palmer, and Larry Ferlazzo. "Rowing the Boat with Two Oars." Working Papers for Comm-Org. 1999.

Campbell, S. J. *A Guide for Training Study Circle Facilitators*. Pomfret, CT: Topsfield Foundation, 1998.

Capraro, James F. "Community Organizing+Community Development=Community Transformation." *Journal of Urban Affairs* 26, no. 2 (2004): 151–62.

Cardwell, Diane. "Protests Come Early by So Do Arrests," 2004.

Carlsson, Chris, ed. *The Political Edge*. San Francisco: City Lights Foundation, 2004.

Cassidy, Robert. *Livable Cities: A Grassroots Guide to Rebuilding Urban America*. New York: Holt, Rinehart and Winston, 1980.

Castelloe, Paul, and Dorothy Gamble. "Participatory Methods in Community Practice." In *The Handbook of Community Practice*, edited by Marie Weil, 261–75. Thousand Oaks, CA: Sage Publications, 2005.

Castells, Manuel. *The City and the Grassroots: A Cross-Cultural Theory of Urban Social Movements*. Berkeley: University of California Press, 1983.

Castillo, Richard Griswold del, and Richard A. Garcia. *César Chavez: A Triumph of Spirit*. Norman, OK: University of Oklahoma Press, 1995.

Center for Community Change. How and Why to Influence Public Policy: An Action Guide for Community Organizations. Washington, DC: Center for Community Change, 1996.

———. *How to Tell and Sell Your Story: Part 1*. Washington, DC: Center for Community Change, 1997.

———. "Issues: The Community Voting Project," 2004. www.communitychange.org/issues/cvp/november-2004.

———. "An Action Guide for Education Organizing." Washington, DC: Center for Community Change, 2005.

Center for Public Finance and Housing. *Status and*

Prospects of the Nonprofit Housing Sector. Report to the U.S. Department of Housing and Urban Development: Office of Policy Development and Research. Washington, DC: Community and Economic Development Program, Urban Institute, 1994.

Center for Reflective Community Practice. *North End Strategic Plan*. Springfield, MA: North End Outreach Network, 2003.

Center on Budget and Policy Priorities. *What Does the Safety Net Accomplish: New Series of Reports Examines Research Findings*. Washington, DC: Center on Budget and Policy Priorities, 2005.

CFED. *Ideas in Development*. Washington, DC: Corporation for Enterprise Development, 1999.

Chambers, Edward T. *Organizing for Family and Congregation*. New York: Industrial Areas Foundation, 1978.

———. *Roots for Radicals: Organizing for Power, Action and Justice*. New York: Continuum, 2003.

Chase, Steve. "Take Action for Willie Fontenot." Colist@coserver.uhw.utoledo.edu. (2005).

Chaskin, Robert J. "Democracy and Bureaucracy in a Community Planning Process." *Journal of Planning Education and Research* 24 (2005): 408–19.

Chaskin, Robert J., Prudence Brown, Sudhir Venkatesh, and Avis Vidal. *Building Community Capacity*. New York: Aldine de Gruyter, 2001.

Chavez, César. "La Causa and La Huegla." In *Community Organizers*, edited by Joan Ecklein, 15–27. New York: John Wiley & Sons, 1984.

Chavez, John R. *Eastside Landmark: A History of the East Los Angeles Community Union, 1968–1993*. Stanford, California: Stanford University Press, 1998.

Checkoway, Barry, and Annette Norsman. "Empowering Citizens with Disabilities." *Community Development Journal*, October 1986, 270–77.

Chung, Amy. *Bridging Sectors: Partnerships Between Nonprofits and Private Developers*. Cambridge, MA: Joint Center for Housing Studies of Harvard University, 2004.

Churchill, Ward, and Jim Vander Wall. *Agents of Repression: The FBI's Secret Wars Against the Black Panther Party and the American Indian Movement*. Boston: South End Press, 1988.

Cincinnati Boycott Council. "Detailed Description of Demands," 2003.

Clavel, Pierre. *The Progressive City: Planning and Participation, 1969–1984*. New Brunswick, NJ: Rutgers University Press, 1986.

Clavel, Pierre, and Wim Wiewell, eds. *Harold Washington and the Neighborhoods: Progressive City Government in Chicago, 1983–1987*. New Brunswick, NJ: Rutgers University Press, 1991.

Cnaan, Ram A. "Neighborhood-Representing Organizations: How Democratic Are They." *Social Services Review*, December 1991, 614–34.

Coalition on Human Needs. *"You've Got to Cut the Butter": Threats to Human Needs Priorities in the FY 2006 Federal Budget*. Washington, DC: Coalition on Human Needs, 2005.

Coastal Enterprises Inc. *Measuring Impact in Practice: Reflections and Recommendations from Coastal Enterprise Inc.'s Experience*. Wiscasset, ME: Coastal Enterprise Inc., 2006.

Cockburn, Alexander, Jeffrey St. Clair, and Allan Sekula. *5 Days That Shook the World: Seattle and Beyond*. London: Verso, 2000.

Cohen, Rick. *Axis of Ideology: Conservative Foundations and Public Policy*. Washington, DC: National Center for Responsive Philanthropy, 2004a.

———. *Community-Based Public Foundations: Small Beacons for Big Ideas*. Washington, DC: National Center for Responsive Philanthropy, 2004b.

———. *Funding the Culture Wars: Philanthropy, Church and State*. Washington, DC: National Center for Responsive Philanthropy, 2005a.

———. *Social Justice Philanthropy: The Latest Trend or a Lasting Lens for Grantmaking?* Washington, DC: National Center for Responsive Philanthropy, 2005b.

Committee for Economic Development. *Rebuilding Inner-City Communities: A New Approach to the Nation's Urban Crisis*. New York: Committee for Economic Development, 1995.

Conway, Brian, and David S. Hachen, Jr. "Attachments, Grievances, Resources and Efficacy: The Determinants of Tenant Association Participation Among Public Housing Tenants." *Journal of Urban Affairs* 27, no. 1 (2005): 25–52.

Cormick, Gerald W. "Strategic Issues in Structuring Multi-Party Public Policy Negotiations." *Negotiation Journal* (1989), 125–32.

Cortes, Ernesto, Jr. "Reweaving the Social Fabric." http://my.Voyager.Net/ttresser/cortes.htm (1996).

Counts, Alex. *Give Us Credit*. New York: Times Books, 1996.

Crenson, Matthew. "Social Networks and Political Processes in Urban Neighborhoods." *Journal of Political Science* 22, no. 3 (578-94 1980).

Crespo, Al. *Protest in the Land of Plenty*. Miami, FL: Center Lane Press, 2002.

Cress, Donald. "Nonprofit Incorporation Among Movements of the Poor: Pathways and Consequences for Homeless Social Movement Organizations." *The Sociological Quarterly* 38, no. 2 (Spring 1997): 343–60.

Crowley, Sheila. "Point of View." Washington, DC: National Low Income Housing Coalition, 2005.

Crozat, Michael. "Are the Times a-Changing? Assessing the Acceptance of Protest in Western Democracies." In *The Social Movement Society*, edited by David Meyer and Sidney Tarrow, 59–82. New York: Rowman & Littlefield, 1998.

Cutler, Ira. "The Working Poor: Sittin' Here Thinkin." www.Handnet.Org/index_show.Htm? Doc _id=15531&Frme_id=1331, June 1999. Handsnet.

Daley, John Michael, and Julio Angulo. "Understanding the Dynamics of Diversity Within Nonprofit Boards." *Journal of the Community Development Society* 25, no. 2 (1994): 172–88.

Danielson, Michael. *The Politics of Exclusion*. New York: Columbia University Press, 1976.

Deckard, Barbara. *The Women's Movement: Political, Socioeconomic and Psychological Issues*. New York: Harper and Row, 1983.

Deegan, Denise. *Managing Activism: A Guide to Dealing with Activists and Pressure Groups*. London: Kogan Page Limited, 2001.

DeFilippis, James. *Unmaking Goliath: Community Control in the Face of Global Capitalism*. New York: Routledge, 2004.

Delgado, Gary. *Organizing the Movement: The Roots and Growth of ACORN*. Philadelphia: Temple University Press, 1986.

DiMaggio, Paul J., and Walter W. Powell. "The Iron Cage Revisited; Institutional Isomorphism and Collective Rationality." In *The New Institutionalism in Organizational Analysis*, eds. Walter W. Powell and Paul J. DiMaggio, 63–82. Chicago: University of Chicago Press, 1991.

Dittmer, John. *Local People: The Struggle for Civil Rights in Mississippi*. Urbana, IL: University of Illinois Press, 1994.

Dolbeare, Cushing N., Barbara Saraf, and Sheila Crowley. *Changing Priorities: The Federal Budget and Housing Assistance 1975–2005*. Washington, DC: National Low Income Housing Coalition, 2004.

Dorius, Noah. "The Social Change Role of Community-Based Development Corporations: A Quiet Transformation of Private Lives and Local Institutions." Manchester, NH: Southern New Hampshire University, 2006.

Dreier, Peter. "Hahn's Failed Promise on L.A. Housing," B-13, 2005.

Dresang, Dennis L., and James J. Gosling. *Politics, Policy & Management in the American States*. New York: Longman, 1989.

Dudley Street Neighborhood Initiative. "DSNI Staff." www.dsni.org/Staff/staff2.htm. (2005).

Eckholm, Erik. "America's 'Near Poor' Are Increasingly at Economic Risks, Experts Say." *The New York Times*, 2006, 5 May 2006, A-14.

Ecklein, Joan. *Community Organizers*. New York: John Wiley & Sons, 1984.

Economic Policy Institute. *Facts and Figures: State of Working American 2004/2005: Inequality*, 2005. www.epinet.org.

Edelman, Murray. *Constructing the Political Spectacle*. Chicago: University of Chicago Press, 1988.

Edelman, Peter, Harry J. Holzer, and Paul Offner. *Reconnecting Disadvantaged Young Men*. Washington, DC: The Urban Institute Press, 2006.

Ehrenreich, John H. *The Altruistic Imagination: A History of Social Work and Social Policy in the United States*. Ithaca, NY: Cornell University Press, 1985.

Eliasoph, Nina. *Avoiding Politics: How Americans Produce Apathy in Everyday Life*. Cambridge, U.K.: Cambridge University Press, 1998.

Engdahl, Lori. "Cuyoga Falls Vs. Buckeye." KnowledgePlex, 2003.

Fabricant, Michael, and Robert Fisher. *Settlement Houses Under Siege: The Struggle to Sustain Community Organizations in New York City*. New York: Columbia University Press, 2002.

Faludi, Susan. *Backlash: The Undeclared War Against Women*. New York: Anchor Books/Doubleday, 1992.

Fantasia, Rick. *Cultures of Solidarity: Consciousness, Action, and Contemporary American Workers*. Berkeley: University of California Press, 1988.

Fellner, Kim. "Hearts and Crafts: Powering the Movement." *Shelterforce* xx, no. 5 (September/October 1998): 20–22.

Feltner, Tom, and Marva Williams. *New Terms for Payday Loans: High Cost Lenders Change Loan Terms to Evade Illinois Protections*. Reinvestment Alert. Chicago: The Woodstock Institute, 2004.

Ferraro, Kathleen. "Policing Woman Battering." *Social Problems* 36, no. 1 (February 1989): 61–74.

Ferree, Myra Marx, and Patricia Martin, Yancey, eds. *Feminist Organizations: Harvest of the New Women's Movement*. Philadelphia: Temple, 1995.

Fetner, Tina. "Working Anita Bryant: The Impact of the Christian Anti-Gay Activism on Lesbian and Gay Movement Claims." *Social Problems* 48, no. 3 (August 2001): 411–27.

Fisher, Robert. *Let the People Decide: Neighborhood Organizing in America*. Boston: Twayne, G. K. Hall, 1984.

———. *Let the People Decide: Neighborhood Organizing in America Updated Edition*. New York: MacMillan, Twayne, 1994.

———. "History, Context, and Emerging Issues for Community Practice." In *The Handbook of Community Practice*, edited by Marie Weil, 34–58. Thousand Oaks, CA: Sage, 2005.

Fisher, Robert, and Joe Kling. "Community Organization and New Social Movement Theory." *Journal of Progressive Human Services* 5, no. 2 (1994): 5–23.

Fisher, Robert, and Eric Schragge. "Challenging Community Organizing: Facing the 21st Century." *Journal of Community Practice* 8, no. 3 (2000): 1–19.

Fitzgerald, Kathleen, and Diane Rodgers. "Radical Social Movement Organizations: A Theoretical Model." *The Sociological Quarterly* 41, no. 4 (Fall 2000): 573–92.

Flanagan, Joan. *The Grass Roots Fund Raising Book: How to Raise Money in Your Community*. Chicago: Contemporary Books, 1982.

Fleischer, Doriz Zames, and Frieda Zames. *The Disability Rights Movement: From Charity to Confrontation*. Philadelphia, PA: Temple University Press, 2001.

Foley, Michael W., and Bob Edwards. "Escape from Politics? Social Theory and the Social Capital Debate." *American Behavioral Scientists* 40, no. 5 (March/April 1997): 550–61.

Foley, Raymond. "University and Four Peace Activists Subpoenaed Over Anti-War Demonstration," 2004. Http://seattlepi.nwsource.com/local/aplocal_story.asp?category=6420&slug=Activist%20Investigation.

Fordham, Christopher C., III. "Shanty-Town Protests: Symbolic Dissent." *The Atlantic Community Quarterly* (1986), 244–47.

Forrester, John. *Planning in the Face of Power*. Berkeley, CA: University of California Press, 1989.

Foster, Mary. "New Orleans Bar Tab Bias." *Chicago Sun Times*, 2005, 17 April 2005.

Frank, Thomas. *What's the Matter with Kansas?* New York: Henry Holt and Company, 2004.

Freeman, Jo, and Victoria Johnson, eds. *Waves of Protest: Social Movements Since the Sixties*. Lanham: Rowman & Littlefield, 1999.

Freire, Paulo. *Pedagogy of the Oppressed*. Translated by Myra Bergman Ramos. New York: Seabury Press, Continuum, 1970.

———. *Education for Critical Consciousness*. New York: Continuum, 1980.

Freudenberg, Nicholas. *Not in Our Backyards! Community Action for Health and the Environment*. New York: Monthly Review Press, 1984.

Fruchter, Norm. "Challenging Failing Schools." *Shelterforce* xxiii (July/August 2001): 10–12; 27.

Fung, Archon. *Empowered Participation: Reinventing Urban Democracy*. Princeton, NJ: Princeton University Press, 2004.

Galaskiewicz, Joseph, and Deborah Stein. "Leadership and Networking Among Neighborhood Human Service Organizations." *Administrative Science Quarterly* 26, no. 3 (1981): 434–48.

Galster, George, Diane Levy, Noah Sawyer, Christopher Tempkin, and Kenneth Walker. *The Impact of Community Development Corporations on Urban Neighborhoods*. The Urban Institute. Washington, DC: 2005.

Gamson, William A. *Talking Politics*. New York: Cambridge University Press, 1992.

———. "The Success of the Unruly." In *Social Movements: Readings on Their Emergence, Mobilization and Dynamics*, edited by Doug McAdam and David A. Snow, 357–64. Los Angeles, CA: Roxbury Publishing, 1997.

Gans, Herbert. *Middle American Individualism: The Future of Liberal Democracy*. New York: The Free Press, MacMillan, 1988.

Gans, Herbert J. *The War Against the Poor: The Underclass and Antipoverty Policy*. New York: Basic, 1995.

Gaventa, John, Barbara Ellen Smith, and Alex Willingham, eds. *Communities in Economic Crisis: Appalachia and the South*. Philadelphia: Temple University Press, 1990.

Gecan, Michael. *Going Public*. Boston: Beacon Press, 2002.

Gibson, Chris L., Jihong Zhao, Nicholas Lovrich, and Michael Gaffney. "Social Integration, Individual Perceptions of Collective Efficacy, and Fear of Crime in Three Cities." *Justice Quarterly* 19, no. 3 (2002): 537–63.

Gilderbloom, John, and R. L. Mullins. *Promise and Betrayal: Universities and the Battle for Sustainable Urban Neighborhoods*. Albany: State University of New York Press, 2005.

Giloth, Robert, ed. *Jobs and Economic Development: Strategies and Practices*. Thousand Oaks, CA: Sage, 1998a.

———. "Jobs, Wealth, Or Place: The Faces of Community Economic Development." *Journal of Community Practice* 5, no. 1/2 (1998b): 11–28.

Gitlin, Todd. *The Sixties: Years of Hope, Days of Rage.* 1987. New York: Bantam, 1989.

———. *Letters to a Young Activist.* New York: Basic Books, 2003.

Gittell, Ross, and Avis Vidal. *Community Organizing: Building Social Capital as a Development Strategy.* Thousand Oaks, CA: Sage, 1998.

Goetz, Edward G. *Shelter Burden: Local Politics and Progressive Housing Policy.* Philadelphia: Temple University Press, 1993.

———. "The Community-Based Housing Movement and Progressive Local Politics." In *Revitalizing Urban Neighborhoods*, edited by W. Dennis Keating, Norman Krumholz, and Philip Star, 164–78. Lawrence, KS: University Press of Kansas, 1996.

Goetz, Edward G., and Mara S. Sidney. *The Impact of the Minneapolis Neighborhood Revitalization Program on Neighborhood Organizations.* Center for Urban and Regional Affairs, Hubert Humphrey Center, 1994.

Goffman, Erving. *Frame Analysis.* Cambridge, MA: Harvard University Press, 1974.

Golden, Olivia. *Assessing the New Federalism: Eight Years Later.* Washington, DC: The Urban Institute, 2005.

Gold, Eva, and Elaine Simon. "Successful Community Organizing for School Reform." In *Successful Community Organizing for School Reform: A Report in The Indicators Project One Education Organizing Series: Strong Neighborhoods, Strong Schools.* COMM-ORG Papers 2003, 2003. http://comm-org.utoledo.edu/papers2003/goldsimon/goldsimon.htm.

Goode, Judith, and Jo Anne Schneider. *Reshaping Ethnic and Racial Relations in Philadelphia: Immigrants in a Divided City.* Philadelphia: Temple, 1994.

Goodnough, Abby. "Tourists to Florida Get Warning as Greeting." *The New York Times*, 2005, 4 October 2005.

Goodpaster, Gary. *A Guide to Negotiation and Mediation.* Irvington-on-Hudson, New York: Transaction, 1997.

Gordon, Jennifer. *Suburban Sweatshops: The Fight for Immigrant Rights.* Cambridge, MA: The Belknap Press of Harvard University Press, 2005.

Gottlieb, Robert. *Forcing the Spring: The Transformation of the American Environmental Movement.* Washington, DC: Island Press, 1993.

Gramsci, Antonio. *Letters from Prison.* New York: Harper and Row, 1973.

Granovetter, Mark. "The Strength of Weak Ties." *American Journal of Sociology* 78, no. 6 (1973): 1360–74.

Greenbaum, Thomas L. *The Handbook for Focus Group Research; Second Edition.* Thousand Oaks, CA: Sage, 1998.

Greenberg, David. *The Ricanne Hadrian Initiative for Community Organizing: CDC Stories of Change.* Boston: Massachusetts Association of Community Development Corporations; Local Initiatives Support Corporation, 2004.

Groenbjerg, Kirsten A. *Understanding Nonprofit Funding: Managing Revenues in Social Services and Community Development Organizations.* San Francisco: Jossey-Bass Publishers, 1993.

Gross, Julian, and Greg LeRoy, with Madeline Janis-Aparicio. *Community Benefits Agreement.* Washington, DC: Good Jobs First and the California Partnership for Working Families, 2005.

Gunn, Christopher. *Third-Sector Development: Making up for the Market.* Ithaca, NY: Cornell University Press, 2004.

Gutierrez, Lorraine, Edith Lewis, Biren Ratnesh Nagda, Laura Wernick, and Nancy Shore. "Multicultural Community Practice Strategies and Intergroup Empowerment." In *The Handbook of Community Practice*, edited by Marie Weil, 341–59. Thousand Oaks, CA: Sage, 2005.

Hanna, Mark G., and Buddy Robinson. *Strategies for Community Empowerment: Direct-Action and Transformative Approaches to Social Change Practice.* Lewiston: Edwin Mellen Press, 1994.

Hardcastle, David A., Stanley Wenocur, and Patricia R. Powers. *Community Practice: Theories and Skills for Social Workers.* New York: Oxford, 1997.

Hardy-Fanta, Carol. *Latina Politics, Latino Politics: Gender, Culture, and Political Participation in Boston.* Philadelphia: Temple University Press, 1993.

Harrison, Bennett, and Marcus Weiss. *Workforce Development Networks: Community-Based Organizations and Regional Alliances.* Newbury Park, CA: Sage, 1998.

Hartman, Chester. "Debating the Low-Income Housing Tax Credit: Feeding the Sparrows by Feeding the Horses." *Shelterforce* xiv, no. 1 (1992 January/February 1992): 12, 15.

Hart, Stephen. *Cultural Dilemmas of Progressive Politics: Styles of Engagement Among Grassroots Activists.* Chicago: University of Chicago Press, 2001.

Hebert, Scott, Kathleen Baron Heintz, Nancy Kay, and James E. Wallace. *Non Profit Housing: Costs and Funding Final Report Volume I-Findings.* Prepared for U.S. Department of Housing and Urban Development Office of Policy Development and Research. Abt Associates with Aspen Systems. Washington, DC, 1993.

Heisey, Ian. "Building Stronger Communities

Through Mediation." *Shelterforce* xxvi (July/August 2004): 22–23.

Hertz, Judy. *Organizing for Change: Stories of Success.* Chicago: Wiebolt Foundation, n.d.

Higgins, Lindley. *Measuring the Economic Impact of Community-Based Homeownership Programs on Neighborhood Revitalization.* LISC Center for Home Ownership and George Mason University's School of Public Policy, 2001.

hooks, bell. *Talking Back: Thinking Feminist, Thinking Black.* Boston: South End Press, 1989.

Horton, John, with the assistance of Joe Calderon, Mary Pardo, Leland Saita, Linda Shaw, and Yen-Fen Tseng. *The Politics of Diversity: Immigration, Resistance, and Change in Monterey Park, California.* Philadelphia: Temple University Press, 1995.

Horwitt, Sanford D. *Let Them Call Me Rebel: Saul Alinsky—His Life and Legacy.* New York: Alfred A. Knopf, 1989.

Hospital Accountability Project. *Separate and Unequal: Racial Redlining in Investment at Advocate Hospitals.* Chicago: Hospital Accountability Project (SEIU), 2004.

Hula, Kevin W. *Lobbying Together: Interest Group Coalitions in Legislative Politics.* Washington, DC: Georgetown University Press, 1999.

Hyde, Cheryl. "The Inclusion of a Feminist Agenda in Community Organization Curriculum." Presented at the 1987 CSWE Community Organizing and Administration Symposium. St. Louis, March, 1987.

———. "A Feminist Response to Rothman's 'The Interweaving of Community Intervention Approaches.'" *Journal of Community Practice* 3, no. 3/4 (1996): 127–46.

———. "The Hybrid Nonprofit: An Examination of Feminist Social Movement Organizations." *Journal of Community Practice* 8, no. 4 (2000): 45–68.

———. "Feminist Community Practice." In *The Handbook of Community Practice*, edited by Marie Weil, 360–71. Thousand Oaks, CA: Sage, 2005.

Iannello, Kathleen. "A Feminist Framework for Organizations." Prepared for delivery at the Annual Meeting of the American Political Science Association. Washington, DC, 1988.

Imbroscio, David L. *Reconstructing City Politics: Alternative Economic Development and Urban Regimes.* Thousand Oaks, CA: Sage, 1997.

Immergluck, Dan. *Credit to the Community: Community Reinvestment and Fair Lending Policy in the United States.* Armonk, NY: M. E. Sharpe, 2004.

———. "The Power of a Community-Based Develop-

ment Coalition." *Shelterforce* xxvii (May/June 2005a): 8–10, 29.

———. "Building Power, Losing Power: The Rise and Fall of a Prominent Economic Development Coalition." *Economic Development Quarterly* 19, no. 3 (August 2005b): 211–24.

Immergluck, Daniel. *Barriers to Nonprofit Advocacy and Public Policy Efforts: Lessons from Michigan Fair Housing Groups.* Report to Michigan Nonprofit Research Program. Grand Rapids, MI: Grand Valley State University, 2004.

Irwin, Bob, and Gorden Faison. *Why Non Violence: Introduction to Nonviolence Theory and Strategy.* New Society Publishers, 1984.

Jackall, Robert. "Paradoxes of Collective Work: A Study of the Cheeseboard, Berkeley, California." In *Worker Cooperatives in America*, edited by Robert Jackall and Henry Levin, 3–15. Berkeley: University of California Press, 1984a.

———. "Work in America and the Cooperative Movement." In *Worker Cooperatives in America*, eds. Robert Jackall and Henry Levin, 277–90. Berkeley: University of California Press, 1984b.

Jacobsen, Dennis A. *Doing Justice: Congregations and Community Organizing.* Minneapolis, MN: Fortpress Press, 2001.

Jacobs, Jill. "For This I Went to Rabbinical School." *Lilith* 29, no. 4 (Winter 2004): 25.

Janis, Irving. *Groupthink: Psychological Studies of Policy Decisions and Fiascoes.* Boston: Houghton Mifflin Company, 1982.

Jaquay, Robert. "Cleveland's Housing Court: A Grassroots Victory 25 Years Ago Paved the Way for a Reliable Much Needed Institution." *Shelterforce* 141 (May/June 2005). www.nhi.org/online/issues/141/housingcourt.html.

Jargowsky, Paul A. *Poverty and Place: Ghettos, Barrios, and the American City.* New York: Russell Sage Foundation, 1997.

Jasper, James. "A Strategic Approach to Collective Action: Looking for Agency in Social Movement Choices." *Mobilization* 9, no. 1 (February 2004): 1–16.

Jasper, James M. *The Art of Moral Protest: Culture, Biography, and Creativity in Social Movements.* Chicago: University of Chicago Press, 1997.

Jenkins, J. Craig. *The Politics of Insurgency: The Farm Worker Movement in the 1960s.* New York: Columbia University Press, 1985.

Jenkins, J. Craig, and Charles Perrow. "Insurgency of the Powerless: Farm Worker Movements 1946–1972." *American Sociological Review* 42, no. 2 (1977): 249–68.

Jennings, James. "The Politics of Black Empowerment

in Urban American: Reflections on Race, Class, and Community." In *Dilemmas of Activism; Class, Community, and the Politics of Local Mobilization*, edited by Joseph M. Kling and Prudence S. Posner, 113–33. Philadelphia: Temple University Press, 1990.

Jezierski, Louise. "Neighborhoods and Public-Private Partnerships in Pittsburgh." *Urban Affairs Quarterly* 26, no. 2 (December 1990): 217–49.

Johnson, Alice, and Alice Rollins Castengera. "Integrated Program Development: A Model for Meeting the Complex Needs of Homeless Persons." *Journal of Community Practice* 1, no. 3 (1994): 29–48.

Joint Center for Housing Studies, Harvard University. *The State of the Nation's Housing 2003*. Cambridge, MA: Joint Center for Housing Studies, Harvard University, 2005.

Jones, Stanley E., Dean C. Barnlund, and Franklyn S. Haiman. *The Dynamics of Discussion: Communication in Small Groups*. New York: Harper & Row, 1980.

Jones, Tim. "The Public Starts SLAPPing Back." *The Chicago Tribune*, 26 December 2005, 11.

Kadushin, Charles, Matthew Lindhold, Ryan Dan, Arhie Brodsky, and Saxe Leonard. "Why It is So Difficult to Form Effective Community Coalitions." *City & Community* 4, no. 3 (September 2005): 255–76.

Kahn, Si. *Organizing: A Guide for Grassroots Leaders*. New York: McGraw Hill, 1982.

Kamin, David, and Isaac Shapiro. *Studies Shed New Light on Effects of Administration's Tax Cuts*. Washington, DC: Center on Budget and Policy Priorities, 2004.

Kaner, Sam, with Linny Lind, Catherine Toldi, Sarah Fisk, and Duane and Berger. *Facilitator's Guide to Participatory Decision-Making*. Gabriola Island, BC: New Society Publishers, 1996.

Karger, Howard. *Shortchanged: Life and Debt in the Fringe Economy*. San Francisco: Berrett-Koehler, 2005.

Karger, Howard Jacob, and David Stoesz. *American Social Welfare Policy: A Pluralist Approach; Fourth Edition*. Boston: Allyn and Bacon, 2002.

Kaufman, Roni. "Coalition Activity of Social Change Organizations in a Public Campaign: The Influence of Motives, Resources, and Processes on Levels of Activity." *Journal of Community Practice* 9, no. 4 (2001): 21–42.

Kingdom, John W. *Agendas, Alternatives and Public Policies, Second Edition*. New York: Longman, 1995.

Kingsley, G. Thomas, and Kathryn Pettit, *Neighborhood Change in Urban America* 2, no. 3 (May 2003): 1–14 *Concentrated Poverty a Change in Course*. Urban Institute.

Klandermans, Bert, and Dirk Oegema. "Potentials, Networks, Motivations, and Barriers: Steps Towards Participation in Social Movements." *American Sociological Review* 52, no. 3 (August 1987): 519–31.

Klein, Kim. *Fundraising for Social Change. Third Edition*. Berkeley, CA: Chardon Press, 1996.

Kleyman, Paul. *Senior Power: Growing Old Rebelliously*. San Francisco: Glide Publications, 1974.

Knoche, Tom. "Organizing Communities—Building Neighborhood Movements for Radical Social Change." In *Globalize Liberation: How to Uproot the System and Build a Better World*, edited by David Solnit, 287–312. San Francisco: City Lights Books, 2004.

Knoke, David, and James Wood. *Organized for Action: Commitment in Voluntary Organizations*. New Brunswick, NJ: Rutgers University Press, 1981.

Kornblum, William. *Blue Collar Community*. Chicago: University of Chicago Press, 1974.

Kowitz, Albert, and Thomas Knutson. *Decision Making in Small Groups: The Search for Alternatives*. Boston: Allyn and Bacon, 1980.

Kramer, Frederica D., Kenneth Finegold, Carol J. DeVita, and Laura Wherry. *Federal Policy on the Ground: Faith-Based Organizations Delivering Local Services*. Assessing the New Federalism. Washington, DC: The Urban Institute, 2005.

Krauss, Celene. "Grass-Roots Consumer Protests and Toxic Wastes: Developing a Critical Political View," *Community Development Journal* 48, (1988) 258–65.

Kretzman, John P., and John L. McKnight. *Building Communities from the Inside Out: A Path Toward Finding and Mobilizing a Community's Assets*. Chicago, IL: Center for Urban Affairs and Policy Research, Neighborhood Innovations Network, Northwestern University, 1993.

Kubisch, Anne C. "Comprehensive Community Initiatives." *Shelterforce* xviii, no. 1 (January/February 1996): 8–11, 8.

Kurtz, Sharon. *Workplace Justice: Organizing Multi-Identity Movements*. Minneapolis, MN: University of Minnesota Press, 2002.

Kweit, Mary Grisez, and Robert Kweit. *Implementing Citizen Participation in a Bureaucratic Society: A Contingency Approach*. New York: Praeger, 1981.

Lang, Robert E., and Steven P. Hornburg. "What Is

Social Capital and Why It Is Important to Public Policy." *Housing Policy Debate* 9, no. 1 (1998): 1–16.

Laraña, Enrique, Hank Johnston, and Joseph Gusfield, Eds. *New Social Movements: From Ideology to Identity.* Philadelphia: Temple University Press, 1994.

Lawler, Edward J. "Power Processes in Bargaining." *The Sociological Quarterly* 33, no. 1 (Spring 1992): 17–34.

Lawless, J. L., and R. Fox. "Political Participation of the Urban Poor." *Social Problems* 48, no. 3 (August 2001): 362–85.

Lawson, Ronald. "Tenant Response to the Urban Housing Crisis, 1970–1984." With the assistance of Reuben B. Johnson, III. In *The Tenant Movement in New York City, 1904–1984,* edited by Ronald Lawson, with the assistance of Mark Naison, 209–78. New Brunswick, NJ: Rutgers University Press, 1986.

Lee, Judith A. B. *The Empowerment Approach to Social Work Practice: Building the Beloved Community, Second Edition.* New York: Columbia University Press, 2001.

Lee, Matthew. "Community Reinvestment In a Globalizing World: To Hold Banks Accountable from the Bronx to Buenos Aires, Beijing and Basil." In *Organizing Access to Capital: Advocacy and the Democratization of Financial Institutions,* edited by Gregory Squires, 135–53. Philadelphia: Temple University Press, 2003.

Lelieveldt, Herman. "Helping Citizens Help Themselves: Neighborhood Improvement Programs and the Impact of Social Networks, Trust, and Norms on Neighborhood-Oriented Forms of Participation." *Urban Affairs Review* 39, no. 5 (2004): 531–51.

Lenz, Thomas J. "Neighborhood Development: Issues and Models." *Social Policy* 19 (Spring 1988): 24–30.

Leondar-Wright, Betsy. *Class Matters: Cross-Cultural Alliance Building for Middle-Class Activists.* Gabriola Island, B.C., Canada: New Society Publishers, 2005.

Leondar-Wright, Betsy, Meizhu Lui, Gloribell Mota, Dedrick Muhammed, and Mara Voukydis. *State of the Dream: Disowned in the Ownership Society.* Boston: United for a Fair Economy, 2005.

Levine, Adeline. *Love Canal: Science, Politics, and People.* Lexington, MA: Lexington, 1982.

Levine, Hillel, and Lawrence Harmon. *The Death of an American Jewish Community: A Tragedy of Good Intentions.* New York: The Free Press, 1992.

Levy, Jacques E. *Cesar Chavez: Autobiography of La Causa.* New York: W. W. Norton, 1975.

Lewis, G. "Style in Revolt: Music, Social Protest, and the Hawaiian Cultural Renaissance." *International Social Science Journal.* 66, No. 4 (1987), 168–77.

Liou, Y. Thomas, and Robert C. Stroh. "Community Development Intermediary Systems in the United States: Origins, Evolution, and Functions." *Housing Policy Debate* 9, no. 3 (1998): 575–94.

Lipsitz, George. *A Life in the Struggle: Ivory Perry and the Culture of Opposition.* Philadelphia: Temple University Press, 1988.

———. *A Life in the Struggle: Ivory Perry and the Culture of Opposition, Revised Edition.* Philadelphia: Temple University Press, 1995.

Logan, John, and John Mollenkopf. *People & Politics in America's Big Cities.* New York: Metropolitan College of New York, 2003.

Lord, Richard. *American Nightmare: Predatory Lending and the Foreclosure of the American Dream.* Monroe, ME: Common Courage Press, 2005.

Louie, Miriam Ching Yoon. *Sweatshop Warriors: Immigrant Women Workers Take on the Global Factory.* Cambridge, MA: South End Press, 2001.

Lowe, Jeffrey S. "Community Foundations: What Do They Offer Community Development?" *Journal of Urban Affairs* 26, no. 2 (2004): 221–40.

Luce, Stephanie. "The Fight for Living Wages." In *From ACT UP to WTO: Urban Protest and Community Building In the Era of Globalization,* eds. Benjamin Shepard and Ronald Hayduk, 342–50. New York: Verso, 2002.

Majka, Theo J., and Patrick G. Donnelly. "Cohesiveness Within a Heterogeneous Urban Neighborhood; Implications for Community in a Diverse Setting." *Journal of Urban Affairs* 10, no. 2 (1988): 141–60.

Maly, Michael. *Beyond Segregation: Multiracial and Multiethnic Neighborhoods in the United States.* Philadelphia: Temple University Press, 2005.

Mancoske, Ronald J., and Jeanne Hunzeker. "Advocating for Community Services Coordination: An Empowerment Perspective for Planning AIDS Services." *Journal of Community Practice* 1, no. 3 (1994): 29–48.

Mann, Eric. "Los Angeles Bus Riders Derail the MTA." In *Highway Robbery: Transportation Racism and New Routes to Equity,* edited by Robert Bullard, Gleen S. Johnson, and Angel Torres, 33–47. Cambridge, MA: South End Press, 2004.

Mansbridge, Jane J. *Beyond Adversary Democracy.* New York: Basic Books, 1980.

———. *Why We Lost the ERA.* Chicago: University of Chicago Press, 1986.

Marciniak, Ed. *Reversing Urban Decline: The Winthrop-*

Kenmore Corridor in the Edgewater and Uptown Communities of Chicago. Washington, DC: National Center for Urban Ethnic Affairs, 1981.

Marcuse, Peter. "Neighborhood Policy and the Distribution of Power: New York City's Community Boards." *Policy Studies Journal* 16, no. 2 (1987–88 Winter 1988): 277–89.

Massey, Douglas S. "The Wall That Keeps Illegal Workers In." *The New York Times*, 4 April 2006, A23.

Massey, Douglas S., and Nancy A. Denton. *American Apartheid: Segregation and the Making of the Underclass.* Cambridge, MA: Harvard University Press, 1993.

Márquez, Benjamin. *Constructing Identities in Mexican-American Political Organizations.* Austin, TX: University of Texas Press, 2003.

Mattera, Philip. Post to co-list at comm-org.edu. Oct. 23, 1997.

McAdam, Doug. "The Decline of the Civil Rights Movement." In *Waves of Protest: Social Movements Since the Sixties*, ed. Jo Freeman, ed. by Victoria Johnson, 325–48. Lanham: Rowman & Littlefield, 1999.

McAdam, Doug, and Ronnelle Paulsen. "Specifying the Relationship Between Social Ties and Activism." *American Journal of Sociology* 99 (1993): 640–67.

McAdam, Douglas. "Culture and Social Movements." In *New Social Movements: From Ideology to Identity*, edited by Enrique Laraña, Hank Johnston, and Joseph R. Gusfield, 36–57. Philadelphia: Temple University Press, 1994.

McCaffrey, Dawn, and Jennifer Keys. "Competitive Framing Processes in the Abortion Debate: Polarization-Vilification, Frame Saving, and Frame Debunking." *The Sociological Quarterly* 41, no. 1 (Winter 2000): 41–62.

McCarthy, John D., and Mayer N. Zald. "Resource Mobilization and Social Movements: A Partial Theory." In *Social Movements in an Organizational Society: Collected Essays*, eds. Mayer N. Zald, John D. McCarthy, 15–42. New Brunswick: Transaction Books, 1987.

McCarthy, John D., and Clark McPhail. "The Institutionalization of Protest in the United States." In *The Social Movement Society*, edited by David S. Meyer and Sidney Tarrow, 83–110. Lanham, MD: Rowman & Littlefield Publishers, 1998.

McCreight, Mac. "Lawsuits for Leverage." In *Roots to Power: A Manual for Grassroots Organizing*, Lee Staples, 181–87. New York: Praeger, 1984.

McDermott, Mark. "National Intermediaries and Local Community Development Corporation Networks: A View from Cleveland." *Journal of Urban Affairs* 26, no. 2 (2004): 171–76.

McKay, Emily Gantz, and Cristina Kanter with Lynn Rothman, Iris Mott, Andrew Saasta, and Timothy Lopez. *Linking Human Services and Economic Development.* Washington, DC: Center for Community Change, 1997.

McKnight, John L., and John P. Kretzman. "Mapping Community Capacity." In *Community Organizing and Community Building for Health*, edited by Meredith Minkler, 158–72. Brunswick, NJ: Rutgers University Press, 2005.

McNichol, Liz, and John Springer. *State Policies to Assist Working Poor Families.* Washington, DC: Center on Budget and Policy Priorities, 2004.

Medoff, Peter, and Holly Sklar. *Streets of Hope: The Fall and Rise of an Urban Neighborhood.* Boston: South End Press, 1994.

Meyer, David S., and Catherine Corrigall-Brown. "Coalitions and Political Contests: U.S. Movements Against Wars in Iraq." *Mobilization* 10, no. 3 (October 2005): 327–44.

Meyer, Diana A., Jennifer L. Blake, Henrique Caine, and Beth Williams Pryor. *On the Ground with Comprehensive Community Initiatives.* Columbia, MD: The Enterprise Foundation, 2000.

Meyer, John W., and Brian Rowan. "Institutionalized Organizations: Formal Structure as Myth and Ceremony." In *The New Institutionalism in Organizational Analysis*, eds. Walter W. Powell and Paul J. DiMaggio, 41–62. Chicago: University of Chicago Press, 1991.

Midwest Academy. *Midwest Academy Organizing Manual.* Chicago: Midwest Academy, various dates.

Milbrath, Lester. *Political Participation.* Chicago: Rand McNally, 1977.

Millennial Housing Commission. "Meeting Our Nation's Housing Challenges: Report of the Bipartisan Millennial Housing Commission Appointed by the Congress of the United States." Washington, DC: Millennial Housing Commission, 2002.

Miller, James. *"Democracy is in the Streets": From Port Huron to the Siege of Chicago.* New York: Simon and Schuster, 1987.

Mills, C. Wright. *The Sociological Imagination.* New York: Oxford University Press, 1959.

Minkler, Meredith. "Organizing with the Elderly Poor." In *Community Organizing and Community Building for Health; 2nd Edition*, edited by Meredith Minkler, 272–87. Rutgers: State University of New Jersey Press, 2005.

Mondros, Jacqueline B., and Scott M. Wilson. *Organizing for Power and Empowerment*. New York: Columbia University Press, 1994.

Monsignor John Egan Campaign for Payday Loan Reform. *Greed: An In-Depth Study of the Debt Collection Practices, Interest Rates, and Customer Base of a Major Illinois Payday Lender*. Chicago: Msgr. John Egan Center, 2004.

Moore, Carl M. *Group Techniques for Idea Building*. Applied Social Research Methods Series. Newbury Park, CA: Sage, 1987.

Morgan, David L. *Focus Groups as Qualitative Research*. Qualitative Research Methods Series. Newbury Park, CA: Sage, 1988.

Morgen, Sandra. " 'It's the Whole Power of the City Against Us!': The Development of Political Consciousness in a Women's Health Care Coalition." In *Women and the Politics of Empowerment*, edited by Ann Bookman and Sandra Morgen, 97–115. Philadelphia: Temple University Press, 1988.

Moss, Jordan. "The Power of the Community Press." *Shelterforce* 124 (July/August 2002): 12–15.

Mott, Andrew. *University Education for Community Change: A Vital Strategy for Progress on Poverty, Race and Community Building*. Washington, DC: Community Learning Project, 2005.

Moyer, Bill. *Doing Democracy: The MAP Model for Organizing Social Movements*. Gabriola Island, BC: New Society Publishers, 2001.

Muhammad, Richard. "Out of the Shadows: Sunflower Community Action March Calls for Fairness for Immigrants." *Disclosure*, no. 203 (March–April 2005): 3.

Murphy, Patricia Watkins, and James V. Cunningham. *Organizing for Community Controlled Development: Renewing Civil Society*. Thousand Oaks, CA: Sage Publishers, 2003.

Nagel, Joane. *American Indian Ethnic Renewal: Red Power and the Resurgence of Identity and Culture*. New York: Oxford, 1996.

Nathan, Richard. "The Newest New Federalism for Welfare." *Rockefeller Institute Bulletin* (1998), 4–11.

National Congress for Community Economic Development. *Reaching New Heights: Trends and Achievements of Community-Based Development Organizations*. Washington, DC: NCCED, 2006.

National Low Income Housing Coalition. *2004 Advocates' Guide to Housing and Community Development Policy*. Washington, DC: National Low Income Housing Coalition, 2004. www.nlihc.com/.

National Neighborhood Coalition. "Forge a New Partnership Between Funders and Grantees." *NNC Voice*, January 2005.

Needleman, Ruth. "Building Relationships for the Long Haul: Unions and Community-Based Groups Working Together to Organize Low-Wage Workers." In *Organizing to Win: New Research on Union Strategies*, edited by Kate Bronfenbrenner, Sheldon Friedman, Richard Hurd, Rudolf Oswald, and Seeber Ronald, 71–86. Ithaca, NY: ILR Press: An imprint of Cornell University Press, 1998.

Nelson, Kathryn P., Mark Treskon, and Danilo Pelletiere. *Losing Ground in the Best of Times: Low Income Renters in the 1990s*. Washington, DC: National Low Income Housing Coalition, 2004.

Nepstad, Sharon Erickson. "Persistent Resistance: Community and Community Kin the Plowshare Movement." *Social Problems* 51, no. 1 (2004): 43–59.

Ness, Immanuel. "Organizing Immigrant Communities: UNITE's Workers Center Strategy." In *Organizing to Win: New Research on Union Strategies*, edited by Kate Bronfenbrenner, Sheldon Friedman, Richard Hurd, Rudolf Oswald, and Seeber Ronald, 87–101. Ithaca, NY: ILR Press: An imprint of Cornell University Press, 1998.

Newman, Kathe, and Elvin Wyly. "Gentrification: Boon or Bane." *Shelterforce* xxvii (July/August 2005): 12–15.

Nickel, Denise R. "The Progressive City? Urban Redevelopment in Minneapolis." *Urban Affairs Review* 30, no. 3 (January 1995): 355–77.

Nissen, Bruce. *Fighting for Jobs: Case Studies of Labor-Community Coalitions Confronting Plant Closings*. Albany: State University of New York Press, 1995.

Nyden, Philip, and Joanne Adams. *Saving Our Homes: The Lessons of Community Struggles to Preserve Affordable Housing in Chicago's Uptown*. A report completed by researchers at Loyola University of Chicago in Collaboration with Organization of the Northeast. Chicago: Loyola University Department of Sociology, 1996.

Nyden, Philip, Anne Figer, Mark Shibley, and Darryl Burrows. *Building Community: Social Science in Action*. Thousand Oaks, CA: Pine Forge Press, 1997.

O'Connor, Brendon. *A Political History of the American Welfare System*. Lanham, MD: Rowman & Littlefield Publishers, 2004.

O'Donnell, Sandra M. "Is Community Organizing 'the Greatest Job' One Could Have? Findings from a Survey of Chicago Organizers." *Journal of Community Practice* 2, no. 1 (1995): 1–20.

————. "Urban African American Community Development in the Progressive Era." *Journal of Community Practice* 2, no. 4 (1995): 7–26.

O'Donnell, Sandra M., and Sokoni Karanja. "Transformative Community Practice: Building a Model for Developing Extremely Low Income African-American Communities." *Journal of Community Practice* 7, no. 3 (2000): 67–84.

O'Donnell, Sandy, Jane Becket, and Jean Rudd. *Promising Practices in Revenue Generation for Community Organizing.* Washington, DC: Center for Community Change, 2005.

Oegema, Dirk, and Bert Klanderman. "Why Social Movement Sympathizers Don't Participate: Erosion and Conversion of Support." *American Sociological Review* 59 (703–22 1994).

Ogilvie, Robert S. *Voluntarism, Community Life and the American Ethic.* Bloomington, IN: Indiana University Press, 2004.

Okamoto, Dina G. *Toward a Theory of Panethnicity: Explaining Asian American Collective Action American Sociological Review* 68, no. 6 (2003): 811–42.

Oliver, Pamela E., and Gregory M. Maney. "Political Processes and Local Newspaper Coverage of Protest Events: From Selection Bias to Triadic Interactions." *American Journal of Sociology* 106, no. 2 (September 2000): 463–505.

OMB Watch. "Report Finds Growing Pattern of Attacks on Nonprofit Speech," 2004.

————. "New PART Score Showcase Contradictions of Program." *OMB Watch* 7 (7 March 2006). *New PART Scores Showcase More Contradictions of Program.*

Orland, Chris. "Economic Human Rights Tribunal." Typescript Department of Sociology, NIU, DeKalb, Illinois, 1998.

Osterman, Paul. *Gathering Power: The Future of Progressive Politics in America.* Boston: Beacon Press, 2002.

Padilla, Felix M. *Puerto Rican Chicago.* Notre Dame, IN: University of Notre Dame Press, 1987.

Pardo, Mary. "Creating Community: Mexican-American Women in Eastside Los Angeles." In *Community Activism and Feminist Politics: Organizing Across Race, Class, and Gender*, edited by Nancy A. Naples, 275–301. New York: Routledge, 1998.

Pardo, Mary S. *Mexican American Women Activists: Identity and Resistance in Two Los Angeles Communities.* Philadelphia: Temple University Press, 1998.

Parzen, Julia Ann, and Michael Hall Kieschnick. *Credit Where It's Due: Development Banking for Communities.* Philadelphia: Temple University Press, 1992.

Passy, Florence. "Socialization, Connection and the Structure/Agency Gap: A Specification of the Impact of Networks on Participation in Social Movements." *Mobilization* 6, no. 2 (2001): 173–92.

Payne, Charles M. *I've Got the Light of Freedom: The Organizing Tradition and the Mississippi Freedom Struggle.* Berkeley: University of California Press, 1995.

Pear, Robert. "Rulings Trim Legal Leeway Given Medicaid Recipients." *New York Times*, 15 August 2005, A12.

Pedriana, Nicholas. "Help Wanted NOW: Legal Resources, the Women's Movement, and the Battle Over Sex-Segregated Job Advertisements." *Social Problems* 51, no. 2 (May 2004): 182–201.

Peirce, Neal R., and Carol F. Steinbach. *Corrective Capitalism: The Rise of America's Community Development Corporations.* New York: Ford Foundation, 1987.

————. *Enterprising Communities: Community-Based Development in America, 1990.* Washington, DC: Council for Community Based Development, 1990.

Pelletiere, Danilo, Keith Wardrip, and Sheila Crowley. *Out of Reach 2005.* Washington, DC: National Low Income Housing Coalition, 2006. www.nlihc.org/oor2005/.

Pellow, David Naguib. *Garbage Wars: The Struggle for Environmental Justice in Chicago.* Cambridge, MA: MIT Press, 2002.

Perkins, D., and M. Zimerman. "Empowerment Theory, Research and Application." *American Journal of Community Psychology* 18 (1995): 569–78.

Perkins, Douglas D. "Speaking Truth to Power: Empowerment Ideology as Social Intervention and Policy." *American Journal of Community Psychology* 23, no. 5 (1995): 765–94.

Perkins, John M. *Beyond Charity: The Call To Christian Community Development.* Grand Rapids, MI: Baker Books, 1993.

Phillips, Kevin. *American Theocracy: The Perils and Politics of Radical Religion, Oil, and Borrowed Money in the 21st Century.* New York: Penguin, 2006.

PICO Network News. April 20, 2005.

Pilisuk, Marc, Joann McAllister, Jack Rothman, and Lauren Larin. "New Contexts of Organizing: Functions, Challenges, and Solutions." In *Community Organizing and Community Building for Health; 2nd Edition*, edited by Meredith Minkler. Brunswick, NJ: Rutgers University Press, 2005.

Piven, Frances Fox, and Richard Cloward. *Poor People's Movements: Why They Succeed, How They Fail.* New York: Pantheon, 1977.

Pogge, Jean. "Reinvestment in Chicago's Neighborhoods: A Twenty Year Struggle." In *From Redlining to Reinvestment: Community Responses to Urban Disinvestment*, edited by Gregory D. Squires, 133–48. Philadelphia: Temple University Press, 1992.

Pogge, Jean, and Maria Choca. *The Long Term Future of Resources for Chicago's Community Development Corporations*. A Report to the John D. and Catherine T. MacArthur Foundation. Chicago: Woodstock Institute, 1991.

Polletta, Francesca. " 'It Was Like a Fever.' Narrative and Identity in Social Protest." *Social Problems* 45, no. 2 (May 1998): 137–59.

Popkin, Susan J., Bruce Katz, Mary K. Cunningham, Karen D. Brown, Jeremy Gustafson, Margaret Turner. *A Decade of HOPE VI: Research Findings and Policy Challenges*. Washington, DC: The Urban Institute; The Brookings Institute, 2004.

Pruitt, Dean. *Negotiation Behavior*. New York: Academic Press, 1981.

Pruitt, Dean G., and Peter J. Carnevale. *Negotiation in Social Conflict*. Pacific Groves, CA: Brooks Cole, 1993.

Purinton, Anna, Nasreen Jilani, Kristen Arant, and Kate Davis. *The Policy Shift to Good Jobs: Cities, States and Counties Attaching Job Quality Standards to Development Subsidies*. Washington, DC: Good Jobs First, 2003.

Putnam, Robert D. *Making Democracy Work: Civic Traditions in Modern Italy*. Princeton, NJ: Princeton University Press, 1993.

Rappaport, Julian. "The Power of Empowerment Language." *Social Policy*, Fall 1985, 15–21.

Reger, Jo, ed. *Different Wavelengths: Studies of the Contemporary Women's Movement*. New York: Routledge, 2005.

Reisch, Michael. "Radical Community Organizing." In *The Handbook of Community Practice*, edited by Marie Weil, 287–304. Thousand Oaks, CA: Sage, 2005.

Reitzes, Donald C., and Dietrich C. Reitzes. *The Alinksy Legacy: Alive and Kicking*. Greenwich, CT: JAI Press, 1987.

Relman, John P. "Taking It to the Courts: Litigation and the Reform of Financial Institutions." In *Organizing Access to Capital: Advocacy and the Democratization of Financial Institutions*, edited by Gregory Squires, 55–71. Philadelphia: Temple University Press, 2003.

Research for Democracy. "Blight Free Philadelphia:." In *Blight Free Philadelphia: A Public-Private Strategy to Create and Enhance Neighborhood Value*. A collaboration between the Eastern Pennsylvania Organizing project and the Temple University Center for Public Policy with assistance from Diamond & Associates, Philadelphia, 2001.

Reynolds, David B. *Taking the High Road; Communities Organize for Economic Change*. Armonk, NY: M. E. Sharpe, 2002.

Reynolds, David B., and Jen Kern. "Labor and the Living Wage Movement." In *Partnering for Change: Unions and Community Groups Build Coalitions for Economic Justice*, edited by David B. Reynolds, 67–87. Armonk, NY: M. E. Sharpe, 2004.

Rich, Michael J. *Federal Policymaking and the Poor: National Goals, Local Choices, and Distributional Outcomes*. Princeton, NJ: Princeton University Press, 1993.

Rivera, Felix G., and John L. Erlich, eds. *Community Organizing in a Diverse Society; Second Edition*. Boston: Allyn and Bacon, 1995.

Roberts-DeGennaro, Maria. "Conceptual Framework of Coalitions in an Organizational Context." In *Community Practice: Models in Action*, edited by Marie Weil, 91–108. New York: Haworth Press, 1997.

Roberts-DeGennaro, Mario. "Internet Resources for Community Practitioners." *Journal of Community Practice* 11, no. 4 (2003): 133–37.

Rogers, David, David Whetten, and Associates. *Interorganizational Coordination: Theory, Research and Implementation*. Ames, IA: Iowa State University, 1982.

Rogers, Mary Beth. *Cold Anger: A Story of Faith and Power Politics*. Denton, Texas: University of North Texas Press, 1990.

Rohe, William. "Building Social Capital Through Community Development." *Journal of the American Planning Association* 70, no. 2 (Spring 2004): 158–64.

Rohe, William M., and Michael Stegman. "The Effects of Homeownership on the Self-Esteem, Perceived Control and Life Satisfaction of Low-Income People." *Journal of the American Planning Association* 60, no. 2 (Spring 1994a): 173–84.

Rohe, William M., and Michael Stegman. "The Impact of Home Ownership on the Social and Political Involvement of Low-Income People." *Urban Affairs Quarterly* 30, no. 1 (September 1994b): 152–72.

Rohe, William M., Lucy S. Gorham, and Roberto G. Querca. "Individual Development Accounts: Participants' Characteristics and Success." *Journal of Urban Affairs* 27, no. 5 (2005): 503–20.

Rooney, Jim. *Organizing the South Bronx*. Albany: State University of New York Press, 1995.

Rose, Fred. *Coalitions Across the Class Divide: Lessons from the Labor, Peace, and Environmental Movements*. Ithaca, NY: Cornell University Press, 2000.

———. "Labor-Environmental Coalitions." In *Partnering for Change: Unions and Community Groups Build Coalitions for Economic Justice*, edited by David B. Reynolds, 3–18. Armonk, NY: M. E. Sharpe, 2004.

Rotella, Sebastian. "SUV War Pumps up The Deflated in Paris," *Chicago Tribune*. Oct 11, 2005.

Roth, Benita. *Separate Roads to Feminism: Black, Chicana and White Feminist Movements in America's Second Wave*. New York: Cambridge University Press, 2004.

Rothman, Jack. "Intent and Content." In *Reflections on Community Organization*, edited by Jack Rothman, 3–26. Itasca, IL: F. E. Peacock, 2000.

Rothschild, Joyce, and J. Allen Whitt. *The Cooperative Workplace: Potentials and Dilemmas of Organizational Democracy and Participation*. Cambridge: Cambridge University Press, 1986.

Rouen, Ethan. "Bootstrap Philanthropy: Housing Works Proves That Charity and Good Business Sense Begin at Home." *Shelterforce* xxv (July/August 2003): 8–12.

Rubin, Herbert J. *Applied Social Research*. Columbus, Ohio: Charles E. Merrill, 1983.

———. "There Aren't Going to be any Bakeries Here If There is no Money to Afford Jellyrolls: The Organic Theory of Community Based Development." *Social Problems* 41, no. 4 (August 1994): 401–24.

———. *Renewing Hope Within Neighborhoods of Despair: The Community-Based Development Model*. Albany, NY: SUNY Press, 2000a.

———. "What Conferences Accomplish for Social Change Organizations: Illustrations from the Community Based Development Movement." *Journal of Community Practice* 7, no. 4 (2000b): 35–55.

Rubin, Herbert J., and Irene S. Rubin. *Qualitative Interviewing: The Art of Hearing Data*, Second Edition. Thousand Oaks, CA: Sage, 2005.

Rubin, Herbert J., and Margaret Sherraden. "Community Economic and Social Development." In *The Handbook of Community Practice*, edited by Marie Weil, 475–93. Thousand Oaks, CA: Sage, 2005.

Rucht, Dieter. "The Structure and Culture of Collective Protest in Germany Since 1950." In *The Social Movement Society*, edited by David Meyer and Sidney Tarrow, 29–58. New York: Rowman & Littlefield, 1998.

Russell, Dick. "The Monkeywrenchers." *The Amicus Journal*, Fall 1987, 28–42.

Ryan, Barbara. *Feminism and the Women's Movement: Dynamics of Change in Social Movement, Ideology, and Activism*. New York: Routledge, 1992.

Ryan, Charlotte. *Prime Time Activism: Media Strategies for Grassroots Organizing*. Boston: South End Press, 1991.

Ryan, Charlotte, Michael Anastario, and Karen Jeffreys. "Start Small, Build Big: Negotiating Opportunities in Media Markets." *Mobilization* 10, no. 1 (February 2005): 111–28.

Sabatier, Paul A., and Hank C. Jenkins-Smith. "The Advocacy-Coalition Framework: Assessment, Revisions, and Implications for Scholars and Practitioners." In *Policy Change and Learning: An Advocacy Coalition Approach*, edited by Paul A. Sabatier and Hank C. Jenkins-Smith, 211–36. Boulder, CO: Westview, 1993.

Saegert, Susan, and Gary Winkel. "Paths to Community Empowerment: Organizing at Home." *American Journal of Community Psychology* 24, no. 4 (1996): 517–50.

Saegert, Susan, and Susan Winkel. "Social Capital and the Revitalization of New York City's Distressed Inner-City Housing." *Housing Policy Debate* 9, no. 1 (1998): 17–60.

Sahd, Brian. "Community Development Corporations and Social Capital: Lessons from the South Bronx." In *Community-Based Organizations: The Intersection of Social Capital and Local Context in Contemporary Urban Society*, edited by Robert Mark Silverman, 85–121. Detroit, MI: Wayne State University Press, 2004.

Salamon, Lester M. *Partners in Public Service: Government-Nonprofit Relations in the Modern Welfare State*. Baltimore: John Hopkins Press, 1995.

Sampson, Robert, Stephen W. Raudenbusch, and Felton Earls. "Neighborhoods and Violent Crime: A Multilevel Study of Collective Efficacy." *Science* 277 (August 1997): 918–24.

Sampson, Robert J. "Crime and Public Safety: Insights from Community-Level Perspectives on Social Capital." In *Social Capital and Poor Communities*, edited by Susan Saegert, J. Phillip Thompson, and Mark Warren, 89–114. New York: Russell Sage Foundation, 2001.

Sanders, Heywood T. "Communities Organized for Public Service and Neighborhood Revitalization in San Antonio." Edited by Robert H. Wilson. In *Public Policy and Community: Activism and Governance in Texas*, 36–68. Austin: University of Texas Press, 1997.

Sard, Barbara, and Douglas Rice. *President's 2007 Bud-*

get Renews Same Number of Housing Vouchers Funded in 2006. Washington, DC: Center for Budget and Policy Priorities, 2006.

Savage, J. A. "Radical Environmentalists: Sabotage in the Name of Ecology." *Business and Society Review* 58 (Summer 1986): 35–37.

Scally, Corianne. "Housing Ex-Offenders." *Shelterforce* xxvii, no. 1 (January/February 2005): 10–11.

Scanlon, Edward. "Low-Income Homeownership Policy as a Community Development Strategy." *Journal of Community Practice* 5, no. 1/2 (1998): 137–54.

Schecter, Susan. *Women and Male Violence: The Visions and Struggles of the Battered Women's Movement.* Boston: South End Press, 1982.

Scheiber, Matthew Schuck. "Home Equity Plan Put Before Local Voters." *The Neighborhood Works* 10, no. 3 (April 1987): 6–7.

Schein, Edgar H. *Organizational Culture and Leadership.* San Francisco: Jossey-Bass, 1985.

Schelling, Thomas. *The Strategy of Conflict.* New York: Oxford University Press, 1960.

Schillinger, Elisabeth. "Dependency, Control, and Isolation: Battered Women and the Welfare System." *Journal of Contemporary Ethnography* 16, no. 4 (January 1988): 469–90.

Schneider, Cathy. "Framing Puerto Rican Identity: Political Opportunity Structures and Neighborhood Organizing in New York City." *Mobilization* 2, no. 2 (September 1997): 227–45.

Schock, Kurt. "Nonviolent Action and Its Misconceptions: Insights for Social Scientists." *PS: Political Science and Politics* xxxvi, no. 6 (October 2003): 705–12.

Schopler, Janice H. "Interorganizational Groups in Human Services: Environmental and Interpersonal Relationships." *Journal of Community Practice* 1, no. 3 (1994): 2–28.

Schwartz, Edward. "NetActivism 2001: How Citizens Use the Internet." In *Advocacy, Activism, and the Internet: Community Organization and Social Policy,* edited by Steven F. Hick and John G. McNutt, 81–93. Chicago: Lyceum, 2002.

Scotch, Richard K. "Disability as the Basis for a Social Movement: Advocacy and the Politics of Definition." *Journal of Social Issues* 44, no. 1 (1988): 159–72.

Scott, Ralph. "Advocates for Healthy Housing." *Shelterforce* xxvii (March/April 2005): 20–23.

Sekul, Joseph D. "Communities Organized for Public Service: Citizen Power and Public Policy in San Antonio." In *The Politics of San Antonio: Community, Progress & Power,* eds. David R. Johnson, John A. Booth and Richard J. Harris, 175–90.

Lincoln, Nebraska: University of Nebraska Press, 1983.

Seltzer, Michael, Kim Klein, with David Barg. *Securing Your Organization's Future: A Complete Guide to Fundraising Strategies; Revised and Expanded Edition.* New York: The Foundation Center, 2001.

Sen, Rinku. *Stir It Up: Lessons in Community Organizing and Advocacy.* San Francisco, CA: Jossey-Bass, 2003.

Servon, Lisa J. "Credit and Social Capital: The Community Development Potential of U.S. Microenterprise Programs." *Housing Policy Debate* 9, no. 1 (1998): 115–50.

"Seven Worth Watching." *Ballotwatch* 3 (September 2004).

Shapiro, Joseph P. *No Pity: People with Disabilities Forging a New Civil Rights Movement.* New York: Times Books, 1993.

Sharp, Gene. *The Dynamics of Nonviolent Action.* Vol. 3 of *The Politics of Nonviolent Action.* Edited by Marina Finkelstein. Boston: Extending Horizons, 1973a.

———. *The Politics of Non-Violent Action.* Boston: Porter Sargent Publisher, 1973b.

Shepard, Benjamin, and Ronald Hayduk, eds. *From ACT UP to the WTO: Urban Protest and Community Building in the Era of Globalization.* New York: Verso, 2002.

Sherkat, Darren E., and T. Jean Block. "Explaining the Political and Personal Consequences of Protest." *Social Forces* 75, no. 3 (March 1997): 1049–76.

Sherraden, Margaret Sherrard, Cynthia K. Sanders, and Michael Sherraden. *Kitchen Capitalism: Microenterprise in Low-Income Households.* Albany, NY: State University of New York Press, 2004.

Sherraden, Michael, Lissa Johnson, Margaret Clancy, Slondra Beverly, Mark Schreiner, Min Zhan, and Jami Curley. *Saving Patterns in IDA Program.* St. Louis: MO: Center for Social Development: George Warren Brown School of Social Work; Washington University in St. Louis, 2000.

Shipler, David K. *The Working Poor: Invisible in America.* New York: Alfred A. Knopf, 2004.

Shirley, Dennis. *Valley Interfaith and School Reform: Organizing for Power in South Texas.* Austin: University of Texas Press, 2002.

Shlay, Anne B., and Gordon Whitman. "Research for Democracy: Linking Community Organizing and Research to Leverage Blight Policy," 2004. comm-org.utoledo.edu/papers2004/shlay/shlay.html.

Shore, Bill. "Powering Social Change." In *Powering Social Change: Lessons on Community Wealth Generation for Nonprofit Sustainability,* edited by Bill

Shore, 7–11. Washington, DC: Commonwealth Ventures Inc., 2003.

Shragge, Eric. *Activism and Social Change: Lessons for Community and Local Organizations.* Petersborough, Ontario: Boadview Press, 2003.

Shuman, Michael. "Why Do Progressive Foundations Give Too Little to Too Many?" *The Nation,* 1919, 12 January 1998.

Shuman, Michael H., and Merrian Fuller. "The Revolution Will not be Grant Funded." *Shelterforce* xxvii (September/October 2005): 9–11.

Sidney, Mara A. *Unfair Housing: How National Policy Shapes Community Action.* Lawrence: University of Kansas Press, 2003.

Simmons, Louise B. *Organizing in Hard Times: Labor and Neighborhoods in Hartford.* Philadelphia: Temple, 1994.

Slayton, Robert A. *Back of the Yards: The Making of a Local Democracy.* Chicago: University of Chicago Press, 1986.

Small, Mario Luis. "Villa Victoria: The Transformation of Social Capital in a Boston Bario." Chicago: University of Chicago Press, 2004.

Smith, Christian. *The Emergence of Liberation Theology: Radical Religion and Social Movement Theory.* Chicago: University of Chicago Press, 1991.

Smith, David Horton, Richard Reddy, and Burt Baldwin, eds. *Participation in Social and Political Activities.* San Francisco: Jossey-Bass, 1980.

Smith, Steven Rathgeb, and Michael Lipsky. *Nonprofits for Hire: The Welfare State in the Age of Contracting.* Cambridge: Harvard University Press, 1993.

Smock, Kristina. "Comprehensive Community Initiatives: A New Generation of Urban Revitalization Strategies." *Comm-Org* (1997).

———. *Democracy in Action: Community Organizing and Social Change.* New York: Columbia University Press, 2003.

Snow, David A., E. Burke Rochford Jr., Steven K. Worden, and Robert D. Benford. "Frame Alignment Processes, Micromobilization, and Movement Participation." *American Sociological Review* 51, no. 3 (August 1986): 464–81.

Solnit, David. "Introduction—the New Radicalism: Uprooting the System and Building a Better World." In *Globalize Liberation: How to Uproot the System and Build a Better World,* edited by David Solnit, xi–xxiv. San Francisco: City Lights Books, 2004.

Soss, Joe. "Making Clients and Citizens: Welfare Policy as a Source of Status, Belief and Action." In *Deserving and Entitled: Social Construction and Public Policy,* 291–328. Albany: State University Press of New York, 2005.

Speer, Paul W., and Joseph Hughey. "Community Organizing: An Ecological Route to Empowerment and Power." *American Journal of Community Psychology* 23, no. 5 (1995): 729–48.

———. "Mechanisms of Empowerment: Psychological Processes for Members of Power-Based Community Organizations." *Journal of Community & Applied Social Psychology* 6, no. 3 (1996): 177–87.

Squires, Gregory D. "The New Redlining." In *Why the Poor Pay More: How to Stop Predatory Lending,* ed. Gregeory D. Squires, 1–24. Westport, CT: Praeger, 2004.

Stall, Susan, and Randy Stoecker. "Toward a Gender Analysis of Community Organizing Models: Liminality and the Intersection of Spheres." In *Community Organizing and Community Building for Health,* edited by Meredith Minkler, 196–217. Brunswick, NJ: Rutgers University Press, 2005.

Stanley, Jay, and Barry Steinhardt. *Bigger Monsters, Weaker Chains: The Growth of an American Surveillance Society.* Washington, DC: American Civil Liberties Union, 2003.

Staples, Lee. "Selecting and Cutting the Issue." In *Community Organizing and Community Building for Health,* edited by Meredith Minkler, 173–95. Brunswick, NJ: Rutgers University Press, 2005.

Starr, Jerold. "The Challenges and Rewards of Coalition Building: Pittsburgh's Alliance for Progressive Action." In *Forging Radical Alliances Across Differences: Coalition Politics for the New Millennium,* edited by Jill M. Bystydzienski and Steven P. Schacht, 107–19. New York: Rowman & Littlefield Publishers, 2001.

Steggert, Frank. *Community Action Groups and City Government.* Cambridge, MA: Ballinger, 1975.

Stoecker, Randy. *Defending Community: The Struggle for Alternative Redevelopment in Cedar Riverside.* Philadelphia: Temple University Press, 1994.

———. "Community, Movement, Organization: The Problem of Identity Convergence in Collective Action." *The Sociological Quarterly* 36, no. 1 (Winter 1995): 111–30.

———. "Empowering Redevelopment: Toward a Different CDC." *Shelterforce,* no. 87 (May/June 1996): 12–16, 27.

———. "The CDC Model of Urban Redevelopment: A Critique and an Alternative." *Journal of Urban Affairs* 19, no. 1 (1997): 1–22.

———. "Are Academics Irrelevant? Roles for Scholars in Participatory Research." http://uac.Rdp .Utoledo.Edu/comm-Org/papers98 (1998).

———. "Understanding the Development-Organizing Dialectic." *Journal of Urban Affairs* 25, no. 4 (2003): 493–512.

———. *Research Methodology for Community Change: A Project Based Approach*. Thousand Oaks, CA: Sage, 2005a.

———. "The Last Line of Defense." *Shelterforce* xxvii (September/October 2005b): 16–18.

Stone, Clarence. *Economic Growth and Neighborhood Discontent: System Bias in the Urban Renewal Program of Atlanta*. Chapel Hill: The University of North Carolina Press, 1976.

———. *Regime Politics*. Lawrence, KS: University of Kansas Press, 1989.

Stone, Michael E. "Housing Affordability: One-Third of a Nation Shelter Poor." In *A Right to Housing: Foundation for a New Social Agenda*, edited by Rachel Bratt, Michael E. Stone, and Chester Hartman, 38–60. Philadelphia: Temple University Press, 2006.

Stone, Rebecca, ed. *Core Issues in Comprehensive Community-Building Initiatives*. Chicago: Chapin Hall Center for Children at the University of Chicago, 1996.

Stout, Linda. *Bridging the Class Divide: And Other Lessons for Grassroots Organizing*. Boston: Beacon Press, 1996.

Struyk, Raymond J., Margery A. Turner, and Makiko Ueno. *Future U.S. Housing Policy: Meeting the Demographic Challenge*. Urban Institute Report 88–2. Washington, DC: The Urban Institute Press, 1988.

Sullivan, Mercer L. *More Than Housing: How Community Development Corporations Go About Changing Lives and Neighborhoods*. New York: Community Development Research Center Graduate School of Management and Urban Policy New School for Social Research, 1993.

Sullivan, Thomas. *Introduction to Social Problems*; 6th Edition. Boston: Allyn and Bacon, 2003.

Susskind, Lawrence, and Jeffrey Cruikshank. *Breaking the Impasse: Consensual Approaches to Resolving Public Disputes*. New York: Basic Books, 1987.

Swanstrom, Todd, Casey, Robert Flack, and Peter Dreier. *Pulling Apart: Economic Segregation Among Suburbs and Central Cities in Major Metropolitan Areas*. Washington, DC: The Brookings Institution, 2004.

Swindell, David. "Issue Representation in Neighborhood Organizations: Questing for Democracy at the Grassroots." *Journal of Urban Affairs* 22, no. 2 (2000): 123–38.

Tait, Vanessa. *Poor Workers' Unions: Rebuilding Labor from Below*. Cambridge, MA: South End Press, 2005.

Tanner, Robert. "States Keep Limiting Access to Public Information." *Daily Chronicle (DeKalb, IL)*, 15 March 2006.

Tarrow, Sidney. *Power in Movement: Social Movements, Collective Action and Politics*. New York: Cambridge University Press, 1994.

Teaford, Jon C. *Post-Suburbia: Government and Politics in the Edge Cities*. Baltimore: John Hopkins University Press, 1997.

Temkin, Kenneth, and William Rohe. "Social Capital and Neighborhood Stability: An Empirical Investigation." *Housing Policy Debate* 9, no. 1 (1998): 61–88.

Teske, Nathan. *Political Activists in America: The Identity Construction Model of Political Participation*. Cambridge, U.K.: Cambridge University Press, 1997.

The National Coalition for the Homeless and The National Law Center on Homelessness & Poverty. *A Dream Denied: The Criminalization of Homelessness in U.S. Cities*. Washington, DC: The National Coalition for the Homeless and The National Law Center on Homelessness & Poverty, 2006.

Thomas, John Clayton. *Between Citizen and City: Neighborhood Organizations and Urban Politics in Cincinnati*. Lawrence KS: University of Kansas Press, 1986.

"Three-Year Housing LA Campaign Culminates in Largest City Housing Trust Fund." *Housing Trust Fund News—Center for Community Change*, Spring 2002, 1–3, 12.

Throgmorton, James A. *Planning as Persuasive Storytelling: The Rhetorical Construction of Chicago's Electric Future*. Chicago: University of Chicago Press, 1996.

Tigges, Leann, M., Irene Browne, and Gary Green. "Social Isolation of the Urban Poor: Race, Class and Neighborhood Effects on Social Resources." *The Sociological Quarterly* 39, no. 1 (1998): 53–77.

Tracy, James, ed. and comp. *The Civil Disobedience Handbook: A Brief History And Practical Advice for the Politically Disadvantaged*. San Francisco: Manic D. Press, 2002.

Trapp, Shel. *Dynamics of Organizing*. Chicago: National Training and Information Center, 1976.

———. *Dynamics of Organizing: Building Power by Developing the Human Spirit*. Chicago, IL: Shel Trapp, n.d.

Traynor, William J., and Jessica Andors. "Network Organizing: A Strategy for Building Community Empowerment." *Shelterforce* xxvii (March/April 2005): 8–11.

Treskon, Mark, and Daniel Pelletiere. *Up Against a*

Wall: Housing Affordability for Renters: An Analysis of the 2003 American Community Survey. Washington, DC: National Low Income Housing Coalition, 2005.

Tulloss, Janice K. "Citizen Participation in Boston's Development Policy: The Political Economy of Participation." *Urban Affairs Review* 30, no. 4 (March 1995): 514–37.

Turner, Allan. "Leaders Listen to ACORN Group's Complaints About Storm Assistance." *Houston Chronicle*, October 8, 2005, B-6.

Turner, Margery Austin, Carla Herbig, Deborah Kaye, Julie Fenderson, and Diane Levy. *Discrimination Against Persons with Disabilities: Barriers at Every Step*. Washington, DC: The Urban Institute, 2005.

Turner, Margery Austin, and Lynette Rawlings. *Overcoming Concentrated Poverty and Isolation*. Washington, DC: The Urban Institute, 2005.

"Two Reports Show Influence of Business Lobbying Spending." *The Watcher* 4 (30 June 2003): 13.

United for a Fair Economy. *The Activist Cookbook: Creative Actions for a Fair Economy*. Boston: United for a Fair Economy, 1997.

———. "Dow Breaks 10,000 But Typical Household Wealth Down Since 1983." www.Stw.Org/html/shifting_fortunes_ Press.Html, April 1999.

U.S. Conference of Mayors. *Rebuilding America's Cities*. Cambridge, MA: Ballinger Publishing, 1986.

Van der Werf, Martin. " 'Sweatshop' Protests Raise Ethical and Practical Issues." *The Chronicle of Higher Education*, 5 March 1999, A38–A39.

Van Dyke, Nella. "Crossing Movement Boundaries: Factors That Facilitate Coalition Protest by American College Students 1930–1990." *Social Problems* 50, no. 2 (May 2003): 226–50.

Van Ryzin, Gregg G. "Residents' Sense of Control and Ownership in a Mutual Housing Association." *Journal of Urban Affairs* 16, no. 3 (1994): 241–53.

Verhovek, Sam Howe. "Growing Popularity of Ballot Initiatives Leads to Questions." *The New York Times*, 1 November 1998, A1, A20.

Von Hoffman, Alexander. *House by House, Block by Block: The Rebirth of America's Urban Neighborhoods*. New York: Oxford University Press, 2003.

Võ, Linda Trinh. *Mobilizing an Asian American Community*. Philadelphia: Temple University Press, 2004.

Wagner, David. "Radical Movements in the Social Services: A Theoretical Perspective." *Social Service Review* 63, no. 2 (June 1989): 264–84.

Walker, Christopher. *Community Development Corporations and Their Changing Support Systems*. Washington, DC: The Urban Institute, 2002.

Wallack, Lawrence. "Media Advocacy: A Strategy for Empowering People and Communities." In *Community Organizing and Community Building for Health Second Edition*, edited by Meredith Minkler, 419–32. Brunswick, NJ: Rutgers University Press, 2005.

Waller, Margy. *Block Grants: Flexibility vs. Stability in Social Services*. Washington, DC: The Brookings Institution, 2005.

Wandersman, Abraham. "A Framework of Participation in Community Organizations." *The Journal of Applied Behavioral Science* 17, no. 1 (1981): 27–58.

Warcquant, Lois, J. D., and William Julius Wilson. "The Cost of Racial and Class Exclusion in the Inner City." *The Annals of the American Academy of Political and Social Science* 501 (January 1989): 8–25.

Warren, Mark R. *Dry Bones Rattling: Community Building to Revitalize American Democracy*. Princeton, NJ: Princeton University Press, 2001.

Warren, Mark R., and Richard L. Wood. "Faith-Based Community Organizing: The State of the Field." Comm-Org, 2001. Http://comm-org.utoldeo.edu/papers2001/faith/faithtm.

Waters, Dane. "The Initiative Process in America: An Overview of How It Works Around the Country," 2000. www.iandrinstitute.org/.

Weicher, John. *Maintaining the Safety Net: Income Redistribution Programs in the Reagan Administration*. Washington, DC: American Enterprise Institute for Public Policy Research, 1984.

Weil, Marie. "Social Planning with Communities." In *The Handbook of Community Practice*, edited by Marie Weil, 215–43. Thousand Oaks, CA: Sage, 2005.

Weil, Marie, and Dorothy N. Gamble. "Community Practice Models." In *Encyclopedia of Social Work*. Nineteenth Edition, edited by R. I. Edward, 577–94. Washington, DC: NASW, 1995.

———. "Evolution, Models, and the Changing Context of Community Practice." In *The Handbook of Community Practice*, edited by Marie Weil, 117–51. Thousand Oaks, CA: Sage, 2005.

Wei, William. *The Asian American Movement*. Philadelphia: Temple, 1993.

Wellman, Barry, and Barry Leighton. "Networks, Neighborhoods, and Communities: Approaches to the Study of the Community Question." *Urban Affairs Quarterly* 14, no. 3 (1979): 363–90.

Wenocur, Stanley, and Michael Reisch. *From Charity to Enterprise: The Development of American Social Work in a Market Economy*. Urbana: University of Illinois Press, 1989.

Whyte, William Foote, and Kathleen King Whyte. *Making Mondragon: The Growth and Dynamics of the Worker Cooperative Complex.* Ithaca, NY: ILR Press, New York State School of Industrial and Labor Relations, 1988.

Wiewel, Wim, and Gerrit-Jan Knaap, eds. *Partnerships for Smart Growth: University-Community Collaboration for Better Public Places.* Armonk, NY: M. E. Sharp, 2005.

Wilcox, Clyde. "The Dynamics of Lobbying the Hill." In *The Interest Group Connection: Electioneering, Lobbying, and Policymaking in Washington,* edited by Paul S. Herrnson, Ronald G. Shaiko, and Clyde Wilcox, 89–99. Chatham, NJ: Chatham, 1998.

Williams, Lynora. "Interview: Harvard Scientist Asks What Makes Neighborhoods Work." *Connectivity: People and Places* 1 (Summer 2004).

Williams, Marva, and Val Sean McLenighan. *Building Community Assets: A Guide to Credit Union Partnerships.* Chicago, IL: The Woodstock Institute, 2004.

Williamson, Thad, David Imbroscio, and Gar Alperovitz. *Making a Place for Community: Local Democracy in a Global Era.* New York: Routledge, 2003.

Wilson, Robert, ed. *Public Policy and Community: Activism and Governance in Texas.* Austin: University of Texas Press, 1997.

Wilson, William Julius. *The Truly Disadvantaged: The Inner City, the Underclass, and Public Policy.* Chicago: University of Chicago Press, 1987.

Woliver, Laura R. *From Outrage to Action: The Politics of Grass-Roots Dissent.* Urbana: University of Illinois Press, 1993.

Wong, Pat. "The Indigent Health Care Package." In *Public Policy and Community: Activism and Governance in Texas,* edited by Robert Wilson, 95–118. Austin: University of Texas Press, 1997.

Wood, Lesley, and Kelly Moore. "Target Practice: Community Activism in a Global Era." In *From ACT UP to the WTO: Urban Protest and Community Building in the Era of Globalization,* edited by Benjamin Shepard and Ronald Hayduk, 21–34. New York: Verso, 2002.

Wood, Richard L. *Faith in Action: Religion, Race, and Democratic, Organizing in America.* Chicago: University of Chicago Press, 2002.

Wright, David J. "Comprehensive Strategies for Community Renewal." *Rockefeller Institute Bulletin* (1998), 48–66.

Wright, Talmadge. *Out of Place: Homeless Mobilizations, Subcities, and Contested Landscapes.* Albany: State University of New York Press, 1997.

Yanow, Dvora. *How Does a Policy Mean? Interpreting Policy and Organizational Action.* Washington, DC: Georgetown University Press, 1996.

Yeich, Susan, and Ralph Levine. "Political Efficacy: Enhancing the Construct and Its Relationship to the Mobilization of People." *Journal of Community Psychology* 22 (July 1994): 259–69.

Yukl, Gary A. *Leadership in Organizations.* Upper Saddle River, N.J.: Prentice Hall, 1989.

Zisk, Betty H. "Coalitions Among Peace and Environmental Groups: A Comparative Study of the Impact of Local Political Culture." Paper presented at the Annual Meeting of the American Political Science Association. Atlanta, GA, 1989.

INDEX